DATE DUE

REF.	REF.	REF.	
	REF.	REF.	

The Harper
Handbook to
Literature

THE HARPER HANDBOOK TO LITERATURE

NORTHROP FRYE
Massey College, University of Toronto

SHERIDAN BAKER
The University of Michigan

GEORGE PERKINS
Eastern Michigan University

With a Chronology of Literature
and World Events
by Barbara M. Perkins
Eastern Michigan University

1817

HARPER & ROW, PUBLISHERS, New York
Cambridge, Philadelphia, San Francisco,
London, Mexico City, São Paulo, Singapore, Sydney

Sponsoring Editor: Phillip Leininger
Project Editor: Nora Helfgott
Text Design: Robert Sugar
Cover Design: 20/20 Services Inc., Mark W. Berghash
Production: Marion Palen
Compositor: The Clarinda Company
Printer and Binder: The Murray Printing Company

The Harper Handbook to Literature

Library of Congress Cataloging in Publication Data

Frye, Northrop.
    The Harper handbook to literature.

    1. Literature—Terminology. 2. Literature—Handbooks,
manuals, etc. 3. English literature—Handbooks, manuals, etc.
I. Baker, Sheridan Warner, 1918-   II. Perkins,
George B., 1930-   III. Title.
PN44.5.F75   1985   802'.02   84-19205
ISBN 0-06-042217-3

84 85 86 87 88 9 8 7 6 5 4 3 2 1

ACKNOWLEDGMENTS

Grateful acknowledgment is made for the use of the following material:

Auden, W. H., lines from "September 1, 1939," from *The English Auden: Poems, Essays and Dramatic Writings, 1927–1939* by W. H. Auden, edited by Edward Mendelson, by permission of Random House, Inc., and Faber and Faber Publishers.

Basho, Matsuo, "A Cove at the 'Lake of the Views,'" from *An Introduction to Haiku* by Harold E. Henderson. Copyright © 1958 by Harold E. Henderson. Reprinted by permission of Doubleday & Company, Inc.

Hardy, Thomas, lines from "I Look into My Glass," from *Collected Poems* by Thomas Hardy, by permission of Macmillan, London and Basingstoke.

Hodgson, Ralph, lines from "Eve," from *Collected Poems* by Ralph Hodgson, 1961, by permission of Macmillan, London and Basingstoke.

MacLeish, Archibald, "Ars Poetica" from *New and Collected Poems 1917–1976* by Archibald MacLeish. Copyright © 1976 by Archibald MacLeish. Reprinted by permission of Houghton Mifflin Company.

Noyes, Alfred, lines from "The Barrel Organ," from *Collected Poems* by Alfred Noyes, 1906, by permission of Hugh Noyes.

Williams, William Carlos, *Pictures from Brueghel and Other Poems.* Copyright 1955 by William Carlos Williams. Reprinted by permission of New Directions Publishing Corporation.

CONTENTS

PREFACE

The Harper Handbook to Literature, arranged in alphabetical order, aims to satisfy curiosity about terms like *syzygy* or *zeugma*, concepts like *structuralism* or *phenomenology* or *unity*, and literary genres and movements like *Afro-American literature* or *Goliardic verse*. It is a supplementary text for college students beginning their literary study, a handy guide for casual readers, and a ready reference for advanced students and instructors. Entries range from a few words to summary essays with bibliographies for further study. Cross-references lead from short definitions to larger concepts. A "Chronology of Literature and World Events," at the end of the text, ranges from the first pictographs to contemporary names and titles. The aim is comprehension, in coverage and in understanding.

We focus on literature in English but include those influences and terms that have flowed in from the great matrix of world literature. *Drama*, for instance, begins with the Greeks; *Romanticism*, with the French Jean Jacques Rousseau. Students may follow the history of *printing* all the way from China, or the more recent story of the *Beat Generation* in the United States or the *Angry Young Men* in England. SMALL CAPITAL LETTERS indicate terms treated elsewhere in the *Handbook*. The entry on **Irony**, for instance, mentions ROMANCE, TRAGEDY, and COMEDY. Terms introduced and discussed under a larger heading are printed in *italics*. *Individualized characters*, for example, appears this way under **Characters**. We have tried to include all useful terms, but not all terms ever used. Readers will find clarified most terms that might puzzle them when encountered elsewhere, or they may browse through the corridors of literary history and critical thought, discovering innumerable surprises and satisfactions within the rich literary heritage of English-speaking people.

Northrop Frye
Sheridan Baker
George Perkins

The Harper
Handbook to
Literature

A

Abbey Theatre. Dublin theater, important to the IRISH RENAIS-SANCE in the early decades of the twentieth century. A conversation between Yeats and Lady Gregory in 1898 led to her support of the annual presentation of "certain Celtic and Irish plays," among which was, in 1899, Yeats's *Countess Kathleen.* By 1902 the Irish National Theatre Society was founded with the help of J. M. Synge and AE (George Russell), and in 1904 plays began to be produced in the Abbey Theatre. In 1910 the theater was purchased for the company by public subscription. Other playwrights whose works were produced include Padraic Colum and, later, Sean O'Casey. Yeats remained as director with Lady Gregory until her death in 1932 and after, until his own death in 1939.

Abecedarius. An ACROSTIC in which each word in each line alliter-ates on successive letters of the alphabet, as in these lines:

> An abecedarius always alliterates,
> Blindly blunders, but blooms:
> Comes crawling craftily, cantering crazily,
> Daring, doubtless, dark dooms.

The term is also more loosely applied to a poem running down the alphabet only in the initial letters of its lines.

Ab Ovo. From the beginning (literally, "from the egg"), a term Hor-ace used for a story that begins with the earliest relevant event, as distinguished from one that begins with middle things, IN MEDIAS RES.

Abridgment. A shortened or condensed version of a work, frequently intended as a substitute. See ABSTRACT.

Absolute. Perfect; without limitation or qualification. A belief in ab-solute standards of aesthetics, ethics, morality, or the like is called AB-SOLUTISM. In grammar, the term is used in several ways, for example, for a word that cannot be qualified (*unique*), or for a portion of a sen-tence that stands apart without the normal syntactical relation to the rest.

Absolutism. In CRITICISM, the belief in irreducible, unchanging val-ues of FORM and content that underlie the tastes of individuals and

1

periods and arise from the stability of an ABSOLUTE hierarchal order. See RELATIVISM.

Abstract. (1) The opposite of CONCRETE—general ideas like *love* and *justice,* or *"Beauty is truth, truth beauty,"* rather than physical tangibles like *stone, house, frog.* (2) A brief summary of a scholarly work; unlike an ABRIDGMENT, it does not serve as a substitute. (3) In art, nonrepresentational.

Abstract Poetry. Edith Sitwell's term for her *Façade* poems, in which she aims at "patterns of sound" equivalent to the nonobjective patterns of abstract painting. See PURE POETRY.

Absurd. Unreasonable, ridiculous. In contemporary literature and philosophy, *the absurd* refers to one fundamental reaction of modern humans when they contemplate their relationship to existence. Unable to accept the traditional religious and philosophical beliefs of the past, and incapable of perceiving a meaningful pattern in their lives or the lives of those around them, they discover they must somehow come to terms with this overwhelming absurdity, and react with laughter or despair (and sometimes with both), or else with resolve or resolution. In philosophy, the most important result of a sense of the absurd is EXISTENTIALISM. In literature, a sense of the absurd is important in the fiction of existentialists like Albert Camus and Jean-Paul Sartre, as well as in that of less overtly philosophical writers like Samuel Beckett, Günter Grass, Joseph Heller, Thomas Pynchon, and Kurt Vonnegut. See ABSURD, THEATER OF THE; ANTI-HERO; ANTI-NOVEL; BLACK HUMOR.

Absurd, Theater of the. A term used to describe a movement in the theater after World War II that created new theatrical conventions by emphasizing the ABSURD in dramatic content and staging techniques. Prominent playwrights included Samuel Beckett, Eugène Ionesco, Jean Genêt, Harold Pinter, and Edward Albee. Blending techniques of EXPRESSIONISM and SURREALISM with content philosophically allied to EXISTENTIALISM, they produced some of the most powerful and influential plays in recent theatrical history.

Reference

Martin Esslin, **The Theatre of the Absurd** (1961).

Academic Drama. See SCHOOL PLAYS.

Academies. Associations established for the advancement of learning or culture. The term is derived from the name of the park near Athens that served as the site of Plato's Greek Academy. It has been widely applied since to many different situations, from local academies serving as public or private secondary schools through the influential national academies that attempt to provide educational guidance for a country.

National academies have sought to advance learning by establishing climates conducive to education and research, to set standards for language by compiling and publishing dictionaries, and to protect and conserve literary classics by overseeing editorial and publishing projects. They have sometimes been publicly supported, sometimes privately, with membership usually by election of peers and strictly limited in number. Noteworthy early academies include the Académie Française and the Royal Society (Great Britain), both dating from the seventeenth century, and the American Academy of Arts and Sciences, founded in Boston in 1780. More recent is the American Academy of Arts and Letters (1904).

Acatalectic. Metrically complete, from the Greek "not leaving off." It refers to a metrical line fulfilling its pattern in the last foot. See METER.

Accent. STRESS or emphasis. *Word accent* denotes where the stress normally falls, as in *áccent*. RHETORICAL ACCENT denotes emphasis for meaning: "*Are* you going?" "Are *you* going?" *Metrical accent* denotes the metrical pattern (˘ —) to which writers fit and adjust accented words and rhetorical emphases, keeping the meter as they substitute word-accented feet and tune their rhetoric.

Accentual-Syllabic Verse. Verse with lines established by counting both ACCENTS and syllables, the dominant basis for verse in English since the fourteenth century. It is distinguished from ACCENTUAL VERSE, which counts only accents; SYLLABIC VERSE, which counts only syllables; and FREE VERSE, which depends on no system of counting. See METER; OLD ENGLISH VERSIFICATION.

Accentual Verse. Verse with lines established by counting ACCENTS only, without regard to the number of unstressed syllables. This was the dominant form of verse in English until the time of Chaucer. See ALLITERATIVE VERSE; OLD ENGLISH VERSIFICATION.

Accidie. Sloth, or listless, spiritual boredom: in the Middle Ages one of the SEVEN DEADLY SINS and now sometimes said to characterize modern alienation.

Accisimus. A kind of irony, an affected and hypocritical refusal of something strongly desired, as when a cardinal, on being offered a bishopric, traditionally says *Nolo episcopari,* "I do not want to be a bishop." Similarly, Caesar in Shakespeare's play and Cromwell in actuality both refused the crown they coveted. See IRONY.

Acephalous. See HEADLESS LINE.

Acronym. An ACROSTIC in which a name is formed by the initial letters of a series of words, as *NATO* for *North American Treaty Organization* or *MASH* for *Mobile Army Surgical Hospital.* The word *cabal,* now a name for any group dedicated to intrigue, is an older acronym, formed by the initials of five ministers of Charles II: *C*lifford, *A*rlington, *B*uckingham, *A*shley, and *L*auderdale.

Acrostic. Words arranged, frequently in a poem or puzzle, to disclose a hidden word or message when the correct combination of letters is read in sequence. *Acrostic* is from Greek roots meaning the end of a line of verse, and an acrostic is most often a poem in which the first letters of the lines deliver the message when read downward. In another form *(telestich),* the last letters of each line are used, while still another *(mesostich)* uses the middle letters. In a *cross acrostic,* the message is formed by the first letter of the first line, the second letter of the second, the third of the third, and so on. Chaucer's "An ABC" is an acrostic beginning each stanza with a new letter. Another example, James Merrill's "The Book of Ephraim" in *Divine Comedies* (1976), begins each section with a new letter. See ABECEDARIUS; ACRONYM.

Act. The larger division into which plays are conventionally divided. SCENES are small divisions. Acts are usually indicated in the modern theater by dropping the curtain. Greek plays were generally divided into five major parts by the appearances of the CHORUS, and in the Roman theater Seneca's tragedies employed five acts, both following basically this DRAMATIC STRUCTURE: EXPOSITION, COMPLICATION, CLIMAX, FALLING ACTION, and CATASTROPHE. In Elizabethan plays the basic five parts were not always so clear, and nineteenth- and twentieth-century dramatists have often ignored the divisions, writing major plays of four, three, or two acts, or with scene divisions only. A one-act play is usually a shorter form.

Action. (1) Broadly, the events of a dramatic work as presented on stage or in film, embodying the PLOT. In this sense, action includes both physical movement and speech. It may be distinguished from the STORY, the events behind the action but not necessarily portrayed for the audience. (2) More narrowly, the movements of the actors on stage or before the camera, as distinguished from speeches and inner, or psychological, movement. (3) Either of these concepts as applied to the events of nondramatic FICTION, presented either dramatically or through NARRATION.

Adage. An old or popular saying. See PROVERB.

Adaptation. A revision of a work for a new purpose, as a novel for a film, a short story for the stage, an older play for a new musical comedy.

Adonic Verse. A Greek and Latin meter combining a DACTYL and a SPONDEE $- \smile \smile \mid - -$ (or $- \smile \smile \mid - \smile$), celebrating the festival of Adonis. See METER.

Adventure Story. A form of POPULAR LITERATURE emphasizing spectacular ACTION and physical danger, frequently at the expense of CHARACTERIZATION or meaning. Classic adventure stories include Robert Louis Stevenson's *Treasure Island* and *Kidnapped* and H. Rider Haggard's *King Solomon's Mines*. In the twentieth century, the GENRE has proved important to Hollywood, an excellent example being the George Lucas and Steven Spielberg film *Raiders of the Lost Ark*.

Aesthetic Criticism. A consideration of a work in isolation, as opposed to MORAL CRITICISM, a consideration of a work in relationship to humanity. See CRITICISM.

Aesthetic Distance. The detachment experienced by an author in creating a work or a reader in responding to it. Wordsworth's "emotion recollected in tranquility" represents one formula for aesthetic distance, as the poet's initial emotion is translated into art through a later, detached contemplation, conducive to the application of a carefully considered technique. For the reader or critic, aesthetic distance represents the achievement of a stance in relation to the work that allows for balancing the initial emotional impact against later, more objective judgment. See DISTANCE; PSYCHIC DISTANCE.

Aestheticism. Devotion to beauty. The term applies particularly to a nineteenth-century literary and artistic movement celebrating beauty as independent from morality, and praising FORM above content; ART FOR ART'S SAKE. The aesthetic movement began early in the century, with philosophic roots still earlier, in Kant's concept of "purposiveness without purpose" in art. Keats's "Beauty is truth, truth beauty" may be understood as an expression of it. In France, Théophile Gautier flatly denied the utility of art in the preface to *Mademoiselle de Maupin* (1835). Poe, in "The Poetic Principle" (1850), emphasized the formal elements of poetry, "the rhythmical creation of Beauty," which he also stressed in his poems. Charles Baudelaire and Stéphane Mallarmé followed, and the movement reached its pinnacle in the 1890s with Oscar Wilde and Aubrey Beardsley. Adherents of the aesthetic movement were opposed to didacticism and tried to live their lives as art, "to burn always with hard, gemlike flame" as Walter Pater expressed it in *Studies in the History of the Renaissance* (1873). Among opponents of these ideas, Tennyson reacted with scorn:

> Art for Art's sake! Hail, truest lord of Hell!
> Hail Genius, Master of the Moral Will!
> "The filthiest of all paintings painted well
> Is Mightier than the purest painted ill!"
> Yes, mightier than the purest painted well,
> So prone are we toward the broad way to Hell.

See DECADENTS.

Aesthetics. The study of the beautiful. Aesthetics is the branch of philosophy concerned with defining the nature of art and establishing criteria of judgment. Objective theorists, like Plato and Aristotle, discovered the source of beauty in the object. The subjective philosophy of Hume found it in the eye of the beholder. See CRITICISM.

Aet., Aetat. Abbreviations for the Latin *aetatis:* "aged" [a given number of years]; at the age of.

Affective Fallacy. Judgment of a literary work by its results, a fallacy by the tenets of the NEW CRITICISM. The term was introduced in *The Verbal Icon* (1954), by W. K. Wimsatt and Monroe C. Beardsley, who defined the affective fallacy as "a confusion between the poem and its *results* (what it *is* and what it *does*)," and argued that criticism should focus on the work.

The danger in too rigid application of this idea was well expressed by David Daiches in *Literary Essays* (1956): "The value of literature surely lies in its actual or potential effect. . . . To deny this is to fall into the 'ontological fallacy' of believing that a work of art fulfills its purpose and achieves its value simply by *being*." See INTENTIONAL FALLACY.

African Literature. See COMMONWEALTH LITERATURE.

Afro-American Literature. Literature in the United States written by Americans of black African descent; also called *black literature*. The term arose in the early 1960s, in the wake of the civil rights movement of the fifties and onward, but the literature began in the eighteenth century with the poems of Jupiter Hammon and Phillis Wheatley, and continued in the nineteenth century with the poetry of George Moses Horton and other slaves, though owners and state laws continued to suppress literacy to prevent communication and escape. Frederick Douglass, whose master's wife taught him the rudiments of reading at eight but stopped on her husband's orders, eventually escaped to lecture on abolition and to write his autobiography in 1845, rewritten as *My Bondage and My Freedom* (1855) and again as *Life and Times of Frederick Douglass* (1882). This is the most distinguished of many SLAVE NARRATIVES. Many pamphlets and sermons also appeared. William Wells Brown, also an escaped slave, published *Clotel, or, The President's Daughter* (1853), the first Afro-American novel.

Charles W. Chesnutt, the first black writer after Emancipation, published more than 50 essays, sketches, and stories, three novels, two collections of stories, and a biography of Douglass between 1885 and 1903. His "The Goophered Grapevine" was the first Afro-American story to appear in *The Atlantic Monthly* (August 1887). Paul Laurence Dunbar was the first black writer to live by his pen and the first to gain national recognition, beginning with his self-published poems *Oak and Ivy* (1893), then with stories and four novels, mostly in dialect with a humorous slant for the white public.

With the HARLEM RENAISSANCE of the 1920s, black literature came fully to racial consciousness. James Weldon Johnson (1871–1938), a Florida lawyer and former high-school principal, was the central inspiration and mentor, having moved to Harlem in 1901 with his brother John, a composer, where they wrote more than two hundred songs for the stage. His novel *Autobiography of an Ex-Colored Man* (1912; reissued, 1927) led the way in breaking black stereotypes. But Langston Hughes's poem "The Negro Speaks of Rivers," published in W. E. B. Du Bois's magazine *Crisis* (1920), and Johnson's anthology, *Book of American Negro Poetry* (1922), with valuable introduction, brought the movement to national recognition. In 1921, jazz pianist Eubie Blake, with his vaudeville teammate Noble Sissle, also a composer, had staged *Shuffle Along*, with the hit tune "I'm Just Wild About Harry," the first Broadway musical written, produced, directed, and performed entirely by blacks. Also highly influential on younger writers was Jean Toomer's *Cane* (1923), a miscellany of sketches, fiction, poems, and drama. Johnson's *God's Trombone* (1927), seven sermons in free verse, is one of the movement's most notable works. Other significant poets were Arna Bontemps—he also wrote three novels, a number of nonfiction books, and edited several anthologies—Zora Neale Hurston, Nella Larson, Claude McKay, and Countee Cullen. McKay's *Harlem Shadows* (1922) contains "If I Must Die," which Winston Churchill was to quote in his appeal to Congress for American aid in World War II. McKay's novel, *Home to Harlem* (1928), about a young black's return from World War I, was a best seller. Cullen's *Color* (1925), *Copper Sun* (1927), *The Black Christ and Other Poems* (1927), and *Caroling Dusk: An Anthology of Verse by Negro Poets* (1927) also won wide respect for the movement.

Richard Wright's *Native Son* (1940), a masterful novel about black alienation, frustration, and violence—the single most influential work of Afro-American literature—started a new surge of black writing. Other significant novelists were Walter White, Zora Neale Hurston, Ann Petry, and Chester Himes. In Chicago, Gwendolyn Brooks established herself as a major poet with her first book, *A Street in Bronzeville* (1945). Her *Annie Allen* (1949) made her the first black Pulitzer Prize-winner. Ralph Ellison, encouraged by Wright, published his classic *Invisible Man* (1952), moving from Wright's naturalism into a more pervasive symbolism. James Baldwin's first novel, *Go Tell It on the Mountain* (1953), established him as a major writer of the fifties and sixties, which also saw a second "Renaissance" in the poetry of LeRoi Jones (Imamu Amiri Baraka), Nikki Giovanni, and Don L. Lee (Haki Madhubuti).

Lorraine Hansberry's *Raisin in the Sun* (1959), which takes its title from a poem by Hughes, was the first Broadway hit by a black playwright. Other significant plays are LeRoi Jones's *Dutchman* (1964)—produced before he changed his name to Baraka—Martin Duberman's documentary *In White America* (1964), and Baldwin's *Blues for Mister Charlie* (1964) and *The Amen Corner* (1965). The protests of the 1960s produced some distinguished nonfiction: *The Autobiography of Malcolm X* (1965), ghostwritten by Alex Haley (whose *Roots: The Saga of an American Family*, 1974, became a classic of the black American experience); Eldridge Cleaver's *Soul on Ice* (1968); and George Jackson's *Soledad Brothers* (1970). In 1977, James McPherson won the Pulitzer Prize with his novel *Elbow Room*. Other prominent black writers are Ernest Gaines, Michael Harper, Robert Hayden, Gayl Jones, Clarence Major, Ishmael Reed, John Wideman, and Alice Walker, 1983 Pulitzer Prize-winner for her novel *The Color Purple*. See AMERICAN LITERATURE, HARLEM RENAISSANCE.

References

M. J. Butcher, **The Negro in American Culture** (1956).
Nathan Irvin Huggins, **Harlem Renaissance** (1971).
James M. McPherson et al., **Blacks in America: Bibliographical Essays** (1971).
Charles D. Peavy, **Afro-American Literature and Culture Since World War II: A Guide to Information Sources** (1979).
Darwin T. Turner, **Afro-American Writers** (1970).
Carl Van Vechten, **Keep A-Inchin' Along: Selected Writings of Carl Van Vechten About Black Arts and Letters** (1979).
Mary Helen Washington, **Midnight Birds: Stories of Contemporary Black Women Writers** (1980).

Ages of Man.   See SEVEN AGES OF MAN.

Age of Reason.   The Neoclassic period, roughly 1660–1800. See ENGLISH LITERATURE, PERIODS OF.

Ages of the World.   First summarized in Hesiod's *Works and Days* (c. 700 B.C.), the four ages declining from perfection into strife and sin—Golden, Silver, Bronze, and Iron. The four ages originated in Indo-Iranian or Indo-European myth, reflecting some perception of humankind's actual technological advance from stone to bronze to iron. The passage from one age to the next was identified and defined as progress in the nineteenth century. The four declining ages represent PRIMITIVISM, a view prevailing from classical times through Christianity until the late eighteenth century.

The Golden Age was perfection, with perpetual spring, fruits in abundance without cultivation, peace, and bliss. It was ruled by Cronos, the creator of life, and located in Arcadia, a mountainous region north of Sparta. Roman mythology had Saturn, the Roman Cronos, come to Italy when ousted by his son Jove, bringing agriculture and the arts of civilization, Saturn being the god of agriculture, his name deriving from *serere*, "to sow." The account of Adam and Eve in Eden in Genesis is another version of the Golden Age.

The Silver Age was ruled by Zeus, who lopped the spring and introduced seasons and hardship. According to the Greeks, he, not Cronos–Saturn, introduced tillage and housing as humans left their solitary caves for civilization, luxury, and discontent. The Bronze Age was fierce and warlike, but, as Ovid says in his summary of the four ages in *Metamorphoses* (I.89–150), "still unstained by crime." The Iron Age, this wretched present, according to Hesiod, had lost all justice and piety. Here sin was born, and murder. Hesiod included a Heroic Age, that of the Trojan War, before the Iron Age.

Agon.   In Greek tragedy, an argument, often with the chorus dividing and taking sides (*agon* means "contest"). In the OLD COMEDY, an *epirrhematic agon* engaged the chorus in stylized responses to the disputants and comments to the audience. Later, *agon* came to mean a major conflict in plot, from which the terms ANTAGONIST, DEUTERAGONIST (a secondary hero), and PROTAGONIST derive.

Agrarians.   A group of writers centered at Vanderbilt University, Nashville, Tennessee, from 1922 until World War II. They opposed both Northern industrialism and "the old high-caste Brahmins of the Old South." Allen Tate (1899–1979), poet, novelist, and initiator of the NEW CRITICISM, was a leader. *The Fugitive* (1922–1925), their poetry magazine, consolidated the group, also known as THE FUGITIVES, consisting of Tate, Robert Penn Warren (1905–   ), John Crowe Ransom (1888–1974), Donald Davidson (1899–1979), and Merrill Moore (1907–1957). Their symposium, *I'll Take My Stand* (1930), was a manifesto for Southern agrarian society as the best hope against industrialism for preserving art. Between 1933 and 1937, *The American Review* represented them, and *The Southern Review* (1935–1942), edited by Warren and Cleanth Brooks, also published their works.

Agroikos.   A STOCK CHARACTER dating from Greek COMEDY: a rustic or country bumpkin. See CHARACTERS.

Alazon.   A deceiving or self-deceived imposter or braggart, a STOCK CHARACTER of COMEDY and TRAGEDY. See BRAGGADOCIO; CHARACTERS; *MILES GLORIOSUS*.

Alba.   A medieval Provençal love lyric, lamenting the coming of the dawn, when lovers must part. See AUBADE; TROUBADOUR.

Alcaic Strophe.   A STANZA after the manner of the Greek poet Alcaeus, consisting of four lines with the first two HENDECASYLLABIC (eleven syllables), the third of nine syllables, and the fourth decasyllabic (ten). Horace used it frequently. Tennyson imitated it in "Milton," which begins

$$\bar{O} \mid \overline{\text{might}}\breve{\text{y}}\text{-} \mid \overline{\text{mouthed}} \text{ in-} \mid \overline{\text{ven}}\breve{\text{tor}} \breve{\text{of}} \mid \overline{\text{harmon-}} \mid \overline{\text{ies,}}$$

$$\bar{O} \mid \overline{\text{skilled to}} \mid \overline{\text{sing of}} \mid \overline{\text{Time or E-}} \mid \overline{\text{tern it-}} \mid \bar{\text{y,}}$$

$\overset{\_}{\text{God-}}$ | $\overset{\_}{\text{gift}}\overset{\smile}{\text{ed}}$ | $\overset{\_}{\text{or}}\overset{\smile}{\text{gan-}}$ | $\overset{\_}{\text{voice}}$ $\overset{\smile}{\text{of}}$ | $\overset{\_}{\text{Eng}}\overset{\smile}{\text{land,}}$

$\overset{\_}{\text{Mil}}\overset{\smile}{\text{ton,}}$ $\overset{\smile}{\text{a}}$ | $\overset{\_}{\text{name}}$ $\overset{\smile}{\text{to}}$ $\overset{\smile}{\text{re-}}$ | $\overset{\_}{\text{sound}}$ $\overset{\smile}{\text{for}}$ | $\overset{\_}{\text{age}}\overset{\smile}{\text{s}}$.

See METER.

Alexandrine. A six-foot iambic pentameter line, characteristic of classic French verse, originating in romances celebrating Alexander the Great. The earliest was *The Pilgrimage to Jerusalem* (c. 1100), describing a fanciful campaign by Charlemagne against Alexander. It was soon followed by the *Roman d'Alexandre*, one of whose authors was Alexandre de Bernais, surnamed de Paris, whose name also contributes to the *Alexandrine* nomenclature. Spenser established it in English as the concluding line to his five-foot iambic stanza. Dryden and Pope added the six-footer for classical emphasis to their iambic pentameter couplets, especially with its balanced CAESURA, precisely in the middle, famously satirized in Pope's own *Essay on Criticism*:

> A *needless Alexandrine* ends the Song,
> That like a wounded Snake, drags its slow length along.

See METER.

Alienation Effect. Associated especially with the dramatic theory of Bertolt Brecht, the *alienation effect (Verfremdungseffekt* in German) results when the audience becomes aware that the play is not real, but only mimics life. Brecht intended that the members of the audience maintain an emotional distance that allowed them to respond critically and objectively to what was occurring on stage. Freed from the complication of sympathetic involvement with the lives of the characters, the playgoers become, at least in theory, more receptive to the intellectual message of the drama. The alienation effect is achieved through various devices that remind the audience of the play's artificiality: stylized acting, nonrepresentational sets, interruptions, slogans, songs. Other playwrights followed; some, like Ionesco, believe that Brecht did not go far enough in abandoning traditional simulations of reality. Some of the same techniques, used for Brecht to further Marxist propaganda, became staples of THEATER OF THE ABSURD. See AESTHETIC DISTANCE, DISTANCE, PSYCHIC DISTANCE.

Allegorical Meaning. A secondary meaning of a NARRATIVE in addition to its primary or LITERAL MEANING. In the Middle Ages, the allegorical meaning was sometimes given a more specialized sense as the broad social application of a story, to be considered along with its

moral and spiritual applications. See FOUR SENSES OF INTERPRETA-
TION.

Allegory. A story that suggests another story. The first part of this
word comes from the Greek *allos*, "other," and an allegory is present
in literature whenever it is clear that the author is saying, "By this I
also mean that." In practice allegory appears when a progression of
events or images suggests a translation of them into conceptual language. Thus when Sir Guyon, the knight of Temperance, enters the
house of Medina, in Book II of Spenser's *Faerie Queene*, and finds
himself attracted to her but not to her two sisters, the prudish Elissa
and the wanton Perissa, the episode is clearly to be taken as an allegory
of Aristotle's doctrine of the ethical mean, as a way intermediate between opposed extremes. Allegory is normally a continuous technique,
like counterpoint in music, and a work of literature that seems to have
a continuous parallel between its narrative and conceptual or moral
ideas, or historical events looked at as illustrations of moral precepts,
may be called an allegory. Examples in English literature would include Spenser's *Faerie Queene* and Bunyan's *Pilgrim's Progress*; in
American literature, some of Hawthorne's stories, such as "The Birth-
mark."

The simplest form of allegory is usually conveyed by personification: thus in the *Pilgrim's Progress* the hero, Christian, with his companion Hopeful, is imprisoned in the castle of Giant Despair, but they
escape by means of a key to the prison door called Promise. This technique is very old in literature: the two characters who bind down Prometheus, in Aeschylus's *Prometheus Bound*, are called Power and
Force. More complex techniques occur when literary criticism examines, say, a sacrosanct myth which does not seem to conform to approved moral standards. Thus the episode in the *Odyssey* of the forni-
cating Aphrodite and Ares caught in the net of Hephaistos,
Aphrodite's husband, was subjected to allegorizing on Plutarch's principle that gods of whom indecent stories can be told are no gods. This
tendency was far enough advanced by Plato's time for Plato to ridicule
it, and it became, despite the ridicule, an important critical trend in
later Alexandrian times. Similarly, when in Exodus 33:23 God turns
his "back parts" to Moses, because a direct view of him would be
destructive, the back parts of God are explained in later commentary
to mean the material world.

Allegory is thus a technique of aligning imaginative constructs,
mythological or poetic, with conceptual or moral models. In the Mid-

dle Ages Dante's *Commedia* was written in continuous allegory because at that time imaginative structures were regarded as rhetorical analogues to the revealed truth, which was communicated more directly in conceptual (and mainly theological) language. As a method of reading Scripture, it was permitted as long as it did not conflict with the "literal" or historical meaning, but there was still a suspicion that it was too flexible to be trustworthy. If A can mean B, the way is open for making it mean C or D as well. In Book I of *The Faerie Queene*, Spenser introduces the character Duessa to represent falsehood and duplicity: her main associations are with the Great Whore of the Apocalypse in the New Testament, identified by Protestant polemic with the Roman Catholic church. When she reappears in Book V she is clearly identified with Mary Queen of Scots. Thus Sir Thomas Browne, in his *Religio Medici*, grants that for some biblical obscurities "allegorical interpretations are also probable," but it is clear that he finds that allegorical interpretations in general as a way of reading Scripture do not apply to allegory in a professedly literary work.

The assumption that it was a primary social function of literature to provide rhetorical analogues to the truths of morality and revelation maintained the prestige of allegorical techniques until, roughly, the seventeenth century. The medieval habit of thinking of nature as a second Word of God produced among other things the bestiaries, catalogues of the habits of animals, mostly fabulous, which illustrated some moral or scriptural truth. Thus the unicorn, which can be hunted only by using a virgin as a decoy, is a type of the Christ who was born of a virgin. The dramatic rise of science from the seventeenth century onward greatly weakened this attitude of mind. With Romanticism came the revolt of the poets themselves, who could no longer accept the view that it was their duty to be an answering chorus to morality. •

If we say that a work of literature "is" an allegory, we mean that allegorical techniques are continuous throughout; but there are many such works which make only an episodic and sporadic use of allegory. Examples may be found in Tasso's *Gerusalemme Liberata*, in the second part of Goethe's *Faust,* and in several plays of Ibsen. The garden scene in *Richard II* seems to be one of Shakespeare's very rare ventures into allegory. But in Melville's *Moby-Dick* it is to be noted, first, that the author, like the majority of post-Romantic writers, deprecates having the book called an allegory, and, second, that while Moby Dick himself clearly represents many things besides an albino whale, the imaginative effect of the book depends on the sense of a great variety of suggested meanings, and would be spoiled by the pinning down of such meanings to explicit alignments with specific conceptions. It would be insensitive to say that Moby Dick represents the noumenal world or the demonic elements in nature or a projection of Captain Ahab's mind.

Hence it is not surprising that in Romantic times a distinction should grow between allegory and SYMBOL, the latter being preferred because of its greater suggestiveness and because it does not suggest that a poem can be fully "explained" in other terms than its own. The effect of the new reliance on symbol is to break down the continuities of allegory, as when Stéphane Mallarmé speaks of avoiding the naming of objects and concentrating instead on the effect produced on the observer by the object. Similarly, such a conception as Eliot's "objective correlative," where an image represents an emotion, tends to turn the allegorical technique inside out, so that instead of images being aligned with concepts, they are aligned with the poet's feelings. In the present day allegory survives chiefly in parody: thus Kafka's *The Castle* is a kind of parody of the quest of the soul in *The Pilgrim's Progress;* and science fiction romances allude, usually in the tone of parody also, to social and political trends on this earth.

Reference

Angus Fletcher, **Allegory: The Theory of a Symbolic Mode** (1964).

Alliteration. "Adding letters" (Latin *ad* + *littera*, "letter"). Two or more words, or accented syllables, chime on the same initial letter: *l*ost *l*ove *a*lone; *a*fter *a*pple-picking, or repeat the same consonant, as in Tennyson's lines

> The *m*oan of doves in i*mm*e*m*orial el*m*s.,
> And *m*ur*m*uring of innu*m*erable bees.

Old English poetry relied chiefly on alliteration:

> *w*adan *w*raeclastas: *w*yrd bith ful araed.

The wanderer "wades the paths of exile: fate is completely inexorable."

Alliterative Revival. The outburst of ALLITERATIVE VERSE that occurred in the second half of the fourteenth century in west and northwest England. Prominent are the four poems of the Gawain Poet, including *Sir Gawain and the Green Knight* and *Pearl*, and William Langland's *Piers Plowman*. See MIDDLE ENGLISH LITERATURE.

Alliterative Romance. A METRICAL ROMANCE in ALLITERATIVE VERSE. Among those that formed a part of the ALLITERATIVE REVIVAL in the second half of the fourteenth century are *William of Palerne* and two from the Arthurian cycle, *Sir Gawain and the Green Knight*, in which stanzas of varying numbers of long alliterative lines conclude with five short rhyming lines, and an alliterative *Morte Arthure* (c. 1360).

Alliterative Verse.   Verse using ALLITERATION on stressed syllables for its fundamental structure. In Old and Middle English, the essential pattern was four stresses to the line, with two, three, or four stresses alliterating and unstressed syllables not counted: "In a summer season, when soft was the sun" (*Piers Plowman*). Ordinarily, alliterative verse did not rhyme, but in the thirteenth and fourteenth centuries it was sometimes combined with rhyme, as in Layamon's *Brut* and the Gawain Poet's *Sir Gawain and the Green Knight* and *Pearl*. In Chaucer and in most other poets in English since the fourteenth century, the usual verse structure has been ACCENTUAL/SYLLABIC VERSE, with rhyme common and alliteration less prominent. See OLD ENGLISH VERSIFICATION.

Allonym.   The name of an actual person adopted as a PSEUDONYM or NOM DE PLUME, as if one were to write letters to the editor signed "Ovid." The term also refers to a work written under an allonym.

Allusion.   A meaningful reference, direct or indirect, as when Yeats writes, "Another Troy must rise and set," calling to the reader's mind the whole tragic history of Troy; or when Shakespeare's Falstaff alludes to the biblical "Dives who lived in purple" to describe the color of Bardolf's face; or when T. S. Eliot in *The Waste Land*, with a cryptic "To Carthage then I came/ Burning," calls up the young St. Augustine's wayward life. See PARADIORTHOSIS.

Almanac.   An annual book forecasting weather and providing lists and tables for astronomy, tides, holidays, and other useful information (from Spanish Arabic *al*, "the," plus *manakh*, "weather"). The medieval almanac was a permanent astrological table. Then came calendars predicting weather, wars, and plagues for several years; then annuals, particularly for farmers. The seventeenth century added coarse jokes, and eventually helpful aphorisms. Harvard College published the earliest American almanac, its first book: *An Almanack for the Year of Our Lord 1639. Calculated for New England. By Mr. William Pierce, Mariner.* Benjamin Franklin's famous *Poor Richard's Almanack*, published under the name of "Richard Saunders" in Philadelphia (1733–1757), is sometimes erroneously thought to be America's first. Following an anonymous facetious English almanac, *Poor Robin* (beginning about

1661), Franklin spoofs predictions and includes witty maxims and homey philosophy. From the mid-eighteenth to the mid-nineteenth centuries, the French *Almanach des Muses* and such German imitators as *Musenalmanach* published the best contemporary poetry. The *Almanach de Gotha,* originating in 1763, summarized the noble families of Europe with additional administrative and political data. Many believe that *The Farmer's Almanac,* beginning in 1793, still beats the Weather Bureau. Since 1868, the annual *World Almanac and Book of Facts* has provided a wealth of data—population of states and nations, rainfall, world leaders, best sellers, automotive production—on almost everything under the sun.

Altar Poem.   Another name for SHAPED POEM.

Ambiguity.   Something suggesting multiple meanings (from Latin *ambigere,* "to wander around, be uncertain"). Unintentional ambiguity bedevils all writing, as in *She held him still,* which can mean either "yet" or "quiet." But literary ambiguity concentrates meanings. Shakespeare, for instance, in his sonnet "When in disgrace with Fortune," first writes of the *state,* or situation, of being an outcast, then of a *state* of mind, then concentrates these two meanings, together with two others, in a magnificent concluding pun:

> For thy sweet love remembered such wealth brings
> That then I scorn to change my *state* with kings.

In the fourfold ambiguity of *state,* the speaker declares that he would now change neither his impoverished and alienated condition nor his state of mind for any monarch's kingdom (national state) and all his pomp and glory as he sits in state.

William Empson has distinguished *Seven Types of Ambiguity* (1931) that add "some nuance to the direct statement of prose": (1) language simultaneously effective in several ways; (2) differing meanings an author finally resolves into one; (3) one word with two apparently unrelated meanings; (4) alternative meanings that illuminate an author's complex feelings; (5) an ambiguous simile, a "fortunate confusion," that shows the author discovering an idea; (6) contradictions or irrelevancies that force readers to interpretation; (7) a contradiction revealing an author's ambivalence. *Multiple meanings* and PLURISIGNATION are synonyms for ambiguity. See AMPHIBOLOGY.

Ambivalence.   Conflicting feelings about something, such as revulsion and fascination, hate and love. The term was coined by Freud. An **AMBIGUITY** may reveal an author's ambivalence.

American Academy and Institute of Arts and Letters. An organization of 250 writers, composers, and artists, elected by the membership for outstanding creative work. It contains an inner Academy of 50 chairs, held for life, election to which is America's highest honor in literature and the arts.

In 1898, the American Social Science Association organized the 250-member National Institute of Arts and Letters. In 1904, the institute organized the American Academy of Arts and Letters, to be elected only from Institute membership. The first 7, who then chose others until the expanding group had elected 50, were, in descending order of votes, William Dean Howells, Augustus Saint-Gaudens, Edmund Clarence Stedman, John LaFarge, Mark Twain, John Hay, and Edward McDowell.

In 1913, an act of Congress, signed by President Taft, incorporated and chartered the Institute. In 1976, the Institute and Academy merged under a single board of directors, adopting its present name. The Academy-Institute annually gives 17 awards of $5000 each; a number of fellowships to young writers, composers, and artists; 13 other named awards, 2 Gold Medals for distinguished achievement; another occasional medal for excellence in speech on the stage, television, or radio; and, every 5 years, the William Dean Howells medal for distinction in American fiction, of which William Faulkner, Eudora Welty, and John Cheever have been recipients. Others among the Academy members are Saul Bellow, Leonard Bernstein, Ralph Ellison, Lillian Hellman, Arthur Miller, Georgia O'Keeffe, Isaac Bashevis Singer, John Updike (also Secretary of the Academy), Robert Penn Warren, and E. B. White.

American Indian Literature. The literature of the earliest inhabitants of North and South America, sometimes called Amerind literature or Native American literature. Prior to the arrival of Europeans in America, most tribal lore was preserved orally, since only the Aztecs and Mayas possessed more than a rudimentary written language. As early as the sixteenth century, native Mexican literature was recorded in native languages by means of Latin script and also in Latin and Spanish by Spanish missionaries and by Indians educated in Spanish schools. This pattern was later repeated in Central and South America and in the British and French settlements to the north. As a result, American Indian literature is polyglot, recorded in many native languages in writing systems brought from Europe, as well as in the European languages, especially Spanish, French, and English, that Indians learned early and have now spoken for several centuries.

Its mixed linguistic and cultural history suggests division of Indian literature (including literature about Indians) into three categories: (1) interpretations of Indians in the words of non-Indians; (2) written records of the Indian oral heritage; (3) adaptations of traditional materials and original creative works by Indians.

For Europeans and Americans of European descent, non-Indian interpretations came first and have remained popular. At first, they were speculative, as in Montaigne's essay "Cannibals," (1580) or historical, as in the Spanish accounts that form the basis for Prescott's *History of the Conquest of Mexico* (1843). The CAPTIVITY NARRATIVE, such as Mary Rowlandson's account of her twelve weeks with the followers of King Philip, formed a popular seventeenth-century GENRE. In the nineteenth century, Cooper portrayed the Indian character in the *Leather-Stocking* series and other novels, and Longfellow interpreted legend and poetry in *The Song of Hiawatha*. Later in the century, the German novelist Karl May helped keep European interest alive with *Winnetou* and other adventure stories. In POPULAR LITERATURE and the movies, the Indian became stereotyped in a few roles, the Apache attacking the settlers, Tonto faithfully serving the Lone Ranger. In recent decades, works such as Gary Snyder's *Myths and Texts* (1960) and David Wagoner's *Who Shall Be the Sun* (1978) have arisen from an increasingly sympathetic response to the richness of Indian lore.

Compared with these views from external perspectives, the traditional poems, tales, and orations of the American Indian, as recorded from oral presentation, have had small circulation, although they exist in numbers that place them with the richest cultural remains of any tribal people. In English, the most extensive collections are found in the *Reports* and *Bulletin* of the Bureau of American Ethnology. Good examples, suggestive of the range, are Washington Matthews, "The Mountain Chant: A Navajo Ceremony," BAE, 5th *Annual Report* (1887); James Mooney, "Sacred Formulas of the Cherokees," BAE, 7th *Annual Report* (1891); Jeremiah Curtin and J. N. B. Hewitt, "Seneca Fiction, Legends, and Myths," BAE, 32d *Annual Report* (1918); Frances Densmore, "Papago Music," BAE, *Bulletin 90* (1929), and Francis La Flesche, "The Osage Tribe: Rite of the Wa-Xó-Be," BAE, 45th *Annual Report* (1930). Prominent among earlier efforts is Henry Rowe Schoolcraft's rendition of the tales of the Algonquian culture hero Manabozho, in his *Algic Researches* (1839).

Within recent years, Indians have become increasingly active in interpreting their folk materials in English for general readers and in creating a new literature by Indians that reflects both the Indian heritage and the Indian's place in contemporary society. Prominent in this effort are Vine Deloria, Jr.; N. Scott Momaday; and James Welch.

References

Gordon Brotherstone, **Image of the New World: The American Continent Portrayed in Native Texts** (1979).
A. Grove Day, **The Sky Clears: Poetry of the American Indians** (1951).
Thomas E. Sanders and Walter W. Peek, **Literature of the American Indian** (1973).
Brian Swann, ed., **Smoothing the Ground: Essays on Native American Oral Literature** (1983).
Stith Thompson, ed., **Tales of the North American Indians** (1929).
Alan R. Velie, ed., **American Indian Literature: An Anthology** (1979).
Shirley Hill Witt and Stan Steiner, eds., **The Way: An Anthology of American Indian Literature** (1972).

American Language (or American English). The language of the United States, with those idioms and intonations that distinguish it from the language of England—its origin—and from that of Canada. The three (excluding French Canadian) are all "English," though each has evolved its characteristics of vocabulary, phrasing, intonation, its typical slang, its regional and ethnic dialects.

In the U.S.A., Americans have retained some forms from their colonial forebears that England has dropped: gotten for got, and "attitude *toward*" for "attitude *to*." Americans pronounce closer to the written letter than the British, tending to enunciate every letter of *extraordinary*, for instance, as against the Britisher's *strórdnr*. The Britisher's *got* and *that* tend to disappear in the throat, so that the modern Londoner sounds like the traditional Scot saying, "Will y' na' come back again." Americans keep those final *t*'s. Virginians even retain something of the old Anglos-Saxon *u* ("oo") in words like *mouse* and *house*, which they pronounce something like "muhoos" and "huhoos."

Many such speechways reflect the region of England, and sometimes the historical period, from which the American colonists came. But since most groups of colonists included people from different Anglo-Saxon dialectical areas, the reasons for Maine's saying *pail* and Pennsylvania's saying *bucket*, for example, remain obscure. *Pail* comes from Anglo-Saxon; *bucket*, from Norman French, 500 years later. Something in that Down East Maine personality reached farther back and endured. But these differences demonstrate how any language, or dialect, will develop independently in regions not consistently communicating with one another. So an American's car has a *hood;* a Britisher's, a *bonnet.* One buys *gas;* the other purchases *petrol. Two-lane traffic* is a *dual carriageway;* an *overpass,* a *flyover;* a *drugstore,* a *chemist's shop. Corn,* in England, is wheat, or any grain; in America, it's on the cob, or is something generally rural and *corny.* And an American's *crotch* is a Britisher's *crutch.*

American English has been highly inventive, and highly absorptive of words from its many ethnic backgrounds. Many Americanisms have gone back to England and around the world. *O.K.,* arising from the Boston newspapers' humorously mispelled "oll korrect" in the 1830s, is probably the world's most universal word. Thomas Jefferson invented *belittle.* Benjamin Russell, newspaper editor, invented *gerrymander* when, in 1912, the Massachusetts legislature, under Governor Elbridge Gerry, rearranged electoral districts so that one of them looked like a salamander. *Cocktail, jackpot, know-how, fizzle, bingo,* and *honk* are all American innovations, as are most of our terms of racial contempt, like *honky,* first applied (in the form *bohunk,* "Bohemian-Hungarian") to Hungarian laborers by established whites, now a term of contempt sometimes used by blacks to refer to whites of any national background.

The most curious thing about American English is the marked difference in pronunciation between New England and the South, though they both remain somewhat nearer England than the rest of the country in dropping the final *r.* New England and the South were settled by people from the old East Anglian region—southeastern England, including London. America's middle coastal area—New Jersey, Delaware, Maryland, Pennsylvania, which generally stretched westward to the Pacific and northwest—came mostly from more northern English regions, where the *r* stayed hard, or even trilled. Consequently, most Americans say *water,* not *watah.*

But New England and the South soon differed in pronunciation. New England tended to nasalize under the influence of Puritan sermonizing. Jonathan Swift gives his ridiculous Calvinist preacher a tongue so subtle "that he could twist it up into his nose, and deliver a strange kind of speech from thence" (*A Tale of a Tub,* XI, 1710), and in 1770 an English visitor reports a "whining cadence" in New England speech (Pyles, p. 241). Contrarily, Southern speech seems to have mellowed.

Some attribute this mellowing to a languid climate and aristocratic leisure. But the greatest distinction between North and South was a large population, frequently a huge majority, of African slaves. Deliberately assorted from different tribes to deprive them of a common language and minimize revolt on shipboard and ashore, slaves, along with their masters, evolved a Pidgin English and eventually a Plantation Creole, with traces of earlier Pidgin Portuguese, like *pickaninny*, *savvy*, and *Negro*. Slaves who escaped to islands offshore South Carolina, Georgia, and Florida developed from the pidgins of Portuguese and English and their native African an independent Creole known as Gullah, which in turn put many Africanisms into BLACK ENGLISH, then into general American usage: *jazz*, most notably, and *tote*, *gumbo*, *buckaroo*, *banjo*, *okra*, *juke*, *bozo*, *voodoo*, and probably other special usages like *man*, *hip*, *hep*, and *cat*.

Thus, even as blacks were acquiring English, and secretly learning to read and write, some of their idioms and intonations were tempering the speech of their white masters. Whites, when giving orders, would imitate blacks to make themselves understood, and some of that imitation eventually remained. Even more significant was the black mammy, and her children, with whom white children spent much of their time from cradle onward. William Faulkner's short story "That Evening Sun" illustrates the process. Conversely, Southern vowels were changing in ways unrelated to West African, Caribbean, or Gullah, and blacks were acquiring them from the white community. From the first, the early pidgins and Plantation Creole moved steadily over toward the evolving American English and moved outward to virtually every state in the union. The dual process continues from coast to coast, as whites pick up black idioms and intonations, and blacks take in the shared standard usages of the daily news. The large Spanish-speaking population of the Southwest, and more recently of New York and Florida and many agricultural areas, remains largely bilingual.

From colonial times, England's cultural priority led Americans to deny any difference in their language. But in 1919, H. L. Mencken finally made the differences a matter of fact, and even of pride, in his *American Language*, which he enlarged until the fourth edition in 1936 and then added two supplements (1946, 1949). George P. Krapp of Columbia University followed Mencken with his more scholarly *English Language in America* (1925). From 1936 to 1943, Sir William Craigie and J. R. Hulbert issued *A Dictionary of American English on Historical Principles*. Milford M. Matthews's *Dictionary of Americanisms* (1951) added colloquial detail. Hans Kurath's monumental *Linguistic Atlas of the United States* (1939–1943) worked out and displayed, with a distinguished team of researchers, the historical progress of American English.

Beginning with James Fenimore Cooper's *The Spy* (1821), American literature began to turn American idiom to account. Whitman's *Leaves of Grass* (1855) lifted it to international stature. In his "Explanatory" note introducing *Huckleberry Finn* (1884), Twain calls attention to his seven American dialects, from "Missouri negro" through "the extremest form of backwoods South-Western" to "Pike-County" with four other modifications, not mentioning the several levels of educated idiom that help to set his magnificent irony before the reader. Salinger's *Catcher in the Rye* (1951) did much the same with adolescent American slang. Ernest Hemingway, Richard Wright, Ralph Ellison, and, particularly, William Faulkner have orchestrated unlettered dialect with learned elegance to exploit the full range of American English, lifting it to worldwide recognition and the Noble Prize.

References

J. L. Dillard, **Black English** (1972).
Albert H. Marckwardt, **American English** (1958).
Thomas Pyles, **Words and Ways of American English** (1952).

American Literature. The literature of the United States from the colonial period to the present.

The Colonies, 1609–1776. The literature of the American colonies was largely utilitarian. Like the early literature of British colonies around the world (see CANADIAN LITERATURE; COMMONWEALTH LITERATURE), it was frequently descriptive of conditions of life in the new country, providing records of hardships and triumphs for those who remained at home and histories to enlighten future generations. It was often heavily religious, especially in New England, where Puritan zeal provided an impetus toward settlement and controlled most governmental and social structures for many generations. No literary geniuses emerged within the first century and a half, and few authors attempted any bellestristic writing, but there were many who wrote clearly and intelligently of a fascinating time.

Plymouth and Massachusetts Bay were also especially fortunate in possessing early governors who were also careful historians. William Bradford's *History of Plymouth Plantation* and John Winthrop's journal, published as *The History of New England from 1630 to 1649,* are readable first-hand accounts by men of great influence. Later, Cotton Mather's *Wonders of the Invisible World* (1693), on witchcraft, and *Magnalia Christi Americana* (1702), a history, contain some brilliant passages, along with much that is ponderous and pedantic. Private diarists and observers include, in New England, Samuel Sewall and Sarah Kemble Knight, and, in Virginia, William Byrd, whose secret diaries provide valuable insights into a plantation life far removed from the Puritanic obsessions to the north. *A Narrative of the Captivity and Restoration of Mrs. Mary Rowlandson* (1682), by a Massachusetts woman carried off in King Philip's War, is a fine example of a once-popular GENRE. Jonathan Edwards (1730–1758), whose sermons spawned the GREAT AWAKENING, was America's first great theologian, less read now in his theological treaties *The Freedom of the Will* (1754) than in sermons such as "A Divine and Supernatural Light" and "Sinners in the Hands of an Angry God." John Woolman's *Journal* (1774) is a classic of Quaker writing and of autobiography, preserving in forthright prose the thoughts of an exemplar of one of the important non-Puritan strains in American life. Just before the Revolution, St. Jean de Crèvecoeur gathered the material for his portrayal of "a land of happy farmers" in his *Letters from an American Farmer* (1782).

Among poets in this early period, Anne Bradstreet (1612?–1672) was first, with some memorable domestic and religious lyrics. Edward Taylor (1645?–1729), later and more accomplished, left his mostly religious poems in manuscript, where they remained until published over two hundred years after his death, acclaimed then for their affinities with the verse of Donne and Herbert. Phillis Wheatley (1754?–1784), a slave born in Africa, published at 19 her *Poems on Various Subjects*.

The Revolution and the New Nation, 1776–1820. For the first half century after 1776, American literature was tinged with the colors of political and intellectual revolution, as well as exploratory of the literary possibilities of the new country. Thomas Paine's *Common Sense* (1776) was a ringing call for a "Declaration for Independence" six months before Jefferson's famous draft. Paine's *American Crisis* (1776–1783) bolstered the morale of Washington's sometimes faltering army. His *Age of Reason* (1794–1795) is a classic of DEISM. The multitalented Benjamin Franklin wrote brilliant satires and light, occasional pieces (his "Bagatelles"), and left in his *Autobiography* one of the finest examples of that GENRE. Washington, Jefferson, Hamilton, and Madison all wrote distinguished political prose, the last two especially in *The Federalist* (1787–1788), essays presenting the case for the central governmental control outlined in the Constitution. In poetry, Philip Freneau's patriotic verse made his reputation, and his later nature poems established him as the best American poet prior to William Cullen Bryant. Other poets of the period include Joel Barlow and the other CONNECTICUT WITS, patriots and satirists. Belles-lettres in addition to poetry emerged in Royall Tyler's comedy *The Contrast* (1787), extolling plain American virtues over British artificialities, and in Charles Brockden Brown's novels, uniting abnormal psychology and American scenery in a gothic mixture impressive to European novelists, including Scott. Best are *Wieland* (1798) and *Edgar Huntly* (1799). Westward exploration is memorably recorded in the *Original Journals of the Lewis and Clark Expedition, 1804–1806*, which were not completely published until a century later. Washington Irving shortly embarked on a more literary exploration, first of the Dutch heritage of New York in his comic *History of New York* (1809), and then of the possibilities of the American short story or tale, in his hands a naturalized hybrid, as in "Rip Van Winkle" and "The Legend of Sleepy Hollow" in *The Sketch Book* (1820).

The Romantic Temper, 1820–1865. The Sketch Book inaugurated the first great period of American literature, an "American Renaissance" as F. O. Matthiessen called it, by analogy with the creative explosion of the English Renaissance. Bryant's first collection, *Poems*, appeared in 1821. After two earlier novels, James Fenimore Cooper began the *Leather-Stocking* series with *The Pioneers* in 1823. Before the end of the decade, Edgar Allan Poe had published his first poems, and his tales and those of Nathaniel Hawthorne began to appear in 1832. Ralph Waldo Emerson's "The American Scholar" in 1837 sounded a ringing call for literary independence from Europe. A year earlier he had provided American TRANSCENDENTALISM a substantial foundation with *Nature* (1836), and his *Essays* (1841), *Essays: Second Series* (1844), and *Poems* (1847) soon followed. Meanwhile, he kept up the journals and voluminous correspondence accepted as a major part of his work by later scholars. Other New England poets of the period included Henry Wadsworth Longfellow, John Greenleaf Whittier, Oliver Wendell Holmes, and James Russell Lowell, all gifted versifiers whose poems were often heavily narrative and didactic. Popular, long-lived humanitarians, they established reputations prior to the Civil War, lived and wrote long after, and set the dominant tone of American poetry until well into the twentieth century. A poet better known for his prose, Henry David Thoreau lived in some ways the life Emerson preached, leaving as monuments to individualism "Civil Disobedience" (1849) and *Walden* (1854). Following Cooper, the great romantic novels of the period, also monuments to individual genius, were those of Hawthorne and Herman Melville, in particular *The Scarlet Letter* (1850) and *Moby-Dick* (1851). And in 1855, with the publication of the first edition of Walt Whitman's *Leaves of Grass*, American poetic Romanticism attained a height that was also a new beginning for poetry. *Leaves of Grass*, however, was not complete until the 1891–1892 edition, and not fully appreciated until many years later.

Serious interest in the American Indians and their literature emerged in this period (see AMERICAN INDIAN LITERATURE), and, in a related development, concern for the unique quality of the American experience produced distinguished historical writing: William Hickling Prescott's *History of the Conquest of Mexico* (1843) and Francis Parkman's *Oregon Trail* (1849) and *History of the Conspiracy of Pontiac* (1851).

Besides the generally Romantic work of the most acclaimed novelists, fiction made some tentative strivings toward REALISM, usually with a humorous or sentimental coloring, in the colloquial humor of Augustus Baldwin Longstreet and George Washington Harris and in Harriet Beecher Stowe's New England stories, eclipsed in fame by her *Uncle Tom's Cabin* (1852). Slavery and the Civil War prompted a vast literature, including, besides much by writers already mentioned, Abraham Lincoln's memorable addresses and the autobiography of the escaped slave Frederick Douglass.

Realism and Naturalism, 1865–1920. After the Civil War, strains of realism and NATURALISM largely replaced the earlier Romantic and transcendental exuberance, but the New England poets were still writing and still popular, Whitman was greatly expanding his *Leaves of Grass*, and Emily Dickinson was quietly composing the brilliant, highly individualistic poems that gained her recognition years after her death. Until the turn of the century, the major novelists were William Dean Howells, Mark Twain, and Henry James, exponents of realism whose works demonstrated the slippery nature of the term and its uneasy alliance with earlier Romance and later naturalism. Stephen Crane, Frank Norris, and Theodore Dreiser introduced naturalism to American literature around the turn of the century and were followed by Upton Sinclair, the MUCKRAKERS, and Jack London. After 1900, the realistic tradition continued in the fiction of Edith Wharton, Willa Cather, and Ellen Glasgow. Most novelists after the Civil War were also short story writers, with the form proving especially useful for such LOCAL COLOR writers as Bret Harte, George Washington Cable, Joel Chandler Harris, Sarah Orne Jewett, Kate Chopin, and Mary E. Wilkins Freeman. Established in the nineteenth century, the American short story continued to develop in the twentieth, toward clever plot contrivance in the stories of O. Henry, and toward psychology and subjectivity in Sherwood Anderson's *Winesburg, Ohio* (1919) and later collections. Other prose was as varied and idiosyncratic as Henry Adam's autobiographical *Education of Henry Adams* (1907) and Gertrude Stein's fictional *Three Lives* (1909).

Poetry in most of these years fared less well than prose. In the early period, besides Dickinson and those poets who had begun their careers before the Civil War, Sidney Lanier remains almost alone among poets of note. Stephen Crane published his few poems in the 1890s. William Vaughn Moody was a successful poet and verse dramatist in the first decade of the new century. Only after 1912 did a number of conditions, including the founding in Chicago of Harriet Monroe's journal *Poetry: A Magazine of Verse*, come together to produce the poetic renaissance apparent in the next few years in major books by Robert Frost, Vachel Lindsay, Ezra Pound, Edgar Lee Masters, Edwin Arlington Robinson, Carl Sandburg, and T. S. Eliot.

As the body of American literature grew larger and more varied, blacks continued their contributions in the stories of Charles W. Chesnutt and the poems of Paul Laurence Dunbar, as well as in their considerable influence after the Civil War on the rapidly growing corpus of native FOLK SONG.

Modern American Literature, 1920–1960. Transatlantic literary currents, rapid changes at home, and the shock of two world wars combined to produce a period of vastly increased literary activity, initiated by the modern masters whose work first received public acclaim in the 1920s. T. S. Eliot's *Waste Land* (1922) and other poems culminating in *The Four Quartets* (1943), together with the appearance of Ezra Pound's *Cantos* in installments throughout the period, went far to establish the allusive, intellectual qualities that dominated American poetry into the 1950s. The genius of Wallace Stevens and William Carlos Williams was at first much less widely appreciated, but by the 1950s both began to be perceived as major poets with visions markedly different from those of Pound and Eliot. Robert Frost continued throughout the period as a popular and critically acclaimed narrative and lyric poet, a master of metaphor and meter. A host of other poets wrote sometimes brilliantly in a variety of voices. Especially notable in the earlier generation were Elinor Wylie, Hilda Doolittle, Robinson Jeffers, Marianne Moore, John Crowe Ransom, Conrad Aiken, Archibald MacLeish, Edna St. Vincent Millay, E. E. Cummings, Hart Crane, and Allen Tate. Among their juniors, whose work emerged as significant largely in the 1940s and 1950s, were Richard Eberhart, Theodore Roethke, Elizabeth Bishop, Delmore Schwartz, Randall Jarrell, Robert Lowell, and Richard Wilbur. In an atmosphere of heightened literary awareness, LITTLE MAGAZINES flourished, black literature enjoyed the exhilaration of the HARLEM RENAISSANCE, and writers formed social and literary alliances such as that of the FUGITIVES.

The best novels and short stories of the early giants, F. Scott Fitzgerald, Ernest Hemingway, and William Faulkner, belong mostly to the two decades between the wars. Their work, a blend of the Romantic, realistic, and naturalistic strains of earlier periods of American literature, but touched by individual genius and the modern spirit evident in Great Britain in the novels of James Joyce and D. H. Lawrence, inspired others both in America and abroad. Other distinguished writers of fiction who established reputations prior to the end of World War II include Sinclair Lewis, John Dos Passos, Thomas Wolfe, John Steinbeck, James T. Farrell, Robert Penn Warren, Richard Wright, and Eudora Welty. Common to most was a strong sense of region, of social consciousness, and of fiction as both an artistic and persuasive instrument. After the war, a new generation emerged, including in its ranks two European immigrants of genius, Vladimir Nabokov and Isaac Bashevis Singer; the Canadian-born Saul Bellow; and also John Cheever, Ralph Ellison, Bernard Malamud, J. D. Salinger, Norman Mailer, James Baldwin, and Flannery O'Connor. The multicultural background of American literature was now more apparent than ever.

In the theater, Eugene O'Neill in the 1920s and 1930s wrote the first American plays to set beside those of the great theatrical traditions of other countries. Other fine playwrights appeared, notably, in the earlier decades, Maxwell Anderson, Elmer Rice, Thornton Wilder, and Lillian Hellman, and, toward the end of the period, Tennessee Williams and Arthur Miller.

American Literature Since 1960. Writers who emerged after 1960 inherited a stronger American literary tradition than belonged to any earlier generation. Some of their work represents a continuation of that tradition, especially as it has been marked by modernism, but much is an attempt to extend or rebel against it, in the ways that distinguish the international POST-MODERN PERIOD.

Beginning their work a decade earlier, the writers of the BEAT GENERATION and the BLACK MOUNTAIN SCHOOL came to prominence with the publication of Allen Ginsberg's *Howl* (1956) and Jack Kerouac's *On The Road* (1957) and influenced many younger writers. The plays of Edward Albee brought the THEATER OF THE ABSURD into American literature in the 1960s. Markedly personal or CONFESSIONAL POETRY emerged as Robert Lowell, the most important poet of his generation, gave sanction to a movement already underway when he turned toward private materials and open forms in *Life Studies* (1959) and later volumes. John Berryman, Anne Sexton, Adrienne Rich, and Sylvia Plath are outstanding among other poets of intimate content. Also prominent among recent poets are William Stafford, Howard Nemerov, Denise Levertov, James Dickey, A. R. Ammons, Robert Bly, James Merrill, W. D. Snodgrass, John Ashbery, Galway Kinnell, W. S. Merwin, James Wright, Gary Snyder, and Imamu Amiri Baraka (LeRoi Jones).

Among recent writers of fiction, John Updike stands out as the great traditionalist. Others are frequently experimental, as in the widely varied work of Joyce Carol Oates and John Gardner, ranging from naturalism to Romantic fantasy, or the extravagant and comic inventions of John Barth and Philip Roth. BLACK HUMOR emerges frequently in the work of many writers, including Joseph Heller and Kurt Vonnegut. Fiction and nonfiction merge in the later work of Truman Capote and Norman Mailer. The conventions of traditional fiction are parodied or subverted by Thomas Pynchon, Donald Barthelme, and Robert Coover. Meanwhile, more traditional approaches to fiction continue in the work of writers more recently emerging, among them Toni Morrison, Anne Tyler, and Tim O'Brien.

See AFRO-AMERICAN LITERATURE.

References

Clarence Gohdes and Sanford E. Marovitz, **Bibliographical Guide to the Study of the Literature of the U.S.A.,** 5th ed. (1984).

James D. Hart, **The Oxford Companion to American Literature,** 5th ed. (1983).

George Perkins, Sculley Bradley, Richmond Croom Beatty, and E. Hudson Long, eds., **The American Tradition in Literature,** 6th ed. (1985).

Arthur Hobson Quinn, ed., **The Literature of the American People** (1951).

Robert E. Spiller and others, eds., **Literary History of the United States,** 4th ed. (1974).

Amerind Literature.   See AMERICAN INDIAN LITERATURE.

Amphibology.   A cryptic and ambiguous statement, as when in *Macbeth* the Apparition says, "none of woman born/ Shall harm Macbeth" indicating that Macduff, delivered by caesarian section, will kill him.

Amphibrach.   A Greek and Roman foot, rare in English: $- \smile -$. It is sometimes missapplied to the FEMININE ENDING of a pentameter line:

$$\text{. . . all things } || \overset{\smile \;-\; \smile}{\text{despising}}$$

$$\text{. . . at dawn } || \overset{\smile \;-\; \smile}{\text{ar is ing}}$$

See METER.

Amphigory. A piece of NONSENSE VERSE, usually a BURLESQUE or PARODY.

Amphimacer. A Greek and Roman three-syllable foot going $-\;\smile\;-$. See METER.

Amplification. A restatement of something more fully and in more detail, especially in oratory, poetry, and music.

Ana. (1) A suffix meaning a collection of sayings, gossip, or other material relating to a person or place, as, for example, *Shakespeariana*. (2) A noun standing for a similar collection. Southey called Boswell's *Johnson* "the *ana* of all *anas*."

Anachronism. Something out of its proper place in time. Anachronisms are sometimes employed intentionally for humor, but occur also in places where no humor is intended, as in Shakespeare's references to clocks in *Julius Caesar* or Scott's references to Shakespeare in *Kenilworth*.

Anacoenosis. A heightening of style as if in urgent consultation with the audience, with frequent RHETORICAL QUESTIONS.

> If I be a father, where is my honor? If I be a master, where is my fear?
> *Mal. 1.6*

Anacoluthon. "Not following." A shift in midsentence, or an incompleted sentence—with rhetorical effect when honored with the term: *He couldn't go, how could he?* Much dramatic writing employs it, as in Shakespeare's song:

> The white sheet bleaching on the hedge—
>   With heigh! the sweet birds, O, how they sing!
> Doth set my pugging tooth on edge. . . .

See APOSIOPESIS.

Anacreontic Verse. Verse after the manner of the Greek poet Anacreon (sixth century B.C.), whose *Anacreontics* is a collection of about sixty short lyrics celebrating wine, women, and song. Thomas Moore translated them as *Odes of Anacreon* (1800).

Anacrusis. One or two additional unstressed syllables prefixed to lines regularly beginning with a stress, as italicized below:

> Tell me where is fancy bred,
> *Or* in the heart or in the head?
> How begot, how nourishèd?
>   *Shakespeare*

> Lost in a haunted wood,
> Children afraid of the night
> *Who have* never been happy or good.
>   *W. H. Auden, "September 1, 1939"*

See METER.

Anadiplosis. Repetition, at or near the beginning of a phrase, of a word from the end of the preceding phrase:

Learn as though you would *live* forever; *live* as though you would die tomorrow.

> Adam lay *iboundyn,*
> *Boundyn* in a bond

Anagnorisis. The Greek term for DISCOVERY or RECOGNITION used by Aristotle in his *Poetics;* from the *anagnorisis* comes the PERIPETEIA, or REVERSAL of fortune. See PLOT; TRAGEDY.

Anagogical Meaning. The spiritual or mystical truth of a work, universal and enduring, one of the FOUR SENSES OF INTERPRETATION in the Middle Ages.

Anagogy (or Anagoge). Spiritual or mystical interpretation leading to ANAGOGICAL MEANING. Anagogy is especially connected with religion. In biblical criticism, for example, it provides the foundation by which events in the Old Testament may be considered as prefiguring events in the New. Similarly, the events of pre-Christian history may be given a mystical significance that unites them with the later history of the Christian church. See FOUR SENSES OF INTERPRETATION; POLYSEMOUS MEANING; TYPOLOGY.

Anagram. A word or phrase made by rearranging the letters of another. *Dame* is an anagram for *made; settler,* for *letters.* An anagram reading the same backward and forward is a PALINDROME.

Analects (or Analecta). Collections of literary sayings or fragments, from a Greek word meaning *gatherings.* An example is the *Analects of Confucius.*

Analogue. A word, episode, story, or plot similar to another. Words in one language frequently have analogues, or cognates, in related languages or dialects: *church, kirk, Kirche*. A story may have analogues in tales from other times and places. The existence of analogues, or parallel story elements, is seldom in itself enough to prove direct influence, but it may, as with words, suggest common ancestry.

Analogy. A comparison between things similar in a number of ways. An analogy is frequently used to explain the unfamiliar by the familiar, as when a camera is compared by analogy to the human eye; strategy in a current armed conflict by analogy to an older struggle already understood; the heart's structure by analogy to a pump's. As a rhetorical device, analogy is sometimes used to justify conclusions logic would not allow, for even in closely analogous situations the differences may be crucial.

The numerous similarities common to analogy tend to differentiate it from SIMILE and METAPHOR, which depend on a few points of similarity in things fundamentally dissimilar. Similes and metaphors, however, are sometimes extended into analogies.

Analysis. A breaking into parts in order to explain the whole or examine the relationship between units. Literary analysis involves an examination of chapters, pages, paragraphs, acts, scenes, stanzas, lines, and words in an effort to understand the author's artistry and its effect on reader or audience. See CRITICISM; *EXPLICATION DE TEXTE*.

Analytical Language. A language that expresses syntax by word order, as in Modern English, as distinguished from a SYNTHETIC LANGUAGE, like Latin or German, that is dependent on inflections.

Analytic Criticism. A consideration of a work in isolation: an analysis of its parts. See CRITICISM.

Anamnesis. A reminder to the audience of former success or catastrophe:

> This is the anniversary of the last recession. Again millions are
> unemployed. Again we are uncertain.

Anapest. A metrical foot going ⌣ ⌣ —. See METER.

Anaphora (also called Epanaphora). The technique of beginning successive clauses, phrases, or lines with the same word:

The voice of the Lord is powerful. The voice of the Lord is full of majestie. The voice of the Lord breaks the cedars.

Psa. 29.4–5

> Laura stretched her gleaming neck,
> Like a rush-embedded swan,
> Like a lily from the beck,
> Like a moonlit poplar branch,
> Like a vessel at the launch
> When the last restraint is gone.
>
> *Christina Rossetti, "Goblin Market"*

Anastrophe.   Greek for "turning backward." The term refers to a reversal of normal word order, often a deliberate stylistic choice but sometimes in poetry a concession to the demands of meter and rhyme. Thomas Lovell Beddoes's "Song by Isbrand" begins

> Squats on a toad-stool under a tree
> A bodiless childfull of life in the gloom. . . .

Less extreme examples include Keats's "Much have I travelled in the realms of gold" and Coleridge's "In Xanadu did Kubla Khan / A stately pleasure-dome decree."

Anathema.   (1) A person or thing cursed or assigned to damnation. (2) A formal denunciation pronounced by the Roman Catholic or Greek church against a person, practice, or doctrine. (3) Any curse.

Anatomy.   Greek for "a cutting up": a dissection, analysis, or systematic study. The term was popular in titles in the sixteenth and seventeenth centuries: Thomas Nash's *Anatomy of Absurdity;* John Lyly's *Euphues: The Anatomy of Wit;* Robert Burton's *Anatomy of Melancholy.*
Recent literary criticism has used the term to signify a particular kind of fiction, adopting the definition given in Northrop Frye's *Anatomy of Criticism:*

> A form of prose fiction, traditionally known as the Menippean or Varronian satire and represented by Burton's *Anatomy of Melancholy,* characterized by a great variety of subject-matter and a strong interest in ideas.

The fictional anatomy differs from the other forms of prose fiction— the NOVEL, ROMANCE, and CONFESSION—by being "extroverted and intellectual." Examples include Swift's *Gulliver's Travels,* Voltaire's *Candide,* and Aldous Huxley's *Brave New World.*

Ancients and Moderns, Quarrel of the. A controversy in France and England boiling up in the 1680s and 1690s as to whether ancient classical or modern writers were superior. Sir Francis Bacon had sounded the new progressive note in his *Advancement of Learning* (1605), which challenged the reverence for the past that was characteristic of medieval and RENAISSANCE thought: "These times are the ancient times, when the world is ancient"—hence modern humans should claim the greater wisdom of experience and age.

The case for the moderns began in France with Charles Perrault's *Parallèles des anciens et des modernes* (1688–1697) and Fontenelle's *Digression sur les anciens et les modernes* (1688). In England, Sir William Temple's *Essay upon the Ancient and Modern Learning* (1690) attacked the idea of progress and the Royal Society (founded in 1660 to promote scientific study) and championed ancient literature. William Wotton answered him in *Reflections upon Ancient and Modern Learning* (1694), stressing the advances of science and showing Temple wrong about the antiquity of Aesop and the *Epistles* of Phalaris (died c. 554 B.C.), a tyrant in Grecian Sicily, which he cited as examples of ancient excellence. Charles Boyle, egged on by Oxford cronies, published an edition of the *Epistles* (1695) to demonstrate their mediocrity and, in passing, attacked Richard Bentley, Royal Librarian at St. James's Library, for discourtesy. Bentley countered with a scholarly demonstration, first in an appendix to the second edition of Wotton's *Reflections* (1697) and then more fully in his famous *Dissertation upon the Epistles of Phalaris* (1699), the cornerstone of modern textual and historical scholarship, that the *Epistles* originated some four centuries after Phalaris's death. Temple's secretary, Jonathan Swift, came to his defense with his playful *Battel Between the Ancient and Modern Books in St. James's Library* (1704). Swift had his uppity moderns claim, as had Francis Bacon in *The Advancement of Learning*, that they are the true ancients, "According to the Modern Paradox," because the world is now older and wiser. The most famous passage in the *Battel* is a debate between the modern spider, who spins everything out of himself from his inner supply of dirt, and the ancient bee, who gathers honey and beeswax from his flights among all the flowers, providing the world with sweetness and light. See PRIMITIVISM.

Android. An artificial human: usually, in SCIENCE FICTION, one made of organic material, as opposed to a mechanical human, or ROBOT. See CYBORG.

Anecdote. From *anékdota,* Greek for "things unpublished." An anecdote is a short narrative, sometimes introduced to give point to a longer work, sometimes presented for its own sake or for its interest in relation to the life of a famous person. Anecdotes are often presented as true, frequently rest on hearsay, and sometimes achieve wide oral circulation before their appearance in print. Focused on single episodes, they lack the careful development of the typical SHORT STORY.

Angels, Orders of. The angelic ranks implied but not specified in the Bible, made more rigid later. Early tradition, fixed especially in *The Divine Hierarchy,* a work attributed to Dionysius the Areopagite (Acts 17.34), specified a hierarchy of nine orders, beginning with the seraphim and cherubim, said to be in the very presence of God, and colored red (seraphim) and blue (cherubim) by medieval painters, suggesting the fire of sun and stars and the blue of the sky. Below these were, in order, thrones, dominions, virtues, powers, principalities, archangels, and angels. But the order is often indefinite, and Milton, for example, seems to have no clear hierarchy in mind. The Old Testament mentions cherubim (especially Gen. 3.24, Ezek. 10) and seraphim (Is. 6.2) and names two archangels, Michael, commanding general of heavenly hosts, and Gabriel, heavenly messenger—who also, as Jibrīl, reveals Allah and the Qur'ān (Koran) to Mohammed. The apocryphal Old Testament names two more: Raphael, the healer, "one of the seven holy angels" (Tobit 12.15), and Uriel, "God's Fire," warden of earth and Hell (II Esdras). Thrones, dominions, powers, and principalities derive from St. Paul's Epistles to the Ephesians (1.21) and Colossians (1.16).

Angevin. See ROYAL HOUSES.

Anglo-Catholic Revival. See OXFORD MOVEMENT.

Anglo-Irish Literature. The literature of English writers living in Ireland, or of Irish writers using English, as most have since the eighteenth century. See IRISH LITERATURE; IRISH RENAISSANCE.

Anglo-Latin Literature. Latin writings in England during Anglo-Saxon and Middle English periods, including religious poems in hexameters, chronicles, scientific treatises, works of theology and law, SAINTS' LIVES, and, in the medieval period, light and satiric verse. Notable works are those of the Venerable Bede (c. 673–735), especially his *Historia Ecclesiastica Gentis Anglorum* (c. 735—"Ecclesiastical History of the English People") and Bishop Asser's *Annales Rerum Ges-*

tarum Alfredi Magni (c. 893—usually known as *The Life of Alfred the Great*). A renaissance of learning after the Norman Conquest brought forth the works of Walter Map (c. 1140–c. 1209), a picaresque figure who ended as archdeacon of Oxford. Map distinguished himself by GOLIARDIC verse and a collection of prose anecdotes, stories, and bright sayings entitled *De Nugis Curialium* (c. 1193–*Courtiers' Trifles*). Geoffrey of Monmouth's *Historia Regum Britanniae* (after 1135—*History of the Kings of Britain*) is known especially as a source for ARTHURIAN LEGEND, and the anonymous thirteenth-century *Gesta Romanorum*, a collection of tales and romances, with morals attached, as a source for many later works, including Chaucer's "Man of Law's Tale" and Shakespeare's *Merchant of Venice*.

Anglo-Norman (Language). The language of upper-class England after the Norman Conquest (1066–1350). It derives from the Norman dialect of French and is also called *Anglo-French* when emphasizing the influence of English idioms. Anglo-Norman literature included treatises, saints' lives, histories, and biographies in prose, and histories, romances, and allegories in verse. Norman French leaves its upper-class imprint on English words like *cordial* as against Anglo-Saxon *hearty* and in other differing pairs: *mansion/house, chamber/room, demand/ask, reply/answer, spirit/ghost, avoid/shun, annual/yearly.* While the Anglo-Saxon peasants herded, in their own language, the lords' *calves, steers, swine,* and *sheep,* and refrained from shooting the *deer,* the Norman lords and ladies dined, in French, on *veal, beef, pork, mutton,* and *venison.* But by the reign of Edward III (1327–1377), even the nobility were speaking English. About 1350, "John Cornwal, maystere of gramere," changed the language of grammar schools from "Freynsch into Englysch." John Gower's *Mirour de l'Omme* (1376—*The Mirror of Man*) is a last, 30,000-line gasp of Anglo-Norman French.

Anglo-Norman Period. The period between 1100 and 1350. Henry I (reigned 1100–1135), William the Conqueror's youngest son, ascended the throne of French-speaking England to introduce a flourishing literary period, of which both his first and second queens were enthusiastic patronesses. Philippe de Thaün, the earliest known Anglo-Norman poet, dedicated his *Bestiary* (c. 1125) to Adelaide of Louvain, Henry's second wife. Henry II (reigned 1154–1189) and his queen, Eleanor of Aquitaine, supported literature and scholarship, both Latin and French, even more energetically. Marie de France dedicated her *Lais* (c. 1175) to Henry; Robert Wace, his *Roman de Brut* (1155) and

Roman de Rou (1161–1174) to Eleanor. Other significant Anglo-Norman poems are the allegorical *Château d'Amour* (c. 1250) by Robert Grosseteste, bishop of Lincoln, and *Manuel des Péchés* (c. 1250), 11,000 lines cataloguing sins, perhaps by one William of Wadington. Robert of Brunne translated the work into English as *Handlyng Synne* (1303), considered one of the liveliest pictures extant of medieval life. Anglo-Norman literature included the FABLIAU and a great number of romances, notably *Gui de Warewic* and *Boeve de Hamtone* (both about 1300), which soon became the immensely popular *Guy of Warwick* and *Bevis of Hampton*. John Gower's latter-day *Mirour de l'Omme* (1376) is the last poem in England in which a French-speaking audience was assumed. Anglo-Norman literature remains in more than 400 texts, ranging from short lyrics to the 22,000-line *Waldef*, an anonymous romance of the twelfth century, and Gower's winning score of 30,000 lines. See ANGLO-NORMAN (LANGUAGE); LAY; ROMANCE.

Anglo-Saxon. The people, culture, and language of the three neighboring tribes—Jutes, Angles, and Saxons—who invaded England, beginning in 449, from the lower part of Denmark's Jutland peninsula, now the Schleswig-Holstein area. The Angles, settling along the eastern seaboard of central and northern England, developed the first literate culture of any Germanic people. Hence England (Angle-land) became the dominant term. Even the West Saxon Alfred the Great called himself *rex Angul-Saxonum* (king of the Anglo-Saxons), and West Saxon writers referred to themselves as *Angelcyn* and their language *Englisc*. Today, *Anglo-Saxon* loosely designates anyone of English derivation. See OLD ENGLISH; OLD ENGLISH LITERATURE; OLD ENGLISH VERSIFICATION.

Angry Young Men. A term applied to a group of writers who appeared in England in the 1950s. Characteristically from lower-class, provincial backgrounds, they directed their anger at the London-centered literary, economic, political, and social structure still prevailing, although already in decline, in the aftermath of World War II. Like the LOST GENERATION and the BEAT GENERATION, they were disillusioned, unable to discover worthwhile causes. Theirs was the world of the ANTI-HERO, of loners out for themselves: "I'm all right, Jack." Never a movement, they were generally not experimental in method, and some denied the applicability of the term to themselves or their works. Leslie Paul's autobiography *Angry Young Man* (1951) provided the name. John Osborne's play *Look Back in Anger* (1956) is usually cited as the paradigmatic work. Other titles include John Wain's *Hurry on Down* (1953), Kingsley Amis's *Lucky Jim* (1954), Colin Wilson's *Outsider* (1956), John Braine's *Room at the Top* (1957), and Alan Sillitoe's *Loneliness of the Long Distance Runner* (1959).

Angst. German for "anxiety" or "anguish." The term is applied sometimes to individual fears, sometimes to the collective anxieties of society since World War II. It is an important element in the literature of EXISTENTIALISM.

Animism. The primitive belief that nonhuman objects like stones, trees, and animals have souls. The concept is distinct from PERSONIFICATION, a consciously imaginative projection of the same concept. More philosophically, the term refers to Pythagoras's and Plato's idea that a soul (*anima*) vitalizes the universe, with its highest consciousness in humans.

Annals. (1) Yearly records of historical events. (2) Papers of a scholarly society, published annually.

Annotation. The addition of notes to a work, in explanation or commentary. An annotated EDITION is one with notes. A VARIORUM EDITION provides the notes of many editors, or else the various readings in different printings of a work. An annotated BIBLIOGRAPHY lists sources and comments upon them.

Annuals. Publications appearing yearly, as, for example, a yearbook published by an ENCYCLOPEDIA: *The Readers' Guide to Periodical Literature* in its annual compilations; and collections of various "bests," such as the *Best American Short Stories* and *Prize Stories: The O. Henry Awards*. Literary annuals were especially popular in nineteenth-century England and America, where they often appeared as GIFT BOOKS, with names like *The Gift, Friendship's Offering,* and *The Token*. In America, gift books provided a stimulus to native productivity, printing writers like Hawthorne and Poe, who had difficulty achieving success in a literary marketplace dominated in their time by writers from England.

Antagonist. In Greek DRAMA, the CHARACTER who opposes the PROTAGONIST, or HERO: therefore, any character who opposes another. In some works, the antagonist is clearly the VILLAIN (Iago in *Othello;* Claggart in *Billy Budd*), but in strict terminology an antagonist is merely an opponent, and may be in the right, like Creon in *Oedipus Rex*. See AGON.

Antanaclasis.   Repetition of a word in a different sense to drive a point home:

> Learn a *craft* to live without *craft.*
> *Care* in your youth so you may live without *care.*

Anthem.   A song of praise and allegiance, especially one officially recognized, like *The Star-Spangled Banner* and *God Save the Queen.* The word comes from Late Greek *antiphonos* through Latin *antiphona* to Old English *antefn* to Middle English *antem,* an antiphonal hymn, or musical responses between priest and choir, with biblical texts, usually from the psalms. See ANTIPHON.

Anthology.   A collection of poems, stories, plays, or other literary pieces by different authors. The term is from Greek and Latin *anthologia,* "a gathering of flowers," after the *Greek Anthology,* a collection of some 4500 poems, inscriptions, and other pieces by 300 writers. The work, dating from about 490 B.C. to A.D. 600, was first collected by Meleager of Gadara about 60 B.C. and called *Stephanos (The Garland),* representing 46 writers with a headnote comparing each to a different flower. The compilation grew through successive editions until the beginning of the tenth century A.D. Other notable anthologies are Tottel's *Miscellany* (1557), containing Wyatt and Surrey; *England's Helicon* (1600), containing Sidney and Spenser; Thomas Percy's *Reliques of Ancient English Poetry* (1765); Palgrave's *Golden Treasury* (1861); and Child's *English and Scottish Popular Ballads* (1883–1898).

Anthropomorphism.   The practice of giving human attributes to animals, plants, rivers, winds, and the like, or to such entities as Grecian urns and abstract ideas. Mythological gods are anthropomorphisms—Zeus with his thunderbolts for natural power, Mercury for swiftness, Athena for wisdom. See PERSONIFICATION.

Antibacchius.   A Greek and Roman foot going − − ◡. See METER.

Anticlimax.   A sudden descent from the impressive to the trivial, especially at the end of an ascending series for ludicrous effect. In *The Rape of the Lock,* Pope constantly and amusingly plays with anticlimax to satirize his heroine's coquettish triviality, as he describes the unknown impending disaster to her hair:

> Whether the Nymph shall break *Diana*'s Law,
> Or some frail *China* Jar receive a flaw,
> Or stain her Honor, or her new Brocade,
> Forget her Pray'rs, or miss a Masquerade,

> Or lose her Heart, or Necklace, at a Ball;
> Or whether Heav'n has doom'd that *Shock* [her lapdog] must fall.

An unintentional anticlimax in a sentence, an essay, or a story can make an author look foolish. See BATHOS.

Anti-Hero. A fictional CHARACTER occupying a central position in the PLOT but possessing qualities antithetical to those of the traditional hero. The anti-hero is not simply a failed hero but a social misfit, graceless, weak, and often comic, the embodiment of ineptitude and bad luck in a world apparently made for others. The term was first applied to such post–World War II characters as Charles Lumley in John Wain's *Hurry On Down* (1953); Jim Dixon in Kingsley Amis's *Lucky Jim* (1954); Sebastian in J. P. Donleavy's *Ginger Man* (1955); Jimmy Porter in John Osborne's play *Look Back in Anger* (1957); and Yossarian in Joseph Heller's *Catch-22* (1961). More recently the anti-hero has been frequent in fiction; earlier, elements of the type may be found in the heroes of *Don Quixote* (1605, 1615) and *Tristram Shandy* (1760–1767) as well as in James Joyce's Leopold Bloom (*Ulysses*, 1922). See ANGRY YOUNG MEN.

Anti-Intellectualism. Distrust of book learning, intellect, reason, and cultivation. In his *Anti-Intellectualism in America* (1969), Richard Hofstadter described the concept as endemic in the United States from the frontier to the present. The twentieth century, insofar as it tends to value feeling, intuition, action, individual experience, and random expression over reason, contemplation, tradition, and order, has been strongly anti-intellectual. Anti-intellectualism can be seen in the eighteenth century's SENTIMENTALISM, in Wordsworth's ROMANTICISM, in POSITIVISM, PRAGMATISM, and UTILITARIANISM.

Antimasque. A coarse comic and parodic interlude, usually by professional dancers. Ben Jonson introduced it into the lofty, delicate matter of his masques, performed by courtly amateurs. See MASQUE.

Antimeria. The use of one part of speech for another: "*Catch* as *catch* can," "*But* me no *buts*," (*Richard II*). *Shelley:* "To *hope* till *hope* creates." Yeats: "Of hammered *gold* and *gold* enamelling." Cummings: "*Anyone* lived in a pretty *how* town." See ENALLAGE.

Antimetabole. The repetition of words in successive phrases in reverse: "One should eat to live, not live to eat" (Molière). See CHIASMUS.

Antinomianism. The belief that Christians are free of the restrictions of moral law, especially as codified in the Old Testament, since faith alone will ensure salvation. The idea was current among the Gnostics (see GNOSTICISM), surfaced at times in the Middle Ages, and was attacked as a heresy by the New England Puritans. Anne Hutchinson was accused of antinomianism when she was expelled from the Massachusetts Bay colony.

Anti-Novel. (1) The French NOUVEAU ROMAN. (2) Any novel that undercuts traditional novelistic conventions and assumptions. The anti-novel has been especially popular in the twentieth century, as writers have frequently attempted to create fictions freed from the constraints of previous expectations concerning technique and subject matter. The desire, of course, goes back much earlier, at least to Laurence Sterne's *Tristram Shandy* (1760–1767).

Antiphon. Part of the liturgy or psalms sung in responses. Medieval drama grew from this musical dialogue. See ANTHEM.

Antiphrasis. Verbal irony—saying the contrary of what is meant; also called *ironia*. See IRONY.

> He was a beauty.
> She is so kind to her friends.
> How thoughtful!

Antiquarianism. Interest in regional antiquities pursued through the study of relics, statuary, coins, inscriptions, manuscripts, and the like. In 1533, Henry VIII sent John Leland as King's Antiquary around England to study and collect old documents. His notes were the nucleus for the Society of Antiquaries (1572–1605), of which Sir Walter Raleigh, John Donne, and Sir Robert Cotton, collector of Old English manuscripts, were members. William Camden (1551–1623), headmaster of Westminster School and the most energetic Elizabethan antiquarian, wrote six successively amplified editions of *Britannia* (1586–1607) and a history of Elizabeth's reign; he also founded and endowed the first chair in history at Oxford. James I, politically suspicious, abolished the Society of Antiquaries, but it was reconstituted in 1717 and chartered in 1751 by George II. Local antiquarians sprang up all over England. The interest in primitive British antiquities, as opposed to the classical ancients, anticipated the Romantic movement and produced Thomas Percy's *Reliques of Ancient English Poetry* (1765); Thomas Chatterton's spurious medieval poems; James Macpherson's equally spurious poems of Ossian, a legendary Gaelic warrior and bard (1760–1763)—see OSSIANIC CONTROVERSY; Thomas Leland's *Longs-*

word (1762); the CELTIC REVIVAL; and such offshoots as the Gothic novel and the general interest in the romantic past. In modern criticism, the term antiquarianism often disparages historical studies that seem to ignore critical and aesthetic problems.

Antirealistic Novel. The fictional counterpart of the twentieth century's Theater of the Absurd, reflecting NIHILISM, EXISTENTIALISM, and alienation in desperately comic fantasies. Samuel Beckett (1906–) is the master of the antirealistic novel with *Molloy* (1951), *Malone Dies* (1956), and *The Unnamable* (1958), paralleling his success on the stage, beginning with *Waiting for Godot* (1952). Franz Kafka (1883–1924) was the significant innovator of antirealistic fiction with nightmarishly realistic stories and his two posthumous masterpieces *The Trial* (1925) and *The Castle* (1926). James Joyce's riotous subconscious Nighttown episode and Molly Bloom's stream-of-consciousness soliloquy in *Ulysses* (1922) are important early examples, as are works of the following decade: Henry Miller's *Tropic of Cancer* (1934) and *Tropic of Capricorn* (1936), Djuna Barnes's *Nightwood* (1936), and Nathaniel West's *Day of the Locust* (1939).

After World War II, the antirealistic novel gained momentum with Malcolm Lowry's *Under the Volcano* (1947), Beckett's fiction, and John Barth's novels of comic frustration reflected in the author's own playful frustrations in his writing, which he claims has no realistic referent other than itself. Other antirealists are John Hawkes, Joseph Heller (in some works), Donald Barthelme, and Thomas Pynchon, all expressing meaninglessness through irrational absurdities. The Argentinian Jorge Luis Borges (1899–), also a dreamlike nonrealist, is nevertheless cryptically affirmative, having asserted on one of his visits to the United States, "All life is a parable, though we do not know what it means." See ABSURD, THEATER OF THE; SURREALISM.

Antispast. A four-syllable Greek and Roman foot found in English only as an IAMBIC FOOT followed by a TROCHAIC FOOT: ⏑ – | – ⏑. See METER.

Antistrophe. (1) The second choral movement and song in Greek tragedy, matching the STROPHE, which preceded it in form and movement. While singing the strophe, the chorus moved from left to right. The antistrophe then reversed the movement back to the starting point. (2) The second part of the triad (strophe, antistrophe, EPODE) constituting a section of a Pindaric ODE. (3) The second STANZA, and those like it, in poems that alternate stanzaic forms. Rhetoricians sometimes refer to a CHIASMUS as an *antistrophe:* "The beauty in the mind; the mind in the beauty."

Antithesis.   (1) A direct contrast or opposition. (2) The second phase of dialectical argument, which considers the opposition—the three steps being thesis, antithesis, synthesis. (3) A RHETORICAL FIGURE sharply contrasting ideas in balanced parallel structures:

> He for God only, she for God in him
> *Milton*

> Though deep, yet clear, though gentle, yet not dull,
> Strong without rage, without o'erflowing, full.
> *John Denham*

> If the flights of Dryden therefore are higher, Pope continues longer on the wing. If of Dryden's fire the blaze is brighter, of Pope's the heat is more regular and constant. Dryden often surpasses expectation, and Pope never falls below it. Dryden is read with frequent astonishment, and Pope with perpetual delight.
>
> *Samuel Johnson*

Antitype.   A later event prefigured by an earlier one. See TYPE.

Antonomasia.   (1) Substitution of a proper name for a general type: "He is an *Elvis Presley,* a *Mickey Mouse,* a *Rock of Gibraltar.*" (2) Substitution of an EPITHET for a proper name: *Mr. President; Her Majesty;* the *Brown Bomber* (for heavyweight champion Joe Louis). See PERIPHRASIS.

Antonyms.   Words opposite in meaning: *good* and *bad, light* and *dark. See* SYNONYMS.

Aphaeresis.   Colloquial or poetic omission of initial unstressed sounds, as in *'bout* for *about, though* for *although, neath* for *beneath, till* for *until.*

Aphorism.   A pithy saying of known authorship, as distinguished from a folk proverb. Hippocrates (c. 460–377 B.C.) invented the term and the form in his medical *Aphorisms* (meaning "delimitations"), which begin:

> Life is short, art is long, opportunity fleeting, experimenting dangerous, reasoning difficult.

References

W. H. Auden and Louis Kronenberger, eds., **The Faber Book of Aphorisms** (1964).
John Gross, ed., **The Oxford Book of Aphorisms** (1983).

Apocalyptic.   Resembling the Apocalypse, the Book of Revelations, the last book of the New Testament, predicting, in cryptic symbols, the end of the world. Judeo-Christian writing between 200 B.C. and A.D. 150 was frequently apocalyptic. Edward Young's *Night Thoughts* (1742–1745), which remained popular into the early twentieth century, is a meditative apocalyptic poem, as are Blake's "prophetic books" (1791–1820), Yeats's "Second Coming" (1921), and Thomas Pynchon's novel *Gravity's Rainbow* (1973). The term loosely denotes any ultimate disaster.

Apocopated Rhyme.   The rhyming of a masculine ending and a feminine ending, with the stressed syllables sounding alike, but not the unstressed syllable: *meet, beaten; come, summer. See* RHYME.

Apocope.   The practice of cutting off the last sound of a word or syllable: *doin'* for *doing, morn* for *morning, t'other* for *the other.*

Apocrypha.   Greek for "things hidden." Certain Old Testament books were excluded by Jews and Protestants as not inspired by God or the Holy Spirit, though included in the Greek Septuagint and in St. Jerome's Latin Vulgate translation. Jerome (A.D. 331–420) first applied the term to excluded books. The Apocrypha, translated as part of the 1611 King James version, consists of 14 books: the 2 books of Esdras; Tobit; Judith; the Additions to Esther; the Wisdom of Solomon; Ecclesiasticus; Baruch, with the Epistle of Jeremiah; the Song of the Three Children; Susanna; Bel and the Dragon; Manasseh; and 2 books of Maccabees. Other apocryphal books are Enoch, the Life of Adam and Eve, the Testament of Abraham, the Psalter of Solomon, the Acts of Matthew, St. Paul's Third Epistle to the Corinthians, the Apocalypse of Peter, and the Gospel of Peter.

Metaphorically, *apocrypha* applies to any works excluded from an author's canon. See BIBLE, TRANSLATIONS OF; PSEUDEPIGRAPHA.

Apodioxis.   Emphatic rejection of an idea, as in "Will this deficit create new jobs? Absurd!"

Apodosis. The concluding clause of a conditional sentence: "If she works on her game, *she will win*." The conditional clause is a PRO-TASIS.

Apollonian. Serene, harmonious, restrained. According to Friedrich Nietzsche (1844–1990), in Greek drama the god Apollo represented rational artistic control, in contrast to the joyous wine and irrationalities of Dionysus. He established the contrast in his *Birth of Tragedy* (1872), his first book, in which he rejected the Apollonian for the ecstatic DIONYSIAN. Ruth Benedict's influential *Patterns of Culture* (1934) applied the contrast to the sociologies of tribal peoples. Nietzsche's terms restate the contrast between CLASSICISM and ROMANTICISM and between Matthew Arnold's HELLENISM and HEBRAISM, a dichotomy also explored in Arthur Schopenhauer's *World as Will and Idea* (1819).

Apologue. A moral tale, like Aesop's fables and Johnson's *Rasselas* (1759).

Apology. A justification (from Greek *apo-*, "defense," plus *logos*, "discourse"), as in Sidney's *Apologie for Poetrie* (1595), Thomas Heywood's *Apology for Actors* (1612), Cibber's *Apology for the Life of Mr. Colley Cibber, Comedian* (1740), and Cardinal Newman's *Apologia pro Vita Sua* (1864).

Apophasis. A "passing over." It is the pretense of not mentioning something in the very act of mentioning it. The device is also called *paralepsis* and *preteritio* (a favorite technique of Cicero's):

> I shall not go into all his broken promises, nor his predictions of success, nor his scandalous treatment of his aged mother. I shall pass over . . . .

Aporia. Ironical hesitation between alternatives:

> Whether he is more negligent than stupid, I hesitate to guess.
> One hardly knows what to call it, folly or forgetfulness, ignominy or ignorance.

Aposiopesis. The sentence left hanging in air—"What if I . . . "—for rhetorical effect. In Laurence Sterne's novel, Tristram Shandy's Uncle Toby achieves a classical example in speculating as to why his sister-in-law resists having a male doctor deliver her child: "My sister, I dare say, added he, does not care to let a man come so near her ★ ★ ★ ★." Tristram's father snaps the stem of his clay pipe in exasperation, for which the world may owe, as Tristram says, "one of the neatest examples of that ornamental figure of oratory, which Rhetoricians stile the *Aposiopesis*." ANACOLUTHON completes the idea ungrammatically; aposiopesis leaves it hanging.

Apostrophe. An address to an imaginary or absent person (or as if the person were absent), a thing, or a personified abstraction:

> Awake, my St. John! leave all meaner things
> To low ambition, and the pride of Kings.

> O wild West Wind, thou breath of Autumn's being

> Milton: thou shouldst be living at this hour

> Ebb, ocean of life, (the flow will return,)
> Cease not your moaning you fierce old mother

See PERSONIFICATION.

Apothegm (or Apophthegm). A pithy, and usually witty saying; a maxim, proverb, or APHORISM. Examples are Samuel Johnson's "Love is the wisdom of the fool and the folly of the wise," or Queen Elizabeth's "Hope is a good breakfast, but it is a bad supper," or Edward Young's "Procrastination is the thief of time."

Apposition. A noun or noun phrase placed in grammatical equivalence to explain another noun or noun phrase:

> Washington, *the first president, a frontiersman and planter,* was born in Westmoreland County, Virginia.

> Fascinated, my eyes reverting from the south, dropt, to follow those
>   slender windrows,
> *Chaff, straw, splinters of wood, weeds,* and *the sea-gluten,*
> *Scum, scales from shining rocks, leaves of salt-lettuce,* left by the
> tide. . . .

Apprenticeship Novel. A novel of learning and growth through experience. See *BILDUNGSROMAN*.

Approximate Rhyme. See SLANT RHYME.

A Priori Judgment. Deductive reasoning from an assumed principle to its effect. Kant applied the term to any principle necessary to make experience intelligible. In criticism, the term is used pejoratively to describe literary analysis based on prior rules and assumptions.

Apron Stage. A stage projecting into the audience, like that of the GLOBE THEATER. In some theaters the apron is the portion of the stage in front of the PROSCENIUM arch. The modern PICTURE FRAME STAGE has little or no apron. See ARENA STAGE.

Ara.   An elaborate, formal CURSE.

Arabesque.   Intricate Moorish mural designs of intertwining vines, flowers, geometrical figures, calligraphy, and, occasionally, animals stylized to avoid the Mohammedan prohibition against representing God's creatures. Renaissance arabesques included animals and humans both grotesque and natural. German Romantic criticism of the early nineteenth century applied the term to the new modes of fiction. In 1827, Thomas Carlyle was the first to apply it in English to literature, in an essay on the German Jean Paul Friedrich Richter: "That his manner of writing is singular, nay, in fact a wild complicated Arabesque, no one can deny" (*Works* [1899], XXVI, 19). Also in 1827, Sir Walter Scott, writing "On the Supernatural in Fictive Composition," observed that the new writing "resembles the arabesque in painting, in which is introduced the most strange and complicated monsters . . . and . . . other creatures of the romantic imagination." Edgar Allan Poe evidently acquired the term from Scott for his tales of strangeness and wonder as distinguished from those of horror, which he termed the GROTESQUE, in his *Tales of the Grotesque and Arabesque* (1840).

Arcadian.   Pastoral, rustic, idyllic, and simple; pertaining to the Golden Age, which the Greeks located, with its shepherds, in the actual Arcadia, a mountainous area north of Sparta. Sir Philip Sidney's PASTORAL ROMANCE *The Countess of Pembroke's Arcadia* (1590) derives from Sannazaro's Italian *Arcadia* (1504). See AGES OF THE WORLD; BUCOLIC; ECLOGUE; IDYLL; PASTORAL.

Archaism.   An archaic or old-fashioned word or expression, like *o'er, ere, shoon,* or *darkling.* Spenser endued his *Faerie Queene* with archaisms of phrase and spelling to suggest a mythic and glamorous past:

> Lo! I the man, whose Muse whylome did maske,
> As time her taught, in lowly shepheards weeds,
> Am now enforst, a farre unfitter taske,
> For trumpets sterne to chaunge mine oaten reeds.

Archetypal Criticism.   The examination of the ARCHETYPE in CHARACTER and PLOT. See CRITICISM.

Archetype.   A term that has come down from Neoplatonic times and has usually meant a standard, pattern, or model. It has been sporadically employed in this sense in literary criticism down to at least the eighteenth century. An archetype differs from a prototype (even though the two words have often been used interchangeably) in that *prototype* refers primarily to a genetic and temporal pattern of relationship. In modern literary criticism *archetype* means a recurring or repeating unit, normally an image, which indicates that a poet is following a certain convention or working in a certain GENRE. For example, the PASTORAL ELEGY is a convention, descending from ritual laments over dying gods, and hence when Milton contributes *Lycidas* to a volume of memorial poems to an acquaintance who was drowned in the Irish Sea, the poem is written as a pastoral elegy, and consequently employs a number of conventional images that had been used earlier by Theocritus, Virgil, and many RENAISSANCE poets. The conventions include imagery of the solar and seasonal cycles, in which autumn frost, the image of premature death, and sunset in the western ocean are prominent; the idea that the subject of the elegy was a shepherd with a recognized pastoral name and an intimate friend of the poet; a satirical passage on the state of the church, with implied puns on *pastor* and *flock* (naturally a post-Virgilian feature); and death and rebirth imagery attached to the cycle of water, symbolized by the legend of Alpheus, the river and river god that went underground in Greece and surfaced again in Sicily in order to join the fountain and fountain nymph Arethusa.

One of the conventional images employed in the pastoral elegy is that of the red or purple flower that is said to have obtained its color from the shed blood of the dying god. *Lycidas* contains a reference to "that sanguine flower inscrib'd with woe," the hyacinth, thought to have obtained red markings resembling the Greek word *ai* ("alas"), when Hyacinthus was accidentally killed by Apollo. Milton could of course just as easily have left out this line: the fact that he included it emphasizes the conventionalizing element in the poem, but criticism that takes account of archetypes is not mere "spotting" of such an image. The critical question concerns the context: What does such an image mean by being where it is? The convention of pastoral elegy continues past Milton to Shelley, Arnold, and Whitman's "When Lilacs Last in Dooryard Bloom'd." Here again are many of the conventional pastoral images, including the purple lilacs: this fact is all the more interesting in that Whitman regarded himself as an anti-archetypal poet, interested in new themes as more appropriate to a new world. In any case the gathering or clustering of pastoral archetypes in his poem indicates to the critic the context within literature that the poem belongs to.

The archetype, as a critical term, has no Platonic associations with a form or idea that embodies itself imperfectly in actual poems: it owes its importance to the fact that in literature everything is new and unique from one point of view, and to the reappearance of what has always been there, from another. The former aspect compels the reader to focus on the distinctive context of each particular poem; the latter indicates that it is recognizable as literature. In other genres there are other kinds of archetypes: a certain type of character, for example, may run through all drama, like the braggart soldier, who with variations has been a comic figure since Aristophanes's *Acharnians*, the first extant comedy. The appearance of a braggart soldier in a comedy by Shakespeare or Molière or O'Casey is quite different each time, but the archetypal basis of the character is as essential as a skeleton is to the performing actor. Thus the archetype is a manifestation of the extraordinary allusiveness of literature: the fact, for example, that all wars in literature gain poetic resonance by being associated with the Trojan War.

In JUNGIAN CRITICISM the term *archetype* is used mainly to describe certain characters and images that appear in the dreams of patients but have their counterparts in literature, in the symbolism of alchemy, in various religious myths. The difference between psychological and literary treatments of archetypes is that in psychology their central context is a private dream. Hence they tell us nothing except that they appear, once we leave the psychological field of dream interpretation. The dream is not primarily a structure of communication: its meaning is normally unknown to the dreamer. The literary archetype, on the other hand, is first of all a unit of communication: primitive literature, for example, is highly conventionalized, featuring formulaic units and other indications of an effort to communicate with the least possible obstruction. In more complex literature the archetype tells the critic primarily that this kind of thing has often been done before, if never quite in this way.

Architechtonics.   By analogy with architecture, the structural design of a literary work when understood as a UNITY, with each part functional in supporting the whole.

Archive.   A repository for items collected, as, for example, public documents or the accumulations of scholarly work: a folklore archive or the archives of the Library of Congress.

Arena Stage.   A stage surrounded by the audience, used for THEATER IN THE ROUND. The arena stage has been popular in the twentieth century with college and LITTLE THEATER groups. It requires different acting and production styles from the APRON STAGE and PICTURE FRAME STAGE, since the actors must enter and leave through the aisles, settings must not obstruct vision, and a curtain is not used.

Areopagus. The oldest council at Athens, which met on a hill of the same name near the city to decide important matters concerning the public welfare. *Areopagitica,* Milton's famous plea for unlicensed printing, signifies by its title "things to be said before the Areopagus." Milton, of course, addressed his remarks to the English Parliament, honoring that body by his classical ALLUSION. In a similar allusion, the name *Areopagus* was used by Edmund Spenser to refer to a group of literary friends—including Spenser, Sir Philip Sidney, and Sir Edward Dyer—that met at Leicester House in London in 1579 and 1580.

Argument. (1) A series of statements intended to establish a position or prove a point. In this sense, argument is one of four major kinds of prose discourse, the others being DESCRIPTION, EXPOSITION, and NARRATION. Another name is *argumentation.* (2) The content of a literary work, sometimes given in a brief summary, or ABSTRACT, at the beginning of its divisions—for example, the prose Argument that precedes each book of Milton's *Paradise Lost.*

Argumentation. See ARGUMENT.

Arianism. One of the major heresies in the history of Christianity: the belief that Jesus was God's first creature, His son, above humans, but not equal to the Father. It took its name from Arius, an Alexandrian priest of the fourth century. Condemned by the First Council of Nicea (325), the concept nevertheless continued to prove troublesome to the church.

Arminianism. Belief in the doctrines of Jacobus Arminius (1560–1609), a Dutch theologian who taught that humans are free even though God is omnipotent, challenging the Calvinistic doctrine of predestined election through divine grace. It followed that salvation could be achieved not through predestination but through good works. To seventeenth- and eighteenth-century Puritans, this was a heresy, challenged especially in America in the writings of Jonathan Edwards (1703–1758). On the other hand, Arminianism became one of the accepted doctrines of Methodism.

Arsis. Metrical stress. In Greek, it was the opposite, the unstressed

or upbeat syllable, derived from the "lift" of the foot in dancing. See
METER; THESIS (3).

Art for Art's Sake. The doctrine that art is valuable in itself, without
reference to religion, politics, ethics, or other considerations. Beauty is
its own excuse for being. See AESTHETICISM.

Arthurian Legend. The lore surrounding King Arthur. Although a
real Arthur probably lived in the west of England or in Wales in the
sixth century, nothing is known of him beyond the fact that many
legends from the great store of Celtic and Germanic folklore became
attached to his name over the next nine hundred years, attaining their
most complete expression in Thomas Malory's *Morte Darthur* (1485).
In the five hundred years since Malory, these legends have maintained
their power, situated with the Greek and Roman myths not far behind
the Bible among the imaginative and allusive resources of Western
writers and thinkers. Spenser used an Arthurian background for his
Faerie Queen. Tennysons's *Idylls of the King* is a nineteenth-century
version of the legend. Richard Wagner derived three solemn operas
from the Arthurian material: *Lohengrin, Tristan and Isolde,* and *Parsi-
fal.* Twain's *Connecticut Yankee in King Arthur's Court* achieves humor
from ANACHRONISM when chivalry meets nineteenth-century progress.
In the twentieth century, Edwin Arlington Robinson wrote three long
Arthurian poems, *Merlin, Lancelot,* and *Tristram,* and T. H. White a
prose tetralogy, *The Once and Future King.* The MUSICAL COMEDY
Camelot has been highly successful on stage and screen. John Steinbeck's last book was *The Acts of King Arthur and His Noble Knights.*

Arthur was first named in a Welsh poem of about 600, the *Gododdin*
(or *Canu Aneurin*), in which a hero is praised, "though he was not
Arthur." Around 800, the Welsh historian Nennius accounted him a
leader in battles against the Anglo-Saxons, crediting him with the sin-
gle-handed slaying of 960 enemies. He appeared again in Welsh in the
tenth century in the *Annales Cambrias* and *The Spoils of Annwn.* Perhaps the first Arthurian ROMANCE was the Welsh *Culhwch and Olwen*
(c. 1100), from the MABINOGION, but here Arthur was still basically a
tribal hero: chivalry had not yet arrived. In England, Arthur appeared
first in histories: William of Malmesbury's *Gesta Regum Anglorum
(Deeds of the Kings of Britain,* 1125) and Geoffrey of Monmouth's *History of the Kings of Britain* (1137). By this time the legendary material
was vast, Geoffrey containing in outline much that was important later.
Robert Wace, in his *Roman de Brut* (1155), expanded upon Geoffrey,
adding details like the Round Table. The Arthurian legend became

important to romance, however, only at the end of the twelfth century, in the five romances of Crétien de Troyes (see MEDIEVAL ROMANCE), where it assumed the chivalric characteristics now associated with it. In Germany in the thirteenth century, Wolfram von Eschenbach in *Parzifal* and Gottfried von Strassburg in *Tristan* added significantly to the canon. Arthur's first appearance in English (as distinct from Welsh or Latin) was in the late twelfth or early thirteenth centuries in Layamon's *Brut,* a work of 30,000 lines, with considerable attention to Arthur. This, with the alliterative *Morte Arthure* (c. 1360) and other poems of the late thirteenth and early fourteenth centuries, made most of the Arthurian tales available in English. The great Arthurian works in English, however, are the fourteenth-century *Sir Gawain and the Green Knight,* an unexcelled telling of one story, and Malory's *Morte Darthur,* printed by Caxton in 1485, the compilation that gave the entire legend the form most familiar since.

Malory pulled stories together, eliminating minor characters and creating thematic unities, chief of which is the establishment of a perfect society, humanistically based in selflessness. Camelot is humanity's nearest approach to the city of God on earth; the Round Table the symbol of equality and friendship; the Grail quest a search for spiritual fulfillment; the Arthur/Guenevere/Lancelot triangle a lesson in love, fidelity, and forgiveness. Arthur's pulling of the sword from the stone reminds us of humankind's continual hope that an unrecognized leader will arise from among the least of us to gather our wasted forces in grand, united purpose. The promise of the leader's return continues to stand, symbolically, for the better hopes we share for times to come.

References

Roger Sherman Loomis, ed., **Arthurian Literature in the Middle Ages: A Collaborative History** (1959).

James W. Spisak and William Matthews, eds., **Caxton's Malory: A New Edition of Sir Thomas Malory's Le Morte Darthur** (1984).

Eugène Vinaver, ed., **The Works of Sir Thomas Malory** (1954).

Article.   (1) An item separate from others, as in the sections of a constitution or other written document. (2) An ESSAY or other piece of expository writing, self-contained, for inclusion with other material in a newspaper, magazine, or book.

Artificiality.   A quality ascribed by critics to writing that seems mannered, forced, or unnatural. Artificiality may be intentional, for effect, or inadvertent, the result of ineptitude or of striving for effects that are not achieved.

Aside. In the theater, a speech directed to the audience but, by dramatic CONVENTION, apparently unheard by the other characters in the play, who continue in their roles without the knowledge thus given the spectators. Much used from the Renaissance to the nineteenth century, the aside permitted a character to reveal thoughts or motives otherwise hidden. It proved a handy device in MELODRAMA. See SOLILOQUY.

Assonance. Repetition of middle vowel sounds: *fight, hive; pane, make.* Assonance, most effective on stressed syllables, is often found within a line of poetry; less frequently it substitutes for END RHYME. Like other sounds of poetry, it is sometimes a useful effect in prose. See ALLITERATION; CONSONANCE; RHYME.

Astrology. The system for predicting the presumed influence of the sun, moon, planets, stars, and their positions on mundane affairs. Derived from the Babylonians, the system arose in Greece about 300 B.C. Beginning the year with March 21, astrologers divided the sun's annual circuit into 12 30° segments, each named for a constellation and given a zodiacal sign. Each segment was also the "house" of a heavenly body. Associations with the four elements (fire, earth, air, water), with parts of the body, and with opposites like day and night or male and female were common. The following table shows some of the connections:

CONSTELLATION	SIGN	DATE	HEAVENLY BODY	SEX	ELEMENT
Aries	Ram	Mar. 21	Mars	male	fire
Taurus	Bull	Apr. 20	Venus	female	earth
Gemini	Twins	May 21	Mercury	male	air
Cancer	Crab	June 22	Moon	female	water
Leo	Lion	July 23	Sun	male	fire
Virgo	Virgin	Aug. 23	Mercury	female	earth
Libra	Scales	Sept. 23	Venus	male	air
Scorpio	Scorpion	Oct. 24	Mars	female	water
Sagittarius	Archer	Nov. 22	Jupiter	male	fire
Capricorn	Goat	Dec. 22	Saturn	female	earth
Aquarius	Water Bearer	Jan. 20	Saturn	male	air
Pisces	Fishes	Feb. 19	Jupiter	female	water

Asyndeton. Omission of conjunctions between coordinate sentence elements: "I came, I saw, I conquered" (Julius Caesar); "I too am not a bit tamed, I too am untranslatable, / I sound my barbaric yawp over the roofs of the world" (Walt Whitman). With conjunctions, the effect is POLYSYNDETON. See PARALLELISM; PARATAXIS.

Atmosphere. The MOOD or general feeling of a literary work, especially as it relates to the physical SETTING. Ordinarily, the atmosphere is established at the beginning. It is related to FORESHADOWING insofar as it proves predictive of the turn events will take, as, in a general way, it often does. But foreshadowing is usually considered a plot device, whereas atmosphere involves much more—characters, clothes, furniture, natural surroundings, patterns of light and shadow. In works heavy with atmosphere, ACTION sometimes seems slow or imperceptible, but in masters of atmosphere such as Dickens, Poe, or Hardy, the action comes quickly enough.

Attic. Classical in style, after the manner of the ancient Greeks: polished, refrained, graceful. Keats's Grecian urn is an "Attic shape." Joseph Addison's style was famed and imitated for its Attic qualities. Attica was a state in ancient Greece, with Athens its capital.

Attic Salt. Refined, delicate, poignant wit. The phrase originated with Pliny the Elder as *sal atticum* in his *Historia Naturalis*, XXXI.87 (A.D. 77). See ATTIC.

Aubade. Dawn song, from French *aube*, for *dawn*, with the suffix *-ade*, as in *serenade*. The aubade originated in the Middle Ages as a song sung by a lover greeting the dawn, ordinarily expressing regret that morning means parting. Chaucer's *Troilus and Criseyde* includes an aubade, as does Shakespeare's *Romeo and Juliet*, when Romeo must leave upon their wedding night. In Provençal verse, such a song is called an *alba*. In German, it is a *Tagelied*.

Aube. An AUBADE.

Augustan Age. The period 1700–1750, following the RESTORATION. Writers continued to emulate the reign of Caesar Augustus (27 B.C.–A.D. 14), pursuing the Neoclassical ideal of rational balance between extremes, translating and imitating Virgil and Horace, comparing London to Rome, hoping for the *pax Romana* of arts and letters they had glimpsed with the restoration of Charles II in 1660, especially when the Treaty of Utrecht ended the War of the Spanish Succession (1701–1713) against Louis XIV. Alexander Pope's *Windsor Forest* (1713) forecast a world peace sailing abroad from the Thames to all nations in ships from the oaks of Windsor. Addison, Steele, Swift, and Pope are the chief Augustans. Irony and satire thrived, criticizing social and moral extremes by rational indirection. Pope's "Epistle to Augustus," imitating *The First Epistle of the Second Book of Horace* (1737), turned the Augustan idea against George II, whose name was George Augustus, with devastating irony. The modern novel began with Defoe's distinctly un-Augustan *Robinson Crusoe* (1719), as an ordinary man makes his place in the world and works out a perception of God. Richardson's *Pamela, or Virtue Rewarded* (1740) made another case for the unnoticed individual and got the novel fully under way with its tremendous popularity. It prompted Fielding's parody, *Shamela* (1741), which immediately led to his *Joseph Andrews* (1742), the first true comic novel in English. Richardson's *Clarissa* (1748) was the first tragic novel. Fielding's *Tom Jones* (1749) concluded the Augustan Age with a rich and balanced CONCORDIA DISCORS in which all apparent evils and random chances harmonize for good in the end. See ENGLISH LITERATURE, PERIODS OF; NEOCLASSICAL PERIOD; and "Chronology of Literature and World Events."

Augustinianism. The doctrines of St. Augustine (354–430) and his followers. More specifically, Augustinianism refers to Augustine's opposition to PELAGIANISM, a doctrine denying original sin and consequently implying that God's grace is not a necessary initial step toward salvation. Augustine's view of humans as innately corrupt and therefore in need of grace is also a tenet of CALVINISM.

Australian Literature. See COMMONWEALTH LITERATURE.

Auteur Theory. In film CRITICISM, the theory that a movie, although obviously a collaboration of many hands—writer, producer, director, camera crew, actors, and make-up and special effects technicians—achieves its essential identity from one person, the director. As *auteur* (French for *author*), the director controls the materials in a manner analogous to the control an author exerts over the materials of a book. The term derives from French film criticism.

Author's Voice. (1) The passages in which an author speaks directly, in his or her own person, as distinct from those in which the writer adopts a role or speaks through a PERSONA. In an AUTOBIOGRAPHY, ESSAY, and LETTERS, the author's voice is generally undisguised. In FICTION, too, authors sometimes speak directly, as when Fielding and Thackeray address the reader in voices we assume to be their own. (2) The characteristic style of a writer, evident in many works even when there is no direct address to the reader. In this sense, Henry James and

Ernest Hemingway, although they seldom speak directly to the reader in their fictions, may both be said to have characteristic voices.

In either sense, the author's voice may change, just as a speaking voice may, for different circumstances; it may not represent the author's permanent self, but only the self of the occasion. Terminology useful to qualify the voice in a given work includes IMPLIED AUTHOR and NARRATOR.

Autobiographical Essay. An ESSAY providing a brief AUTOBIOGRAPHY or a portion of one. James Baldwin's "Notes of a Native Son," for example, describes and attempts to explain the events surrounding his father's funeral.

Autobiography. The description of a life, or a portion of one, written by the person who has lived it, in contrast to a BIOGRAPHY, which presents a life as written by another person. Ordinarily, an autobiography is intended for public readership, as opposed to the private account of a life found in a DIARY, JOURNAL, or LETTERS. MEMOIRS are a form of autobiography, usually limited in scope and dwelling on the private side of public events.

The first great autobiography was the *Confessions* of St. Augustine (354–430). Recounting his backsliding youth, spiritual enlightenment, and embracing of Christianity, Augustine established a pattern for later writers, who often present the interplay of external events and interior growth, especially in their early years, as they attempt to explain or justify the conditions of their being. For some later writers, external events are most important, as these authors provide permanent witness to a passing historical moment or transient social conditions. For others, self-reflection seems most vital. The *Autobiography* of Benvenuto Cellini (1500–1571) reports the turbulent life of an Italian Renaissance sculptor. The *Autobiography* of Benjamin Franklin (1706–1790) provides insight into the personality of one of the great public men of the eighteenth century. In *The Education of Henry Adams*, the historian Adams (1838–1918) speculates on the human implications of the material and spiritual changes of his time.

An autobiographical element is often important in fiction, as in Melville's *Typee* and *Omoo*, Joyce's *Portrait of the Artist as a Young Man*, and D. H. Lawrence's *Sons and Lovers*. On the stage, Eugene O'Neill's *Long Day's Journey into Night* explores tragic personal relationships. In poetry, Wordsworth's *Prelude* records, the poet said, "the growth of my own mind," and Whitman's *Leaves of Grass* is in part an intellectual or spiritual autobiography.

In recent times, autobiography has sometimes merged with fiction and journalism. Writers of literary autobiographies, increasingly aware of the fictions forced into their art by faulty memories and changing perspectives, have obscured traditional lines between GENRES, as in Vladimir Nabokov's *Speak, Memory*, which uses some of the techniques and illuminates the themes of his fictions. Novels like James Baldwin's *Go Tell It on the Mountain* would require few changes to pass as autobiography. Literary journalists, also, have ignored distinctions once rigidly observed, in books such as Norman Mailer's *Armies of the Night*, which mixes objective reporting and personal involvement as it describes the 1967 peace march on the Pentagon. Autobiographies more traditional in form continue to be written, however, and have recently proliferated, recording the lives of ordinary people as well as of politicians and dignitaries, entertainment and sports figures, artists, scientists, business and religious leaders.

Automatic Writing.   Writing produced in a trancelike state, without intellectual control, so that the words flow from the subconscious or from inspiration, as from the spirit world. A device sometimes used by spiritualists in their attempts to communicate with the dead, automatic writing has appeared occasionally in LITERATURE, especially among writers influenced by spiritualism.

Autotelic.   Greek for "self-completing." The term, from the NEW CRITICISM, is used to describe a literary work whose value lies in itself—a work that serves no nonliterary ends. For instance, an autotelic poem imparts no moral; its only purpose is to be.

Auxesis.   Ironic OVERSTATEMENT, or exaggeration:

> The little devil found the cookies.
> She is a saint when you are looking.

Avant-Garde.   Experimental, innovative, at the forefront of a literary or artistic trend or movement. The term is French for *vanguard*, the advance unit of an army. It frequently suggests a struggle with tradition and convention, as the *avant-garde* writer attempts to win acceptance for new ideas or techniques.

Awakening, the Great.   See GREAT AWAKENING.

Axiom.   (1) A self-evident MAXIM, or APHORISM. (2) An established principle. (3) In logic and mathematics, either an accepted principle or an undemonstrated postulate to be proved.

B

Bacchius. A Greek and Roman foot going $\smile - -$. See METER.

Background. As in painting, the surroundings against which literary action is pictured, or the cultural and educational circumstances from which authors derive their ideas and viewpoints.

Baconian Theory. The belief that Sir Francis Bacon wrote Shakespeare's plays. Herbert Lawrence originated the idea in *The Life and Adventures of Common Sense* (1769); it was wholly ignored until revived by Joseph C. Hart's *Romance of Yachting* (1848). W. H. Smith mused more elaborately in *Was Bacon the Author of Shakespeare's Plays?* (1856). Delia Bacon, an American schoolteacher, brought it to passionate prominence, first in an article in *Putnam's Monthly Magazine* (1856), then in her *Philosophy of the Plays of Shakespeare Unfolded* (1857), with preface by Nathaniel Hawthorne. She attacked the "Stratford poacher" with his "dirty, doggish group of players" as a "vulgar, illiterate man" wholly incapable of the immortal plays. She believed that a group of intellectuals, which she called "Raleigh's school," wrote the plays under Bacon's guidance to expound his philosophy allegorically. Delia Bacon traveled to England shortly before her book's publication, became convinced that secret proofs lay under Shakespeare's alleged tombstone, went insane, and died in a hospital in 1859.

Nevertheless, the Bacon Society, which still exists, arose in England in 1885 and started its journal, *Baconiana*, in 1892. In *The Great Cryptogram* (1888), Ignatius Donnelly followed hints from Delia Bacon and her disciple, Mrs. C. F. Ashmead Windle, to establish a mathematical-alphabetical cipher that revealed in letters threading down the lines "I Francis Bacon wrote this play." His cipher showed to Donnelly that Bacon wrote not only all of Shakespeare's plays, but also all of Marlowe's works, Montaigne's essays, and Robert Burton's *Anatomy of Melancholy* (1621). Mark Twain was a believer in Donnelly's theory, writing *Is Shakespeare Dead?* (1909). Sir Edwin Durning-Lawrence also supported Donnelly in *Bacon Is Shakespeare* (1910), finding in the comic word *honorificabilitudinitatibus* (*Love's Labour's Lost*, V.i.44) the Latin statement HI LUDI F. BACON NATI TUITI ORBI, "These plays, offspring of F. Bacon, are preserved for the world."

References

Oscar James Campbell and Edward G. Quinn, eds., **The Reader's Encyclopedia of Shakespeare** (1966).

John Crow, "Heretics Observed," **Times Literary Supplement** (23 April 1964).

W. Friedman and E. Friedman, **The Shakespearean Ciphers Examined** (1957).

Frank W. Wadsworth, **The Poacher from Stratford** (1958).

Balance. A common RHETORICAL FIGURE in which phrases of identical grammatical construction are balanced against each other in prose or poetry, especially in the HEROIC COUPLET.

Ballad. A narrative poem in short stanzas, with or without music. The term derives by way of French *ballade* from Latin *ballare*, "to dance," and once meant a simple song of any kind, lyric or narrative, especially one to accompany a dance. As ballads evolved, most lost their direct association with dance, although they kept their strong rhythms. Modern usage distinguishes three major kinds: the *traditional ballad* (*popular ballad* or *folk ballad*), a song of anonymous authorship, transmitted orally; the *broadside ballad*, printed and sold on single sheets; and the *literary ballad*, a sophisticated imitation of the traditional ballad.

The first traditional ballad recorded in English is "Judas," from a manuscript of about 1300. Although only a few others survive in manuscripts older than the seventeenth century, many certainly originated in the Middle Ages, the oral tradition keeping songs alive, without benefit of print, sometimes for hundreds of years. After ballads began to be printed, they continued to circulate orally, maintaining a tradition separate from print well into the twentieth century. Interest in the traditional ballad as literature began in Great Britain in the eighteenth century. The first great collection was Thomas Percy's *Reliques of Ancient English Poetry* (1765). Sir Walter Scott followed, with *Minstrelsy of the Scottish Border* (1802). Francis J. Child's *English and Scottish Popular Ballads* (5 vols., 1882–1898) defined the canon accepted today, the 305 songs known as the *Child Ballads*. These, carried throughout the world by English-speaking people, constitute the major corpus of the traditional ballad in English. Ballads in English native to Ireland, the United States, Canada, or Australia have some of the same qualities, but are much newer.

The subject matter of the Child ballads is the common experience and belief of the community, essentially as it existed from feudal times to the beginning of the industrial revolution. The world depicted is rural and strife-torn, a castle- or manor-centered land of lords and ladies, servingmen and handmaidens, carpenters and weavers, gypsies and outlaws. Religion is important, as in "Judas" or "The Cherry-Tree Carol." Ghosts and other supernatural beings are common, as sons returned from the dead in "The Wife of Usher's Well" or the demon lover in "James Harris." Many ballads are grounded in history or treat historical people in legendary fashion: "The Bonny Earl of Murray," "Mary Hamilton," "Queen Eleanor's Confession." Some have analogues in the MEDIEVAL ROMANCE: "King Horn," "King Orfeo." Outlaws figure in many, including over three dozen involving Robin Hood. Death is a frequent subject, as in "Sir Patrick Spens" and "The Twa Corbies," and often involves murder between lovers or within the family, as in "Lord Randal" and "Edward." Unhappy or betrayed love figures prominently: "The Twa Sisters," "Bonny Barbara Allan," "Lord Thomas and Fair Annet."

Traditional ballads share important formal characteristics. The most common stanza is the BALLAD STANZA, four lines alternating iambic tetrameter and iambic trimeter in a 4/3/4/3 pattern, rhyming on the second and fourth lines, *abcb* (see RHYME SCHEME). Less common, but still frequent, are stanzas with four iambic tetrameter lines and stanzas in iambic tetrameter couplets. A burden, or REFRAIN, is common. Development of incident or theme is often by INCREMENTAL REPETITION. Within these structural limits, most ballads share characteristics most readily explained as products of oral transmission. Typically, one incident is developed in a few stanzas, sometimes elliptically, as though a longer tale has been stripped by repetition of all but essentials. Narration is objective. Exposition is reduced to a line or two, or missing entirely. Individuals speak without introduction, and there is no transition between speakers. Language is archaic and formulaic, with phrases and even an entire FLOATING STANZA repeated from ballad to ballad.

Broadside ballads originated in the sixteenth century and were especially popular in the eighteenth and nineteenth centuries. Printed on single sheets, ornamented by woodcuts, they were sold by street vendors. Occasionally, they served to fix in print, for a time, a version of a traditional ballad. More often, they were written to commemorate sensational news: a fire, robbery, murder, or hanging. Seldom the work of skillful poets, most lack the polished intensity of traditional ballads, but some have passed into oral tradition, acquiring folk song qualities.

The literary ballad was popular in the nineteenth century as sophisticated poets tried to imitate the traditional ballads, often at much greater length. Noteworthy examples are Keats's "La Belle Dame sans Merci," Coleridge's "Rime of the Ancient Mariner," Longfellow's "Wreck of the Hesperus," and Kipling's "Ballad of East and West."

In North America, the traditional ballad has been primarily English and Scottish, the old songs continuing in oral tradition from the earliest settlements. Over 100 Child ballads have been discovered in living tradition in the United States and Canada in the twentieth century. Here the songs have often changed to suit new conditions, Lord Randal becoming Jimmy Randal and references to knights and castles less common than in Great Britain. At the same time, many native ballads have been created, these directly reflecting the American experience. Among the best are "Springfield Mountain," the story of a farm boy bitten by a snake; "Little Omie Wise," a North Carolina murder ballad; "The Jam at Gerry's Rock," a lumberjack song; "The Buffalo Skinners," a western range song; and "Jesse James" and "John Henry," tales of an outlaw and an heroic steel driver. "Springfield Mountain" is eighteenth century, the others nineteenth. Within the twentieth century, ballads have continued to be created, but print, records, radio, movies, and television have tended to fix the texts, protecting them from the changes of the traditional folk process.

References

Bertrand H. Bronson, **The Ballad as Song** (1969).
Tristram P. Coffin, **The British Traditional Ballad in North America** (1963).
D. C. Fowler, **A Literary History of the Popular Ballad** (1968).
Gordon H. Gerould, **The Ballad of Tradition** (1932).
James Kinsley, ed., **The Oxford Book of Ballads** (1971).
G. Malcolm Laws, Jr., **Native American Balladry** (1964).
Alan Lomax, **The Folksongs of North America in the English Language** (1960).

Ballade. One of the VERSE FORMS (not to be confused with the BALLAD) popular in France in the fourteenth and fifteenth centuries, also sometimes written in English. The most common type consists of three eight-line stanzas, rhyming *ababbcbc*, and a four-line ENVOY, rhyming *bcbc*, with the last line of each STANZA and the envoy repeated as a REFRAIN. Other types are also found, including ballades with ten-line stanzas and five-line envoys. Line lengths vary, with iambic or anapestic tetrameter frequent. The envoy is typically addressed to a prince or patron. Examples in English include Chaucer's "Truth" and "Lak of

Stedfastnesse," both in RHYME ROYAL, and Dante Gabriel Rossetti's translation of François Villon's "Ballad of Dead Ladies," which begins and ends

> Tell me now in what hidden way is
>   Lady Flora the lovely Roman?
> Where's Hipparchia, and where is Thais,
>   Neither of them the fairer woman?
> Where is Echo, beheld of no man,
> Only heard on river and mere,—
>   She whose beauty was more than human? . . .
> But where are the snows of yesteryear?
>   · · ·
> Nay, never ask this week, fair lord,
>   Where they are gone, nor yet this year,
> Except with this for an overword,—
>   But where are the snows of yesteryear?

Ballad Opera.   A politically satirical musical comedy, a form initiated by John Gay's tremendously popular *Beggar's Opera* (1728). Gay set his songs to ballad tunes to parody the rage for Handel's Italian operas. Jonathan Swift had suggested that Gay write a "Newgate pastoral," in which the London underworld would satirize the royal establishment— Newgate being London's central prison. These mock pastorals, to which Henry Fielding was a major contributor, flourished for the next decade, until Sir Robert Walpole's government shut out Fielding from the stage with the Licensing Act of 1737.

Ballad Stanza.   The name for COMMON METER as found in ballads: a QUATRAIN in iambic METER, alternating tetrameter and trimeter lines, usually rhyming *abcb* (see RHYME SCHEME):

> There lived a wife at Usher's Well,
>   And a wealthy wife was she;
> She had three stout and stalwart sons,
>   And sent them o'er the sea.

In the traditional BALLAD, essentially a song, the musical structure allows considerable freedom with syllable count, since an underlying and fundamental four beats to the line is carried by the music. Thus the music provides the fourth beat at the end of lines two and four in the 4/3/4/3 pattern given above and is accompanied by the lyrics in the 4/4/4/4 pattern of LONG METER. Against this musical four beats, the iambics of standard metrical SCANSION frequently appear very irregular in folk songs. Occasionally in the stanzas of folk songs, and frequently in more sophisticated poems, the basic rhyme scheme is complicated by the addition of rhyme in the first and third lines in an *abab* pattern. A shorter version of the same stanza is known as SHORT METER.

Banal.   Flat, trite, hackneyed, uninteresting.

Barbarism.   (1) A nonstandard usage: *youse, hisn, hern, usuns*. (2) A falsely coined word, like *irregardless* (for regardless), *preventative* (for *preventive*), or *antidotic* (for *anecdotic*).

Bard.   An ancient Celtic singer of the culture's lore in epic form; a poetic term for any poet, particularly after Thomas Gray's pre-Romantic poem *The Bard* (1757).

Baroque.   (1) A richly ornamented style in architecture and art. Founded in Rome by Frederigo Barocci about 1550, and characterized by swirling allegorical frescoes on ceilings and walls, it flourished throughout Europe until 1700. Bernini's great bronze canopy with twisting columns at St. Peter's and his fountains are striking examples. (2) A chromatic musical style with strict forms containing similar exuberant ornamentation, flourishing from 1600 to 1750.

In England, Sir Anthony Van Dyck's portraits of Charles I and his court are considered the acme of baroque style. Inigo Jones (1573–1652) introduced baroque architecture in the settings he designed for the court masques of Ben Jonson and others. His Neoclassical buildings, notably the Banqueting House, Whitehall (1622), and St. Paul's Church, Covent Garden (c. 1630) contain baroque elements and are called baroque, as are the subsequent works of Sir Christopher Wren (1632–1723) and Sir John Vanbrugh (1664–1726).

In literature, Richard Crashaw's bizarre imagery and the conceits and rhythms of John Donne and other metaphysical poets are sometimes called baroque, sometimes mannerist. Some literary historians designate a Baroque Age from 1580 to 1680, between the RENAISSANCE and the ENLIGHTENMENT. Some include Milton in the baroque period, considering *Paradise Lost* (1667) the supreme baroque achievement. *See* CONCEIT; MANNERISM; METAPHYSICAL POETRY; ROCOCO.

Basic English.   A vocabulary of 850 words—600 nouns, 150 adjectives, 100 "operators" (verbs, adverbs, prepositions, conjunctions)— selected by the British linguist C. K. Ogden (1889–1957) for foreign learners, following a suggestion found in Jeremy Bentham (1748–1832). Ogden first outlined the vocabulary in his quarterly, *The Cambridge Magazine*, in 1919 and presented it in 1928. In 1943, Winston

Churchill appointed a committee to promulgate Basic English as an international common language. I. A. Richards, co-author with Ogden of *The Meaning of Meaning* (1923) and then teaching at Harvard, published *Basic English and Its Use* (1943) to popularize it in America. Franklin D. Roosevelt became an advocate. Books in Basic English include *The Basic Bible* (1944) and some of Plato.

Bathos. (1) A sudden slippage from the sublime to the ridiculous. Alexander Pope invented the term in parody of Longinus's famous work περι ὕψους (*Peri Hypsos*, literally "about height," known as "On the Sublime") in Pope's περι βάθος [*Peri Bathos*, "about depth"], *or the Art of Sinking in Poetry* (1728): "While a plain and direct road is paved to their ὕψος; no track has yet been chalked out to arrive at our βάθος." (2) Any anticlimax. (3) Sentimental pathos. (4) Triteness or dullness.

Battle of the Books, the. A term for the dispute as to whether ancient classical writers or modern writers were superior. The debate arose in France and England in the 1680s and 1690s; the term itself was taken from the most famous document in the quarrel, Jonathan Swift's *Battel Between the Ancient and the Modern Books in St. James's Library*, written 1697, published 1704. See ANCIENTS AND MODERNS, QUARREL OF THE.

Beast Epic. Probably an elaboration of Aesop's fables (sixth century B.C.) and similar folklore in which talking animals satirize human foibles and institutions, particularly church and court. Paulus Diaconus (c. 720–c. 800), an Italian monk respected by Charlemagne, is said to have written the earliest known beast epic, but the form flourished in northern France, western Germany, and Flanders in the twelfth and thirteenth centuries. A central story, like one of Reynard the Fox's tricks on King Lion, usually branches out into related tales. Isegrym the wolf, Chanticleer the cock, Tybert the cat, Bruin the bear, and Courtoys the hound are prominent characters. The *Roman de Renard* (c. 1200–1250), 30,000 lines and 27 stories, is the most famous.

Beast Fable. A short tale about talking animals, making a moral point, like those or Aesop (sixth century B.C.) See APOLOGUE; BEAST EPIC.

Beat Generation. The group of writers coming to maturity in the 1950s and 1960s and rebelling against literary and social conventions, pursuing ecstatic states through meditation and hallucinogens. Allen

Ginsberg, the leading poet, was a close friend of novelists Jack Kerouac and William Burroughs in New York, and the three sparked the movement in San Francisco in 1954. Ginsberg's long dithyrambic poem *Howl*, published in San Francisco in 1956, is a major work, proclaiming that society and insanity have destroyed the "best minds of my generation." Kerouac's *On The Road* (1957) was also of major importance in spreading the Beat gospel. *Beat* suggests being beaten into weariness, the beat of the jazz to which the poets often read their works, and the beatitude they claimed to achieve through freedom, poetry, and drugs.

Belief, Problem of.   (1) The question of whether the reader's prior beliefs color evaluation of a work of literature. The NEW CRITICISM answers, "Probably, but they should not: the work's aesthetic and intellectual power should radiate its own merits." (2) More broadly, the modern inability or the wish to find a belief. See AUTOTELIC.

Belles-Lettres.   "Beautiful letters, fine writing" (French). (1) IMAGINATIVE as opposed to EXPOSITORY WRITING. (2) Literature as aesthetic rather than didactic. (3) Light literature, or all literature, viewed as trivial, especially in the adjective *belletristic*. Swift first applied the term in English in *Tatler* 230 (1710)—"The Traders in History and Politics, and the Belles Lettres"—giving it from the start its pejorative connotation ("Traders").

Benthamism.   The utilitarian philosophy of Jeremy Bentham (1748–1832): the belief that the basis for morality is the greatest happiness for the greatest number. See UTILITARIANISM.

Bestiary.   A medieval collection of allegorical poems about animals and their habits, for moral and satirical point. The bestiary originated in folk tales about talking creatures like those of Aesop (sixth century B.C.). The term also refers to treatises on natural history. The *Physiologi*, after the Greek moralist Physiologus (c. A.D. 150), arising about A.D. 900, were unnatural natural histories with a religious point, popularizing lore about the phoenix rising from its ashes and the bear licking its cubs into shape.

Bibelot.   A literary trinket, especially a beautifully bound miniature edition.

Bible.   The Holy Scriptures, the Old and New Testament, "The Book." The word derives from the Greek *biblion*, "book," originally a diminutive form of Byblos, Syria, the ancient world's chief exporter of

papyrus after the sedges died out along the lower Egyptian Nile. The
Torah ("The Law"), the Prophets, and the Writings (including the
Psalter and ending with Chronicles) comprise the Jewish Bible, which
evolved from ancient times into the Hebrew Masoretic, the traditional
text of the tenth century. St. Paul designated the Jewish Holy Scriptures as the Old Testament, to distinguish them from the new covenant
with God through Christ. Consequently, the early Christian writings,
all in Greek—the common Mediterranean language of the first century—eventually became the New Testament.

The Old Testament consists of the Pentateuch ("the five papyrus
boxes" containing the Torah—Genesis, Exodus, Leviticus, Numbers,
Deuteronomy), the various chronicles, Job, Psalms, Proverbs, the
Song of Solomon, and the Prophets.

The New Testament is composed of the Gospels (Matthew, Mark,
Luke, John), Acts, Epistles, the Book of Revelation. The New Testament Scriptures began about A.D. 50 with St. Paul's two epistles to the
Thessalonians, followed by a *Logia*, or collection of Christ's sayings,
by Matthew, then the Gospel of Mark (c. 64–70). The Gospels of Luke
and Matthew combine Matthew's *Logia* and the Gospel of Mark, probably drawing from other sources as well. John wrote a decade or two
later, before the close of the first century.

The Septuagint is a third-century B.C. Greek Old Testament, translated by the "Seventy" (Latin, *septuaginta*) Jewish scholars, supposedly
in seventy-two days, on the island of Pharos in Alexandrine Egypt.
The Vulgate (Latin, "the popular," "the people's") is the Latin version
by St. Jerome (c. A.D. 340–420). The Vulgate was finished about A.D.
400, revised from an older Latin version with careful research and aid
from Jewish scholars. This, with many unauthorized changes, became
the standard Bible throughout the Middle Ages until the Reformation
prompted vernacular versions. See BIBLE AS LITERATURE; BIBLE,
TRANSLATIONS OF; and DEAD SEA SCROLLS.

Bible as Literature.   The Bible considered for its narrative and imaginative qualities, as distinct from its religious content. Studies of the
Bible as literature often treat the Bible as a kind of anthology, concentrating on parts of it, such as the Book of Job, that seem analogous to
the reader's other literary experiences. But this does violence both to
the Bible and to the traditional way of reading it. The Bible has always
been regarded as a self-consistent unit and not as a miscellaneous pile
of small books, and its cultural influence, including its literary influence, has derived from that view of it.

While it is not possible to say that the Bible simply "is" a work of literature, no book could have exerted its immense literary influence without having literary qualities. Its narrative is submerged for the most part, but still the Christian Bible begins with the beginning of time at the Creation, ends with the end of time at the Last Judgment, and surveys the history of humankind—under the symbolic names of Adam and Israel—in between. Its climax is reached near the end with the revelation in the Gospels of the hero of the story. Again, the language of the Bible is metaphorical and figurative throughout, and proceeds by a repetition of concrete images (sheep, mountains, rivers, bread, wine, bride and bridegroom, trees, serpents, monsters, cities, gardens, etc.) which recur so often that they clearly point to some kind of overall structure of imagery.

The fact that the Bible includes a kind of total narrative, with a beginning at Creation and an end at the Last Judgment, has enabled it to form an imaginative framework for later Christian centuries. For example, Shakespeare's *Richard II* begins with a scene in which Bolingbroke accuses his enemy Mowbray of a murder he compares to Cain's murder of Abel. It ends with Henry IV (the same Bolingbroke) dissociating himself from the murder of Richard II that he had ordered himself, and sentencing the actual murderer to banishment "with Cain." In between comes a scene with a gardener who discourses allegorically on the proper way to govern a country and who is addressed by the queen as "old Adam's likeness"—that is, Adam after the fall, tilling resisting ground. There are also several references to the trial of Christ during Richard's abdication. None of this makes *Richard II* a Christian allegory, but it puts the story into a frame of reference that the original audience might be assumed to have brought into the theater with them. The same is true of the opening description of the London fog in Dickens's *Bleak House,* recalling the Flood, and the references to the judgments of the law courts as a kind of parody of the trial and judgment metaphor in the Bible.

All through the history of literature, there have been two major modes of organization of imagery. The model for one mode is the cycle of nature: images are arranged in cyclical patterns corresponding to the daily cycle of the sun, the yearly cycle of seasons, the lunar cycle, and the larger historical cycles in which empires decline and fall and others arise. This arrangement suggests an environment of death and rebirth, with despondency accompanying every decline and hope attached to every return. Cyclical imagery, though present in the Bible, is not the dominating pattern there: the Bible seems to insist on an absolute beginning and end. The second organizing mode is that of polarity, in which images of an ideal world are separated from and opposed to demonic images of a hideous or repulsive world. The latter, after separation, seem to be parodies of their ideal counterparts. This polarized imagery is the mode on which the Bible is primarily based: the trees and water of Eden are contrasted with the wasteland and dead seas of heathen kingdoms, Jerusalem is contrasted with Babylon, lambs and sheep are contrasted with beasts of prey or dragons, and the like. This polarized imagery, where instead of death followed by rebirth we have eternal death and permanent resurrection—or what later Christianity identified as heaven and hell—is the major contribution of the Bible to literary craft, as classical literature's major contribution was cyclical imagery.

Actual literature is purely hypothetical: the poet makes certain assumptions that readers must accept if they are to read at all. The assumptions themselves are not questioned, and it is only what the poet does with them that is relevant to criticism. The Bible can hardly be confined to the hypothetical literary world in this way. But there is an intermediate form between the imaginative or literary and the discursive or direct-address use of words: this is the form traditionally known as rhetoric, where there is an element of persuasion bound up with the figurative use of language. Rhetoric is often (and often rightly) distrusted, but the style of the Bible can hardly be separated from rhetorical address. The term *kerygma*, "proclamation," applied by biblical scholars in particular to the New Testament, seems to apply to the whole of the Bible so far as its figuration of language is concerned.

Bible, Translations of. Renditions of the Bible in languages other than those of its first composition. The Christian Bible consists of an Old Testament, a New Testament, and a body of writings known as the Old Testament APOCRYPHA. The Old Testament was written in Hebrew (except for a few passages in Aramaic, the language which succeeded Hebrew in biblical countries), and its text was established in the New Testament period. It is known as the Masoretic, or traditional text. The greatest difficulty in achieving it lay in the fact that the 22 letters of the Hebrew alphabet are all consonants, and hence practically all the vowels are editorial. Some centuries earlier, the Old Testament had been translated into Greek for the benefit of Jews living in various parts of the Greek-speaking world. This translation is known as the Septuagint (abbreviated LXX), from the traditional number of

translators. Because it is earlier than the final Masoretic text, it sometimes preserves earlier and more primitive readings. The recent discovery of DEAD SEA SCROLLS, which include versions of most books of
the Old Testament, indicates that the textual tradition was far more
conservative than many scholars had previously considered it to be.

The New Testament was written in the colloquial and conversa-
tional Greek, known as *koiné,* which was the general linguistic medium
of the Near East at the time. Its writers were doubtless familiar to
varying degrees with the Hebrew text, but when they quoted from the
Old Testament they tended to use the Septuagint. Throughout its history Christianity has been more dependent on translation than either
Judaism or Islam. As the center of Christianity shifted to Rome, the
need for a Latin Bible became urgent, and this was supplied by St.
Jerome in the fifth century A.D., in the version known as the Vulgate,
or version in common use. In Western Europe, Jerome's Latin or Vulgate Bible *was* the Bible for the next thousand years.

The Apocrypha consists of 14 books excluded by Hebrew scholars
from the canon because, although most if not all of them were almost
certainly originally written in Hebrew, the Hebrew original had disappeared, and they could be read only in Greek or Latin. Jerome translated the Apocrypha, but placed it in a separate section. The Catholic
church overruled him on this point, but Protestant Bibles also put it
in a separate section, when they bother to include it at all. Hence the
Old Testament ends with Malachi in Protestant Bibles, and with II
Maccabees in Catholic ones, both versions deriving their order from
the Septuagint. The Jewish arrangement of the books is much more
schematic: 5 books of the Law, as in Christian Bibles; 4 "Former
Prophets" (Joshua, Judges, Samuel, Kings); 4 "Latter Prophets"
(Isaiah, Jeremiah, Ezekiel, and the 12 minor prophets); and a miscellaneous group called the "Writings," including the Psalter and ending
with Chronicles.

In England, the followers of the reformer John Wyclif, in the fourteenth century, translated the Vulgate into English. The fact that the
move to translate the Bible into the vernacular was associated with
reforming or heretical sects led to great resistance to such translation
among church authorities, and caused great bitterness on both sides.
A translation of the Bible from Greek and Hebrew originals was made
under the direction of Martin Luther in Germany, as one of the first
efforts of the Reformation, and this German version is a cornerstone of
German literature as well. In the reign of Henry VIII, William Tyndale, a refugee working on the Continent, made the first attempt to

translate the Bible into English from Greek and Hebrew, but he was kidnapped by Henry's secret police and taken to England, where he was burnt along with many copies of his translation. However, Henry changed his mind and his policy, and by the time of his death a complete English Bible, edited mainly by Miles Coverdale, was available for use in English churches.

Under Elizabeth I there were two English Bibles: one the "Bishop's Bible," a product of conservative scholarship and approved by the Church of England; the other the "Geneva Bible," produced by Puritan scholars working on the Continent as refugees, like Tyndale earlier, during the reign of Mary I. It was also called the "Breeches Bible," because of its rendering of Genesis 3:7. Its scholarship was not in question, but its strongly polemical marginal notes brought it under official disapproval. Shakespeare is thought to have used a Bishop's Bible for his earlier plays and a Geneva Bible for the later ones, almost certainly by pure chance. When James I succeeded Elizabeth in 1603, one of his first acts was to call a conference at Hampton Court in an effort to reconcile Episcopalian and Puritan wings of the Church of England. The conference accomplished little beyond a resolution to provide an "authorized" translation of the complete Bible, including the Apocrypha, which would be a joint effort of the two bodies of scholars. This translation appeared in 1611, and has been known ever since as the Authorized Version or King James' Bible.

This version was an astonishing literary success. It was conceived as a traditional rather than a scholarly translation, and it keeps very close to the Vulgate tradition. The translators thought of it as primarily a version to be read aloud in churches, and their sensitivity to the rhythms and sounds of spoken language was very keen. Among Christian groups only the Roman Catholics attempted to rival it for many centuries. Once again working as refugees on the Continent, they produced an English New Testament at Rheims in 1582, and a complete English Bible at Douai in France in 1609. These were translations of the Vulgate, following the directive of the Council of Trent, which had declared that version to be the authentic one. Because of this the Douai Bible is further removed from ordinary speech, and contains a greater number of learned and abstract words.

It was not until the nineteenth century that a need for new translations made itself felt: by that time there had been many discoveries of new manuscripts and of historical and archeological material, along with greatly increased scholarly knowledge of such matters as the nature of Hebrew poetry. The earlier revised versions (English in 1881–

1885, American in 1900) were not very successful; considering what was available, the improvements in scholarship were not enough, and the prestige of the Authorized Version was more of a hindrance than a help. Twentieth-century translations are too numerous to be considered here: of Protestant Bibles, the Revised Standard Version of 1952 and the New English Bible of 1970 may be mentioned; among Catholic translations, the Jerusalem Bible, and the Anchor Bible, employing Jewish, Protestant, and Catholic scholars, is an ambitious though still incomplete project.

Bibliographical Description.   A system to describe a book materially, as to title page, collation, and contents.

Title page. The copy is recorded line by line, with rule lines between sections, vertical slashes making line ends, and brackets enclosing details such as ornaments. For instance, to describe Hogarth's *Analysis of Beauty* (1753), the following is included:

> | *Curl'd many a wanton wreath, in sight of Eve,* | *To lure her eye.*
> ------Milton. | — | [ornament] | [ornamental rule line] |
> LONDON: | Printed by *J. Reeves* for the *AUTHOR.* |

Collation. The book's size (folio, quarto, octavo—see BOOK SIZES) is followed by its physical assembly, its gatherings, or "signatures," as the printer marks them to keep the job straight. Octavos, for instance, have 8-leaf (16-page) signatures, usually signed at the bottom of the first 4 leaves of each gathering by a capital letter and number: A, A2, A3, A4. Descriptions include plusses and minuses for missing or substituted leaves, and the puzzling $, an abbreviation for "signatures." Brackets enclose unnumbered pages.

Contents. Each part is recorded on the leaf where it begins—title page, dedication, preface, text, major divisions—and where the major divisions end, including publisher's advertisements and blank pages. A superscribed ^{r} means *recto*, the front of a leaf; a ^{v} means *verso*, the back.

Here is a bibliographical description of Fielding's *Tom Jones*, first edition, printed in duodecimo (12°), first volume:

FIRST EDITION (1749), Six Volumes
THE | HISTORY | OF | *TOM JONES,* | A | Foundling. | — | In
SIX VOLUMES. | — | By HENRY FIELDING, Esq; | — |
—*Mores hominum multorum vidit.*— | = | *LONDON:* | Printed for
A. MILLAR, over-against | *Catharine-street* in the *Strand.* |
MDCCXLIX.

Collation: VOL. I. 12°: A^{12} b^{12} c^8 B^{12} (-B9,10 + B9,10) C-K^{12}, 140 leaves ($6 signed), pp. [i–ii] iii–lxii [lxiii–lxiv], [1] 2–214 [215–216]
Contents: VOL. I. A1: title, verso blank; A2: dedication, "═ | To the HONOURABLE | George Lyttleton, *Esq;* | One of the Lords Commissioners of | the TREASURY.", subscribed on A8^v, "Henry Fielding."; A9; contents of the six volumes; c8: "The Reader is desired to correct the following | ERRATA." (errata for Vols. I–V); c8^v: blank. B1: text, headed "═ | THE | HISTORY OF A FOUNDLING. | — | ", ending with Book III, Chap. 10, on K11^v with "*The End of the* First Volume. | [ornament]"; K12^{r-v}: blank.

The *collation* would translate: "This is a duodecimo (12mo). The first signature, A, has twelve leaves; the second, marked b, has twelve; the third, marked c, has eight. Then follows signature B, with the usual twelve, but the original leaves 9 and 10 were cancelled and removed (these are termed *cancellanda*) and corrected leaves (*cancellans*) were substituted. Then signatures C through K proceed, all with the usual twelve leaves. The book totals 140 leaves, with signatures ($) "6-signed"—that is, the first six leaves of each signature bear its letter and sequential numbers: B, B1, B2, B3, B4, B5, B6, on front side. The introductory matter fills 64 pages, of which i, ii, lxiii, and lxiv are unnumbered. Page 1 of the text is also unnumbered, as are concluding pages 215 and 216, the blank leaf that fills out the last gathering.

The *contents* would translate: Leaf A1 is the title page, blank on back. The dedication, headed as shown, begins on the face of leaf A2 and is signed "Henry Fielding" on the back of A8. The table of contents begins on A9; c8, with its back blank, gives a page of errata, or printer's errors, the reader is asked to correct. The novel itself begins on B1, headed as shown, and ends, as shown, on the back of K11, with the final leaf of gathering K blank.

A shorthand way to mark rule lines in transcribing the title page is to stand them on end and save space. Thus | — | becomes ‖ , and | ═ | becomes ⦀ .

References

Fredson T. Bowers, **Principles of Bibliographical Description** (1949). ———, **Bibliography and Textual Criticism** (1964).

Bibliography. (1) A list of works by an author or publisher, or on an author or subject. (2) The occupation of making bibliographies. Bibliographies concluding scholarly essays and books list alphabetically, by author, the works cited. A *subject bibliography* may be comprehensive or selective, listing only important works. An *enumerative bibliography* lists works by country (a "national" bibliography), by printer (a "trade" bibliography), or by author.

Bildungsroman.   A novel of education from youth to experience, such as Goethe's *Wilhelm Meisters Lehrjahr* (1830–"William Meister's Learning-year"), from which the term originates. Other examples are Charles Dickens's *David Copperfield* (1849–1850), Samuel Butler's posthumous *Way of All Flesh* (1903), Somerset Maugham's *Of Human Bondage* (1915), James Joyce's *Portrait of the Artist as a Young Man* (1916), Herman Hesse's *Demian* (1919; translated, 1923), Thomas Wolfe's *Look Homeward, Angel* (1929), and Saul Bellow's *Adventures of Augie March* (1953). Also called an APPRENTICESHIP NOVEL, an *Entwicklungsgeschichte*, "a story of development," and an *Erziehungs-roman*, "a novel of education." When it concerns an artist, like Joyce's *Portrait*, it becomes a KÜNSTLERROMAN, an "artist novel."

Billingsgate.   Coarse, violent, abusive language. The term alludes to the language of London's Billingsgate fish market, noted for its vulgarity.

Biographical Criticism.   An examination of a literary work in relation to the life of the writer. See CRITICISM.

Biographical Essay.   An ESSAY providing a brief history of a person's life—as, for example, in an ENCYCLOPEDIA or other reference book.

Biographical Fallacy.   Reliance on an understanding of the life of a writer to explain the meaning of a literary work. Such an approach is viewed as a fallacy according to the NEW CRITICISM, which holds that the work contains its own meaning, without reference to biography. See GENETIC FALLACY; INTENTIONAL FALLACY.

Biography.   A life of one person written by another, as compared to an AUTOBIOGRAPHY, a life written by the person who has lived it. The impetus to record people's lives, especially great people's, is ancient and can be seen in the records of the deeds of kings carved in stone centuries before Christ, in various sites of the ancient world. Early literature in such forms as BALLAD, CHRONICLE, EPIC, and LEGEND is often partly biographical in intent. A modern biography, however, is generally more detailed and more accurate than these accounts.

Among forerunners of modern biography, Plutarch's *Parallel Lives* (second century) ranks high for its comparative portraits of Greeks and Romans, supplying, in the English translation of Sir Thomas North, material for Shakespeare's *Coriolanus, Julius Caesar, Antony and Cleopatra,* and *Timon of Athens.* In the Middle Ages, biography is best represented in the SAINTS' LIVES and in the individual portraits in chronicles like Jean Froissart's. In the sixteenth century, the works often called the first English biographies began to appear: Cardinal Morton's *Life of Richard III,* William Roper's *Life of Sir Thomas More,* and George Cavendish's *Life of Wolsey.* The seventeenth century produced Izaak Walton's *Lives* and John Aubrey's *Lives of Eminent Men,* but biography really came into its own in the eighteenth century, with Samuel Johnson's *Lives of the Poets* and James Boswell's *Life of Johnson.* Boswell's, especially, has provided the standard against which later biographies are measured.

In the nineteenth and twentieth centuries, biographies have often been more carefully researched than in earlier times, and are sometimes massive and scholarly, but the biography has also become a form of POPULAR LITERATURE, breezy and anecdotal. Among works especially admired, for various qualities, are John G. Lockhart's *Life of Sir Walter Scott,* Lytton Strachey's *Eminent Victorians* and *Queen Victoria,* André Maurois's *Ariel* (a life of Shelley), Carl Sandburg's *Abraham Lincoln,* and Dumas Malone's *Thomas Jefferson.*

Biographies have been written for at least five purposes: to commemorate a life, to reward curiosity, to explain creative or public life by reference to the private background, to illuminate a period or movement by examination of the people within it, or to illustrate a thesis. Commemorative biographies sometimes take the form of a life in letters, or an accumulation of documents, with minimal narrative interspersed. Rewarding curiosity is often the primary motivation of the popular biography—of a movie star or sports figure, for example. Biographies aimed at explanation of works of a writer or artist, or of the career of a public servant, have often in the twentieth century taken a marked psychological turn, explaining the outer life in terms of the inner. Period or movement biographies examine selected individual lives for the light they shed on the history of a time or place. Thesis biographies date from the Middle Ages, when Saints' Lives glorified God; in the twentieth century such biographies illustrate a variety of philosophical, psychological, or sociological positions—as, for example, Marxism.

Biographies purport to tell the truth, or to construct a different kind of truth from the fictional truth of other literary genres. Increasingly in the twentieth century, however, biographers have become aware of the selective nature of their art and the elusive nature of truth. Consequently, biography, like autobiography, has sometimes moved closer to FICTION, as biographers frequently adopt the methods of novelists, and novelists write books based upon real people and events.

Among biographical reference books, the *Dictionary of National Biography* (English) and the *Dictionary of American Biography* are standard for persons no longer living. Recently there has been a proliferation of books providing short summaries of the lives of distinguished people, or of members of a given industry or discipline. Film and television documentaries are also forms of contemporary biography.

References

Leon Edel, **Literary Biography** (1959).
André Maurois, **Aspects of Biography** (trans. 1966).
H. G. Nicolson, **The Development of English Biography** (1928).
E. H. O'Neill, **A History of American Biography** (1961).

Black and White Characters.   Another name for FLAT CHARACTERS, two-dimensional, all good or all bad, as illustrated in the black horse and black outfit of the VILLAIN in a WESTERN, who opposes the HERO, dressed in light clothing and riding a white horse. More realistic characters are GRAY (or GRAYED) CHARACTERS. See CHARACTERS.

Black English.   The DIALECT of American blacks. Its roots are in the languages brought from Africa, the special circumstances of a slave population (the need for coded communication and the linguistic confusion of differing African languages and dialects spoken on a single plantation), and the white English of the American South. Spoken, at least part of the time, by a large percentage of the black population of the United States, it has also influenced Standard English as some elements of its vocabulary and syntax have been absorbed into the general language.

Among the characteristics of Black English are the following:

1. A vocabulary largely identical to that of Standard English, but with some shared words used in quite different senses. *Jazz* is music in Standard English, but originated in Black English as a sexual term. The Standard English *bad* can mean "strong" or "powerful" in Black English, and can connote admiration or even awe. The confusion that can result was illustrated when Muhammad Ali was widely quoted as saying, "There are two bad white men in the

world, the Russian white man and the American white man. They are the two baddest men in the history of the world."

2. Patterns of pronunciation that include the tendency, common in Southern English, to lengthen vowels to diphthongs, producing the Southern drawl; substitution of *f* for *th* at the end and in the middle of words ("maf" for "math," "birfday" for "birthday"); and elimination, in some circumstances, of the sounds of *r, l, t,* and *d* ("fote" for "fort," "toe" for "toll," "firs" for "first," "men" for "mend").

3. Special treatment of the verb *"to be"* including the use of *be* to indicate continual or habitual action ("He be working" means "He is employed" but does not necessarily mean "He is working at this moment"), and elimination of some forms of *to be* ("She my momma," "He always angry").

4. Special treatment of other verb forms, including the elimination of final *s* from the third-person singular ("He like dogs"), the addition of *s* to the first-person singular ("I likes him"), and the dropping of the final *ed* in the past tense ("She walk to work last week").

5. Possession indicated without inflectional *s* ("Her momma dress").

6. Use of *it* in place of *there* ("It's an empty house down the street," "It ain't nobody I know would take that job").

See AMERICAN LANGUAGE.

References

D. Dalby, **Black Through White: Patterns of Communication in Africa and the New World** (1969).

J. L. Dillard, **Lexicon of Black English** (1977).

William Labov, **Language in the Inner City** (1972).

C. Major, **Dictionary of Afro-American Slang** (1970).

Black Humor. Humor discovered in pain, despair, horror, or a generally pessimistic view of the world. Vladimir Nabokov's *Laughter in the Dark* and Nathanael West's *Miss Lonelyhearts* are examples from the 1930s, but the term is most frequently applied to post–World War II writers, especially in America, who present a sense of alienation heightened by laughter. Joseph Heller, Kurt Vonnegut, and Thomas Pynchon are often cited. See ABSURB; GALLOWS HUMOR.

Black Letter. A heavy typeface, called also *Gothic, Old English,* and *German,* characterized by angular lines and ornamental scrolls. This type, derived from handwriting, was the first used in printing in Europe. Lighter styles came in later, although black letter type has remained an alternative into the twentieth century, especially in Germany. The phrase *black letter book* commonly suggests an old one.

Black Literature.   See AFRO-AMERICAN LITERATURE.

Black Mountain School.   A name applied to poets associated in the 1950s with Black Mountain College, an experimental school in North Carolina. The poet Charles Olson, rector of the college from 1951 to 1956, brought the poets Robert Duncan, Robert Creeley, and Edward Dorn, as well as innovators in the other arts, to the school. Anti-establishment and AVANT-GARDE, they published the *Black Mountain Review* and influenced others, including Cid Corman, Joel Oppenheimer, LeRoi Jones (Imamu Amiri Baraka), and Denise Levertov. Olson's essay "Projective Verse" remains their most important statement. See PROJECTIVE VERSE.

Blank Verse.   Unrhymed iambic pentameter. See METER. Henry Howard, earl of Surrey, seems to have originated it in English as the equivalent of Virgil's unrhymed dactylic hexameter, his translations from the *Aeneid* appearing sometime before 1547. In *Gorboduc* (1561), Thomas Sackville and Thomas Norton introduced blank verse into the drama, whence it soared with Marlowe and Shakespeare in the 1590s. In 1576, Gascoigne's *Steele Glas* put blank verse to discursive satiric use. Milton forged it anew for the epic in *Paradise Lost* (1667).

Bleed.   In printing and bookbinding, the technique of printing a page so that, after the sheets have been trimmed, the type or illustration runs off the page, leaving no margin. A page treated this way is called a *bleed page*.

Block Book.   A book printed from an engraved wooden block, as opposed to one printed from movable type. A few block books were printed in Europe in the fifteenth century, but the technique was more common in the Orient, where the languages, composed of characters rather than alphabets, made printing from movable type more difficult.

Bloomsbury Group.   An informal social and intellectual group associated with Bloomsbury, a London residential district near the British Museum, from about 1904 until the outbreak of World War II. Virginia Woolf was a principal member. With her husband, Leonard Woolf, she established the Hogarth Press, which published works by many of their friends. The group was loosely knit, but famed, especially in the 1920s, for its exclusiveness, AESTHETICISM, and snobbishness. Members included, at various times, Lytton Strachey, Clive Bell,

Victoria Sackville-West, Roger Fry, John Maynard Keynes, E. M. Forster, Christopher Isherwood, and David Garnett.

Reference

Quentin Bell, **Bloomsbury** (1969).

Blues. A form of jazz, melancholy and plaintive. The blues style is characterized by 12 bars of melody, supported by 3 chords (tonic, dominant, and subdominant), with the *blue notes* provided by flatted thirds and sevenths. The 12 bars divide into 3 units of 4: a statement, repetition with or without variation, and conclusion.

> That gal is so low down, I often wonder why—
> That gal is so low down, I often wonder why—
> She keeps on livin', 'cause she's just too mean to die.

Sometimes blues are sung, but many works are purely instrumental. In *talking blues,* the lyrics are spoken to musical accompaniment. Blues are often traditional, like the BALLAD, originating anonymously and developing through oral transmission, although some can be identified with a particular composer or performer. Important writers and singers include W. C. Handy, Jimmie Rodgers, Woody Guthrie, Blind Lemon Jefferson, Huddie Ledbetter, Lightnin' Sam Hopkins, Ma Rainey, and Bessie Smith.

Bluestocking. A term applied, disparagingly, to learned or literary women. It was first used in the eighteenth century in reference to women who attended literary gatherings, among them Elizabeth Montagu, Hannah More, and Fanny Burney. James Boswell, in his *Life of Johnson,* says the term derives from the blue (rather than the customary black) stockings worn by one of the men who also attended.

Blurb. A publisher's extravagant description of or advertisement for a book, often printed on the jacket. The term originated in America, and is generally credited to Gelett Burgess.

Boasting Poem. One in which a hero boasts of his exploits. Boasting poems are often incorporated into an EPIC, as in *Beowulf.*

Bob and Wheel. A unit of verse combining a very short line with a few somewhat longer ones. A *bob* is a short, or "bobbed," line, frequently of only two syllables. A *wheel* is a set of short lines, typically with three or four stresses each, ending a STANZA. A *bob and wheel* combines the two, typically in five lines, with the bob first, rhyming *ababa.* The most famous example is the bob and wheel that ends each stanza of *Sir Gawain and the Green Knight.*

Boldface.   Type with a **heavy black face.**

Bombast.   Originally, raw cotton or other material used as stuffing or padding in clothing, and hence, since the sixteenth century also used as a name for inflated, pompous language. The adjective is *bombastic.*

Bon Mot.   French for "good word": an apt, clever saying or witticism.

Book Sizes.   Term referring to physical dimensions of volumes. Whatever their finished sizes, books are first printed on large sheets, which are then folded one or more times, sewn (or, sometimes in modern books, glued), and cut to make the pages. The large sheets, called FOOLSCAP, were once of a uniform size, 13½ inches by 17 inches. When folded once, each sheet produced a section, called a SIGNATURE, with 2 leaves (4 pages), which was then bound with other signatures to produce a large book called a FOLIO. When the foolscap was folded twice, the same procedure produced a smaller book, with 4 leaves (8 pages) in each signature, called a QUARTO. One more folding produced a signature of 8 leaves (16 pages) and a still smaller book, called an *octavo.* Another method of folding produced a *duodecimo* volume, with signatures each of 12 leaves (24 pages). Still other foldings produced *sixteenmo* (16 leaves, 32 pages), *thirty-twomo* (32 leaves, 64 pages), and *sixty-fourmo* (64 leaves, 128 pages), each size smaller than the last.

Modern printers do not always begin with stock of the older, standard size. Consequently, for modern books the terms *folio, quarto, octavo,* and so on have become more relative than precise as indicators of size. In modern practice also, these terms are not necessarily reliable guides to the number of leaves in a signature.

Bourgeois Drama.   Modern realistic DRAMA with middle-class CHARACTERS and problems. See SOCIAL DRAMA.

Bourgeois Literature.   Literature appealing to the middle classes. In this and other applications, the term *bourgeois* is used by Marxist critics to suggest a preoccupation with middle-class values and a lack of concern for the problems of the lower classes. See CRITICISM.

Bourgeois Tragedy.   TRAGEDY with a middle-class PROTAGONIST. See DOMESTIC TRAGEDY; SOCIAL DRAMA.

Bouts-rimés.   French for "rhyming ends": a game in which participants are presented a list of rhyme words and must use them in a poem in the order given. Originating in Paris in the seventeenth century, the game was long popular in France and England.

Bowdlerize.   To alter a book by deleting passages considered immoral or indelicate. The practice takes its name from Thomas Bowdler (1754–1825), English editor, whose expurgated *Family Shakespeare* was long popular.

Box Set.   A stage set in the form of a box, representing three walls of a room, with the fourth wall, invisible, understood as separating the actors from the audience. See PICTURE FRAME STAGE.

Brachycatalectic.   A metrical line short (*brachy-*) two syllables, as in the fourth line of this stanza from Ralph Hodgson's "Eve":

> Eve, with her basket, was
> Deep in the bells and grass
> Wading in bells and grass
> Up to her knees.

See METER.

Braggadocio.   A name for the STOCK CHARACTER of the boasting, cowardly soldier, taken from the character of that name in Spenser's *Fairie Queene*. Another name is MILES GLORIOSUS. See CHARACTERS.

Brahmins.   Among Hindus, the highest, or priestly, caste. In American literature, a term applied to the highest level of New England society, first used in that sense by Oliver Wendell Holmes in "The Brahmin Caste of New England," Chapter I of *Elsie Venner* (1861).

Breton Lay.   A short MEDIEVAL ROMANCE, typically concerning love and magic, and including folklore motifs, perhaps originally sung. The precise original meaning of the term is obscure, but it suggests an early connection with Celtic Brittany. Early Breton lays, if they existed, no longer survive. Some of the poems of Marie de France, a twelfth-century French poet who lived at the English court of Henry II, were said to be based on Breton lays, and the term is used for later poems adapted from or similar to hers. In English, *Sir Orfeo* and Chaucer's *Franklin's Tale* are examples.

Breve.   In SCANSION, the mark ˘ set above a syllable to indicate that it is short or unstressed. A long or stressed syllable is indicated by a MACRON ‾.

Breviary.   The book of Divine Offices for members of Roman Catholic orders. It contains a calendar, list of Saints' Days, Psalter, lessons, recitations, Hours of the Virgin, and burial services, but not the Communion service.

Brief. (1) A writing issued by an official or legal authority. (2) A papal letter, less solemn than a BULL. (3) An ABRIDGMENT or EPITOME. (4) In legal practice, a summary of the main points of law affecting a case.

British Museum. The national repository for British treasures in art, science, and literature, located in Bloomsbury, in West Central London. Founded by an act of Parliament in 1753, it opened its doors in 1759. It is both a museum and a library, its Reading Room one of the world's great research centers. It possesses the only manuscript of *Beowulf*, and manuscripts of the *Magna Carta*, Jean Froissart's *Chroniques*, and a unique papyrus Aristotle, as well as entire collections important to scholars, such as the Cotton and Harleian collections of books, manuscripts, coins, and antiquities. Among other treasures are the Rosetta Stone, the Elgin Marbles, and the remains of the Sutton Hoo ship burial. As a copyright deposit library, it receives copies of every book printed in Great Britain, and its holdings from elsewhere are vast.

Broadside. A sheet of paper printed on one side only. Broadsides containing a BALLAD or tract were once commonly sold on the streets like newspapers.

Broadside Ballad. A BALLAD printed and sold on single sheets.

Brochure. A short, printed work, consisting of a few pages stitched together, or any short work, regardless of binding. See PAMPHLET.

Broken Rhyme. RHYME created by breaking a word at the end of a line: *head- / strong* so broken rhymes with *bread.*

Bronze Age. The third of the four AGES OF THE WORLD.

Brook Farm. An experiment in communal living in West Roxbury, Massachusetts, not far from Boston, lasting from 1841 to 1846. Brook Farm was one of the most famous practical results of TRANSCENDENTALISM, as modified by Fourierism, a social system proposed by François Fourier (1772–1837). Brook Farm brought together intellectuals and farmers in an attempt to construct an ideal, self-sufficient society. Founded by George Ripley, it was a joint-stock company, involving, among others, Nathaniel Hawthorne. Emerson visitied the farm, but did not join. Hawthorne's *Blithedale Romance* (1852) recapitulates the experiment in FICTION. See DIAL, THE; UTOPIA.

Bucolic. Greek for "concerning cowherds," but synonymous with PASTORAL for poems about shepherds, their flocks, and the simple rural life. Virgil's *Eclogues*, about pastoral life, and his *Georgics*, concerning the farmer's yearly planting, tillage, herds, flocks, and bees, are both referred to as his "Bucolics." Loosely, the term applies to anything rustic or countrified.

Bull. From Latin *bulla*, a "knob" or "seal": a papal edict or the seal affixed to it.

Burden. (1) A REFRAIN, a set phrase repeated at intervals throughout a song or poem. (2) A base accompaniment, the "load" carried by the melody, the origin of the term. (3) A bagpipe's drone, the monotone accompaniment to the melody.

Burlesque. (1) A ridicule, especially on the stage, treating the lofty in low style and absurd episode, or the low in grandiose style. (2) A bawdy vaudeville, with obscene clowning and stripteasing.

The *Batrachomyomachia*, "The Battle of the Frogs and the Mice," widely attributed to Homer but probably dating about 450 B.C., a comic epic burlesquing the *Iliad*, is the earliest known. Aristophanes's comedies (427–388 B.C.) are burlesques of Greek tragedy, politics, and philosophy. Chaucer's "Tale of Sir Thopas" in *The Canterbury Tales* (c. 1387) and Cervantes's *Don Quixote* (1605, 1615) burlesque chivalric romances, as does an episode in Thomas Nash's *Unfortunate Traveler, or The Life of Jacke Wilton* (1594). *The Rehearsal* (1672) by George Villiers, duke of Buckingham, burlesques the HEROIC PLAY as popularized by Dryden, and held the stage for a century.

Burlesque flowered in the early eighteenth century, particularly in the Scriblerus Club of Pope, Swift, John Gay, John Arbuthnot (1667–1735), and others, producing *The Memoirs of the Extraordinary Life, Works, and Discoveries of Martinus Scriblerus,* eventually published in Pope's prose *Works* (1741). Three of the period's greatest works spun off independently from this short-lived collaboration in spoofing in 1712–1713: Swift's *Gulliver's Travels* (1726), Gay's *Beggar's Opera* (1728), and Pope's *Dunciad* (1728, 1743). In the decade between Gay's *Beggar's Opera* and the Licensing Act of 1737, when Robert Walpole's government had had enough, particularly from Henry Fielding, ballad opera (burlesquing current Italian opera in satirical songs to ballad tunes) and other political burlesques and farces dominated the stage. Burlesque ridicules a literary form; PARODY burlesques a specific work. See TRAVESTY.

Burletta. A farcical musical play (from the diminutive of Italian *burla*, "mockery"). Horace Walpole records the term for the first time in 1748, in a letter: "The burletta are begun: I think not decisively liked or condemned yet" (*Correspondence*, 5th ed., II.cxcv.243). George Colman the younger (1726–1836), who wrote the burletta *Turk and No Turk* (1785) and sponsored others as manager of the Haymarket Theater, defined the form as "a drama in rhyme, entirely musical—a short comick piece consisting of recitative and singing, wholly accompanied, more or less, by the orchestra."

Burns Stanza. A STANZA in 6 lines, rhyming *aaabab*, with a 4/4/4/2/4/2 stress pattern. A variety of TAIL-RHYME, it was used frequently by Robert Burns, as in these lines from "To a Mouse":

> Wee, sleeket, cowran, tim'rous *beastie*,
> O, what a panic's in thy breastie!
> Thou need na start awa sae hasty,
>   Wi' bickering brattle!
> I wad be laith to rin an' chase thee,
>   Wi' murd'ring *pattle*!

Buskin. The boot worn by Greek tragic actors. The term metaphorically means "tragedy." The boot, reaching halfway up the calf, had thick soles to give tragedians stature, just as the SOCK kept comic actors comically low. The Greek term was *cothurnus*. *Buskin*, as a general word for "boot," deriving from Spanish or other European cognates, first appeared in English in 1503 and as a technical term for the cothurnus in 1570.

C

Cabal, the. An inner group of unofficial advisors to Charles II: *C*lifford, *A*shley, *B*uckingham, *A*rlington, and *L*auderdale. The ACRONYM punned on CABALA, implying secret and sinister power.

Cabala. A secret system of interpreting Scripture, said to have been handed down orally by Abraham but actually formulated from Gnostic sources in early medieval Europe, especially in France and Spain. Words, letters, and accents contained mysterious and magical powers. See GNOSTICISM.

Cacophony. "Bad-sounding." The opposite of EUPHONY, the term signifies discordant, jarring, unharmonious language. It is a pejorative term for deliberate dissonances in poetry or prose.

Cadence. (1) In poetry, a flowing, irregular pulse, as opposed to METER. Whitman set the example, to be recommended by Ezra Pound and William Carlos Williams and followed in much modern FREE VERSE. (2) The dropping of the voice at punctuational pauses, or the general modulation of the voice.

Caesura. A pause in a metrical line, indicated by punctuation, momentarily suspending the beat (from Latin "a cutting off"). Caesuras are *masculine* at the end of a foot, and *feminine* in mid-foot. Pope's opening lines in "An Epistle to Dr. Arbuthnot," spaced out to indicate the foot pause, have five feminine caesuras and three masculines, all marked ‖ :

> Shut, ‖ shut   the door, ‖ good *John:* ‖ fatigu'd   I said,
> Tye up   the knock-   er, ‖ say   I'm sick, ‖ I'm dead,
> The Dog-   star rage-   s: ‖ nay   'tis past   a doubt,
> All *Bed-   lam,* ‖ or   *Parnas-   sus,* ‖ is   let out.

See FEMININE CAESURA; MASCULINE CAESURA.

Calendar. A scheme dividing the year into days, weeks, and months, especially important for literary historians in distinguishing Old Style from New Style. Julius Caesar introduced the Julian calendar, now known as the Old Style, in 46 B.C. The ancient Roman year of 10 months began in March, naming the last 4 months September, October, November, December. The reign of Numa (715–672 B.C.) added 2 months: January at the beginning—from the god Janus, the door opener—and February at the end, from the *februa* festival of purification. When Julius Caesar came along, January and February had been shifted to the first of the year, but calculating months by the moon had thrown the year out of kilter. The Julian calendar recalculated for the solar year and later renamed 2 summer months *July* and *August*, after Julius and Augustus Caesar. Caesar set the year at 365¼ days, with months 1, 3, 5, 7, 9, and 11 having 31 days, as against 30 for the other 6, with February, the shortest, having normally 29, but 30 every fourth year. Augustus Caesar, jealous of his adoptive father, made his month 31 days and chopped 1 day from February.

But Caesar's calendar calculated the year too long by 11 minutes and 14 seconds, amounting to a full day every 128 years. To restore the vernal equinox at about 21 March, Pope Gregory XIII dropped 10 days from the calendar in 1582, with other calculations to manage the leap year. The Gregorian calendar is "New Style," finally adopted by the British and their American colonies in 1752. Consequently, all British annual dates before 25 March 1752, the Feast of the Annunciation, or "Lady Day," belong to the year later: "February 1742" is Old Style ("O.S.") for February 1743 New Style ("N.S."). Dates printed as "1 March, 1748/49" or "3 January, 1749/50" refer to the later year, here 1749 and 1750. From 1582 until 1752, all British dates are 10 days later than their European counterparts, unless adjusted (as most historians do). For a most useful "perpetual calendar" to calculate the date of any day in the week, Old Style or New Style, see "Appendix III," *The Oxford Companion to English Literature* (1932 and following).

Calligraphy. "Beautiful writing." The term means fine handwriting or penmanship. Oriental and Arabic calligraphy treasured aesthetic effects, and medieval scribes similarly developed their handwriting to achieve an artistic quality.

Calvinism. The severe Protestant theology propounded in Geneva by John Calvin (1509–1564), an emigrant Frenchman, notably in his *Institutes of the Christian Religion* (1536). All is predestined, and humans, totally depraved from Adam's fall, have no free will. God has elected some for salvation, though the rest are damned. Good works count neither for the elect nor for the damned. God's grace, ordained from the beginning, descends only on the elect. Christ's atonement for corrupt humanity visits only the elect, as the Holy Spirit helps them to try to do God's will as revealed in Scripture.

The Puritans in England and America, and the Presbyterians in Scotland, were among the earliest Calvinists. COVENANT THEOLOGY mitigated Calvin's harshness, proposing a contract between God and humans for working out salvation. Especially in New England, the covenant urged responsibility for public confession to keep the community whole. New England Calvinists considered education a religious duty, establishing colleges, public schools, and printing presses, much to the new country's advantage. The early twentieth-century sociologist Max Weber pointed out the strange alliance of Calvinism and capitalism, wherein commercial success indicated an "elect" in God's "calling." Calvinist thought is broadly evident in literature, in Defoe's *Robinson Crusoe*, for instance, in Hawthorne, in Faulkner, and in others who attack the Southern Calvinist's division of the elect and the damned along racial lines.

References

Page Smith, **As a City upon a Hill** (1966).
R. H. Tawney, **Religion and the Rise of Capitalism** (1926).
Max Weber, **The Protestant Ethic and the Spirit of Capitalism** (1930—originally in German, 1904–1905).

Calypso.   A rhythmic, improvised style of song originating among the blacks of Trinidad and named after the Greek nymph Calypso, "she who conceals." Calypso songs are often satirical, always topical.

Cambridge Platonists.   A group of Puritan thinkers at Cambridge University, who, led by Benjamin Whichcote (1609–1683) and inspired by his sermons, rejected both Calvinist determinism and the Church of England in favor of a Christian humanism that insisted on reason as the basis for morality and an innate love of goodness. See HUMANISM; PLATONISM; RATIONALISM.

Canadian Literature.   The literature of Canada from the first European explorations to the present. Early Canadian literature, apart from the oral songs and tales of the region's native inhabitants, was a literature of exploration and report. In this, it resembled the early literature of the American colonies to the south, as well as the European literature sent home from other far-flung places in the world during the centuries of great colonial expansion (see COMMONWEALTH LITERATURE). Hakluyt's *Principal Navigations* (1598–1600) preserves accounts of some of the first English explorers, but they were not settlers. The language of the first European settlers (apart from some sparse settlements in Newfoundland, Nova Scotia, and Prince Edward Island) was French; the first great report was *The Jesuit Relations*, begun in 1632 by Paul Le Jeune (1591–1664) and continued by others to 1673, an annual compendium of missionary reports, letters, and journals detailing the travels, religious and social contacts, and conflicts with the Indians of these hardy priests. Significant literature in English by residents of Canada did not begin until after the British conquest of New France in 1759, and then it developed slowly.

In the first half of the nineteenth century, when Americans to the south were asserting their new political independence with a rising national literature, a distinctive Canadian literature in English began to emerge also. Some of it, inevitably, was written by visitors, as when the Scottish novelist John Galt came over long enough to found Guelph, Ontario, and secure material for his portrayals of upstate New York and wilderness Ontario in *Lawrie Todd* (1830) and *Bogle Corbet* (1831). John Richardson (1796–1852) was the first native novelist in English. *Wacousta* (1832), his best novel, is a HISTORICAL ROMANCE based upon Pontiac's siege of Detroit in 1763. Memorable native humor began in the work of Thomas Chandler Haliburton (1796–1865), called by Artemus Ward "the father of American humor." His *Clockmaker* (1836) introduced Sam Slick, the Yankee peddler, a comic creation in the line of colloquial humor leading directly to Twain. Susanna Moodie (1803–1885) described pioneering life in Ontario in two autobiographies, the first one more appreciated today: *Life in the Bush* (1852) and *Life in the Clearing* (1853). Poetry at this time was less distinguished, but Charles Sangster (1822–1893) and Charles Heavysege (1816–1876) earned some notice at home and abroad.

After the Confederation in 1867, Canadian literature did not immediately reflect the unity suggested by the changed political situation. Writers continued to derive their sense of place in part from provincial homes strung out in a long, narrow line from east to west between the imposing borders of the United States below and the frozen north above, in part from their awareness of their isolation from the mother country across the Atlantic. Post-Confederation poets took as their models the English writers of the ROMANTIC PERIOD and the VICTORIAN PERIOD, and such Americans as Longfellow, bringing Canadian materials into traditional verse forms; among the best are Isabella Valency Crawford (1850–1887), Charles G. D. Roberts (1860–1943), Archibald Lampman (1861–1899), Bliss Carman (1861–1929), and Duncan Campbell Scott (1862–1947). Later, Robert Service (1847–1958), who lived most of his life abroad, gained an immense popularity with his poems of the Yukon, beginning with *Songs of a Sourdough* (1907). The novel of this period was typically a popular adventure or RO-

MANCE, displaying Canada as a land of challenging extremes, aimed as much at publishers in London or New York as at the audience at home. Among the best and most popular were those by Ralph Connor (pseudonym of Charles William Gordon, 1860–1937), including *Black Rock* (1898) and *The Man from Glengarry* (1901). A different kind of prose writer, Stephen Leacock (1869–1944) gained an international following with the humorous pieces gathered in *Sunshine Sketches of a Little Town* (1912), *Arcadian Adventures of the Idle Rich* (1914), and other volumes.

From the 1920s onward, at a pace accelerating in recent decades, Canadian literature has moved toward a stronger position in world literature. In a series of striking narrative poems, E. J. Pratt (1882–1964) raised conflicts in nature to a mythic scale. His "Cachalot" (in *Titans*, 1926) depicts a struggle between a squid and a whale; his *Titanic* (1935), the famous sinking; his *Brébeuf and His Brethren* (1940), the martyrdom of a Jesuit priest. Among poets in the generation immediately following, Earle Birney (1904–   ) is perhaps most admired, but F. R. Scott (1899–   ), A. J. M. Smith (1902–   ), A. M. Klein (1909–1972), Dorothy Livesay (1909–   ), and Irving Layton (1912–   ) are all accomplished poets. Margaret Atwood (1939–   ), also a novelist of note, and Michael Ondaatje (1942–   ) are more recent. In the years since the First World War, Canadian writers have produced some excellent short stories, among them those by Morley Callaghan (1903–   ), author also of a number of novels and of the memoir *That Summer in Paris* (1963), chronicling his friendship with Hemingway, Fitzgerald, and others; Mavis Gallant (1922–   ), writer for the *New Yorker* magazine and long resident in Paris; and Alice Munro (1931–   ). Robertson Davies (1913–   ), prolific playwright and critic, achieved wide readership as a novelist with the richly complex trilogy composed of *Fifth Business* (1970), *The Manticore* (1972), and *World of Wonders* (1975). Younger novelists include Brian Moore (1921–   ), author of *The Luck of Ginger Coffey* (1960), and Mordecai Richler (1931–   ), author of *The Apprenticeship of Dudley Kravitz* (1959) and *St. Urbain's Horseman* (1971).

References

Carl F. Klinck, ed., **Literary History of Canada** (1965).
William Toye, ed., **The Oxford Companion to Canadian Literature** (1983).
Robert Weaver and William Toye, eds., **The Oxford Anthology of Canadian Literature** (1973).

Canon. (1) The books of the Bible that are officially recognized. (2) An author's works similarly accepted. The word is from Greek *kanon,* "rod, rule."

Canso. A Provençal love song of the twelfth and thirteenth centuries. A northern French version is the *canzo.* See CANZONE; TROUBADOUR.

Cant. Hypocritical, argumentative, self-righteous, or professional language. The term is from beggars' monotonous pleas (Latin, *cantare,* "to sing").

Canto. A major division in a long poem. The Italian expression is from Latin *cantus,* "song," a section singable in one sitting.

Canzo. A northern French version of the Provençal CANSO. See CANZONE; TROUBADOUR.

Canzone. A lyric in stanzas, in various patterns, usually with an EN-VOY, or conclusion, of fewer lines. Giraud de Broneil established, or invented, the form in Provence, whence it migrated to Italy and then into the hands of Petrarch, Dante, Tasso (1544–1595), and others. See CANSO; TROUBADOUR.

Captivity Narrative. An account by or about Europeans held captive by American Indians, a popular GENRE during the seventeenth and eighteenth centuries. John Smith's rescue by Pocahontas passed into LEGEND after his accounts in *A True Relation of Such Occurrences and Accidents of Note as Hath Happened in Virginia* (1608) and, with significant differences, *The General History of Virginia* (1624). Among many other captivity narratives, outstanding is *A Narrative of the Captivity and Restoration of Mrs. Mary Rowlandson* (1682), a Massachusetts woman's story of her three months with the Wampanoags during King Philip's War.

Caricature. Literary cartooning, depicting characters with exaggerated physical traits such as huge noses and bellies, short stature, squints, tics, humped backs, and so forth. Sir Thomas Browne seems to have introduced the term into English in 1682 from the Italian *caricatura.* In his Preface to *Joseph Andrews* (1742), Henry Fielding identifies his kind of comic description with that of Hogarth, "a Comic History-Painter" who copies "Nature," as distinct from "those Performances which the *Italians* call *Caricatura,*" which admits all kinds of exaggeration. But his descriptions of Mrs. Slipslop and Parson Trulliber are clearly caricatures in their grotesque comic detail, as are those typical of Tobias Smollett and of his inspired admirer, Dickens.

Carmen Figuratum. A SHAPED POEM. See CONCRETE POETRY.

Carol. A joyous religious or secular song of folk origin, especially celebrating Christmas. It originated in ancient choral song. In France, a *carole* became a dance, with a soloist singing stanzas and the dancing chorus singing the REFRAIN. The tunes moved into the medieval church in the twelfth and thirteenth centuries. The French Christmas carol is a *noël*. See CAROL STANZA.

Caroline Period (1625–1642). The reign of Charles I, from *Carolus,* Latin for "Charles." The period marked the end of the Renaissance in England. The CAVALIER POETS—Herrick, Carew, Lovelace, Suckling—came into glory, as did the creators of METAPHYSICAL POETRY, Donne and Cowley. Drama declined, becoming gloomy and macabre, frequently reflecting the growing political and religious tension, but with some good comedy looking toward the RESTORATION. The Puritan Parliament ousted Charles I in January, and closed the theaters in September, 1642, because of "the distracted estate of England, threatened with a cloud of blood by a civil war." See ENGLISH LITERATURE, PERIODS OF, and the "Chronology of Literature and World Events."

Carol Stanza. The STANZA of a medieval CAROL, a QUATRAIN with three tetrameter lines on one rhyme and a fourth line that is usually shorter and leads into or rhymes with a *burden,* or REFRAIN. The folksong "The Fox and the Goose" has preserved the carol form into the twentieth century:

> The fox went out one winter night,
> And prayed the moon to give him light,
> For he'd many a mile to go that night,
> Before he reached his den, O!

See METER.

Carpe Diem. "Seize the day"—the theme of poems urging a young woman to live and love, since time is short and youth fleeting. The expression comes from the concluding line of Horace's ode to Leuconoë: ". . . *carpe diem, quam minimum credula postero*": "seize the day; trust tomorrow as little as possible," since envious time will have fled even as we talk. Catullus's earlier "Let's live, my Lesbia, and love" (no. 5) is more outspoken. The theme became popular in the sixteenth century and was especially so in the seventeenth century. Ben Jonson's song to Celia in *Volpone* is a virtual translation of Catullus, and Catullus continues to echo more strongly than Horace in Robert Herrick's famous "Gather ye rosebuds while ye may," his "Corinna's

Going A-Maying," Marvell's "To His Coy Mistress," and others. Generally, *carpe diem* means "make the most of every opportunity."

Catalexis.   The absense of a syllable or two at the end of a verse; the opposite of ANACRUSIS. An *acatalectic* line is one not lacking, or complete. See BRACHYCATALECTIC.

Catalog.   In literature, an enumeration of ancestors, of ships, of warriors, of a woman's beauties, and the like, a standard feature of the classical EPIC. Modern poets like Whitman, Sandburg, and Vachel Lindsay catalog at length. Whitman's "There Was a Child Went Forth," for instance, is virtually a catalog of the elements forming the child's experience: "The early lilacs . . . And grass . . . And the fish . . . And the old drunkard . . . And the schoolmistress . . . And the friendly boys . . . And the tidy and fresh-cheeked girls. . . ."

Catastasis.   The FALLING ACTION in drama. See DRAMATIC STRUCTURE. In oratory, the term refers to a narrative part of the introduction.

Catastrophe.   The final disaster of a tragedy, usually including a resolution back to order. In older usage, the word also referred to the DENOUEMENT of a comedy, as Edmund observes in *King Lear*: "Edgar—and pat: he comes, like the catastrophe of the old comedy" (I.ii.145–146). See DRAMATIC STRUCTURE.

Catch.   (1) A ROUND for three or more singers, each catching the lines canonically in turn, starting the line after the preceding singer has gotten midway. The intricate rhythms of the round were popular in the seventeenth and eighteenth centuries. (2) A song for strong and weak voices, with the strong adding something bawdy. Swift wrote a few catches. (3) An ANACRUSIS, an extra unstressed syllable at a line's beginning.

Catch Word.   (1) A slogan or a character's habitual word or phrase. (2) A word at the top of a column or page in a dictionary to aid the reader's search, like the CATALEXIS at the top of this page. (3) In books printed before 1810 or so, a word placed at the end of each page, below the text, bottom right: it is the first word on the next page, guiding printer and reader.

Catharsis.   Purification, purgation, cleansing, specifically of the bowels, metaphorically of emotions. Aristotle introduced *catharsis* as essential to tragedy in the *Poetics* (1449b.28): "incidents arousing pity and terror to achieve a catharsis of these emotions." Critics have interpreted this differently: as (1) a discovery that pity and terror destroy, and thus should be disciplined; (2) a vicarious experience that unloads pity and terror on the hero as scapegoat; (3) a detached pity and an involved terror that leave the spectator, like Milton's Samson, with "calm of mind all passion spent." Plato, Aristotle's teacher, had several times called catharsis the soul's collection from the body's senses to be "alone by itself, freed from the body as from fetters."

Causerie. An informal ESSAY or chatty discussion, especially one of a series on literary topics. The term is associated with the *Causeries du lundi (Monday talks)*, weekly articles by the nineteenth-century French critic Charles Augustin Sainte-Beuve.

Cavalier Poets. Lyricists flourishing in light, smooth, and amorous verse during the last fifteen years of Charles I (1625–1649), associated with his court as Cavaliers, as opposed to the Puritan Roundheads. The Cavaliers were Robert Herrick (1591–1674), Thomas Carew (c. 1598–c. 1639), Sir John Suckling (1609–1642), and Richard Lovelace (1618–1658). See CAROLINE PERIOD.

Celtic Literature. See IRISH LITERATURE.

Celtic Renaissance. See IRISH RENAISSANCE.

Celtic Revival. In the eighteenth century, a groundswell of the Romantic movement in discovering the power in ancient, primitive poetry, particularly Welsh and Scottish Gaelic, as distinct from that of the classics. John Home's tragedy *Douglas* (1756), derived from a Scots ballad, had a flurry of popularity under David Garrick's energetic sponsorship. Thomas Gray's *Bard* (1757), a Pindaric ODE concerning the last Welsh bard doomed under British conquest (c. 1300), contributed significantly to the new interest. James Macpherson's *Fragments of Ancient Poetry Collected in the Highlands of Scotland, and Translated from the Gaelic or Erse Language* (1760) fired the rage for his subsequent spurious poems by Ossian. See OSSIANIC CONTROVERSY.

Center for Editions of American Authors (CEAA). See CENTER FOR SCHOLARLY EDITIONS (CSE).

Center for Scholarly Editions (CSE). A center for information and advice on scholarly editing, supervised by a committee of the Modern Language Association of America, established in 1976 to replace the Center of Editions of American Authors (CEAA). The CEAA, funded by the National Endowment for the Humanities, had originated in the American Literature Section of the Modern Language Association to edit definitive editions of nineteenth-century American authors, establish editorial principles, set meticulous standards, and award its seal on publication. Before funding expired in 1975, it had sponsored editions of Charles Brockden Brown, Stephen Crane, Emerson, William Dean Howells, William James, Washington Irving, Twain, Melville, William Gilmore Simms, Thoreau, and Whitman. The CSE extended its range to all authors and periods, and reduced its mission to counseling and to awarding its seal to meritorious editions.

Center of Consciousness. A term derived from Henry James, although not expressed quite that way in his work (he wrote of "the centre of the subject in . . . consciousness"). It refers to the tendency of James and other modern novelists to place the center of interest in the mind of a character rather than in actions outside the mind. The high points of such novels come as the mind, or consciousness, reflects upon events, as in Chapter 42 of James's *Portrait of a Lady*. The center of consciousness in a novel of this type is the most reflective mind. See NARRATIVE PERSPECTIVE.

Cento. Latin for "patchwork": a literary work, usually in verse, made up of scraps from other works; a PASTICHE. Homer and Virgil were once popular sources of lines rearranged to new purpose. Most modern centos are humorous. A PARODY is often, at least in part, a cento.

Chain Line. One of the thin, translucent, perpendicular lines, spaced about an inch apart, left by the metal grid on which the pulp of laid paper settles to form a sheet. See WATERMARK; WIRE LINE.

Chain of Being. See GREAT CHAIN OF BEING.

Chain Rhyme. See CHAIN VERSE.

Chain Verse. (1) POETRY using *chain rhyme:* two lines linked by repeating the last syllable of the first line as the first syllable of the second, but with a different meaning. Chain verse is occasionally found in French verse, but is rare in English. (2) Poetry with each STANZA linked by repetition of lines, words, or rhymes to another stanza. In the simplest chain, the last line of the first stanza becomes the first line of the second:

My spirit longs for Thee
Within my troubled breast,
Though I unworthy be
Of so divine a guest:

Of so divine a guest
Unworthy though I be,
Yet has my heart no rest,
Unless it come from Thee.

Unless it come from Thee,
In vain I look around:
In all that I can see
No rest is to be found. . . .
                              John Byrom

A VILLANELLE forms a more complex chain.

Chanson.   (1) A medieval French song in couplets (two rhymed metrical lines) with REFRAIN. (2) A French cabaret song. (3) Any small poem reflecting French song.

Chanson De Geste.   French for "song of deeds"; French EPIC poem centering on Charlemagne and his times. Part history, part legend, the form was popular from the eleventh through the fourteenth centuries. Most famous of the eighty or so that survive is the eleventh-century *Chanson de Roland,* based on a defeat inflicted by Basque mountaineers on a rear guard of Charlemagne's army as the warriors returned from Spain in 778.

The *chanson de geste* emphasizes the ideals of chivalry, with courage and loyalty frequent themes. Duty to God, to feudal lord, and to king and country are important; hatred of pagans is a recurring motif. Three main cycles may be distinguished: (1) the cycle of William of Orange, the largest group, consisting of about 24 poems; (2) the cycle of Charlemagne, including the *Chanson de Roland*; (3) the cycle of the barons in revolt, a group of chansons unified only by the common theme of rebellion. Most *chansons de geste* were written in ten-syllable lines, with a CAESURA after the fourth syllable. Anonymous in authorship, they were transmitted orally by *jongleurs,* or wandering musical entertainers, who may have improvised as they sang. See MEDIEVAL ROMANCE.

Chant.   (1) Any song. (2) Words intoned, without much melody, often to a musical or rhythmic accompaniment. The chant is a form of

POETRY among tribal peoples and has sometimes been a feature of poetic presentation in the twentieth century, as, for example, by Vachel Lindsay and Allen Ginsberg. Chants are also used in religious ceremonies and are heard at political and sports gatherings. REPETITION is a prominent feature.

Chantey.   See SHANTY.

Chapbook.   A small book or pamphlet. The chapbook derives its name from being sold on the streets by *chapmen* (merchants or peddlers). Inexpensive, chapbooks were outlets for the POPULAR LITERATURE of the sixteenth, seventeenth, and eighteenth centuries, including the BALLAD, crime story, BIOGRAPHY, children's tale, and religious tract.

Character.   (1) A person in a work of FICTION. See CHARACTERS. (2) The moral qualities, personality traits, or other distinctive attributes of a real or fictional person. (3) A short prose description of a type of person. The *Characters* of Theophrastus (c. 372–c. 287 B.C.) pictured thirty unattractive Greek types. Writers in seventeenth-century England revived the form in books like Joseph Hall's *Characters of Virtues and Vices* (1608). The *Characters* (1614) by Sir Thomas Overbury and others was especially popular in many editions during the century.

Characterization.   The delineation of a real person or the creation of an imaginary one. In a BIOGRAPHY, AUTOBIOGRAPHY, or HISTORICAL NOVEL, characterization provides the identifying traits of an actual person. Henry VIII, Thomas Jefferson, Lord Byron, or Ernest Hemingway—indeed any historical figure—may emerge with distinctly different characteristics in different books. In a novel, short story, poem, or play, characterization creates a lasting identity for an imagined person—sometimes, paradoxically, making the fictional character more "real" than people who have lived. The character of a fictional creation—the Wife of Bath, Hamlet, Emma Woodhouse, Huckleberry Finn, Leopold Bloom, Willy Loman— is fixed forever in the words of the creator, though it is open to differing interpretations by readers or, in the case of plays, actors and directors. The character from history is subject to potentially radical revision with each new book.

Summary characterization is the simplest method. With words, sentences, or paragraphs the author summarizes a person's distinguishing features and personality traits. Frequently one or more characters will summarize another. When summaries differ, a CHORUS CHARACTER may give a trustworthy perspective. *Naming,* sometimes complicated by irony, allusiveness, or symbol, is often a kind of summary, as in *Squire Allworthy, Murdstone, Daisy Miller, Ishmael, Joe Christmas.* Tag lines, or repeated words and phrases, also summarize as they identify and express character: Dicken's Uriah Heep is forever " 'umble"; Scott's Meg Dods asks repeatedly, "And what for no?" Lawyers, sailors, doctors, ministers and innkeepers identify and characterize themselves by speaking in metaphors drawn from their trades in Scott, Cooper, and Dickens. Tricks of speech—the persistent failure of certain characters in Austen to finish their sentences, dialect in Twain, Holden Caulfield's use of the word "phony"—help to summarize by providing a sense of character in brief. Gestures and actions also summarize: Bitzer in Dickens's *Hard Times* places his knuckles to his forehead; John Updike's Rabbit runs.

NARRATIVE PERSPECTIVE is important. First-person narrators define themselves through their presentation and tint their reports of others with the palette of their own personality: Huckleberry Finn and Holden Caulfield are examples. Omniscient narrators sometimes discuss characters in direct address to the reader, as Thackeray does in *Vanity Fair.* Third-person limited omniscient narrators construct their stories in scenes expressive of character, as in Austen's *Emma.* Sometimes third-person narration makes use of a *reflector,* a character whose special angle of vision helps to illuminate another—a frequent device in the novels of Henry James. Both first-person and third-person narrators may emphasize thoughts as keys to personality, reporting them directly, summarizing them ("I thought. . . .," "She thought. . . ."), or presenting interior monologue or stream of consciousness. The *dramatic method* of characterization forces attention to action and speech. Characters are defined by what they say and do, even when this evidence conflicts with the judgment of the narrator or other characters. Sometimes the difference between seeming (the character as viewed by others) and being (the character as revealed dramatically) is crucial in fiction, as it may be in life. This is frequently so with the *alazon* or *eiron* (braggart or trickster), but it may also be true of characters without exaggerated or ironic dimensions who are nevertheless widely misunderstood. In these instances chorus characters may help. In complex narratives, the dramatic portions serve as important checks against misreading of character arising from untrustworthy narrative perspectives, authorial ironies, and ambiguities.

A final element of characterization is the world, or ETHOS, created within the fiction. This begins with the setting: Thomas Hardy's Egdon Heath in *The Return of the Native,* Charlotte Brontë's moors in

Jane Eyre, Melville's ship and ocean in *Moby-Dick*, all characterize the people associated with them. Houses in James, Dickens, and other writers are extensions of personality. Clothes, of course, characterize—in Dreiser, for example. People characterize each other just by inhabiting the same community; so the characters in Austen, Dickens, Chekhov, George Eliot, Joyce, Hemingway or John Cheever are known to us in part, as soon as they appear, by the company they keep. The art of characterization is finally the art of creating a world—or a convincing corner of one. See CHARACTERS; INTERIOR MONOLOGUE; PLOT; STREAM OF CONSCIOUSNESS.

References

E. M. Forster, **Aspects of the Novel** (1927).
Northrop Frye, **Anatomy of Criticism** (1957).
W. J. Harvey, **Character and the Novel** (1965).

Characters.   The people in a work of literature. Characters in literature, whether based on history or original with the author, may be classified by function in a number of ways. The HERO and HEROINE are central to the PLOT and generally, though not always, to be admired by the reader. The VILLAIN is set in evil opposition. These terms suggest a simple approach to character, appropriate to MELODRAMA, ROMANCE, and various forms of POPULAR LITERATURE, but less useful for the NOVEL unless carefully qualified to allow for the usual human mixture of good and bad traits. The Greek terms PROTAGONIST, for the principal actor in a drama, and ANTAGONIST, for a second actor opposing the first, are also useful for nondramatic works and carry less of a connotative burden than "hero" and "villain." A CHORUS CHARACTER, originally a member of the chorus in a Greek play, is now any character in fiction who stands apart from the central action, commenting on it with a wisdom that is presumably the author's or is representative of the best moral standards of the community. A FICELLE is a character whose primary function in a narrative is to manipulate other characters for the purposes of the author, like a string on a puppet. A CONFIDANT serves a similar purpose, accepting the confidences of a more central character at least partially so the reader may overhear.

Literary characters may also be classified by the degree or quality of their resemblance to real people. E. M. Forster distinguishes the *flat* from the *round*. *Flat characters*, often vivid in outline, are *two-dimensional*, like cardboard cutouts, lacking the depth and complexity of living humans. *Round characters*, sometimes called *three-dimensional*, have the depths and complexities of real life. Flat characters are sometimes called *black and white*, as opposed to *grayed* for more rounded characters. *Individualized characters* stand out as individuals; *type characters* represent a class—the lawyer; the preacher; the salesman.

Stock characters, type characters repeated as the stock in trade of many writers of different times and places, may be identified under five major headings: *agroikos, alazon, eiron, pharmakos*, and *vice*. The *agroikos*, dating from Greek comedy, is the rustic, farmer, or country bumpkin, sometimes churlish and sometimes good-natured, continually tricked and bewildered: Malvolio in *Twelfth Night* is an example. The *alazon*, or imposter, is the braggart of Greek comedy, a man who pretends to be greater than he is. Later appearing in many forms, he is often pompous, pedantic, and long-winded. The *miles gloriosus*, originating in Plautus's *Miles Gloriosus*, is the boasting soldier, of which type Shakespeare's Falstaff is the most famous representative. In Spenser's *Faerie Queene* the alazon is the bragging coward *Braggadocio*, whose name has also become generic for the type. The *eiron* in Greek comedy is the self-effacing trickster who undermines the alazon, bringing him down. An opposite to the alazon, who pretends to be more than he is, the eiron pretends to be less. Ironically feigning ignorance, he manipulates those more highly placed or who appear on the surface more clever than he; in tragedy, Hamlet is a kind of eiron. The *pharmakos* is the victim or scapegoat, sacrificed not because he has done anything wrong but because an inscrutable fate positions him to atone for society's ills. Melville's Billy Budd is a fine example. The *vice* originated in the medieval morality plays and is a playful, even comic tempter, whose mischief is usually not serious or long-lasting: Puck in *A Midsummer Night's Dream* and Ariel in *The Tempest* are examples. Taken together, the five basic stock characters form a schematized view of society. On the center and major axis is the alazon at the top, ready for a fall, and the eiron at the bottom, seeking to rise by his wits. On the tragic side of the axis stands the pharmakos, not actor, but victim. On the comic side awaits the vice with his pranks and temptations to folly. Somewhere in the center, neither rising nor falling, wanders the agroikos, the perpetual gull.

ALLEGORY requires type characters, abstractions of virtues and vices, perhaps even so named, as *Truth* or *Falsehood*, as in *Everyman*, *The Faerie Queene*, or *Pilgrim's Progress*. Any partly allegorical or mythical literature tends toward such type characters, as in *Billy Budd* and *Lord of the Flies*. Indeed, to the extent that all narrative is allegoric (all stories remind us of some other story), all characters are more or less typical. In fantasy and science fiction, this is particularly true: Tolkien's Frodo and Gollum resemble no one the reader knows, but in sum are human in unmistakably typical ways; the rabbits of Richard Adam's *Watership Down* engage the reader's attention as both animals and human types; the sensate ocean of Stanislaw Lem's *Solaris* evokes human analogies. Detective fiction, popular romances, and Westerns all thrive on types. Plays bring typically human roles, larger than life, to the stage. Even the most sturdily realistic fiction succeeds in part because of its illustration of types through individuals: Jane Austen's, Emma Woodhouse, Flaubert's Madame Bovary, James Joyce's Stephen Dedalus, John Updike's Harry Angstrom. The difficult but crucial job for criticism is to recognize individual and type at the same time, giving both their proportionate due.

Finally, literary characters are usefully classified as either *static* or *changing*. Static characters retain essentially the same qualities throughout a work. They may respond superficially to the passing of time, sprouting white hairs or putting on spectacles, but they retain in age the personalities they had in youth. Again, the reader may come to understand them differently as the work progresses, but discovers on reflection that it is not they who have changed, but only the reader's knowledge of them: Gilbert Osmond of *The Portrait of a Lady* is an example. Comic characters are necessarily static, never learning to see beyond their characteristic comic blindness. Some characters do change, however, in response to their experiences. The Pip who narrates *Great Expectations* is much less shallow than the young Pip he describes, and the reader can see the change coming as the work progresses. Moll Flanders says at the end that she has changed, but her argument fails to convince. Emma Woodhouse clearly changes in that she makes more sophisticated mistakes in the last two books of *Emma* than she does in the first, but it is questionable how deeply the change runs; she is still fundamentally Emma. Indeed, sometimes a narrative's greatness can be measured in part by the reader's sense that characters have changed significantly in response to experiences, but have changed in ways fully compatible with their immutable personalities. See CHARACTERIZATION.

References

E. M. Forster, **Aspects of the Novel** (1927).
Northrop Frye, **Anatomy of Criticism** (1957).
W. J. Harvey, **Character and the Novel** (1965).

Chartism. A working-class reform movement in England, 1838–1848. In May 1838, the London Working Men's Association published the People's Charter, asking for voting by ballot, universal male suffrage, annual Parliaments, equal electoral districts, payment for members of Parliament, and no property qualifications for membership. William Lovett and others had formed the association in 1836. Feargus O'Connor was the most energetic promoter of the Charter, traveling widely and speaking to discontented workers. The Chartists held several conventions and twice presented their petition to Parliament. In July 1839, riots broke out. In November, Chartist miners in Wales faced the army, and the government arrested most of the Chartist leaders by the end of 1839. An economic crisis in 1847–1848 stimulated a new Chartist convention and demonstration called for April 1848 in London. But the police were out in force, the demonstration was rained out, and Chartism fizzled out completely. Thomas Carlyle's *Chartism* (1839) attacked the movement. Charles Kingsley's *Alton Locke* (1850) presented it sympathetically. See INDUSTRIAL REVOLUTION.

Chaucer, Age of. The period, 1369–1400, dominated by one of England's four or five greatest poets, and the greatest in Middle English. It was a sophisticated period, when the new learning of the early Italian Renaissance flowered in an England equally at home in French and English, and learned in Latin. The period began with Chaucer's *Book of the Duchess* (1369) and ended with his death (1400). His *Canterbury Tales* (1387–1395) was the period's great achievement. Chaucer's friend John Gower (c. 1330–1408) wrote three immense moralistic poems: one in French, the *Mirour de l'Omme* (1376—*The Mirror of Man,* later retitled *Speculum Meditandis*); one in Latin, *Vox Clamantis* (c. 1382—*The Voice of Crying Out,* directed against the Peasants' Revolt of 1381); one in English, *Confessio Amantis* (1390—*The Lover's Confession*). Also noteworthy are the work of the Gawain Poet and William Langland, the anonymous and fabulous *Travels of Sir John Mandeville* (1366–1371) and the Wycliffe Bible (c. 1395), the earliest complete English translation, by the followers of John Wycliffe (c. 1320–1384), a biblical fundamentalist much disturbing to Chaucer's contemporaries. See ENGLISH LITERATURE, PERIODS OF; MIDDLE ENGLISH LITERATURE; and the "Chronology of Literature and World Events."

Chaucerian Stanza. See RHYME ROYAL.

Chiaroscuro. From Italian, meaning "bright dark," a term referring to the effect obtained in a painting or literary work when light and dark IMAGES or patterns of IMAGERY are emphasized. Excellent examples may be found in *Macbeth* and *The Scarlet Letter*.

Chiasmus.   Greek for a "placing crosswise," from the letter *X*, or *chi*. Chiasmus is a rhetorical BALANCE created by the inversion of one of two parallel phrases or clauses: "Destroying others, by himself destroy'd" (Pope, *An Essay on Man*); "Ask not what your country can do for you: ask what you can do for your country" (President John F. Kennedy); "He is the cook of kings and the king of cooks" (Kaiser Wilhelm, said of Auguste Escoffier). See ANTIMETABOLE.

Chicago Critics.   A group of critics associated with the University of Chicago from the 1930s to the 1950s and later. The term was originally applied to the authors of *Critics and Criticism: Ancient and Modern* (1952), but later included others influenced by them. They were pluralists in approach to CRITICISM, believing that no single approach has greater merit than others, but that different approaches may be appropriate to different circumstance. This RELATIVISM was partly contradicted by their early attraction to Aristotle's *Poetics*, which earned them the name *Neo-Aristotelian*. In Aristotle's concern for FORM they saw an approach useful for their time, when there was much talk about a need of a poetics for forms that Aristotle did not discuss. They were anticipated or parallelled in some of their concerns, especially as they applied their observations to particular works, by I. A. Richards's *Practical Criticism* (1929) and by the NEW CRITICISM. Important among their number were Ronald S. Crane, Elder Olson, Wayne Booth, and Norman Friedman.

Child Ballad.   Any of the 305 ballads printed by Francis J. Child in *English and Scottish Popular Ballads* (5 vols., 1882–1898), the definitive collection. They are frequently referred to by the numbers given them by Child. "Sir Patrick Spens," for example, is Child 58. See BALLAD.

Children's Literature.   Literature specifically written and printed for children, as distinct from the oral tales and rhymes of the nursery. The form began with the CHAPBOOK. By the late eighteenth century, children's literature had grown into a fair-size industry, with much emphasis on the inculcation of moral values to offset the supposed bad influences of the ROMANCE and the FAIRY TALE, also widely available. DIDACTICISM continued important in the nineteenth century, a time that also gave rise to the first CLASSICS of children's literature: Lewis Carroll's *Alice's Adventures in Wonderland* (1865), Louisa May Alcott's *Little Women* (1868–1869), Mark Twain's *Adventures of Tom Sawyer*

(1876), and Robert Louis Stevenson's *Treasure Island* (1883). In the twentieth century, writing for children has attracted scores of talented authors, as books for younger children have proven especially distinguished, including Kenneth Grahame's *Wind in the Willows* (1908), A. A. Milne's *Winnie-the-Pooh* (1926), and E. B. White's *Charlotte's Web* (1952). The adult GENRES, especially in POPULAR LITERATURE, have all been duplicated for children.

Chiliasm.   Another name for MILLENARIANISM, from Greek *chilioi* ("thousand").

Chivalry.   A term, meaning originally "men on horseback," used in the Middle Ages as a collective noun for knights, especially when arrayed for battle. In later times, it came to stand for the ideal social, moral, and religious code associated in the popular imagination with knightly quests, adventures, and love relationships. See ARTHURIAN LEGEND; COURTLY LOVE; MEDIEVAL ROMANCE.

Choriambus.   A four-syllable Greek and Latin foot going $-\ \smile\ \smile\ -$, occurring in English only as a TROCHEE plus an IAMBUS, a very common line opener. See METER. Swinburne frequently tried for the classic choriambic effect, as in "The Heptalogia":

$$\overline{\text{Leaves}}\ \breve{\text{love}}\ |\ \breve{\text{last}}\ \overline{\text{year}}\ |\ \overline{\text{smelt}}\ \breve{\text{now}}\ |\ \breve{\text{feel}}\ \overline{\text{dead}}$$

$$\breve{\text{love's}}\ \overline{\text{tears}}\ |\ \overline{\text{melt}}\text{—}\breve{\text{flies}}\ |\ \breve{\text{caught}}\ \overline{\text{in}}$$

$$\breve{\text{time's}}\ \overline{\text{mesh!}}$$

Chorus.   In Greek DRAMA, the group of singers and dancers that appears at intervals within a play to comment on the action or the antagonists, or sing the praises of the gods. Generally, the chorus expresses the judgment of objective bystanders, compassionate and intelligent, representative of the best morality of the community, but not directly involved in the passions of the PROTAGONIST and the other major CHARACTERS. In later times, the chorus is sometimes one person, as in Shakespeare's *Henry V*, where the chorus introduces and concludes the play.

Chorus Character.   A CHARACTER that functions as a CHORUS in a literary work, without necessarily being named as such. Standing apart from the central action, the chorus character observes and comments on it. A common device in the construction of a NOVEL, the chorus character provides a guide to interpretation, especially when the author's choice of NARRATIVE PERSPECTIVE has diminished or eliminated the writer's own direct commentary from without. See CONFIDANT.

Chrestomathy.   Greek for "useful learning": a collection or ANTHOLOGY of passages, especially one for learning a language or studying its literature.

Christabel Meter.   The METER of Coleridge's "Christabel": four-stress lines, mostly in couplets (rhymed pairs of lines), with varying syllable count. The result is a kind of ACCENTUAL VERSE, but in Coleridge's poem tending toward iambs and anapests.

Christ Figure.   A literary character reminiscent of Christ, enriching the work in which he appears by suggesting typological or allegorical interpretations. Examples include Melville's Billy Budd, Faulkner's Joe Christmas (*Light in August*), and Steinbeck's Jim Casy (*The Grapes of Wrath*). See ALLEGORY; SYMBOL; TYPOLOGY.

Christianity, Early English.   A force important to the history of early English literature for its influence in creating, shaping, and preserving the texts that have come down to us.

There were certainly individual Christians in Roman Britain as early as the third century A.D., but religion there at the time was almost entirely either that of pagan Rome or of the northern tribes for whom the Romans served as overlords. By the fourth century, Christianity was well enough established to allow bishops from London and York to attend a church conference in Gaul in 314; a decade later, in 324, Christianity became the official religion of the Roman Empire, but the new religion made few converts among the barbarians of the north, particularly as the Romans were having difficulty holding their lands. In 407 the legions withdrew from Britain.

Meanwhile, around 397 in southwestern Scotland, St. Ninian, a Romanized Briton, began a Christian settlement that had far-reaching influence, and St. Patrick arrived in Ireland not much later, in 432. Following the general breakup of the Roman Empire in the fifth century, the Celtic Christians maintained for several centuries a strong tradition of learning in Europe, with Ireland the major center. Christianity eventually returned to England in 597, with a mission sent by Pope Gregory the Great. Early in the sixth century, King Edwin of Northumbria accepted conversion, as recorded memorably by Bede in his *Ecclesiastical History of the English Nation*. Under the influence, primarily, of the Celtic Christians, Northumbria achieved then its remarkable literary flowering of the seventh and eighth centuries. That was followed in the next three centuries by the dominance of Wessex as a literary center, after the unification of the kingdom under Alfred the Great.

During these centuries of growth and assimilation, pagan literature, much of it oral, and church literature flourished side by side. *Beowulf,* set in a pagan time, shows the Christianity of its seventh or eighth century author. The ARTHURIAN LEGEND, pagan in origins, slowly accepted the Christian coloring characteristic of the versions found in Middle English (by the tenth century, under the date 516 in the *Annales Cambriae,* Arthur wears a cross on his shield). Much literature in these times was in Latin, the church language, but increasingly the different vernaculars came to be used. See IRISH LITERATURE; OLD ENGLISH LITERATURE.

Chronicle.   A kind of history, with the emphasis, as the name suggests, on *time* (Greek *chronos*). Events are described in order as they occurred. The chronicles of the Middle Ages provided material for later writers and serve now as important sources of knowledge about the period. *The Anglo-Saxon Chronicle,* for example, begun in the ninth century under Alfred the Great, compiled records from earlier sources to reach back as far as the Roman invasion of Britain in 55 B.C. It was then continued by various hands until 1154. Geoffrey of Monmouth's *History of the Kings of Britain* (1137) is a Latin chronicle mixing fact and legend as it recounts English history from the supposed founding of the nation by the great-grandson of Aeneas, thus linking England with Troy. In Geoffrey's *History* much of the early ARTHURIAN LEGEND is recorded. Layamon's *Brut* is a verse chronicle in English, adding to material found in earlier writers, including a long account of King Lear and his daughters. One of the most famous chronicles of the Middle Ages, Jean Froissart's *Chroniques,* covers events in Western Europe from 1325 to 1400, with much drawn from personal observation. Chronicles continued to be written in later periods as well. Raphael Holinshed's *Chronicle* (1577) is especially famous as the immediate source of much of Shakespeare's knowledge of English history.

Chronicle Play.   A play dramatizing historical events, as from a CHRONICLE. Chronicle plays tend to stress time order, presenting the reign of a king, for example, with much emphasis on pageantry and little on the UNITY of ACTION and dramatic CONFLICT necessary for a TRAGEDY. The form was popular in Elizabethan England. Shakespeare's dramatic works of this kind usually go by the name HISTORY PLAY.

Chronological Primitivism.   The belief that each succeeding age is worse. See PRIMITIVISM.

Ciceronian Style.   Dignified, balanced, rhythmical prose style, after the manner of the Roman orator Cicero (106–43 B.C.). See SENECAN STYLE.

Cinema Vérité.   A French critical term, meaning "film truth," designating a style of moviemaking that takes to the streets and uses such devices as hand-held cameras, improvisation, natural lighting, and minimally controlled sound.

Cinquain.   (1) A medieval STANZA with varying meter and rhyme. (2) Any stanza of five lines. (3) The stanza invented by Adelaide Crapsey (1878–1914): five lines, unrhymed, with, in order, two, four, six, eight, and two syllables.

Classic.   Among the best of a class, of the highest quality in a group. The concept has roots in the class structure of ancient Rome, where a *scriptor classicus,* who wrote for the upper classes, was distinguished from a *scriptor proletarius,* who wrote for the lower. Something of this earliest sense remains in the high price or snobbishness often associated with the term, as a *classic car,* for example, is likely to be beyond the means of people of modest income. In literature, at least in literate societies, classics have been, since the invention of printing, increasingly available to all. Today, a classic book is often available in a number of inexpensive paperback editions, although the original sense of exclusiveness remains in the expensive bindings sometimes found in editions for collectors.

A literary classic, then, ranks with the best of its kind that have been produced. As T. S. Eliot observed in "What Is a Classic?" (1945), an important test is time, for a classic is recognized "only by hindsight and in historical perspective" (the same is true of cars). A classic is a work that endures. It is inherently rich, capable, it has been suggested, of sustaining diverse interpretations simultaneously. The qualities that distinguish it as ranking with the best are those that educated people have come most to value. It is the job of CRITICISM to define and apply the standards. See CLASSICISM.

Classical Literature.   (1) The literature of ancient Greece and Rome. (2) Later literature reflecting the qualities of classical Greece or Rome. See CLASSICISM; NEOCLASSICISM. (3) The CLASSIC literature of any time or place, as, for example, classical American literature or classical Japanese literature.

Classical Tragedy. (1) The TRAGEDY of Greece and Rome. (2) Later tragedy imitative of Greek or Roman tragedy or reflecting the qualities of CLASSICISM.

Classicism. A principle in art and conduct reflecting the ethos of ancient Greece and Rome: balance, form, proportion, propriety, dignity, simplicity, objectivity, rationality, restraint, responsibility rather than self-expression, unity rather than diversity. In English literature, classicism emerged with Erasmus (1466–1536) and his fellow humanists. The largely Romantic Elizabethans also showed classical inspiration, as Spenser designed his *Faerie Queen* (1589) on Aristotelian virtues, and Philip Sidney wrote his *Defence of Poesie* in 1580. Ben Jonson, in his criticism, his polished verse, and his plays ordered and staged in one place, was a thorough classicist. Inigo Jones (1573–1652), under the influence of Andrea Palladio (1508–1580) and a visit to the ruins of Rome, founded classical architecture in England, particularly with his royal Banqueting House at Whitehall (1622) and his beautiful little church of St. Paul's, Covent Garden (c. 1630), which included London's first "square," or urban park, soon to predominate throughout the city. Grecian facades, pillars, and squares revived strongly in the eighteenth century and prevailed through the nineteenth and into the twentieth to give most public buildings their classical lines. In the RESTORATION and eighteenth century, classicism, or NEOCLASSICISM, expressed society's deep need for balance and restraint after the shattering Civil War and Puritan COMMONWEALTH, which, in 1649, had dared to behead an anointed king. Charles I stepped to the block from one of the windows of Inigo Jones's classic Banqueting House.

The seventeenth-century French were strongly classicists, strengthening the classical tendency in England. Dryden imitated and translated Virgil; Pope translated Homer and modeled his satires and himself on Horace. Classicism continued in the nineteenth century, after the ROMANTIC PERIOD, particularly in the work of Matthew Arnold. T. E. Hulme, Ezra Pound, and T. S. Eliot expressed it for the twentieth.

Clerihew. A VERSE FORM invented by Edmund Clerihew Bentley (1875–1956). It is usually two jingling couplets (rhymed pairs of lines) of LIGHT VERSE beginning with a person's name and rhyming on it in playful characterization. In 1891, Bentley, age 16, studying Caesar at St. Paul's School in London, suddenly found drifting across his mind "the valiant figure of Sir Humphrey Davy." He continued (though misspelling Humphry): "The pen was in my hand. Musing, I hardly knew what it was tracing on the page. Then, with a start, I saw that I had written:

> Sir Humphrey Davy
> Detested gravy.
> He lived in odium
> Of having discovered sodium."

G. K. Chesterton and others caught the craze. Bentley published his first collection in 1905, including the following:

> Edgar Allan Poe
> Was passionately fond of roe.
> He also liked to chew some
> When writing anything gruesome.

Cliché. An overused expression, once clever or metaphorical, but now trite and timeworn: *brown as a berry, working like a dog, run of the mill, acid test*. The term derives from the French word for a stereotype plate, used for printing, and suggests unimaginative repetition.

Climactic Order. Ideas arranged in the order of least to most important, a strategy common in composing an ARGUMENT.

Climax. Greek *klimax, "ladder."* (1) A point of high emotional intensity, the CRISIS or turning point in a DRAMA or STORY. In the tightly constructed PLOT of a TRAGEDY, there is often one major climax, but in an EPISODIC STRUCTURE there may be a series of climaxes of varying intensities. See DRAMATIC STRUCTURE. (2) The high point of an ARGUMENT, reached by arranging ideas in a CLIMACTIC ORDER of importance. (3) The point of greatest interest in any piece of writing. (4) A rhetorical FIGURE OF SPEECH repeating the same word or sound in each succeeding phrase or clause—an intensified form of ANADIPLOSIS: "Knowing that tribulation works patience, and patience experience, and experience hope" (Rom. 5.3–4).

Cloak-and-Dagger. Romantic melodrama of intrigue and espionage, originating on the stage in Spanish or Italian settings of the late Renaissance. The term includes any such romantic thriller, like the novels of John Buchan, Ian Fleming, and Helen MacInnes. See CLOAK-AND-SWORD.

Cloak-and-Sword. A swashbuckling play or novel, usually with an early Spanish, Italian, or French setting, originating in the Spanish *comedia de capa y espada* of Lope de Vega (1562–1635). Alexandre Dumas's *Three Musketeers* (1844) is a famous example. Cloak-and-sword romances were in vogue in America from 1890 to 1915.

Closed Couplet. The HEROIC COUPLET, especially when the thought and grammar are complete in the two iambic pentameter lines, as in Pope's:

> A *little Learning* is a dang'rous Thing;
> Drink deep, or taste not the *Pierian* Spring.

See METER.

Closet Drama. A play written for reading in the "closet," or private study. Closet dramas were usually in verse, like Shelley's *The Cenci* (1819) and *Prometheus Unbound* (1820) and Browning's *Pippa Passes* (1841). Poetic plays more often read than acted—Milton's *Samson Agonistes* (1671), Browning's *Stafford* (1837), Swinburne's *Atalanta in Calydon* (1865), Tennyson's *Becket* (1884)—are also loosely called closet dramas. William Dean Howells wrote a number of one-act closet dramas in prose for *The Atlantic Monthly*.

Club, The. Samuel Johnson's informal literary group. Sir Joshua Reynolds proposed it in February 1764, and Johnson agreed. Other original members were Edmund Burke, Dr. Christopher Nugent (Burke's father-in-law), Topham Beauclerk, Bennet Langton, Oliver Goldsmith, Anthony Chamier, and Sir John Hawkins. They met for dinner once a week at seven at the Turk's Head tavern, Gerrard Street, Soho, "and generally continued their conversation till a pretty late hour," as Boswell reports. After a decade, they met fortnightly, and moved several times. The membership gradually increased, numbering 35 by the time of Boswell's account in June 1792, 8 years after Johnson's death. Later members included David Garrick, Thomas Percy, Adam Smith, and Edward Gibbon. They took no name at first, merely referring to "our Club," but became The Literary Club at the time of Garrick's death in 1779.

Cock-and-Bull Story. A rambling, absurd tale deliberately pointless, told as a joke on the listener; a shaggy-dog story. Originally, a medieval animal fable was told about a cock changed into a bull, with the usual moral of the story missing at the end. Robert Burton, summarizing pastimes, wrote: "Some men's whole delight is to take Tobacco, and drink all day long in a Tavern or Ale-house, to discourse, sing, jest, roar, talk of a Cock and Bull over a pot . . ." (*Anatomy of Mel-*

ancholy, 1621, II.ii.4; Dell-Jordan-Smith ed., 1941, p. 449). Laurence Sterne ends his *Tristram Shandy* (1767) in the following manner:

> L——d! said my mother, what is all this story about?——
> A COCK and a BULL, said *Yorick*——And one of the best of its kind, I ever heard.

Cockney. A native of central London, the East End, "born within the sound of Bow bells"—that is, of St. Mary-le-Bow Church near Gresham Street and the Guildhall. The term originally meant "cocks' eggs" (Middle English *coken*, genitive plural, plus *ey*, "egg"), a rural term of contempt for city softies and fools. Cockneys are London's ingenious street peddlers, speaking a dialect rich with an inventive rhyming slang, dropping and adding aitches, turning long *a* to *i* (*May Day* becomes *My Die*), and, in Dicken's day, interchanging *w* and *v* (*very well* becomes *wery vell*). On Lord Mayor's Day and others, cockneys don costumes laden with myriad white buttons.

Cockney School of Poetry. John Lockhart's contemptuous term for Leigh Hunt's poetry, which aimed for "free and idiomatic use of language," run-on couplets, and flexible meter, and that of his young friends Keats and Shelley. Writing in *Blackwood's Magazine*, October 1817, Lockhart observed that to rhyme *name* with *time* and *vista* with *sister* could suit only a cockney ear. He found the group vulgar, "by far the vilest vermin that ever dared to creep upon the hem of the majestic garment of the English muse." His attack on Keats (August 1818) linked bad poetry with the radical politics of Hunt and Shelley and Keats's lowly apothecary's apprenticeship.

Coda. A section added in final summary (Italian for "tail," borrowed from music). The term originally referred to the addition of two or more lines to a sonnet.

Codex. A manuscript volume, especially of a Greek or Roman work, or of Holy Scriptures. Originally, a stack of four or six wooden writing tablets—shallow trays containing wax to be written on with a stylus and then rubbed out—ringed together at the long edges, was called a *codex*, a "stump," looking like the block from which it was sawed. Codices with parchment leaves between boards appeared in the first century A.D., but the codex, with leaves written on both sides, did not predominate over the parchment *volumena*, or rolls, written only on one side, until about A.D. 300.

Coffee Houses. Eighteenth-century taverns serving coffee and, by extension, chocolate. British enterprise brought coffee to England sometime in the 1630s and 1640s. The earliest coffee house on record, unnamed, was in existence in 1652 in St. Michael's Alley, Cornhill. Charles II tried unsuccessfully to suppress coffee houses as political hotbeds. Will's Coffee House, No. 1 Bow Street, at the corner of Russell Street, Covent Garden, was named for its proprietor, William Urwin, and accommodated Dryden, Wycherley, Addison, Pope, and Congreve. Steele's first *Tatler* (April 1709) assigned poetry to Will's gallantry to White's, politics to St. James's, and learning to The Grecian. White's Chocolate House, in St. James's Street near the palace, was an aristocratic haunt notorious for big gambling. St. James's, more Whiggish, was across and up the street. The Grecian, the lawyers' favorite, was near the Inns of Court. Button's, backed by Addison, challenged Will's across Russell Street for Tory patronage.

Coherence. "Clinging together"—the flowing along of words, phrases, ideas in logical sequence.

Coincidence. A happenstance, unplanned, accidental. Though frequent in life, coincidence in literature may seem a straining against probability and Aristotle's "illusion of reality," producing MELO-DRAMA. Critics challenge Thomas Hardy's fatalistic tragedies as hinging too incredibly on coincidence. But comedy exploits coincidence for its happy ends.

Coined Words. Words invented and becoming current, like Freud's *Ambivalenz* or Maury Maverick's *gobbledygook*. Many commercial words become accepted coinages: *telephone, frigidaire, xerox*. Many words, of course, are coined but do not circulate.

Collage. "A pasting" (French). A collage is a picture harmoniously pasted together of colorful odds and ends, including print. In literature, the term refers to writing approaching this coincidental harmony, like the poetry of Pound and Eliot. A PASTICHE is an unsuccessful collage, for some critics.

Collate. (1) To compare texts word by word and point by point, recording variations. (2) To verify the order of pages, sheets, and gatherings of a book.

Collective Unconscious. According to Carl Jung (1875–1961), the universal instinctive patterns manifest in images, behavior, and religious belief. Jung, Freud's early colleague, later dissented from him about dreams, believing they came not from personal repressions but from a collective unconscious built into the brain's caverns by evolution and shared by everyone. See ARCHETYPE; CRITICISM; JUNGIAN CRITICISM; MYTH.

Colloquialism.   An informal expression characteristic of speech and acceptable in informal writing. See SLANG.

Colloquy.   A formal or mannered conversation, or a written argumentative dialogue, as in Erasmus's *Colloquies* (1518). See DIALOGUE.

Colophon.   (1) A publisher's emblem. (2) Facts about a book's publication, originally put at the end of the work. The term is from Greek *kolophon*, "a summit, an ending."

Comedy.   One of the typical literary structures, originating as a form of drama and later extending into prose fiction and other genres as well. The word is usually derived from *komos*, "a revel," suggesting that comedy sprang from the kind of festival which, like the Roman Saturnalia, inverted normal social customs in memory of a lost Golden Age. Comedy has preserved throughout its history the sense of two levels of existence, one an absurd reversal of the normal order, the other pragmatically more sensible. The first comedies extant are those of Aristophanes (438?–380? B.C.); they belong mainly to what is called *Old Comedy*, a highly conventionalized form that included personal attacks, Socrates and Euripides being among the targets. Later came *New Comedy*, of which the best-known Greek practitioner was Menander (342?–291 B.C.), whose work is known only by fragments except for one complete play recently discovered. The Greek New Comedy dramatists were imitated and adapted by Plautus (c. 254–184 B.C.) and Terence in Rome, and about two dozen plays from them survive. When drama revived in the Renaissance period, these plays served as the main classical models for comedy.

What frequently happens in a New Comedy is that a young man wants to marry or become sexually allied to a young woman; that other characters with more money, influence, pretenses, or social position are opposed to this; and that toward the end of the story some device in the plot reverses the current of the action and allows hero and heroine to be united. A tricky or resourceful servant is often the hero's ally; the hero's father or a rival supported by his father is often in the opposition. Thus in New Comedy an absurd or obviously unjust situation forms most of the comic action, and a more sensible order of things is reached at the end of a teleological plot. In comic drama there is, as a rule, a final scene in which everyone is assembled on the stage, forming a new society that crystalizes around the united pair.

The characterization of New Comedy fits the plot. The hero and heroine are usually likable but not very interesting people, because their real lives are assumed to begin just after the play stops. The chief character interest thus falls on the blocking characters. In Molière, for example, the central blocking character—a miser, a hypochondriac, a snob, or a hypocrite—usually has the play named after him. Earlier than Molière, Ben Jonson's theory of "humors" had described the character appropriate to a New Comedy plot. A humor, Jonson, said, is a person dominated by a single obsession, and is thus confined to a simple repetitive and mechanical behavior, which is the source of the amusement caused by the character.

The New Comedy formulas held the stage until the nineteenth century, and were disseminated also by the half-improvised type of drama known as the COMMEDIA DELL'ARTE which was a major influence on Shakespeare, Molière, and Carlo Goldoni (1707–1793). In the eighteenth century the comic formulas expanded into the genre of prose fiction, and can be found in Henry Fielding, Jane Austen, and Dickens. With Oscar Wilde and the Gilbert and Sullivan operas, the formulas are presented in the form of parody, indicating that the conventions were wearing out. Flanking New Comedy are variants which take it in either a romantic or an ironic direction. A mystery of birth, affecting either hero or heroine, is often the means of bringing about the comic resolution. This theme is central in *Tom Jones* and is frequent in Dickens. In Shakespeare's comedies a symbolic representation of the freer world reached at the end is often hidden within the action, where it takes the form of a forest or enchanted island or a world connected with mystery, magic, fairies, identical twins, dreams, or wish fulfillment. This romantic development of a "green world" comedy was taken over by Shakespeare from his predecessors—Peele, Greene, Lyly, Nashe—but tends to the spectacular and operatic rather than the purely verbal.

The other direction is the ironic or realistic direction, in which the blocking activities of stupid or obsessed characters are triumphant and the hero's efforts are crushed in frustration and despair. In the twentieth century, when writers became weary of the rigidities of New Comedy plots with their compulsory happy endings, this ironic structure has predominated. The darker comedies that begin with Ibsen, Strindberg, and Chekhov present anything from farce to brutality or terror, but remain within the general comic area because the dominant impression they leave is one of absurdity—in fact, many such black comedies belong explicitly to the THEATER OF THE ABSURD.

Characterization in comic drama is somewhat limited in scope, because comedy deals with people in groups rather than concentrating on

isolated figures of heroic size. The most fully realized comic figure in
Shakespeare is Falstaff, because he appears in history plays. Prose fiction has more scope to develop full-scale comic characters: the most
notable example is Don Quixote, whose dream of a chivalric society,
however ridiculous, is still not discreditable, and suggests again another order of things behind the absurdity. See TRAGEDY.

Comedy of Humors.   A kind of play popular in the late sixteenth and
early seventeenth centuries in England, in which the COMEDY was derived from characters driven by their dominant HUMORS. Ben Jonson's
Every Man in His Humor (1598) and *Every Man Out of His Humor*
(1599) are most remembered, but plays on this model were also written
by John Fletcher, Thomas Middleton, and Philip Massinger. In the
late seventeenth century Thomas Shadwell was still using the idea in
plays like *The Sullen Lovers* (1668) and *The Squire of Alsatia* (1688).

Comedy of Intrigue.   A term applied especially to a type of play popular in Spain in the seventeenth century, written by Lope de Vega and
others. Much of the interest comes from intricate twists, turns, and
surprises in the plot, with characterization of secondary importance. In
England, Aphra Behn (1640–1689) is sometimes cited as writing comedies of intrigue.

Comedy of Manners.   A term used to describe a play deriving its
COMEDY from the social habits (manners and mores) of a given society,
usually the dominant one at the time the play is written. A comedy of
manners typically chronicles the foibles of the upper classes, with some
attention to the lower classes as they interact with the gentry in their
roles as servants, tradespeople, and the like. In the seventeenth century
George Etherege, William Wycherley, and William Congreve made the
comedy of manners one of the characteristic dramatic forms of the RES-
TORATION. In France, Molière's plays are outstanding. Richard Sheridan's *School for Scandal* (1777) is a famous eighteenth-century example, imitated in the first American comedy, Royall Tyler's *Contrast*
(1787). Later, Oscar Wilde's *Importance of Being Earnest* (1895) and
Noel Coward's *Private Lives* (1930) continued the tradition.

Comic Opera.   A comedy with spoken dialogue, songs, choruses,
dancing, and orchestral accompaniment; an OPERETTA or MUSICAL
COMEDY. The form gained popularity in the 1730s with the BALLAD
OPERA, following Gay's success with *The Beggar's Opera* (1728). The
musical comedy, like Sheridan's *Duenna* (1775) and others of the nineteenth century, has original music rather than ballad tunes. New

York's first comic opera was *The Black Crook*, a spectacular extravaganza staged by William Wheatley using a magical melodrama by Charles M. Barras, adopted music, trap doors, elaborate scenery and machines, and French dancers with filmy garments and suggestive antics. Its opening on 12 September 1866 was attended by some ladies in masks, and after its 474 performances it netted over a $1 million. It set the pattern for later Broadway musicals. In England, W. S. Gilbert and Arthur Sullivan started their Golden Age of comic opera in 1871 with *Thespis, or The Gods Grown Old*. Richard D'Oyly Carte soon staged their work, beginning with *The Sorcerer* (1877). He built the Savoy Theater specifically for their operettas, which became known as the "Savoy Operas," opening with *Patience* in October 1881.

Comic Relief. A humorous scene or speech in a tragedy by some simple soul unaware of the surrounding, or impending, horror. Examples are the "Hell porter" in *Macbeth*, the gravedigger in *Hamlet*, and the rustic with his basket of asps in *Antony and Cleopatra*. These comic interjections, characteristic of Shakespeare's mastery, deepen the tragedy even as they relieve it, reminding the audience of the breadth of life along with the isolation of death.

Commedia Dell'Arte. Italian comedy with improvised dialogue and masked characters, flourishing from the sixteenth to the eighteenth centuries, probably deriving from ancient Oscan folk plays as well as from Byzantine mimes of the Eastern Roman Empire. Plautus (c. 254–184 B.C.) evidently drew his early Roman comedies from these folk sources of the commedia dell'arte.

Traditional characters were the *zanni*—servants (originally clever slaves) who hatched plots—particularly Arlecchino, or Harlequin, a naïve amatory wit and acrobat in black feline mask, motley clothes (later stitched in blue, red, and green diamonds), with wooden sword or slapstick; and Pulcinella, the ancestor of British Punch and Judy shows, a cruel humpbacked dwarf with hooked nose and an eye for the ladies. Pedrolino was a white-masked, moony dreamer, ancestor of French Pierrot. Pantalone, or Pantaloon (named for a Venetian saint, and hence the source of the words *pantaloons* and *pants*), was a rich retired Venetian merchant with baggy pants, a pointed beard, and a young wife or bumptious daughter. Il Dottore was Pantalone's friendly physician, the archetype of all the greedy and ignorant doctors of Molière and Fielding. Il Capitano, the cowardly boastful soldier, had already crystalized in Plautus's *MILES GLORIOSUS* (c. 100 B.C.) to be immortalized in Shakespeare's Falstaff. The lovers, Inamorato and Inamorata, wore no masks. Inamorata's servant, or soubrette, witty and intriguing, was beloved by Harlequin. She became a popular type in eighteenth-century comedy, particularly in plays Fielding wrote for Kitty Clive. Under the inspired pantomiming of John Rich (1692–1761), known as John Lun, Harlequin captured the London audiences in the 1720s and 1730s.

Common Meter. The BALLAD STANZA as found in hymns (abbreviated *C.M.* in hymn books) and other poems: a quatrain (four-line stanza) in iambic METER, alternating tetrameter and trimeter, rhyming *abcb* or *abab*. It is used with perfect regularity in Wordsworth's "A Slumber Did My Spirit Seal":

> A slumber did my spirit seal;
> I had no human fears:
> She seemed a thing that could not feel
> The touch of earthly years.

Other examples, with varied effects, include "Western Wind," Burns's "The Banks o' Doon," Dickinson's "I Heard a Fly Buzz—When I Died," and Hardy's "The Oxen." See LONG METER; SHORT METER.

Commonplace Book. A journal collecting quotations, poems, excerpts, memorable facts, and comments, usually in sections under headings for ready reference. Many authors and educated people kept them throughout the eighteenth century and later to enrich their conversation and writing. Milton's is extant. Fielding refers to his, now lost. Edward Bysshe's *Art of English Poetry* (1702) is the first commonplace book for the general public, with quotations arranged under headings like *Astonishment, Despair, Rage, Death, Life, Departing*. It went through many editions and augmentations, the 1714 edition being entitled *The British Parnassus; or, A Compleat Commonplace-Book of English Poetry*. Bysshe's work originated dictionaries of quotations, with many imitators, leading up to John Bartlett's enduring *Familiar Quotations* (Boston, 1855). Personal collections like the Elizabethan miscellanies of poetry, or W. H. Auden's *Certain World*, or R. W. Stallman's *Critic's Notebook* of the NEW CRITICISM are loosely called commonplace books.

Commonwealth. The Puritan Interregnum (1649–1660), under the leadership of Oliver Cromwell, who died in 1658. The Commonwealth spanned the period between the execution of Charles I and the restoration of Charles II. Milton, Latin Secretary, wrote his prose pamphlets, though he had drafted part of *Paradise Lost* as early as 1642,

resuming it only after the RESTORATION. Sir William Davenant wrote
an incomplete epic, *Gondibert* (1650), as did Abraham Cowley, *Davideis* (1656). Henry Vaughan, Abraham Cowley, and Andrew Marvell
were the chief lyricists of the period. Sir John Denham and Edmund
Waller established the heroic couplet, first put to dramatic use in Davenant's *Siege of Rhodes* (1656), forerunner of the HEROIC PLAY. Prose
flourished in Thomas Hobbes's *Leviathan* (1651), Jeremy Taylor's *Holy
Dying* and *Holy Living* (1650, 1651), and Izaak Walton's *Compleat Angler* (1653). Translations of Madeleine de Scudéry's and La Calprenède's huge French romances poured into England to influence English speech and manners and the future English novel, remaining
popular well past 1750. Roger Boyle's *Parthenissa* (1654) was the first
English imitation.

Commonwealth Literature.   The literature of countries once part of
the British Empire and since 1931 associated with Great Britain in the
Commonwealth of Nations, including many sovereign states in Africa
and the West Indies, as well as Canada, Australia, New Zealand, Indian, Malta, Malaysia, Singapore, and others. Most have preserved at
least some of the folk and learned literatures of their native languages;
in India, especially, the non-English tradition is ancient, rich, and varied. In some, a non-English tradition has remained active, but all have
also used English as a literary medium, creating a large body of literature unique to each country, but in some ways marked by a commonality of interest and outlook. Students of Commonwealth literature
concerned with particular countries must familiarize themselves with
the literature of the native languages. Students of Commonwealth literature as worldwide phenomenon find much to interest them in English.

Commonwealth literature in English includes the writings of English-speaking visitors and settlers and their descendants and also the
descendants of original inhabitants for whom English is an adopted
language. Its subjects are often insistently local, recording images of
the past in a land rapidly changing or depicting the stress of adjustment for newcomers and old inhabitants. Style varies widely, including
nostalgic imitations of the language of the English at home, efforts to
construct a literary language around the idiomatic English of a given
time and place, and attempts to bring into English the verbal and syntactical richness of a native vernacular.

For India, some major writers are Rudyard Kipling (1865–1936)
and Ruth Prawer Jhabvala (1927–   ), Western novelists long resi-

dent in India; R. K. Narayan (1906–   ) and Raja Rao (1909–   ),
native-born novelists; and Mahatma Gandhi (1869–1948) and Jawahar-
lal Nehru (1889–1964), political leaders who wrote remarkable biographies. Joyce Cary (1888–1957), looking back on eight years in Nigeria,
wrote four African novels, with *Mister Johnson* the best. Native Nige-
rian novelists include Amos Tutuola (1920–   ), Cyprian Ekwensi
(1921–   ), and Chinua Achebe (1930–   ). Achebe's *Things Fall
Apart* has won especially widespread admiration. Doris Lessing (1919–
) has remembered her early years in Rhodesia (now Zimbabwe) in
a number of novels and short stories. South Africa's fiction writers
include Alan Paton (1903–   ), Jack Cope (1913–   ), Ezekiel
Mphahlele (1919–   ), Nadine Gordimer (1923–   ), and Dan Jacobson (1929–   ). Roy Campbell (1901–1957) and William Plomer
(1903–   ) are South African poets, expatriates much of their lives.
Australian literature includes the novels of Henry Handel Richardson
(1870–1946), Christina Stead (1902–   ), and Patrick White (1912–
) and the poems of Christopher Brennan (1870–1932), A. D. Hope
(1907–   ), and Judith Wright (1915–   ). Katherine Mansfield
(1888–1932) emigrated early from New Zealand, but set some of her
fine short stories there. The novelists Wilson Harris (1921–   ), from
Guyana, and V. S. Naipaul (1932–   ), from Trinidad, write in England of the West Indies. Derek Walcott (1930–   ), West Indian
poet and playwright, has written mostly in Trinidad. See CANADIAN
LITERATURE.

Companion Piece. A work by the same artist or writer treating a
previous subject from a different angle. Notable companion pieces are
Plato's dialogues *Lysis* and *Laches*; and poems like Wordsworth's "Ex-
postulation and Reply" and "The Tables Turned"; Browning's "Meeting at Night" and "Parting at Morning," "Fra Lippo Lippi" and "Andrea del Sarto," and others; and Arnold's two poems "To Marguerite."

Comparative Literature. The study of writings of the same period
and kind in different languages to discover common sources and influences, shared traits, cultural differences, and the like, and to examine
movements, developments, and critical theories. It arose in the nineteenth century as linguists began to compare languages, and anthropologists, religions. Abel François Villemain (1790–1870) was a pioneer
in his *Cours de littérature française* (1830). Other historical critics followed: Charles Augustin Sainte-Beuve, Hippolyte Taine, Ferdinand
Brunetière, and particularly the Danish scholar George Brandes, with
his *Main Currents in Nineteenth-Century Literature* (1872–1890). Ameri-

can universities began to establish departments and centers of comparative literature after World War II.

Comparison.   Latin for "with an equal": a consideration of separate things in the light of their similarities. In RHETORIC, comparison is frequently paired with CONTRAST as a device for explanation or clarification. See ANALOGY; METAPHOR; SIMILE.

Compendium.   Latin for "weighing together": a collection, briefly presented, of essential information about a subject.

Compensation.   The technique of filling out a metrical line with pauses to make it equivalent to the regular meter, as Tennyson does in the first line of his famous

> Break, break, break,
> On thy cold grey stones, O Sea!

Complaint.   A kind of lyric poem, popular in the Middle Ages and the Renaissance, in which the poet expresses unhappiness because of unrequited love, or the poet's personal situation, or the state of the world. "The Complaynt of Chaucer to His Purse" mocks the tradition, beginning:

> To yow, my purse, and to noon other wight
> Complayne I, for ye be my lady dere!
> I am so sorry, now that ye been lyght;
> For certes, but ye make me hevy chere,
> Me were as leef be layd upon my bere;
> For which unto your mercy thus I crye:
> Beth hevy ageyn, or elles mot I dye!

Complete Rhyme.   See EXACT RHYME.

Complication.   (1) In a narrative or dramatic work, the introduction of PLOT elements after the EXPOSITION of the initial situation, entangling them so that they must be untangled at the end, in the RESOLUTION. (2) A plot element so introduced. See DRAMATIC STRUCTURE.

Comstockery.   Zealous suppression of literature considered offensive or obscene. Its coinage attributed to George Bernard Shaw, the term refers to the activities of Anthony Comstock (1844–1915), leading figure in the New York Society for the Suppression of Vice.

Concatenation.   Union by linking together, as with chains; hence sometimes a term for CHAIN VERSE.

Conceit. Any fanciful, ingenious expression or idea, but especially one in the form of an extended METAPHOR. A PETRARCHAN CONCEIT, imitating those of Petrarch (1304–1374), generally involves unsurprising comparisons to such things as gardens, stars, ships. A METAPHYSICAL CONCEIT is a more startling or unlikely comparison, typical of METAPHYSICAL POETRY, such as John Donne's likening of lover's souls to a drawing compass in "A Valediction: Forbidding Mourning."

Concordance. An alphabetical index to words in a given work or body of work, with line or page references to the places they are used. Examples include concordances to the Bible, the works of Shakespeare, and the massive *Microfiche Concordance to Old English* (1980), comprising over 125,000 pages.

Concordia Discors. "Discordant harmony," a phrase expressing for the eighteenth century the harmonious diversity of nature, a pleasing balance of opposites. It originated with Horace, the eighteenth century's most quoted Latin poet (*Epistles* I.xii.19):

> Quid velit et possit rerum concordia discors?
> What wills and enables the discordant harmony of things?

His next line mentions the philosopher Empedocles (c. 444 B.C.), who, according to Aristotle (*Metaphysics* I.4), was the first to see the world originating in two opposing principles, fire as against earth, water, and air, evidently Horace's source for the idea of opposites combining. Ovid soon followed (*Metamorphoses* I.432–433—first decade A.D.), reversing Horace's phrase to describe how warm sun on wet banks spontaneously created the first nonhuman life, since procreation seems to entail the harmonious discord of opposites:

> cumque sit ignis aquae pugnax, vapor umidus omnes res creat, et
>   discors concordia fetibus apta est.
> Though fire and water are pugnacious, a humid vapor created all
>   things, and a harmonious discord was joined in offspring.

Finally, Lucan (*Pharsalia* I.93—c. 60 A.D.) again played with Horace's phrase, calling the feigned friendship between Caesar and Pompey a concordia discors.

In the eighteenth century, Pope echoed the idea to describe the new Eden of Windsor Forest:

> Here Hills and Vales, the Woodland and the Plain,
> Here Earth and Water seem to strive again,

> Not *Chaos*-like together crush'd and bruis'd,
> But as the World, harmoniously confus'd:
> Where Order in Variety we see,
> And where tho' all things differ, all agree.
>
> *Windsor Forest,* 11–16

And again in *An Essay on Man:*

> All Nature is but Art, unknown to thee;
> All Chance, Direction, which thou canst not see;
> All Discord, Harmony, not understood;
> All partial Evil, universal Good.
>
> *I.289–294*

Samuel Johnson played on the idea to disparage the metaphysical CON-CEIT, emphasizing discord, as Ovid did:

> But Wit, abstracted from its effects upon the hearer, may be more rigorously and philosophically considered as a kind of *discordia concors;* a combination of dissimilar images, or discovery of occult resemblances in things apparently unlike.
>
> *Life of Cowley*

Concrete. Possessing physical existence, capable of being experienced by the senses; the opposite of ABSTRACT. Many concrete words or phrases can be defined by touching, pointing, or acting: *chair, sun, skate on ice.* In practice, abstract terms may be used concretely, as in "this beauty" for a specific beautiful object, and concrete terms may be used abstractly, as in "my house" for a dwelling planned but not yet built.

Concrete Poetry. Poetry that attempts a CONCRETE embodiment of its idea, expressing itself physically apart from the meaning of the words. A recent relative of the much older SHAPED POEM, the concrete poem typically places heavy emphasis on the picture and little on the words, so that the visual experience is more interesting than the linguistic. An interesting example, combining concrete visual and sound IMAGERY, is Edwin Morgan's "Siesta of a Hungarian Snake," a linear representation of a snake, stretched out at rest, narrow at the ends and thicker in the middle, made entirely by repeating the letters *SZ.*

References

Mary Ellen Solt, **Concrete Poetry: A World View** (1969).
Emmett Williams, ed., **Anthology of Concrete Poetry** (1967).

Concrete Universal.   A concept used in CRITICISM to suggest that a literary work achieves some of its power by a union of the contradictory qualities of concreteness and universal appeal. The POEM, STORY, or DRAMA is CONCRETE and specific, a thing that can be experienced, the only one of its kind. At the same time, it is universal and ABSTRACT, representing ideas permanently true that cannot be experienced except in particular examples. Hawthorne's "Young Goodman Brown" tells its own story, but it also tells of the reader. Tennyson's "In Memoriam" expresses one sorrow, but stands for many. We all wait for Beckett's Godot.

This fundamental PARADOX, that literature can be itself and also something else, has been much debated in the twentieth century. Some critics have insisted on the concreteness or separate identity of the work, denying the value or even the possibility of universality. Others have discovered concrete universals in some works, or in parts of works, but not in all. Still others insist that the universal is necessarily present in any poetic use of language. See ALLEGORY; ARCHETYPE.

Condensation.   A shortened form of a literary work, an ABRIDGMENT.

Confession.   (1) An AUTOBIOGRAPHY that emphasizes private, personal matters in order to discover a pattern of coherence in a life, as opposed to one that is primarily a record of public activities. Famous examples include the *Confessions* of St. Augustine and Jean Jacques Rousseau. (2) A prose FICTION modeled on autobiography. It is distinguished in that respect from the NOVEL, ROMANCE, and ANATOMY, but the types frequently merge under the inclusive heading *novel*. *Moll Flanders* (entirely fictional) and *The Portrait of the Artist as a Young Man* (fiction modeled on life) are examples.

Confessional Poetry.   A term applied to the work of American poets—all friends, students, teachers of one another—who, especially in the 1960s, derived much of their subject matter from personal anguish. Key works include W. D. Snodgrass, *Heart's Needle* (1959); Robert Lowell, *Life Studies* (1959); Anne Sexton, *All My Pretty Ones* (1962) and *Live or Die* (1967); Sylvia Plath, *Ariel* (1965); and John Berryman, *The Dream Songs* (1969). In a less specialized sense, earlier very personal poetry, such as Wordsworth's *Prelude*, may also be seen as to some degree confessional.

Confidant (fem., **Confidante**).   A secondary CHARACTER who advises or befriends the PROTAGONIST of a work of FICTION. As Henry James expressed it, the confidant is sometimes also "the reader's friend," whose conversations with the HERO reveal MOTIVATION or provide EXPOSITION that might otherwise remain unclear. Examples include Horatio in *Hamlet*, Watson in the Sherlock Holmes stories, and Maria Gostrey in *The Ambassadors*. See CHORUS CHARACTER; FICELLE.

Conflict. (1) An opposition between a CHARACTER in a work of FICTION and some other force: (a) between PROTAGONIST and ANTAGONIST, as, for example, Othello and Iago; (b) between protagonist and society as a whole, as in Molière's *Misanthrope;* (c) between protagonist and external forces, such as the FATES or the deterministic forces of NATURALISM, as in *Oedipus Rex* and Crane's *Maggie: A Girl of the Streets*. (2) The opposition of forces within a character, or *inner conflict*. According to Faulkner, in his Nobel Prize address, the one thing worth writing about is "the human heart in conflict with itself." (3) An opposition of ideas, values, or ways of life, as objectified in the conflicts between persons or within them. Sir Walter Scott's novels characteristically involve a conflict between the ideals of past and present. Henry James's works frequently involve a conflict between the values of the Old World and the New.

Congregationalism. A movement of Separatist Puritans originating with Robert Browne, who drew together a congregation in Norwich, England, in 1579 or 1580, asserting the independence of each congregation from ecclesiastical governance. See PURITANISM.

Connecticut Wits. A group of writers and intellectuals of the late eighteenth and early nineteenth centuries, also known as the *Hartford Wits*. Most important are John Trumbull (1750–1831), Timothy Dwight (1752–1817), and Joel Barlow (1754–1812). Trumbull is remembered for a satire on American education, *The Progress of Dulness*, and one on Tories in the American Revolution, *M'Fingal*. Dwight, who became president of Yale, wrote a biblical epic, *The Conquest of Canaan*, and a pastoral, *Greenfield Hill*. Barlow, a distinguished diplomat, wrote *The Columbiad*, a lengthy celebration of America, and the delightful MOCK EPIC *The Hasty-Pudding*.

Connotation. The ideas, attitudes, or emotions associated with a word in the mind of speaker or listener, writer or reader. It is contrasted with the DENOTATION, the thing the word stands for, the dictionary definition, an objective concept without emotional coloring. The denotation of the word *cat* is either a specific animal or a general definition. The connotation is the feeling aroused by the word, which may be quite different for people fond of cats and others who are afraid of them or allergic to them. Broadly speaking, connotations are favorable, neutral, or unfavorable, but the range within these categories is as wide as the range of human emotion and thought. CONCRETE words have readily defined denotations, and, frequently, little or no connotative value, as, for instance, the word *chair* arouses no emotion in most circumstances. ABSTRACT words like *liberty* and *justice* have denotations more difficult to define and are frequently highly connotative. Words like *liberal* and *conservative* are notorious for their shifting connotations, ranging widely from favorable to unfavorable depending on user, hearer, and circumstances.

Denotative language is important to scientific and scholarly discourse, or to any writing requiring accurate, objective description of the external world. Connotative language is important wherever a large part of the communication is emotional—in politics and advertising, as well as in all forms of imaginative literature.

See SIGNIFIED, SIGNIFIER, related concepts placing the emphasis on word and user.

Consonance   (1) Repetition of inner or end consonant sounds, as, for example, the *r* and *s* sounds in this phrase from Gerard Manley Hopkins's "God's Grandeur": "*broods* with *warm breast.*" Frequently found within a line of poetry, consonance also substitutes at times for END RHYME, as when Emily Dickinson rhymes *up, step* / *peer, pare* / *while, hill* / and *star, door* in "I Like to See It Lap the Miles." In the end position, it is often called SLANT RHYME. See ALLITERATION; ASSONANCE; RHYME. (2) In a broader sense, a generally pleasing combination of sounds or ideas; things that sound well together.

Conte.   French for "story" or "tale." The term applies especially to the prose or verse stories of the Middle Ages, or to a tightly constructed, concise SHORT STORY, such as those of Guy de Maupassant.

Contentio.   See ENANTIOSIS.

Context.   The verbal or physical surroundings of a literary work or of a portion of one. Both verbal and physical contexts may be narrow (the immediate surroundings) or broad (those farther away).

The verbal context of a word in a POEM, for example, consists, in the narrowest sense, of the other words in the same line, and, more broadly, of the words in other lines nearby and in the poem as a whole. More broadly still, there are the contexts of the author's work as a whole, as well as the writings of other authors of the time, or of other times. A scene in a PLAY exists in the immediate context of the scenes just before and after, and in the broader contexts of the act, the entire play, and other plays. Any portion of a STORY or NOVEL has similar narrow and broad verbal contexts.

Physical contexts are also varied. A work may be examined in the context of its creation, considering such things as the author's life in relation to the composition; the publishing conventions of the time; the expectations of the public; and the social, economic, and cultural history of the age. It may also be examined in some entirely different physical context, as a play by Shakespeare, for example, may be understood differently in a modern television production from the way the viewer imagines it to have been understood in the Globe Theater of the seventeenth century. A classroom discussion of *The Scarlet Letter* may shed a light, not necessarily invalid, that would have been unlikely in Hawthorne's time.

CRITICISM must consider context. In the twentieth century, verbal context has generally received most attention in the direct examination of a literary work, with physical context considered separately, in relation to the author's biography and to literary and social history. See NEW CRITICISM; SEMIOTICS; STRUCTURALISM, POST-STRUCTURALISM.

Contrapuntal. See COUNTERPOINT RHYTHM.

Contrast. Latin for "standing against": IMAGES, ideas, or other literary elements standing in opposition to one another, or considered for their differences. In RHETORIC, contrast is frequently paired with COMPARISON as a device for explanation and clarification.

Controlling Image (or **Controlling Metaphor**). An image or metaphor that dominates a literary work, especially with respect to STRUCTURE or THEME. See FUNDAMENTAL IMAGE.

Convention. A "coming together" (the meaning of the Latin roots): an unwritten but widely accepted agreement or compact about the terms of communication.

Stage conventions are most obvious, as the DRAMA requires clear rules to govern the direct communication between players and audience. For example, by a common convention of dramatic REALISM, the actors on stage are not aware that they are actors or that they play before an audience. By an entirely different dramatic convention, the ASIDE, the actor speaks to the audience, but the others on stage do not hear. So, too, VERSE on stage is accepted by actors and audience as though it were everyday speech, and dimming the lights or dropping the curtain stops physical action in its tracks as effectively as shutting the pages of a book.

POETRY and prose FICTION have their conventions also, as when Robert Frost's New England farmers cast their homely observations in impeccable BLANK VERSE, or techniques for communication between author and reader differ dramatically from the nineteenth century, in the novels of Sir Walter Scott and Charles Dickens, to the twentieth, in those of James Joyce and Ernest Hemingway.

Copernican Universe. The sun-centered universe as perceived by Nicolaus Copernicus (1473–1543), in contrast to the PTOLEMAIC UNIVERSE, world-centered, accepted before Copernicus's time, and, by some, for long after. Copernicus's work, published in 1543, established a basis for later advances, such as Kepler's law of planetary motion and Newton's theory of gravitation.

Copy. (1) A single book or set of books. (2) A MANUSCRIPT from which type is set. A used manuscript, marked by proofreader, editor, and printer, is called *foul copy.* See FAIR COPY.

Copyright. The legal right to publish a literary or artistic work. Copyright is a form of property protection, designed to secure a fair monetary return for the creator of the work and the company that assumes the risk of publication. In pursuit of these basic aims, the law becomes quite complex, with copyright assigned in the first place sometimes to the author, sometimes to the publisher, and qualified by numerous contractual agreements concerning reprints, new editions, foreign markets, and subsidiary rights such as movies and television.

Copyright laws developed slowly, arising out of common law after the invention of printing. By 1710, England had a specific copyright act, the model for the first in the United States in 1790. In the nineteenth century, in the absence of international copyright laws, American writers like Hawthorne and Melville were forced to compete at home against pirated editions of Dickens (less expensive because Dickens received no royalties), and were frequently themselves pirated in England. Meanwhile, Dickens and other English writers received little from their U.S. sales. By the late nineteenth century, some progress had been made, but problems have remained even after the Universal Copyright Convention of Geneva, accepted by the United States in 1955.

British law (since 1911) and United States law (since 1978) now agree in providing copyright for the author's life and fifty years more, thus protecting, for a period, the interests of the heirs.

Copy Text. The text used by an editor or textual scholar as the basis for an EDITION of a work. Another PRINTING, the MANUSCRIPT, FOUL COPY, galley and page PROOF, and so on are compared with the copy text to arrive at the most satisfactory reading for the new edition. In simple cases, the author's HOLOGRAPH manuscript, if it exists, or the TYPESCRIPT, if its authenticity can be determined, is taken as the copy text. In more complicated instances, authors have made corrections on proof, or perhaps on the pages of their own copy of the printed book, which must be considered. In some instances, an author has personally supervised more than one edition, and in these the new editor must choose between an early and a late version, each representing the author's intention at different stages of his or her life, as in many of the works of Henry James.

Coronach. A Celtic lament or dirge for the dead, from Ireland or the Scottish Highlands, sung or played on bagpipes. See KEENING; PIBROCH.

Corpus Christi Plays. Medieval plays presented in celebration of the feast of Corpus Christi. See MEDIEVAL DRAMA; MYSTERY PLAY.

Correlative Verse. Poetry employing an abbreviated sentence matching two or more parallel elements in the first half with two or more in the second. The *Greek Anthology,* for example, describes wine as "boldness, youth, strength, wealth, country / To the shy, the old, the weak, the poor, the foreign." See PARALLELISM.

Cosmic Irony. A kind of situational IRONY, throwing humans into insignificance as against an infinite or empty universe, as when in Stephen Crane's poem "A Man Said to the Universe," the man says, "I exist," and the universe replies that this fact has not created in the universe a sense of obligation.

Counterplayers. CHARACTERS in a DRAMA who conspire against the PROTAGONIST.

Counterpoint. By analogy with music, a technique in literature whereby independent elements are woven into a harmonious whole. Separate PLOT threads may be counterpointed, or separate THEMES, each generally illuminating the others. See MONTAGE.

Counterpoint Rhythm. A second rhythm imposed on a poem's basic metrical pattern. Gerard Manley Hopkins originated the term to describe what he saw as a natural evolution on the way to his SPRUNG

RHYTHM, which obliterated the basic meter in favor of the counterpoint:

> . . . the reversal of the first foot and of some middle foot after a strong
> pause is a thing so natural that our poets have generally done it, from
> Chaucer down, without remark. . . . If however the reversal is repeated
> in two feet running, especially so as to include the sensitive second foot, it
> must be due either to a great want of ear or else is a calculated effect, the
> super-inducing or *mounting* of a new rhythm upon the old; and since the
> new or mounted rhythm is actually heard and at the same time the mind
> naturally supplies the natural or standard foregoing rhythm, for we do not
> forget what the rhythm is that by rights we should be hearing, two
> rhythms are in some manner running at once and we have something
> answerable to counterpoint in music, which is two or more strains of tune
> going on together, and this is Counterpoint Rhythm. Of this kind of verse
> Milton is the great master and the choruses of *Samson Agonistes* are
> written throughout in it—but with the disadvantage that he does not let
> the reader clearly know what the ground-rhythm is meant to be and so
> they have struck most readers as merely irregular.
>
> *"Author's Preface," Poems*, 1930

Karl Shapiro is one of those, finding that Milton's verse in *Samson Agonistes* "flows by the count of ear and no more scans . . . than Hebrew." See SYNCOPATION.

Coup de Théâtre.   A surprising theatrical effect or gimmick.

Couplet.   A pair of rhymed metrical lines, usually in iambic tetrameter or pentameter. Sometimes the two lines are of different length. See CLOSED COUPLET; HEROIC COUPLET; METER.

Court Comedy.   Comedy written for the royal court, like Shakespeare's *Love's Labour's Lost* and John Lyly's *Endimion* and *Alexander and Campaspe,* akin to the MASQUE in its spectacular staging, music, and stylized plot and characters, but written in prose, with much wit and verbal bravura. See COMEDY.

Courtesy Book.   A book outlining the education, conduct, and duties of a courtier or prince. Baldassare Castiglione's *Cortegiano* (1528; translated by Sir Thomas Hoby as *The Book of the Courtier,* 1561), written as a DIALOGUE, made him the Renaissance Emily Post of aristocratic manners, wherein everything must be done with *sprezzatura,* a seeming negligence and easy grace. Sir Thomas Elyot's *Book Named the Governour* (1531) was England's first and most famous. Written for Henry VIII, it "treateth of the education of them that hereafter may be deemed worthy to be governors of the public weal under your highness." Henry Peacham's *Compleat Gentleman* (1622), Richard Braithwait's Puritan *English Gentleman* (1622), and Francis Osborne's *Advice to a Son* (1658) continued the GENRE in the seventeenth century and pretty well concluded it.

Giovanni Della Casa's *Galateo* (1558; translated by Robert Peterson in 1576) initiated a slightly different line from Castiglione's, that of etiquette in polite society rather than courtly manners. *The Babees Book* and *The Boke of Curtasye* (1450) were similar etiquette books in English.

Courtly Love. A code for chivalrous adultery originating in the twelfth century in the lyrics of the troubadours of northern Italy and Provence, probably deriving from Ovid and popular Oriental ideas. A lover, smitten from afar by a beautiful married woman of equal or higher status, must long agonize and weep in sleepless silence; then reveal his love; then prove it in mighty exploits, adhering to pledges of secrecy and faithfulness until death; then, finally, he achieves consummation. The cult of the Virgin Mary and Neo-Platonism contributed to a heightening of the ideal over the sensual.

Andreas Capellanus wrote three volumes of *Liber de arte honeste amandi et reprobatione inhonesti amoris* (c. 1185, *Book of the Art of Loving Nobly and the Reprobation of Dishonorable Love*) outlining 31 rules in imaginary conversations. The soliloquies and debates in courtly-love poems drew both from Andreas and from scholastic philosophy. The Countess Maria, daughter of Eleanor of Aquitaine, who had established the courtly-love tradition in France and England, asked Andreas, evidently her chaplain, to write his book. At about the same time, she also commanded the romances of Chrétien de Troyes, including the famous courtly-love *Lancelot*. Guillaume de Loris's influential *Roman de la Rose* (c. 1230) drew directly from Andreas's *Liber*. Chaucer's *Troilus and Criseyde* (c. 1386), though not adulterous, is essentially a courtly-love poem. Indeed, the pattern became a standard framework for romances and romantic comedies, with the woman purified into a virgin high above the worthy squire of low degree and unknown origin with his lute at the base of the tower. See COURTS OF LOVE; ROMANCE.

Reference

C. S. Lewis, **The Allegory of Love** (1936).

Courtly Makers. Poets (Greek, "makers") of Henry VIII's court, notably Sir Thomas Wyatt (c. 1503–1542) and Henry Howard, earl of Surrey (c. 1517–1547), who together introduced the sonnet to England from Italy, particularly on the model of the fourteenth-century Petrarch. Surrey also originated blank verse in English in his *Aeneid*, Book IV, "translated into English, and drawn into a straunge meter" (1554). In 1557, Richard Tottel published his *Miscellany* containing Wyatt's and Surrey's poems, including *Aeneid*, Book II, along with Book IV. Others of the group were Francis Bryan, Sir Thomas Chaloner, Robert Cooper, William Cornish, Robert Fairfax, John Heywood, Lord Morley (Henry Parker), Sir Anthony St. Leger, Lord Rochford (George Boleyn, Anne's brother—Wyatt had been her lover before her marriage), and Lord Vaux. Most of their works have vanished, since gentlemen wrote only for private amusement and circulation.

Courts of Love. Tribunals of lords and ladies to decide amatory questions like "Can a lover love two ladies at once?" and "Are lovers or married couples more affectionate?" The courts were thought to have existed in medieval Languedoc and Provence, but probably were only a literary convention in which a lady, or Venus herself, presided as judge hearing the case debated.

Covenanters. Scottish Presbyterians who signed a covenant (1557) as a "godly band" to stand together to resist the Anglican church and the English establishment. The Bishops' Wars (1639–1640) successfully resisted English royal armies. In the English Civil War, Parliament accepted the Scottish Solemn League and Covenant (1643), constituting the Presbyterian church in England, Scotland, and Ireland. Because the pact was never implemented, the Covenanters fought Charles I, but Cromwell, also fighting Charles, conquered Scotland in 1650–1651 and suppressed them. After the RESTORATION, in 1660, Charles II, who had landed in Scotland in 1650 and sworn allegiance to Presbyterian covenants, abrogated his oath and declared Anglican episcopacy throughout the kingdom, enforcing it with savage bloodshed. The Glorious Revolution of 1688, overthrowing James II's return to Catholicism and allowing religious tolerance, established the Presbyterian church in Scotland.

Covenant Theology. An adjustment of Calvinist doctrine. God's absolute determination of election for heaven or damnation was replaced by God's promise of salvation in exchange for obedience, as that of Noah and Abraham, promising the possibility of perfection through effort. Jesus became the new covenant. Johannes Cocceius (1603–1669), a German theologian and Hebraic philologist, formulated the theory already expressed independently by others in other countries. The New England Puritans enacted covenant theology in seeing themselves as God's chosen people, with the true covenant to found the new theology in the new and promised land. In their view, sinners broke the community's covenant with God, but public confession restored the community and the covenant. The GREAT AWAKENING, stirred by Jonathan Edwards in 1743, swept the American colonies with a return from the Covenant to a stricter CALVINISM.

Creative Criticism. A personal approach to literature that treats the critic's job as a form of IMAGINATIVE WRITING, emphasizing the critic's response, however, individual or idiosyncratic, as valid for others, or at least as offered to them, like any other literature, to accept or reject. See CRITICISM.

Creative Writing. See IMAGINATIVE WRITING.

Crisis. In a play or novel, the "turning point" (Greek, *krisis*, "a separation," "a judging or determining"), for better or worse. *Crisis* refers to the episode or events where the protagonist's choices go right or wrong; CLIMAX, to the peak of the audience's emotional response. The two do not always coincide, since the PROTAGONIST may choose quite casually in innocuous circumstances. See DRAMATIC STRUCTURE.

Critic. Literally, a judging person; a literary analyst, evaluator, or theorist. See CRITICISM.

Critical Realism. REALISM used to express criticism of society. The term has been applied especially to American works at the end of the nineteenth and beginning of the twentieth centuries, like those of Upton Sinclair and the MUCKRAKERS. Vernon L. Parrington coined the term in his posthumous *Beginnings of Critical Realism in America* (1930), the third volume of his *Main Currents in American Thought* (1927–1930).

Criticism. From Greek *kritikos*, with the root meanings of "discernment" and "decision": the analysis, interpretation, evaluation, and classification of literary works, or, in Matthew Arnold's words, "a disinterested endeavor to learn and propagate the best that is known and thought in the world."

With respect to a given literary work, the areas for critical examination are essentially five: (1) the work in isolation, with primary focus on its form, as opposed to its content; (2) its relationship to its own time and place, including the writer; the social, economic, and intellectual MILIEU surrounding it; the method of its printing or other dissemination; and the assumptions of the audience that first received it; (3) its relationship to literary and social history before its time, as it repeats, extends, or departs from the traditions that preceded it; (4) its relationship to the future, as represented by those works and events that come after it, as it forms a part of the large body of literature, influencing the reading, writing, and thinking of later generations; (5) its relationship to some eternal concept of being, absolute standards of art, or immutable truths of existence.

In practice, two or more of these areas are often joined in a single critical effort. It is very difficult, for example, to consider the form of a short story in isolation, without considering how that form relates to some abstract standard of construction. Similarly, a consideration of a story's content inevitably implies some involvement with time and place, and perhaps also with the problem of immutable truth. As another example, a poem's relationship to its own time may be clarified by measuring contemporary assumptions against the expectations of some earlier or later period. In any critical effort, the relative importance of each area may depend upon whether the aim of the critic is primarily theoretical or practical. *Theoretical criticism* is concerned with establishing the value of art in general and explaining the principles that underlie its achievement. It defines the goals, illustrates the methods, and supplies the tools for the practical critic. *Practical criticism* is concerned with justifying or explaining a work, with establishing guidelines for the creation of art, and with setting standards of taste. It applies the insights of the theorist.

There are other ways to delineate the territory. For M. H. Abrams, the "work" lies at the center of a triangle formed by the "universe" at the apex above and the "artist" and "audience" at either end of the base below. This conceptualization leads to a consideration of four basic critical orientations, which Abrams designates as (1) *mimetic*, emphasizing the universe as the subject of art's imitative function; (2) *pragmatic*, emphasizing the effect on the audience; (3) *expressive*, emphasizing the individuality of the artist; (4) *objective*, emphasizing the work itself. Not immediately obvious in this scheme is the effect of time on a literary work, although it is present by implication and becomes an immediate and unavoidable concern as soon as the critic turns to the mimetic category and asks what precisely is being imitated, or to the pragmatic category and considers the audiences of different times and places.

Whatever orientation the critic chooses, the approach is usually directed in part by internal guidelines that may be described as either *moral* or *aesthetic*. The moral critic takes humanity as the measure of art, seeing literature as a reflection of life and in some way a comment upon it; such a critic believes that literature has an effect upon the way people lead their lives—perhaps only minimally, perhaps to a very great extent—and it follows that one of the legitimate concerns of criticism is the appropriate response to that belief. For the aesthetic critic, the literary work is quite separate from life. This may mean that art has no direct relationship to the way humans conduct themselves, or it may mean that, whatever the relationship, it is not the business of the literary critic to deal with it. Among major types of criticism, only TEXTUAL CRITICISM, the attempt to establish the precise words the author intended for the work, remains largely outside the dichotomy between morality and aesthetics.

Criticism's concern with morality began with Plato, who emphasized the power of poetry to move humanity, and distrusted it enough to ban it from his ideal commonwealth. Without being necessarily Platonic, many kinds of criticism since ancient times display a similar commitment to the idea that literature and life are closely related. *Biographical criticism,* for example, seeks the clues to the work in the life of the writer. *Psychoanalytical criticism* uses the tools of psychology to probe the relationship between the writer's psyche and his or her creation (see FREUDIAN CRITICISM). *Historical criticism* examines the time in which the work was produced, seeing literature as the result of the human forces of a particular milieu, or, in a wider sense, as the result of traditions arising over a long period of time. *Marxist criticism* interprets literature in terms of class struggle. *Humanistic criticism* is a broad term embracing any critical posture that is essentially centered on humanity, as, for example, the *new humanism* (see HUMANISM, NEW). *Impressionistic criticism* stresses the personal reaction of the critic. In extreme form, it becomes *creative criticism,* wherein the critic creates a new work, imposing his or her imagination upon the literature at hand, as in the "strong readings" advocated by Harold Bloom. *Rhetorical criti-*

cism combines an interest in aesthetics with a concern for moral effect, analyzing the formal elements of a work to show how the writer arranges material for the most effective communication of feelings and ideas to the reader.

Aristotle is the father of aesthetic or *analytic criticism*, which stresses a consideration of the elements that distinguish one kind of work from another or give to an individual work its peculiar characteristics. *Genre criticism* is of this kind; it examines the characteristics of a typical COMEDY, EPIC, LYRIC, TRAGEDY, or other GENRE, or, reversing the process, it illuminates a particular poem or story with reference to the characteristics of the genre to which it belongs. *Archetypal criticism* proceeds by identifying the ARCHETYPE in character and plot that reappears regularly in literature, identifying it sometimes with the symbolic structures in JUNGIAN CRITICISM, which examines humanity's widely shared experience of dream and MYTH. *Formal criticism* is a general term, embracing any critical approach that considers the form of the work without particular reference to its content, as one may speak of the form of a sonnet, for example, or a short story, without discussing its subject matter. AESTHETICISM, the formal criticism of the nineteenth century, stressed the importance of beauty in form above moral content. In the twentieth century, the NEW CRITICISM suggested that form and content are inseparable, analyzing form as the expression of content. *Structural criticism* is a general name for an illumination of a work by an analysis of the way its pieces go together, as in an examination of the principles of DRAMATIC STRUCTURE. SEMIOTICS, a form of structural criticism, approaches structure by considering the verbal signs at the heart of a literary work. STRUCTURALISM, another form, applies to literature the insights of structural linguistics and cultural anthropology. POST-STRUCTURALISM considers the words in isolation, stripping them of interpretations based on preconceptions. See CHICAGO CRITICS; EXEGESIS; HERMENEUTICS; YALE CRITICS.

References

M. H. Abrams, **The Mirror and the Lamp** (1953).
Walter J. Bate, ed., **Criticism: The Major Texts** (1948).
M. C. Beardsley, **Aesthetics from Classical Greece to the Present** (1966).
Harold Bloom, **Agon: Towards a Theory of Literary Revisionism** (1982).
R. S. Crane, **Critical and Historical Principles of Literary History** (1967).
Jonathan Culler, **Structuralist Poetics** (1975).

David Daiches, **Critical Approaches to Literature** (1956).
Terry Eagleton, **Literary Theory: An Introduction** (1983).
Northrop Frye, **Anatomy of Criticism** (1957).
Ann Jefferson and David Robey, eds., **Modern Literary Theory: A Comparative Introduction** (1983).
René Wellek, **A History of Modern Criticism,** 4 vols. (1955–1965).
René Wellek and Austin Warren, **Theory of Literature,** 2nd ed. (1956).
W. K. Wimsatt and Cleanth Brooks, **Literary Criticism: A Short History** (1957).
Yvor Winters, **The Function of Criticism** (1957).

Critique.   A brief criticism, more closely analytical than a REVIEW.

Cross Acrostic.   See ACROSTIC.

Cross-Cutting.   In film, the technique of shifting back and forth from one place or object to another during a sequence to show simultaneous, parallel, and suspenseful events. It was developed by D. W. Griffith and used by him masterfully in *Birth of a Nation* (1915). See MONTAGE.

Crossed Rhyme (or **Interlaced Rhyme**).   Internal rhyme and end rhyme combined in an interlaced pattern. See RHYME.

Crown of Sonnets.   A SONNET SEQUENCE with seven sonnets linked by using the last line of each sonnet as the first line of the next until the sequence ends, with the closing line of the last sonnet the same as the opening line of the first. Donne used a crown of sonnets as the prologue to his *Holy Sonnets*.

Cruelty, Theater of.   Plays designed to purge erotic cruelty by portraying it in ceremonial religious acts. Antonin Artaud gave rise to the genre in the 1930s with several manifestoes and uncompleted plays about Blue Beard and the Marquis de Sade. Peter Brook, Jean-Louis Barrault, Roger Blin, Jean Genet, and others produced Artaudian plays, the most successful being Peter Weiss's *The Persecution and Assassination of Jean Paul Marat as Performed by Inmates of the Asylum of Charenton under the Direction of the Marquis de Sade* (1964). The play, originally in German, is known more conveniently as *Marat/Sade*. See ABSURD, THEATER OF THE.

Cubist Poetry.   Poetry that imitates cubist painting by fragmenting perceptions (Picasso's "destructions") and reassembling them meaningfully (Picasso's "sum of destructions"). The most notable example is the poetry of E. E. Cummings. Kenneth Patchen, Kenneth Rexroth, and many others followed Cummings's lead.

Cultural Primitivism. The belief that nature and freedom are superior to art, reason, and any aesthetic or political controls. See PRIMITIVISM.

Curse. A call upon the gods, or God, to bring down evil on someone—also called a *malediction*, an *imprecation*. If formal, as by the Roman Catholic or Greek Orthodox church, it is called an ANATHEMA: *Si quis dixerit . . . anathema sit* ("If someone should say . . . let him be an anathema.") Sterne reproduces and translates a memorable curse in *Tristram Shandy*, III.xi.

Curtain. A drapery separating the stage from the audience. Orginally covering only the inner stage in the open Elizabethan theater, developing with the PROSCENIUM ARCH in the early seventeenth century, the curtain came into general use after the RESTORATION in 1660. A rising and falling curtain marks the opening and closing of acts and scenes. A "curtain speech" comes just before the last curtain, or is delivered in front of the curtain, after the action closes. A "quick curtain" is a sudden ending; a "strong curtain," an emotionally powerful one. Douglas Jerrold's *Mrs. Caudle's Curtain Lectures*, published in *Punch* during 1845 and contributing greatly to the magazine's success, are delivered at bedside to Mr. Caudle just as he wants to lower the curtain on the day and go to sleep.

Curtain Raiser. (1) A one-act play or skit before the main play. (2) Any preliminary entertainment.

Curtal Sonnet. A verse form invented by Gerard Manley Hopkins, with the sonnet form curtailed to ten lines, plus a shorter tail. A sestet rhyming *abcabc* is followed by a quartet linked by rhyme to the sestet, *dbcd* or *dcbd*. The tail rhymes on *c*. "Pied Beauty" is an example. See SONNET; VERSE FORMS.

Cut. In film, (1) a switch from one scene or object to another, or (2) an interrupted sequence.

Cyborg. In SCIENCE FICTION, a cybernetic organism: a combination of human and machine. The idea of the cyborg began with the actual practice of grafting artificial limbs or hearts onto humans, but is extended in science fiction to humans so rebuilt as to lose their humanity. See ANDROID; ROBOT.

Cycle. A group of poems, plays, epics, or romances concerning a notable subject, like the Trojan War or Charlemagne's court, or a person like Sir Lancelot, by a succession of writers. The Cyclic Poets were late Greeks extending the Trojan lore.

Cycle Plays. The Medieval MIRACLE PLAY presented in great cycles as part of holiday pageants. See MEDIEVAL DRAMA.

Cynicism. Literally, "doggishness." (1) The belief that all motives are selfish. (2) The doctrine of Antisthenes (c. 444–371 B.C.), embraced by Diogenes (c. 412–323 B.C.), that virtue is the only good, and ascetic self-control and poverty, the shunning of pleasure and social conventions, the only way to virtue. Antisthenes believed that individuals were unique and morally responsible for their acts, which they can control by will. Consequently, most modernist movements and many individualistic writers contemptuous of conventional society—Beckett, Kerouac, Jean Genet, Imamu Amiri Baraka—are called cynical. See ANTIREALISTIC NOVEL; ABSURD, THEATER OF THE; CRUELTY, THEATER OF; DADISM; MODERNISM; NIHILISM; STOICISM.

D

Dactyl. A three-syllable metrical foot: — ◡ ◡. It is the basic foot of dactylic hexameter, the six-foot line of Greek and Roman epic poetry. See METER.

Dactylic Hexameter. The classical or HEROIC LINE of the EPIC. A line based on six dactylic feet, with spondees substituted, and always ending — ◡ ◡ | — —. In English, the last syllable tends to be light rather than heavy, but ending in what British schoolboys still call the

$$\overset{—}{\text{. . . straw}}\overset{◡}{\text{berry}} \mid \overset{—}{\text{jam}} \overset{◡}{\text{pot}} \mid .$$

English-speaking writers have tried to match it, notably Gabriel Harvey, working on classical metrics with Spenser (who nevertheless went for iambic pentameter as the best English equivalent); Arthur Hugh Clough ("The Bothie of Tober-na-Voulich," 1848); and Longfellow (*Evangeline*, 1849). See METER.

Dadaism. A nihilistic artistic movement from 1916 to 1924, originating in Zürich in repugnance to World War I and the bourgeoisie and in response to the poetry of Tristan Zara, a Rumanian. The name, variously explained by Dadaists, evidently originated at the Cabaret Voltaire, Zürich, when a group of young war resisters and artists, including Jean Arp and Zara, stuck a paper knife into a French-German dictionary to find it pointing to *dada*, the French baby-talk word for "hobbyhorse." The nonsense fitted their intent to eradicate all aesthetic and philosophical order through outrageous nonsense in protest against the insanity of the war. At least one Dada exhibit offered viewers hatchets to destroy the already chopped-up assemblages.

In France, Marcel Duchamp, already an anti-artist with a bicycle wheel mounted on a stool (1913), became the leader of a Dada group including writers Zara, in from Zürich, André Breton, and Louis Aragon. From this group, Duchamp, Francis Picabia, and Man Ray imported Dada to New York. Picabia edited a Dada periodical, *291*, published in New York, Zürich, Paris, and Barcelona (1917–1924). In Berlin, Dada became more political, creating photomontages jumbled with messages. Max Ernst, in Cologne, was the leading painter. The movement began to wane in 1922, supplanted by SURREALISM. See

136

ABSURD, THEATER OF THE; CRUELTY, THEATER OF; MODERNISM; NIHILISM.

Dark Ages. The Middle Ages, especially the early part. Petrarch (1304–1374), at the dawn of the RENAISSANCE, originated this misnomer for a colorful and intellectually lively period. See GOTHIC.

Dead Metaphor. A METAPHOR accepted without its figurative picture: "a jacket," for the paper around a book, with no mental picture of the human coat that prompted the original metaphor; "a tie," for a business or social relationship, with no picture of a knot under the collar nor of two teams bound equally in rope.

Dead Sea Scrolls. Ancient Hebrew scrolls discovered by shepherds in 1947 in jars in caves near the Dead Sea. The findings led to others, all evidently from the library of the Qumran sect hidden under Roman duress. They contain every book of the Hebrew Scriptures (the Old Testament) except Esther, copied between the first century B.C. and A.D. 50. Two copies of Isaiah are nearly 1000 years earlier than previous texts. Other scrolls contain documents of the sect and some religious poems. Parallels between the Qumran texts and the New Testament suggest Essene influence on Christianity. See ESSENES.

Débat. A medieval poetical debate, perhaps arising from the pastoral contests in Theocritus, like the twelfth-century *Debate between the Body and the Soul* and *The Owl and the Nightengale*.

Decadence. Latin for "falling away": a decay of values or decline in literary excellence after a period of major accomplishment. The term has been used in connection with later Greek literature (c. 300–c. 30 B.C.) after the period of Hellenic excellence; Roman literature after the death of Augustus (14 A.D.); English drama after Shakespeare; and French and English literature at the end of the nineteenth century. Qualities common to periods of decadence include an uncertain grasp of FORM, a lack of serious subject matter, and a fondness for perverse or outrageous effects.

Decadents. Writers marked by qualities of DECADENCE. The term has been applied especially to writers in France and England at the end of the nineteenth century. In France, the journal *Le Décadent* in the 1880s displayed admiration for Baudelaire and the French Symbolists. In England, the important journal was the *Yellow Book* of the 1890s. The literature of the decadents was not so much a falling away from earlier artistic and social standards as it was a rejection of respected values in art and a documentation of spiritual and moral uncertainty in life. Partly, the literature was a protest against the dominance of REALISM and NATURALISM. Oscar Wilde's *Picture of Dorian Gray* (1891) is a memorable portrait of a decadent. See AESTHETICISM; ART FOR ART'S SAKE.

Decasyllabic. Having ten-syllables. An iambic pentameter line is decasyllabic. See METER.

Deconstruction. A technique of CRITICISM, central to POST-STRUCTURALISM, by which each element of a literary text is examined for its possible signification when isolated from preconceptions imposed from without. Each word is a sign, each phrase a combination of signs linguistically at odds in their possibilities. The emphasis is on objective examination and analysis, without the intrusion of the subjective element of interpretation. See SEMIOTICS.

Decorum. Latin for "becoming": propriety in behavior or speech, appropriateness of action to a situation and of conduct to a character. Decorum as a literary quality was highly valued in classical and Neoclassical CRITICISM, as it was understood that each CHARACTER should speak and act in a manner appropriate to his or her station. For example, Shakespeare's kings speak in BLANK VERSE, his fools in rhymes or prose. Writers display decorum by suiting character to action and also by their choice of PLOT elements, setting, and STYLE.

Decorum is defined by taste, changing as time change. Horace's *dulce et decorum est pro patria mori* ("sweet and fitting it is to die for one's country") becomes heavily ironic when quoted at the end of Wilfred Owen's *"Dulce et Decorum Est,"* a poem about gas warfare. Neoclassical ideas about decorum in poetic language and subject matter are challenged by the English Romantics, with their theory expressed, for example, in Wordsworth's Prefaces to the 1798 and 1800 editions of *Lyrical Ballads*.

Deep Focus. In filmmaking, a method that presents objects both near and far in clear focus, rendering sharp images of things close to the camera and, simultaneously, of things in the distance.

Deep Image. A term sometimes applied to an image derived from a writer's subconsciousness. When such images are perceived as arising from widespread human mental patterns, the concept of the deep image bears a close relationship to the DEEP STRUCTURE postulated for language by linguists and for behavior by cultural anthropologists. See ARCHETYPE; IMAGERY; JUNGIAN CRITICISM.

Deep Structure.   A basic language structure postulated by structural linguists as innate in all humans, existing below the level of verbal communication. The deep structure allows different surface structures or verbal utterances, as, for example, in different languages, or within the syntactical possibilities of one language. The term applies also to fundamental patterns of behavior postulated by cultural anthropologists as common to all human societies. See ARCHETYPE; JUNGIAN CRITICISM; TRANSFORMATIONAL GRAMMAR.

Definition.   A description of a word's MEANING. Definition frequently proceeds in two stages: first, a classification in a familiar category ("a *hoe* is a garden tool"), and second, a differentiation specifying special qualities ("with a metal blade set crosswise at the end of a long handle, used for weeding or loosening soil").

Deism.   A rational philosophy of religion beginning with Lord Herbert of Cherbury, the "Father of Deism," in his *De Veritate* (1624); reflected in *The Philosophical Works* (1752) of Henry St. John, Lord Bolingbroke; and championed in Thomas Paine's *Age of Reason* (1794–1795). It arose from the new scientific view of the universe beginning with Copernicus's *De Revolutionibus Orbium Coelestium* (1543) and the new empiricism of Francis Bacon (*Novum Organum*, 1620), encouraged further by Newton's discovery of gravity and the mathematical refraction of light (God's primary creation) into its constituent colors by prisms. Deism reached its peak between 1688, the "Glorious Revolution" that deposed the Catholic rule of James II, and 1742, a period of relative religious freedom, but deism remained influential throughout the eighteenth century. Much orthodox religion was qualified by deistic rationalism, and deists differed considerably in their beliefs. They generally held the following tenets: (1) a natural religion, as opposed to a revealed religion, is either innate through God's dispensation or to be acquired by reason from observing God's rationally ordered universe; (2) God, the supreme Artisan, created a perfect clock of a universe, withdrew, and left it running, not to return to intervene in its natural works nor the life of humankind; (3) the Bible is a moral guide, but neither historically accurate nor divinely authentic; (4) Christ's divinity, the Trinity, miracles, and the atonement for sin are merely human superstitions; (5) reason guides human beings to virtuous conduct; (6) humans may move toward God's perfection through rational education. In the early years of the United States, deism was especially important, as Benjamin Franklin, George Washington,

Paine, and Thomas Jefferson all subscribed to its ideas. Paine's *Age of Reason*, attacked as atheistic, continued long popular in America as a kind of freethinker's bible. Prominent European deists included Voltaire and Rousseau. See ARIANISM (opposition to the Trinity) and ARMINIAMISM (opposition to Calvinist election and predestination).

References

Ernst Cassirer, **The Philosophy of the Enlightenment** (English trans., 1951).
James Collins, **God in Modern Philosophy** (1959).
John Orr, **English Deism: Its Roots and Its Fruits** (1934).

Demotic Style. The language of common people in their everyday discourse. See HIERATIC STYLE; STYLE.

Denotation. The thing a word stands for, the dictionary definition, an objective concept without emotional coloring. It is contrasted with the CONNOTATION, the ideas, attitudes, or emotions associated with the word in the mind of user or hearer.

Denouement. French for "unknotting": the unraveling of PLOT threads toward the end of a PLAY, NOVEL, or other NARRATIVE.

Description. A rendition in words, especially of observations of the human or natural environment. Description is often classified as one of four major types of prose, the others being ARGUMENT, EXPOSITION, and NARRATION, which, however, all use description. In a narrative FORM such as the STORY or NOVEL, description involves especially setting down the visible qualities of CHARACTER and SETTING, as passages of description are frequently distinguished from passages of ACTION or DIALOGUE.

Detective Story (or **Detective Novel**). A type of POPULAR LITERATURE following a detective through the solution of a crime. Although earlier examples of the GENRE can be found (one of the earliest is the story of Bel and the Dragon in the APOCRYPHA), the modern detective story began with Poe's "tales of ratiocination," including "The Murders in the Rue Morgue" and "The Purloined Letter." Typically, the detective is an amateur, like Poe's, whose mental prowess and idiosyncratic fund of information allow him to solve a mystery baffling to the professional police. A CONFIDANT assists him in his labors. Sir Arthur Conan Doyle's Sherlock Holmes is a famous example, with Watson the archetypal confidant.

In the twentieth century the FORM has proliferated. Dorothy Sayers's Lord Peter Wimsey and Bunter carry on the Holmes–Watson tradition. Ian Fleming extended the form to international espionage, with his HERO, James Bond, distinguished for his esoteric knowledge and equipment, aided by various beautiful women as confidantes. Many writers in the twentieth century follow the police in their work, emphasizing the underworld of the big city. The *hard-boiled detective story* of Dashiell Hammett and Mickey Spillane removes many of the admirable qualities of the earlier heroes and frequently adds violence and sex to the world of the *private eye*.

References

Jacques Barzun and W. H. Taylor, **A Catalogue of Crime** (1971).
Howard Haycraft, **Murder for Pleasure** (rev. ed., 1968).
Julian Symons, **Mortal Consequences: A History from the Detective Story to the Crime Novel** (1972).

Determinism. The philosophical belief that events are shaped by forces beyond the control of human beings. In earlier times, the question was one of PREDESTINATION as opposed to free will. This question arises in *Oedipus Rex,* with regard to the FATES, and in literature, especially of the seventeenth and eighteenth centuries, that reflects the theological debates over ANTINOMIANISM and ARMINIANISM. More recently, the question has revolved around events as they occur, or as the shaping forces emerge, without reference to ideas of predestination. *Scientific determinism,* important to literature at the end of the nineteenth century (see NATURALISM), assigns control especially to heredity and environment, without seeking their origins further than science can trace. MARXISM looks to economic determinants. Both shift the old discussion of free will from a theological to a social basis, suggesting, paradoxically, that environmental or economic forces beyond the control of humans can be controlled collectively by humankind. EXISTENTIALISM frees human beings from deterministic bondage, endowing them with the responsibility for shaping their lives.

Deus Ex Machina. Latin for "god out of the machine." The term refers to the practice in the Greek theater of lowering a god from the heavens by a crane or other mechanical device when the play required his presence on stage. More generally, it is a term for any unlikely PLOT contrivance or solution to a NARRATIVE problem, as though the author had called upon the gods for assistance.

Deuteragonist. The second player in a Greek DRAMA, after the PROTAGONIST. Prior to Aeschylus, there was only one actor in a Greek PLAY. Aeschylus added the second, the deuteragonist. In later plays, a deuteragonist is any secondary CHARACTER, often, but not necessarily, the ANTAGONIST.

Devil's Advocate. One who pleads the devil's case. In the process of canonization, the devil's advocate presents the evidence of sin, making the case that the person considered for sainthood does not deserve it. The term is widely used for any person who argues from a position judged wrong or seen as belonging to the devil.

Diachronic. Across time, as in the diachronic analysis of linguistic structures, considering those of the past as well as the present. See LINGUISTICS; SYNCHRONIC.

Dial, The. (1) A Boston PERIODICAL disseminating TRANSCENDENTALISM, edited by Margaret Fuller from 1840 to 1842 and Emerson from 1842 to 1844. Among its contributors were Bronson Alcott, James Russell Lowell, Thoreau, and Jones Very. BROOK FARM was discussed within its pages in essays like Elizabeth P. Peabody's "Plan of the West Roxbury Community" (January 1842). (2) Later American periodicals of the same name, especially an influential literary monthly of the 1920s. In 1922 *The Dial* published *The Waste Land* (first printed in London a month earlier in T. S. Eliot's own journal, *The Criterion*), awarding it a prize of $2000. Among its other contributors was Marianne Moore, who edited it from 1926 to 1929.

Dialect. A variety of language belonging to a particular time, place, or social group, as, for example, an eighteenth-century cockney dialect, a New England dialect, or a coal miners' dialect. A language other than one's own is for the most part unintelligible without study or translation. A dialect other than one's own can generally be understood, although pronunciation, vocabulary, and syntax seem strange. Within a language there may be a wide range of dialects, with some differences apparent only to an expert and some so great that the line between another dialect and another language becomes difficult to draw.

Dialectic. Greek for "the art of conversation," or of logical, analytical discussion or ARGUMENT. The SOCRATIC method of reasoning through question and answer is an example. *Hegelian dialectic* is a philosophical system of reasoning through thesis, ANTITHESIS, and synthesis. *Dialectical materialism* is the Communist philosophy that explains history as a progress of thesis, antithesis, and synthesis produced by conflicting economic forces. *Dialectic* is also used as a term describing the intellectual argument of a NOVEL, PLAY, or other literary work. See HEGELIANISM; MARXISM.

Dialogue. Conversation between two or more persons, as represented in prose fiction, drama, or essays, as opposed to MONOLOGUE, the speech of one person. Good dialogue characterizes each speaker by idiom and attitude as it advances the dramatic conflict. Shakespeare managed this, even though he cast the dialogue of eminent personages, and of tragedy, in BLANK VERSE, and that of the lower classes, and of comedy, in prose. The medieval verse DÉBAT is another form of dialogue.

The dialogue as a form of speculative exposition, or dialectical argument, is often less careful to distinguish the diction and character of the speakers. Famous speculative dialogues are Plato's *Dialogues*, Cicero's *De Oratore*, Lucian's *Dialogues of the Dead*, Dryden's *Essay of Dramatick Poesie*, Berkeley's *Dialogues between Hylas and Philonous*, and Walter Savage Landor's *Imaginary Conversations*.

Dialogue also refers to continuing discussions in different works or over a long period of time, between persons of opposing opinions, as, for example, a dialogue between liberals and conservatives over fundamental taxation policies, or between schools of literary CRITICISM over the value of BIOGRAPHY as an aid to interpretation of a POEM.

Diary. A daily record of events and observations, especially personal ones. Examples include the diaries of Samuel Pepys, providing a portrait of everyday life in seventeenth-century England; Samuel Sewall, portraying seventeenth- and eighteenth-century life in colonial Massachusetts; and Anne Frank, recording events prior to her death in a concentration camp in World War II. See AUTOBIOGRAPHY; JOURNAL; MEMOIRS.

Diatribe. Greek for "a wearing away": a bitter and abusive criticism or INVECTIVE, often lengthy, directed against a person, institution, or work.

Dibrach. A Greek and Latin metrical foot of two unstressed syllables; also called a PYRRHIC foot.

Diction. Word choice in speech or writing, an important element of STYLE.

Dictionary. A list of words in alphabetical order, with useful information given for each. A comprehensive modern dictionary of the English language provides pronunciations, definitions in historical order, synonyms and antonyms, and examples of usage. Some dictionaries are prescriptive, giving correct or standard usage as judged by the editors on such grounds as etymology or taste. Others are descriptive, giving usage as it has been recorded, without judgment as to correctness. Specialized dictionaries serve special purposes, such as a dictionary of legal or medical terms, a dictionary of slang, or a foreign language dictionary. See GLOSSARY.

Didactic. Greek for "teaching": instructive, or having the qualities of a teacher. Since ancient times, literature has been assumed to have two functions, instruction and entertainment, with sometimes one and sometimes the other dominant in a particular work. Literature intended primarily for instruction or containing an important moralistic element is didactic, but the range in emphasis and quality is wide, from Michael Wigglesworth's *Day of Doom* to Milton's *Paradise Lost*.

One kind of didactic literature upholds the widely accepted moral or religious standards of a community, inculcating in its members proper behavior and belief. Much primitive literature is at least partly didactic in this sense, as is much of the literature of ancient Greece and Rome. SAINTS' LIVES, the MIRACLE PLAY, and the MORALITY PLAY performed this function in the Middle Ages. Elizabethan literature frequently supported Elizabethan values. Much POPULAR LITERATURE since, especially CHILDREN'S LITERATURE, has also been heavily didactic in this important way. A second kind of didactic literature opposes widespread belief or practice, soberly exposing injustice, as in Harriet Beecher Stowe's *Uncle Tom's Cabin*, Dickens's *Hard Times*, Upton Sinclair's *The Jungle*, or Steinbeck's *The Grapes of Wrath*, or ripping it with SATIRE, as in Swift's *Gulliver's Travels*, Aldous Huxley's *Brave New World*, or George Orwell's *1984*. See AESTHETICISM; ART FOR ART'S SAKE; AUTOTELIC; FICTION; POETRY.

Dieresis. (1) Separation of two consecutive vowels into two syllables (also the mark that distinguishes them or indicates special pronunciation): coöperation, Brontë. (2) In prosody, a slight pause when the end of a word coincides with the end of a foot.

Digression. A temporary departure of deviation from the main subject of a literary work. Digressions are common in a loose FORM like the EPIC, FAMILIAR ESSAY, or PICARESQUE NOVEL, but generally considered less acceptable in DRAMA, the SHORT STORY, and novels tightly organized around a unified PLOT.

Dilettante. Originally, a lover of the arts, but now primarily a literary or artistic hanger-on, superficial or amateurish.

Dime Novel. A FORM of POPULAR LITERATURE in nineteenth-century America, featuring fast-paced adventures, generally of the American Revolution, the frontier, the Civil War, the Wild West, or crime and outlaws. The publishers Beadle and Adams initiated the form in 1860 with *Malaeska: The Indian Wife of the White Hunter,* which sold perhaps 300,000 copies in its first year. Some later dime novels were presented as true adventures of men like Buffalo Bill Cody and Ned Buntline. Others were series adventures, like the Deadwood Dick dime novels by Edward L. Wheeler and the thousand or more Nick Carter titles, written by various hands and published by the firm of Street and Smith. By the 1890s dime novels began to be less popular, eventually giving way to other popular forms in PULP MAGAZINES, boys' books like the Frank Merriwell series, and newspaper comic strips. See PENNY DREADFUL.

References

Albert Johannsen, **The House of Beadle and Adams and Its Dime and Nickel Novels** (3 vols., 1962).
Edmund Pearson, **Dime Novels** (1929).

Dimeter. Metrical lines of two feet. See METER.

Dionysian. Sensuous, irrational, ecstatic. See APOLLONIAN.

Diorama. A peep show in a box containing miniature figures arranged in a three-dimensional scene. Hawthorne's "Ethan Brand" features a diorama, a popular entertainment of the time.

Dipodic Verse. "Two-footed." Surviving from Old English poetry, dipodic verse is a lighthearted rocking meter in two half-lines, each with two stresses falling among scattered light syllables. Nursery rhymes picked up the pattern from Old English:

There was | an old woman ‖ who lived | in a shoe |
She had | so many children ‖ she did- | n't know what to do. |

Today, critics apply the term to a more patterned derivative that scans in alternating heavy and light iambic feet: ta-DA/ ta-da/ ta-DA/ ta-da:

Go down | to Kew | in li- | lac-time, ‖ in li- | lac-time, | in li- |
lac-time |

But it really rollicks better when read more quickly in the old dipodic way:

˘ ‾ | ˘ ˘ ˘ ‾˘ ˘ || ˘ ‾˘ ˘ | ˘ ‾˘ ˘ |
Go down | to Kew in lilac-time, || in lilac-time, | in lilac time |

˘ ‾ | ˘ ˘ ˘ ‾˘ ˘ || ˘ ‾ | n' ˘ ˘ ˘ ‾ ˘
Go down | to Kew in lilac-time || (it is | n' t far from London!) |

Alfred Noyes, "The Barrel-Organ"

Direct Camera. The technique of taking film directly with portable cameras in documentaries, as in CINEMA VÉRITÉ.

Dirge. A lamenting funeral song. See CORONACH; ELEGY; MONODY; PASTORAL ELEGY; THRENODY.

Discordia Concors. See CONCORDIA DISCORS.

Discovery. Revelation of the truth toward the end of a play, Aristotle's ANAGNORISIS, a discovery, like Oedipus's discovery of the awful truth that he has murdered his father and slept with his mother, or the happy discovery in comedy of the orphan's true identity. See DRAMATIC STRUCTURE.

Disguising. See MUMMING.

Dissenter. A term arising in the 1640s for a member of the clergy or a follower who dissented from the forms of the Anglican established church, particularly Puritans. The Toleration Act (1689), answering the Catholic repression of James II (1685–1688), granted freedom of worship to "Protestant Dissenters," confirming the term's usage in place of "Puritans." Dissenters generally came from the lower middle classes, merchants who disapproved of aristocratic frivolity and ecclesiastical pomp.

Dissertation. A book-length scholarly exposition written to fulfill the requirements of the Ph.D.; a doctoral thesis. The term also refers to a less formal disquisition on a subject, such as Charles Lamb's famous "Dissertation on Roast Pig" or Newton's scientific dissertations.

Dissimile. The technique of emphasizing some condition by saying how dissimilar it is from the usual run of things:

> The foxes have holes, and the fowls of the air their nests, but the son of man has nowhere to lay his head.

Luke 9.58

One generation passeth away, and another generation cometh; but the earth abideth forever.

Eccles. 1.2

Dissociation of Sensibility. T. S. Eliot's phrase for the detachment of feeling from thought in poets coming after Donne and Marvell, roughly from the RESTORATION of 1660 onward. Eliot developed the idea in two essays, "The Metaphysical Poets" and "Andrew Marvell," first published in 1921, collected in *Selected Essays, 1917–32* (1932). Before Milton and Dryden, he argued, thought and feelings ("sensibility") were one, but in Milton and Dryden intellect took charge in a poetry so commanding that feeling seemed to have no part in it at all. Their successors in the eighteenth and nineteenth centuries did not experience their thought as feeling, and could no longer experience feeling as thought or thought as feeling. Consequently, they expressed their dissociated feelings more crudely.

Dissonance. (1) Harsh and jarring sound; discord. It is frequently an intentional effect, as in Browning. (2) Occasionally a term for half rhyme or SLANT RHYME, like *hand / fond*, as an antonym for ASSONANCE.

Distance. The author's, or the audience's, detachment from characters and action. In tragedy the distance is small because sympathetic; in comedy, greater in varying degrees. Writers achieve AESTHETIC DISTANCE when their artistry and aesthetic devices objectify their personal experience into an independent creation. Readers achieve a so-called PSYCHIC DISTANCE in realizing that art and reality are different and distinct.

Distich. A couplet, or pair of rhymed metrical lines.

Distributed Stress. In free, cadenced verse with no regular metrical beat, a stress falling on two successive syllables (what would be a SPONDEE in regular METER). It is also called HOVERING STRESS and RESOLVED STRESS.

All else continuing, the stars shining,

The winds blowing, the notes of the bird continuous echoing

Walt Whitman, "Out of the Cradle Endlessly Rocking"

Dithyramb. A frenzied choral song and dance to honor Dionysus, Greek god of wine and the power of fertility. The CHORUS, and TRAG-

EDY itself, originated in these wild celebrations. Any irregular, impassioned poetry may be called dithyramic. The irregular ODE also evolved from the dithyramb.

Ditty.   A simple song, usually traditional, like sailors' songs.

Divine Afflatus.   Divine INSPIRATION, which Plato recommended and in which Shelley believed. The term is often ironic for overblown writing, *afflatus* meaning "breath."

Doctrinaire.   (1) Writing too closely bound by a particular political or critical doctrine. (2) An impractical theory, or one who holds it; the term originated in 1815 in France to describe a group holding the impractical doctrine that authority and royalty could be reconciled with liberty and representative government.

Documentary Novel.   A novel loaded with contemporary documentation—from newspapers, legal transcripts, popular songs, and the like. F. O. Matthiessen coined the phrase to describe Theodore Dreiser's factual novels (*Theodore Dreiser*, 1951).

Doggerel.   Trivial verse clumsily aiming at meter.

Domestic Tragedy.   A tragedy of domestic, middle-class life. It appears first on the Elizabethan stage: the anonymous *Tragedy of Mr. Arden of Feversham* (1592); Thomas Heywood's *Woman Kilde with Kindnesse* (1607); the anonymous *Yorkshire Tragedy* (1608), claiming Shakespeare's authorship fraudulently on its title page. They tended, like folk gossip and ballads, to pluck the heartstrings. But George Lillo (1693–1739) established domestic tragedy in the eighteenth century with *The London Merchant, or The History of George Barnwell* (1731), based on the ballad of "George Barnwell" (Thomas Percy's *Reliques of Ancient English Poetry*, 3rd ser., III.iv). Edward Moore's *Gamester* (1753) was even more successful.

But if London temporarily admired *George Barnwell*, Europe was captivated. Gotthold Lessing modeled his *Miss Sara Sampson* (1755) on it, leading directly to Ibsen's domestic masterpieces a century later (1877–1900). John Masefield's *Tragedy of Nan* (1909) recaptured the genre for England, and Eugene O'Neill's many domestic masterpieces, beginning with *Beyond the Horizon* (1920), for America. Arthur Miller's *Death of a Salesman* (1949) is America's classic example.

Donnée.   French "the given". Henry James initiated and repeated the word in his prefaces for the character, situation, or theme from which the writer begins to create a work. Whatever *donnée* first struck him, of it James frequently said, "something might be made of that."

Doppelgänger. An alter ego; a second passional self haunting one's rational psyche; from German, "double-goer." G. H. Schubert, a follower of Franz Mesmer's psychotherapy and forerunner of Freud in seeing dreams as symbolic of repressed subconsciousness, predicted this psychic doubleness in *Die Symbolik des Traumes* (Bamberg, 1814— *The Symbolism of Dreams*). Immanuel Kant (1724–1804) had already seen a perpetual contention between humankind's evil heart and rational head, and romances had for centuries paired good and evil identities, as Fielding did with Blifil and his good half-brother Jones (1749). Nevertheless, E. T. A. Hoffmann (1776–1822) specifically embodied Schubert's psychology in his supernatural tales collected as *Die Serapionsbrüder* (4 vols., 1819–1821—*The Serapion Brethren*) and *Die Lebensansichten des Katers Murr* (2 vols., 1820–1822—*Katers Murr's Views of Life*), widely translated, and much of nineteenth-century fiction followed suit. Mary Shelley's *Frankenstein* (1818), for instance, grew out of reading ghost stories—among them presumably Hoffmann's—with Byron and Shelley during a rainy Swiss summer, with all three trying a hand at writing some. James Hogg's *Private Memoirs and Confessions of a Justified Sinner* (1824) and Robert Louis Stevenson's *Dr. Jekyll and Mr. Hyde* (1886) are notable examples of the shadowy Doppelgänger that haunts a great deal of subsequent fiction, as in Dostoevsky's *Crime and Punishment* (1866) and Conrad's great story "The Secret Sharer" (1912).

Dorian Mode. Originally a Greek musical mode, simple and solemn, contrasted to the softer, more voluptuous LYDIAN MODE. Milton's *Lycidas* is sung by an "uncouth swain" who "touched the tender stops of various quills, / With eager thought warbling his Doric lay." See DORIC.

Doric. Referring to the oldest Greek civilization, in northern Greece between Mount Parnassus and Mount Oeta; hence "rustic" or "primitive." Doric columns are the oldest and simplest of the three Greek styles, topped by a smooth capital ring as compared to the leafy Corinthian and the scrolled Ionian. Hence the connotations of simplicity and strength. See ATTIC, by contrast.

Double Dactyls. A playful form of verse, as in Anthony Hecht and John Hollander's *Jiggery-Pokery*. Each line is two DACTYLS. Each poem has two four-line stanzas. The first line is a nonsensical jingle (*Jiggery-pokery*). The second line is a name (*Anthony Hollander*). The second stanza must have one one-word line (*oxyacetylene*). The last lines of the two stanzas must rhyme.

Double Entendre. French for "double meaning." A risqué pun: "The bawdy hand of the dial is now upon the prick of noon" (*Romeo and Juliet* II.iv.119). The term came into English from archaic, or mistaken, French for *double entente*, first recorded in Dryden's play *Marriage à la Mode* (1673; III.i.36). Now long naturalized, it should not be italicized as a foreign phrase.

Double rhyme. See FEMININE RHYME.

Downstage. Toward the front part of the stage; the opposite of UP-STAGE.

Drama. A form of FICTION, distinguished from POETRY and from prose fictions like the NOVEL and SHORT STORY by being acted in front of an audience. More than other fictions, drama is collaborative, communal, and immediate. In Aristotelian terms "an imitation of an action," often written in verse, drama differs from prose fiction and nondramatic poetry by its presentation through actors playing roles.

Drama need not be verbal, as prose fiction and poetry must be. PANTOMIME presents drama silently, through action, and may carry the entire burden of a play, or an important part of it, as in the dumb show in Act III of *Hamlet*. Silences between lines sometimes speak volumes. Actions on stage may clarify dramatic intent through traditional or newly invented details of production not available in printed play texts. SPECTACLE is especially important in a PAGEANT, a Shakespeare HISTORY PLAY, or a movie like *Star Wars*. Visual effects are powerfully augmented by music in OPERA and MUSICAL COMEDY. Yet, although words are not a consideration in the dramatic effect of a pantomime or a parade, and remain of secondary interest in opera and in some movies, they constitute the dramatic heart at the center of the world's serious plays.

Drama is inherently ritual and communal, stressing conventions of belief, behavior, and presentation important to a community in a given time and place. The collaboration between playwright, producer, and actors necessary to secure a receptive audience in today's professional theater is a specialized, sophisticated form of the group effort that in a primitive setting defined drama as a ritualized prayer to the gods or a celebration of the deeds of a culture hero. The history of drama is therefore, in part, like the history of poetry and prose fiction, a history of the accomplishments of individual genius: Sophocles, Shakespeare, Molière, Chekhov, O'Neill, Beckett. But it is also, in ways unique to the GENRE, a history of the conditions of presentation: theaters, directors, actors and acting companies, stage equipment, audience expectations. Drama has always emphasized stories known to the audience, mining its ore from the mountains of religious belief and cultural myth of a people, reshaping and polishing old nuggets to make each presentation new. Hence the vital theater of any time is likely to include revivals of past works, as a new *Othello* or *Waiting for Godot* is imaginatively reconstituted through a new production.

Role playing is essential to drama. The Asian or American Indian shaman wears a mask to assist in communication with the spirit world. The masks of the ancient Greek theater provided visual identity for characters and passions. In O'Neill's *Great God Brown* personalities are defined by masks, and psychological truths revealed when characters speak without them. Hamlet feigns madness. Willy Loman's truth is lies. These instances point toward the central core of pretense in drama. Not only are the actors pretending, but the characters they portray are caught in roles they must endure, although they struggle against them, to the end. The structured world of theater, stage, actor, lights, and lines captures the members of an audience in a shared experience that reminds them of how they, too, respond in role playing to the situations surrounding them in life. Questions of illusion and reality are important to all literature, but vital to drama.

Drama is present action embodied in live actors. Narrative unfolds in the past, but the action of a play, even though set in the Greece of *Medea* or the Scotland of *Macbeth*, is insistently present before the audience. Cleopatra applies the asp to her breast now. We are still waiting for Godot. This is related to the magic through which all art remains timeless, but it is given in the theater the added and essential dimension of the living actor. Thus, a poem read on stage becomes a kind of drama as the audience reacts not merely to the words but to the living presence of the reader. In the same way, prose stories adapted for stage or film become drama, some more successfully than others. Conversely, a play read in a book is drama stripped of important elements; consequently, accomplished readers of plays learn to supply imaginatively the theatrical ingredients not present on the page.

The dramatic tradition of the Western world began in Greece, where it seems to have originated in Dionysian religious rites. From celebrations of fertility came COMEDY; from rites associated with death, TRAGEDY. Song and dance were important, as the CHORUS praised or propitiated a god, but there was at first no dramatic inter-

change. According to tradition, in 534 B.C. Thespis added an actor to
the festivities, and tragedy was born in the dialogue between actor and
chorus. Aeschylus (525–456 B.C.) added a second actor, and Sophocles
(496?–406 B.C.) a third. Greek Old Comedy began in the fifth century
B.C. and survives in the plays of Aristophanes (438?–380? B.C.). Roman
drama was often imitative of the Greek, although Seneca (4 B.C.–
A.D. 65) added a lurid emphasis influential in the RENAISSANCE on
plays like Thomas Kyd's *Spanish Tragedy* (c. 1586), and the comedies
of Plautus (254?–184 B.C.) and Terence (190?–159? B.C.) inspired many
later imitations and adaptations. In England, sword dances and mummer's plays preserved pagan folk dramas associated, perhaps, with pre-
historic vegetation rituals, but the mainstream of later drama there, as
elsewhere in Europe, was produced in the blend of communal and ec-
clesiastic influences that gave rise to the MIRACLE PLAY and the MO-
RALITY PLAY. The burst of creative energy in the Renaissance included
individual playwrights of genius, among them Lope de Vega (1562–
1635), Shakespeare (1564–1616), and Calderón (1600–1681). In the
seventeenth and eighteenth centuries, CLASSICISM dictated the form
and content of the plays of Corneille (1606–1684), Molière (1622–
1673), Congreve (1670–1729), Dryden (1631–1700), Racine (1639–
1699), and Sheridan (1751–1816). The nineteenth century was replete
with MELODRAMA, but produced also the ROMANTICISM of Goethe
(1749–1832) and Pushkin (1799–1837) and the REALISM and NATURAL-
ISM of Gogol (1809–1852), Tolstoy (1828–1910), Ibsen (1828–1906),
and Chekhov (1860–1904).

Under one guise or another, SOCIAL DRAMA dominated the stage in
the years around 1900, as the nineteenth century turned into the twentieth. Strindberg (1849–1912), Wilde (1854–1900), Shaw (1856–1950),
Hauptmann (1862–1946), and Synge (1871–1909) ranged from naturalism through EXPRESSIONISM to comedy and FARCE, preparing the way
for Pirandello (1867–1936), O'Neill (1888–1953), and Brecht (1898–
1956). More recently, playwrights like Tennessee Williams (1911–1983)
and Arthur Miller (1915–   ) have made brilliant use of the technical
possibilities of the modern theater, while Beckett (1906–   ), Ionesco
(1912–   ), and Pinter (1930–   ) have breathed new life into the
old game of dramatic illusion by fracturing traditional dramatic expectations in plays sometimes collectively designated theater of the absurd
(see ABSURD, THEATER OF THE).

Among other types of drama, dance forms such as ballet and musical forms such as opera have their own histories. Pageants, parades,
the MASQUE, circuses, sideshows, and puppets each have their dramatic interest and traditions. NŌ DRAMA and KABUKI plays illustrate

Oriental theatrical conventions. Within the twentieth century, movies, radio, and television have created new forms of drama, allied to the stage play but bowing to different social and aesthetic laws. See DRA-MATIC STRUCTURE; THEATERS.

References

John Gassner and Edward Quinn, eds., **The Reader's Encyclopedia of World Drama** (1969).
Richard Gilman, **The Making of Modern Drama** (1974).
H. D. F. Kitto, **Form and Meaning in Drama** (1956).
Allardyce Nicoll, **World Drama** (1950).

Dramatic Irony.   A situation in which a character in drama or fiction unknowingly says or does something in ironic contrast to an awareness possessed by an audience or reader. It may be comic, as when Laurel and Hardy, in full confidence, try horrendously to move a piano, or when Groucho Marx, told he will be seated on his hostess's right hand, asks, "How will she eat?" It may be tragic, as when Oedipus vows he will smoke out the villain and save the city while he himself, unbe-knownst, is the guilty cause. It may be feigned, as when carefree fat Jack Falstaff claims: "When I was about thy years, Hal, I was not an eagle's talon in the waist; I could have crept into an alderman's thumb-ring. A plague of sighing and grief! It blows a man up like a bladder." It may be retrospective, as when, looking back, we find Oedipus's boasted skill in solving problems growing more and more dramatically ironic. See IRONY.

Dramatic Method.   A technique of writing a NOVEL or SHORT STORY in a manner that provides the reader with only the information avail-able to the viewer of a realistic PLAY: SETTING, CHARACTER descrip-tion, ACTION, and DIALOGUE. All other elements usual in narrations are eliminated—as, for example, the author's commentaries and sum-maries, and the thoughts of the characters, except as they express them aloud. See NARRATIVE PERSPECTIVE.

Dramatic Monologue.   A monologue in verse. A speaker addresses a silent listener, revealing, in DRAMATIC IRONY, things about himself or herself of which the speaker is unaware. In Robert Browning's "My Last Duchess," for instance, a duke, bargaining for a new duchess, reveals himself as a cold aesthete and materialist, who has murdered his innocent young "last duchess," quite evidently not the first. Lyric monologues appear from the Middle Ages onward, particularly in bal-lads, but Browning brought the form to its full ironic potential, and is usually credited with inventing it. T. S. Eliot's "Love Song of J. Alfred

Prufrock" is notable among a number of modern examples, as are works by Carl Sandburg, Conrad Aiken, Edwin A. Robinson, Robert Frost, Allen Tate, and others.

Dramatic Poetry. Poetry in dialogue or monologue, particularly DRAMATIC MONOLOGUE, frequently concerning intense "dramatic" situations. Loosely, the term sometimes refers to poetry in drama, to BLANK VERSE, to lyrics in plays, to POETIC DRAMA like Shakespeare's *The Tempest,* or to CLOSET DRAMA like Browning's *Pippa Passes.*

Dramatic Propriety. A term from the NEW CRITICISM for judging the propriety of a statement only within its literary context, without reference to considerations of its abstract truth. Keats's "Beauty is truth, truth beauty" and Shakespeare's "Ripeness is all" are, according to Cleanth Brooks, appropriate only to Keats's Grecian urn and *King Lear*'s Edgar within the contexts of their works, and no more.

Dramatic Situation. A situation inherently dramatic, as is frequently the case even with LYRIC poems. In assessing the dramatic situation, a critic considers who is speaking, to whom, and in what circumstances. See PERSONA.

Dramatic Structure. In conventional understandings, arising primarily from TRAGEDY, a focus on elements suggested by the simple NARRATIVE outline of a PROTAGONIST, or HERO, in CONFLICT with an ANTAGONIST, or opposing CHARACTER. This scheme gives rise to FREYTAG'S PYRAMID, a diagrammatic way of presenting the action in five units: (1) EXPOSITION, the unfolding of events necessary to understand later PLOT development; (2) RISING ACTION, the complication of events after the exciting force has initiated the conflict between protagonist and antagonist; (3) CLIMAX, the high point of the pyramid, the major CRISIS that brings about the turn in the fortunes of the protagonist; (4) falling action, the events leading away from the climax, as the protagonist attempts to escape his or her fate; (5) CATASTROPHE, the final disaster, involving also, usually, a RESOLUTION, or restoration of order to the disturbed world of the play. In this way of understanding dramatic structure, the five essential movements of the action are reflected in the five ACT structure of a tragedy, but it must be remembered that the scheme is only generally applicable, for not all tragedies have five acts and those with five do not always follow the pattern precisely as outlined. In COMEDY, FARCE, SOCIAL DRAMA, and other forms, including nondramatic ones such as the NOVEL, the same pattern can be observed, provided proper allowances are made.

Conventional understandings aside, thorough discussions of dramatic structure involve both literary and nonliterary elements, for a play is both a construction in words and a physical presentation before an audience. Words may be examined in a book, by considering the structure in methods similar to those used for a poem, short story, or novel. A play may also be considered as it appears on the stage, with attention to the spectacular, or visual, elements, and little or no consideration given to the verbal text. For dramas that are not in large measure verbal, or not verbal at all (as, for example, PANTOMIME), the stage presentation is paramount. The structural elements then have to do with such things as ACTION, pace, entrances and exits, setting, make-up, lighting, musical accompaniment, STORY or narrative line, and so on, and some of these things change, of course, in different productions. For the great plays of the Western tradition, which are literary texts as well as stage presentations, structural considerations may apply first to the verbal texture, but the reader's thoughts are often modified, sometimes surprisingly, when the play is seen on stage.

Dramatis Personae. "The persons of the drama." (1) The list of characters in a play, printed under this Latin heading before the text and in program notes, frequently with phrases describing each role: "a tyrannical father"; "Malwit's daughter, in love with Goodbody." (2) Any listing of characters in a short story, novel, poem, or play. (3) A metaphorical reference to "all the characters."

Dramatism. Kenneth Burke's system for analyzing literature in terms of the active sentence, which he sees as the essential pattern of all literary activity: "Somebody [subject] is always doing [verb] something [object] to somebody else [indirect object]." Literature is "symbolic action" perceived through the symbols of language. Thus, two of his basic works are *A Grammar of Motives* (1945; new edition, 1969) and *A Rhetoric of Motives* (1950; new edition, 1969). All literary works, Burke believes, consist of five essential elements—the pentad: *act* (what happened), *scene* (where), *agent* (who did it), *agency* (how), and *purpose* (why).

Drame. An eighteenth-century French play of serious intent blending tragedy and comedy for, usually, a happy outcome; a TRAGICOMEDY. See PROBLEM PLAY.

Drawing-Room Comedy. A comedy of high society and witty banter set chiefly in a drawing room. It is a form of COMEDY OF MANNERS. See WELL-MADE PLAY.

Dream Vision. A narrative, frequently an ALLEGORY, within the frame of a dream or vision, a form especially popular in the Middle Ages. Cicero's *Somnium Scipionis* (*The Dream of Scipio*, first century

B.C.) and the commentary on it by Macrobius (c. A.D. 400) were influential on the GENRE. Typically, the dreamer, in the midst of a spiritual crisis, falls asleep in a garden and dreams of a mysterious journey, perhaps to heaven or hell, interpreted for the sleeper by a guide. The dreamer then awakes to a renewed sense of spiritual wholeness. The thirteenth-century *Roman de la Rose* set a model for much that followed. In the late fourteenth century the device was used by Chaucer in *The Book of the Duchess* (1369), *The House of Fame*, *The Parliament of Fowls*, and the prologue to *The Legend of Good Women* (all between 1369 and 1386); by Langland in *Piers Plowman* (c. 1362–c.1390); and by the Gawain Poet in *The Pearl*. John Bunyan's *Pilgrim's Progress* (1678) is a famous later example.

Dreams as entries to existences future, past, or fantastic are common in more recent literature, with or without significant allegorical dimension. Examples include Keats's *Fall of Hyperion: A Dream* (1819), Lewis Carroll's *Alice's Adventures in Wonderland* (1865), Edward Bellamy's *Looking Backward* (1888), and Twain's *Connecticut Yankee in King Arthur's Court* (1889).

Droll. A short farce, or comic scene from an earlier play, adapted or invented by actors on extemporaneous stages in taverns and at fairs from the closing of the London Theaters after 2 September 1642 until after the Restoration of Charles II in 1660. Falstaff, the grave diggers from *Hamlet*, and Bottom from *A Midsummer Night's Dream* were popular subjects. It is also called "droll-humours."

Dumb Show. A PANTOMIME enacted within a play, often by allegorical figures, to foreshadow or comment upon the principal action. It originated in SENECAN TRAGEDY of the early Elizabethan period and continued well into the seventeenth century. The dumb show preceding the play-within-the-play in *Hamlet* is the most famous example.

Duodecimo. Also called *twelvemo*, abbreviated 12mo, 12°: a book made from sheets folded to give a SIGNATURE of 12 leaves (32 pages). See BOOK SIZES.

Duologue. A DIALOGUE limited to two people, especially when it constitutes an entire SCENE or PLAY.

Duple Meter. A two-syllable line. See METER.

Dystopia. Greek for "bad place": an anti-UTOPIA, such as Aldous Huxley's *Brave New World* (1932) or George Orwell's *Nineteen Eighty-Four* (1949).

E

Echo Verse. A VERSE (or a POEM of such verses) in which the final syllables of a line are echoed, frequently with different meaning. Jonathan Swift's "Gentle Echo on Woman" is an example, as in the lines that follow:

> How shall I please her, who ne'er loved before?
> > Be fore.
> What most moves women when we them address?
> > A dress.
> Say, what can keep her chaste whom I adore?
> > A door.

Eclogue. A short POEM, usually a PASTORAL, and often in the form of a DIALOGUE or SOLILOQUY. In ancient Greece, an *ecloga* was a "selection," a choice poem or passage. An association of the term with shepherds began with the *Eclogues* of Virgil (70–19 B.C.), who modeled them on the *Idylls* of Theocritus (third century B.C.). In the RENAISSANCE, in the works of Dante, Petrarch, Boccaccio, Spenser (*The Shepheardes Calender*), and others, the eclogue became a major form of verse, with shepherds exchanging verses of love, LAMENT, or EULOGY. In the eighteenth century, Jonathan Swift moved the form to the city, writing *A Town Eclogue* (1710), and the term began to mean a form of verse that could be set anywhere, with an eclogue in the country more commonly a pastoral, as with Pope. The term continues to be used, as in Louis MacNeice's "Eclogue from Iceland" and Allen Tate's "Eclogue of the Liberal and the Poet."

Ecphonesis. A crying out against something, often in an APOSTROPHE:

> O wicked speed, to post with such dexterity to incestuous sheets
> > *Shakespeare, Hamlet*

Edinburgh Review. Quarterly journal published 1802–1929, an important force in nineteenth-century politics and CRITICISM. Its motto (*Judex damnatur, cum nocens absolvitur;* "The judge is condemned when the guilty one is acquitted") encouraged scathing attacks and strong, mostly Whig, opinions. Byron's *English Bards and Scotch Reviewers* (1809) was a response to a harsh review of his *Hours of Idleness*

(1807). Sydney Smith's famous *Edinburgh Review* question, "In the four quarters of the globe, who reads an American book?" (January 1820) was answered by the almost immediate emergence of Washington Irving and James Fenimore Cooper as world-famous writers. See QUARTERLY REVIEW.

Editing. (1) The process of selecting and arranging the elements of a literary work, as, for example, poems for an ANTHOLOGY, ESSAYS for a JOURNAL, or the MANUSCRIPT or previous PRINTING, among several possible, to be used in a new EDITION of a writer's work. (2) The process of correcting a manuscript for the printer. (3) In the film industry, the selection and arrangement of the various shots to create the structure of the final version. See COPY TEXT.

Edition. The form in which a book is published, including its physical qualities and its content. A *first edition* is the first form of a book, printed and bound. A *second edition* is a later form, usually with substantial changes in content. Between the two, there may be more than one PRINTING or IMPRESSION of the first edition, sometimes with minor corrections. The term *edition* also refers to the format of a book. For example, an *illustrated edition* or a *two-volume edition* may be identical in verbal content to one without pictures or bound in a single volume. See STANDARD EDITION; VARIORUM EDITION.

Editorial. A newspaper or MAGAZINE commentary on an issue of public concern. Frequently unsigned, an editorial carries the weight of the editor or staff, and is generally identified as a matter of opinion by its placement or STYLE. *Editorializing* is a term used frequently to describe the presentation of opinions in a similar authoritative manner in, for example, a news story, ESSAY, or work of FICTION.

Education Novel. A NOVEL presenting the intellectual or moral education of a young person as a model for other youth. Following the pattern set in Rousseau's *Émile* (1762), education novels were popular in England in the late eighteenth century and in England and America in the nineteenth. A British example is Thomas Day's *Sandford and Merton* (1783–1789). See *BILDUNGSROMAN*.

Edwardian Period (1901–1914). From the death of Queen Victoria to the outbreak of World War I, named for the reign of Victoria's son, Edward VII (1901–1910), a period generally reacting against Victorian propriety and convention. Operetta and musical comedy had a heyday, while Shaw's comedies and Galsworthy's starker plays dramatized intellectual and social conflict. James Barrie's *Admirable Crichton* (1902) and *Peter Pan* (1904) both delightfully challenged conformity. Ireland contributed not only the emigrant Shaw but the native CELTIC RENAISSANCE, flowering in the ABBEY THEATRE, Dublin, with Yeats's mythic and symbolic plays forecasting his eventual achievement in poetry. James Stephens's fairy novel, *The Crock of Gold* (1912), and James Joyce's collection of stories, *Dubliners* (1914), signaled Ireland's new literary awareness.

Arnold Bennett, Galsworthy, and H. G. Wells made their mark with realistic novels of moral and social criticism. Conrad was preeminent with *Lord Jim* (1900), *Youth* and *Heart of Darkness* (1902), *Nostromo* (1904), and others leading to his posthumous *Suspense* (1925). Samuel Butler's posthumous *Way of All Flesh* (1903) was a permanent achievement. W. H. Hudson's *Green Mansions* (1904) and Kenneth Grahame's *Wind in the Willows* (1908) are classics of the romantic fancy.

John Masefield, Alfred Noyes, and Robert Bridges (named Poet Laureate in 1913) were the leading poets, with AE (George William Russell) and Yeats beginning to make their mark. Thomas Hardy, after *Jude the Obscure* (1895), abandoned prose for a second career in poetry. In 1914, the war blew apart the Victorian remnants.

Effect. The impression made by a literary work on a reader or on society. Effect in either sense is difficult to measure, its use as a tool of CRITICISM much debated. As an indication of the effect of literature on society, President Lincoln is reported to have greeted Harriet Beecher Stowe, author of *Uncle Tom's Cabin*, with the words "So, this is the little lady who made this big war!" A phrase from W. H. Auden's "In Memory of W. B. Yeats," however, says that "poetry makes nothing happen." And Upton Sinclair reminds us that the author's intent may miscarry, stating that in *The Jungle* he aimed for the public's heart, but miscalculated and hit people in the stomach instead, giving great impetus to the passage of the Pure Food and Drugs Act, but doing little to alleviate the misery of the workers in the stockyards and packing plants of Chicago. Effect on an individual is an equally slippery concept, since a reader must be aware that the effect on one person, either intellectual or emotional, may be different for others, or for the same person at another time.

From the perspective of the writer, however, effect remains a necessary consideration, as the writer must assume that the work will impress someone in some way. Edgar Allan Poe is much cited for his concept of the *single effect* that should govern the construction of a POEM or SHORT STORY. For Poe, there is no such thing as a long poem, but only short poems, each organized around one effect, a long poem like *Paradise Lost* being but a succession of shorter poems. For the short story, his idea is condensed in the following passage from his review of Hawthorne's *Twice-Told Tales:*

> A skilful literary artist has constructed a tale. If wise, he has not fashioned his thoughts to accommodate his incidents; but having conceived, with deliberate care, a certain unique or single *effect* to be wrought out, he then invents such incidents—he then combines such events as may best aid him in establishing this preconceived effect. If his very initial sentence tend not to the outbringing of this effect, then he has failed in his first step. In the whole composition there should be no word written, of which the tendency, direct or indirect, is not to the one pre-established design. And by such means, with such care and skill, a picture is at length painted which leaves in the mind of him who contemplates it with a kindred art, a sense of the fullest satisfaction.

Modern criticism frequently avoids discussions of effect, invoking the INTENTIONAL FALLACY and the AFFECTIVE FALLACY as reasons to examine STRUCTURE apart from considerations of impact either intended or felt.

Eiron.   A STOCK CHARACTER in Greek COMEDY, a self-effacing trickster, opposed to the *alazon*. In TRAGEDY, the *eiron* often acts as agent to bring down the *alazon*. See CHARACTERS.

Eisteddfod.   Originally an assembly of members of Welsh bardic, or poetic, guilds, to establish rules, issue licenses, and award prizes. The International Musical Eisteddfod and The Royal National Eisteddfod (the latter conducted in Welsh) are now annual festivals in Wales, promoting a variety of cultural activities.

Elaboration.   Latin for "a working out": careful, thorough explanation or expansion of an idea, IMAGE, or other literary element. In RHETORIC, elaboration can apply either to subject matter or to STYLE. Overelaboration of subject matter can become tedious, an overelaborate style a barrier to communication.

Electra Complex.   A term from psychoanalysis for a mental condition involving a daughter's obsessive love for her father and hatred of her mother; the female version of an OEDIPUS COMPLEX. In Greek MYTH, Electra avenged the death of Agamemnon, her father, by encouraging or assisting in the killing of her mother, Clytemnestra, who had been involved in the murder of Agamemnon. Aeschylus, Sophocles, and Euripides all dramatized the story. O'Neill's *Mourning Becomes Electra* (1931) retells it in a Civil War setting.

Elegiac Meter.   A COUPLET of two dactylic lines, hexameter followed by pentameter, used for epitaphs and laments. Coleridge translated an imitation by Schiller as:

> In the hexameter rises the fountain's silvery column,
> In the pentameter aye falling back.

Originating in Greek verse, the form was widely used by Roman poets like Catullus and has been imitated in English by Sir Philip Sidney, Edmund Spenser, Algernon Charles Swinburne, and others. See METER.

Elegiac Stanza.   A STANZA in four lines of iambic pentameter METER, rhyming *abab*. Taking its name from Thomas Gray's "Elegy Written in a Country Churchyard" (1751), it is identical to the HEROIC QUATRAIN. The separate name has a special appropriateness for the use of the stanza in Gray's and other eighteenth- and nineteenth-century elegies.

Elegy.   Greek for "lament": A POEM on death or other serious loss, characteristically a sustained meditation containing an expression of sorrow and, frequently, an explicit or implied consolation. Elegies in English on the death of individuals include Chaucer's *Book of the Duchess*, a DREAM VISION; Milton's "Lycidas," a PASTORAL ELEGY; Tennyson's "In Memoriam"; and Auden's "In Memory of W. B. Yeats." Whitman's "When Lilacs Last in the Dooryard Bloom'd" begins with the death of Lincoln and expands to include the deaths of soldiers killed in the Civil War. Gray's "Elegy Written in a Country Churchyard" ponders the deaths of many ordinary people. Poems using the *UBI SUNT* theme are usually elegiac in mood.

Elements.   See FOUR ELEMENTS.

Elision.   Latin for "striking out": the omission or slurring of an unstressed vowel sound at the end of a word to bring a line of poetry closer to a prescribed metrical pattern. Milton's "Lycidas" provides an example: "Tempered to th' oaten flute." See METER; SYNCOPE.

Elizabethan Drama.   English DRAMA of the reign of Elizabeth I (1558–1603). Strictly speaking, drama from the reign of James I (1603–1625) belongs to the JACOBEAN PERIOD and that from the reign of

Charles I (1625–1642) is CAROLINE PERIOD, but the term *Elizabethan* is sometimes extended to include the works of later reigns, prior to the closing of the theaters in 1642.

Modern English drama began in the latter part of Elizabeth's reign. The native tradition seen earlier in the MIRACLE PLAY and the MORAL- ITY PLAY merged with CLASSICAL tradition (see CLASSICISM) as wit- nessed in England in the SCHOOL PLAYS of the earlier sixteenth century to produce the great Elizabethan plays. Major dramatists are Thomas Kyd (1558–1594), Christopher Marlowe (1564–1593), William Shake- speare (1564–1616), Thomas Dekker (c. 1570–1632), Ben Jonson (1572–1637), Thomas Heywood (1573–1641), John Fletcher (1579– 1625), John Webster (c. 1580–c. 1630), and Francis Beaumont (c. 1585–1616). See COMEDY; HISTORY PLAY; REVENGE TRAGEDY; TRAGEDY.

Elizabethan Period (1558–1603). A period marked by the reign of Elizabeth I, the literary culmination of the Renaissance, the "Golden Age of English Literature," especially in lyric poetry and the drama, with Marlowe, Spenser, Sidney, Shakespeare, and the early Jonson and Donne. See ENGLISH LITERATURE, PERIODS OF and the "Chronology of Literature and World Events."

Elizabethan Theaters. See THEATERS.

Ellipsis. (1) The omission of words for rhetorical effect: *Drop dead* for "You drop dead." (2) Three spaced dots . . . to indicate words omitted from quotations.

Emblem. (1) A DIDACTIC pictorial and literary form consisting of a word or phrase *(mot* or *motto),* a symbolic woodcut or engraving, and a brief moralistic POEM *(explicatio). Emblem books* were collections of emblems, popular in the sixteenth and seventeenth centuries, such as Francis Quarles's *Emblemes* (1635). They served as sources of IMAGERY for Spenser, Shakespeare, Donne, and other poets. (2) A TYPE or SYM- BOL. The word is used in this sense, for example, in the works of Nathaniel Hawthorne.

Emendation. Latin for "fault removal": a change made in a literary text to remove faults that have appeared through tampering or by er- rors in reading, transcription, or printing from the MANUSCRIPT.

Empathy. Greek for "feeling with": identification with the feelings or passions of another person, natural creature, or even an inanimate ob- ject conceived of as possessing human attributes. Empathy suggests emotional identification, whereas SYMPATHY may be largely an intellectual appreciation of another's situation.

Emphasis. Stress placed on words, phrases, or ideas to show their importance in a literary text. Emphasis may be achieved in many ways, ranging from mechanical devices like *italics*, **boldface**, and punctuation!!!, through poetical devices like FIGURATIVE LANGUAGE, METER, and RHYME, to strategies of RHETORIC, like CLIMATIC ORDER, CONTRAST, REPETITION, and position in a sentence, paragraph, or ESSAY (first and last positions generally carrying the most weight).

Empiricism. Greek for "experience": the belief that all knowledge comes from experience, that human understanding of general truth can be founded only on observation of particular instances. Empiricism is important to the scientific method and was influential in forming the theoretical background for literary NATURALISM. As a philosophy, it is opposed to RATIONALISM, which discovers truth through reason alone, without regard to experience. Important empirical philosophers include John Locke (1632–1704), George Berkeley (1685–1783), David Hume (1711–1776), and John Stuart Mill (1806–1873).

Enallage. A synonym for ANTIMERIA: the technique of putting one part of speech for another—"*head* the class" "*toe* the line."

Enantiosis. The practice of emphasizing contraries, often with ANTIMETABOLE or CHIASMUS; also called *contentio:*

> One wouldn't hurt her; the other couldn't help her.
> Could not go on, would not go back.
> Serious in silly things, silly in serious.

Enchiridion. A handbook or manual.

Enclosed Rhyme. A couplet, or pair of rhyming lines, enclosed in rhyming lines to give the pattern *abba*. Examples include the "IN MEMORIAM" STANZA and the two halves of the OCTAVE of an Italian sonnet.

Encomium. Originally, a Greek choral song in praise of a hero; later, any formal expression of praise, in verse or prose.

Encyclopedia (or **Encyclopaedia**). "All-encompassing education" (Greek *enkuklios*, "circular, general," and *paideia*, "education")—an alphabetical compendium of knowledge. The word first appeared in English in Sir Thomas Elyot's *Boke of the Governour* (1531). *The En-*

cyclopaedia Britannica began in 1771 to survey all knowledge. Works like *The New Columbia Encyclopedia* do it in one volume. Works like the *Catholic Encyclopaedia* and the *Encyclopedia of Banking and Finance* cover particular fields.

End Rhyme. RHYME at the end of a line of verse (the usual placement), as distinguished from *initial rhyme*, at the beginning, or INTERNAL RHYME, within the line.

End-Stopped Line. A line marked with a grammatical pause at the end. It is the opposite of a RUN-ON LINE, or ENJAMBMENT, where the grammatical phrase runs from one line of poetry onto the next, without pause (i.e., no punctuation).

English Language. The language of Great Britain, Canada, and other members of the Commonwealth of Nations, as well as of the United States; widely used as an international language. The English language arrived in Britain in A.D. 449. Romans, and Latin, had ruled Britain for almost 500 years, pushing the native Celts and Celtic into the hinterland. In 409, Emperor Honarius, besieged by Alaric the Goth, wrote the British cities that Rome could no longer defend them, and the Roman legions and many citizens withdrew from England. The native chieftains squabbled to fill the vacuum. One, Vortigern, invited two "Saxon" lords to help fend off Picts and Irish. Hengist and Horsa, two brothers (the first means "stallion," the second "horse's"), sailed from their native Jutland—the Danish peninsula—to land at Ebbsfleet, Kent, south of the Thames. The Anglo-Saxon language had arrived.

The Jutes went on to dominate Kent, and soon Saxons and Angles, neighboring tribes in Jutland closely related in race and language, followed, landing first on the southern coast, then on the northeast. The invaders soon prevailed over the scattered Celtish fragments left by the Romans—Saxons in the south and west, Angles in Mercia and Northumberland, north of the Thames. Here the first literature arose in *Anglisc* or *Englisc*, the earliest among any of the Germanic languages, now completely lost except for later Saxon versions. These are what is called Old English, or Anglo-Saxon.

Two centuries later, invaders again altered the language. Danish Vikings began raiding on the south coast in 789, and in Northumbria in 793, destroying monasteries, the literature, and the culture of the Angles, eventually settling and dominating central England and Northumbria by the late 800s. The influence of the Old Norse of the Danes began the long modification of Anglo-Saxon into Modern English. Because Old Norse and Old English had similar structure but differing word endings, grammatical complexities began to disappear as speakers went for the word and forgot the endings. Nevertheless, only about 40 Norse words appear in written Anglo-Saxon, among them *lagu*, "law"; *husbonda*, "householder"; and *þræl*, "thrall" ("slave," now in *enthrall*). King Alfred, who created the Saxon literature which replaced that of the Angles, defeated the Danes and partitioned the country at the Peace of Wedmore (878), keeping the two peoples somewhat separate. But when Middle English began to emerge after 1100, many Norse words appear well established, picked up from the spoken language— *die*, *egg*, *she*, *sky*, *take*, for instance, and a considerable number of others beginning in *sk* and the *skr* sound: *skew*, *skill*, *skin*, *skirt* (alongside Anglo-Saxon *shirt*), *scrap*, *scrape*, *scream*.

Old English had case endings for nouns, pronouns, adjectives, and participles. The noun *daeg*, "day," for instance, declined in the singular as *daeg* (nominative and accusative), *daeges* (genitive), *daege* (dative and instrumental), and in the plural as *dagas*, *daga*, *dagum*. Verbs conjugated. *Singan*, "to sing," for instance, ran *singe*, *singest*, *singeð* in the three persons singular (ð being pronounced "th"), and *singað* for all plurals. Word order was characteristically Germanic, with the verb coming late or last. The four major dialects, Northumbrian, Mercian, West Saxon, and Kentish, differed, of course, but Alfred's West Saxon prevailed in writing. The earliest writing had been in Germanic runes, but missionaries re-introduced Christianity and the Roman alphabet, beginning with Augustine's landing from Rome in 597, a process completed by one French missionary and a number from Ireland by 686.

Norse Vikings also effected the second and most significant change in English. While the Danes were raiding England, other Norse people were invading France, most prominently in Normandy, which bears their name. They depopulated the country, but intermarried (as in England) and soon adopted the more civilized French culture and language. Two centuries later, when William the Conqueror, the Norman, landed in England, about the only Norse remaining was his battle cry, *Tur ai!* ("Thor, aid!"). The Norman Conquest of 1066 made the language of England French. Anglo-Saxon went underground, the speech of peasants, who herded *calves*, *steers*, *swine*, and *sheep* as the French lords and ladies ate their *veal*, *beef*, *pork*, and *mutton*. The Norman Conquest not only rebuilt the English vocabulary but also erased inflectional endings and changed the Germanic word order to the subject–verb–object order we use today.

But English, as it evolved from Anglo-Saxon, continued to work upward until, by the reign of Edward III (1327–1377), the nobility were speaking English. About 1350, teaching in the schools shifted from French to English. Nothing remained of the old inflectional endings but a meaningless final *e*, pronounced "uh" or not at all. Though Anglo-Saxon had acquired many Latin words from Romans on the Continent—the originals of *butter, copper, kitchen, peas, pepper, wall, wine,* for instance—by the middle 1300s Latin and related French words had flooded in. From the Conquest to 1500 is the Middle English period, usually rounded as 1100–1500.

Modern English (1500 onward) began when William Caxton, a retired English merchant in Belgium, returned to London with his new printing press in 1476. In his remaining 14 years, Caxton translated and printed almost 80 books, confirming the English of London as the national standard. But English was still exploring and experimenting in Shakespeare's day, borrowing easily from the Latin in which all educated people were bilingual. After the civil wars in the middle 1600s and the RESTORATION of 1660, the language settled into recognizably modern form. The Bloodless Revolution of 1688 provides a convenient watershed into modernity, as the language attained a new smoothness under John Dryden's fluent pen. Samuel Johnson's *Dictionary* (1755) stabilized English spelling, and Bishop Robert Lowth's *Short Introduction to English Grammar* (1762) did much the same for grammar, setting the pattern for school texts almost down to our own time.

Some 60 percent of the English vocabulary comes, in one way or another, from Latin, another 12 percent from other languages, notably Greek in scientific words, prefixes, and suffixes. But the reamining 25 percent, from Anglo-Saxon, gives the framework, the repeated common verbs, pronouns, articles, and connectives. Tough monosyllabic Anglo-Saxon plays against pliant polysyllabic Latin to give English an unusual range of sound and feeling, as in Faulkner's "only the indomitable skeleton was left rising like a ruin or a landmark above the somnolent and impervious guts." Faulkner's latinate words set a resonant contrast for the pungent and punning Anglo-Saxon *guts* at the end. The passage also illustrates how Anglo-Saxon predominates in spite of its minor percentage of the vocabulary. Fourteen of the nineteen words are Anglo-Saxon; only five come from Latin: *indomitable, skeleton* (Latin from Greek), *ruin, somnolent, impervious.* English also retains the old Germanic habit of accenting first syllables, still dropping endings, so that people say, and write, *could care less* when they mean *couldn't care less.* But English continues to borrow from most of the world's major languages, and continues to innovate to meet new social and scientific needs. See AMERICAN ENGLISH; MIDDLE ENGLISH; MIDDLE ENGLISH LITERATURE; OLD ENGLISH; OLD ENGLISH LITERATURE.

References

A. C. Baugh, **A History of the English Language** (2nd ed., 1963).
Henry Bradley, **The Making of English** (1904; rev. by Simeon Potter, 1968).
W. N. Francis, **The English Language, an Introduction** (1965).
J. O. H. Jesperson, **Growth and Structure of the English Language** (1905; repr. 1971).
Thomas Pyles and John Algeo, **The Origins and Development of the English Language,** 3rd ed. (1982).
B. M. H. Strang, **A History of English** (1971).

English Literature, Periods of. The time spans into which English literature can be divided. The movement of literature does not suddenly veer, nor halt, when the literary historian cracks the periodic whip. The historian is not yet there, but only centuries later looks back to discover periods and to describe movements as an aid to understanding particular works in their social and intellectual climates. The generalization then made will also always apply to works that anticipate or continue a period's central impulse. New aspirations and old yearnings will always eddy through the current, complicating or contradicting the historian's descriptions, which have also skipped some stretches of indistinction. Labels have differed, but the table below gives those that have stuck. This *Handbook* includes, at the end, a more detailed "Chronology of Literature and World Events," and summarizes each period in its alphabetical place.

PERIODS OF ENGLISH LITERATURE

449–1100	Old English	
1100–1150	Middle English	
	1100–1350	Anglo-Norman
	1369–1400	The Age of Chaucer
1500–1660	The Renaissance	
	1485–1558	The Early Tudors
	1558–1603	Elizabethan
	1603–1625	Jacobean
	1625–1642	Caroline
	1649–1660	The Commonwealth
1660–1800	Neoclassical (The Age of Reason)	
	1660–1700	The Restoration

1700–1750   Augustan (The Augustan Age)
1750–1789   The Age of Johnson
1798–1832   Romantic
1837–1901   Victorian
1837–1870   Early Victorian
1870–1901   Late Victorian
1901–1914   Edwardian
1914–1965   Modern
1965–   Post-Modern

English Sonnet.   Another name for a SHAKESPEAREAN SONNET.

Enjambment.   RUN-ON LINES. The opposite of END-STOPPED LINE. In enjambment the grammatical sense runs from one line of poetry to the next without pause or punctuation. The ending of Wordsworth's "Lines Composed a Few Miles Above Tintern Abbey" shows enjambment (the second and fourth lines below) alternating with end-stopped lines:

> Nor wilt thou then forget,
> That after many wanderings, many years
> Of absence, these steep woods, and lofty cliffs,
> And this green pastoral landscape, were to me
> More dear, both for themselves and for thy sake!

Enlightenment.   A philosophical movement in the seventeenth and eighteenth centuries, particularly in France, characterized by the conviction that reason could achieve all knowledge, supplant organized religion, and ensure progress toward happiness and perfection. In 1543, Copernicus had launched God's stable world into orbit. Kepler (1571–1630), Tycho Brahe (1546–1601), Galileo (1564–1642), and, later, Newton (1642–1727) described God's ancient universe in mathematical terms. In 1605, Francis Bacon's *Advancement of Learning* announced the new empirical science. In 1637, Descartes, inquiring empirically into the mind, threw reality inward to individual consciousness, and Locke, in 1690, confirmed the tenuous psychological lines by which humans perceived external reality. The idea of progress began more and more insistently to erode the older PRIMITIVISM, which saw humans falling downhill from a perfect Golden Age or Eden into mere cycles of better and worse. DEISM, or rational religion, challenged divine mysteries with a rational Clockmaker, whose vast mechanism ticked on, needing neither His immanence nor intercession, though His existence underwrote both universal and social order.

In France, the PHILOSOPHES emphasized rational and political progress, characterized by Denis Diderot's *Encyclopédie* (1751–1776), in which leading authorities sought to describe all fields of knowledge, and by Voltaire's militant Deism, which led him, in the 1760s, to defend several people cruelly executed or condemned for religious offenses, crying, "Every sensible man, every honorable man, must hold the Christian sect in horror." In England, on the other hand, every major writer satirized the proud faith in reason, which blinded human beings to their ordained limits, suggesting the higher reason of knowing their limitations, in spite of "Pride" and "erring Reason," in Pope's words (*An Essay on Man* I.293). Only toward the end of the century did England match French optimism in the PERFECTIBILIANS ("perfectibilitarianism"), notably William Godwin and Thomas Paine, who believed, in Paine's words, "there is a morning of reason rising upon the world," wherein the liberty, equality, and fraternity of the French Revolution would arise from a rational education, in an environment rationally purged of crime and injustice. Paine's *Age of Reason* (1794–1795) urged Enlightenment thinking: reason and a natural religion should eradicate monarchy and its ally, Christianity. Enlightenment thought is clearly evident in the Declaration of Independence and the U.S. Constitution.

Enthymeme. (1) An informal SYLLOGISM omitting, but implying, either the major or the minor premise. "Too many cooks spoil the broth. I quit"—the speaker omits the minor premise that he is a cook. (2) In Aristotelian terms, a persuasive and probable syllogism that is not necessarily valid.

Entr'acte. An interlude, usually musical, between acts of a play.

Entropy. In physics, the quantity of randomness or disorder in any system containing energy. Increased entropy means less energy available for work. In information theory, entropy serves as a measure of the amount of random error or disorder hindering communication. Thomas Pynchon's story "Entropy" plays on both meanings.

Entwicklungsgeschichte. "Development story." See *BILDUNGSROMAN.*

Entwicklungsroman. "Development novel"—a novel tracing a young person's maturation through experience. See *BILDUNGSROMAN.*

Envelope Construction. In poetry, the enclosing of several lines in an envelope of two or more repeated or similar lines, or even repeated stanzas, as in John Lennon and Paul McCartney's "Eleanor Rigby." Two lines repeating, "Ah, look at all the lonely people!" enclose the whole song at beginning and end, and a four-line repeated stanza about lonely people encloses the inner narrative stanzas. Tennyson's "IN MEMORIAM" STANZA is sometimes called an "envelope stanza" because its outer rhyming lines enclose the inner:

> I sometimes hold it half a sin
>   To put in words the grief I feel;
>   For words, like Nature, half reveal
> And half conceal the Soul within.

Envoy (or **Envoi**).   A concluding STANZA, generally shorter than the earlier stanzas of a poem, normally linked to them by rhyme, and bringing about a formal conclusion in brief summary of theme, address to a prince or patron, or return to a REFRAIN. The BALLADE and SESTINA are VERSE FORMS employing envoys.

Epanados.   (1) Any rhetorical repetition. (2) An ANTIMETABOLE, a repetition in reverse order. (3) Repetition to distinguish: "Both played well, Emily wisely, Augusta adventurously." (4) A return after a digression, or temporary departure from the main subject.

Epanalepsis.   The technique of ending the second clause with the same word or sound that began the first. Similar to ANTIMETABOLE and CHIASMUS:

> A fool with his friends, and with his wife a fool.
> In sorrow was I born, and will die in sorrow.

Epanaphora.   Synonym of ANAPHORA.

Epanorthosis.   "A correction"; the device of seeming to correct oneself to reinforce an idea:

> Written not in tables of stone but in the fleshy tables of the heart.
>
> *II Cor. 3.3*

> He asks, or rather demands, an answer.
> A gift horse—no, a white elephant.

Epic.   A long narrative poem, typically a recounting of history or legend or of the deeds of a national hero. In the earliest poetry of Greece, long poems were delivered on specific occasions, usually religious ritual, which were normally not written down but delivered orally, and were improvised or partly improvised, perhaps by poets who did not read or write. They were known as *epos* or, in the plural, *ta epe*. Improvised poetry of this sort demands a strict meter and a number of fixed epithets, known as formulaic units, which fitted into an established meter. Even as late as Homer one can see the importance of these formulaic epithets in giving to the long dactylic hexameter line an impression of masterly ease. Formulaic poetry still survives, mainly in Slavic countries, and the study of it is illuminating in understanding the background of Homer (see Albert B. Lord, *The Singer of Tales*, 1960). The so-called Homeric Hymns illustrate a related type of epos, poems celebrating the birth and accomplishments of a god. The most familiar type of epic now is a presentation of a heroic event in the past, where the material is partly historical and partly legendary. The two great poems ascribed to Homer, the *Iliad* and the *Odyssey*, are the only early epics to survive intact, although we are told of many "cyclical" poets who filled out the total body of traditional history and legend with other poems.

Epic poetry ever since has reflected the overwhelming influence of Homer. In Greek literature the best-known surviving example of post-Homeric epic is the *Argonautica* of Apollonius Rhodius (c. 250 B.C.). Roman literature produced a similar dominating influence in Virgil, whose *Aeneid* owes much to Homer, particularly the *Odyssey*. Virgil was followed, in the Silver Age of Latin, by Lucan (A.D. 39–65), whose *Pharsalia* deals with the wars of Caesar, and Statius (A.D. c. 45–c. 96), whose *Thebais* goes back to the Greek legends about Thebes. The latter gained a considerable reputation in the Middle Ages through the legend that he had been converted to Christianity. Such epics, whatever their diversity, tend to be organized on a basis of straightforward narrative: what makes the *Iliad*, *Odyssey*, and *Aeneid* attain a distinctive rank in epic is the careful shaping of the foreground action of the poem in relation to a total action that covers the whole story of Troy. The *Odyssey* and the *Aeneid* begin in the middle of the total action, with the hero far from his home and the end of the quest, and then work forward and backward to the end and the beginning of the total action. Alexandrian editors divided the *Iliad* and the *Odyssey* into 24 books each; the *Aeneid* has 12 books, and it seems clear that these divisions correspond to a genuine symmetry in the poems as a whole.

Another great semilegendary figure in early Greek poetry is Hesiod (eighth century B.C.), often paired with Homer. Hesiod's *Theogony* is concerned with myths of the gods; *Works and Days*, despite its personal tone, indicates one of the primitive social functions of the poet, who in times before writing was the walking encyclopedia of society, the one who knew the myths, legends, maxims, proverbs, magic, and practical science of the community. The poet held this function be-cause verse provides the simplest framework for memorization. Hesiod is more closely related than Homer to the tradition of the DIDACTIC poem, the poem on a philosophical or scientific subject, of which Lu-cretius's *De Rerum Natura* (*On the Nature of Things*) is the supreme classical example. The combination of the long didactic poem and the long heroic narrative produced what became in Renaissance critical theory the supreme GENRE that only the greatest poets could hope to succeed with: the encyclopedic epic poem, the poem that summarizes the learning of its time as well as telling one of the central stories in its society's mythology.

This encyclopedic quality is already present in Virgil, where the story of Aeneas is embedded in a profound Stoic philosophy of history (see STOICISM) and of the role of the Roman Empire in that history. In the Middle Ages the encyclopedic survey of all knowledge, whether in verse or in prose, was a fairly frequent form, partly because of the interlocking shape of the different disciplines of the time, dependent as they all were on the axioms of the Christian faith. The encyclopedic shape of the Bible, which runs from the beginning of time, at the Cre-ation, to the end of time, at the Apocalypse, and surveys the history of mankind in between under the symbolic names of Adam and Israel, became the model for such surveys as the *Cursor Mundi* in fourteenth-century England. The supreme medieval example, however, is of course the *Divine Comedy* of Dante, which covers the entire "comedy" or mythology of Christianity in the three great journeys through hell, purgatory, and paradise.

In the RENAISSANCE, critical theory emphasized two assumptions glanced at above: (1) the encyclopedic knowledge needed for major poetry, an ideal fostered by the belief that the oldest poets were the most learned people of their time and by such models of scholarly vir-tuosity as those of Cicero's *De Oratore*, and (2) an aristocracy of genres, according to which epic and TRAGEDY, because they deal with heroes and ruling-class figures, were reserved for major poets. The in-fluence of these views is clear in Milton, for whom the encyclopedic epic, achieved in *Paradise Lost*, was the supreme effort of his life, "long choosing and beginning late," as he says, and one that could be made only once. In the next age came a change of taste, epitomized in the antimythological attitude of Boileau (1636–1711) and in Pope's ax-iom that "the proper study of mankind is man," which meant that long poems in the age of Dryden and Pope tended to be satires.

ROMANTICISM revived both the long mythological poem and the verse romance, but the prestige of the encyclopedic epic still lingered, and when Byron speaks of "an epic from Bob Southey every spring," the implication is that Southey's romances are too facile to be called genuine epics. Victor Hugo's *Légende des Siècles* (1859–1883) is perhaps the most impressive epic achievement in nineteenth-century poetry, though it is not a unified work but a procession of episodes on a loosely chronological basis. The influence of such critical views as that of Poe in his *Poetic Principle,* that poetry is essentially discontinuous, and that long poems are poetic passages connected by versified prose, led to a technique of fragmentation, in which separate poems or episodes imply an unwritten epic framework holding them together. T. S. Eliot's *Waste Land* is a familiar example. Contemporary with Eliot were James Joyce and Ezra Pound, both of them writers of great erudition interested in history and in comparative mythology. The *Finnegans Wake* of the former and the *Cantos* of the latter are once again encyclopedic epics, and *Finnegans Wake* in particular, written in a synthetic associative language based on English but incorporating echoes from many other languages, seems to have reached a kind of limit in the genre.

Epic Simile. See HEROIC SIMILE.

Epicurean. Hedonistic (see HEDONISM)—devoted to sensual pleasure and ease. Actually, Epicurus (c. 341–270 B.C.) was a kind of puritanical Stoic, recommending detachment from pleasure and pain to avoid life's inevitable suffering, hence advocating serenity as the highest happiness, intellect over the senses. He believed, with Democritus, that randomly colliding atoms created life. He rejected the gods and an afterlife. Honesty, prudence, and justice were his means to the most serene society.

Epideictic Poetry. Poetry celebrating public occasions—victories, birthdays of eminent people, holidays, and the like. Aristotle saw rhetoric as (1) deliberative (arguing a cause), (2) forensic (condemning or praising), and (3) epideictic (praising ceremonially). See ENCOMIUM; EPITHALAMIUM; and PROTHALAMIUM.

Epigone. A second-rate imitator. The Epigonoi ("those born after") were the sons of the Seven against Thebes, all of whom died in attacking that city. Ten years later, their sons conquered Thebes and leveled it to the ground. The term unaccountably acquired its negative connotation in the mid-nineteenth century.

Epigram. (1) A brief poetic and witty couching of a home truth. (2) An equivalent statement in prose.

Epigraph. (1) An inscription on a monument or building. (2) A quotation or motto heading a book or chapter.

Epigraphy. Inscriptions and their study, particularly of ancient ones.

Epilogue. (1) A poetic address to the audience at the end of a play. (2) The actor performing the address. (3) Any similar appendage to a literary work, usually describing what happens to the characters in the future. Dramatic epilogues, standard in the RESTORATION and eighteenth century, had disappeared by about 1850.

Epiphany. (1) In Greek mythology and literature, a god's (or goddess's) revealing his (or her) true divinity to a mortal, by throwing off some disguise or concealing vapor (literally, "a showing forth"). (2) The Christian festival of Epiphany, January 6, when Christ's divinity was revealed to the Gentiles—the gift-bearing Magi; also called Twelfth Night, because it occurred 12 nights after the Nativity. (3) Any moment of profound or spiritual revelation, as James Joyce adapted the term in *Stephen Hero*, when even the stroke of a clock or a noise in the street brings sudden illumination, and "its soul, its whatness leaps to us from the vestment of its appearance." For Joyce, art was an epiphany, and his stories themselves are sometimes called epiphanies.

Episode. An incident in a play or novel—a continuous event in action and dialogue. Originally, the term referred to a section in Greek tragedy between two choric songs.

Episodic Structure. In narration, the incidental stringing of one EPISODE upon another, as in *Don Quixote* or *Moll Flanders*, where one episode follows another with no necessary causal connection or plot. The structure is characteristic of the PICARESQUE NOVEL and the ROMANCE.

Epistle. (1) A letter, usually a formal or artistic one, like St. Paul's Epistles in the New Testament, or Horace's verse *Epistles*, widely imitated in the late seventeenth and eighteenth centuries, most notably by Pope. (2) A dedication in a prefatory epistle to a play or book.

Epistolary Novel. A NOVEL written in letters, or epistles, presented as an actual correspondence, frequently with the author posing as an editor who has substituted fictitious names for protection. Nicholas

Breton's *Poste with a Packet of Mad Letters* (1602) seems to be the earliest. Others were soon to appear in France, moving into England after 1660 with Charles II, and influencing such racy works as Roger L'Estrange's *Five Love-letters from a Nun to a Cavalier* (1678) and Aphra Behn's *Love Letters Between a Nobleman and His Sister* (1684). The anonymous *Adventures of Lindamira, a Lady of Quality* (1702), revised by Tom Brown, is the first epistolary attempt at serious fiction.

But the short reign of the epistolary novel began with Samuel Richardson's *Pamela* (1740), as the pursued servant girl writes home about her mounting troubles. In *Clarissa* (1747–1748), Richardson expands the correspondence to include both villain and heroine, each with a correspondent in turn, carrying this first tragic novel in English through intense psychological immediacies and seven full volumes. His *Sir Charles Grandison* (1754), endeavoring to portray an ideal man, is less successful. Tobias Smollett in *Humphry Clinker* (1771) turns the epistolary novel comic as he contrasts views of a traveling entourage and omits replies. Fanny Burney's *Evelina* (1778), a comedy of youthful uncertainty, is the last significant epistolary novel.

Epistrophe. The technique of ending successive phrases, clauses, or lines with the same words, usually stated three times:

> Are they Hebrews? *so am I*. Are they Israelites? *so am I*. Are they the seed of Abraham? *so am I*.
>
> *(2 Cor. 11.22)*

> They loved *football*. They ate *football*. They slept *football*.

Epitaph. (1) An inscription on a tombstone or monument memorializing the person, or persons, buried there. (2) A literary epigram or brief poem epitomizing the dead, like A. E. Housman's "Epitaph on an Army of Mercenaries"; or Milton's "On the University Carrier," which begins, "Here lies old Hobson, Death hath broke his girt"; or Herrick's "Upon Prue his Maid":

> In this little urne is laid
> Prewdence Baldwin (once my maid)
> From this happy spark here let
> Spring the purple violet.

Ben Jonson's, in a small paving stone in Westminster Abbey, is famous: "O RARE BEN JONSON," which may contain a pun, or a mason's mistake for *orare*, "pray for." That of Richard Burbage, the leading actor in Shakespeare's company, is neatly explicit: "*Exit* Burbage." Swift wrote his own: *Ubi saeva indignatio ulterius cor lacerare nequit*, "Where savage indignation can no longer tear his heart." And Pope wrote one "Intended for Sir Isaac Newton, In Westminster Abbey":

> Nature, and Nature's Laws lay hid in Night.
> God said, *Let Newton be!* and All was *Light*.

Epithalamium (or **Epithalamion**).   A lyric ode honoring a bride and groom. Pindar, Sappho, and Theocritus wrote them to be sung by a chorus *epithalamos*, "at the bridal chamber." Catullus wrote an elegant Latin adaptation (No. 61) in which he himself calls forth the bride and accompanies the procession to the groom's house, including the traditional teasing of the groom about his now having to give up his slave boy. Ronsard revived the form in France to celebrate the marriage of King Charles IX to Elizabeth of Austria in 1571. Spenser's *Epithalamion* (1595), celebrating his own marriage to "my beloved love," is perhaps the most beautiful of all, and certainly the most famous.

Epithet.   A term characterizing a person or thing: *sweet Fortune's minion*, for Shakespeare's Henry Percy, also called by the epithet *Hotspur*. *Richard the Lion-Hearted* and the *Iron Duke* (for Wellington) are well-known epithets. Satirical epithets, like Pope's *that mere white Curd of Ass's milk* for Lord Hervey, have given the word *epithet* its secondary, negative connotation: "He hurled *epithets* at him." A HOMERIC EPITHET characterizes with a hyphenated adjective: "*rosy-fingered* dawn," "*wine-dark* sea," "*swift-footed* Achilles." A TRANSFERRED EPITHET is an adjective modifying a noun not usually associated with it: a "*cold* war," "*iron* curtain," "*dry* wit," Milton's "*blind* mouths," Shakespeare's "*that glib and oily* art," Keats's "*snarling* trumpets," Eliot's "*muttering* retreats."

Epitome.   (1) A summary, an abridgment, an abstract. (2) One that supremely represents an entire class: "The Gettysburg Address is the *epitome* of memorial orations; Lincoln, the *epitome* of presidents."

Epitrope.   The ironical granting of permission:

> Let her go, let her go, God bless her!
> All right, go on, have a good time, kill yourself.

Epizeuxis.   The doubling of a word for emphasis:

> Romeo, Romeo, wherefore art thou Romeo?
> Bargains, bargains, bargains will keep you broke.

Epode. (1) The last STROPHE in the unitary triad (strophe, antistrophe, epode) of a Pindaric ODE. (2) A poem based on couplets with a long line, usually dactylic hexameter, followed by a shorter one; invented in Greek by Archilochus, adopted by Horace in Latin for his *Epodes*, which are related in neither substance nor form to the original Pindaric ode.

Eponym. (1) A personage whose name is the source for a place name: *Romulus* for *Rome*, King *George* II for *Georgetown*, Queen *Mary II* for *Maryland*. (2) A personage representing an EPITOME: a Mickey Mouse, a Hitler, a Helen, a Fred Astaire.

Epyllion. Greek for "little song": since the nineteenth century, most often used to describe a miniature EPIC or short narrative poem such as Matthew Arnold's *Sohrab and Rustum*.

Equivalence. The substitution of another kind of metrical foot in the regular pattern. In iambic writing, the TROCHEE and the SPONDEE are equivalents for the IAMBUS, and the double IONIC FOOT ($\smile\ \smile\ |\ -\ -$) for two iambics. In classical QUANTITATIVE VERSE, one long syllable was equivalent to two shorts. Hence a spondee ($-\ -$) was equivalent to a dactyl ($-\ \smile\ \smile$). See METER.

Equivocation. Latin for "equal speaking": speaking or writing ambiguously; hedging one's words to conceal or mislead. See AMBIGUITY.

Equivoque. A verbal AMBIGUITY, double meaning, or PUN.

Erastianism. The belief that the church should leave punishment of sin to civil authority and, by extension, that the state should dominate the church in all matters. The concept takes its name from Thomas Erastus (1524–1583), Swiss Protestant theologian. It is an important part of the thought of Thomas Hobbes's *Leviathan* (1651) and became an issue in the OXFORD MOVEMENT in nineteenth-century England.

Erotesis. The RHETORICAL QUESTION:

Is this the best course? Will this pave the streets?

Erotica. See PORNOGRAPHY.

Erotic Literature. From Eros, Greek god of love: the literature of sensual love; more particularly, literature treating sex in explicit detail or calculated to arouse an erotic response in the reader. Erotic literature occupies a middle ground between the literature of love as a spiritual quality (or as a combination of spiritual and physical elements) and the literature of PORNOGRAPHY.

Erziehungsroman.   See BILDUNGSROMAN.

Escape Literature.   Literature designed to provide an escape from the everyday world of the reader. Most escape literature is fast-paced and unrealistic, intended to provide an emotional or intellectual stimulus far removed from the ordinary world that dominates the literature of REALISM or the traditional NOVEL. Much POPULAR LITERATURE is fundamentally escapist, as, for example, the ADVENTURE STORY; DETECTIVE STORY; POPULAR ROMANCE; SCIENCE FICTION; and WESTERN.

Esemplastic Power.   A term used by Samuel Taylor Coleridge to describe the ability of the IMAGINATION to create unity out of diversity. *Esemplastic* derives from Greek and means "molding into unity."

Esperanto.   An artificial language invented in the late nineteenth century and intended to serve as an international language. It derives from the languages of Western Europe: Greek, Latin, and the Romance and Germanic tongues. Other attempts at international languages include *Interlingua*, created in 1951 and based on English and the Romance languages, and BASIC ENGLISH.

Essay.   A literary composition on a single subject; usually short, in prose, and nonexhaustive. The word derives from French *essai*, "an attempt," first used in the modern sense by Michel de Montaigne, whose *Essais* (1580–1588) are CLASSICS of the GENRE. Francis Bacon's *Essays* (1597) brought the term and form to English. Writers in English who are especially identified with the essay include Joseph Addison, Richard Steele, Charles Lamb, William Hazlitt, Ralph Waldo Emerson, Walter Pater, G. K. Chesterton, H. L. Mencken, and E. B. White. The essay is sometimes ranked with POETRY, PROSE FICTION, and DRAMA as a fourth literary genre. For the wide range covered by the term, see AUTOBIOGRAPHICAL ESSAY; BIOGRAPHICAL ESSAY; *CAUSERIE*; FAMILIAR ESSAY; FORMAL ESSAY; INFORMAL ESSAY; NARRATIVE ESSAY; PERIODICAL ESSAY.

Essenes.   A small, rigorous Jewish sect, established near the Dead Sea and the Jordan River, flourishing from about 200 B.C. to about A.D. 150. The Essenes celebrated purity, cleanliness, sensual abstinence, and ritual observance of the Sabbath. They practiced baptism, believed in immortality, wore only white, shared ownership, and forbade oaths, untruthfulness, commerce, and slavery. The DEAD SEA SCROLLS were evidently an Essene library, hidden from attackers. Christ's teachings, particularly the Sermon on the Mount, show Essene influence, perhaps through John the Baptist, who baptized Him in the Jordan and who may have been an Essene probationer or outcast.

Establishing Shot.   In motion pictures, a shot that establishes the location of the following SCENE. Usually a long shot, it may also be a close-up when it contains a clue to the location.

Ethos.   Greek for "character": the prevailing or characteristic TONE or sentiment of a people or community. In CRITICISM, ethos is the prevailing tone or character of a work considered in its social context or as a reflection of the character of the author. It is manifested in FICTION primarily through CHARACTERIZATION and SETTING. Contrasted with PATHOS, ethos suggests the stable, ideal, or permanent truths of a NARRATIVE or DRAMATIC work, as opposed to the temporary passions expressed in the PLOT. In discussions of RHETORIC, ethos may be thought of, simply, as the character the author projects through the work, the IMPLIED AUTHOR.

Etiquette Book.   A book offering instruction on manners in society. Popular in the RENAISSANCE in the form of instructions to young noblemen or princes, etiquette books have continued to appear at intervals since, offering their advice to a wider audience, as, in the twentieth century, those by Emily Post, Amy Vanderbilt, and Judith Martin (*Miss Manners*). See COURTESY BOOK.

Eulogy.   Greek for "good speaking": a speech or composition of praise, especially of a deceased person.

Euphemism.   Greek for "good speech": an attractive substitute for a harsh or unpleasant word or concept; FIGURATIVE LANGUAGE or circumlocution substituting an indirect or oblique reference for a direct one. Examples are *passed away* or *gone to the great beyond* for *died, earthly remains* for *corpse*.

Euphony.   Melodious sound, the opposite of CACOPHONY. A major feature of VERSE, but also a consideration in PROSE, euphony results from smooth-flowing METER or sentence RHYTHM as well as attractive sounds, with emphasis on vowels and on liquid consonants and semivowels (*l, m, n, r, w, y*), as opposed to the harsher sounds of stops (*b, d, g, k, p, t*) and fricatives (*f, s, v, z*).

Euphuism. An artificial, affected STYLE that takes its name from John Lyly's *Euphues: The Anatomy of Wit* (1578) and its sequel *Euphues and his England* (1580), both enormously popular well into the seventeenth century. Euphuism is a highly elaborate style, characterized by heavy use of rhetorical devices such as BALANCE and ANTITHESIS, by much attention to ALLITERATION and other sound patterns, and by learned ALLUSION. The following passage is from *Euphues: The Anatomy of Wit:*

> As therefore the sweetest rose hath his prickle, the finest velvet his brack, the fairest flour his bran, so the sharpest wit hath his wanton will, and the holiest head his wicked way. And true it is that some write and most men believe that in all perfect shapes a blemish bringeth rather a liking every way to the eyes than a loathing any way to the mind. Venus had her mole in her cheek which made her more amiable; Helen her scar on her chin which Paris called *Cos amoris,* the whetstone of love, Aristippus his wart, Lycurgus his wen. So likewise in the disposition of the mind, either virtue is overshadowed with some vice, or vice overcast with some virtue. Alexander valiant in war, yet given to wine. Tully eloquent in his gloses, yet vainglorious. Solomon wise, yet too wanton. David holy but yet an homicide. None more witty than Euphues, yet at the first none more wicked.

Especially influential in Elizabethan England, euphuism also helped shape later English prose style. See MANNERISM.

Exact Rhyme. Also called *full, true, perfect, complete, whole*: RHYME that repeats the sound precisely (except for the initial consonant), as *fine, dine; heather, weather*.

Exciting Force. In DRAMA, the agent that initiates the CONFLICT between PROTAGONIST and ANTAGONIST. See DRAMATIC STRUCTURE.

Excursus. (1) A lengthy discussion of a point, appended to a literary work. (2) A long DIGRESSION.

Exegesis. (1) A detailed ANALYSIS, explanation, and interpretation of a difficult text, especially the Bible. (2) A RHETORICAL FIGURE, also called *explicatio*, which clarifies a thought in the same sentence: "Time is both short and long, short when you are happy, long when in pain."

Exemplum. Latin for "example": a story used to illustrate a moral point. *Exempla*, many drawn from the GESTA ROMANORUM (*Deeds of the Romans*), a late thirteenth- or early fourteenth-century collection of tales, were a characteristic feature of medieval sermons. Chaucer's *Pardoner's Tale* and *Nun's Priest's Tale* are famous secular examples.

Exergasia. "A polishing"—the technique of putting the same thing several ways:

A beauty, a dream, a vision, a phantom of delight.

Existential Criticism. The CRITICISM of Jean-Paul Sartre and his followers considering how a literary work deals with existential questions and its effect on the reader's existential consciousness. See EXISTENTIALISM; PHENOMENOLOGY.

Existentialism. A philosophy centered on individual existence as unique and unrepeatable, hence rejecting the past for present existence and its unique dilemmas. The Greeks asked, "What is Man?" With Job and St. Augustine, the existentialist asks, "Who am I?" Existentialism rose to prominence in the 1930s and 1940s, particularly in France after World War II in the work of Jean-Paul Sartre (1905–1980).

Søren Kierkegaard (1813–1855), a Dane, is considered the founder of existentialism, though preceded by the subjective queryings in St. Augustine (A.D. 354–430), Michel de Montaigne (1533–1592), and Blaise Pascal (1623–1662). Kierkegaard turned nineteenth-century Romantic optimism upside down by finding existence meaningful only in the possible, to which dread, rather than hope, is the key, and despair the path to the minimal possibilities among the specters of frustration, sickness, pain, and death in God's inscrutable world. In 1882, Friedrich Wilhelm Nietzsche (1844–1900) presented the world with *Die fröhliche Wissenschafte* (*The Joyful Knowledge*) that God was dead, giving future existentialists an even bleaker prospect. In *Was ist Metaphysik?* (*What Is Metaphysics?* 1929), Martin Heidegger (1889–1976) averred that existence could exist only in the midst of nothingness.

The persistence under torture of the French underground in World War II gave Sartre the ultimate negative from which the only positives of existence can grow. Alone, powerless under torturers, the self can still assert its existence by a defiant "No!" As Sartre suggested, René Descartes (1596–1650) might qualify two centuries before Kierkegaard as the first existentialist. Starting in doubt, shutting himself in darkness to discover what, if anything, could supply belief, Descartes found that he could not doubt that he was doubting, thus verifying his existence: *Je pense, donc je suis*—or, as he translated it more famously into Latin, *Cogito, ergo sum* ("I think, therefore I am"). Sartre, with his back to the black wall of nothingness, similarly found in his negatives his base for affirmation. In saying, "No!" he exists: "Non!, donc je suis," as it were.

As Gordon Bigelow has pointed out, existentialism, whether in the theological branch of Kierkegaard or the atheistic branch of Sartre, shares six essential aspects.

1. Existence before essence. An essential human nature, shared in all times and climes and assumed from Plato and Aristotle forward, does not exist. All individuals are unique in ever new circumstances, in which they must act on their desperate choices. Through their choices and acts, they create their unique existence, their individual essence.

2. Impotence of Reason. Humankind's presumed rationality cannot deal with the subterranean reaches of existence. In the *Phaedrus*, Plato's charioteer, Reason, reins in the white horses of emotion and the black horses of passion. But the existentialist sees reason powerless until merged with the irrational to make humans whole.

3. Alienation. Scientific rationalism and a collective industrial materialism have alienated humans (a) from God, (b) from nature, (c) from society, and (d) from self. God is dead. We encase ourselves in shoes and walls, out of touch with nature. Cities produce what sociologist David Riesman termed *The Lonely Crowd* (1950), each person alone and unknown to those with whom he or she rubs elbows in the elevator. The self is fragmented into superego, ego, and id. "We are the Hollow Men," says T. S. Eliot's mournful chorus.

4. Anxiety. Lost in the crowd, alienated even from self, yet faced with desperate choices even to exist, we live in what W. H. Auden called the Age of Anxiety. Kierkegaard's *Fear and Trembling* (1843) describes "the anguish of Abraham" as typical of the existential choice. In the Old Testament, God orders Abraham to sacrifice his son Isaac to demonstrate his superior love of God. In anguish, Abraham chooses to break God's imperative "Thou shalt not kill" and to go against his natural love and fatherhood to serve God's higher command. God saves Isaac, of course, but Kierkegaard's point is that we must choose one abstract imperative over another, not in arrogance but in fear and trembling, only hoping the choice is right where moral laws contradict each other or fade altogether. In fear and trembling, we must frequently choose the exception to the rule because each existence is unique, each circumstance exceptional.

5. Nothingness. NIHILISM, "nothing-ism," first appeared among the disaffected Russian students of Ivan Turgenev's *Fathers and Sons*

(1862). In *A Confession* (1882—the year of Nietzsche's cheerful news of God's death), Count Leo Tolstoy described his own earlier nihilistic crisis. At the height of his creative powers, with health, wealth, fame, position, a beautiful wife, and children, he felt a creeping uneasiness:

> I felt the ground on which I stood was crumbling, that there was nothing for me to stand on, that what I had been living for was nothing, that I had no reason for living. . . . To stop was impossible, to go back was impossible; and it was impossible to shut my eyes so as not to see that there was nothing before me but suffering and actual death, absolute annihilation.

Kierkegaard called this *The Sickness Unto Death* (1849), the ultimate Christian dilemma of doubt and a dread that wishes for death but cannot die.

6. Awful freedom. Since human beings are free to become anything, to make their existential being through the acts they must choose, their freedom is awesome and awful, in Kierkegaard's terms. The Christian existentialists fill the void with faith. Sartre filled it with will. Humans must move forward from black nothing into the moral void by choosing for themselves as if they were choosing for all, creating for themselves the essence of their being, and rediscovering, oddly, the old verities like "Love thy neighbor as thyself," which Sartre believed have vanished.

Existentialism pervades the works of Franz Kafka, Sartre, Camus, Simone de Beauvoir, Samuel Beckett, and Eugéne Ionesco. Stephen Crane and Hemingway are strongly existentialist.

References

Nicola Abbagnano, "Existentialism," **Encyclopaedia Britannica** (1980), VII.73–79.

Hazel E. Barnes, **The Literature of Possibility** (1959).

Gordon E. Bigelow, "A Primer of Existentialism," **College English** 23 (1961), 171–178.

Arturo Fallico, **Art and Existentialism** (1962).

Rollo May (with Ernest Angel and Henri F. Ellenburger), **Existence: A New Dimension in Psychiatry and Psychology** (1958).

Walter Odajnyk, **Marxism and Existentialism** (1965).

Exordium.   Latin for "beginning": the opening invitation or introduction to a speech, sermon, or treatise. See ORATION.

Exotica. See PORNOGRAPHY.

Expatriate. Latin for "out of the fatherland": a person who lives long in a place other than his or her native country. Many famous writers within the last century have been expatriates, including Henry James, Joseph Conrad, Gertrude Stein, Thomas Mann, James Joyce, Ezra Pound, T. S. Eliot, Ernest Hemingway, Vladimir Nabokov, Isaac Bashevis Singer, Samuel Beckett, W. H. Auden, Richard Wright, Alexander Solzhenitsyn, and James Baldwin.

Expletive. Latin for "filling out." (1) An unnecessary word or phrase used as a filler in speaking and writing ("you know") or as an aid to metrical regularity in VERSE ("oh"). (2) An exclamation or oath.

Explicatio. See EXEGESIS.

Explication. An explanation or interpretation. See EXEGESIS; EXPLICATION DE TEXTE.

Explication de Texte. A French term for close ANALYSIS, "unfolding" the text of a literary work by detailed examination of its smallest structural elements—words, linguistic patterns, IMAGES, MOTIFS. See NEW CRITICISM.

Exposition. (1) In DRAMA or NARRATION, the unfolding or explanation of present events or past history necessary to understand the PLOT development. In schematic renderings of DRAMATIC STRUCTURE, like FREYTAG'S PYRAMID, exposition comes early, but in practice it often continues throughout the play or story as present action reveals more and more of the past. (2) Also, in RHETORIC, one of four major kinds of prose discourse, the others being ARGUMENT, DESCRIPTION, and NARRATION. Exposition explains an idea or develops a thought.

Expository Writing. Explanatory writing, the presentation of facts, ideas, or opinions, as in short forms like the ARTICLE or ESSAY, or in longer nonfictional forms like the history, scientific treatise, travel book, BIOGRAPHY, or AUTOBIOGRAPHY. Expository writing is often treated as a large category, including EXPOSITION as a major element, but making use also of ARGUMENT, DESCRIPTION, and NARRATION. It is contrasted with *imaginative writing* or *creative writing*.

Expressionism. An early twentieth-century movement in art and literature, best understood as a reaction against REALISM and NATURALISM and as an extension of the aims and methods of IMPRESSIONISM. The impressionist presented a subjective impression of a scene one might actually observe, structuring a painting, for example, around certain dominant colors, shapes, or patterns in a real landscape, or structuring a prose FICTION, such as Stephen Crane's *Maggie* (1893) or *Red Badge of Courage* (1895), around dominant but highly subjective colors, images, or ironies, omitting the accumulated details that support VERISIMILITUDE. The expressionist looked inward for images, expressing in paint, on stage, or in prose or verse a distorted, nightmarish vision of reality, things dreamed about rather than actually existing. Prominent among early expressionist painters were the Russian Wassily Kandinsky (1866–1944) and the German Oskar Kokoschka (1886–1980). Jackson Pollock's *abstract expressionism* was a much later extension of the idea to abstract representation of interior images without clear pictorial counterparts in the outer world, an extension not very successful, thus far, in literature. In literature, expressionism has been most successful on the stage, where the physical presence of actors and sets provides an objective reality similar to that of paint on canvas. August Strindberg's *A Dream Play* (1902) is an early example. Eugene O'Neill's *Emperor Jones* (1920) and *Hairy Ape* (1922) were the first successful American plays to make substantial use of expressionism. Other examples include Elmer Rice's *Adding Machine* (1923) and, much later, Tennessee Williams's *Camino Real* (1953).

STREAM OF CONSCIOUSNESS is sometimes considered a technique of expressionism, as in James Joyce's *Ulysses* (1922) and *Finnegans Wake* (1939).

Expressive Criticism. Emphasis on the individuality of the artist, as opposed to a focus on the audience, the subject, or the work itself. See CRITICISM.

Extended Image. In motion pictures, a composition that draws the viewer's attention beyond the frame of the picture, suggesting a relevant image that lies outside the camera range. A shot of marching feet, for example, is suggestive of the bodies that march but are not depicted.

Extravaganza. An extravagant, spectacular theatrical or literary production. On stage or in film, the extravaganza usually incorporates exuberant music and dance, ornate costumes and sets, and elaborate special effects.

Eye Dialect. Dialect for the eye rather than the ear, a device of comic writing. Eye dialect occurs when a word is misspelled to suggest a dialect even though the resulting pronunciation is standard. For example, George Washington Harris, in "Sut Lovingood's Daddy, Acting Horse," writes, "Them words toch dad tu the hart," using eye dialect for *heart* and, perhaps, *to*. In this instance, as often, eye dialect has the added function of suggesting ignorance, indicating the spelling the CHARACTER might use.

Eye Rhyme.   A RHYME of words that look but do not sound the same: *one, stone; word, lord; teak, break.* Sometimes eye rhyme is intentional, sometimes the result of dialect or of a change in pronunciation, as with *proved* and *loved* (rhyming in sound for Shakespeare but not for modern readers).

F

Fable. (1) A short, allegorical STORY in VERSE or PROSE, frequently of animals, told to illustrate a moral. The most famous fables are those of Aesop (c. 620–560 B.C.) and Jean de La Fontaine (1621–1695), the latter excellently translated in our time by Marianne Moore. More recent examples include Rudyard Kipling's *Just So Stories* (1902) and James Thurber's *Fables for Our Time* (1940) and *More Fables for Our Time* (1956). George Orwell's *Animal Farm* (1945) is a longer fable. (2) The story line or PLOT of a narrative or DRAMA. See *FABULA*. (3) Loosely, any legendary or fabulous account.

Fabliau. A medieval tale in octosyllabic couplets, often bawdy, French in origin but superbly adapted in Chaucer's tales of the Miller, Reeve, Friar, Summoner, Merchant, and others.

Fabula. The events of a NARRATIVE considered in chronological order, the order in which they may be supposed to have happened. The *fabula* of a work is distinguished from its *sujet*, the events in the order of presentation. Both terms derive from Russian FORMALISM. In essence, they are equivalent to STORY and PLOT in the distinction common in CRITICISM in English since E. M. Forster's *Aspects of the Novel* (1927), but they have been used much more methodically in formalist criticism.

Fair Copy. An exact copy of the final version of a document, with earlier corrections and changes incorporated. See COPY; FOUL COPY.

Fairy Tale. A story of dire trials and rescue by witches, ogres, fairies, and other magical beings. Charles Perrault's collection for his son, *Contes de ma Mere l'Oye* (1697—perhaps written down by his son from nurses' tales and edited by the father), was the basic collection, soon translated into English as *Mother Goose's Tales*. The philologists Jacob and Wilhelm Grimm published their famous German fairy tales from 1812 to 1815, translated into English, with illustrations by George Cruikshank, in 1823. Hans Christian Andersen's Danish fairy tales appeared in 1835, translated into English in 1835. John Ruskin, Charles Kingsley, Robert Louis Stevenson, Oscar Wilde, and Rudyard Kipling have inverted modern fairy tales. See FOLKLORE; FOLK TALE.

Falling Action.   The second half of a dramatic plot, when things go from bad to worse after the central CLIMAX of perplexities. See DRAMATIC STRUCTURE.

Falling Meter.   A meter beginning with a stress, running from heavy to light, as Coleridge described it:

> Trochee is in falling duple,
> Dactyl is falling, like—Tripoli.

See METER.

Familiar Essay.   An ESSAY dealing with personal matters or subjective opinions or prejudices, often light or humorous, with a familiar or intimate TONE. The *Essais* of Montaigne remains the model collection. See PERIODICAL ESSAY.

Fancy.   Day-dreaming wish fulfillment; building castles in air. As Shakespeare's lovesick Orsino says in *Twelfth Night:* "So full of shapes is fancy / That it alone is high fantastical." Coleridge saw fancy as a "mechanical" associative function "emancipated from the order of time and space" as contrasted with the IMAGINATION, which penetrates sensory images to an essential reality.

Fantasy.   (1) Make-believe, a daydream, a reverie. (2) A story following this make-believe pattern—James Barrie's *Peter Pan*, Tolkien's *Lord of the Rings*, *E.T.* from outer space.

Fanzine.   A magazine produced by fans (short for fanatics). The term applies especially to the many such magazines associated with FANTASY and SCIENCE FICTION. A fanzine is distinguished from a professional magazine that also caters to the GENRE.

Farce.   A wildly comic play, mocking dramatic and social conventions, frequently with satiric intent. The term comes from Latin *farsus*, "stuffed," originally any extemporaneous stuffing in regular liturgy or written plays, especially jocular ribaldry.

Fascicle.   "A little bundle"—one of a series of published installments, with paper covers, of a larger work.

Fatalism.   The belief, and its acceptance, that all events are predetermined. For the Greeks, the Moirai assigned at birth a measure of misfortune to be endured. For the Romans, the Parcae, the three FATES, spun out human destiny. Islam is ruled by Kismet. Calvinism decrees everyone predestined to be among either the elect or the damned. Secular fatalism shrugs its shoulders: *Que sera sera*, "What will be will be," taking chances as they come without any sense of divine destiny.

Fates.   The three sisters (Roman) spinning the thread of life. Clotho held the distaff of birth; Lachesis spun the thread; Atropos cut it at the end.

Fellowships and Grants.   Monetary awards and honors from numerous foundations and societies to support scholarly research, professional development, or creative effort. For useful details see "Fellowships and Grants" in the annual *PMLA* Directory, September issue.

Feminine Caesura.   A syntactic pause (‖) in the middle of a metrical foot, or one following an unstressed syllable within a line:

$$\text{S}\bar{\text{h}}\text{ut,} \; \| \; \text{sh}\bar{\text{u}}\text{t} \; | \; \text{th}\breve{\text{e}} \; \bar{\text{d}}\text{oor,} \; | \; \text{g}\breve{\text{o}}\text{od} \; \bar{\text{J}}\text{ohn}$$

$$\breve{\text{I}} \; \bar{\text{knew}} \; | \; \breve{\text{a}} \; \bar{\text{wom-}} \; | \; \text{an,} \; \| \; \text{love-} \; | \; \text{ly in} \; | \; \text{her bones}$$

$$\bar{\text{Dad}}\breve{\text{dy,}} \; \| \; | \; \bar{\text{I}} \; \text{have} \; | \; \text{had to} \; | \; \text{kill you.}$$

See CAESURA; MASCULINE CAESURA.

Feminine Ending.   An extra unstressed syllable at the end of a metrical line, usually iambic. Frequent in BLANK VERSE, as in the first line of this famous passage from Shakespeare's *The Tempest:*

$$\breve{\text{Our}} \; \bar{\text{rev-}} \; | \; \breve{\text{els}} \; \bar{\text{now}} \; | \; \breve{\text{are}} \; \bar{\text{end-}} \; | \; \breve{\text{ed.}} \; \bar{\text{These}} \; | \; \textit{our } \bar{\text{act}}\breve{\text{ors,}}$$

As I foretold you, were all spirits and
Are melted into air, into thin air

In Oliver Goldsmith's "When Lovely Woman Stoops to Folly," feminine and masculine endings are alternated, continuing the pattern begun in the first two lines:

$$\breve{\text{When}} \; \bar{\text{love-}} \; | \; \breve{\text{ly}} \; \bar{\text{wo-}} \; | \; \breve{\text{man}} \; \bar{\text{stoops}} \; | \; \breve{\text{to}} \; \bar{\text{fol-}} \; | \; \breve{\text{ly,}}$$

$$\breve{\text{And}} \; \bar{\text{finds}} \; | \; \breve{\text{too}} \; \bar{\text{late}} \; | \; \breve{\text{that}} \; \bar{\text{men}} \; | \; \breve{\text{be}}\bar{\text{tray,}} \; |$$

See MASCULINE ENDING.

Feminine Rhyme.   A rhyme of both the stressed and unstressed syllables of one FEMININE ENDING with another:

> Yet in these thoughts myself almost *despising*,
> Haply I think on thee,—and then my state,
> Like to the lark at break of day *arising*
> From sullen earth, sings hymns at heaven's gate.

Also called *double rhyme*.

Femme Fatale.   A woman seductively dangerous or fatal.

Festschrift.   "Festival writings" (German). A collection of scholarly articles written in honor of a distinguished scholar by colleagues, former students, and admirers.

Feudalism.   The political and social system prevailing in Europe from the fragmenting of Charlemagne's empire after 814 until the 1400s. It was a system of independent holdings (*feud* is Germanic for "estate") in which autonomous lords pledged fealty and service to those more powerful in exchange for protection, as did villagers to the neighboring lord of the manor. Villeins (free tenants) and serfs (bondservants) were sharply distinct from the "prayers and fighters," clergy, knights, lords of church and castle. A lord might pledge fealty to two kings or barons, choosing his best bet if the two went to war, and kings might owe fealty to powerful bishops or barons. From feudalism arose the conventions and ideals of chivalry and COURTLY LOVE portrayed in the ROMANCE, ROMANTIC EPIC, and other medieval and RENAISSANCE literature. Chaucer's Canterbury pilgrims represent the feudal social order in its middle ranks. *Piers Plowman* (c. 1362–c. 1390) includes the laborer in its allegorical social protest against the times.

Ficelle.   Henry James's term for a CONFIDANT, a friend of the PROTAGONIST through whom a novelist may convey the protagonist's private thinking without becoming omniscient. *Ficelle* is French for "string." The *ficelle* character is hence a kind of string with which the puppeteering novelist can manipulate the protagonist.

Fiction.   An imagined creation in verse, drama, or prose. Fiction is a thing made, an invention. It is distinguished from nonfiction by its essentially imaginative nature, but elements of fiction appear in fundamentally nonfictional constructions such as essays, biographies, autobiographies, and histories. Fictional anecdotes and illustrations abound in the works of politicians, business leaders, the clergy, philosophers, and scientists. Although any invented person, place, event, or condition is a fiction, the term is now most frequently used to mean "prose fiction," as distinct from verse or drama.

Early fictions were often in verse, recited to an audience, or drama, acted in front of one. Early prose fictions were short, easily memorized, suited to oral delivery: fables, parables, folk tales, jokes, anecdotes. The spread of print encouraged the development of longer and more complex prose fictions in various versions of the SHORT STORY, NOVELLA, and NOVEL. In time, these, with their emphasis on narrative, became the dominant forms, but even in the twentieth century verse narratives have continued to be written, notably by Edwin Arlington Robinson, Robert Frost, Robinson Jeffers, and Robert Penn Warren. And drama has continued popular, with writers such as Shaw, O'Neill, and Arthur Miller borrowing from prose fiction to include in the printed versions of their plays important prose sections that can be read in the privacy of an armchair, but are not spoken on stage.

Fiction may be classified according to the object of imitation, or invention, as either mimetic or self-reflexive. *Mimetic fictions* reflect the actual world, sustaining an illusion of reality, life as it is lived or could be, the way things are or might be. This is the fiction of realism, ranging from the small scale of an EPIPHANY by Joyce or a short story by Chekhov, Katherine Mansfield, or Hemingway, to the broad panoramas of Tolstoy's *War and Peace*, Proust's *A la recherche du temps perdu*, or Joyce's *Ulysses*. It is also the fiction resulting from earlier theories and conventions that aimed at the imitation of life, as seen in works as varied as *Oedipus Rex*, *The Canterbury Tales*, and *Hamlet*. More recently it is the fiction of the great romances, or of those serious novels heavy with romantic elements: some of Walter Scott, much of James Fenimore Cooper, Nathaniel Hawthorne, and Herman Melville. *Self-reflexive fictions* describe worlds governed primarily by an internal logic, so they reflect life much less insistently than they reflect themselves or other fictions. FANTASY is one large area of self-reflexive fiction, seen in *Alice in Wonderland*, *At the Back of the North Wind*, and *The Lord of the Rings*. SCIENCE FICTION postulates a world unlike the real world in at least one significant way, usually projected far into the future or outer space, and then extrapolates from the invented premise. Other forms of POPULAR LITERATURE, such as the DETECTIVE STORY, POPULAR ROMANCE, and WESTERN, are self-reflexive both internally within each work and externally to conventions shared by others of the same genre. Of course, all fictions are mimetic if one assumes that nature, the object of mimesis, encompasses all inventions humans are capable of making. In any case, the terms *mimetic* and *self-reflexive* should be seen not as isolated boxes into which literary works may be thrust, but as opposite ends of the same long box. At one end are those works most like life in every detail, at the other those most unlike. Toward the middle of the box, many writings share qualities of both extremes: Jorge Luis Borges's short stories, Vladimir Nabokov's *Ada*, Thomas Pynchon's *V.* and *Gravity's Rainbow*.

Mimetic fictions classified according to the general qualities of the world they imitate are either *real* or *ideal*. Realistic fiction imitates the experiential world of the here and now, seeking truth in life observed as though reflected in a mirror. Chaucer's "Miller's Tale" is an early example, John Updike's *Rabbit* trilogy a recent one. Idealistic fiction imitates a transcendent reality, a higher truth standing behind the forms of the corporeal world like Plato's ideal chair. Before the novel in the eighteenth century popularized a physically detailed realism, an ideal mimesis was the rule, in Greek or Elizabethan tragedy, for example. In the nineteenth century, the serious ROMANCE, as distinguished from novel, pursued the truth of the ideal, as in *The Scarlet Letter* and *Moby-Dick*. Again the categories merge. Strains of the real and the ideal are observable in twentieth-century writers as diverse as D. H. Lawrence and Faulkner, John Fowles and Nabokov.

Fictions classified according to the hero's relationship to the world are either *high mimetic* or *low mimetic*. In high mimetic fiction the hero stands above us, but is subject to the same natural laws as other humans (unlike, for example, the heroes of self-reflexive fictions, for whom no consistently real laws seem to apply). Medea and Lear are larger than life, but succumb to laws all-encompassing and immutable. In low mimetic fiction the hero interacts with the world on a level with other humans, as in comedy from Greek times to the present. The world of high mimesis tends generally toward the ideal, the world of low mimesis toward the real.

The purpose of fiction, as traditionally understood since expressed by Horace in *Ars Poetica*, is "to inform or delight" or to combine the two. A helpful subdivision gives didactic and mimetic fictions, which inform, and aesthetic and popular fictions, which delight. *Didactic fiction* informs through an emphasis on teaching: *Pilgrim's Progress, Uncle Tom's Cabin, Nineteen Eighty-Four, The Grapes of Wrath*. *Mimetic fiction* informs through a careful representation of life, either real or ideal: *Madame Bovary, Moby-Dick, Middlemarch, Lord Jim*. *Aesthetic fiction* places artistic considerations first, avoiding didacticism and treating mimesis as a byproduct of form, as in some of the late works of Henry James, and, more or less, in Gertrude Stein, Joyce, Beckett, and Nabokov. *Popular fiction* stresses delight through a flight from reality rather than the pleasure of art and informs only superficially, as in the display of esoteric knowledge in a Sherlock Holmes or James Bond story, or the smattering of history or geography woven into a popular romance.

The fictional urge is basic. Humans dream in stories, daydream in stories; express hope for the future, account for the present, and recapture the past in stories. Fictional literature is an extension of life. It begins in tale telling, assumes widely divergent forms in different times and cultures, feeds upon itself in imitation or rejection of its constantly changing past, and takes specific shape in the print of an individual work. A phenomenon so varied may be approached in numerous ways. As passive receptors, readers are informed by its didactic or mimetic qualities, delighted by its aesthetic or popular qualities. Students' relationship to fiction becomes more thoughtfully methodical. See CRITICISM; DRAMA; GENRE; MIMESIS; MODE; MYTH; NOVEL; POETRY; POPULAR LITERATURE; SHORT STORY; STRUCTURE; STRUCTURALISM.

References

Wayne Booth, **The Rhetoric of Fiction** (1961).
Northrup Frye, **Anatomy of Criticism** (1957).
Frank Kermode, **The Sense of an Ending** (1967).
David Lodge, **Language of Fiction** (1966).
Sheldon Sacks, **Fiction and the Shape of Belief** (1964).
Robert Scholes and Robert Kellogg, **The Nature of Narrative** (1966).
Mark Spilka, ed., **Towards a Poetics of Fiction** (1977).

Figurative Language.   Language that is not literal, being either metaphorical or rhetorically patterned. See also FIGURE OF SPEECH; IMAGERY; METAPHOR; TROPE; RHETORICAL FIGURE.

Figure of Speech.   An expression extending language beyond its literal meaning, either pictorially through METAPHOR, SIMILE, ALLUSION, and the like, or rhetorically through REPETITION, BALANCE, ANTITHESIS, and the like. A figure of speech is also called a TROPE. The most common pictorial figures are metaphor, simile, METONYMY, SYNECDOCHE, and PERSONIFICATION. The most common rhetorical figures are simple repetition, PARALLELISM, antithesis, CLIMAX, HYPERBOLE, and IRONY. APOSTROPHE is a RHETORICAL FIGURE very nearly a metaphor. See IMAGERY.

Figure Poem.   Another name for SHAPED POEM.

Filid (or *Filidh*).   Gaelic: the professional poets or seers of the ancient Irish. The singular form is *file* or *fili*.

Film.   A motion picture, a cinema. American FILM CRITICISM prefers the term *film* to the earlier French *cinema*.

Film Criticism.   An analysis and evaluation of movies. Criticism ranges from an examination of the director's technical and innovative skill with the camera and cutting room in juxtaposing the scenes and images, to a study of the quality of the story and the acting.

Film Theory.   The theoretical aesthetics evolved from FILM CRITICISM, including the AUTEUR THEORY and others.

Final Suspense, Moment of.   The glimmer of hope just before the CATASTROPHE in a TRAGEDY, as when Hamlet accepts the "divinity that shapes our ends" and the "special Providence in the fall of a sparrow" just before the fatal duel.

Fin de Siècle.   "The end of the century," especially the last decade of the nineteenth. The Victorian period was fading into the twentieth century with the DECADENCE and AESTHETICISM of Oscar Wilde, Aubrey Beardsley, and Walter Pater. But the REALISM, the "sense of fact," of Shaw, George Gissing, and George Moore reacted against Victorian sentimentalism, along with socialist ideas and the independence of the "new woman" seeking suffrage and sexual freedom. The term *fin de siècle*, acquired with the French influence of the SYMBOLISTS Stéphane Mallarmé and Charles Baudelaire, connotes PRECIOSITY and decadence. See EDWARDIAN PERIOD.

First Folio.   The first collected edition of Shakespeare's plays (1623), edited by his friends and fellow actors John Heminge and Henry Condell, and printed in FOLIO by Edward Blount and William Jaggard at Jaggard's shop. It contains 36 plays—all except *Pericles*—half never before printed. In their epistle "To the Great Variety of Readers," Heminge and Condell state that previous readers have been "abus'd with diuerse stolne, and surreptitious copies, maimed, and deformed by the frauds and stealthes of iniurious imposters," indicating that they themselves were working directly from Shakespeare's manuscripts:

> His mind and hand went together: And what he thought, he vttered with that easinesse, that wee haue scarce receiued from him a blot in his papers.

The edition is estimated at 1000 copies, of which 238 remain, some in very poor condition.

References

Oscar James Campbell and Edward G. Quinn, eds., **The Reader's Encyclopedia of Shakespeare** (1966).
W. W. Greg, **The Shakespeare First Folio** (1955).

First-Person Narration. Narration by a CHARACTER involved in a STORY. See NARRATIVE PERSPECTIVE.

Fixed Verse Forms. A term sometimes used for rigidly prescribed verse patterns, as, for example, the SONNET, VILLANELLE, SESTINA. See VERSE FORMS.

Flashback. A reversion to events in the past from the present action in a narrative or film, either directly, through recollections recounted by a character, or through reveries, or dreams. A mode of EXPOSITION, flashback is also called "cut back."

Flat Character. In a literary work, a character that is two-dimensional, without the depth and complexity of a living person; the opposite of a *round character*. See CHARACTERS.

Fleshly School of Poetry. Algernon Charles Swinburne, William Morris, and Dante Gabriel Rossetti, so dubbed by Robert W. Buchanan writing under the name of "Thomas Maitland" in *The Contemporary Review*, October 1871. In reviewing Rossetti's poems, Buchanan accused the three of lauding each other's poems in a "Mutual Admiration School." "The fleshly gentlemen have bound themselves by solemn league and covenant," he wrote, "to extol fleshliness," and to imply that "the body is greater than the soul, and sound superior to sense," that the poet, to develop his or her powers, "must be an intellectual hermaphrodite." Rossetti responded in "The Stealthy School of Criticism," *The Athenaeum*, 16 December 1871. See PRE-RAPHAELITE.

Floating Stanza. A STANZA found more or less intact in different folk songs, as it suits a variety of situations. The Scottish folk song, "Waly, Waly," for example, published by Allan Ramsay in his *Tea-Table Miscellany* (1723–1740), contains stanzas found also in "Jamie Douglas" (Child 204) and other songs. The following is one of those stanzas, as given by Ramsay:

> Oh, oh, if my young babe were born,
>   And set upon the nurse's knee,
> And I my sell were dead and gane!
>   For a maid again I'll never be.

See FOLK SONG.

Fly on the Wall Technique. Narration, or story telling, by DRA-
MATIC METHOD. The author places the reader in relation to the story
similar to the position of a fly on the wall: the reader sees and hears
what is happening but cannot tell what the CHARACTERS are thinking,
and the author does not interpret for the reader. See NARRATIVE PER-
SPECTIVE.

Flyting. Scottish for "scolding": a form of invective, or violent verbal
assault, in VERSE, possibly originally Celtic, traditional in SCOTTISH
LITERATURE. Typically, two poets exchange scurrilous and often exhaustive abuse, as in "The Flyting of Dunbar and Kennedy" (1508).
Loosely, the term means an abusive exchange between characters.

Foil. A contrasting character who helps illuminate the PROTAGONIST,
like a metallic foil under a diamond. "I am resolved my husband shall
not be a rival, but a foil to me" (Charlotte Brontë). Laertes and For-
tinbras are foils to Hamlet; Sancho, to Don Quixote.

Folio. From Latin for "leaf." (1) A sheet of paper, folded once. (2)
The largest of the BOOK SIZES, made from standard printing sheets,
folded once before trimming and binding. Shakespeare's First Folio,
containing all his plays but *Pericles*, appeared in 1623. (3) A number
of words taken as a unit (72 or 90 in England, 100 in the U.S.), used
in estimating the length of a document.

Folk Ballad. Another name for the *traditional ballad* or *popular ballad*, a song of anonymous authorship, transmitted orally. See BALLAD.

Folk Drama. (1) DRAMA created through the folk process of anonymous contribution and accretion, remaining outside the literary tradition because transmitted directly by experience and word of mouth.
MEDIEVAL DRAMA, especially in the CYCLE PLAYS, was heavily influenced by folk drama. Purer instances include the morris dance, the
mummers' play, the MASQUE, and Punch and Judy shows. (2) Drama
based on folk material or imitating folk presentations. Examples include some of the plays of Lope de Vega, John Millington Synge, and
Frederico Garcia Lorca. In the twentieth century, national theaters like
Dublin's ABBEY THEATRE and regional and university theaters have all
been active in promoting dramas drawn from local history and tradition.

Folklore. The lore, or learning, of the folk, a body of information
traditional in a community and passed on from generation to generation by experience and word of mouth. Folklore is traditional wisdom
and belief forming an important part of the ETHOS of a group. It

ranges from song, story, and drama through RIDDLE and PROVERB to traditional ways of ploughing, weaving, curing illnesses, and building chimneys. From the eighteenth century onward, folklore study has increased, as scholars have attempted to record and interpret older ways threatened everywhere by the rapid changes following upon industrialization. Recently, urban folklore has arisen as a significant branch of study as scholars now recognize that the city, too, has its changing patterns.

Folklore has always formed an important part of literature, in earlier times shaped into the MYTH, FOLK SONG, FOLK TALE, and LEGEND recorded in anonymous manuscripts, later serving as important source material for individual literary artists—in English, as early as Chaucer, as recently as Faulkner. See ARTHURIAN LEGEND; BALLAD; FAIRY TALE; FOLK DRAMA; MIDDLE ENGLISH LITERATURE; OLD ENGLISH LITERATURE.

References

Jan Harold Brunvand, **The Story of American Folklore: An Introduction** (1968).
Richard M. Dorson, ed., **Folklore and Folklife: An Introduction** (1972).
Richard M. Dorson, ed., **Handbook of American Folklore** (1983).

Folk Song.   A song forming part of the FOLKLORE of a community. Like the FOLK TALE and the LEGEND, a folk song is a traditional creative expression, characteristically shaped by oral tradition into the form in which it is later recorded in MANUSCRIPT or print. Most folk songs probably had single authors to begin with (scholars, however, used to theorize about communal origins), but changed with time, responding to the conditions of different communities and the genius of individual singers. Books, magazines, and the BROADSIDE, from the eighteenth century onward, and radios, records, tapes, and television, in the twentieth, have changed the way of the folk song, sometimes putting back into oral circulation songs apparently forgotten, or impressing new ones on the folk mind. Hence, some recent songs, accepted into oral tradition and sometimes changed there, are by authors whose names are known. The BALLAD has been most studied, but another very large category is the folk LYRIC. Children's songs and NURSERY RHYMES are also important. The BLUES is a contemporary American form.

The first major collection was Thomas Percy's *Reliques of Ancient English Poetry* (1765). Sir Walter Scott's *Minstrelsy of the Scottish Border*

(1802) followed. Francis J. Child's *English and Scottish Popular Ballads* (5 vols., 1882–1898) formed the canon now generally accepted for ballads of English and Scottish origin, including many widely known in North America. Among the best regional collections including songs native to America are Vance Randolph, *Ozark Folksongs* (1946–1950); *The Frank C. Brown Collection of North Carolina Folklore*, general editor Newman Ivey White (1952–1964); and H. M. Belden, *Ballads and Songs Collected by the Missouri Folk Song Society* (1940). A broad general collection is Alan Lomax, *The Folksongs of North America in the English Language* (1960).

Folk Tale. A STORY forming part of the FOLKLORE of a community, generally less serious than the stories called *myths*. In preliterate societies, virtually all narratives were either myths or folk tales: oral histories of real wars, kings, heroes, great families, and the like accumulating large amounts of legendary material. Of course in such societies there were also the moral and religious tales of gods, heroes, and animals, emphasizing beginnings and conduct; these tales were as "true"—in the sense of gaining widespread acceptance—as the ones more clearly based in historical facts. Early recorded literature was therefore largely folkloristic: a national EPIC like the *Iliad*, the *Odyssey*, or *Beowulf* was compounded to a great extent of folk tales, and much later collections like Boccaccio's *Decameron* and Chaucer's *Canterbury Tales* still relied heavily on the GENRE.

The most famous collection of non-Western folk tales is the *Thousand and One Nights*, or *Arabian Nights*, first translated into European languages in the eighteenth century and enormously influential thereafter. *Grimm's Fairy Tales* (1812–1815), German tales collected by Jakob and Wilhelm Grimm, did much to spur interest in the form in the nineteenth century. Andrew Lang's *Blue Fairy Book* (1889) and others with similar titles presented translated and adapted versions from different languages to readers of English at the end of the nineteenth century. Many twentieth century collections exist.

An invaluable tool for comparing folk tales and other narratives from different periods and cultures is Stith Thompson's *Motif-Index of Folk Literature* (6 vols., 1932–1936). See AMERICAN INDIAN LITERATURE; ARTHURIAN LEGEND; BEAST FABLE; EPIC; FABLE; FAIRY TALE; MIDDLE ENGLISH LITERATURE; MYTH; OLD ENGLISH LITERATURE; TALL TALE.

References

Richard M. Dorson, **America in Legend** (1974).
Stith Thompson, **The Folktale** (1946).

Foolscap. In printing, the large sheet on which a book is printed. The size now varies, but was formerly 13½ inches by 17 inches. See BOOK SIZES.

Foot. The metrical unit; in English, an accented syllable with accompanying light syllable or syllables. See METER.

Foreshadowing. The technique of suggesting or prefiguring a development in a literary work before it occurs. Foreshadowing applies primarily to PLOT, as a significant later event is prepared for by information provided earlier. A minor EPISODE may foreshadow a major later one. A subplot often parallels and may foreshadow a main plot. A DIALOGUE may suggest a later ACTION. A SYMBOL early in a STORY may sow the seed of understanding for the end. The ATMOSPHERE of a work, established early, is a major element of foreshadowing.

Foreword. A "word before": a brief introductory comment on a literary work, often written by a person other than the author of the work.

Forgery, Literary. A literary work falsely attributed by the writer to someone who had no hand in it. Literary forgery is the opposite of PLAGIARISM, in which a writer lays claim to someone else's work. Literary forgeries have been frequent in history, sometimes intended for personal gain, sometimes to advance a political cause or religious doctrine, and sometimes, apparently, for sheer amusement. A famous instance resulted in the OSSIANIC CONTROVERSY of the eighteenth century. More recently, Clifford Irving's *Howard Hughes* raised issues of fraud that ultimately sent the author to jail.

Literary forgeries come in all ranges of seriousness, depending upon property rights, issues of personal privacy, and considerations of artistic and scholarly integrity. A minor sin, or no sin at all, for example, is commited by the GHOSTWRITER, who creates works to be presented by agreement with another person as that person's, in a kind of literary forgery considered acceptable by modern literary CONVENTION.

Form. The shape or STRUCTURE of a literary work, or of a part of one. Form is frequently distinguished from content, the point being that the writer's idea has no shape until the work is written, in the form, say, of a short story, a novel, a poem, or a play. Form, in this first sense, is synonymous with GENRE, but the term is also used to suggest the distinction between works in verse and prose (in the form of verse or the form of prose), as well as to describe the smaller units of a work (as the form of its lines—metrical or free verse; or of its stanzas—the ballad stanza, for example).

Coleridge originated the useful distinction between ORGANIC FORM, a shape arising naturally out of the writer's conception, and mechanical (conventional, or fixed) form, a shape imposed from without.

Formal Criticism. A general term for any approach that considers FORM more important than content. See CRITICISM.

Formal Essay. An ESSAY dealing seriously with a subject, characterized by careful organization and formal diction, or word choice, and sentence structure. Francis Bacon's *Essays* were more formal than the FAMILIAR ESSAY of Montaigne.

Formalism. A Russian literary movement of the 1920s and 1930s. Formalists such as Victor Shklovsky, Boris Eichenbaum, and Boris Tomaschevsky emphasized theoretical considerations of FORM as they sought to develop a science or poetics of literature. Formalism evolved into STRUCTURALISM. See *FABULA*; *SUJET*.

Format. (1) The physical shape, dimensions, or appearance of a book, magazine, newspaper, or other printed work, as, for example, its paper, page size, type size, column arrangement, margins, binding, and cover. (2) Any general structural arrangement, as the format of a debate, interview, or television program.

Formula. A PLOT outline or set of characteristic ingredients used in the construction of a literary work or applied to a portion of one. Formula FICTION is written to the requirements of a particular market, usually undistinguished by much imagination or originality in applying the formula. Much POPULAR LITERATURE is essentially formulaic.

Fortune's Wheel. A wheel of fortune as an image for fate. In medieval literature, a person's destiny was often portrayed as lying at the mercy of Fortuna, a goddess who, by one sudden spin of her wheel, could send one upward to bliss or downward to misery. In illustrations such as one accompanying a 1544 edition of John Lydgate's *Fall of Princes*, Dame Fortune spins a wheel to which individuals cling helplessly, kings and bishops along with less exalted folk. The concept appears in Boethius's *Consolation of Philosophy*, a sixth-century Latin work translated by Alfred the Great, Chaucer, and others, and widely influential in the Middle Ages. As a consolation following from Christian belief, the wheel could be seen as embracing both this life and the next, sinners punished after death by one quick downward spin, saints and other good Christians rewarded by the upward movement to heaven.

Foul Copy. A MANUSCRIPT that has been used for printing, bearing marks of proofreader, editor, and printer, as well as, frequently, the author's queries and comments. See COPY; FAIR COPY.

Foul Proof. A PROOF sheet or sheets bearing marks for correction in final printing.

Four Elements. In ancient and medieval cosmology, earth, air, fire, and water—the four ultimate, exclusive, and eternal constituents that, according to Empedocles (c. 493–c. 433 B.C.) made up the world. After earlier philosophers had conceived the world in terms of opposites such as Void and Earth or Light and Night, Empedocles originated the concept of physical elements. His four elements were often seen as each combining two of the following qualities: cold, hot, moist, dry. Earth was therefore cold and dry, air hot and moist, fire hot and dry, and water cold and moist. To the basic four there was sometimes added a fifth, quintessence, the immortal substance of the heavenly bodies, latent in all things. The four elements were often related to the four HUMORS.

Four Senses of Interpretation. A mode of medieval CRITICISM in which a work is examined for four kinds of meaning. The *literal meaning* is related to fact or history, things that actually occur. The *moral* or *tropological meaning* is the lesson of the work as applied to individual behavior, what people do. The *allegorical meaning* is the particular story in its application to people generally, with emphasis on their beliefs as opposed to their actions. The *anagogical meaning* is its spiritual or mystical truth, its universal significance. After the literal, each of the others represents a broader form of what is usually called ALLEGORY, moving from individual morality to social organization to God. Dante summarized the four in the *Convivio* (c. 1304), an allegory drawing together love and science. See POLYSEMOUS MEANING.

Fourteeners. Lines of 14 syllables—7 iambic feet. Introduced by the Earl of Surrey, they became popular with the Elizabethans. Thomas Sternhold translated a number of the Psalms in fourteeners (1549), and George Chapman's *Iliad* (1598, 1611)—which Keats eventually looked into—was in fourteener couplets. See HEPTAMETER; METER; POULTER'S MEASURE.

Fourth Wall. The area of the PROSCENIUM arch on a PICTURE FRAME STAGE, treated by the actors as an invisible fourth wall through which the audience views the action in a BOX SET.

Frame Narrative. A narrative enclosing one or more separate stories. Characteristically, the frame narrative is created as a vehicle for the stories it contains. In Boccaccio's *Decameron,* people fleeing the plague assemble outside Florence and tell stories to pass the time. Chaucer's *Canterbury Tales* are told within the framework of a pilgrimage to Canterbury. *The Thousand and One Nights* involves the fate of Scheherazade with her skill as a narrator. See ENVELOPE CONSTRUCTION; STORY WITHIN A STORY.

Free Verse. French *vers libre;* poetry free of traditional metrical and stanzaic patterns. Free verse does not lend itself readily to SCANSION by methods used for ACCENTUAL-SYLLABIC VERSE, ACCENTUAL VERSE, or SYLLABIC VERSE. On the other hand, freedom from traditional patterns does not mean that free verse has no patterns at all. Rhythmical repetition of some sort is necessary to distinguish verse from prose. In this sense, the term *free verse* is a misnomer, as poets have long understood. In the words of T. S. Eliot, "no verse is free for the man who wants to do a good job," or, more explicitly,

> . . . only a bad poet could welcome free verse as a liberation from form. It was a revolt against dead form, and a preparation for new form or for a renewal of the old; it was an insistence upon the inner unity which is unique to every poem, against the outer unity which is typical.

As William Carlos Williams expressed it, "No verse can be free, it must be governed by some measure, but not by the old measure."

Verse has always appeared free when poets strayed further than usual from traditional meters. In this sense, forerunners of modern free verse lines can be found sometimes in medieval ALLITERATIVE VERSE, in the King James Bible in Psalms and the Song of Songs, in Milton's *Lycidas* and *Samson Agonistes,* and in some of the poems of William Blake and Christopher Smart. As a movement, however, free verse came into its own in the nineteenth century, with Walt Whitman and the French Symbolists the great progenitors of free verse in the twentieth century.

For the strict rhythmical repetition of traditional verse, free verse substitutes a looser CADENCE, securing repetition in a variety of ways.

1. In Whitman, as in some later poets, the fundamental line is END-STOPPED, so that the end of a line is always signaled by a pause. In Allen Ginsberg's *Howl,* for example, the pause allows the reader to take in breath; in Ginsberg's words, "Ideally, each line of *Howl* is a single breath unit."

2. In Whitman, and others also, PARALLELISM becomes an element of rhythmic technique, as the same structures, with the same stress patterns, repeat in line after line.

3. Simple repetition of words and phrases is common, and achieves a similar effect.

4. The stress pattern is often repeated. In the VARIABLE FOOT of William Carlos Williams, the pattern is frequently one to a line, with the lines in units of three, as in most of the poems of *The Desert Music and Other Poems* (1954) and *Journey to Love* (1955). In other examples of free verse, the pattern is frequently two stresses to a line. The foot tends to be long, as a short foot would fall more easily into the rhythms of traditional scansion.

5. In some free verse poems, repetition is visual, as the length of lines and their placement on the page create a continuing pattern.

6. Sound repeats, as in traditional poetry, but generally with no fixed pattern of rhyme.

7. Images repeat, as in traditional poetry, enforcing the sense of verse as a circular movement, turning back upon itself, as opposed to the linear movement of prose.

Robert Bly has said that the term *free verse* "implies not a technique, but a longing." For some poets, this longing extends beyond meter into the contents of the poem, so that *free verse* comes to mean verse freed not simply from the restrictions of traditional meter but also from the restrictions of traditional syntax and logic. In such verse, intellectual content is disjointed, fragmented, shaped by the techniques of STREAM OF CONSCIOUSNESS and free association. See PROSE POETRY; SPRUNG RHYTHM.

Freeze Frame (also **Stop Frame, Hold Frame**). In motion pictures, a single frame, or picture, reprinted on the film so that movement stops, holding the image on the screen, although the projector continues to operate.

French Forms. Complex VERSE FORMS, many of which originated with the troubadours. Some forms were especially popular with nineteenth-century English poets. See BALLADE; RONDEAU; RONDEAU REDOUBLÉ; RONDEL; SESTINA; TRIOLET; VILLANELLE.

Freudian Criticism. The analysis of literature based on Freudian principles. Freud changed directions often during his life, but each change seems to have had important effects on the criticism of literature. His great pioneering work on *The Interpretation of Dreams* (1900) was accompanied by various other conceptions that explained a good many mysterious literary phenomena. The dream was treated in that book as a construct of wish fulfillment made by the repressed unconscious: the repression, and the fact that the wishes are often forbidden in ordinary experience, made it an oblique symbolic construct, subject to certain mechanisms called "condensation" and "displacement," which enabled it to get past the socially disapproving attitude in the mind called the "censor." Along with this view of the dream came the view of wit as an escape of something normally repressed or subordinated from the unconscious, and the conception of the Oedipus complex as an infantile impulse to get rid of the father and possess the mother. Sophocles's *Oedipus Rex* was seen as owing its power to its dramatization of a forbidden or buried impulse, and one of Freud's followers, Ernest Jones, interpreted *Hamlet* as a play in which Hamlet is unable to kill Claudius because Claudius has done precisely what something in Hamlet wanted to do—kill his father and go to bed with his mother. Such critical works as D. H. Lawrence's *Studies in Classic American Literature* and Leslie Fiedler's *Love and Death in the American Novel,* as well as many works by Kenneth Burke and Norman Holland, show how Freud's view of the crucial importance of repressed sexuality in social life can be made a valuable instrument for literary criticism. There is also what might be called vulgar Freudianism, the attempt to explain literary works by a hypothetical psychoanalysis of their authors, but this is out of fashion and has seldom produced anything of permanent value.

Freud's later work, represented by such books as *The Future of an Illusion* and *Civilization and its Discontents,* took a somewhat stoic and pessimistic view of society, partly because Freud came to think of the sexual driving force as closely related to a death instinct. However, this attitude was transformed into a revolutionary doctrine by Norman O. Brown in *Life Against Death* and *Love's Body,* and by Herbert Marcuse in *Eros and Civilization.* In other writers, such as Lionel Trilling, the influence of Freud operates in a more conservative direction, stressing the Freudian connection between sanity and the sense of self-limitation. Freud's later view of narcissism as the means by which the ego maintains its autonomy has been combined with the Oedipus theme in some of Harold Bloom's criticism, notably *The Anxiety of Influence.* Narcissism again bulks large in some of the Freudian conceptions brought to literary criticism by Jacques Lacan, notably his view of the *stade du miroir* and his conception of the myth of the lost phallus. Lacan has also suggested that the unconscious is itself linguistically structured, which is the factor that enables dialogue to form part of psychoanalytical treatment, and naturally such a view of the unconscious, if established, would have far-reaching implications for criticism.

Freytag's Pyramid.   A diagram presenting DRAMATIC STRUCTURE as a pyramid, as suggested by Gustav Freytag in *Technik des Dramas* (1863). A PLAY begins at the bottom of the pyramid with the EXPOSITION, moves up one side through the RISING ACTION to the CLIMAX at the top, and then down the FALLING ACTION of the other side to the CATASTROPHE at the bottom.

Frontier Literature.   The literature of the frontier in North America, reflecting conditions of frontier life and the conflicts of the settlers with the native inhabitants. Frontier literature moves westward with European settlement, beginning with the seventeenth century accounts by John Smith of exploration in New England and Virginia and by William Bradford and John Winthrop of the early Puritan settlements in Massachusetts. Most early accounts were utilitarian—diaries, journals, histories. Belletristic examination of the frontier began with Charles Brockden Brown's *Wieland* (1798) and became a permanent part of world literature with James Fenimore Cooper's *Pioneers* (1823) and subsequent *Leather-Stocking Tales.* John Galt's *Bogle Corbet* (1831) portrays early settlement in Ontario. William Gilmore Simms's *Yemassee* (1835) depicts warfare with the Indians in the colonial Carolinas. In the nineteenth century, Eastern writers like William Cullen Bryant ("The Prairies," 1833), Washington Irving (*A Tour on the Prairies,* 1835), and Francis Parkman (*The California and Oregon Trail* [in later editions, *The Oregon Trail*], 1849) brought back observations from trips to the West. Mark Twain's *Roughing It* (1872) tells of visits to western mining camps, and *Tom Sawyer* (1876) and *Huckleberry Finn* (1884) portray settlements not long removed from the frontier. Much nineteenth-century colloquial humor and LOCAL COLOR are similarly close to the frontier, in the works of writers like A. B. Longstreet, George Washington Harris, and Bret Harte. Meanwhile, people like Meriwether Lewis and William Clark (Reuben G. Thwaites, ed., *Original Journals of the Lewis and Clark Expedition, 1804–1806,* 8 vols., 1904–1905) and Davy Crockett (*A Narrative of the Life of David Crockett,* 1834) helped push the frontier westward. The West also produced a substantial body of FOLK SONG and FOLK TALE and, from the American Indian side, some memorable oratory on the confrontation between cultures to place beside the stores of Indian FOLKLORE. The West, important to the DIME NOVEL, also constituted one of the major subject areas of POPULAR LITERATURE since the later nineteenth century. Among accounts of later pioneers, outstanding are those by Hamlin Garland (*Main-Travelled Roads*, 1891) and Willa Cather, whose *My Ántonia* (1918) is one of the finest examples of the genre.

In a larger sense, frontier literature has emerged from many other situations where cultures have clashed after exploration and conquest, from the Romans in Gaul to the Europeans in South America, Africa, and Asia. See COMMONWEALTH LITERATURE.

Fugitives. The group of writers and critics who first came together at Vanderbilt University, Nashville, Tennessee, in the 1920s, publishing the journal *The Fugitive* (1922–1925). John Crowe Ransom (1888–1974) and Donald Davidson (1893–1968) were English instructors, Allen Tate (1899–1979) and Robert Penn Warren (1905–   ) at first their students. See AGRARIANS.

Full Rhyme. See EXACT RHYME.

Funambulism. Tightrope walking in art (from Latin *fūnis*, "rope," and *ambulāre*, "to walk"). The term has been applied to the sense of difficulty and danger apparent in much twentieth-century writing, as authors have felt an anxiety derived from uncertainty as to their aesthetic, religious, or moral ground. See Georgio Melchiori, *The Tightrope Walkers* (1956).

Fundamental Image. An IMAGE (or *metaphor*) basic to the STRUCTURE of a work, as, for example, the sea in *Moby-Dick* or the scarlet *A* in *The Scarlet Letter*. When an image or metaphor becomes not merely fundamental to the structure but actually seems to control it, it is sometimes called a CONTROLLING IMAGE. An example is the scaffold that supports three crucial scenes in *The Scarlet Letter*.

Fustian. (1) A coarse, short-napped cotton cloth. (2) Turgid speech or writing; BOMBAST. In his *Epistle to Dr. Arbuthnot*, Pope refers to a writer "whose fustian's so sublimely bad, / It is not poetry, but prose run mad."

G

Gaelic Movement. See IRISH RENAISSANCE.

Galley Proof (or **Galleys**). See PROOF.

Gallicism. A word, phrase, or manner derived from France or the French language; sometimes an English word or phrase used in the French way. Examples include self-conscious translations of terms familiar in English, like *reason for being* for *raison d'être*, and comic usages derived from French, like *my old* for *mon vieux*. The term *gallicism* is not generally applied to actual French words or phrases used in a natural way in English, but only to affected usages.

Gallows Humor. Humor based on the idea of death, especially in a threatening situation. See BLACK HUMOR.

Gasconade. Extravagant boasting, like the bragging of a Gascon, a native of Gascony (in France). Gascons were proverbial braggarts. See *MILES GLORIOSUS*.

Gathering. In printing, sometimes another name for SIGNATURE, the unit formed by one printed sheet after folding. In a sense that is more common today, the term *gathering* is also the process of assembling signatures to make a book.

Generative Grammar. An approach to grammar that examines a particular linguistic structure in the light of the essential kernel of meaning that generated it. See TRANSFORMATIONAL GRAMMAR.

Genetic Fallacy. Reliance on an understanding of the conditions in which a work was created to explain its meaning. Such an approach is viewed as a fallacy according to the NEW CRITICISM, which holds that the work stands apart from its genesis. See BIOGRAPHICAL FALLACY; INTENTIONAL FALLACY.

Geneva School of Criticism. A group of critics active in the 1940s and 1950s, including the Belgian Georges Poulet, the Swiss critic Jean Starobinski, the Frenchman Jean-Pierre Richard, and (in his early work) the American J. Hillis Miller. They saw a literary work as successive expressions of the author's consciousness and its reading as a recapturing of that consciousness. Approached in this way, a literary work has its unifying force in the mind of the author, which can be understood only as it is manifested in the text. Like the adherents of the NEW CRITICISM, the Geneva school critics distrusted evidence outside the text. See YALE CRITICS.

Genre.   A term often applied loosely to the larger forms of literary convention, a kind of analogy to "species" in biology. The root of the conception of genre, however, seems to be the relation of the literary work to its audience. The Greeks spoke of three main genres of poetry—lyric, epic, and drama—each of which indicates a specific and distinct form of presentation. The EPIC developed out of *epos*, poetry which takes the form of an oral recitation by the poet, or rhapsode, directly confronting the listening audience. DRAMA is marked by the concealment of the author from the audience behind an external MIMESIS of plot and characters. LYRIC is marked by the concealment of the audience from the poet, who internalizes the mimesis of sound and imagery, presenting it in relation to self only. Since the Greeks, literature has developed a fourth relationship, the presentation by means of a written text that we have in prose fiction.

Clearly these forms of presentation readily merge into one another: for example, anything written down can be read aloud. The epic is a development of the genre of oral presentation by a reciter. In Homer, the written text is closely related to conventions of oral presentation, whereas Milton's *Paradise Lost* is, in practice, a poem to be read in a book. But because Milton preserves certain *epos* conventions—such as the invocation to a Muse at the opening, the assumption that the poem is "dictated" to him by her, and references to himself as singing—he is indicating what tradition he associates with his poem. Hence to clarify the notion of genre it is necessary to speak of a *radical* of presentation, which relates to the origin of the tradition within which the poet is operating rather than to what in practice would be the poet's mode of communication. The dramas of Shakespeare are practical plays for the stage; Milton's *Samson Agonistes* is not intended for the stage, according to Milton himself, although it could be acted; Shelley's *Prometheus Unbound* would probably be impossible to stage, yet in its form it is clearly being associated with the dramatic genre. Again, a novel of Dickens is generically fiction, though readings from it to an audience would turn it, or some of it, into *epos*, and of course, stage or movie adaptations of it would assimilate it to drama.

Because of this relationship to the form of presentation, genre must be an aspect of RHETORIC. In *epos* there is normally a uniform meter throughout: dactylic hexameter in Homer, the four-beat alliterative line in *Beowulf*, blank verse in Milton. In the lyric there is an associative rhythm distinct from the material, the lyric being a discontinuous form which, so to speak, revolves around itself and does not propel the reader into a narrative movement. In written fiction the semantic rhythms of prose tend to dominate, and drama possesses what may be called a rhythm of decorum, where the rhythmical movement is continually adapted to changing characters or moods, as Shakespeare in *Henry IV* switches from blank verse to prose for the Falstaff scenes.

Within each major genre there are, naturally, subgenres. In written forms dominated by prose, for example, there is a broad distinction between works of FICTION (e.g., the novel) and thematic works (e.g. the essay). Within the fictional category we note, first, a distinction between NOVEL and ROMANCE, the latter featuring greater emphasis on plot, more flexibility about including fantastic or supernatural elements, greater emphasis on pacing, which often means using a narrator, and the like. Then there are forms that seem to be literary but emphasize intellectual rather than social conditioning, such as the MENIPPEAN SATIRE, which comes down through Lucian in Greek, Petronius in Latin, Erasmus in Renaissance times, Voltaire and Swift in the eighteenth century, Thomas Love Peacock in the Romantic period. The CONFESSION form used by St. Augustine and Rousseau also seems to have literary affinities. In drama, besides the TRAGEDY and COMEDY inherited from the Greeks, there are ironic plays, black comedies, and the like, where the boundary between comedy and tragedy seems to disappear; we have the subgenre of MIRACLE PLAY in the Middle Ages, which continues in Calderón in seventeenth-century Spain, and a group of spectacular dramatic forms, the MASQUE, the OPERA, many movies, the puppet play among others. The object of making these distinctions in literary tradition is not simply to classify, but to judge authors in terms of the conventions they themselves chose. Readers accept Jane Austen because they are familiar with the novel form, but Peacock is often regarded as dull or fantastic or amateurish because the convention he worked in is not recognized.

Genre Criticism. A consideration of the characteristics that distinguish one GENRE from another or that define a particular work within a genre. See CRITICISM.

Genteel Comedy. Addison's term for the increasingly sentimental comedy beginning with Colley Cibber's *Love's Last Shift* (1696), in which the essential benevolence in the human heart effects the rake's reform in the last act. Jeremy Collier's attack on RESTORATION comedy, *A Short View of the Immorality and Profaneness of the English Stage* (1698), accelerated the movement.

Genteel Tradition. A tradition in American literature, particularly poetry, emanating Victorian taste and propriety in the last three decades of the nineteenth and the early years of the twentieth centuries. It centered in the New York home of Richard H. Stoddard, poet, critic, and editor of several New York newspapers and magazines, together with his wife, Elizabeth, also a poet, and included poets Edward R. Sill, Edmund C. Stedman, and Bayard Taylor, also a correspondent for the *New York Tribune*, who lectured and wrote travel books on California, Mexico, Africa, and China. Thomas Bailey Aldrich, novelist and editor of *The Atlantic Monthly*, represented the tradition among the BRAHMINS of Boston. REALISM and NATURALISM were more vital movements during the same period.

Georgian. (1) Pertaining to the reigns of the four Georges—1714–1830. Particularly in silver work, furniture, architecture, and design, the term refers to the reigns of the first three, up to the close of the eighteenth century. The Romantic poets from Wordsworth to Keats and Shelley were once called "Georgians." The "second Georgian school" of Thomas Lovell Beddoes, Thomas Hood, and Winthrop Mackworth Praed, from the 1820s to early 1840s, was considered transitional to the VICTORIAN PERIOD. (2) Pertaining to the reign of George V, 1910–1936, especially because of Edward Marsh's anthology of contemporary poets, *Georgian Poetry* (1912), continuing for four more volumes, the last in 1922. Marsh declared that poetry was "once again putting on new strength and beauty" and initiating a new "Georgian" period in the work of Rupert Brooke, John Masefield, Walter de la Mare, Wilfred Wilson Gibson, Harold Munro, and others, including the conservative G. K. Chesterton and the liberal D. H. Lawrence. They took on a quiet rusticity, reacting to the hedonistic DECADENTS, and encouraged by the verbal coincidence with Virgil's *Georgics*. But the notion of a "Georgian Age," sometimes defined as the years between the two world wars (1914–1940), has not survived the strong association of "Georgian" with the eighteenth century.

Georgic. A poem about farming and annual rural labors, after Virgil's *Georgics*. See BUCOLIC.

Gest. A notable feat of arms, or tale thereof. The medieval term was borrowed probably from the French CHANSON DE GESTE, "song of heroic deeds," and from the Latin GESTA ROMANORUM.

Gestalt. German for "form". A unified configuration signifying more than the sum of its parts, especially in *Gestalt* psychology, originated, with the term, by Charles von Ehrenfels in 1890. The idea of the complete structure immediately and intuitively perceived entered literary criticism. The *Gestalt* critic sees a "whole" experience of a work preceding any analysis, with each item bearing meaning only relative to its position in the whole. Herbert Read has suggested that Coleridge's view of art is consonant with *Gestalt* theory.

Gesta Romanorum. *Deeds of the Romans,* a medieval Latin collection of moral tales, a source of stories for later writers, including Chaucer and Shakespeare. See ANGLO-LATIN LITERATURE; EXEMPLUM.

Ghostwriter. An anonymous person paid to write in the name of an employer, often a celebrity with no literary skill. A notable example is Alex Haley, who wrote *The Autobiography of Malcolm X* (1965).

Gift Books. Annual collections of poems, stories, or essays published for the Christmas trade in the early and middle nineteenth century, important as outlets for such writers as Poe and Hawthorne. See ANNUALS.

Gleeman. A medieval itinerant minstrel, especially in Anglo-Saxon times. The SCOP, a king's official singer composed new songs and sang the old. The gleeman sang the songs of others, sometimes finding a secondary place at court.

Globe Theater. Shakespeare's most famous theater, built in 1599 by Richard and Cuthbert Burbage at Bankside, Southwark, south of the Thames, west of London Bridge. Its sign was Atlas holding up the globe, a concept upon which Shakespeare frequently played:

> All the world's a stage. . . .
>
> *As You Like It*

> . . . the baseless fabric of this vision,
> The cloud-capped towers, the gorgeous palaces,
> The solemn temples, the great globe itself,
> Yea, all which it inherit shall dissolve,
> And, like this insubstantial pageant faded,
> Leave not a rack behind.
>
> *The Tempest*

It was probably octagonal, or nearly round. Shakespeare refers to it as an "O":

> Can this cockpit hold
> The vasty fields of France? or may we cram
> Within this wooden O the very casques
> That did afright the air at Agincourt?
>   *Henry V*

See THEATERS.

Gloss. An explanation (from Greek *glōssa*, "tongue, language")—originally, Latin synonyms in the margins of Greek manuscripts, and vernacular synonyms in later manuscripts, as scribes gave the reader some help. Early medieval Latin manuscripts, for instance, carried some of the earliest written Irish in margins and between lines. Extended marginal commentaries, or *glosses*, then appeared in the margins of Scriptural manuscripts. "E. K.," probably Spenser's friend Edward Kirke, supplied *The Shepheardes Calender* (1579) with an even more elaborate explanatory and literary gloss, and Coleridge added a running narrative gloss to his *Rime of the Ancient Mariner* (1798), presumably to lend an air of romantic antiquity. To *gloss over*, "to explain away or ignore," evidently borrowed its negative connotation from another *gloss* (Icelandic *glossi*, "spark"), "to put a shine, or deceptive surface, on."

Glossary. A list of words, with explanations or definitions. A glossary is ordinarily a partial DICTIONARY, appended to the end of a book to explain technical or unfamiliar terms.

Glossolalia. (1) "To speak with tongues" (Greek, *glōssais lalein*), also called the "gift of tongues," when, in some Christian congregations, people seem possessed with the Holy Spirit and utter unintelligible speech. At the miracle of the Pentecost, the Apostles "were all filled with the Holy Ghost, and began to speak with other tongues, as the Spirit gave them utterance" (Acts 2.4). (2) In psychology, meaningless speech associated with schizophrenia.

Gnomic. Aphoristic, as in pithy sayings or maxims, a term derived from the *gnome*, or aphorisms, of the Greek "Gnomic Poets" (sixth century B.C.). The WISDOM LITERATURE of the Bible and Apocrypha is *gnomic*, as are the Latin *sententiae*, the Icelandic Saemundian *Edda*, and the Old English *gnomic* verses. Some of the poems of Francis Quarles (1592–1644) and some of Francis Bacon's essays are called *gnomic*.

Gnosticism. The system of belief of those Christian sects of the second century A.D. who trusted in a direct, inner spiritual knowledge, divinely implanted or revealed, simply *there*, apart from faith, wisdom, or teaching. The term comes from Greek *gnōstikos*, "one who knows," the mystical knowledge being *gnōsis*. Theologians of the emerging church attacked Gnosticism strenuously as pagan and as a negation of Christ. Its roots seem to lie in Iranian Mithraism, a dualism between good Ormazd and evil Ahriman, and in similar beliefs in Mesopotamia and Egypt, assimilated by later Platonists.

Gnostic beliefs include revelation by a demiurge (Platonic creator), divine knowledge for an elite only, the immateriality and illusory (or evil) nature of the physical world and cosmos, Christ as a unique non-corporeal force *(aeon)* sent with redeeming *gnosis* for the elite. Some gnostic teachers considered themselves sent as saviors. Some developed an extreme asceticism, based on Jesus's presumed rejection of the world and women; others were extremely permissive, since *gnosis* was all.

Any belief in a personally revealed divine knowledge of salvation is sometimes called *gnostic*.

Golden Age. (1) The first, and perfect, of the AGES OF THE WORLD. (2) The period of Latin literature from 80 B.C. to A.D. 14, including Cicero, Caesar, Lucretius, Catullus, Salust, Virgil, Horace, Livy, and Ovid.

Golden Line. (1) A line of Latin poetry, particularly in Virgil's *Georgics*—composed of two adjectives, the verb, then the two substantives the adjectives modify:

> mollia luteolā pingit vaccinia calthā
> ". . . embroiders soft blueberries with the light-yellow marigold."
>
> *Eclogues II.50*

(2) In English, a similar line, considered Virgilian, of adjective with noun, verb, adjective with noun, as in Gray's "Elegy Written in a Country Churchyard":

> And drowsy tinklings lull the distant folds (8)
>
> Or busy housewife ply her evening care (22)
>
> Chill Penury repressed their noble rage (51)

Variations are also considered "golden":

> Can storied urn or animated bust (41)
>
> With uncouth rhymes and shapeless sculpture decked (79)

Golden Mean. Moderation between two extremes. The term derives from Horace, *Odes* II.x.5:

> auream quisquis mediocritatem
> diligit, tutus caret obsoleti
> sordibus tecti, caret invidenda
>   sobrius aula.

"Whoever cherishes the golden mean safely avoids the sordidness of a neglected house and more wisely avoids the envied hall."

The phrase *golden mean* first appeared in English in *A Mirror for Magistrates* (1587 version, I.52).

Golem. In Jewish folklore, an artificial person supernaturally brought to life.

Goliardic Verse. Scurrilous, amorous, satirical, irreverent, bibulous Latin verse composed by wandering students, called goliards, in Germany, France, and England in the twelfth and thirteenth centuries. The term probably derives from Old French *gole*, "throat," a glutton or trickster, also related to the gullet of drinking, but the verses purport to originate from a Bishop (or *pontifex*) Golias, a merry fellow with many children, or disciples. Walter Map, an Englishman, wrote many and is credited with many more. The students' drinking song, *Gaudeamus Igitur*, originating about 1276, popular and somewhat revised through the centuries, is representative:

> Gaudeamus igitur
> Juvenes dum sumus;
> Post jucundam juventutem,
> Post molestam senectutem,
>   Nos habemus humus.
>   *first verse*

> "Therefore let's be glad
> While we still are young;
> After jocund youth,
> After burdened age,
>   We will get the sod."

Gongorism. A florid and highly mannered style, with neologisms, paradoxes, conceits, puns, and grammatical inventions, popularized by the Spanish poet Luis de Gongora y Argote (1561–1627), a kind of Spanish EUPHUISM. See MARINISM.

Gothic.   Originally, pertaining to the Goths, then to any Germanic, or Teutonic, people. Because the Goths began warring with the Roman empire in the third century A.D., eventually sacking Rome itself (410), *Gothic* later became a synonym for "barbaric," which the eighteenth century next applied to anything medieval, of the Dark Ages. To the Neoclassical mind, medieval architecture was Gothic, though the style had no connection with the Goths. In 1702, for instance, John Evelyn said erroneously that classical buildings were "demolished by the Goths or Vandals, who introduced their own licentious style now called modern or Gothic." The Gothic cathedral, with its pointed arches and lofty vaultings, contrasts with the lower rounded arches of the older Romanesque style, as do its spires, its flying buttresses, stained-glass windows, and great variety in carved ornamentation, including fruit and vines, apes and devils, and grotesque gargoyles. As the ROMANTIC PERIOD approached, *Gothic* became a term of praise for richness in variety and aspiration, as in Spenser and Shakespeare. *Gothic* meant freedom, natural wildness, the mysterious, the awesome, the romantic, the sublime. It was manifested in a new respect for such medieval literary types as the BALLAD and the ROMANCE, and the works of Chaucer, now freed from judgment based on Neoclassical principles. John Ruskin and Walter Pater praised the Gothic. See GOTHIC NOVEL.

Gothic Novel.   A type of fiction introduced and named by Horace Walpole's *Castle of Otranto, A Gothic Story* (1764). Walpole wanted "to blend the two kinds of romance, the ancient and the modern," having wearied of the "strict adherence to common life" in Richardson and Fielding (his "modern romances"). He wanted to revive the mysterious and supernatural from the huge seventeenth-century French romances while cutting them down to modern form. But he chose medieval Italy as his setting, making it standard for his successors, along with his wily monk (his presumed author) and the spectral castle, or abbey, with subterranean vaults and sudden drafts.

The stage had already invented Gothic terror. William Congreve's *Mourning Bride* (1697), frequently revived, presents a castle, and vaults, that Samuel Johnson thought unequaled in "the whole mass of English poetry." Here, in a subterranean cell, a Moorish queen, embracing a headless corpse, mourns and takes poison. Here originates the scary midnight noise explained away as only the wind, a required ingredient from Walpole onward. Nicholas Rowe's *Fair Penitent* (1703), popular through most of the century, concludes in a black-draped room with skull and bones, the hero's corpse, and the disheveled heroine intoning "Ah—how Pale he looks! / How Grim with clotted Blood, and those dead Eyes." The ghost of Hamlet and his battlements contributed, as did the GRAVEYARD SCHOOL of poetry.

In the novel, Richardson's *Clarissa* (1747–1748) provides a prison, and a coffin for writing desk, and Smollett's *Ferdinand, Count Fathom* has distinctly Gothic scenes. But Walpole introduced supernatural terror, with a huge mysterious helmet, portraits that walk abroad, and statues with nosebleeds. Ann Radcliffe's five Gothic thrillers, notably *The Mysteries of Udolpho* (1794), rejected Walpole's supernatural and rationalized the mysteries, as her English girls, like Nancy Drews, encounter spooky French or Italian castles and ruined abbeys. William Beckford's *Vathek, an Arabian Tale* (1786) introduced the mysterious East, to be inherited by Wilkie Collins's *Moonstone* (1868) and Sax Rohmer's *Dr. Fu Manchu* (1913). William Godwin's *Caleb Williams* (1794) and Charles Brockden Brown's *Wieland* (1798), the first notable American novel, evoke Gothic mystery and terror in modern settings. Byron's dramatic poem *Manfred* (1817) descends directly from the evil Manfred in Walpole's *Otranto*. Mary Shelley's *Frankenstein* (1818) transformed the Gothic into moral science fiction. Indeed, all mystery stories derive from the Gothic, and those that evoke terror, like Poe's, or novels like Daphne du Maurier's *Rebecca* (1938), are frequently called Gothic. See GOTHIC.

Götterdämmerung. *The Twilight of the Gods*, the title of Wagner's fourth and concluding opera in his tetralogy, *The Ring of the Nibelung* (1857–1874); hence, any stormy and apocalyptic ending.

Graces. The three sister-goddesses of Greek mythology who dispense comeliness and charm: Aglaia ("Splendor"), Euphrosyne ("Cheerfulness"), Thalia ("Abundance").

Grail, Holy. In medieval LEGEND, the cup or dish used by Christ at the Last Supper, also used by Joseph of Arimathea to catch drops of Christ's blood at the Crucifixion. According to one tradition, it was brought to England by Joseph of Arimathea. In ARTHURIAN LEGEND, it was sought by the knights of the Round Table.

Graveyard School. A grouping of several early Romantic, eighteenth-century poets meditating on death and immortality. Thomas Parnell's *Night Piece on Death* (1722) is the earliest example, followed by Robert Blair's *Grave* (1743). Most notable of these long poems, Edward Youngs, *Complaint, or Night Thoughts on Life, Death, and*

Immortality (1745), remained popular into the early twentieth century. Young's *Night Thoughts* argues from personal loss, through dreams, to immortality, anticipating Wordsworth in suggesting that the mind half-creates reality, and making proverbial the expression "Procrastination is the thief of time." Gray's "Elegy Written in a Country Churchyard" (1751), briefer and more lyrical in its melancholy, is one of the most renowned poems in English. They all reflect the somber pleasures of melancholy, characteristic of SENTIMENTALISM. In America, Philip Freneau's "House of Night" (1779) and William Cullen Bryant's "Thanatopsis" (1817) represent the GENRE.

Gray (or Grayed) Characters.   Characters realistically shaded as mixtures of good and bad, the opposite of BLACK AND WHITE CHARACTERS. See CHARACTERS.

Great Awakening.   An emotional religious revival in the American colonies, aroused by Jonathan Edwards's preaching in 1734, though other revivals had been stirring. It fired new fervor for essential Calvinist Grace and individual experience as against the more benign COVENANT THEOLOGY of the older Puritans. George Whitefield, the English Methodist, preached in America on seven trips from 1738 to 1759, fanning Calvinist enthusiasm, trances, faintings, shoutings, and rendings of clothes. The Baptist faith spread in the South. The "New Lights" were enthusiastic Calvinists; the "Old Lights," COVENANTERS. Missionaries fanned westward. New Lighters founded Princeton, Brown, Rutgers, Dartmouth, and the University of Pennsylvania. Their democratic, though Calvinist, spirit helped to fuel the American Revolution. See CALVINISM.

Great Chain of Being.   The cosmos conceived hierarchically as stretching, like a chain, from God, as Infinity, downward through ranks of angels (see ANGELS, ORDERS OF) to humans and on downward through ranks of animals to Nothing, each creature in its proper place. Ideas of hierarchies of being, ranked under their leaders, are almost as old as society itself. They appear in Plato's *Timaeus* and *Republic*, in medieval perceptions of the earthly kingdom reflecting the ranks of the heavenly, of the lion as king of the beasts, and all other notions of rank. But the image of the chain probably originated with Milton in *Paradise Lost:*

> And fast by hanging in a golden Chain
> This pendant world . . . .
>
> *II.1051–1052*

The concept of the Great Chain of Being, with its order, and humans properly balanced in the middle between God and beast, caught the imagination of the late seventeenth and early eighteenth centuries. Pope gave it its fullest expression and widest currency in his *Essay on Man* (1732–1734):

> Vast chain of being, which from God began,
> Natures aethereal, human, angel, man,
> Beast, bird, fish, insect; what no eye can see,
> No glass can reach! from Infinite to thee,
> From thee to Nothing!—On superior pow'rs
> Were we to press, inferior might on ours:
> Or in the full creation leave a void,
> Where, one step broken, the great scale's destroy'd:
> From Nature's chain whatever link you strike,
> Tenth or ten thousandth, breaks the chain alike.
>
> *I.237–246*

The idea of progress, with the metaphor of *steps* upward, began to replace the metaphor of the static chain by the end of the eighteenth century, but it persists in the concept of a missing *link* between apes and human beings.

Great Mother. Perhaps the most ancient conception of divinity, the Mother of the Gods, the Earth, Cybele, Mā (or Ammas), the primal creative power, symbol of all fertility; worshipped earliest in the Middle East, but also in most parts of the world. In Babylonia and Assyria, she was Ishtar; in Syria and Palestine, Astarte; in Egypt, Isis. In Greece, she was Gaea, the Earth, later Rhea, wife of Chronos, becoming also Hera, Demeter, and Aphrodite. In Rome, she was Maia, Ops, Tellus, Ceres, and Venus. Cybele and Isis acquired sons who became lovers, Attis and Osiris, who died to be reborn, symbolizing the natural cycle of winter and spring, death and rebirth. Aphrodite and Persephone, queen of the underworld, both loved the beautiful youth Adonis, child of an incestuous union, though not either of theirs. Zeus ruled that Adonis must spend half the year with each, descending to the underworld, to return to earth reborn each spring. The Virgin Mary became the Christian equivalent, the beneficent and fertile virgin, the mother of a God who dies to be resurrected. Robert Graves's *White Goddess: A Historical Grammar of a Poetic Myth* makes the case for the Great Mother as the primeval source for all myth, and especially for artistic creation as the Muse, later divided into nine, whom the poet addresses for inspiration.

Reference

E. O. James, **The Cult of the Mother Goddess** (1959; repr., 1961).

Greats. A colloquialism for the final examination (until the nineteenth century, the *great go*) for the B.A. degree at British universities, especially Oxford; sometimes applied specifically to the honors examination in literature.

Greek Theater. See THEATERS.

Grotesque. (1) Fanciful fresco or sculptural decorations mixing and distorting parts of human and animal figures amid flowers and linear vines and swirls with open spaces, a Roman style of the first century A.D. The word is from Italian *grottesca*, "grotto-ish," because the decorations were discovered in the excavated "grottoes"—the rooms—of Roman mansions such as Nero's Golden House, about 1500. In Renaissance Italy, Raphael (1483–1520) immediately adopted the style, the popularity of which spread throughout Europe until the nineteenth century. (2) Anything unnaturally distorted, ugly, ludicrous, fanciful, or bizarre, especially, in the nineteenth century, literature exploiting the abnormal, like Stevenson's *Strange Case of Dr. Jekyll and Mr. Hyde* (1886). Walter Bagehot (1826–1877) took Wordsworth, Tennyson, and Browning to represent the pure, the ornate, and the *grotesque* in poetry (*Literary Studies*, 1879). (3) In twentieth-century literature, a distorted merging of the comic, which assumes social norms, and the tragic, which assumes cosmic order, in a frustrated response to a meaningless universe. Thomas Mann (1875–1955) declared it the modern world's "most genuine style," the "only guise in which the sublime may [now] appear." Günter Grass is a recent German example. Sherwood Anderson began his *Winesburg, Ohio* (1919) with the introductory "The Book of the Grotesque," suggesting that the small town warps the inhabitant, who, by clasping only one truth, becomes "a grotesque and the truth he embraced a falsehood." William Van O'Connor called the *grotesque* an American genre. Frank Norris, William Faulkner, Erskine Caldwell, Flannery O'Connor, Eudora Welty, Nathanael West, Kurt Vonnegut, and Thomas Pynchon would all qualify in their various ways. See ABSURD; NIHILISM.

Groundlings. Spectators in the Elizabethan theater who stood on the ground in the pit, or orchestra, where there were no seats, for the cheapest price. They were shopkeepers, artisans, and apprentices, usually considered less perceptive than the gentry, as Hamlet indicates:

O! it offends me to the soul to hear a robustious periwig-pated
fellow tear a passion to tatters, to very rags, to split the ears of the
groundlings, who for the most part are capable of nothing but inexplicable
dumb-shows and noise.

III.ii

Against this informed evidence, O. J. Campbell avers that they were
mostly "solid, well-behaved citizens, in no sense an undisciplined rab-
ble," with a strong representation of apprentices, who "were intelligent
and well-bred, for they always came from well-to-do families and had
usually enjoyed a grammar-school education," and who provided "an
enthusiasm for which both playwright and actor were grateful" (*The
Reader's Encyclopedia of Shakespeare*, 1966, p. 50).

Grub Street.   The home of literary hacks and impecunious writers in
early eighteenth-century London; hence, the dregs of literary endeavor. Grub Street became Milton Street in 1830.

Grundy, Mrs.   In Thomas Morton's melodrama *Speed the Plough*
(1798), a character who never appears. She is the neighbor of Dame
Ashfield, who constantly asks, "What will Mrs. Grundy say?" She thus
represents the cream of propriety and snobbish disapproval.

H

Hagiography. (1) The biography of saints, from Greek *hagios*, "holy." Eusebius (c. 263–339?), of Caesarea, in Asia Minor (now Turkey), was the originator, with his *Martyrs of Palestine*, but his *Ecclesiastical History* (312–324) includes more. Gregory I ("the Great") in the sixth century and the Venerable Bede in eighth-century England are next in importance as sources for the glorified saints' lives of the Middle Ages. A group of Belgian Jesuit scholars—called the "Bollandists," after Father John Bolland, who carried on the encyclopedia initiated by Father Heribert Rosweyde—published volumes of manuscripts edited with notes as the *Acta Sanctorum* from 1643 until 1770, with later volumes continuing until 1883. (2) Any glorified biography.

Haiku (also **Hokku,** an older term). A Japanese lyric verse form in three lines, unrhymed, with a syllable count of 5/7/5. Typically, a Japanese haiku presents a natural image that gains symbolic or spiritual force from Japanese literary or religious tradition. Imitations in English often present an image accompanied with a more general statement. Haiku influenced the IMAGISTS, and something of the effect, although not the form, can be seen in Ezra Pound's "In a Station of the Metro." The following haiku shows a strict syllable count, in a translation of "A Cove at the 'Lake of the Views' " by Matsuo Bashō (1644–1694):

> From all four quarters
> cherry petals blowing in
> to Biwa's waters!
> *Translated by Harold G. Henderson*

See VERSE FORMS.

Half Rhyme. Another term for *slant rhyme*. See RHYME.

Hamartia. The *tragic flaw* or *error of judgment* considered by Aristotle to form a necessary part of the CHARACTER of a tragic HERO. The hero must be good, but not perfect: "a man who is not eminently good and just, yet whose misfortune is brought about not by vice or depravity, but by some error or frailty" (translated by S. H. Butcher).

Hanover. See ROYAL HOUSES.

Harlem Renaissance. The literary awakening of black creative consciousness in the 1920s in Harlem, New York City, sparked by James

Weldon Johnson (1871–1938) and Langston Hughes (1902–1967), including artists and musicians as well. White society supported the movement with grants and fellowships, and danced to Duke Ellington's jazz at the Cotton Club. Alain Locke, the first black Rhodes Scholar (1907–1910), a Harvard Ph.D. (1918), and chair of the philosophy department at Howard University, celebrated and defined the movement in his anthology *The New Negro: An Interpretation* (1925), as did the white writer Carl Van Vechten in his novel *Nigger Heaven* (1926). Countee Cullen published two important books of poems, *Color* (1925) and *Copper Sun* (1927), and gained further national interest with his *Caroling Dusk: An Anthology of Verse by Negro Poets* (1927). Langston Hughes collected his poems in *The Weary Blues* (1926) and published a novel, *Not Without Laughter* (1930). Wallace Thurman and William Jordan Rapp produced a successful play, *Harlem*, in 1929. Thurman's novel *The Blacker the Berry* (1929) satirizes the movement. Arna Bontemps's first novel, *God Sends Sunday* (1931), is usually taken as the movement's last work, as writers dispersed into the Depression. See AFRO-AMERICAN LITERATURE.

Reference

Nathan Irvin Huggins, **Harlem Renaissance** (1971).

Harlequinade.   A play featuring the character Harlequin. See COMMEDIA DELL'ARTE; PANTOMIME.

Hartford Wits.   See CONNECTICUT WITS.

Headless Line.   An iambic line with the initial unstressed syllable missing, sometimes called, from the Greek, *acephalous*. See CATALEXIS; METER.

Hebraism.   An attitude subordinating other aspects of life to the ideal of obedience to a strict moral code, like that of Old Testament Judaism. Hebraism is the opposite of HELLENISM; the dichotomy has been widely employed since it was formulated by Matthew Arnold in Chapters Four and Five of *Culture and Anarchy* (1869). In Arnold's view, the nineteenth century had inherited too much Hebraism—in the form of Puritan morality and the work ethic—from a tradition that includes Pauline Christianity, medieval asceticism, and Puritanism.

Hedge Club.   An early name for the TRANSCENDENTAL CLUB. Frederic Henry Hedge (1805–1890), Unitarian clergyman, was one of the original members.

Hedonism. A philosophy that sees pleasure as the highest good. In earlier times, this goal was subject to two approaches. (1) The early Cyrenaics, followers of Aristippus (c. 435–c. 360 B.C.), believed in gratification of all sensual desires, with virtue equivalent to the ability to enjoy. (2) The Epicureans, followers of Epicurus (341–270 B.C.), taught that pain could be avoided and pleasure attained by rational control of desires. Serenity, they believed, is more likely to result from the pursuit of intellectual rather than physical pleasure. See CARPE DIEM; EPICUREAN.

Hegelianism. The philosophy of G. W. F. Hegel (1770–1831), who developed the system of thought known as Hegelian DIALECTIC. According to this system, a given concept, or *thesis*, generates its opposite, or *antithesis*, and from the interaction of the two arises a *synthesis*. The synthesis then forms a thesis for a new cycle. Hegelian dialectic suggests that history is not static but contains a rational progression, an idea influential on many later thinkers. As modified by Karl Marx, it is the basis for dialectical materialism, in which social change is seen as a "struggle of opposites."

Hellenism. According to Matthew Arnold in Chapters Four and Five of *Culture and Anarchy* (1869), *"spontaneity of consciousness,"* the opposite of the *"strictness of conscience"* he attributes to HEBRAISM. Hellenism is intellectual and aesthetic, seeking "to see things as they really are" in accordance with Greek ideals of "the *best* nature." It is opposed to the moral rigor of Hebraism. Arnold's call for more Hellenism in nineteenth-century England was an important influence on AESTHETICISM. See SWEETNESS AND LIGHT.

Hell Fire Club. The name taken early in the eighteenth century by several groups of young hellions. One group called itself "The Hell Fire Club, kept by a Society of Blasphemers," recorded in 1721, a year in which three Hell Fire clubs were suppressed. Sometime in midcentury, Sir Francis Dashwood founded the notorious "Franciscans, or The Hell Fire Club" at Medmenham Abbey, rebuilt from ruins left by Henry VIII, his estate on the Thames near Marlow, Buckinghamshire. The club was less riotous but no less drunken than its predecessors. The name "Franciscans" was derived from their founder's name, and the members adopted from Rabelais's Abbey of Thelma the motto *Fay ce que voudrais* ("Do what you want"). John Wilkes and George Bubb Dodington, members of Parliament, belonged to the club. Charles Johnstone's satiric novel *Chrystal, or the Adventures of a Guinea* (1760–1765) describes the club in several chapters.

Hemistich.   A half-line.

Hendecasyllabic Verse.   A 5-foot, 11-syllable line invented by the Greek epigrammatic poet Phalaecus, popularized by Catullus, and standard in Italian. Basically *trochaic*, with the second foot invariably a *dactyl:* $- \cup | - \cup \cup | - \cup | - \cup | - \cup$. Tennyson and some others have tried hendecasyllables in English. See METER.

Hendiadys.   "One through two." An adjective and noun changed into two nouns connected by *and:*

> We drank from cups and gold [*golden cups*].
> He looked with eyes and anger [*angry eyes*].

Heptameter.   Seven-foot lines. In English it is found principally in the Elizabethan FOURTEENER, but occasionally later, as in Whittier's "Massachusetts to Virginia":

> The blast from Freedom's Northern hills, upon its Southern way,
> Bears greeting to Virginia from Massachusetts Bay.

When iambic heptameter couplets are divided into four lines, this becomes the BALLAD STANZA, or COMMON METER.

Heptastich.   A unit of verse in seven lines.

Hermeneutics.   The science or art of interpretation, originally of Scripture, but now of any text. See EXEGESIS, the practical application of principles of hermeneutics.

Hero or **Heroine.**   In classical mythology, a person of superhuman powers, sometimes a demigod, perhaps attaining immortality. Later, the term came to mean a brave leader or a person of great physical or moral strength, a sense it often still carries today. Thackeray was thinking of this sense when he subtitled *Vanity Fair* "A Novel without a Hero," and it survives, frequently with a touch of IRONY, in many nineteenth-century references to "our hero." Used with reference to works of REALISM or NATURALISM, however, the term is often diminished to mean no more than "leading character," carrying with it no sense of superiority to others, a neutral sense conveyed less ambiguously by the term PROTAGONIST. In the twentieth century, the concept of the hero has produced its antithesis, the ANTI-HERO. In comic fiction, the hero may be an amusing bumbler, like Swift's Gulliver or Kingsley Amis's (anti-hero) Jim Dixon, in *Lucky Jim* (1954).

Heroic Couplet.   The closed and balanced iambic pentameter couplet typical of the HEROIC PLAY of Dryden; hence, any CLOSED COUPLET.

Chaucer originated the iambic pentameter couplet in English. Edmund Waller and John Denham polished it in the mid-seventeenth century, giving it balance and antithesis, as in Denham's famous APOSTROPHE to the Thames from *Cooper's Hill* (1642):

> O could I flow like thee, and make thy stream
> My great example, as it is my theme:
> Tho' deep, yet clear; tho' gentle, yet not dull;
> Strong without rage; without o'erflowing, full.

Dryden mastered the heroic couplet in full and easy lines with relatively few balancing caesuras (see CAESURA). Pope gave it its final perfection, with more of Denham's antithesis and balance, yet with remarkable variety of phrase, tone, and colloquial ease, as in the opening lines of his *Dunciad*, Book IV:

> Yet, yet a moment, one dim Ray of Light
> Indulge, dread Chaos, and eternal Night!
> Of darkness visible so much be lent
> As half to shew, half veil the deep Intent.
> Ye Powers: whose Mysteries restor'd I sing,
> To whom Time bears me on his rapid wing,
> Suspend awhile your Force inertly strong,
> Then take at once the Poet and the Song.

Heroic Line. In English, the iambic pentameter line of the HEROIC COUPLET (see METER); in Greek and Latin, the DACTYLIC HEXAMETER of the epic; in French, the ALEXANDRINE.

Heroic Play. A grandiose romantic tragedy using the HEROIC COUPLET, arising in the RESTORATION. The heroic plays are set in far-off places and times, as in Montezuma's Mexico or Aurengzebe's India, with lavish costuming and scenery and orchestral accompaniment; mighty conflicts of war, love, honor, and loyalty rend the lofty heroes, as when Dryden's Almanzor in *The Conquest of Granada* (1670, 1671), condemned to death, says: "Stand off; I have not leisure yet to die."

The heroic play originated when Sir William D'Avenent, to get around the Commonwealth's ban on the theaters (1642–1660), asked permission to stage an *opera*—a "work," using the word in English for the first time—"an entertainment after the manner of the ancients," *The Siege of Rhodes* (1656). Restaged in several versions until its full two-part presentation in 1661, it introduced passages in couplets, which became characteristic, along with the general epic elevation of language and grand romantic conflicts. Orrery's *Henry V* and Dryden and Howard's *Indian Queen*, both of 1664, established the GENRE.

Dryden dominated the stage with four more heroic plays—*The Indian Emperor* (1665), *Tyrannick Love* (1669), *The Conquest of Granada* (Part I, 1670; Part II, 1671), *Aureng-Zebe* (1675)—before turning to BLANK VERSE, in *All for Love* (1677), which dominated Restoration tragedy henceforth. But the heroic plays continued on the stage until the early 1680s. Other writers of heroic plays were John Crowne, Sir Robert Howard (Dryden's brother-in-law), Nathaniel Lee, Elkanah Settle, and Nahum Tate. *The Rehearsal* (1671), written by George Villiers, second Duke of Buckingham, with some collaboration from others, burlesqued the heroic play and Dryden hilariously, and remained popular for more than a century.

Heroic Quatrain. A STANZA in four lines of iambic pentameter, rhyming *abab* (see METER). Also known as the *heroic stanza* and the ELEGIAC STANZA, this is the form of the QUATRAIN in a Shakespearean SONNET and in poems like A. E. Housman's "The Chestnut Casts His Flambeaux" and John Crowe Ransom's "Winter Remembered." Without stanzaic divisions, it is embedded five times within lines 235 to 256 of T. S. Eliot's *Waste Land*.

Hexameter. Six-foot lines. Homer established *dactylic hexameter* as the epic line, the "heroic line," in his *Iliad* and *Odyssey*. Virgil followed suit in his *Aeneid*. See METER.

Hexastich. A unit of verse in six lines. See SEXAIN.

Hiatus. A break or gap. (1) A gap in a literary work, as in a MANUSCRIPT from which pages have been lost or lines dropped in copying. (2) A pause between two vowels not separated by a consonant, but pronounced separately: *we enter, reinvest;* the opposite of ELISION. (3) A missing step necessary to complete the logic of an ARGUMENT.

Hieratic Style. Greek for "priestly": a style, intended for an educated class or a group of initiates, that is often self-consciously learned or elaborate. See DEMOTIC STYLE; STYLE.

High Comedy. George Meredith's term, from *The Idea of Comedy* (1877), for COMEDY arising from MANNERS and characterized by wit, grace, and elegance. Its appeal is predominantly intellectual. High comedy may be found in the COMEDY OF MANNERS, the NOVEL OF MANNERS, and such poems as Pope's *Rape of the Lock*. Its opposite is LOW COMEDY.

Higher Criticism. A term associated with nineteenth-century biblical studies, where it was applied to rigorous scholarly attempts to provide accurate information concerning the historical background of the Scriptures: their date, authorship, circumstances of composition, and so on. Higher Criticism was distinguished from *Lower Criticism*, the establishment of accurate texts.

High Mimetic. A term applied to literature in which the characters are above the reader in power and authority, but still subject to natural laws, as the characters in MYTH (and, frequently, ROMANCE) are not. Examples of high mimetic literature include most examples of the EPIC and of classical TRAGEDY. See LOW MIMETIC; MIMESIS.

Hirmos. The technique of heaping a series of appositives: Everyone, rich, poor, tall, short, young, old, loves it.

Historical Criticism. Any CRITICISM linking history and literature, as, for example, the study of the textual history of a work, or the examination of the social, economic, political, cultural, or intellectual history of the time in which it was written. *Biographical criticism* is a special branch of historical criticism. An intensive, methodical approach to historical criticism, or a strong belief in its value, is sometimes called HISTORICISM. For objections sometimes made to the uses of historical criticism, see AFFECTIVE FALLACY; BIOGRAPHICAL FALLACY; GENETIC FALLACY. See also TEXTUAL CRITICISM.

Historical Fiction. FICTION that attempts to re-create the past, as opposed to fiction that reflects the present time of its author. The term avoids the distinction, sometimes difficult to make, between HISTORICAL NOVEL and HISTORICAL ROMANCE.

Historical Novel. A NOVEL set in a time prior to that available to the author's direct experience or one that makes significant use of a major historical event or bygone ETHOS. Sir Walter Scott set the CLASSIC pattern in *Waverley* (1814) and subsequent works. Scott's novels are characteristically set in a time of rapid change, with old ways succumbing to new ones against a background of warfare or other civil turmoil. Actual figures from history appear, generally in minor roles, and major historic events form an important part of the background. The major CHARACTERS and central PLOT are usually invented, but are subordinated to the commentary presented by the novel upon the larger social issues of the time. Although the historical novel has remained popular, authors since Scott have mostly failed to match his success with this FORMULA. James Fenimore Cooper, usually taken as the originator of the American historical novel, prided himself on his greater "invention," caring less for historical accuracy than Scott, and wrote more often of his own times, as in *The Pioneers* (1823), set in the Cooperstown of his boyhood. Among later historical novelists are William Makepeace Thackeray, Alexandre Dumas, Victor Hugo, Leo Tolstoy, and Kenneth Roberts (1885–1957). Recently, the historical novel has sometimes appeared in the guise of an ironic or parodic version of earlier novel STYLE, as in John Barth's *Sot-Weed Factor* (1960) or in John Fowles's *French Lieutenant's Woman* (1969).

Historical Romance.   Terminology generally reserved for POPULAR LITERATURE set in the past. In this sense, a historical romance may be a costume piece, emphasizing seduction and swordplay. Nathaniel Hawthorne called *The Scarlet Letter* "A Romance," however, and it is set two centuries before its publication in 1850.

Historicism.   (1) Historical relativism, founded by Wilhelm Dilthey, especially in his *Einleitung in die Geisteswissenschaften* (*Introduction to Human Sciences*, 1883). Dilthey believed that human beings were part of an inevitable historical process by which they can be understood but which renders all past perceptions and values relative and, in effect, obsolete: "The prototype 'man' disintegrates during the process of history." According to Dilthey, the past must be studied without value judgments because absolute values and the permanency of human nature are illusions. (2) An approach to literature that emphasizes its historical environment, the climate of ideas, belief, and literary conventions surrounding and influencing the writer. It is intensive HISTORICAL CRITICISM, arising from a conviction of the tight bond between history and literature, history influencing the literary text and providing an understanding beyond, or supplemental to, that available in the text alone. Literary texts also shed light on history, being artifacts produced by history, which help to elucidate past cultures and each other. See AFFECTIVE FALLACY; ANTIQUARIANISM; BIOGRAPHICAL FALLACY; CRITICISM; GENETIC FALLACY.

History as Literature.   Factual accounts considered for their literary value. The ancient dichotomy between historical and belletristic literature rests in the popular assumption that history is fact and literature is FICTION. As Aristotle expressed it, "it is not the function of the poet to relate what has happened, but what may happen. . . . Poetry, therefore, is a more philosophical and a higher thing than history: for poetry tends to express the universal, history the particular" (translated by S. H. Butcher). Yet, popular assumptions and Aristotle aside, in practice the division between historical and belletristic writing is not always clear. Early histories in the form of CHRONICLE or LEGEND treat fact and fiction as belonging to the same body of received truth. In later times, an artistic selection and arrangement of facts or a highly literary use of language gives to some histories an alliance with the universals of literature that may be as interesting to the reader as the particulars that serve as their subjects. Some twentieth-century theory tends to blur or remove the borderline between history and literature.

Among earlier historians whose writings stand up well beside the belletristic works of their times are Herodotus, Thucydides, Caesar, and Tacitus. The Venerable Bede's *Ecclesiastical History* was one of the important literary works of medieval England. Later, Edward Gibbon, in the eighteenth century, and Thomas Carlyle and Thomas Babington Macaulay, in the nineteenth, were important English historians. At least three American historians of the nineteenth century were important to the literature of their time: William Hickling Prescott, Francis Parkman, and Henry Adams. Twentieth-century historians of note include Charles and Mary Beard, Oswald Spengler, Samuel Eliot Morison, and Arnold Toynbee. See AUTOBIOGRAPHY; BIOGRAPHY; MEMOIRS.

History Play. A PLAY with history as its subject. The most famous are the ten plays by Shakespeare called, in the FIRST FOLIO, histories, as opposed to comedies or tragedies. See CHRONICLE PLAY.

Hold Frame. See FREEZE FRAME.

Holograph. A MANUSCRIPT, letter, or other document wholly in the author's handwriting. Holographic evidence is important in establishing an author's intention. See COPY TEXT.

Homeoteleuton. The technique of ending successive phrases with the same sound:

> In activity commend*able*, in commonwealth formid*able*, in war ter-*rible*.

> She spoke witt*ily*, praised the president might*ily*, and ended hap-*pily*.

Homeric. Having the literary characteristics of Homer's *Iliad* and *Odyssey*, or of the world they describe; grand, heroic, imposing.

Homeric Epithet. A hyphenated adjective linked to a noun and repeated, as in Homer, so that they are remembered together: "rosy-fingered dawn," "swift-footed Achilles," "wine-dark sea." See EPITHET.

Homeric Simile. Sometimes called an *epic simile:* an extended SIM-
ILE, comparing one thing with another by lengthy description of the
second, often beginning with "as when." Homer's practice was echoed
by many later writers, including Milton. Here is Satan's entry into
Eden, from Book IV of *Paradise Lost:*

> Due entrance he disdained, and, in contempt,
> At one slight bound high overleaped all bound
> Of hill or highest wall, and sheer within
> Lights on his feet. As when a prowling wolf,
> Whom hunger drives to seek new haunt for prey,
> Watching where shepherds pen their flocks at eve,
> In hurdled cotes amid the field secure,
> Leaps o'er the fence with ease into the fold;
> Or as a thief, bent to unhoard the cash
> Of some rich burgher, whose substantial doors,
> Cross-barred and bolted fast, fear no assault,
> In at the window climbs, or o'er the tiles;
> So clomb this first grand Thief into God's fold. . . .

Homily. A religious discourse or sermon, especially one emphasizing
practical spiritual or moral advice, as opposed to a discussion of questions of doctrine.

Homostrophic. Composed of structurally identical STROPHES.

Horatian Satire. Gentle SATIRE, wittily amused at humankind's follies, after the manner of the Latin poet Horace (65–8 B.C.). Horatian
satire is contrasted with JUVENALIAN SATIRE. See MENIPPEAN SATIRE.

Horismos. The technique of elaborating a concept by defining it:

> Beauty is transitory, a snare for the unwary, an invitation to disaster.

Hornbook. A primer composed of a sheet of parchment or paper carrying the alphabet, numerals, Lord's Prayer, or other lesson, protec-
tively covered with a transparent sheet of thin horn, and mounted on
a board with a projecting handle. Such books were in use from the
fifteenth to the eighteenth centuries. From them was derived the secondary meaning of a hornbook as any primer or introductory text, as
in Thomas Dekker's *Gull's Hornbook* (1609).

Hubris. From Greek *hybris,* "pride": prideful arrogance or insolence
of the kind that causes the tragic HERO to ignore the warnings that
might turn aside the ACTION that leads to disaster. See HAMARTIA;
TRAGEDY.

Hudibrastic Verse. VERSE in the STYLE of Samuel Butler's *Hudibras,* a MOCK EPIC poem in couplets, or rhymed pairs of lines, in tetrameter (see METER). Using DOGGEREL rhyme and rhythm, *Hudibras* satirized the Puritans.

Humanism. A literary and philosophical view emphasizing humankind as the center of its concerns. Humanism originated in the RENAISSANCE, as writers and thinkers turned from an acceptance of received values to a renewed study of the humanities, the Classical literature of Greece and Rome, and the Bible. Renaissance humanists were concerned with people in this world, rather than with the natural or supernatural world central to the studies of scientists and religious thinkers who were not humanists. They replaced the medieval concern with the hereafter and its accompanying emphasis on spiritual values with their own emphasis on the actual or potential accomplishments of humanity. Opposing the medieval view of life on this earth as a preparation for eternity, Renaissance humanists imagined a perfect, civilized life in the here and now, brought about by the intellectual and cultural achievements of humankind.

Humanism is an attitude rather than a system of thought, a suggested direction rather than a prescription of method. Since the Renaissance, the term has been used in many ways, but always suggests humanity as the central concern, with the natural world (science) and the spiritual world (religion) valued for their relation to people. Classics are studied as repositories of human values and culture, great men and women perceived as models of achievement for all people.

Humanism, New. The brand of HUMANISM advocated in America in the first decades of the twentieth century by Irving Babbitt and Paul Elmer More. The New Humanists preached a rejection of the loosely nature-centered thinking and literary practice of ROMANTICISM and NATURALISM, asking instead for a return to a CLASSICISM centered in the humanities, with human beings perceived as subject to a higher law and most human when their accomplishments are measured not against their circumstances but against their potential.

Humanistic Criticism. Broadly, any CRITICISM centered on humanity. See HUMANISM; HUMANISM, NEW.

Humors. The *cardinal humors* of ancient medical theory: blood, phlegm, yellow bile (choler), black bile (melancholy). From ancient times until the nineteenth century, the humors were believed largely responsible for health and disposition. Hippocrates (c. 460–c. 370 B.C.)

thought an imbalance produced illness. Galen (c. A.D. 130–200) suggested that CHARACTER types are produced by dominance of fluids: *sanguine*, or kindly, cheerful, amorous; *phlegmatic*, or sluggish, unresponsive; *choleric*, or quick-tempered; *melancholic*, or brooding, dejected. In literature, especially in the RENAISSANCE, characters were portrayed according to the humors that dominated them, as in the COMEDY OF HUMORS, like Ben Jonson's *Every Man in His Humor* (1598) and *Every Man out of His Humor* (1599). See WIT AND HUMOR.

Hybris.   See HUBRIS.

Hymn.   From Greek *hymnos*, a song of praise, thanksgiving, or devotion. Medieval Christian hymns were mainly in Latin, with vernacular hymnals appearing in the sixteenth century, including, in English, Thomas Sternhold's *Psalter*, published in Geneva in 1556. The first American hymnal was the *Bay Psalm Book* (1640). Among noteworthy writers of hymns in the eighteenth and nineteenth centuries were Charles and John Wesley, Isaac Watts, William Cowper, Henry Wadsworth Longfellow, John Greenleaf Whittier, and Oliver Wendell Holmes.

Hymnal Stanza.   The COMMON METER of hymn books, identical to the BALLAD STANZA.

Hypallage.   The technique of exchanging syntactic relations, as in converting "When in the course of human events" to "When in event of the human course."

Hyperbaton.   The technique of transposing idiomatic order: "Of Man's First Disobedience . . . / Sing Heav'nly Muse" for "Heav'nly Muse, sing of Man's first disobedience."

Hyperbole.   OVERSTATEMENT to make a point, either direct or ironical.

Hypercatalectic.   Having an extra metrical syllable at the end; also called a *hypermetrical* line. The term is from Greek *hyper*, "over," and *katalegein*, "to leave off." See FEMININE ENDING.

Hypermetrical.   See HYPERCATALECTIC.

Hypotaxis.   Subordination of clauses and phrases. It is the opposite of PARATAXIS, in which phrases or clauses are joined with *and* or another coordinating conjunction. Erich Auerbach proposes a crucial and historic distinction between *paratactic* style (*and . . . and . . . and*)

and *hypotactic* style (*although . . . after . . . because . . . if . . .*) in his *Mimesis: The Representation of Reality in Western Literature* (German, 1946; trans., 1953).

Hypothesis. (1) An assertion or assumption to be verified or acted upon. (2) A RHETORICAL FIGURE that illustrates with an impossible supposition:

> If salt lose its savor, wherewith shall it be salted?

> Even if he had a million dollars, he would be unhappy.

> I'll come to thee by moonlight, though Hell should bar the way.

Hysteron Proteron. "Last first." The term refers to the placement of the cart before the horse in logic or phrasing: *bred and born* instead of *born and bred.*

I

Iambus (or **Iamb**). A metrical foot going ⌣ ⎯. See METER.

Ictus. A metrical stress; an accent.

Idealism. (1) In philosophy and ethics, an emphasis on ideas and ideals, as opposed to the sensory emphasis of MATERIALISM. Plato's idealistic philosophy assumed that the world of experience is only an imperfect shadow of a more real, permanent, ideal world. George Berkeley's eighteenth-century idealism, opposed to philosophic REALISM, assumed that the only reality is in the mind. Immanuel Kant (1724–1804), Georg Wilhelm Friedrich Hegel (1770–1831), and other later idealists also explored the possibilities of the mind as the source of reality. Ethical idealism seeks perfect patterns of behavior in a spiritual or mental realm apart from the physical world.

(2) Literary idealism follows from philosophical precepts, emphasizing a world in which the most important reality is a spiritual or transcendent truth not always reflected in the world of sense perception. See TRANSCENDENTALISM.

Identical Rhyme. Repetition of the entire sound, including the initial consonant, sometimes by repeating the same word (*fate, fate*), sometimes, as in *rime riche,* by repeating the sound with two senses: *pair, pare.* See RHYME.

Ideolect. Each person's distinctive DIALECT. Linguists observe that each person in any dialectic community has a characteristic vocabulary, habit of phrasing, and intonation as individually marked as fingerprints.

Idiom. An expression peculiar to a language, not literally translatable. In French, *Il n'y a pas de quoi* translates literally as "It has nothing here of what," but as a polite response to thanks, it means, idiomatically, "Please don't mention it," "Not at all," "It was a pleasure," "Forget it."

Idyll. A short poem of rustic pastoral serenity (from Greek *eidullion,* "little picture"). Theocritus (third century B.C.) invented the GENRE and the term in his *Idylls,* the first pastoral poems, in which he idealized the shepherds of his native Sicily for his Alexandrian audience.

234

Tennyson took the term for his long narrative poem, *The Idylls of the King*, published between 1842 and 1885. See ARCADIAN; PASTORAL.

Illumination. (1) In DRAMA, a DISCOVERY or RECOGNITION (ANAGNORISIS). (2) More generally, an intellectual or spiritual enlightenment; an EPIPHANY. (3) An illustration in a medieval manuscript.

Illusion of Reality. The sensation that literary events are real though known to be fictitious, the result of what Coleridge called the "willing suspension of disbelief" as even the simplest comic strip or "Once upon a time" draws the reader or listener in. With whatever people, animals, or extraterrestrial creatures, the illusion holds if, in Aristotle's terms, that kind of personage would probably do or say that kind of thing, and if events would necessarily or probably follow from whatever impossible circumstances (*Poetics*, 1454a). The illusion breaks when probability fails. Cervantes and some modern authors like John Barth break the illusion playfully with authorial comments and shifts in NARRATIVE PERSPECTIVE, reminding the reader comically of the illusion's powerful charm.

Image. A concrete picture, either literally descriptive, as in "Red roses covered the white wall," or figurative, as in "She is a rose," each carrying a sensual and emotive connotation. Critics speak of "tied" images, with connotations closely similar for all readers, and "free" images, open to various associations. A figurative image may be an ANALOGY, METAPHOR, SIMILE, PERSONIFICATION, or the like. Both literal and figurative images may serve as SYMBOL: "The doves cooed peacefully around the temple"; "The dove of peace flies no more." See ABSTRACT; CONCRETE; IMAGERY.

Imagery. Collectively, the images of a literary work (see IMAGE). The images, taken individually, are representative of things accessible to the five senses: sight, hearing, touch, taste, and smell. Thus, the water imagery of a work may be *visual*, suggesting a picture; *auditory*, representing the sounds of a running brook; *tactile*, if wetness or temperature is brought to mind; or even *gustatory* or *olfactory*, if the water is given a taste or smell.

Imagery is fundamental to literature in the primary sense that art is an imitation of nature (see MIMESIS), and an emphasis on imagery is one of the characteristics that distinguishes IMAGINATIVE WRITING from EXPOSITORY WRITING, although that, too, may employ imagery in significant ways. Of course, this primary relation to sense impressions does not mean that the images of literature are limited to the immediate sensory experiences of the writer. It is not necessary to have a swan in view in order to create the image of a swan in a poem, and just as things not experienced may be presented through imagery, so may things beyond experience, as when literature turns to FANTASY or MYTH for its materials. In this sense, the IMAGINATION is free to create images that cannot be directly experienced except through literature.

Images standing for single things in nature tend to represent the world in simple, primary terms. When an image is made to stand for two things, as when a rose represents itself and also the color in a young woman's cheeks, the image turns into a METAPHOR, SIMILE, or other form of FIGURATIVE LANGUAGE. When an image is used so as to suggest complex or multiple meanings, as when a rose represents itself, young women generally, and also beauty and fragility, it becomes a SYMBOL.

Within many works and for many writers, patterns of imagery are important, as when Shakespeare in *Macbeth* and Hawthorne in *The Scarlet Letter* bring the reader back repeatedly to patterns of light and dark, with occasionally a flash of red. So some writers are characterized by their fondness for the roots, tendrils, and budding shoots of nature; others by repeated reference to clothes; still others to the bricks, concrete, and glass of the modern city.

The array of images in a literary work may range from literal descriptions to metaphors with the physical picture only lightly implied, as in "The *run* of luck," but made significant by repetition and mutual reinforcement, as with the many images of animal savagery in *King Lear*. The NEW CRITICISM called attention to imagery as the essence of meaning. Unconscious imagery may reveal more about a poem, or novel—or its author—than its deliberate effects, and may reflect the communal unconscious of ARCHETYPE and MYTH. Patterns of images may contradict ostensible meaning. See ABSTRACT; ALLEGORY; CONCRETE; IMAGISTS; SYNAESTHESIA; TROPE.

Imagination.   The forming of mental images, originally with negative wishful connotations: "travails my saule in vayn ymagynacioun" (*Psalter*, 1340, xxxvii). Francis Bacon associated it with literature: "History has reference to the memory, poetry to the imagination, philosophy to the reason," as did Shakespeare (though the poet shares it with the lunatic and the lover):

> And as imagination bodies forth
> The forms of things unknown, the poet's pen

> Turns them to shapes, and gives to airy nothing
> A local habitation and a name.
> *Midsummer Night's Dream, V.i.14–17*

For the eighteenth century, particularly under Locke's influence, the term *imagination* referred to the picturing of objects from the physical world: "When we speak of Justice or Gratitude, we frame to our selves no Imagination of any thing" (*Essay Concerning Human Understanding*, 1690, III.v). Addison explored "The Pleasures of the Imagination" in eleven successive *Spectator* papers (1712, Nos. 411–421), asserting that we "cannot, indeed, have a single image in the fancy that did not make its first entrance through the sight; but we have the power of retaining, altering, and compounding those images, which we have once received, into all the varieties of picture and vision that are agreeable to the imagination" (No. 411). Later writers saw *imagination* as a higher power, distinguishing it from FANCY. Mark Akenside's poem *Pleasures of the Imagination* (1744) aimed to "pierce divine Philosophy's retreats" through the primary imaginative pleasures of the sublime, the wonderful, the beautiful, with their moral implications, and the secondary pleasures of the passions of the heart, including "ennobling sorrows."

In *The Prelude* (1805), Wordsworth raised the imagination even higher, seeing it as the divinely endowed means of perceiving the divine Love at the heart of nature and the mind's experience:

> This spiritual Love acts not nor can exist
> Without Imagination, which, in truth,
> Is but another name for absolute power
> And clearest insight, amplitude of mind,
> And Reason in her most exalted mood.
> *XIV.188–192*

The human mind becomes "A thousand times more beautiful than the earth/ On which he dwells . . ./ In beauty exalted, as it is itself/ Of quality and fabric more divine" (XIV.449–454).

Coleridge, discussing Wordsworth's poetry in *Biographia Literaria* (1817), distinguished Fancy as a mere "mode of Memory emancipated from the order of time and space," operating, like Memory, through association, from Imagination, the "shaping and modifying" power, which transcends the senses to an ultimate reality. In the same year, Keats wrote Benjamin Bailey (8 October 1817), "A long poem is a test of invention which I take to be the Polar star of poetry, as fancy is the sails, and imagination the rudder." On 22 November 1817, he wrote Bailey, "I am certain of nothing but the holiness of the heart's affections and the truth of imagination—what the imagination seizes as beauty must be truth—whether it existed before or not."

Imagination remains the higher power, giving literature and art authority. Fancy is lighter, associative, amusing, *fanciful*, as in reverie. See FANTASY.

Imaginative Writing.   Creative writing, or writing of prose FICTION, POETRY, or DRAMA. See EXPOSITORY WRITING.

Imagists.   Early twentieth-century American poets revolting against Romantic idealism and Victorian moralism. Their first anthology, *Des Imagistes* (1914), took its title from contemporary French poetry termed *imagistic*. In *Tendencies in Modern American Poetry* (1917), Amy Lowell defined their aims: (1) to use the exact word from common speech; (2) to avoid clichés; (3) to invent new rhythms for the new mood; (4) to have freedom to choose any subject; (5) to create a concrete IMAGE, sharply outlined; (6) to achieve concentration—the essence of poetry; (7) to suggest rather than to state. The principle imagists were Ezra Pound, Amy Lowell, H. D (Hilda Doolittle), John Gould Fletcher, Carl Sandburg, and William Carlos Williams. Chinese ideographic poetry and the Japanese HAIKU, the terse picture with no comment, were influential.

Imitation.   See MIMESIS.

Immaculate Conception.   Frequently mistaken as the mysterious conception of Jesus in the Virgin Mary's womb, but actually the dogma Pope Pius IX proclaimed in 1854 freeing "the Blessed Virgin Mary, from the first instant of conception [in *her* mother's womb], . . . from all stain of Original Sin" because she was destined to become the mother of Christ.

Imperfect Rhyme.   See SLANT RHYME.

Implied Author.   Wayne Booth's term for the Aristotelian ETHOS, the authorial PERSONA, of a novel—the authorial personality as gathered from the voice behind the words—distinct from the biographical person of the writer, which may inhere only partially, tangentially, or not at all (*The Rhetoric of Fiction*, 1961).

Imprecation.   An entreaty to the gods to visit evil on someone; a CURSE.

Impression.   All the copies of a publication printed from the same setting of type; also called a *printing*. See EDITION.

Impressionism.   A literary style conveying subjective impressions rather than objective reality, taking its name from the movement in French painting in the mid-nineteenth century, principally the work of Manet, Monet, Degas, and Renoir. The IMAGISTS represented impressionism in poetry; in fiction, Dorothy Richardson, Virginia Woolf, James Joyce, and John Dos Passos in his "Camera Eye" sections of *U.S.A.* See EXPRESSIONISM.

Impressionistic Criticism.   An emphasis on the personal reaction of the critic. See CRITICISM.

Imprimatur.   "Let it be printed"—the Roman Catholic church's official stamp of approval on a manuscript, or similar official sanction, especially under terms of censorship. Metaphorically, the term refers to any authoritarian critical approval.

Incantation.   A ritualistic charm or spell, chanted or repeated to produce a magical effect, like the witches' chant in *Macbeth* or Ariel's "Full fathom five" in *The Tempest.*

Incident.   An event, the smallest unit in a fictive action or set of occurrences, either a complete EPISODE in a string of adventures, or one happening in a larger episode.

Inciting Moment.   Gustav Freytag's term for the event or impulse that starts a play's RISING ACTION. See FREYTAG'S PYRAMID.

Incremental Repetition.   The restating of a line of poetry, usually with slight variation, so that each repetition accumulates meaning or effect. It is frequent in ballads, as in "Lord Randal," where each of the six stanzas begins with a variation of the question "Where have you been to, Randal my son" and each ends with the same two lines:

> Make my bed soon, for I'm sick to the heart,
> And I fain would lie down.

The repetition of these two lines is especially incremental, since by the last stanza, from the minimal details added at each step, we gather that Randal's heartsickness is not merely from disappointed love but from his sweetheart's poisoning him with eel broth. Shakespeare incrementally repeats the word *state* in his sonnet "When in disgrace with Fortune" so that it gathers meaning from "outcast *state*," or mere condition, to *state* of mind, to some glorious kingdom of love: "I would not change my *state* with kings." Poe's "Nevermore" in "The Raven" and

Tennyson's "Rode the six hundred" in "The Charge of the Light Brigade" are other notable examples.

Incrementum. The arrangement of items from lowest to highest:

> The law will be kept in the shacks of the farms, in the tenements of the slums, in the bungalows and homes of the suburbs, and in the mansions of the countryside.

Incunabulum. A book printed from movable type before 1501 (from Latin *incunabula*, "swaddling clothes"—infancy). Incunabula, designed after illuminated manuscript books, are frequently large and beautiful in print and binding. Many are extant, including about 360 printed in England, among them William Caxton's famous editions of Chaucer's *Canterbury Tales* (1483) and of Malory's *Morte Darthur* (1485).

Index Expurgatorius. The list of passages expunged by Roman Catholic censors.

Index Librorum Prohibitorum. The catalog, formerly published by the church, of books forbidden to Roman Catholic readers, or restricted from general use; called "The Index."

Indian Literature. See AMERICAN INDIAN LITERATURE; COMMONWEALTH LITERATURE.

Individualized Characters. Ones endowed with traits that mark them as individuals, as opposed to TYPE CHARACTERS. Individualized characters belong, generally speaking, to REALISM, as opposed to the type characters of ROMANCE. See CHARACTERS.

Induction. An introduction to a literary work; sixteenth-century usage. Thomas Sackville's "Induction" to *A Mirror for Magistrates* (1563) tells of Sorrow leading the poet to the kingdom of the dead, where he meets the shades who tell their tragic stories in each of the subsequent sections. Shakespeare's Induction to *The Taming of the Shrew* (1594) has Christopher Sly, a drunken tinker, persuaded that he is a lord for whom the following play is privately performed.

Industrial Revolution. The accelerated change, beginning in the 1760s, from an agricultural-shopkeeping society, using hand tools, to an industrial-mechanized one. By 1760, blast furnaces were turning out iron in quantity. Between 1764 and 1767, James Hargreaves invented the spinning jenny, by which one person could spin sixteen or more threads simultaneously. In 1785, Dr. Edmund Cartwright, a clergyman, patented the first of his progressively improved power looms, which, with the spinning jenny, instituted the automated factory system. By 1800, English looms had increased from 3,000 to 100,000. Roads, canals, and railroads, especially after Richard Trevithick invented the heavy locomotive in 1804, sped the transportation necessary for industry. By 1826, two-thirds of the farm population had left to seek work in the industrial cities, many dying jobless and diseased. The machine displaced the craftworker; the factory, handwork in the home. Many villages were virtually deserted. Men, women, and children entered the new capitalist mills of the middle class.

These were the "dark Satanic Mills" Blake abhorred in "England's green & pleasant Land." This is the new London of "each charter'd street" by the "charter'd Thames" where "the Chimney-sweeper's cry" appalls "Every black'ning Church," where the midnight streets echo the curse of the youthful harlot, no longer merrily tumbling in Shakespearean hay. Dickens addressed himself to the new disoriented poor and the waifs, like Oliver Twist, in "the cold, wet, shelterless midnight streets of London." Oliver Goldsmith's poem *The Deserted Village* (1770) had nostalgically noted the rural depopulation. Crabbe's poem *The Village* (1783) pictured rural poverty more glumly, as did Charles Kingsley's novel *Yeast* (1848). In *Alton Locke* (1850), Kingsley portrayed London's working poor and the early revolutionary stirrings of CHARTISM. Elizabeth Gaskell studied the "hungry forties" and the bitterness of trade unionism in industrial Manchester in her novel *Mary Barton* (1848). From 1860 onward, John Ruskin addressed himself to a number of social and economic reforms, advocating organized labor and trying several industrial improvements, including the revival of handmade linen. Thomas Carlyle similarly considered the problems of labor and advocated a return to a medieval system. Matthew Arnold condemned the new Philistines, who equated money with greatness. Jeremy Bentham had addressed himself to the new social and political problems as early as 1776, with his anonymous *Fragment on Government*, a forerunner of UTILITARIANISM. In 1798, Thomas Malthus published *An Essay on the Principle of Population*, his famous case for restraining population, followed by *Principles of Political Economy* (1820). Robert Owen, a prosperous owner of a cotton-spinning mill in Manchester, sought socialist and cooperative solutions in his *New View of Society* (1813) and *Revolution in Mind and Practice* (1849). John Stuart Mill's *Principles of Political Economy* (1848) is perhaps the definitive social–economic work of the period.

Influence. The apparent effect of literary works on subsequent writers and their work, as in Browning's influence on T. S. Eliot. Tracing influence—the German *einfluss*—was widespread among literary historians and critics in the early decades of the twentieth century.

Informal Essay. An ESSAY less serious in TONE and purpose than the FORMAL ESSAY; one loosely organized and with informal diction, or word choice, and sentence structure.

Initial Rhyme. RHYME at the beginnings of lines.

Inkhorn Terms. Erudite coinages from Greek and Latin to make English more elegant by writers caught up in the new learning of the early sixteenth century. Bishop John Bale was the first to look on the new fashion as pedantry: "Soche are your Ynkehorne termes" (*Yet a Course*, 1543). See HUMANISM; PURIST.

In Medias Res. Horace's advice to start with the "middle things," usually translated "in the midst of things."

> nec gemino bellum Troianum orditur ab ovo;
> sempter ad eventum festinat et in medias res
> non secus ac notas auditorem rapit.
> *Ars Poetica, 147–149*

"[And the good poet] does not begin the Trojan war from the twin egg; he always hastens to the event and rushes his listener into the middle matters, just as if known."

In other words, Homer did not begin with the egg that Leda produced after her encounter with Zeus disguised as a swan, explaining that the egg hatched Helen, who caused the Trojan War, along with the twin brothers Castor and Pollux. See *AB OVO*.

"In Memoriam" Stanza. The STANZA of Tennyson's "In Memoriam": four iambic tetrameter lines, rhyming *abba*. See ENVELOPE CONSTRUCTION; METER.

Inner Conflict. See CONFLICT.

Inns of Court. England's four legal societies, and their buildings, founded about 1300: Gray's Inn, Lincoln's Inn, the Inner Temple, the Middle Temple. They function as law schools, operated by practicing barristers, and have the exclusive right to award the degree of barrister.

Innuendo. An indirect remark or gesture, especially one implying something derogatory; an insinuation. *Innuendo* was formerly a legal term used to introduce explanatory material in a document, especially when listing the reasons for complaint in a case of libel or slander. Its Latin meaning is "nodding to" or "intimating."

Inscape and **Instress.** Terminology inverted by Gerard Manley Hopkins to express his philosophy of the relationship between nature and POETRY. *Inscape*, in either nature or poetry, is the totality of individual elements joined in one beautiful object, giving to it its essential oneness. It is "the very soul of art." *Instress* is the energy that combines the elements of being in a unified design. In part natural, in part supernatural, it is an inner tension belonging to both object and poem. Both inscape and instress act through the senses and are experienced in the mind in a kind of mystic illumination, or EPIPHANY, so they are interior as well as exterior, subjective within humanity as well as objective in the world outside.

Inspiration. A stimulus to creativity. Since ancient times inspiration has been associated with *breath*, in the sense of being alive or drawing air into the lungs, and *spirit*, in the sense of something from without that enters and inhabits, if only temporarily, the physical being. Thus, the inspiration for creative works is sometimes seen as unique to individual writers, connected with their personal existence or being, engendered within them in the time and place in which they draw the breath of life. Inspiration was originally and traditionally seen, however, as something external to the writer, a force that enters from God or nature or whatever, an eternal something not always present within and not always prompt to come when convenient or necessary. This idea was expressed by the ancients in their concept of the divine madness— or DIVINE AFFLATUS—of poets, who can write only when the gods are within them, and it survives in popular conceptions of poets as either mad (not themselves) or in tune with some universal principle or force. A more individualistic, more modern view surfaces in the idea that inspiration is only hard work ("perspiration"), or that it arises from within, from the depths of the subconscious mind.

Intentional Fallacy. The idea that the meaning of a work can be explained by considering the author's intention, a fallacy according to the NEW CRITICISM. The term was introduced by W. K. Wimsatt and Monroe C. Beardsley in their essay "The Intentional Fallacy," reprinted in *The Verbal Icon* (1954). In brief, their point is that "the poem is not the critic's own and not the author's (it is detached from the author at birth and goes about the world beyond his power to intend about it or control it). The poem belongs to the public. . . ."

Critics who emphasize the intentional fallacy are attempting to minimize the effect of too much reliance on Alexander Pope's advice, long standard in criticism:

> In every work regard the writer's end,
> Since none can compass more than they intend.

Just as Pope's position can be carried to extremes, however, so can that of the New Critics. Between the extremes of either position lies an approach derived from complementary assumptions: (1) Despite Pope's observation, writers may accomplish more than they intend, or even something quite different. (2) Despite the warnings of the New Criticism, a consideration of the author's intention can sometimes lead to an understanding perfectly compatible with close ANALYSIS, but overlooked without the external clue. Similar cautions may be suggested for each of the other New Critical fallacies. See AFFECTIVE FALLACY; BIOGRAPHICAL FALLACY; GENETIC FALLACY.

Interior Monologue. A fictional presentation of unspoken thoughts as though delivered in monologue, typically characterized by STREAM OF CONSCIOUSNESS content and technique. James Joyce, Virginia Woolf, and William Faulkner are masters. Édouard Dujardin's *Les Lauriers sont coupés* (1887) is often cited as the first example. *Direct interior monologue* presents thoughts in first-person narration directly to the reader, excluding any sense of participation by an author or external narrator, as in Faulkner's *As I Lay Dying. Indirect interior monologue,* a form of third-person limited omniscient narration, presents thoughts as seen from within the mind but expressed in the words of an external narrator, as frequently in Joyce's *Ulysses* and Woolf's *Mrs. Dalloway* and *To the Lighthouse.* The conventions of interior monologue have earlier roots, in Shakespeare's soliloquies and Sterne's *Tristram Shandy*, for example. An interesting transitional passage is Chapter 42 of Henry James's *Portrait of a Lady* (1881). See NARRATIVE PERSPECTIVE.

Interlaced Rhyme. See CROSSED RHYME.

Interlingua. See ESPERANTO.

Interlocking Rhyme. RHYME between stanzas, using a word unrhymed in one as a rhyme for the next, as in TERZA RIMA: *aba bcb cdc* and so on.

Interlude. Latin for "between play." An interlude is a brief form of DRAMA, a short PLAY, MASQUE, or some other entertainment, as, for example, by jugglers, jesters, mimes, or dancers, providing a break during a feast or between the acts of a longer play. Interludes were common in the RENAISSANCE.

Internal Rhyme. RHYME within a line, rather than at the beginning *(initial rhyme)* or end *(end rhyme);* also, rhyme matching sounds at the middle of a line with sounds at the end.

Intrigue. A secret plot or scheme; hence, in literature, a PLOT constructed on hidden motives, frequently complex and underhanded. A COMEDY of intrigue is one complicated by the scheming of its CHARACTERS, as, for example, William Congreve's *Way of the World* (1700).

Introduction. A portion of a literary work placed at the beginning to introduce the matter to follow later. For a book, the introduction may take the form of an ESSAY providing an overview or explaining the conditions of writing and be placed before the first chapter, or the first chapter itself may contain the introduction. For an essay or speech, the introduction comes within the first section, or within the first paragraph. See FOREWORD; PREAMBLE; PREFACE; PROEM; PROLEGOMENON.

Intrusive Narrator. A narrator, or story teller, whose explanatory comments, opinions, or prejudices form an important part of the story being told—a story, strictly speaking, about someone else. The THIRD-PERSON OMNISCIENT narrator of a typical novel by Henry Fielding, Sir Walter Scott, or Charles Dickens, for example, is intrusive by contrast with the narrator of a novel by Henry James, James Joyce, or Ernest Hemingway. See NARRATIVE PERSPECTIVE; SELF-EFFACING AUTHOR.

Invective. Violent verbal assault, vehement denunciation, vituperation.

Invention. According to ancient theories of RHETORIC, the first step in ORATION, applying primarily to the discovery of material. Invention was then followed by arrangement of the material in an effective order, by development of an appropriate style, by memorization, and, finally, by delivery. In literary CRITICISM, invention has often echoed this early sense that authors must first invent or discover their material before they can express it in words. Still, the nature and source of invention has remained open for discussion. It is sometimes contrasted with *imitation,* in the sense of following models in nature or art (the sense in which James Fenimore Cooper, for example, thought his invention superior to Walter Scott's). In this later sense of invention, the emphasis

is on originality: creating the material rather than finding it. See IMAG-
INATION; INSPIRATION; MIMESIS.

Inversion.   A reversal of sequence or position, as when the normal
order of elements within a sentence is inverted for poetic or rhetorical
effect, or when the logical order of an ARGUMENT is reversed. See
CHIASMUS; INVERTED FOOT.

Inverted Foot.   A trochee in an iambic line. See METER.

Invocation.   From Latin *vocāre,* "to call": a prayer addressed to a
god, one of the MUSES, or patron. In an ancient poetic CONVENTION,
less common since the eighteenth century, poets invoked assistance or
blessing at the beginning of a poem, before turning to its proper subject matter.

Ionic Foot.   A Greek and Latin foot going ˘ ˘ — —. In English
iambics, the term refers to a *double foot* one of the three recurrent
substitutions, along with the *trochee* and the *spondee.* It is the farthest
stretch of iambic meter, as in the second line of Marvell's couplet:

$$
\text{Ănni- | hĭlat- | ĭng all | thăt's máde |}
$$
$$
\text{Tŏ ă | green thought | ĭn ă | green shade. |}
$$

Or in Pope's:

$$
\text{Ă per- | fĕct Júdge | wĭll réad | eăch Work | ŏf Wit |}
$$
$$
\text{Wĭth the | săme Spir- | ĭt that | ĭts Auth- | ŏr writ. |}
$$

Or Blake's:

$$
\text{Yŏu throw | the sand | ă gainst | the wind, |}
$$
$$
\text{Ănd the | wind blows | ĭt back | ă gain. |}
$$

Or in Shakespeare's line:

$$
\text{Let me | not to | the mar- | riage of | true minds |}
$$

See METER.

Ipse Dixit.   Latin for "he himself (or she herself) said it": a dogmatic
assertion, without proof.

Irish Literary Movement.   See IRISH RENAISSANCE.

Irish Literature. The writing produced in Ireland. In addition to numerous Latin writings, religious and secular, medieval Ireland produced in Gaelic one of the earliest, largest, and most interesting bodies of literature in any vernacular language of the Middle Ages in Europe. By the fourteenth century, however, English began to make its way into the speech of Ireland, and from the eighteenth century onward English has been the language of Ireland's major literary accomplishments.

For several centuries after the breakup of the Roman empire in the fifth century, Ireland was Europe's major center of Christian learning, with Irish clerics playing a major role in preserving the literature of the ancient Celts. The most important manuscripts came late, the *Book of the Dun Cow* (before 1106), the *Book of Leinster* (c. 1160), and the *Yellow Book of Lecan* (late fourteenth century). In these is preserved the three major cycles of the Irish sagas, the bulk in prose, with verse passages. The Ulster Cycle presents history, legend, and myth from about the first century B.C., frequently in simple stories of one episode each, relating to the hero Cuchulain. *The Cattle Raid of Cooley*, from this cycle, is a long, complex account of armed conflict, slaughter, single combat, a fairy curse, and divine intervention. *Briciu's Feast* displays Cuchulain accepting a beheading challenge like that in *Sir Gawain and the Green Knight*. The Finn Cycle centers on Finn, a hero of about the third century A.D. Within this cycle, *The Flight of Diarmaid and Grainne* is an important analogue, perhaps source, for *Tristan and Isolde*. The Historical and Mythological Cycle has traits in common with the others, but lacks the focus on a single hero. Events are loosely historical, or deal with magic and the supernatural shape-shifting of gods, demigods, fairies, and wizards. Dagda, king of the fairies, and Lug of the Long Arm, divine father of Cuchulain, figure in a number of them. In addition to the sagas preserved in the cycles, Ireland in the Middle Ages had many adventure stories and visions, often in Latin, and a bardic tradition in Gaelic verse, often in the form of praise, lamentation, or satire. Gaelic literature continued to be written as late as the eighteenth century, but declined rapidly in the nineteenth, to be revived in the twentieth century by writers like Patrick Pearse (1879–1916), executed for his part in the 1916 Easter Rebellion, and Flann O'Brien, pseudonym for Brian O'Nolan (1911–1966), author of *At Swim-Two-Birds* (1939), who wrote sometimes in Gaelic, but more often in English.

Irish literature in English has been at times indistinguishable from the literature of England, at times forcefully shaped by Irish conditions and heritage. Prominent Anglo-Irish writers who seem most clearly to belong to the English tradition include Jonathan Swift (1667–1745), Oliver Goldsmith (1728–1774), Oscar Wilde (1854–1900), George Bernard Shaw (1856–1950), Cecil Day Lewis (1904–1972), and Louis MacNeice (1907–1963).

Among writers in English more closely identified with Ireland, Maria Edgeworth (1767–1849) is remembered as the creator of *Castle Rackrent* (1800), one of the first regional novels, admired by Scott. Thomas Moore (1779–1852), born and educated in Ireland, spent most of his life abroad but became the chief Irish poet of his time with *Irish Melodies* (1808–1834). Sheridan Le Fanu (1814–1873) wrote novels and short stories, including some classic supernatural tales. The late nineteenth and early twentieth centuries saw an astonishing flowering of Irish literature, especially in drama and in the poems of Yeats (see IRISH RENAISSANCE). Largely apart from this movement, but greatly in debt to it, James Joyce (1882–1941), writing in Trieste, Zürich, and Paris, created in *A Portrait of the Artist as a Young Man* (1916), *Ulysses* (1922), and *Finnegans Wake* (1939) novels quintessentially Irish that are also masterworks of our time. The short stories of *Dubliners* (1914) have become classics, and Joyce's fine lyrical gift, apparent in his prose, was displayed also in two volumes of poems. Samuel Beckett (1906–   ), closely associated with Joyce in Paris, has written chiefly in French, self-translated into English. His principal works include the novels *Murphy* (1938), *Molloy* (1951), *Malone Dies* (1956), *The Unnamable* (1958), and *Watt* (1953), and the plays *Waiting for Godot* (1952) and *Happy Days* (1961). Yeats, Joyce, and Beckett are the Irish giants of this century. Other recent writers of distinguished achievement include, among the older generation, Liam O'Flaherty (1896–   ), Sean O'Faolain (1900–   ), Frank O'Connor (1903–1966), and Mary Lavin (1912–   ), all especially effective in the short story form. Another exceptional writer of fiction, Edna O'Brien (1932–   ), has seen her sexually liberated novels banned in Ireland, like the works of Joyce and others earlier. Brendan Behan (1923–1964) was noteworthy for his fictionalized autobiography *Borstal Boy* (1958) and the play *The Quare Fellow* (1954). Accomplished poets since Yeats include Patrick Kavanagh (1905–   ), Thomas Kinsella (1927–   ), Desmond O'Grady (1935–   ), and Seamus Heaney (1939–   ). See IRISH RENAISSANCE.

References

Myles Dillon, **Early Irish Literature** (1948).
Robin Flower, **The Irish Tradition** (1947).

Douglas Hyde, **A Literary History of Ireland** (1899).
Patrick Rafroidi, **Irish Literature in English: The Romantic Period** (2 vols., 1980).

Irish Renaissance.   A term used to describe the literary and political history of Ireland from about 1880 to 1930. Other terms for this period, or elements within it, include *Celtic Renaissance, Gaelic Movement,* and *Irish Literary Movement.* Politically, the period began with a rising nationalism that led to the Easter Rebellion of 1916 and the establishment of the Irish Free State in 1922. In literature, it began with a revival of interest in the folk traditions and literary remains of the past, coupled with a patriotic attempt to create a new, unmistakably Irish literature. Standish O'Grady's *History of Ireland: Heroic Period* (1878) gave impetus to this movement with its focus on ancient heroes such as Cuchulain and Finn. Other workers followed, collecting, translating, reinterpreting, creating anew. Although some writing was done in Gaelic, the most impressive achievements were in English.

William Butler Yeats (1865–1939) was the leading poet of this movement and one of the great poets in any language. His *Wanderings of Oisin* (1889) powerfully demonstrated the uses of Irish legendary material in English. Two years later, he helped found the Irish Literary Society in London, and the next year (1892), the Irish National Literary Society in Dublin. In 1898, with Lady Gregory, George Moore, and Edward Martyn he began the movement that culminated in the famous ABBEY THEATRE of Dublin. Multitalented, Yeats wrote many plays, some short stories, and much miscellaneous prose. As a poet, he improved with age, turning to less romantic, more nearly universal themes, the lyric expression of a powerful symbolic vision. His *Collected Poems,* Definitive Edition (1956), is convenient and authoritative.

The Abbey Theatre gave rise to many fine playwrights. Lady Augusta Gregory (1859–1932) served as guiding spirit and contributed plays such as *The Rising of the Moon* (1907). John Millington Synge (1871–1907) created two classics of modern drama, *Riders to the Sea* (1904) and *The Playboy of the Western World* (1907). *The Shadow of a Gunman* (1923), *Juno and the Paycock* (1924), and *The Plough and the Stars* (1926) by Sean O'Casey (1880–1964) deal memorably with the trials of the lower classes in wartime.

Among other writers associated with the movement, George Moore (1852–1933) is remembered chiefly for his novel *Esther Waters* (1894), and George William Russell (1867–1935), who wrote under the pseudonym AE, for his poems. Padraic Colum (1882–1972) possessed a lyr-

ical poetic voice that sometimes echoed folk materials. See IRISH LIT-
ERATURE.

References

Una Ellis-Fermor, **The Irish Dramatic Movement,** 2nd ed. (1954).
Phillip L. Marcus, **Yeats and the Beginning of the Irish Renaissance** (1970).

Iron Age.   The fourth and last of the AGES OF THE WORLD.

Ironia.   See ANTIPHRASIS.

Ironic Mode.   A mode of literature in which the CHARACTERS are
viewed from above, with detached IRONY, as possessing powers inferior to those assumed to belong to author and reader. See LOW MI-
METIC.

Irony.   A term originating in the *eiron* of Greek comedy, a clever self-
effacer whose assumed simplicity and humility triumph over the loud-
mouthed *alazon*. (see CHARACTERS). Plato cast Socrates as a constant
eiron in his *Dialogues,* the truly wise man who pretends ignorance and
poses simple questions to lead the *alazons* to expose their fallacies in
what he ironically praises as wisdom. Both Plato (c. 427–347 B.C.) and
Aristophanes (c. 448–380 B.C.) used the word *eironeia* somewhat re-
proachfully to indicate a mocking pretence and deception. In his *Ethics,* Aristotle (384–322 B.C.) gave the term more breadth and respect-
ability, setting Truth as the mean between the Alazon's loud
exaggerations and the Eiron's humble concealment. Cicero (106–43
B.C.) and Quintilian (c. A.D. 35–96) distinguished between irony as a
figure of speech and as a mode of discourse. Irony came into its own
in the early eighteenth century, with Swift—perhaps the world's greatest ironist—and his circle, though the word itself was not widely current. All admired "Cervantes' serious air"—Pope's phrase for Swift's
pervasive mock gravity, especially in his *Modest Proposal* and *Gulliver's
Travels*—and many, including Pope, Gay, and Fielding, practiced it.

In general, irony is the perception of a clash between appearance
and reality, between *seems* and *is,* or between *ought* and *is.* The myriad
shadings of irony seem to fall into three categories: (1) verbal, (2) dramatic, (3) situational.

1. *Verbal irony*—saying something contrary to what it means. The
appearance is what the words say; the reality, their contrary meaning.
Both speaker and listener are aware of the contrast, mutually understanding the situation and each other. "A marvelous time" means a

boring time. "A great guy" is a petty sniveler. "A truth universally acknowledged" is a self-interested opinion. The listener must know that the party was boring to get the irony in the speaker's "marvelous." The listener must know that it is raining to get the irony in the speaker's "What a great day for a picnic!" Speaker and listener enjoy a silent compact. They are in cahoots. This silent ironic understanding may flow between author and reader, as it does between reader and Jane Austen. Or it may flow between characters within a story, as someone stands by in ignorance, all of which the reader enjoys by listening in. ACCISIMUS, LITOTES, MEIOSIS, OVERSTATEMENT, and *understatement* are types of verbal irony.

2. *Dramatic irony*—saying or doing something while unaware of its ironic contrast with the whole truth. Dramatic irony, named for its frequency in DRAMA, is a verbal irony with the speaker's awareness erased. The speaker's, or doer's, assumptions are the appearance, to him or her; the true situation is the reality, which the audience knows. Someone says, "This is the happiest day of my life," and dances a jig, while members of the audience, and perhaps some of the people on stage, know that his mortgage has been foreclosed and his family wiped out at the intersection. When someone goes to open a door behind which the audience knows disaster awaits, the audience has dramatic irony in action alone. An ignorant person in company with verbal ironists embodies a dramatic irony by a blank face and no movement at all. Or the ignorant one may understand only the surface of what the verbal ironists say. An even better variation occurs when two characters exchange verbal ironies, enjoying what they think is superior knowledge, while the audience knows how blind they are to the awful truth. Furthermore, FICTION and drama abound in a kind of retrospective dramatic irony, as, looking back, the reader or watcher realizes that the speaker's "happiest day of my life" is now being rendered painfully or comically ironic. When in Act I, Hamlet tells his father's ghost that he will sweep to his revenge with wings as swift as meditation or the thoughts of love, his words gather more and more dramatic irony as he dawdles on and on through most of the play.

3. *Situational irony*—events turning to the opposite of what is expected or what should be (also called *circumstantial irony* and the *irony of fate* or, in some circumstances, COSMIC IRONY), as when it rains on the Weather Bureau's annual picnic. The ironic situation—the *ought* upended by the *is*—is integral to dramatic irony. The ironic situation turns the speaker's unknowing words ironic. Situational irony is the

very essence of both comedy and tragedy. The young lovers run into the worst possible luck, until everything clears up happily. The most noble spirits go to their death, while the featherheads survive.

In *Anatomy of Criticism* (1957), Northrop Frye sees Irony as one of the four archetypal *mythoi*, or ways, in which we perceive the world and its works. Irony, or SATIRE, is the polar opposite of ROMANCE, the wry realities opposite the wishful dream, just as TRAGEDY is the opposite of COMEDY. If we think of a circle, with Romance at the top and Irony at the bottom, Tragedy at the right and Comedy at the left, we can see how the four modes blend. The arcs of Romance and Irony have their tragic or comic tinges at one end or the other.

Irony also blends with SARCASM, with which it is frequently confused. Sarcasm has a cutting edge. It derives from Greek *sarkazein*, "to tear the flesh." The tearing may be ironic, but it may also be straight malice, a remark intended to hurt where it hurts most. "Well, little man, what now?" is straight sarcasm when a dwarf interrupts the class; it is ironic sarcasm when a seven-footer bursts in.

References

Wayne C. Booth, **A Rhetoric of Irony** (1974).
Northrop Frye, **Anatomy of Criticism** (1957).
Norman Knox, **The Word Irony in Its Context, 1500–1755** (1961).
G. G. Sedgewick, **Of Irony, Especially in Drama** (1948).
F. McD. C. Turner, **The Element of Irony in English Literature** (1926).

Issue. (1) Copies of a publication put forth at one time, as, for example, the June issue of a magazine. (2) Copies of a book differing in some way from others in the same EDITION, as, for example, by being printed on different paper.

Italian Sonnet (or **Petrarchan Sonnet**).   A SONNET composed of an OCTAVE and SESTET, rhyming *abbaabba cdecde* (or *cdcdcd* or some variant, without a closing couplet).

Italic (or **Italics**).   Type slanting upward to the right. *This is italic.*

J

Jacobean Period (1603–1625). The reign of James I, *Jacobus* being the Latin for "James." A certain skepticism and even cynicism seeped into Elizabethan joy. The Puritans and the court party, the Cavaliers, grew more antagonistic. But it was in the Jacobean period that Shakespeare wrote his greatest tragedies and tragi-comedies, and Ben Jonson did his major work, along with Beaumont and Fletcher, George Chapman, John Webster, Philip Massinger, and Thomas Middleton. Thomas Dekker achieved his starkest London realism in his two-part play, *The Honest Whore* (1604, 1608). METAPHYSICAL POETRY flourished with Donne, and the CAVALIER POETS, and the TRIBE OF BEN wrote some of the best lyrics in English. The King James translation of the Bible appeared in 1611. Bacon's work and Burton's *Anatomy of Melancholy* are also notable. See ENGLISH LITERATURE, PERIODS OF and the "Chronology of Literature and World Events."

Jargon. (1) Language peculiar to a trade or calling, as, for example, the jargon of astronauts, lawyers, or literary critics. Jargon of this kind is useful for communication among those within the group, but frequently remains mysterious to outsiders, (2) Confused or confusing language. This kind of jargon communicates to nobody.

Jeremiad. A LAMENT or COMPLAINT, especially one enumerating transgressions and predicting destruction of a people, of the kind found in the Old Testament book Jeremiah.

Jest Books. Collections of jokes, witticisms, and humorous EPIGRAMS. Such books have been common from the sixteenth century onward, deriving their contents from FOLKLORE and from the FABLIAUX and EXEMPLA of the Middle Ages, and later culling humorous anecdotes, verses, and other materials from longer works. Perhaps the earliest in English is *A Hundred Merry Tales* (c. 1526). *Joe Miller's Jest-book* (1739) was long popular.

Jesuits. Members of the Society of Jesus (abbreviated *S.J.*), a religious order of the Roman Catholic church. Founded by St. Ignatius of Loyola in the sixteenth century, the Jesuits have been famous missionaries, scholars, and educators, founding numerous schools, colleges, and universities. Members take vows of poverty, chastity, and obedience and are organized as soldiers in the service of God, highly disciplined, under a leader called a "general," with headquarters in Rome. Frequently controversial, the order was dissolved in 1773 by Pope Clement XIV, but reestablished in 1814 by Pius VII. The poet Gerard Manley Hopkins (1844–1899) was a Jesuit, as was the distinguished twentieth-century paleontologist and philosopher Pierre Teilhard de Chardin (1881–1955).

Jeu d'Esprit. French for "play of the mind": a playful, witty comment or piece of writing.

Jeu Parti. See PARTIMEN.

Joc Parti (or **Jeu Parti**). See PARTIMEN; TROUBADOUR.

Johnson, Age of (1750–1789). A period from the beginning of Samuel Johnson's literary eminence to the French Revolution. Johnson (1709–1784), in mind, personality, and accomplishment, dominated the second half of the eighteenth century, a diverse and newly skeptical period following the Augustan optimism of Pope's *Essay on Man* (1731) and Fielding's *Tom Jones* (1749). Johnson's *Rambler* papers (1750–1752) meditated on the moral and social problems that engaged the Neoclassical attention—self-love, procrastination, old age, friendship, and the like—and set a pungent and Latinate prose style that continued to echo through most of the nineteenth century. His *Dictionary* (1755) helped to realize a long-standing Neoclassical wish for stability in language. Boswell's *Life of Johnson* (1791) established Johnson's fame.

A new burst of comedy took the stage, giving rise in 1777 to two plays still perennially favored, Goldsmith's *She Stoops to Conquer* and Sheridan's *School for Scandal*. Gibbon achieved a landmark in history, *The Decline and Fall of the Roman Empire* (1776–1788). Horace Walpole originated a new wave of romances in *The Castle of Otranto: A Gothic Story* (1764), from which the GOTHIC NOVEL and all modern mystery fiction derives. The most notable novel of the period was Sterne's comically haphazard *Tristram Shandy* (1759–1767). Thomas Gray was the leading poet. Robert Burns, in his Scottish lyrics, represented at once a version of the eighteenth century's admired noble savage, a natural rustic genius, and the Romantic movement soon to emerge in Wordsworth and Coleridge's *Lyrical Ballads* (1798). See ENGLISH LITERATURE, PERIODS OF and the "Chronology of Literature and World Events."

Jongleur. Literally, a juggler or trickster: in medieval France, a wandering MINSTREL, who entertained with songs, tales, jests, juggling, and tumbling.

Journal. (1) A daily record of events or observations, similar to a DIARY, but generally less personal, as, for example, a travel or business journal. The *Original Journals of the Lewis and Clark Expedition: 1804–1806* (Reuben G. Thwaites, ed., 8 vols., 1904–1905) presents in detail the records of two years of historic exploration. (2) A daily publication, such as a newspaper, or, by extension, any PERIODICAL publication, such as a scholarly journal.

Jungian Criticism. Literary examination based on the writings of Carl Jung. Jung, beginning as an associate of Freud, broke with Freud over the conception of the unconscious, which Jung thought of not as the individual's repressed unconscious but as a COLLECTIVE UNCONSCIOUS which all individuals possessed in common. The process of what Freud called psychoanalysis and Jung analytical psychology thus moved, for Jung, in the direction of reaching certain archetypes common to all experience and recorded in literature and in various occult studies, notably alchemy. Jung regarded this as a crucial step in achieving what he called "individuation," a process in which individuals shift their center of gravity from the reasoning and sensational ego to that of a fully integrated human being. Jungian psychology, while it cannot compare in extent or influence with FREUDIAN CRITICISM or Marxist CRITICISM, has nonetheless had a considerable influence, if perhaps more in the area of comparative religion than in literary criticism. It is, however, notably represented in literary criticism by Maud Bodkin's *Archetypal Patterns in Poetry* (1934) and Joseph Campbell's *Hero with a Thousand Faces* (1949). See ARCHETYPE.

Juvenalia. Youthful literary products: for instance, Dryden's "Upon the Death of Lord Hastings," Pope's *Pastorals*, Jane Austen's *Love and Freindship* and *Volume the First*, Byron's *Hours of Idleness*, the Brontës' *Angria* and *Glondal Chronicle*, Poe's *Tamerlane and Other Poems*.

Juvenalian Satire. Biting SATIRE, harshly critical and contemptuous of human folly, after the manner of the Roman satirist Juvenal (50?–after 127? A.D.). Juvenalian satire is contrasted with HORATIAN SATIRE.

K

Kabbala. See CABALA.

Kabuki. A popular stylized form of Japanese drama, with all-male companies impersonating the female roles, deriving from the formal NŌ DRAMA, with melodramatic folk and historic themes. The name means "singing and dancing," and emphasizes the spectacular in setting, costume, farce, acrobatics, and bloody crisis, with chalk-white faces and furious eyebrows. Originating in the mid-seventeenth century, it is now traditional, with national stars, especially among the female impersonators.

Kailyard School. The school of the cabbage patch, denoting the Scottish dialectical, down-to-earth fiction of the 1890s of Sir James Barrie, S. R. Crockett, and particularly of "Ian Maclaren" (John Watson), author of *Beside the Bonnie Briar Bush* (1894) and *The Days of Auld Lang Syne* (1895).

Keening. Irish wailing or lamentation for the dead. See CORONACH.

Kenning. A compound figurative metaphor, a circumlocution, in Old English and Old Norse poetry: *hronrād*, "whale-road," for the sea; *fugles wynn*, "bird's delight," for feather; *eardstapa*, "land-stepper," for wanderer or outcast.

Key Novel. A novel using fictitious names for real people. See RO-MAN À CLEF.

Kit-Cat Club. A Whig literary and political group, meeting at Christopher Cat's pub in Shire Lane, London, from about 1703 to 1733. Its more than 40 members generally supported the Protestant and Hanoverian succession and opposed Queen Anne's Tory ministry. Cat's mutton pies were called "kit-cats," after their creator, and from these, writes Addison in *Spectator* No. 9 (10 March 1711), the club took its name. Members included Addison; Steele; Congreve; Sir Robert Walpole; Marlborough (John Churchill); John Vanbrugh; Samuel Garth, who wrote the verses for their toasting glasses; Jacob Tonson, publisher, who served as secretary and built a gallery in his house at Barn Elms for club dinners; and Sir Godfrey Kneller, who painted portraits of many of the members to suit the low ceiling of Tonson's room at less than half-length, all 36 x 28 inches, which became known as the kit-cat size.

Knickerbocker Group. New York writers of the early nineteenth century who challenged the literary primacy of Boston. The name comes from Washington Irving's satirical spoof, *A History of New York* (1809), published under the pseudonymous Dutch name of Diedrich Knickerbocker. Irving, James Fenimore Cooper, and William Cullen Bryant were the most prominent of the group and represent its diversity. Others were Joseph Rodman Drake, Fitzgreene Halleck, John Howard Payne, Samuel Woodworth, George P. Morris, Bayard Taylor, and Clement Moore, author of "'Twas the Night Before Christmas" (1823). Lewis G. and Willis G. Clark edited *The Knickerbocker Magazine* (1833–1865), a monthly that published some of the works of these loosely associated New Yorkers.

Knittelvers. "Badly knit verse": DOGGEREL. A derogatory term used by seventeenth-century German classical poets for a verse form popular in fifteenth- and sixteenth-century Germany: ACCENTUAL VERSE in couplets, or rhymed pairs of lines, of four stresses per line. *Knittelvers* has been used both comically and seriously by later poets seeking a popular effect, including Goethe, Schiller, and Hauptmann. See CHRISTABEL METER.

Koran. The Moslem sacred text, a "reading" (Arabic *qur'an*) compiled and edited A.D. 632, after Mohammed's death, from God's revelations to him. It presents, in God's words, theology, moral teachings, and ceremonial instructions.

Künstlerroman. The "artist novel," a form of BILDUNGSROMAN ("formation novel"), *Erziehungsroman* ("education novel"), or *Entwicklungsgeschichte* ("development story")—a novel detailing an artist's awakening and development, as symbolizing all social and spiritual awakening. Goethe's *Wilhelm Meisters Lehrjahr* (1830) is primary. Three others are classic: Samuel Butler's *Way of All Flesh* (1903), James Joyce's *Portrait of the Artist as a Young Man* (1916), Hermann Hesse's *Demian* (1919; translated, 1923).

L

Lacuna (plural, **Lacunae**). A gap or HIATUS in a MANUSCRIPT or book.

Lake School. Wordsworth, Coleridge, and Southey. The EDINBURGH REVIEW contemptuously called these three poets "the lakers" and "The Lake School" (August 1817) because they lived in England's "Lake District" at the intersections of Cumberland, Westmorland, and Lancashire counties.

Lallans. Lowland Scots, the linguistic descendant of the Middle Ages's Northern English: the language of the ballads and of Burns and other colloquial Scottish writers. See SCOTTISH LITERATURE.

Lament. A grieving poem, an elegy, in Anglo-Saxon, or RENAISSANCE times. "Deor's Lament" (c. 980) records the actual grief of a scop, or court poet, at being displaced in his lord's hall. A number of fifteenth-century lyrics concerning the Virgin's grief over her Babe's future death, or her Son's actual death, are called the "Laments of the Virgin." The Scots poet William Dunbar wrote a famous "Lament for the Makaris" (1508), mourning how Death has devoured Chaucer and others and concluding each stanza with *Timor mortis conturbat me* ("Fear of death disturbs me"). Thomas Sackville's "Complaint of Buckingham" in *A Mirror for Magistrates* (1563) was considered a "lament." See COMPLAINT.

Lampoon. A satirical, personal ridicule in verse or prose. The term probably derives from the French *lampons*, "Let's guzzle," a refrain in seventeenth-century drinking songs.

Lancaster. See ROYAL HOUSES.

Laureate. See POET LAUREATE.

Lay (or **Lai**). (1) A ballad or related metrical ROMANCE originating with the BRETON LAY of French Brittany and retaining some of its Celtic magic and folklore. French poets adopted the stories in the twelfth century, first in octosyllabic couplets, then in TAIL-RHYME stanzas. Marie de France, patronized by the highly literate English court of Henry II (reigned 1154–1189) and his queen, Eleanor of Aquitaine, wrote the earliest collection of *Lais* (c. 1175), some of them dealing with Arthurian matter, most notably one concerning Sir Landeval and

258

his invisible fairy mistress, redone anonymously in English as *Sir Landeval* and expanded by Thomas of Chester as *Sir Launfal* (c. 1430). Other English metrical romances deriving from Breton lays are *Sir Orfeo* (about Orpheus and Eurydice), *Sir Gowther*, and Chaucer's *Franklin's Tale*, all fourteenth century. See ANGLO-NORMAN PERIOD. (2) A medieval French poem or song in one or more nine-line stanzas rhymed *aabaabaab*, continuing only the two rhymes throughout. The *a* lines have five syllables; the *b* lines, two. See VIRELAY. (3) Loosely, any BALLAD.

Legend. (1) A folk story concerning historical or reputedly historical figures, with less of the supernatural and more authenticity than MYTH. (2) An inscription, title, or explanatory caption to a coat of arms, map, or the like.

Legitimate Theater. Regular staged drama as distinct from street theater, COMMEDIA DELL'ARTE, puppet shows, and the like. The term originates with the Patent Theaters (see THEATERS) of the Restoration period (1660 onward).

Leitmotif. A repeated phrase, word, or theme running through and unifying a novel or play, like "tomorrow and tomorrow" and "time" in Faulkner's *Sound and the Fury;* "rain" in Hemingway's *Farewell to Arms;* or "God" in Margaret Drabble's *Realms of Gold*. Literary criticism has borrowed the term for the repeated musical phrases in Wagner's operas ("leading motif") that denote characters and themes as they recur.

Leonine Rhyme. Strictly, a disyllabic RHYME pairing the last word before the CAESURA with the end word of a hexameter or pentameter line in Latin: *Quot caelum **stellas**, tot habet tua Roma **puellas*** (Ovid, *Ars amat.* I.59). In classical Latin verse, this was probably only the accidence of grammar and meaning, not an intentional rhyme, as it became in a history of the Old Testament of uncertain date supposedly written by Leoninus or Leonius, a perhaps fictitious canon of St. Victor in Paris. The *Regimen Sanitas* or *Schola Salernitana* from the medical school of Salerno, Italy, of which Arnaldus de Villanova wrote one of the earliest versions in 1480, provides a memorable example: *Mingere cum bumbis, res est saluberrima lumbis* ("To urinate with booming sounds is a most healthful thing for the loins"). Swift incorporated this and annotated it in his "Strephon and Chloe" (1731). Another famous example is Bernard of Cluny's *De Contemptu Mundi* (1595). See INTERNAL RHYME.

Letterpress.   Anything printed from raised, inked type and cuts, as distinct from offset, photographic, and modern electronic methods of printing.

Letters.   (1) Literature in general (see BELLES-LETTRES). (2) Personal correspondence, like Chesterfield's famous letters to his son, or the collected correspondence of distinguished people like Pope, Byron, Carlyle, Stevenson, or Hemingway. The EPISTLE is a more formal letter intended at least partly for a public audience.

Lexicography.   The compilation of lexicons or dictionaries. The oldest known lexicon is *Homeric Words,* a Greek dictionary by Apollonius the Sophist in the reign of Augustus (27 B.C.–A.D. 14). See DICTIONARY.

Lexicon.   A word list, a vocabulary, a DICTIONARY. In linguistics, the term refers to the total morphemes (the smallest meaningful units) of a language. Sometimes the word *lexicon* is limited to dictionaries of Greek or Hebrew. See LEXICOGRAPHY.

Libretto.   "The little book" (Italian)—the text of an opera, operetta, cantata, or other musical drama.

Life in Letters.   A BIOGRAPHY made by presenting letters, or selections of letters, usually with commentary.

Light Opera.   (1) A comic and romantic OPERA. (2) An operetta, including spoken dialogue, slightly more serious than a MUSICAL COMEDY.

Light Verse.   Playful, witty, sophisticated short poems suave in meter and rhyme, though including parodic playfulness like that of the CLERIHEW and of Ogden Nash, and other forms like the LIMERICK, NONSENSE VERSE, VERS DE SOCIÉTÉ, and sometimes the EPIGRAM and OCCASIONAL VERSE. Many serious poets from Aristophanes through Shakespeare and on to T. S. Eliot have indulged in light verse.

Limerick.   One of the VERSE FORMS, used only for NONSENSE VERSE or LIGHT VERSE, in five lines, predominantly anapestic, (see METER), with a stress pattern 3/3/2/2/3 and rhyming *aabba:*

> The limerick's an art form complex,
> Whose contents run chiefly to sex;
>   It's famous for virgins
>   And masculine urgins
> And vulgar erotic effects.

Its origin is conjectural. One theory sees an old French form brought to the Irish town of Limerick by veterans returning from mercenary service in France about 1700. Some songs in William Congreve's *Way of the World* (1700) have a limerick-like beat. Congreve, the son of a British soldier, was educated in Ireland and visited his parents there during his productive years. Another congruent theory suggests that these oral folk poems, sometimes sung, gave their name to the form from a common refrain "Will you come up to Limerick?" Another theory sees them originating from the nursery rhymes collected by John Newbery as *Mother Goose's Melody; or Sonnets for the Cradle* (London, 1781).

They first saw print in *Anecdotes and Adventures of Fifteen Young Ladies* (1820), soon to be followed by *The History of Sixteen Wonderful Old Women* (1821) and then by *Anecdotes and Adventures of Fifteen Gentlemen* (c. 1822), perhaps written by the prolific light-verse writer, Richard Scrafton Sharpe. Edward Lear credited this last book as the inspiration for his *Book of Nonsense* (1846), which put the limerick into permanent circulation, with items like this:

> There was a fat man of Bombay,
> Who was smoking one very hot day,
>   A bird called a snipe
>   Flew away with his pipe,
> Which vexed the fat man from Bombay.

But most limericks since Lear take a witty turn in the last line. Traditionally, limericks in print have been much less bawdy than those in oral circulation, but Gershon Legman has collected and printed large numbers previously considered unprintable.

Linguistics. The empirical study and description of language, particularly as to its structures of sound and form, sometimes defined to include PHILOLOGY, the historical study of ancient languages and literatures. Structural linguistics originated with Ferdinand de Saussure (1857–1913) in a succession of three university courses at Geneva, Switzerland, in alternate years from 1906 to 1911, reconstructed by his students from notes as *Course in General Linguistics* (1961). Saussure rediscovered what John Locke had perceived in 1690 as the "arbitrary," or wholly accidental, connection between sounds and their meanings, each language having very different words for the same object. He distinguished *synchronic* from *diachronic* analysis—the study of a language at the present moment, considering the elements that appear together in time (synchronic), as opposed to an examination of the evolution of particles across the years, from past to present (diachronic). The new linguistics was to be synchronic, describing the structures of the present system and eschewing the past. Saussure also distinguished *signifieds*, the speaker's ideas, from the *signifiers*, the word-symbols expressing them. He distinguished *la langue* ("the language"), the total system of structures and vocabulary in a society's collective consciousness, from *la parole* ("the speaking"), a particular utterance. Language is speech, with writing a cumbersome and distorting representation of the real thing. In America, Franz Boas and Edward Sapir instituted structural linguistics in recording and studying American Indian languages, and Leonard Bloomfield's *Language* (1933) became the bedrock of structural methodology. Bloomfield banished "mentalism"—ideas and meaning—and embraced mechanics: "Mechanism is the necessary form of scientific discourse." Soon Benjamin Lee Whorf, a fire-insurance engineer and self-trained linguist, disagreed: "The very essence of linguistics is the quest for meaning." Whorf also believed what the German Wilhelm von Humboldt had suggested in the 1820s: that each language guides its culture to perceive the world differently. In 1957, Noam Chomsky challenged both Bloomfield's mechanism and Whorf's cultural relativism by proposing a universal structure underlying all languages, as the seventeenth-century Cartesian rationalists had assumed. His transformational-generative grammar applies the concept locally in seeing in each language also a deep structure, containing basic patterns and concepts, and the several surface structures, or actual sentences, generated and transformed from the deep concept. Linguists have moved into sociolinguistics, studying the idioms of social class, into SEMANTICS and SEMIOTICS to study the ways of meaning, and into the problems of teaching foreign languages and of bilingualism. See TRANSFORMATIONAL GRAMMAR.

References

Noam Chomsky, **Aspects of the Theory of Syntax** (1969); **Chomsky: Selected Readings** (1971).
Henry A. Gleason, **Introduction to Descriptive Linguistics** (rev. 1961).
John Lyons, **Introduction to Theoretical Linguistics** (1968).
Ferdinand de Saussure, **Course in General Linguistics** (tr. 1966).
John T. Waterman, **Perspectives in Linguistics** (2nd ed., 1971).
Benjamin Lee Whorf, **Language, Thought, and Reality** (1956).

Linked Rhyme.   A device from Welsh verse borrowed in English by Gerard Manley Hopkins. See RHYME.

Link Sonnet. See SPENSERIAN SONNET.

Litany. A prayer with phrases spoken or sung by a leader alternated with responses from congregation or choir. "The Litany" is a group of such prayers in the Book of Common Prayer. Poets have imitated the form, as with the two parts of Christopher Smart's *Jubilate Agno* (c. 1763).

Literal. According to the letter (of the alphabet): (1) The precise, plain meaning of a word or phrase in its simplest, original sense, considered apart from its sense as a METAPHOR or other figure of speech. Literal language is the opposite of FIGURATIVE LANGUAGE. (2) In TRANSLATION, a rendering as close as possible to the word-for-word plain sense of the original.

Literal Meaning. Words examined for what they say in their first or ordinary sense, without consideration of their metaphorical, suggestive sense. Literal language is opposed to FIGURATIVE LANGUAGE. In the Middle Ages, literal meaning was one of FOUR SENSES OF INTERPRETATION.

Literary Ballad. A sophisticated imitation of the traditional BALLAD.

Literary Club, The. See CLUB, THE.

Literature. Strictly, anything written. Therefore, the oral culture of a people—its FOLKLORE, FOLK SONGS, FOLK TALES, and so on—is not literature until it is written down. The movies are not literature except in their printed scripts. By the same strict meaning, business documents, legal papers, historical records, telephone books, and the like are all literature because they are written in letters of the alphabet, although they are not taught as literature in schools.

In contrast to this strict, literal meaning, literature has come to be equated with *creative writing* or works of the IMAGINATION: chiefly POETRY, prose FICTION, and DRAMA (categories that embrace much folklore, whether written down or not, and leave out business documents). But the ESSAY is also frequently imaginative, as are, sometimes, such utilitarian writings as the JOURNAL, histories, and religious and scientific treatises. In the effort to define the difference between literature and other writings, one consideration is widespread acceptance. Literature expresses the cultural identity of a people. Another consideration is time. Literature is writing that lasts. Still another consideration is aesthetic quality. Literature is writing regarded more highly than other writing. These three considerations do not always point to the same

works. See CRITICISM; HISTORY AS LITERATURE; POPULAR LITERA-
TURE.

Litotes.   A kind of IRONY: the assertion of something by the denial
of its opposite: "Not bad." "This is no small matter." "She was not
supremely happy." "He was not unmindful of it." It is characteristic
of Old English poetry: "He did not need the outcry of joined swords"
(of a dying warrior).

Littérateur.   A writer or critic or other person associated with literature. The term frequently carries a disparaging CONNOTATION: a po-
seur or DILETTANTE.

Little Magazine.   A MAGAZINE of small circulation, devoted to LIT-
ERATURE or the other arts. Since the rise of the mass circulation mag-
azine at the beginning of the twentieth century, the little magazine has
responded to the need for publishing outlets hospitable to AVANT
GARDE, untried, or less popular authors. The list of major writers who
have published significant work in little magazines is extensive, includ-
ing Sherwood Anderson, John Ashbery, Saul Bellow, T. S. Eliot,
Ralph Ellison, William Faulkner, Ernest Hemingway, James Joyce, D.
H. Lawrence, Joyce Carol Oates, Ezra Pound, Gertrude Stein, Wallace
Stevens, Dylan Thomas, William Carlos Williams, and Richard
Wright.

   Forerunners of the little magazine include the American transcen-
dentalist journal *THE DIAL* and *Savoy* (an English journal of the 1890s).
First and most influential in America in the twentieth century was Harriet Monroe's *Poetry: A Magazine of Verse*, founded in Chicago in 1912
and still continuing. Important little magazines between 1912 and
World War II include *The Little Review* (Chicago, San Francisco, New
York, Paris, 1914–1929), *The Egoist* (London, 1914–1919), *The Criterion* (London, 1922–1939), *The Fugitive* (Nashville, 1922–1925; see FU-
GITIVES), *Southwest Review* (1924–   ), *This Quarter* (Paris, Milan,
1925–1932), *New Masses* (1926–1948), *transition* (Paris, 1927–1938),
Prairie Schooner (1927–   ), and *The Partisan Review* (1933–   ).

   Since World War II, little magazines have proliferated, numbering
in the hundreds, supported by individuals, colleges, or universities on
small, or sometimes lavish, budgets. Some, long successful, or well
funded, have attained major status, rivaling the more established magazines of large circulation. Among those most important in recent decades are *Accent, Epoch, The Evergreen Review, The New American Review* (later *The American Review*), *Paris Review, The Sewanee Review*,

Triquarterly. A comprehensive listing of current titles is available in the *International Directory of Little Magazines and Small Presses.*

Reference

Elliott Anderson and Mary Kinzie, **The Little Magazine in America: A Documentary History** (1978).

Little Theater. Experimental theater for the production of noncommercial plays (new, experimental, or revivals) and the encouragement of actors, technicians, and playwrights. Little theater is generally a twentieth-century phenomenon, parallel to the development of the LITTLE MAGAZINE. In New York, Off-Broadway (and, later, Off-Off-Broadway) was founded to provide alternatives to the requirements of large, popular theater. Elsewhere, in smaller cities, little theaters have emphasized local or regional talent. Colleges and universities have been active supporters of the idea of little theater.

The flowering of American theater in the 1920s owed much to the success of little theaters. The Washington Square players, formed in New York in 1914, was transformed in 1919 into the extraordinarily successful Theatre Guild. The PROVINCETOWN PLAYERS began in Provincetown, Massachusetts, in 1916, producing Eugene O'Neill's *Bound East for Cardiff,* and soon moved to New York to work with the Greenwich Village Theatre.

Liturgical Drama. DRAMA arising from or developed in connection with church rites or services. The term is used especially for the European development of drama associated with the medieval Christian church. The *Quem quaeritis?* came first, a Latin dialogue chanted in connection with the Easter service. This and dramatic renderings of the Nativity scene led by the thirteenth century to full plays acted outside the church. Beginning with the Christ story, drama reached outward to the rest of the Bible, SAINTS' LIVES, and moral lessons in MYSTERY PLAY, MIRACLE PLAY, and MORALITY PLAY. See MEDIEVAL DRAMA.

Local Color Writing. Writing that emphasizes the *color,* or distinctive attributes, of a particular locality. SETTING is described as unique, CHARACTERS are representative of place, DIALECT is frequent, and PLOT is closely tied to local circumstances. All REALISM, of course, tends toward local color as it reaches for VERISIMILITUDE, but the term is usually reserved for works in which the color provides a major part of the interest; indeed, local color writing, in its singleminded pursuit of one area of truth, often violates other canons of realism, constructing stories too sentimental or coincidental to fit comfortably into the larger body of realism.

The term is most used in connection with American literature from 1870 to 1890, the so-called *local color movement*. William Dean Howells, first at the *Atlantic* and then at *Harper's*, fostered realism at the same time that American interest in the country's many regions was increasing as a result of the sectional division dramatized by the Civil War, the opening of the West, and the rapidly increasing contrast between urban and rural life. Important writers included Bret Harte (for California), George Washington Cable (Louisiana), Joe Chandler Harris (the old South), Sarah Orne Jewett (Maine), Mary Noailles Murfree (Tennessee), Kate Chopin (Louisiana), Mary E. Wilkins Freeman (Massachusetts and Vermont), and Hamlin Garland (the Middle Border: Minnesota, Wisconsin, Nebraska, the Dakotas). Too early to form a part of the movement, but leading in its direction, is the village humor of A. B. Longstreet (Georgia), Harriet Beecher Stowe (especially in *Oldtown Folks*, Massachusetts), and George Washington Harris (the old Southwest).

At its best, when not too singleminded, local color writing is more accurately described as *regional realism*. Its elements are found in many other American writers during and after the heyday of local color, most notably Mark Twain, Willa Cather, Sherwood Anderson, William Faulkner, John Steinbeck, Eudora Welty, John Cheever, and Flannery O'Connor. Earlier, before the rise of realism, local color was one of the ingredients forming a large part of the immediate and permanent attraction in the Waverley novels of Sir Walter Scott. Other countries, too, have their local colorists and regional realists: see COMMONWEALTH LITERATURE.

Locale.   The SETTING of a STORY or PLAY. The term generally denotes the simpler elements of time and place, as in a small town in Ohio around 1900.

Locution.   A word or phrase; a particular style of speech.

Logaoedic.   Literally, "prose song": any mixed METER.

Logical Positivism.   A modern philosophical movement based on scientific EMPIRICISM. Begun at the University of Vienna in the 1920s, in a group that included Rudolf Carnap, logical positivism was at its height as a movement from then until 1940. With Ludwig Wittgenstein, logical positivists considered the object of philosophy to be the logical clarification of thought, which they attempted to bring about by applying a methodical precision drawn from mathematics and the physical sciences. Considering philosophy to be analytical, rather than speculative, they turned away from metaphysics and morals toward an analysis of language and its relation to meaning.

Lollards. From Middle Dutch, literally, "mumblers"; a derisive term applied to the followers of John Wyclif (c. 1328–1384), the reformer behind the Wyclif Bible (1385), the first in English. Lollards preached against the abuses of the medieval church, setting up a standard of poverty and individual service as against wealth and hierarchical privilege, in a view of the English situation similar to that in *Piers Plowman*. Teaching that people could intrepret the Bible for themselves, in 1395 they presented a document to Parliament denying transubstantiation, condemning the church's use of images and the office of confession, opposing war as un-Christian, and declaring unnatural the celibacy and chastity of priests and nuns. Repression, including some burning at the stake, put an end to the movement after abortive rebellions in 1414 and 1431, but it remained underground to emerge again during the English Reformation.

Long Meter. A STANZA expanding the second and fourth lines of COMMON METER to make four lines of iambic tetrameter (see METER), keeping the common meter rhyme schemes, *abcb* or *abab*. Long meter (abbreviated L.M. in hymn books) is found in many ballads, hymns, and other poems. The following stanza, from the folk song "Waly, Waly," shows the form:

> I leant my back upon an oak,
>   I thought it was a trusty tree;
> But first it bent, and then it broke,
>   Just as my love proved false to me.

Other examples include Donne's "Valediction: Forbidding Mourning." Blake's "London," and Hardy's "Channel Firing."

Long Take. In motion pictures, a single shot or camera run that is held for an extended period before the CUT to the next shot.

Loose and Periodic Sentences. Two types of sentences. A *loose sentence* is one that continues in phrases and clauses beyond the point where it is grammatically complete, the point where a period may be placed, one that continues to add explanatory or qualifying material, like this one. A sentence grammatically incomplete until it reaches or comes close to the period is a *periodic sentence*. As an extreme example, in Melville's *Moby-Dick,* in Chapter 42, "The Whiteness of the Whale," the entire third paragraph is one long periodic sentence.

Lost Generation.   Gertrude Stein's phrase for the younger expatriates in Paris in the early 1920s, their lives disrupted and their values shaken as a result of World War I and its aftermath. "You are all a lost generation," she said to Ernest Hemingway, who used the comment as an epigraph for *The Sun Also Rises* (1926).

Reference

Malcolm Cowley, **A Second Flowering: Works and Days of the Lost Generation** (1973).

Low Comedy.   Humor at the other end of the comedic scale from HIGH COMEDY, with the immediate appeal of SLAPSTICK, buffoonery, and BURLESQUE. More physical than intellectual, and sometimes coarse or violent, it appeared at least as early as the plays of Aristophanes, turned up in the work of poets like Chaucer, served sometimes for COMIC RELIEF in tragedies such as Shakespeare's, and has remained a staple of the movies since the earliest films of Charlie Chaplin.

Lower Criticism.   See HIGHER CRITICISM.

Low Mimetic.   A term applied to literature in which the characters possess a power and authority similar to that of the average reader. Examples include most works of COMEDY and realistic FICTION. Characters with more power than the reader, like kings and princes, belong to the HIGH MIMETIC mode. Characters with less power, observed from a detached, superior position by author and reader, belong to an IRONIC MODE characteristic of much modern fiction. See MIMESIS.

Lydian Mode.   Originally a Greek musical mode, soft and gentle, sometimes with sensuous or voluptuous connotations, contrasted to the simple and solemn DORIAN MODE. Milton's *L'Allegro* includes a request to "Lap me in soft Lydian airs, / Married to immortal verse."

Lyric.   A poem, brief and discontinuous, emphasizing sound and pictorial imagery rather than narrative or dramatic movement. Lyrical poetry began in ancient Greece in connection with music, as poetry sung, for the most part, to the accompaniment of a lyre. The earliest Greek poets were markedly individualized writers (Anacreon, Sappho, Archilocus), but the lyrical cannot be identified with the subjective. Many long continuous poems are subjective (Wordsworth's *Prelude*, Byron's *Childe Harold*), and many lyrics are connected with public occasions, such as the Pindaric ODE and the Old Testament Psalms. The lyric is, rather, a discontinuous poem, in contrast to the continuous epic and dramatic forms. In the lyric we can, so to speak, hear the end in the beginning; the rhythm revolves around a center instead of thrusting forward in a narrative linear motion. In contrast to *epos*, in which the poet, or rhapsode, faces an audience directly, or drama, in which the poet is concealed behind the production, the lyric is a GENRE in which the audience is concealed from the poet. That is, lyric poets normally pretend to be talking to themselves, to a Muse, to a god, to another person not the reader; or else, as in the Psalms, they represent the collective "I" of the group.

The study of literature makes us aware of its position between music, the art of the ear alone, and the pictorial arts, which address the eye alone. The lyric emphasizes the musical and pictorial contexts of words most clearly. Apart from the great number of lyrics that can be or have been set to music, lyric continually relapses from sense into sound: refrains full of "fa la" or "hey nonny nonny," and elaborate schematic arrangements of sound in the VILLANELLE, TRIOLET, BAL-LADE, and RONDEAU. On the other side are lyrics focused on a particular image, as with Keats's Grecian urn or Hopkins's windhover. In early Greece much lyrical poetry was "melic," or sung to music; much of it, too, was in the epitaph convention frequent in the *Greek Anthology*, where we are suddenly confronted by a poem thought of as inscribed on a visible object. As late as Mallarmé we have lyrics thought of as a "Toast Funèbre," or an epitaph on a tomb, and Rimbaud's "Illuminations" represent not a psychological but a strictly pictorial metaphor.

This suggests that lyric is the genre of arrested movement, in contrast to the narrative genres of linear progress. If this is true, it would account for the characteristic brevity of the lyric and for its frequent sense of the inadequacy of purely verbal elements of communication. Even when brief, a lyric is usually divided up still further into stanzas, and the word "stanza" suggests "room," a part of something else that is nonetheless complete in itself. The rhetorical device known as imitative harmony, or making the sound, in Pope's phrase, an echo to the sense, is most common in lyric, where it helps to suggest a self-contained world withdrawn from that of the ordinary external environment.

Lyric was for long generally regarded as a relatively minor form of poetry, better adapted to lesser poets than epic or drama. As a historical fact, many lyrical poets have reached the height of their powers in early life, whereas drama, for example, has never been a genre for infant prodigies. But in the nineteenth century Poe's essay *The Poetic Principle* reacted against this and set forth the thesis that continuous poems were, strictly speaking, fakes, being moments of genuine lyrical emotion strung together with versified prose. This essay had a profound influence on the school of French poetry that runs from Baudelaire to Valéry, and to such English adherents of it as Eliot and Pound. Many of these developed techniques of "fragmentation," or presenting only vivid flashes of poetic experience, leaving it up to the reader to make the connections. Among the critical axioms that sprang from this movement are Eliot's conception of "unified sensibility," Mallarmé's dictum that poets should not name or describe objects but deal only with their effect on the poet; Joyce's conception of "epiphany," or vivid flash from actual experience that illuminates the work of imagination as well; and Hopkins's conception of "inscape" and "instress," which are intuitions of the inwardness or "this-ness" of something, and hence separate it from its surroundings. See DRAMA; EPIC.

M

Mabinogion. Welsh for "youthful careers": the name given in the nineteenth century by Lady Charlotte Guest (later Schreiber) to her translations of old Welsh tales, a name used also by later translators. *The Mabinogion* includes the *Four Branches of the Mabinogi,* hero tales of battle and the supernatural; the ARTHURIAN LEGEND *Culhwch and Olwen* (c. 1100); *Rhonabwy's Dream* (twelfth or thirteenth century), a parodic or satiric Arthurian story; *Lludd and Llefelys,* a dragon story; and three romances similar to three of Crètien de Troyes, drawing on the same sources or traditions (see ROMANCE). Lady Guest's source was the *Red Book of Hergest* (c. 1375–1425). The *White Book of Rhydderch* (c. 1300–1325), discovered later, includes some older and better versions. Composite translations have been made by T. P. Ellis and J. Lloyd (2 vols., 1929) and Gwyn Jones and Thomas Jones (1949). See WELSH LITERATURE.

Macaronic Verse. (1) Strictly, verse mixing words in a writer's native language with endings, phrases, and syntax of another language, usually Latin or Greek, creating a comic or burlesque effect. Such verse was popular in RENAISSANCE Italy, France, and Germany, but not so common in England. A good example, from seventeenth-century Scotland, is *Polemo-Middinia inter Vitarvam et Nebernam,* a lively dispute between two communities over a right of way, sometimes attributed to William Drummond of Hawthornden. (2) Loosely, any verse mingling two or more languages. Among many examples in English are William Dunbar's "Lament for the Makaris" (1508) and Byron's "Maid of Athens" (1812).

Machinery. (1) Literally, mechanical contrivances for dramatic effect used in the production of a play. (2) In a common figurative sense, a supernatural agent in a play or poem. In the preface to *The Rape of the Lock,* Pope defined *machinery* as "a term invented by the critics to signify that part which the deities, angels or demons are made to act in a poem." See *DEUS EX MACHINA*.

Macron. In SCANSION, a mark, ¯, set above a syllable to indicate it is long or stressed. A short or unstresed syllable is indicated by a BREVE, ˘.

Madrigal.   A song form originating in Italy in the fourteenth century. Most madrigals are polyphonic, using from two to five voices, but some are for solo singing. The verbal text characteristically employs two to four identical STROPHES (originally of three lines each), followed by a rhyming COUPLET. Content is PASTORAL, concerning nature and love. Madrigals were popular in England in the ELIZABETHAN PERIOD.

Magazine.   Since the eighteenth century, a term for a PERIODICAL containing miscellaneous ARTICLES for the general reader. The word comes from Arabic via Old French and means, literally, "storehouse."

Magnum Opus (plural, *Magna Opera*).   Latin for "great work": a writer's *magnum opus* is his or her most important work.

Malapropism.   A ludicrous misuse of words. From Latin roots meaning "ill-suited to the purpose," the term derives from Mrs. Malaprop, in Sheridan's *Rivals* (1775), whose malapropisms include "progeny of learning," "reprehend the true meaning," "derangement of epitaphs," and "illiterate . . . him from your memory."

Malediction.   A CURSE.

Manichaeism (or **Manichaeanism**)   The religion founded by Mani (c. 216–c. 276), a Persian who called himself an Apostle of Christ and claimed Buddha, Zoroaster, Hermes, and Plato as predecessors. Drawing on Zoroastrianism and GNOSTICISM as well as Christianity, Mani preached a dualistic religion, with God, light, and spiritualism eternally opposed to Satan, darkness, and materialism. According to Manichaeism, humans who are not part of the elect class are trapped in the misery of darkness and the material world, from which they must seek to extricate themselves by enlightened renunciation, hoping to be reborn, through metempsychosis, among the elect. St. Augustine described his conversion from Manichaeism in his *Confessions*. Manichaeism ceased to be important in the West as early as the sixth century, but survived in the East until the thirteenth. In the Middle Ages, any belief perceived as a dualist heresy was termed Manichaean. See SATANISM.

Mannerism, Mannerist.   (1) In architecture and painting, a style elongating and distorting human figures and spaces, deliberately confusing scale and perspective, as in the work of El Greco, Tintoretto, and others. Originating in Italy, it flourished from about 1520 to 1600, when it gave way to the BAROQUE. In the late eighteenth century, Henry Fuseli (1741–1825) brought the mannerist style to England from his studies in Italy. His eerie and distorted paintings, especially his famous *Nightmare* (1782), greatly influenced his friend William Blake. Some seventeenth-century metaphysical poetry, like Blake's, is sometimes called mannerist. (2) Literary or artistic affectation; a stylistic quality produced by excessive peculiar, ornamental, or ingenious devices. See EUPHUISM.

Manners. Social behavior. In usages like COMEDY OF MANNERS and NOVEL OF MANNERS, the term suggests an examination of the behavior, morals, and values of a particular time, place, or social class. A writer concerned with manners may treat the surface of life, documenting passing social trivia, but may also explore more deeply, revealing serious human choices rooted in the characteristics of an age. Jane Austen and Henry James managed to do both.

Manuscript. Literally, "written by hand": any handwritten document, as, for example, a letter or diary. In this strict sense, a *manuscript* is also a handwritten work submitted for publication, but in modern practice the term is not thus limited, being used as a synonym for *typescript*, or typed copy of a literary work.

Manuscript, Medieval. A MANUSCRIPT from the Middle Ages. Prior to the fifteenth century, all European literature was recorded in manuscript. Until paper began to appear in the eleventh century, manuscripts were of parchment, with vellum (from calfskin) the finest kind. Because of the value of the material, both sides were used. Enormous effort was frequently employed in coloring elaborate illustrations, or *illuminations*. Monasteries were major centers of learning, with most manuscript copying or illumination done by monks or professional scribes. Manuscript books were formed by binding the manuscript pages in covers of wood and leather, sometimes elegantly tooled and studded with jewels. Despite the later destruction or loss of many medieval manuscripts, thousands still exist, in numerous libraries. See PALIMPSEST.

Märchen. German for a FAIRY TALE or FOLK TALE.

Marginalia. Commentary, references, or other material written by a reader in the margins of a MANUSCRIPT or book.

Marinism. An ornate, BAROQUE poetic style named after the Italian poet Giambattista Marino (1569–1625). His most famous work is *L'Adone,* an elaborately metaphoric poem of over 40,000 lines rambling through classical mythology in pursuit of the story of Venus and

Adonis, with many digressions and catalogs. A skilled, mellifluous poet, he was also known for his sensual love lyrics. In Great Britain, he influenced, among others, William Drummond of Hawthornden, Thomas Carew, and Richard Crashaw. See EUPHUISM; GONGORISM; MANNERISM; ROCOCO.

Marprelate Controversy. An English religious controversy of the late sixteenth century. "Martin Marprelate" was the pseudonym used in 1588 and 1589 by the Puritan author or authors of several satiric pamphlets issued in defiance of censorship regulations and attacking the authority of the church of England hierarchy under Archbishop John Whitgift. Although much is known of the circumstances under which the pamphlets were printed and distributed, Martin Marprelate's true identity remains hidden.

Martyria. "Witnessing." The confirmation of something from experience:

> I have seen thousands standing with their rice bowls.
> Many times I have found the parking lot completely empty.

Marxism. The economic and political philosophy of Karl Marx (1818–1883) and Friedrich Engels (1820–1895) and their followers. The classic texts are *The Communist Manifesto* (1848), by Marx and Engels, and Marx's *Kapital* (1867). Modern Communism is derived from Marxism, and much socialist thought is related to it. *Dialectical materialism* is the name given to its system of logical analysis.

According to Marxism, history is a class struggle activated by economic forces. The class that controls production controls society, but the ultimate value of goods derives from labor. The ideal society would be classless, with the production and consumption of wealth shared in accordance with ability and need. Marxism has proven an important influence on some writers and critics—within Russia, but also in England and the United States, particularly in the 1930s. See DIALECTIC.

Marxist Criticism. A consideration of literature from the perspective of MARXISM. See CRITICISM.

Masculine Caesura. A CAESURA (‖) following a stressed syllable at the end of a metrical foot. Three are in this line:

˘ ‾ ‖ ˘ ‾ ‖ ˘‾ ‖ ‾ ˘ ˘ ‾
Came loud— ‖ and hark, ‖ again: ‖ loud as | before. |

See FEMININE CAESURA.

Masculine Ending. The usual iambic ending, on the accented foot: ⌣ — . See FEMININE ENDING; METER.

Masculine Rhyme. RHYME on the last syllable of a line, the most common rhyme in English. See FEMININE RHYME; TRIPLE RHYME.

Masked Comedy. A COMEDY in which characters wear characterizing masks, deriving from the COMMEDIA DELL'ARTE.

Masque. An allegorical, poetic, and musical dramatic spectacle popular in the English courts and mansions of the sixteenth and early seventeenth centuries. It evolved from the folk MUMMING with elements from civic and chivalric spectacles and from religious drama. Henry VIII's *Epiphany* spectacle, in which he himself took part (1512), is credited as the first masque. The masque reached its heights in the reigns of James I (1603–1625) and Charles I (1625–1649) through the collaborative talents of Ben Jonson and Inigo Jones, court architect, who contrived elaborate settings and MACHINERY.

Figures from mythology, history, and romance mingled in a pastoral fantasy with fairies, fauns, satyrs, and witches, as masked amateurs from the court (including kings and queens) participated in dances and scenes. Jonson emphasized a thread of meaningful drama as against the spectacle favored by Samuel Daniel and Inigo Jones. Masques were featured at weddings, coronations, entertainments at the INNS OF COURT, and other occasions.

Milton's *Comus* (1634) culminated the masque. The masque influenced Spenser to include a procession of the Seven Deadly Sins and a masque of Cupid in his *Faerie Queen* (I.iv; III.xii). Many dramatists, also writing masques, were influenced. George Peele's *Arraignment of Paris* (c. 1581), a fully dramatized pastoral masque celebrating Queen Elizabeth's beauty, was presented to her in splendor. Shakespeare's *Tempest* includes a masque of Ceres to celebrate the engagement of Ferdinand and Miranda.

Materialism. In philosophy, an emphasis upon the material world as the ultimate reality, with no truth or knowledge thought to exist apart from it. Its opposite is IDEALISM. In English literature, Thomas Hobbes (1588–1679) was an early materialist. In the nineteenth century, NATURALISM emerged as an especially materialistic form of REALISM.

Matin. A morning song, rising with the birds. The matin is the service celebrating the first, or "morning," of the seven canonical hours, technically at midnight, sometimes at dawn.

Maxim. A pithy rule (from Latin *propositio maxima,* "greatest proposition"): for instance, "Neither a borrower nor a lender be." See APHORISM; PROVERB.

Meaning. Signification; import. Medieval scholastics saw four levels: (1) *historical* (literal), (2) *allegorical* (figurative), (3) *tropological* (moral), and (4) *anagogical* (mystical); I. A. Richards (*The Meaning of Meaning,* 1923), also noted four kinds: (1) *sense,* the denotative fact; (2) *feeling,* the writer's attitude toward the fact; (3) *tone,* the writer's attitude toward the audience; and (4) the writer's *intention,* conscious or unconscious, to convey *feeling* and *tone.* Semantically, meaning consists of DENOTATION and CONNOTATION. See FOUR SENSES OF INTERPRETATION; POLYSEMOUS MEANING.

Measure. METER, as in *common measure* or *long measure* (see COMMON METER and LONG METER). Musical prosodists count *measure* from one accented syllable to the next, as in music from bar to bar.

Medieval Drama. The drama of the Middle Ages. Within this period in Europe, drama developed from primitive forms into a complex tradition that helped shape the works of Shakespeare and other RENAISSANCE playwrights. For several hundred years after the fall of Rome in the fifth century, the great classical tradition, debased in the decadent period of the Roman Empire, was forgotten. Drama existed in pagan rituals and seasonal celebrations, in revels, minstrelsy, and mime, but little is known of these forms beyond what can be inferred from later records. Church ritual kept alive a kind of incipient drama, and from this and folk tradition the medieval drama arose.

By the tenth century, church ritual had added the crucial ingredient of role playing in the *Quem quaeritis?,* a TROPE for Easter. In this small play, the Marys and an angel exchange in Latin at the tomb of Jesus a simple, chanted dialogue, the essence of which is: "Whom do you seek?" "Jesus of Nazareth, who was crucified." "He is not here. He is risen." From this and the Nativity scene, for Christmas, came longer tropes and eventually full plays. By the end of the thirteenth century, they were acted outside the church, where they absorbed some of the characteristics of folk and seasonal celebrations dating from pagan times.

One of the most important forms of medieval drama was the MIRACLE PLAY, a dramatization of religious history as found in the Bible and the lives of saints (the term MYSTERY PLAY has been used, especially by French critics, for Bible stories, with the term *miracle play* then reserved for SAINTS' LIVES). By the fourteenth century, miracle plays were being performed in the vernacular by lay actors in elaborate productions that ran through entire cycles, dramatizing the Bible from the Creation to the Last Judgment, and centering on the essentials of the Christ story: the Nativity, Passion, and Resurrection. Frequently, these cycles were presented in Great Britain as pageants in connection with the feast of Corpus Christi, in May or June. Many have not survived, and although miracle plays were acted in Ireland and Scotland as well as in England, our principal information concerns the Chester, York, and Wakefield (or Towneley) cycles. Numbering as many as 48 in the York cycle, these plays were presented on pageant wagons drawn about the city, with each play acted before a series of different audiences stationed at a number of stops at church, inn, or market. A wagon could be very elaborate, with a changing room, an acting area, a painted dragon's head for a "hell mouth," and a balcony for heaven. The actors appeared in masks, wigs, costumes, and painted faces, and they were supported by stage MACHINERY and sound effects, including gunpowder explosions to herald Judgment Day. Typically, each pageant seems to have become the responsibility of a particular craft guild, as, at York, the *Fall of Man* was presented by the coopers and the *Last Supper* by the bakers. In some such fashion as this, with greater or less elaboration, the cycle plays continued in performance at least until the late sixteenth century. As time passed, they developed by a folk process that interpreted the Bible stories in a homely idiom, frequently adding humorous or satiric touches drawn from the secular dramatic tradition. Only a few seem to be by the same hand, notably those of the anonymous Wakefield Master, probably of the early fifteenth century. His realism, humor, accomplished versification, and occasional irreverence may be observed especially in *Noah* and in the most famous English miracle play, *The Second Shepherds' Play*.

The MORALITY PLAY developed later, originating toward the end of the fourteenth century and flourishing in the fifteenth and sixteenth. Whereas miracle plays centered on God's plan as revealed in the Bible and through the lives of saints, morality plays took as their theme the human search for salvation. Generally peopled by abstractions such as Vice, Death, Dame Sensuality, the SEVEN DEADLY SINS, or the SEVEN CARDINAL VIRTUES, they presented dramatic allegories of the journey from youth to age or the strife between Good and Evil for possession of the human soul. Of these, an especially elaborate example is *The Castle of Perseverance*, an early fifteenth-century play of 3650 lines and 34 characters. Its manuscript includes a plan for staging in a complex outdoor arena, surrounded by a moat, with spectators on all sides. Better known is the frequently reprinted *Everyman* (c. 1500), a journey in the face of Death, with Everyman assisted to his just end by Good Deeds. In Scotland, David Lyndsay's *Satire of the Three Estates* (1540) carried on the morality play tradition, also apparent in the procession of the Seven Deadly Sins in Marlowe's *Dr. Faustus* (c. 1588).

The secular drama of the Middle Ages is mostly lost. In England, two brief scenes survive from a late thirteenth-century INTERLUDE called *Cleric and Maiden*. Robin Hood existed in plays as well as ballads. The SWORD DANCE and mummer's plays (see MUMMING) recorded later have early origins. Court jesters, jugglers, minstrels, and common people at spring and harvest festivals expressed themselves in dramatic fashion both spontaneous and traditional. See DRAMA; FOLK DRAMA; LITURGICAL DRAMA.

References

E. K. Chambers, **The Medieval Stage** (1903).
Hardin Craig. **English Religious Drama of the Middle Ages** (1955).
Arnold Williams, **The Drama of Medieval England** (1961).

Medieval Romance.   Typically, a long, fictional narrative, in verse or prose (but usually in verse), intended primarily for entertainment. It differs from the BALLAD in length and, often, in having more complicated content and technique; from MEDIEVAL DRAMA in using narration and emphasizing secular as opposed to religious subjects; from the CHRONICLE in presenting a looser treatment of history and relying more on legend and folklore. Unlike the SAINTS' LIVES, sermons, and religious meditations of the Middle Ages, it displays no considerable interest in church doctrine or moral teaching. It lacks the earthy humor of the FABLIAU. An important ancestor of the NOVEL, the romance was the response of the Middle Ages to the human desire for a substantial imaginative tale, well told. Later, Spenser's *Faerie Queene* captured many of its qualities for the RENAISSANCE. *Don Quixote* began as a parody of romances, but did not put an end to them, as they continued to be popular, often in debased form, into the seventeenth and eighteenth centuries.

The surviving medieval romances of the twelfth through fifteenth centuries depict a chivalric age of idealized loyalties, knight to lord, and lover to lady. Quests are important, with the archetypal quest the search for the Holy Grail—or, symbolically, the search for ideal human and spiritual relationships. The world of the romances is partly Christian, partly pagan, heavy with folk customs and beliefs. Magic and the supernatural are common, and the settings, seldom effectively localized, are in some remote castle, field, or wood, perhaps in another country or an ancient time. Women play central roles. Love is an important theme. Structure is episodic, with much borrowing of episodes and motifs from one tale to another, from one language to another, and sometimes with attribution of an old event to a new set of characters. As in other medieval genres, tales are seldom original with the writer, but are drawn from the common stock of literary and folk tradition. In the best romances, literary merit results from an inspired combination of traditional materials and individual narrative skill.

The medieval romances fall traditionally into four major categories, the first three generally European and the fourth more specifically English: Matter of Antiquity, Matter of France, Matter of Britain, and Matter of England. Besides these, it is convenient to speak of two minor categories: The BRETON LAY and Miscellaneous Romances.

The Matter of Antiquity (sometimes called Matter of Rome) designates the subject matter of romances that perpetuated in the Middle Ages in Europe the stories of ancient Greece and Rome. Most important were tales of Alexander the Great, the Trojan War, Thebes, and Aeneas. For these romances, unlike most of the others, earlier written sources were important, although in medieval telling the stories frequently reflect the influence of medieval thought or tradition. Chaucer's *Knight's Tale* and *Troilus and Criseyde* are examples. The Matter of France consists primarily of stories found in the CHANSON DE GESTE. The Matter of Britain, by far the most important romance category, includes important sources of the ARTHURIAN LEGEND and other stories of Celtic origin. Their earliest sources are Celtic folklore, from Ireland, Wales, North Britain, and Cornwall, but they were widely known elsewhere in Europe by the twelfth century, when the French writer Chrétien de Troyes gave them forms influential on many later writers. His five Arthurian romances include *Yvain: The Knight of the Lion* and the unfinished *Conte del Graal* (or *Perceval*), the story of the Holy Grail. In Germany in the thirteenth century, Wolfram von Eschenbach's *Parzifal* and Gottfried von Strassburg's *Tristan* were powerful renditions, later inspiring Richard Wagner. In England, the two great Arthurian works are *Sir Gawain and the Green Knight*, a fourteenth-century anonymous poem equal to the best of Chaucer, but in a dialect much more difficult for most modern readers, and Thomas Malory's prose *Morte Darthur*, the fifteenth-century work that gave the

Arthurian legends their most complete and enduring form. The Matter of England is distinguished from the Matter of Britain by its later, non-Celtic origin. *King Horn* and *Havelock the Dane* are good thirteenth-century examples. Breton lays are short romances, often dwelling on love and magic, such as the Middle English *Sir Orfeo*. Finally, some Miscellaneous Romances fit into no convenient category. Examples from England are *Floris and Blancheflour*, a tale of two lovers separated; *Amis and Amiloun*, of male friendship; and *The Squire of Low Degree*, a late (fifteenth century) story of a squire in love with a king's daughter. In Scotland, John Barbour's *Bruce* (1376) celebrated the deeds of a national hero in romance form. See METRICAL ROMANCE; MIDDLE ENGLISH LITERATURE; ROMANCE.

References

Walter H. French and C. B. Hale, eds., **Middle English Metrical Romances** (1930).
Eugene Vinaver, **The Rise of Romance** (1971).
John Stevens, **Medieval Romance: Themes and Approaches** (1973).

Meditative Poetry.   METAPHYSICAL POETRY of the sixteenth and seventeenth centuries that expresses religious meditation. Ignatius Loyola's *Spiritual Exercises* (1548) had become a basic manual for meditation, followed by others such as Edward Dawson's *Practical Method of Meditation* (1614). Meditative poetry reflects those methods and moments of religious experience in "an interior drama," as Louis L. Martz describes it, "in which a man projects a self upon a mental stage, and there comes to understand that self in the light of a divine presence" (*The Poetry of Meditation*, 1954). Edward Taylor, colonial America's leading poet, wrote some two hundred "Spiritual Meditations" from 1682 to 1725, which he referred to as "Preparatory Meditations Before My Approach to the Lord's Supper." In England, Robert Southwell (1561–1595), John Donne (1572–1631), George Herbert (1593–1633), Richard Crashaw (c. 1612–1649), Henry Vaughan (c. 1622–1695), and Thomas Traherne (1637–1674) wrote significant meditative poetry.

Meiosis.   A kind of ironic understatement. It is the technique of making big things seem trifles by substituting a lighter word for ironic effect, as when in *Romeo and Juliet* Mercutio, knowing himself mortally wounded, replies to Benvolio's belief that the wound can't be that bad, "Ay, ay, *a scratch, a scratch* . . . 'tis not so deep as a well, nor so wide as a church door; but *'tis enough, 'twill serve*." See IRONY.

Melic Poetry. Greek POETRY intended for singing to lyre or flute. Melic poetry is essentially the LYRIC poetry of the seventh to fifth centuries B.C., including the works of Sappho and Pindar. The Greek ELEGY and EPIC were not melic; the HYMN, the PAEAN, and the EPITHALAMIUM were.

Meliorism. The belief that society improves innately, especially with conscious assistance, however humble and minute. George Eliot professes the faith at the end of *Middlemarch* (1872): ". . . the growing good of the world is partly dependent on unhistoric acts; and that things are not so ill with you and me as they might have been, is half owing to the number who lived faithfully a hidden life, and rest in unvisited tombs." In his "Apology," *Late Lyrics and Earlier* (1922), Thomas Hardy puts the faith more bleakly: "Whether the human and kindred animal races survive till exhaustion or destruction of the globe . . . , pain to all upon it, tongued or dumb, shall be kept down to a minimum by loving-kindness, operating through scientific knowledge, and actuated by the modicum of free will conjecturally possessed by organic life when the necessitating forces . . . happen to be in equilibrium, which may or may not be often."

Melodrama. A play with dire ingredients—the mortgage foreclosed, the daughter tied to the railroad tracks—but with happy ending: emotion indulged for romantic tremors with no tragic pity and terror. See SENTIMENTALISM. The term originated in the early nineteenth century from the French *melodrame*, "musical drama" (from Greek *melos*, song), for "melodramatic" plays with songs and musical accompaniment with conventional conflicts of good and bad, and happy endings.

Robert Heilman differentiates melodrama from tragedy not by its happy ending but by its external disasters as against the internal conflicts of tragedy. Thus, some authentic tragedies, like George Lillo's *London Merchant* (1731), are trivial, and are called "melodramatic," because unconvincingly portrayed. Some melodramas, like *Richard III*, convincingly convey tragic emotion. Tragedy, Heilman argues, derives from the divided self, the good person torn by a personal tragic flaw, true values clashing. Melodrama results from single-minded commitment, however admirable, conflicting with outer forces.

Reference

Robert Bechtold Heilman, **Tragedy and Melodrama: Versions of Experience** (1968).

Memento Mori. Latin for "Remember [that you have] to die"—any reminder of that fact, particularly a ring or other jewelry featuring skulls and bones, to keep medieval and Renaissance Christians properly humble and promptly confessed of their sins. Mary Queen of Scots had a pendant gold watch in the shape of a coffin.

Memoirs. Personal recollections of significant events and personages. The focus on public matters distinguishes memoirs from the more private AUTOBIOGRAPHY.

Menippean Satire. SATIRE on pedants, bigots, rapacious professional people, and other persons or institutions perceiving the world from a single framework or acting habitually from an occupational rather than a social orientation. The focus is on intellectual limitations and mental attitudes. Typical ingredients include a rambling narrative (or, in short forms, a DIALOGUE or COLLOQUY); unusual settings; displays of erudition; and long DIGRESSIONS. Menippean satire originated with Menippus (third century B.C.), and is sometimes called *Varronian satire* after his follower Varro. Examples in English include Burton's *Anatomy of Melancholy*, Swift's *Gulliver's Travels*, and Lewis Carroll's *Alice* books. See ANATOMY.

Mesostich. An ACROSTIC using the middle letter of each line.

Meta-. A prefix in modern criticism designating something "beyond" or of new and higher type, especially an analysis of theories, methods, and assumptions. See METACRITICISM.

Metabasis. "Transition"; a brief reminder to the audience of where they are, where they have been, and where they are going:

> We have just seen some of radiation's immediate effects; now let us consider the long-term effects.

Metacriticism. "CRITICISM beyond criticism"—criticism of critical assumptions, methods, theories, or principles.

Metafiction. FICTION that plays with the nature and process of fiction, as in John Barth's "Lost in the Funhouse" and his novels; John Fowles's *French Lieutenant's Woman;* Doris Lessing's *Golden Notebook;* Kurt Vonnegut's novels; and, to a lesser degree, several of Margaret Drabble's novels. See META-; POST-MODERN PERIOD.

Metaphor. Greek for "transfer" (*meta* and *trans* meaning "across"; *phor* and *fer* meaning "carry"): to carry something across. Hence a metaphor treats something as if it were something else. Money becomes a *nest egg;* a person who fails, a *washout;* a sandwich, a *submarine.* I. A. Richards describes this metaphorical transfer as *tenor* and *vehicle,* the general idea and its pictorial image. Shakespeare wrote:

> That time of year thou mayst in me behold
> When yellow leaves, or none, or few, do hang
> Upon those boughs which shake against the cold. . . .

The *tenor* is the loneliness and loss of age. The *vehicle* is a tree (or trees) in autumn. A metaphor implies a comparison. If Shakespeare had written "I am like a tree losing its leaves," he would have stated the comparison and made a SIMILE.

Metaphor seems to work at four levels, each with a different force. Suppose we write, "He swelled and displayed his finery." We have cast a man in the image of a peacock to make his appearance and personality vivid. We have chosen one of the four ways to make our metaphor:

1. Simile:	He was *like* a peacock.
	He displayed himself *like* a peacock.
	He strutted *as if* he were a peacock.
2. Plain metaphor:	He was a peacock.
3. Implied metaphor:	He swelled and displayed his finery.
	He swelled and ruffled his plumage.
4. Dead metaphor:	He strutted.

Metaphor is how we picture things. Language is a tissue of dead metaphors. Language seems to have moved from specific names for things, like *lion,* to "he is a lion." Consequently, all languages express many general ideas in dead metaphors. *Transfer* is a dead metaphor, in which the ferrying across on a haphazard raft resolves into the idea of carrying-across-ness. The writer's gift is to revive the dead metaphor, to reveal the pictorial image sleeping like a seed in the living word. See PERSONIFICATION.

Metaphysical Conceit. See CONCEIT.

Metaphysical Poetry. (1) Seventeenth-century poetry of wit and startling extended metaphor. In his "Discourse Concerning the Original and Progress of Satire" (1693), Dryden labeled John Donne (1572–1631) *metaphysical,* originating the term in deploring Donne's admirable but excessive wit. Johnson gave the term currency in his "Life of Cowley" (1779): "About the beginning of the seventeenth century appeared a race of writers that may be termed the metaphysical poets," who "were men of learning, and to shew their learning was their whole endeavour; but, unluckily resolving to shew it in rhyme, instead of writing poetry, they only wrote verses. . . ." Borrowing Ovid's term, he found their wit a *discordia concors* ("harmonious discord") rather than the approved Horatian CONCORDIA DISCORS ("discordant harmony"):

> But Wit, abstracted from its effects upon the hearer, may be more rigorously and philosophically considered as a kind of *discordia concors;* a combination of dissimilar images, or discovery of occult resemblances in things apparently unlike. Of wit, thus defined, they have more than enough. The most heterogeneous ideas are yoked by violence together; nature and art are ransacked for illustrations, comparisons, and allusions; their learning instructs, and their subtlety surprises; but the reader commonly thinks his improvement dearly bought, and, though he sometimes admires, is seldom pleased.

Donne is the outstanding metaphysical poet, followed by Abraham Cowley (1618–1667), Richard Crashaw (1613–1649), and the lesser poet John Cleveland. The Protestant mystics George Herbert (1593–1633), Henry Vaughan (c. 1622–1695), and Thomas Traherne (1637–1674) are classed as metaphysicals, as are the CAVALIER POETS, Thomas Carew (c. 1598–c. 1639) and Richard Lovelace (1618–1658), and the American Puritan minister Edward Taylor (1645?–1729). The twentieth century rediscovered the metaphysicals, who influenced the work of T. S. Eliot, John Crowe Ransom, and Allen Tate.

(2) A term used by some critics, such as H. J. C. Grierson and Herbert Read, more accurately and broadly than Dryden and Johnson, in the sense of "philosophical" or, in Read's definition, as "emotional apprehension of thought," but with no effect on general critical usage. See BAROQUE; CONCEIT; CONCORDIA DISCORS; CONTROLLING IMAGE.

Metathesis.   The interchanging of letters, sounds, or syllables within a word: Old English *acsian* becomes *ascian* and *ask;* Old English *brid* becomes *bird; relevant* becomes confused as *revelant*. The SPOONERISM is founded in metathesis.

Meter.   The measured pulse of poetry. English meters derive from four Greek and Roman quantitative meters (see QUANTITATIVE VERSE), which English stresses more sharply, though the patterns are the same. The unit of each pattern is the *foot,* containing one stressed syllable and one or two light ones. RISING METER goes from light to heavy; FALLING METER, from heavy to light. One meter—iambic—has dominated English poetry, with the three others lending an occasional foot, for variety, and producing a few poems.

RISING METERS

Iambic: ˘ — (the iambus)
Anapestic: ˘ ˘ — (the anapest)

FALLING METERS

Trochaic: — ˘ (the trochee)
Dactylic: — ˘ ˘ (the dactyl)

The number of feet in a line also gives the verse a name:

1 foot: monometer
2 feet: dimeter
3 feet: trimeter
4 feet: tetrameter
5 feet: pentameter
6 feet: hexameter
7 feet: heptameter (rare)

All meters will show some variations, and substitutions of other kinds of feet, but three variations in iambic writing are virtually standard:

Inverted foot: — ˘ (a trochee)
Spondee: — —
Ionic double foot: ˘ ˘ | — —

The *pyrrhic foot* of classical meters, two light syllables (˘˘), lives in the English line only in the Ionic double foot (see IONIC FOOT), though some prosodists will scan a relatively light iambus as pyrrhic. See DIPODIC VERSE and SCANSION.

Examples of meters and scansion:

IAMBIC TETRAMETER

˘ — | ˘ — | ˘ — | ˘ —
An-ni- | hil-a- | ting all | that's made |

— ˘ | — — | ˘ ˘ | — —
To a | green thought | in a | green shade. |

Andrew Marvell, "The Garden"

IAMBIC TETRAMETER
(with two inverted feet)

— ˘ | ˘ — | ˘ — | ˘ —
Close to | the sun | in lone- | ly lands, |

— ˘ | ˘ — | ˘ — | ˘ —
Ringed with | the az- | ure world, | he stands. |

Alfred, Lord Tennyson, "The Eagle"

IAMBIC PENTAMETER

Love's not | Time's fool, | though ros- | y lips | and cheeks |

Within | his bend- | ing sick- | le's com- | pass come |

Shakespeare, Sonnet 116

When to | the ses- | sions of | sweet si- | lent thought |

Shakespeare, Sonnet 30

ANAPESTIC TETRAMETER
(trochees substituted)

The pop- | lars are felled; | farewell | to the shade |

And the whis- | pering sound | of the cool | colonnade |

William Cowper, "The Poplar Field"

TROCHAIC TETRAMETER

Tell me | not in | mournful | numbers |

Longfellow, "A Psalm of Life"

DACTYLIC HEXAMETER

This is the | forest prim- | eval. The | murmuring | pines and the | hemlocks |

Bearded with | moss. . . .

Longfellow, "Evangeline"

Metonymy. "Substitute naming." An associated idea names the item: "*Homer* is *hard*" for "Reading Homer's poems is difficult," or "The *pen* is mightier than the *sword*" for "Literature and propaganda accomplish more and survice longer than warfare," or "The *White House* announced" for "The President announced." See SYNECDOCHE.

Metrical Accent. See ACCENT.

Metrical Romance. A MEDIEVAL ROMANCE in verse or a later poem displaying similar characteristics. *Sir Gawain and the Green Knight* and Chaucer's *Troilus and Criseyde* are excellent fourteenth-century examples. Scott's *Marmion*, Byron's *Giaour*, James Russell Lowell's *Vision of Sir Launfal*, and Tennyson's *Idylls of the King* (an attempt to create an EPIC from Arthurian materials) are examples of the nineteenth-century revival of interest in the form.

Reference

Walter H. French and C. B. Hale, eds., **Middle English Metrical Romances**
   (1930).

Metrics.   The analysis and description of METER. It is also called
PROSODY.

Middle English.   The language of England from the middle of the
twelfth century, when entries made in the *Peterborough Chronicle* first
showed characteristics significantly different from those of Old English, to approximately 1500, the date of *Everyman*. English began to
lose its inflectional endings and accepted many French words into its
vocabulary, especially terms associated with the new social, legal, and
governmental structures (*baron, judge, jury, marshal, parliament,
prince*), and those in common use by the French upper classes (*mansion, chamber, veal, beef*). See ANGLO-NORMAN LANGUAGE; ENGLISH
LANGUAGE; MIDDLE ENGLISH LITERATURE; OLD ENGLISH.

Middle English Literature.   The literature of medieval England from
1150 to 1500. Despite the rich literary heritage of Old English, little
vernacular literature remains from the first century of assimilation following the Norman Conquest in 1066. From the twelfth century onward, Middle English literature developed slowly, in dialects inherited
from Old English, but increasingly influenced by French. Literary
forms and content also showed a heavy continental influence. Toward
the end of the fourteenth century, Middle English literature flourished
briefly and brilliantly in the works of Chaucer, the Gawain Poet, and
Langland. Malory was the only later writer of the period to compare
with them. After the fourteenth century, the West Midland dialect of
the Gawain Poet was no longer important for literature. By the fifteenth century, Northern English was developing in the works of the
SCOTS MAKARS into the Lowland Scots, or Lallans, later used by
Burns and MacDiarmid. The London dialect of Chaucer became the
dominant literary language of English, evolving into Modern English.

   The three and a half centuries of the Middle English period produced a rich, varied literature, much now lost, but much also remaining. Ballads, folk lyrics, romances, and miracle plays were in oral tradition, sometimes for centuries, before they were preserved, frequently
incomplete, in manuscript or print. Religious and didactic verse and
prose fared better in the hands of scribes trained in monasteries than
did the more secular forms of literature. Printing arrived in England
only in the last quarter of the fifteenth century, when William Caxton
set up his press at Westminster.

Of the four authors of most permanent interest in the period, Geoffrey Chaucer (c. 1343–1400) is the only one whose life is known in any detail, at least partly because of his long royal service. A court poet, traveler, and man of affairs, he created in *The Canterbury Tales* a broad panorama of English life at the end of the fourteenth century. His *Troilus and Criseyde* is a metrical romance combining an ancient story, a medieval concept of fate based largely on Boethius, and an astonishingly modern grasp of human psychology. *The Book of the Duchess*, *The House of Fame*, and *The Parliament of Fowls* are fine examples of DREAM VISION.

Of the Gawain Poet almost nothing is known beyond the fact that he wrote as a devout Christian in the West Midlands in the last quarter of the fourteenth century. His *Sir Gawain and the Green Knight* is a great metrical romance from the Arthurian cycle, complex in versification, psychology, and narrative technique. The same poet's *Pearl* is unmatched in its perfected form as a religious dream allegory.

Little is known of William Langland (c. 1332–c. 1400), who is usually credited with the three versions of *Piers Plowman*, an alliterative dream allegory immensely ambitious in its scope, valuable both as satire and social history.

Sir Thomas Malory, of uncertain identity, is credited with *Le Morte Darthur* (1485), one of the most subtly complex of early prose narratives and by far the most important rendition of the Arthurian tales as a whole.

Besides these individual writers of genius, many other authors can be identified by name or by characteristics of their work. The Wakefield Master has left his mark on a few plays. Other individuals of especially significant accomplishment are John Gower (c. 1330–1408), Thomas Hoccleve (c. 1368–c. 1430), John Lydgate (c. 1370–1450), and the Scots poets Robert Henryson (c. 1420–c. 1490) and William Dunbar (c. 1460–c. 1513). Apart from the work of these individuals, Middle English literature is most conveniently considered in generic categories.

Anonymous verse includes many fine lyrics and carols, both religious and secular, such as "Fowls in the Frith," "Ubi Sunt Qui Ante Nos Fuerunt?" ("Where Are Those That Were Before Us?"), "The Fox and the Goose," "Western Wind," and "I Sing of a Maiden." Verse debates were popular and include "The Owl and the Nightingale" and "The Debate between the Body and the Soul." Longer religious verse includes *The Cursor Mundi*, a compilation of Bible stories and early Christian legends; and Robert Mannyng's *Handlyng Synne*, a moral treatise enlivened with examples drawn from English life of the early fourteenth century. Prominent among important prose works are several translations: *The Travels of Sir John Mandeville,* a fabulous account of travels in the Holy Land, India, and China; John Wyclif's Bible; John of Trevisa's translation of Higdon's *Polychronicon,* a popular history of the world from the Creation to the mid-fourteenth century; and William Caxton's translation of the *History of Reynard the Fox. The Paston Letters* is an important collection of family documents recording fifteenth-century life.

Some of the most important Middle English literature was narrative and dramatic. See BALLAD; MEDIEVAL DRAMA; MEDIEVAL ROMANCE.

References

E. K. Chambers, **English Literature at the Close of the Middle Ages** (1954).
George Kane, **Middle English Literature** (1951).
W. L. Renwick and H. Orton, **The Beginnings of English Literature to Skelton,** 3rd ed. (1966).
R. M. Wilson, **Early Middle English Literature** (1939).
David M. Zesmer, **Guide to English Literature from Beowulf through Chaucer and Medieval Drama** (1961).

Miles Gloriosus. The *stock character* of the boasting soldier, originating in Plautus's *Miles Gloriosus.* Shakespeare's Falstaff is a famous example. The *miles glorious* is a subtype of the *alazon.* Another name is BRAGGADOCIO. See CHARACTERS; GASCONADE.

Milesian Tale. A kind of short, erotic story, its origins associated with Aristides of Miletus (c. 100 B.C.). Aristides' Milesian tales are lost, but the term became generic for other tales and collections in the ancient world. Lucius Apuleius (second century A.D.), for example, called his *Golden Ass* a Milesian composition. See SYBARITIC FABLES.

Milieu. French, for "surroundings" or "environment." The milieu created for the CHARACTERS within a literary work is an important part of its ETHOS. In relation to the interpretation of literature, the milieu in which the author worked has been an important consideration for some critics at least since it was emphasized by the French critic Hippolyte Taine (1828–1893) as one of the three most important formative elements, the others being the author's heredity and the historical moments of his or her life. Taine's theories gave important support to NATURALISM.

Millenarianism. The doctrine of the millenium, the belief that Christ will return and reign for one thousand years on earth, derived from Rev. xx.1–5.

Miltonic Sonnet. An ITALIAN SONNET with no pause, or VOLTA, between OCTAVE and SESTET.

Mime. (1) A form of DRAMA that communicates primarily through the actor's gestures and facial expressions, in mimicry of life, LEGEND, or MYTH. (2) A performer of such drama. Common among tribal people, mime was well established in Greece and Rome by the fifth century B.C. Xenophon mentioned a mime of Dionysus and Ariadne that was performed in dance, and Plato wrote in *The Republic* of mimes of neighing horses, bellowing bulls, murmuring rivers, and the like. Generally considered a low class of drama and given to clowning and BURLESQUE, mime was frequently indecent and sometimes accompanied by words spoken or sung. In imperial Rome it was hugely popular, along with other forms of SPECTACLE. In the middle ages, its elements appeared in the entertainments of the JONGLEUR and in the SWORD DANCE and morris dance of Great Britain. Later, mime was a feature of COMMEDIA DELL'ARTE in Italy and of the MUMMING and MASQUE of England.

In the twentieth century, famous mimes like Charlie Chaplin and Marcel Marceau have drawn attention once again to the art, which was important to VAUDEVILLE and the silent movie and has continued as a feature of sound films and of stage and television shows.

Mimesis. A term meaning "imitation." It has been central to literary criticism since Aristotle's *Poetics*, which included, or at least implied, a critique of the conception of mimesis in Plato, more particularly in the last book of the *Republic*, that made Socrates exclude poets from his ideal state. The ordinary meaning of *imitation* as creating a resemblance to something else is clearly involved in Aristotle's definition of dramatic plot as *mimesis praxeos*, the imitation of an action. But there are many things that a work of literature may imitate, and hence many contexts of imitation.

Socrates remarks in Plato's *Phaedrus* that a *logos*, or discourse, should resemble a *zoon*, or organism, a unity from which nothing can be taken away without injury. This organic conception of verbal structure recurs in Romantic criticism: in Coleridge, for instance, a literary work resembles or imitates nature in being an organic unity. At the same time there is a pervasive resemblance in the literary work as a whole to something in the external environment; otherwise, it would be impossible to understand. Similarly in the art of photography, the resemblance in the picture to its original "subject" is the first aspect of it to strike us, though this is reinforced by a corresponding sense of the differences between a photograph and an ordinary sense impression. Literature too may appear as "realistic," or like what the reader knows, though the differences created by its literary structure are at least equally important.

In Aristotle himself *imitation* appears to mean, not an external relation of a copy to its original, but an internal relation of form to content: a tragedy, for example, is a form that has some aspect of "nature," or actual experience, for its content. From this point of view literature surrounds an aspect of experience and transforms it into its own shape. We are aware of the resemblance of the tragic action to human behavior, but we are also aware of the containing conventions of tragic drama that differentiate that action from all other forms of action.

Works of literature may imitate other works of literature: this is the aspect of literature that comes into such conceptions as CONVENTION and GENRE. Thus when Milton is asked for a memorial poem to an acquaintance drowned in the Irish Sea and produces *Lycidas*, he is imitating the convention of the PASTORAL ELEGY established by Theocritus and Virgil, and makes this point very explicitly in the course of the poem. Sometimes the title of, say, a novel, such as Tolstoy's *Resurrection* or Faulkner's *Sound and the Fury*, will indicate a relationship to something within literature that the author is calling attention to. Here again the difference between what is produced and what is being imitated or recalled is as important as the point made by the resemblance or connection.

In a larger sense every work of literature imitates, or finds its identity in, the entire "world of words," in Wallace Stevens's phrase, the sense of the whole of reality as potentially literary, as finding its end in a book, as Mallarmé says. Such a world is in one sense bigger than the "reality" it started by reflecting, because the limits of the verbal imagination are not the real but the conceivable, and may include fantasy or nonsense as readily as analogies to previous experience. See FICTION.

Mimetic Criticism.   CRITICISM that emphasizes the universe as the subject of art, as distinguished from criticism that stresses the work itself, the artist, or the audience.

Minnesinger.   German for *"love singer"*: a German poet and singer of
the twelfth or thirteenth century. The tradition derived partly from the
TROUBADOUR and partly from previous German secular poetry. A
characteristic poetic form was the TAGELIED. The most famous minnesinger was Walther von der Vogelweide (c. 1170– c. 1230).

Minstrel.   A professional musician of the Middle Ages. The minstrel
played and sang the secular lyrics, folk songs, and ballads of the time,
sometimes wandering in search of an audience, but often attached to a
particular court. The term now often includes the JONGLEUR, but *minstrel* came into use later and is sometimes reserved for a musician of
higher social status than the more plebeian *jongleur*. See BALLAD; FOLK
SONG.

Minstrel Show.   A form of American popular entertainment characterized by whites in blackface performing singing, dancing, and comedy routines. Thomas Dartmouth Rice began to perform in blackface
around 1828 and developed the *Jim Crow* song and dance act. From
this developed the minstrel show of the 1840s and later, at first in the
hands of the Virginia Minstrels and, especially, the Christy Minstrels.
Much of the contents became traditional: an initial parade around the
stage; a master of ceremonies, or "interlocutor," who introduced acts
and cracked jokes with the "end-men," "Mr. Tambo" and "Mr.
Bones"; a BURLESQUE on a well-known play or opera.

Miracle Play.   A medieval play based on a saint's life or a Bible story.
In French usage, the term is reserved for a play on a saint's life, with
a Bible story termed a MYSTERY PLAY. See MEDIEVAL DRAMA.

Miscellany.   A collection of various things. A literary miscellany is
therefore a book collecting varied works, usually poems by different
authors, a kind of ANTHOLOGY. The term is applied especially to the
many books of this kind that appeared in the ELIZABETHAN PERIOD,
beginning with Richard Tottel's *Songs and Sonnets* (1557), commonly
called *Tottel's Miscellany*. Others from the same period are *The Paradise
of Dainty Devices* (1576), *The Phoenix Nest* (1593), and *England's Helicon* (1600), the latter containing many of the best lyrics of the period.
The miscellanies were frequently carelessly edited, omitting the names
of authors or attributing poems to the wrong authors, but they gave
wide circulation to the work of such poets as Wyatt, Surrey, Raleigh,
Sidney, Spenser, Nicholas Breton (1545?–1626?), Thomas Lodge
(1558?–1625), Marlowe, and Shakespeare, as well as to anonymous
songs and ballads.

Mise en Abyme. Interior duplication within a story or play of the larger plot or theme, created by placing a brief, separate narrative within the main one. The result is a STORY-WITHIN-A-STORY with the added complication that the interior story reflects upon and illuminates the larger one that encloses it. Examples include the play-within-a-play in *Hamlet* and Poe's poem "The Haunted Palace," placed at the midpoint of "The Fall of the House of Usher." The term originated with André Gide and gained wider currency in discussions of the French NOUVEAU ROMAN in the 1960s.

Mise en Scène. French for "placing on stage." (1) The staging of a PLAY, including stage sets, properties, and the like. Modern playwrights like Chekhov and O'Neill have paid much more attention to *mise en scène* than did earlier ones like Sophocles and Shakespeare. (2) By extension, the surroundings or setting of any event.

Mixed Metaphor. A METAPHOR not consistent with the physical world: for instance, "The population explosion has paved the way for new intellectual growth." It looks good. But then we realize that explosions do not pave and that grass does not sprout through pavement. If the statement had said "cleared" instead of "paved," the picture would not have been scrambled and the metaphor would not have been mixed.

Mock Drama. A PLAY that mocks a literary CONVENTION of its time. Examples include *The Rehearsal* (1671), by George Villiers, duke of Buckingham, and Henry Fielding's *Tragedy of Tragedies; or, the Life and Death of Tom Thumb the Great* (1730), both spoofs of the HEROIC PLAY.

Mock Epic. A poem in EPIC form and manner ludicrously elevating some trivial subject to epic grandeur, echoing Virgil's "Arms and the man I sing," invoking the Muse, describing boasts, legendary armor, battles, supernatural intervention, celebrative games, a descent to the underworld (the *descensus Averno* of the *Aeneid* VI.126), and the like, with much HOMERIC SIMILE and elevated style. The earliest known is the lost *Margites,* whose hero was a fool *(margos)*; Aristotle and Zeno attributed the work to Homer himself. Three notable romances of the Charlemagne cycle, each of the last two much indebted to its predecessor, show amusing mock epic characteristics in chivalric costume: Luigi Pulci's *Morgante Maggiore* (1481), about a Christianized giant, companion to Orlando (Roland); Matteo Boiardo's *Orlando Innamorato* (1494); and Ludovico Ariosto's *Orlando Furioso* (1516–

1532). Chaucer's "Nun's Priest's Tale" (1387), about a cocky rooster, and Spenser's *Muipotomos, or the Fate of the Butterfly* (1591) draw amusingly from the mock epic. Pope's *Rape of the Lock* (1714) is the best in the language, and his *Dunciad* (1743) is a brilliant extended example. Gray's "Ode on the Death of a Favourite Cat, Drowned in a Tub of Gold Fishes" (1747) is a gem. Mock-epic poems and style are also called "mock-heroic."

Mode. A CONVENTION or fashion. Modes in literature are determined by conventional attitudes toward the contents of a work or the audience for which it is written. For FICTION, this means primarily the attitude assumed about the powers of the PROTAGONIST or HERO with respect to other people and the environment. Five significant modes may be discerned: (1) MYTH, with the hero a god or possessing the powers of one; (2) ROMANCE, with the hero less than a god, but possessing more than ordinary human powers, and prodigious in courage and endurance; (3) HIGH MIMETIC, with the hero positioned above other people, as, for example, a king or a prince, but subject to the same natural laws; (4) LOW MIMETIC, a protagonist of average capabilities, as in realistic fiction; (5) *ironic*, with a protagonist considered as possessing less than the average powers of normal people, below both author and reader, helpless and frustrated.

Thus considered, the modes of European literature have succeeded one another in dominance, in the order given, from pre-medieval times to the present. The characteristic literary expression of a given period has taken the coloration of its mode: for example, we have Shakespeare's high mimetic protagonists and Jane Austen's and George Eliot's low mimetic ones. The subject is explored at greater length in Northrop Frye's *Anatomy of Criticism* (1957).

Modernism. A movement characterized by inner individual perceptions, solipsism, NIHILISM, alienation, EXISTENTIALISM, beginning with the French Symbolists as early as Baudelaire's *Fleurs du Mal* (1857). The Impressionists turned from objective reality to subjective impressions. The Cubists continued the revolt. The followers of DADAISM turned art to destruction. The movement continued with the "found" art of the 1960s, constructed of old tires or plumbing or soup cans signed by the nonartist; with the silent nonmusic of John Cage; and with happenings stressing momentary, accidental experience as the only reality. In literature, STREAM OF CONSCIOUSNESS fragments superseded objective narration, and scattered words and lines displayed the poet's inner impressions. See MODERN PERIOD.

Modern Period (1914–1965). As designated by critics, the period that began when World War I blasted the past and history into apparent oblivion. As Matthew Arnold sensed a half a century earlier ("Dover Beach," 1867), the darkling plain was here, in mud and barbed wire, with no joy, love, light, certitude, peace, nor help for pain, where ignorant armies clashed by night. Only a bleak solipsism survived, each sole self projecting its only reality, unsure of its match with any other. The past was dead. God was dead. People were alienated from all community. One could create one's self only by existing, by moving one's existential reality up from the black wall of terror and nothing, acting and choosing, as Sartre said somewhat illogically, as if for all humanity. Individual consciousness reigned, though the unconscious, as Freud and Jung suggested, outweighed the conscious. Emotion and self-will superseded reason and virtue, in this dire extension of the anti-intellectual but optimistic Romantic ethos.

These assumptions, partially suppressed, or expressed, fostered experiments in poetry and prose, as the streams of individual consciousness floated the inner chaos of modern uncertainty. Virginia Woolf, T. S. Eliot, and James Joyce created modern masterpieces from this fragmented surge. After World War II, solipsism intensified with the drugs, hallucinating lights, bombs, and rebellion of the POST-MODERN PERIOD (1965–   ). Americans Thomas Pynchon, Kurt Vonnegut, and John Barth have written fictions satirizing fiction, and Britishers John Fowles and Margaret Drabble have included the author's creative problems in their created account. The puzzled self is the center. See EXISTENTIALISM; MODERNISM.

Modulation. In poetry, variation of the regular METER by the substitution of another kind of foot or by the dropping or adding of light syllables.

Monodrama. (1) A play with one character. (2) A similar CLOSET DRAMA or DRAMATIC MONOLOGUE. Critics have referred to Robert Browning's dramatic monologues as *monodramas*. Tennyson called his *Maud* (1855)—in which a narrator, in sections of different meter, recounts his tragic story—a *monodrama*.

Monody. (1) A Greek ODE for one voice. (2) An elegiac LAMENT, a DIRGE, in poetic SOLILOQUY, like Matthew Arnold's *Thyrsis, a Monody* (1866). See ELEGY; THRENODY.

Monologue. (1) A poem or story in the form of a SOLILOQUY. (2) Any extended speech. See DRAMATIC MONOLOGUE; INTERIOR MONOLOGUE; MONODRAMA.

Monometer. A line containing one metrical foot. See METER.

Monorhyme. A poem, STANZA, or STROPHE on one RHYME. Dante Gabriel Rossetti's "The Woodspurge" is an example, in monorhyme stanzas.

Monostich. A single line, or poem of one line.

Monostrophic. (1) A poem with one STROPHE or STANZA. (2) A poem composed of structurally identical strophes; *homostrophic*.

Montage. (1) An illustration made of many pieces of pictures, designs, printed fragments, and the like jumbled closely and superimposed. (2) A film with rapid sequences and scenes fading into one another. The Russian director Sergei Eisenstein (1898–1948) rhythmically contrasted shots to evoke meaning in a way now called "Soviet montage." In America, quick stylized transitions are called both *dynamic cutting* and *montage*. (3) Similar quick shifts in FICTION, like those in Dickens that influenced D. W. Griffith and, through him, later filmmakers; or, in the twentieth century, the rapid transitions found in the "Newsreels" in John Dos Passos's *U.S.A.*, in Joyce's *Ulysses*, and in STREAM OF CONSCIOUSNESS.

Mood. (1) Verb form conveying the speaker's attitude toward factuality or likelihood: the *indicative* mood for fact; the *subjunctive* mood for the doubtful, conditional, or unlikely; the *imperative* mood for command. (2) The emotive attitude conveyed by a literary work—gaiety, gloom, resignation, IRONY. Rather than the author's projecting a mood, Willa Cather saw the work's mood as dominating the author: the "language, the stresses, the very structure of the sentences are imposed upon the writer by the special mood of the piece." Mood and TONE are virtually synonymous, though some distinguish *mood*—the author's attitude toward the subject—from *tone*, the writer's attitude toward the audience. In works of DRAMATIC IRONY the speaker's mood is probably serious, earnest, or self-important, in contrast with the author's view of the speaker, amused, condescending, contemptuous, wry, or whatever.

Mora. Latin for "delay." A term for the duration of a short syllable in QUANTITATIVE VERSE, indicated in SCANSION by a breve: ˘. Two morae equal one long syllable, indicated by a macron: —.

Moral Criticism. A consideration of the work in relationship to humanity, as opposed to AESTHETIC CRITICISM, a consideration of the work in isolation. See CRITICISM.

Morality Play. A form of late MEDIEVAL DRAMA characterized by an allegoric presentation of the human search for salvation; distinguished from the MIRACLE PLAY and the MYSTERY PLAY, which present Saints' lives and Bible stories. The most famous example is *Everyman* (c. 1500).

Moral Meaning. Another name for *tropological meaning*, in the Middle Ages one of FOUR SENSES OF INTERPRETATION, the one concerned with behavior.

Mosaic Rhyme. Two words rhyming with one word, or two with two: *unit, soon hit; save us, shave us.* See RHYME.

Moscow Art Theater. See STANISLAVSKY METHOD.

Motif (or **Motive**). (1) A recurrent thematic element—word, image, symbol, object, phrase, action. (2) A conventional incident, situation, or device like the unknown knight of mysterious origin and low degree in the ROMANCE, the excruciating riddle in fairy tales, or the virgin tied to the railroad track. (3) In FOLKLORE studies, the smallest identifiable narrative element, often one of several in a tale, as compiled in Stith Thompson's *Motif-Index of Folk Literature* (6 vols., 1932–1936).

Motivation. The forces that move a character to action, including the character's own nature and the circumstances. Motivation is slighter in MELODRAMA, COMEDY, and ROMANCE; deeper and more psychologically involved in more realistic works and TRAGEDY.

Muckrakers. American journalists and novelists in the first decade of the twentieth century who exposed corruption in big business and government. Mass-circulation magazines—*The Arena, Collier's, Cosmopolitan, Everybody's, The Independent, McClure's*—financed the investigations and published the work of Lincoln Steffens, Ida Tarbell, David Graham Phillips, Ray Stannard Baker, T. W. Lawson, Mark Sullivan, and Samuel Hopkins Adams. Phillips's *Great God Success* (1901), Upton Sinclair's *Jungle* (1901), which depicted the Chicago stockyards and led to reforming federal laws for inspecting food, and the later books of the American Winston Churchill are muckraking novels. Theodore Roosevelt invented the term in a speech in 1906, agreeing with some of the findings but deploring the methods as irresponsible sensationalism. He alluded to the "man with a Muck-rake," in John Bunyan's *Pilgrim's Progress* (1678), who could look only downward as he stirred the filth, unable to see the heavenly crown held above him.

Mummery. (1) A performance by mummers, often a farcical PAN-TOMIME. (2) Any pretentious ceremony or display. See MUMMING.

Mumming. A medieval folk entertainment at Christmastide, evidently deriving from ancient celebrations of the death and resurrection of the year, in which a silent ("mum") procession of masked people enters homes and halls, plays dice ("mumchance"), and departs. *The Mummers' Play,* or *St. George Play,* was a popular development throughout England, Scotland, Ireland, and Wales, incorporating the ancient SWORD DANCE, a similar year-end ritual. The principal characters are St. George, the Turkish knight, and the Doctor. St. George and the Turkish Knight introduce themselves boastfully and fight several times until one is killed (usually St. George). The Doctor enters, boasts his skill, and resurrects the loser. Other grotesque characters enter, and then take up a collection.

Muses. (1) The nine daughters of Zeus and Mnemosyne ("Memory") presiding over the arts and sciences: Calliope (epic poetry), Clio (history), Erato (love poetry, lyrics), Euterpe (music), Melpomene (tragedy), Polyhymnia (sacred poetry), Terpsichore (dancing and choral singing), Thalia (comedy), Urania (astronomy). Mt. Helicon in Boeotia, with fountains Hippocrene and Aganippe, was thought to be the home of the Muses. Mt. Parnassus, north of Delphi, was also sacred to the Muses, and to Apollo, as was the Pierian Spring near Mt. Olympus. (2) The Muse: generalized and sometimes not capitalized, the inspirer of poetry, on whom the poet calls for assistance. See PEGASUS.

Musical Comedy. An OPERETTA or COMIC OPERA with dialogue, songs, dancing, and orchestral accompaniment, particularly of the sentimental and romantic type brought to the New York stage by the Europeans Victor Herbert, Rudolf Friml, and Sigmund Romberg in the 1890s and early twentieth century. Herbert's *Naughty Marietta* (1910) and Romberg's *Student Prince* (1924) and *Desert Song* (1926) are notable.

Mystery Play. Medieval religious drama beginning in the church with the *Quem quaeritis?* ("Whom do you seek?"), a chanted dialogue with the angel at Christ's tomb during the Easter service, and leading by the thirteenth century to plays concerning other parts of the Bible acted outside the church. Mystery plays were performed eventually in elaborate cycles of plays acted on the PAGEANT wagons or stages throughout the city streets, with different guilds of artisans and merchants responsible for each. Old Testament plays dramatized the Creation, the fall of the angels, and of Adam and Eve, Cain's killing of Abel, Abraham and Isaac, and the prophets. New Testament plays presented the Annunication, the birth of Christ, the shepherds, the magi, the visit to the temple, the entry into Jerusalem, betrayal by Judas, trial and Crucifixion, Mary's lamentation, visit to the tomb, Resurrection, appearances to disciples, Pentecost, and occasionally the Last Judgment. Extant cycles are the York, the Chester, the Coventry, and the Wakefield or Towneley, the most considerable, especially with its *Second Shepherds' Play*, with its adroit admixture of rough comedy, which is also characteristic of the other cycles. Archdeacon Rogers of the sixteenth century left a frequently quoted description of the Chester cycle at Whitsuntide:

> Every company had its pageant, or part, which pageants were a high scaffold with two rooms, a higher and a lower upon four wheels. In the lower they appareled themselves, and in the higher room they played, being all open on the top, that all beholders might hear and see them. The places where they played them was in every street. They began first at the Abbey gates, and when the first pageant was played it was wheeled to the high cross before the mayor, and so to every street; and so every street had a pageant playing before them at one time, till all the pageants for the day appointed were played: and when one pageant was near ended, word was brought from street to street, that so they might come in place thereof exceeding orderly, and all the streets have their pageants afore them all at one time playing together; to see which players there was great resort, and also scaffolds and stages made in the streets in those places where they determined to play their pageants.

These cycles were usually called *Corpus Christi plays* because performed at the Corpus Christi procession (the first Thursday after Pentecost), or *Whitsuntide plays* because performed at Pentecost (Whitsunday), the seventh Sunday after Easter. Robert Dodsley, the eighteenth-century editor, first called them *mystery plays* (1744), adopting the French term *mystère* for Scriptural plays. See LITURGICAL DRAMA; MIRACLE PLAY; MEDIEVAL DRAMA; MORALITY PLAY.

Mystery Story (or **Mystery Novel**).   A thriller fraught with suspenseful terror, originating in Horace Walpole's *Castle of Otranto: A Gothic Story* (1764) and evolving into the popular DETECTIVE STORY, with a murder to be solved.

Mysticism.   A spiritual discipline to expunge sensory experience and evacuate the mind through deep contemplation and reach a transcendental union with God. W. T. Stace defines five characteristics and accepts some drug-induced experiences as authentically mystical: (1) a sense of objectivity or reality in the mystic state; (2) a sense of peace or blessedness; (3) a feeling of holiness, sacredness, or divinity; (4) a paradoxical quality; (5) an ineffability (*Mysticism and Philosophy*, 1960). The Christian mystic's stages are (1) the purgative way, purifying the soul; (2) the illuminative way, finding illumination in God's love; (3) the unitive way, the soul's finally reaching union with God; (4) the spiritual marriage, reaching an ecstasy in perfect knowledge of God; (5) the dark night of the soul, losing God altogether and sinking into alienation.

Richard Rolle of Hampole (c. 1300–1349) wrote extensively in Latin of his mystical experiences. William Blake (1757–1827) was an intuitive mystic. Whitman recorded a mystical experience in *Leaves of Grass*, as does Allen Ginsberg in several poems.

Myth. From Greek *mythos*, "plot" or "narrative." The verbal culture of most if not all human societies began with stories, and certain stories have achieved a distinctive importance as being connected with what the society feels it most needs to know: stories illustrating the society's religion, history, class structure, or the origin of peculiar features of the natural environment. A distinction arises between "serious" stories and stories told for amusement, and this distinction develops into the literary distinction between myth and FOLK TALE. The difference between myth and folk tale is thus one of social function rather than structure: in structure there are many analogues to myths in folk tales, and vice versa. But the specific social function of myth gives it two characteristics of its own. First, it defines a cultural area and gives it a shared legacy of ALLUSION, as the Homeric epics did for Greek culture and the writings that eventually became the Old Testament did for Hebrew culture. Second, they link with one another to form a *mythology*, an interconnected body of stories that verbalizes a society's major concerns in religion and history particularly. Folk tales, by contrast, lead a nomadic life, passing from one culture to another through all barriers of language. A literature develops mainly out of mythology, but as it develops it tends to absorb the secular or folk tale aspect of verbal culture as well, an expansion made easy by the structural similarity of folk tales to myths. In the Western world, Dante and Milton devoted their main efforts to re-creating the Christian mythology; Chaucer and Shakespeare drew rather from folk tale and legend.

A third factor in this development is the taking over by poets of a mythology which is no longer "believed in," as the Greek and Roman mythologies were taken over by Western European poets after Jupiter or Venus had ceased to be connected with temples or cults. This process indicates the close association of the literary and the mythological: mythology goes on being re-created by poets whatever the degree of its social acceptance. The myths of Christianity possessed a distinctive status in Western Europe until about the eighteenth century; for the last two centuries such mythological material has been used or referred to by poets who may or may not be writing from a commitment of belief.

For many reasons the great bulk of myths are stories about gods or other beings beyond the orbit of ordinary experience (dragons, human heroes of supernormal powers, etc.). As literature develops, there comes a greater demand for stories that conform to plausibility or likelihood; but these often use the same themes as myth, adapted to a greater demand for "realism." Thus the theme of the mysterious or portentous birth of a divine infant, like Zeus or Dionysus in Greek mythology or Jesus in the Gospels, is carried on in ROMANCE, and eventually into the fictions of novelists. Fielding's Tom Jones, like many of Dickens's heroes, is a foundling of mysterious parentage, and the mystery is cleared up only at the very end. One important implication from this is that myths have much the relation to realistic stories that abstract or stylized pictures have to representational painting. As the characters are usually gods, who by definition can do anything, myth normally conveys the kind of events that happen only in stories, just as highly stylized paintings present the visual formal relationships that occur only in pictures. Hence, a movement toward abstraction in twentieth-century painting and a deliberately self-conscious use of mythical patterns (for instance, the *Odyssey* in James Joyce's *Ulysses*) in twentieth-century fiction are part of the same cultural development.

The social function of myth divides into two aspects. First, it is a structure of concern, telling a particular society what that society most wants to know: the names and relationships of its gods, its laws, and the origins of its class structure, its legends and historical reminiscences, and the like. Second, it is a means of symbolizing the ideals and aims of an established spiritual or temporal hierarchy. Thus MEDIEVAL ROMANCE embodies the ideals of a chivalric aristocracy, or, in the Grail stories, of a religious intellectual elite, along with being distantly related to universal mythical themes. If the ideals of an ascendant class are distrusted by a large proportion of the society, mythology acquires the sense of something not true, stories told merely to advance an ideology or rationalize the existing social structure. In contemporary society there is an acute awareness of the false or interested type of mythology that is communicated through advertising and propaganda (see Roland Barthes's *Mythologies*, 1957).

N

Naïve Narrator. A narrator who tells a story without fully understanding its implications, which are, of course, understood by the author and, presumably, by the reader. The tension between the limited comprehension of the narrator and the wider vision shared by author and reader creates the DRAMATIC IRONY that is an important part of the effect in such works. Examples include Mark Twain's *Huckleberry Finn*, Sherwood Anderson's "I'm a Fool," and Ring Lardner's "Haircut." See NARRATIVE PERSPECTIVE.

Narration. One of the four modes of prose writing. It is the telling of a story. See ARGUMENT; DESCRIPTION; EXPOSITION; NARRATIVE PERSPECTIVE; ORATION; PERSUASION.

Narrative. An account of real or imagined events, a STORY.

Narrative Essay. An ESSAY in the shape of a narrative, or story, as, for example, Addison's "Vision of Mirza." The narrative essay differs from the SHORT STORY primarily in the essay's greater concern for ideas.

Narrative Hook. A fictive opener to catch the reader's attention.

Narrative Perspective. The standpoint from which a story is told. *Perspective*, from the Latin for "to look through," first meant in English an optical glass or telescope. The narrative perspective is the lens, or eye (and by extension the mind behind the eye), through which a story is presented. It is sometimes called *point of view*, a term useful to focus attention on the mental processes of the narrator rather than on the physical relation to the story, as "She narrates from a feminist point of view."

The *narrator*, or teller of the story, may stand within the story or outside it, narrating as it occurs, shortly after, or much later, providing in each instance a different narrative perspective in space and time. The reader sees the story through a narrative perspective close to the events or removed from them by various kinds and degrees of DISTANCE, examining, as it were, with a microscope, field glass, or telescope.

Narrative perspective in time is a question of how long after the events the narration occurs. This leads to a much more important question: does the narrator display qualities owing to the time lapse between events and narration? In unusual cases, there is no time lapse, the narration transmitting events as they occur and thereby removing from consideration the reflections of the narrator, as in Alain Robbe-Grillet's *Jealousy*. Usually, however, the narration occurs later, through a mind perhaps altered by subsequent reflection, greater knowledge, or maturity. In an EPISTOLARY NOVEL, such as Samuel Richardson's *Clarissa*, each narrator reflects by letter on recent events but remains in ignorance within each letter of the events of the following days. In J. D. Salinger's *Catcher in the Rye*, Holden Caulfield narrates after the events are over, but not long after, with a boy's vision and vocabulary, of "this madman stuff that happened to me around Christmas." In Dickens's *Great Expectations*, most of the events are years in the past, the Pip who narrates being a man of much wider understanding and sympathy than the Pip of most of the story.

The two chief *narrative perspectives in space*, within the story or outside it, take their names from the grammatical stance employed by the narrator: *first-person narration* for a narrative perspective inside the story, *third-person narration* for one outside. The *first-person narrator* speaks as an "I" and may be identified in one of three roles: *first person as protagonist*, the hero or heroine of the story; *first person as participant*, a character in a subsidiary role; *first person as observer*, a character without essential function except to observe and record, sometimes developed fully as an individual with a name, history, and personality, sometimes almost nonexistent except for the "I" that appears occasionally as a reminder of the individual's personal relation to the story. In those instances where the "I" narrator carries no marks of individuality except for a more or less distinctive narrative voice, the *first person as observer* shifts easily and naturally into a *third-person narrator*, one who stands outside the story, speaking of those within it in the grammatical third person (*he, she, they*).

First-person narration involves the creation of a PERSONA, or mask, through which the author tells the story. In *Huckleberry Finn*, Mark Twain adopts the persona of Huck, who narrates: "You don't know about me, without you have read a book by the name of 'The Adventures of Tom Sawyer,' but that ain't no matter." Because Huck Finn is a *naïve narrator*, much less informed about the world and much less experienced in its ways than the author, the method allows for frequent ironic tension between the narrator's views and those of the author, an effect crucial to the success of the book. Other first-person narrators may be closer in understanding to their authors, or still farther removed from them; in any case the author is bound by the conditions of the persona, presenting only knowledge available to the persona, within the limits of the persona's understanding, and expressed in terms appropriate to the persona's personality and vocabulary. A persona who complicates a story with elements or attitudes the reader assumes the author would consider untrue or immoral is sometimes called an UNRELIABLE NARRATOR, who presents a picture distorted in significant ways from the one that would be presented by the author writing in his or her own voice. In his attitudes toward slavery and religion, Huck Finn is at times in this sense unreliable, although his underlying good sense generally triumphs.

Because most people are not professional story tellers, much less novel writers, first-person narration sometimes takes the form of letters or journals. At times it imitates the oral tale, with the words on the page representing the words as they would be spoken directly to a listener, as in some of the stories of Sherwood Anderson. At times, extending the logic a step further, it imitates the unspoken thoughts of the characters, in extended INTERIOR MONOLOGUE, as in Faulkner's *As I Lay Dying*. The use of several narrators exchanging letters or revealing thoughts removes from first-person narration some of the difficulties associated with a single narrative perspective, but imposes on the author the necessity of devising styles appropriate to more than one persona. In order to increase the range of observation and understanding, the first-person narrative of letters and journals is sometimes combined with sections of third-person narration, as in Walter Scott's *Redgauntlet* and Dickens's *Bleak House*.

The third-person narrator came first, in the form of the anonymous story teller who pretends no personal relation to the tale beyond the fact of knowing it and perhaps contributing to its shape. "'There was once upon a time a poor miller who had a very beautiful daughter"— or it may be a king with three sons or a group of soldiers returning from the wars. The narrative perspective in such traditional tales is called THIRD-PERSON OMNISCIENCE, because the narrator assumes the privileges of omniscience, moving about in time and space, entering freely into the unverbalized thoughts and motives of the characters: "The king was pleased beyond measure at the sight, but his greed for gold was still not satisfied." But the method is not limited to folk tales. The third-person omniscient narrative perspective has remained an important tool of modern novelists and short story writers, from Henry Fielding through Scott, Dickens, and George Eliot, to D. H. Lawrence, John Steinbeck, and Faulkner. All-knowing should not, however, be confused with all-revealing, in either traditional or modern tales. The story teller's art, even when story tellers assume the privileges of omniscience, dictates that they will not reveal much that might be told—what the characters had for breakfast, or what their political views might be—but only information helpful to the story. Most important, the third-person omniscient narrator will seldom reveal the mysteries and secret motives of the story before the moment of greatest effect. Knowing all, the story teller teases the reader with bits and pieces until all comes together at the end.

In THIRD-PERSON LIMITED OMNISCIENCE, the narrator frequently limits the revelation of thoughts to those of one character, presenting the other characters only externally. As a result, the reader's experience is conditioned by the mental state, the qualities of perception, ignorance, or bias of the filtering or reflecting mind. REFLECTOR, Henry James's helpful term for such a character in his own work, is useful in describing the work of others as well. Similarly, CENTER OF CONSCIOUSNESS (shorthand for James's "the centre of the subject in . . . consciousness") describes well the focal point in works where the mental processes of a character are especially important. In another common form of limited omniscience, the narrator follows one character throughout a story, presenting only scenes involving the chosen character while ignoring the privileges of omniscience that would allow attention to other times and places. The two forms are sometimes combined in a focus on mind and scene, as in James's relatively easy *Daisy Miller* or his more complex *The Ambassadors*. Other permutations limit the focus, for example, to two or more minds or to the scenes involving two or more selected characters. Because of its many possible forms, third-person limited omniscience is a term most useful in criticism when accompanied by a detailed description of the kind of limitation in the work at hand.

The *objective method* or *objective point of view* is a form of third-person limited omniscience widely used by novelists from the late nineteenth-century onward. This narrative strategy rules out subjective commentary by the author but still allows the omniscient privileges of movement in time and space as well as into and out of the minds of the characters. Joyce's *Ulysses* is the most famous example. The term SELF-EFFACING AUTHOR has frequently been applied to such a writer.

DRAMATIC METHOD is a term used to describe a severely limited form of third-person narration where the privileges of omniscience are sacrificed almost entirely. Using this method, a writer of fiction limits communication to the kind of evidence available to the viewers of a realistic stage play or to an invisible watcher positioned near the scene of the action. The dramatic method is sometimes called the SCENIC METHOD, because it unfolds the story in scenes like a play, or the FLY ON THE WALL TECHNIQUE, for its alert, observant detachment. By any name, the method, a form of the objective method, is characterized by complete objectivity in description of characters and scenes and in reporting of action and speech. Motives remain unexamined, thoughts unexpressed except insofar as they are spoken aloud. The narrator never comments or moralizes and avoids adjectives and adverbs that suggest attitudes in the observer. The author is self-effacing. Hemingway's "The Killers" is an excellent example. See STREAM OF CONSCIOUSNESS.

References

Wayne C. Booth, **The Rhetoric of Fiction** (1961).
E. M. Forster, **Aspects of the Novel** (1927).
Percy Lubbock, **The Craft of Fiction** (1921).
Meir Sternberg, **Expositional Modes and Temporal Ordering in Fiction** (1978).

Narrative Poem. One that tells a story, particularly the EPICS, METRICAL ROMANCE, and shorter narratives, like those ballads and William Morris's "The Haystack in the Floods" (1858) that eschew dialogue and first-person narrative. See BALLAD; NARRATIVE PERSPECTIVE.

Narrator. One who tells a STORY. See NARRATIVE PERSPECTIVE.

National Institute of Arts and Letters. See AMERICAN ACADEMY AND INSTITUTE OF ARTS AND LETTERS.

Native American Literature. See AMERICAN INDIAN LITERATURE.

Naturalism. (1) Broadly, according to nature. In this sense, naturalism is opposed to IDEALISM, emphasizing things accessible to the senses in this world in contrast to permanent or spiritual truths presumed to lie outside it. Thus defined, naturalism is virtually synonymous with REALISM. (2) More specifically, a literary movement of the late nineteenth century, influential on the twentieth. It was an extension of realism, a reaction against the restrictions inherent in the realistic emphasis on the ordinary, as naturalists insisted that the extraordinary is real, too. In place of the middle-class realities of a George Eliot or a William Dean Howells, the naturalists presented the fringes of society, the criminal, the fallen, the down-and-out, earning as one definition of their work the phrase *sordid realism*.

Naturalism came largely from scientific DETERMINISM. Darwinism was especially important, as the naturalists perceived a person's fate as the product of blind external or biological forces, chiefly heredity and environment, but in the typical naturalistic novel chance played a large part as well, suggesting a formula something like $H + E + C = F$ (Heredity plus Environment plus Chance equals Fate).

The naturalists started with the realists' techniques, but they extended and applied them differently. Their pose as scientists allowed a different selection. Rather than a mirror reflecting all life, they chose a lens focused on what interested them. Imitating the experimental scientist rather than the observer, they manipulated their CHARACTERS and PLOT, displaying a fondness for SYMBOL to clarify their social message. For all their claims of objectivity, the result was often a curious subjectivity of vision somewhat akin to earlier ROMANTICISM.

Naturalism began in France, with the Goncourt brothers' *Germinie Lacerteux* (1865) and Émile Zola's *Thérèse Raquin* (1868) and *L'Assommoir* (1877). Zola's essay *"Le Roman expérimental"* ("The Experimental Novel," 1880) remains a central statement for naturalism, picturing the novelist as a scientist in a laboratory, testing hypotheses. In the United States, naturalism reacted against Howellsian realism in the 1890s and the early years of the twentieth century. Stephen Crane's *Maggie* (1893) was the first novel—designed, he wrote, "to show that environment is a tremendous thing in the world and frequently shapes lives regardless." Frank Norris, Theodore Dreiser, Upton Sinclair, and the MUCK-RAKERS followed. Naturalism also appears in the plays of Eugene O'Neill and the novels of James T. Farrell. In England, naturalism was less visible, but its effects are perceptible in the novels of Thomas Hardy, George Moore, and George Gissing.

Nature. In literature and CRITICISM, a concept with multiple meanings applied both to subject matter and technique. To use nature as subject matter has generally meant to describe things in the natural world (see NATURALISM [1]). To write naturally has generally meant to look to the world of nature for models or into oneself (one's human nature) rather than to literature for principles of guidance. Beyond these general senses, however, the specific characteristics of nature in literature are determined by the different views held in different times and by different people about nature itself.

Neoclassical thought of the eighteenth century saw nature as carefully ordered, according to a plan not in all ways accessible to human beings. Natural literature, then, would reflect this ordered world through the application of ordered, because natural, techniques. RO-MANTICISM at the end of the eighteenth century and the beginning of the nineteenth broke with this view by emphasizing the lack of order, or wildness, in nature, and therefore in literature. These fundamentally different views will stand for others as well, from different times, respecting the idea of nature; and all depend, in part, upon one's understanding of the place of a divine being or beings with reference to the world. *Natural law,* for example, is perhaps the ideal of perfect harmony as seen in Eden before the first transgression and the Fall. Or else it is the law of nature as viewed in the world we now inhabit, imperfect, but still God's. Or, perhaps, giving it another emphasis, it is the law of the jungle in a world of scientific DETERMINISM, with the deity absent or nonexistent. *Human nature* is inborn, naturally depraved, says CALVINISM, naturally good, said Rousseau.

Finally, there is the ancient question whether nature represents reality, as Aristotle believed, or is only illusory, in the Platonic sense of deceptive appearances. Writers who emphasize nature have accepted the proposition that the truth is in it or can be discovered through it. Writers who turn aside from nature, or downplay it, seek to transcend it through reason or inspiration. See MIMESIS.

Near Rhyme.   See SLANT RHYME.

Negative Capability.   An expression used by John Keats in a letter (December 21, 27[?], 1817) to his brothers George and Thomas:

> I had not a dispute but a disquistion with Dilke, on various subjects; several things dovetailed in my mind, & at once it struck me, what quality went to form a Man of Achievement especially in Literature & which Shakespeare possessed so enormously—I mean *Negative Capability,* that is when man is capable of being in uncertainties, Mysteries, doubts, without any irritable reaching after fact & reason—Coleridge, for instance, would let go by a fine isolated verisimilitude caught from the Penetralium of mystery, from being incapable of remaining content with half knowledge. This pursued through Volumes would perhaps take us no further than this, that with a great poet the sense of Beauty overcomes every other consideration, or rather obliterates all consideration.

Keats emphasizes here his sense that the best poets remain objective about their work, isolating it from their personal concerns or values, in contrast to the more subjective practice of many of his contemporaries, including Coleridge, whom he specifically cites. The work exists as an entity, its beauty as art entirely separate from considerations of actuality, including the further pursuit of knowledge glimpsed within it. Earlier in the same letter, Keats wrote:

> . . . the excellence of every Art is its intensity, capable of making all disagreeables evaporate, from their being in close relationship with Beauty & Truth—Examine King Lear & you will find this exemplified throughout. . . .

Nemesis. Greek goddess of vengeance; the personification of righteous indignation. Nemesis pursues and punishes those who have displeased the gods. Later, the term became associated with any agent of fate or bringer of just retribution. See TRAGEDY.

Neoclassical Period. Generally, the span of time from the restoration of Charles II to his father's throne in 1660 until Wordsworth and Coleridge's *Lyrical Ballads* (1798). The period is conventionally divided into the RESTORATION (1660–1700), the AUGUSTAN AGE (1700–1750), and the Age of Johnson (1750–1798; see JOHNSON, AGE OF).

Seeking a balance between the extremes that had shattered England during the Civil War and the COMMONWEALTH (1642–1660), writers hoped to revive something like the classical Pax Romana, the century of peace and literary excellence under Augustus, beginning in 30 B.C. Dialectical reasoning dominated, as poets, chiefly Dryden, sought to establish a reasonable, dignified, colloquial, and urbane footing for a society badly shaken ever since Copernicus threw the solid earth into orbit in 1543. SATIRE and IRONY, both ways of asserting the unstated and attacking fanaticism while avoiding it, thrived. The HEROIC COUPLET balanced the dialectical contrasts in iambic pentameter lines thought to represent both the classical hexameters of Virgil and the colloquial measures of Horace. The irregular ODE, developed earlier by Abraham Cowley (1618–1667), offered a classical release from restriction. Criticism, deriving from French rationalizations of Aristotle, prescribed RULES for the three UNITIES for drama: (1) action—everything coherent and whole; (2) time—one day only, preferably 12 hours; (3) place—all action in one place only, the rest reported. The rule of DECORUM demanded propriety—no horrors on stage—especially in characterization: kings should act and speak like kings; beggars, like beggars.

This Age of Reason sought to establish, through DEISM, the acceptance of God's rationally ordered universe, and yet to attack humankind's pride in its rational superiority to the rest of creation. The highest reason was to know the limits of reason, to discover a modest common sense. In spite of discoveries in science and emerging ideas of progress, the period was strongly conservative, holding on to what was known, and primitivistic, assuming that humankind had slipped downhill from some Golden Age in Eden or Arcadia and that change was likely to be for the worse.

Charles II soon proved no Augustus. Wars and the threat of civil war persisted. The Glorious Revolution of 1688 established the balanced double reign of William and Mary, and marked the watershed into Modern English under the puissant pen of John Dryden. Normality, detachment, urbanity, abhorrence of any *enthusiasm*, was the keynote. Classical architecture reproduced the serenity, balance, and proportion sought in art and daily life. But individualism and inner consciousness soon began to percolate under the classical calm, to erupt eventually in the ROMANTIC PERIOD and the modern world.

New Augustan hopes arose with the Treaty of Utrecht under Anne, in 1713, and with each new George. Prose, after Elizabethan uncertainties and seventeenth-century extremities, settled into a flexible colloquial urbanity, notably with the *Tatler* and *Spectator* papers of Addison and Steele and the new novel. REALISM entered, serious in Defoe, comic in Fielding, and the old romantic paradigm of the unknown nobody who discovers himself or herself somebody, and lives happily ever after, dominated the rising novel as it reflected social aspirations. As the period progressed, SENTIMENTALISM emerged on its way to the inner emphasis of the Romantic period.

Neologism. A word newly coined or newly introduced into a language, or a new meaning given to an old word. Some neologisms are accepted and become part of the standard vocabulary, as, in English, *magazine* (Arabic, via Old French) in its now common sense of *periodical*, introduced in the eighteenth century, and *robot* (Czech), an import of the 1920s. See COINED WORDS; NONCE WORD; PORTMANTEAU WORD.

Neo-Platonism. The philosophy of Plotinus and his followers (third century to sixth century A.D.). A form of IDEALISM, Neo-Platonism rejected theories of dualism, suggesting that there is one order of existence in the universe. From the fountain of the One flows the Divine Mind, which, in the form of a World Soul, unites with the material world. Religion, or contemplation, is the means by which humans seek union with the One. Sin is a negation of union, a turning away from the central idealistic principle. For literary theorists, Neo-Platonism provides support for the idea of the poet as inspired seer, mystically in tune with the One, bringing transcendent truth to a world deceived by the forms of physical reality. See INSPIRATION; PLATONISM.

New Comedy. See COMEDY.

New Criticism. An approach to CRITICISM prominent in the United States after the publication of John Crowe Ransom's *New Criticism* (1941) and fostered in colleges and universities by the phenomenal success over several decades of Cleanth Brooks's and Robert Penn Warren's introductory textbook *Understanding Poetry* (1938). Generally, the New Critics were agreed that a poem or story should be considered an organic unit, with each part working to support the whole. They worked by close ANALYSIS, considering the text as the final authority, and were distrustful, though not wholly neglectful, of considerations brought from outside the text, as, for example, from biography or history. Besides Ransom, Brooks, and Warren, critics writing from a New Critical bias included Allen Tate, R. P. Blackmur, Yvor Winters, and Kenneth Burke. Among earlier critics pointing in the New Critical direction were T. S. Eliot and, especially, the English writers I. A. Richards and William Empson.

In the 1950s, the New Critical approach came under mild attack, especially by the CHICAGO CRITICS, as too restrictive.

For explanations of specific New Critical positions see AFFECTIVE FALLACY; BIOGRAPHICAL FALLACY; GENETIC FALLACY; INTENTIONAL FALLACY. For later critical movements in some ways related to the New Criticism, see STRUCTURALISM; POST-STRUCTURALISM.

Newgate. London prison dating from the twelfth century, originally in the main west gate to the city, torn down in 1902. Burned in the Peasants' Revolt of 1381, it was rebuilt in the fifteenth century. Executions were held outside, attracting huge crowds until they were moved inside in 1868. The *Newgate Calendar* was a publication providing accounts of prisoners.

New Journalism. A style of reporting arising in the 1960s in the United States, associated especially with Tom Wolfe and Norman Mailer. The new journalists abandoned traditional journalistic objectivity to create a literature characterized by strong evidences of the author's personality and opinions, with the author sometimes also a character involved in the events being reported. Examples include Wolfe's *Electric Kool-Aid Acid Test* (1968) and Mailer's *Armies of the Night* (1968). See NON-FICTION NOVEL, an alternate term applied especially to works of reportage cast in the shape of novels.

New Novel. See *NOUVEAU ROMAN*.

Nihilism. "Nothing-ism": a theory of revolution popular among extremists in Russia from the mid-nineteenth century until the abdication of the czar in 1917. Nihilists believed that before new structures could be built, the old had to be completely torn down. Revolutionaries were encouraged to act independently, destroying through assassination, arson, and other acts of terrorism. Ivan Turgenev gave the movement a name in his novel *Fathers and Sons* (1861). The term is also used to refer to similar later movements in other countries. As a philosophy, nihilism involves a belief in nothing, or the total invalidity of traditional ideas of reality and value. In this sense, it is related to EXISTENTIALISM.

Nihil Obstat. Latin for "nothing hinders": a phrase used within the Roman Catholic church to indicate that a book has been judged free of doctrinal or moral error. The phrase is printed on the reverse of the title page. See IMPRIMATUR.

Nine Worthies. As listed in William Caxton's preface to Malory's *Morte Darthur* (1485), "the best that ever were": three pagans (Hector, Alexander the Great, and Julius Caesar), three Jews (Joshua, David, and Judas Maccabeus), and three Christians (Arthur, Charlemagne, and Godfrey of Boulogne).

Nobel Prize. The most prestigious international award for outstanding achievement in literature, as well as in chemistry, economics, medicine, peace, and physics. The awards were established in the will of Alfred Nobel (1833–1896), Swedish inventor of dynamite, and were first given in 1901. Ordinarily, the prizes are annual, with no restrictions as to nationality, with an emphasis on long-term rather than short-term accomplishment.

Noble Savage. A phrase suggesting that humans are inherently good and live moral lives in a savage state, apart from the corrupting influence of civilization. The term appeared first in Dryden's HEROIC PLAY *The Conquest of Granada* (1670):

> I am as free as nature first made man,
> Ere the base laws of servitude began,
> When wild in woods the noble savage ran.

But the idea is especially associated with Jean Jacques Rousseau (1712–1778), whose works were widely influential in the eighteenth and nineteenth centuries. During this time, the American Indian was seen by many Europeans as the most interesting example of the noble savage. See PRIMITIVISM; ROMANTICISM; ROMANTIC PERIOD.

Nocturne. A night piece: writing evocative of evening or night.

Nō (or Noh) Drama. A form of Japanese DRAMA developed in the fourteenth century. Zeami Motokiyo (1363–1443) is usually considered the greatest *Nō* dramatist. The plays are highly stylized, presenting traditional materials, often religious, through a combination of prose, poetry, MIME, music, and dance. Masks and a chorus are used, as in Greek drama. Plays are short, lyrically tragic, slow in movement, and almost plotless. Language is imagistic and symbolic. *Nō* drama has greatly influenced twentieth-century poets and dramatists in English, beginning with Ezra Pound and William Butler Yeats. See KABUKI.

References

Donald Keene, ed., **Twenty Plays of the No Theatre** (1970).
L. C. Pronko, **Guide to Japanese Drama** (1973).

Nom de Plume. French for "pen name": a PSEUDONYM.

Nominalism. In the Middle Ages, the belief that universals have no real being, but are only names, their existence limited to their presence in the minds and language of humans. This belief, advanced by William of Ockham (c. 1295–c. 1349) and others, was opposed to the beliefs of medieval realists, including St. Thomas Aquinas (1225–1274), who held that universals have an independent existence, at least in the mind of God. See REALISM (IN PHILOSOPHY).

Nonce Word. A word coined for a single occasion, from Middle English *for the nones:* "for the once." A nonce word is sometimes used only by the coiner and not repeated in the useage of others.

Nonfiction Novel. A journalistic account of actual events dramatized novelistically. The method originated in the NEW JOURNALISM of Tom Wolfe's *Kandy-Kolored Tangerine-Flake Streamline Baby,* a collection of shorter pieces, and Truman Capote's more novel-like *In Cold Blood,* both in 1965.

Nonsense Verse. (1) Verse written to amuse by its sounds and rhythms, with little or no attention paid to sense, as often in NURSERY RHYMES and other verse for children. Edward Lear and Lewis Carroll were famous authors of nonsense verse. (2) Sometimes in FOLK SONG, a verse or REFRAIN that has lost its meaning through oral transmission, nonsense syllables replacing meaningful lines imperfectly remembered or originating in another language or DIALECT.

Norman Conquest.   The period of English history in which the Normans consolidated their hold on England after the defeat of the Saxon King Harold by William, duke of Normandy, in 1066. French became the court language and Norman lords gained control of English lands, but Anglo-Saxon administrative and judicial systems remained largely in place. See ANGLO-NORMAN (LANGUAGE); ENGLISH LANGUAGE; MIDDLE ENGLISH LITERATURE.

Nouveau Roman.   French for "new novel": a term applied to the work of French experimental writers, especially Nathalie Sarraute, Claude Simon, Alain Robbe-Grillet, and Michael Butor, who attained international fame and influence in the 1950s and 1960s. The new novel rejects earlier novelistic emphases on story, character, theme, chronology, and the like in favor of an objective reporting of uninterpreted facts and images, with no authorial interpretation or order imposed. Robbe-Grillet's work is central, as seen, for example, in *Les Gommes* (1953; translated as *The Erasers*, 1964) and *La Jalousie* (1957; translated as *Jealousy*, 1959). For an explanation of his theories, see his *Pour un nouveau roman* (1963), translated in *Snapshots* (1965). See ANTI-NOVEL.

Nouvelle.   French for SHORT STORY or TALE (but not for NOVEL, which in French is a *roman*).

Novel.   The extended prose fiction that arose in the eighteenth century to become the major literary expression of the modern world. The term comes from the Italian *novella*, the short "new" tale of intrigue and moral comeuppance most eminently collected in, and disseminated by, Boccaccio's *Decameron* (1348–1353). Novellas characteristically are morally illustrative tales inserted for diversion in longer prose works. The terms *novel* and *romance*, from the French *roman*, competed interchangeably for most of the eighteenth century.

The novel compounds two opposite ways of looking at experience, two narrative lines evolving with story telling from the most distant past: (1) the romance and (2) the picaresque tale. Story telling doubtless began as soon as language became sociable, in about 40,000 B.C., as anthropologist Louis S. B. Leakey has estimated, when the group could kindle fire and no longer had to lie low and alert for the creeping cat. From this talk, probably arose accounts of past heroes, of gods, of creation—the lore of the EPIC, which celebrates the culture, taken as history. Then came romances, still with some historical base, as in the medieval cycles concerning the ARTHURIAN LEGEND and Charlemagne, but known and enjoyed as fanciful, once upon a time, long ago and far away—wish fulfillments about mighty deeds and unknown squires who adore ladies impossibly high above them and who discover noble identity, marry high, and live happily ever after. Longus's *Daphnis and Chloe* (third century A.D.), a Greek pastoral tale of two infant foundlings, a boy and a girl, who eventually discover their noble identities and happiness in marriage, is the earliest example, complete with the unknown nobody becoming somebody. The romance indulged in elevation—noble people, noble deeds, noble ideals, noble language, recounted, like the epic, in the third person: "A gentle knight was pricking on the plaine." The romance made its impression on the novel, directly and through Henry Fielding's Cervantic reaction, with the huge French volumes of Madeleine de Scudéry (*The Grand Cyrus, Clelia, Almahide*) and Gauthier de La Calprenède (*Cleopatra, Cassandra, Pharamond*), dating between 1640 and 1663 and immediately translated into English, elaborate fancies about the ancient world and Middle East in chivalric armor.

The picaresque tale takes the opposite view, portraying the nether side of life: low people, low tricks, low language; instead of high seriousness, low comedy; instead of ideals, scatology and wiles; instead of ideal love, sex; instead of the far away and long ago, the here and now; instead of fancy, rough reality. The first picaresque tale was the anonymous Spanish *Lazarillo de Tormes* (1553), "The Little Beggar of Tormes," giving the GENRE its name from the Spanish word for "rogue," *picaro*. But the mode originated with the lost Greek MILESIAN TALE of Aristides of Miletus (c. 100 B.C.), preceding the romance of Longus by several centuries, becoming the medieval FABLIAU, and still surviving virtually unchanged as the dirty joke continues to exhibit humankind's comic lusts and animalities. Petronius's *Satyricon* (c. A.D. 60) and Apuleius's *Golden Ass* (c. A.D. 150), both in Latin, are other early examples.

Like the romance, the picaresque tale is peripatetic, as the hero moves from one place and escapade to the next. Hence it is also satiric, since the hero travels through the social strata, exposing their undersides. Thomas Nashe's *Unfortunate Traveller, or the Life of Jack Wilton* (1594) is England's first picaresque novel, also containing the earliest burlesque of chivalric romance. Other collections of Spanish rogue tales were known to the eighteenth-century novelists. Thomas Deloney's *Jack of Newberry, Thomas of Reading,* and *The Gentle Craft* (all c. 1597) extol the middle-class virtues of clothiers, weavers, and shoe-makers among picaresque episodes, forecasting the middle-class ethos of Defoe and Richardson.

In 1605, Cervantes confronted the world of romance with the pic-aresque realities of the road in *Don Quixote* (second part, 1615), cre-ating an everlasting comic amalgam of the lofty ideal and the grimy real that was to form the English novel in varying proportions, partic-ularly through Fielding's Cervantic transformation in *Joseph Andrews* (1742), and was to continue on through *Huckleberry Finn* and *The Great Gatsby* and out into future Space. Paul Scarron's *Roman Comique* (1651, 1657)—translated by Tom Brown as *The Comical Romance* (1700)—itself indebted to Cervantes as Scarron laughed at the ro-mances of Scudéry and La Calprenède, also contributed to Fielding's *Joseph Andrews.* Other French fiction influencing the new romantic-realistic novel was the Countess de La Fayette's *Princesse de Clèves* (1678), Le Sage's *Gil Blas* (1715, 1735, a new picaresque, strongly influencing Tobias Smollett), Marivaux's *Marianne* (1731) and *La Pay-san parvenu* (1735), and Prévost's *Manon Lescaut* (1731).

Aphra Behn's *Oroonoko, or The Royal Slave* (1688), the first anti-slavery novel, portrays a noble black paragon, the equal of La Cal-prenède's Oroöndates in *Cassandra,* in the romantic and exotic setting of Surinam, probably drawn from actuality, even as Behn claimed. Its romantic power probably lent some features to Crusoe's man Friday and probably led Defoe to move Alexander Selkirk's island from the Pacific to the Caribbean in the confluence of the "Oroonooko" River, as he spells it. *Robinson Crusoe* (1719), the world classic Defoe derived from Selkirk's marooning, may stand as the first fully fledged modern novel, bringing together the three attributes that will characterize the genre: (1) contemporaneity, (2) verisimilitude, (3) philosophical signif-icance. In a romantic, actualized setting, the comic outcast picaresque "I" has become serious: the modern individual seeking a place and identity in God's universe and society.

But Samuel Richardson's *Pamela* (1740), the world's first best seller, an EPISTOLARY NOVEL, really set the new genre on its way. A virtuous serving girl, a Miss Andrews named for a princess in Sidney's romance, *Arcadia,* is again the noble romantic nobody finding her place in triumph and high marriage. Fielding parodied Richardson in his *Life of Mrs. Shamela Andrews* (1741) and again in *Joseph Andrews* (1741), England's first comic novel, "Written in Imitation of the Man-ner of Cervantes." Richardson followed with *Clarissa* (1748), the first tragic novel and his masterpiece, and Fielding with his masterpiece *Tom Jones* (1749). Smollett, beginning with *Roderick Random* (1748) and ending with *Humphry Clinker* and his death in 1771, concluded the first great period of the novel, which included Sterne's *Tristram Shandy* (1759–1767), a Rabelaisian masterpiece of eccentricity on the comic inability of human beings to achieve their aims.

In 1764, Horace Walpole, tiring of the new novel's comic realism, launched a new wave of romances with *The Castle of Otranto, A Gothic Story* (see GOTHIC NOVEL). In 1766, the SENTIMENTAL NOVEL emerged from the comic shell with Goldsmith's *Vicar of Wakefield*, reaching a high-water mark with Henry Mackenzie's *Man of Feeling* (1771), derived directly from Sterne's technique of comic fragmentation which Sterne had acquired, in turn, from Swift's *Tale of a Tub*. In the 1790s, Jane Austen, like Cervantes and Fielding, began by parodying the romances of her day, specifically the Gothics of Ann Radcliffe, and produced her quietly comic masterpieces between 1811 and 1818.

Although William Hill Brown's *Power of Sympathy* (1789), a Richardsonian story of seduction, was America's first novel, Charles Brockden Brown's *Wieland* (1798) was second only in time. It was the first to gain recognition abroad and to remain a significant and powerful work. The nineteenth century produced masterpieces on both sides of the Atlantic as the novel became the leading international form. See ANTI-NOVEL; ANTIREALISTIC NOVEL; *BILDUNGSROMAN*; DIME NOVEL; HISTORICAL NOVEL; *KÜNSTLERROMAN*; PICARESQUE NOVEL; PSYCHOLOGICAL NOVEL; *ROMAN À CLEF*.

Novelette. A short novel or long short story, like Stevenson's *Dr. Jekyll and Mr. Hyde*, Melville's *Billy Budd*, James's *Turn of the Screw*, Conrad's "Heart of Darkness," and Bellow's *Seize the Day*.

Novelization. A novel made from a film script.

Novella. A short tale, like those in Boccaccio's *Decameron* (1348–1353) and the poetic *Contes de la Reine de Navarre* compiled by Marguerite D'Angoulême (Marguerite de Valois), queen of Navarre, published in 1558, 10 years after her death. The work was later called the *Heptameron*, 72 short stories told by ladies and gentlemen detained by a flood. Cervantes in *Don Quixote* (1605, 1615) and Fielding, his disciple in English, introduced the short interruptive tale into the novel, though it was also characteristic of the ROMANCE Cervantes and Fielding parodied. The term *novel*, deriving from the Italian word *novella*, slowly gained predominance in the late eighteenth century over the terms *romance* and *history*.

Novel of Character.   One emphasizing character rather than plot or excitement.

Novel of Incident.   One in which incidents follow one another with little causal relation, easily interchangeable, as in Defoe's *Moll Flanders* (1722).

Novel of Manners.   A term adopted from the COMEDY OF MANNERS to describe novels emphasizing manners and mores, usually comically and satirically, as in Fielding and Austen, but also seriously, as in Edith Wharton, J. P. Marquand, or John Cheever.

Novel of Sensibility.   One implying unusual sensitivity to suffering in characters and readers, as in Richardson's *Pamela* (1740), *Clarissa* (1748), and *Sir Charles Grandison* (1754). The term also includes the even more emotive SENTIMENTAL NOVEL.

Novel of the Soil.   One about life wrested from untamed land, as in Knut Hamsun's *Growth of the Soil* (1920), Ellen Glasgow's *Barren Ground* (1925), and Ole Rölvaag's *Giants in the Earth* (1927).

Nursery Rhymes.   Traditional songs for children, some dating from early vernacular times but most added to the tradition in the sixteenth, seventeenth, and especially the eighteenth centuries, a few with veiled historical and satirical allusions. A French version of "Thirty days hath September" was known in the thirteenth century. European parallels for "Ladybird, ladybird, fly away home," "London Bridge is falling down," and "Humpty Dumpty" point to ancient common sources. Ann and Jane Taylor added "Twinkle, twinkle, little star" to the canon in 1806; Sarah Josepha Hale, "Mary had a little lamb" in 1830.

Many people have proposed historical and political bases, but probability sustains only a few. One rhyme names an eighteenth-century alewife in county Durham:

> Elsie Marley is grown so fine
> She won't get up to feed the swine.

Somerset tradition identifies "Little Jack Horner" (printed 1725) with Thomas Horner of Mells, who pulled out several rich plums when Henry VIII dissolved the monasteries.

The earliest-known collection is *Tommy Thumb's Pretty Song Book* (2 vols., London, 1744); the most influential, *Mother Goose's Melody: or Sonnets for the Cradle*, published 1781 by the firm of John Newbery (died 1767). Isaiah Thomas reprinted this in the United States in 1785, giving America its first edition and the popular appellation "Mother Goose rhymes." The Newbery company acquired "Mother Goose" from the subtitle of Charles Perrault's collection of fairy tales ("Little Red Ridinghood," "Cinderella," "Sleeping Beauty"): *Contes de ma mere l'oye* (1697, "Tales of My Mother Goose"), a French phrase equivalent to the English "old wive's tales." An unfounded American legend identifies Mother Goose as Elizabeth Goose (Vergoose, Vertigoose), buried in Old Granary Burying Ground, Boston, claiming that she wrote and published the rhymes in 1719. See FAIRY TALE.

O

Obiter Dicta. "Statements in passing"—incidental remarks, particularly those in a judge's opinion that are not central and binding, or an author's casual observations. Augustine Birrell published a series of three *Obiter Dicta* (1884, 1887, 1924).

Objective Camera. In film terminology, a camera positioned to place the viewer as an observer of the action, but not a participant. See POINT OF VIEW SHOT; SUBJECTIVE CAMERA.

Objective Correlative. T. S. Eliot's term for the objective events in an artistic work that represent its essential emotion. Eliot found *Hamlet* a disquieting artistic failure because Shakespeare could find no *"objective correlative"* for the emotional significance he himself could not grasp:

> The only way of expressing emotion in the form of art is by finding an "objective correlative"; in other words, a set of objects, a situation, a chain of events which shall be the formula of that *particular* emotion; such that when the external facts, which must terminate in sensory experience, are given, the emotion is immediately evoked.
>
> *"Hamlet and His Problems," Athenaeum 26
> (September 1919), repr. The Sacred Wood
> (London, 1920), and later in Collected Essays*

Eliot's quotation marks suggest that he has borrowed the term. George P. Winston points to Washington Allston's *Lectures on Art* (1850) in "Washington Allston and the Objective Correlative," *Bucknell Review* 11 (1962), 95–108.

Objective Criticism. CRITICISM that emphasizes the work itself, paying little attention to the artist, the subject matter, or the audience.

Objective Method (or **Objective Point of View**). Narration, or story telling, from a completely objective stance, eliminating all traces of authorial subjectivity. See NARRATIVE PERSPECTIVE; SELF-EFFACING AUTHOR.

Objectivity. A quality achieved in writing when an author omits or suppresses the writer's personal emotions, attitudes, or opinions. Objectivity is much prized in mid-twentieth-century CRITICISM. See SUBJECTIVITY.

320

Obligatory Scene. A scene so inevitable as a play progresses as to seem mandatory, as in the WELL-MADE PLAY; the French *Scène à faire*.

Oblique Rhyme. See SLANT RHYME.

Obscenity. Anything offensive to general standards of decency, especially lewdness in language or action. See PORNOGRAPHY. On 6 December 1933, Judge John M. Woolsey ruled that Joyce's *Ulysses* was not obscene and could therefore be admitted into the United States. "The meaning of the word 'obscene' as legally defined by the Courts is: tending to stir the sex impulses or to lead to sexually impure and lustful thoughts," wrote Woolsey. He had checked his own reaction with two independent readers and found no excitation but only "a somewhat tragic and very powerful commentary on the inner lives of men and women." But in 1973, the Supreme Court somewhat tightened the limits Woolsey had broadened, ruling that prurient material without serious literary, artistic, political, or scientific value could be banned as obscene by communities finding it offensive to their standards.

Reference

H. M. Clor, **Obscenity and Public Morality** (1969).

Occasional Verse. Poetry celebrating an occasion, like Marvell's "Horation Ode upon Cromwell's Return from Ireland" (1650), Dryden's "Astrea Redux" (1660), or the many odes turned out by Poets Laureate to commemorate coronations and rulers' birthdays. Personal love poems, the EPITHALAMIUM, and the ELEGY are also sometimes designated "occasional."

Octastich. A unit of verse in eight lines. See OCTAVE.

Octave. (1) The first unit in an Italian SONNET: eight lines of iambic pentameter, rhyming *abbaabba*. See METER. (2) A STANZA in eight lines. Examples include OTTAVA RIMA and doubled four-line stanzas, as in Burns's "John Anderson My Jo," Edwin Arlington Robinson's "The Mill," and Robert Frost's "Two Tramps in Mud Time."

Octavo. (Abbreviated 8vo, 8°): a book made from sheets folded to give signatures of 8 leaves (16 pages), a book of average size. See BOOK SIZES; SIGNATURE.

Octet. An OCTASTICH or OCTAVE.

Octosyllabic. Eight-syllable. Iambic tetrameter is octosyllabic. See METER.

Ode. A long, stately lyric poem in stanzas of varied metrical pattern. The Greek ode began in choral celebrations of songs danced to measure, which the Greek drama adopted. Pindar (c. 522–443 B.C.) took over the dramatic ode to celebrate the feats of athletes: a STROPHE and an ANTISTROPHE in identical pattern, concluded with a differing EPODE. Horace and Catullus followed the simpler stanzaic patterns and meters of Sappho, Anacreon, and Alcaeus, along with their personal subjects, repeating the same stanza (usually four lines) throughout. Ronsard (1524–85) revived the ode in France, with Pindarics for public occasions and Horatians for private. Horatian odes influenced Jonson, Herrick, and Marvell. Milton's "On the Morning of Christ's Nativity" evolved from the Pindaric ode in four matched stanzas. Abraham Cowley (1618–1667) developed an irregular ode with stanzas and lines changing freely. The Cowleyan ode bequeathed the eighteenth century with a classical escape for sublimity and emotion from the sophisticated restraints of the couplet, but the later eighteenth century reembraced Pindar. Famous examples of the three types of ode are:

> Pindaric ("regular")—Thomas Gray's "The Progress of Poetry" (1759)
> Horatian ("homostrophic")—Keats's "To Autumn" (1820)
> Cowleyan ("irregular")—Wordsworth's "Ode: Intimations of Immortality from Recollections of Early Childhood" (1807)

Allen Tate's "Ode to the Confederate Dead" and Wallace Stevens's "The Idea of Order at Key West" are distinguished examples of the infrequent ode in the twentieth century.

Oedipus Complex. Freud's basic concept that the male child between the ages of three and six suppresses his sexual urge to kill his father and sleep with his mother. Freud named it after Oedipus, the legendary Greek king who unwittingly did just that. See ELECTRA COMPLEX for its female opposite, and FREUDIAN CRITICISM.

Off Rhyme. See SLANT RHYME.

Old Comedy. See COMEDY.

Old English. The language brought to England, beginning in 449, by the Jute, Angle, and Saxon invaders from Denmark's Jutland peninsula; the language base from which modern English evolved. Old English is a Low West Germanic language of the Indo-European family, related most closely to Flemish, Dutch, and Frisian. It had already acquired some words from Latin before arrival: *copor* (copper), *win* (wine), *weall* (wall), *pund* (pound), *cuppe* (cup), *flasce* (flask), and *segl* (sail), for instance. It soon picked up place names from the native Celts, like *York*, for instance, and the names of rivers, like Shakespeare's Avon, the Usk, Ouse, Stour, and many others. The Romans had already named their base camp on the Thames *Londinium*, from the Celtic *londos* (wild).

Old English is a "synthetic," or inflected, language, signaling its grammar by word endings, as in German or Latin, with the usual Germanic order of verb before subject and object after verb:

Þā Þæs on sumera on ðysum gērē tōfōr sē here.
"Then thus in summer in this year dispersed the army."
Ond Þā sē here eft hāmweard wende Þe Exanceaster beseten hæfde.
"And then the army back homeward wended that Exeter beset had."

After the Conquest (1066), Norman French rubbed off what remained of inflectional endings, already slowly eroding, and reversed the old synthetic Germanic order into the analytic subject-verb-object order of today. Except for simple concrete words like *stone, tree, man,* and *house,* and connectives like *in, to, what, how,* and *the,* Old English traded a major portion of its old vocabulary for new acquisitions from French and Latin. See ENGLISH LANGUAGE.

Old English Literature.   The literature of England from the Anglo-Saxon invasion of the mid-fifth century until the beginning of the Middle English period in the mid-twelfth century. Old English (Anglo-Saxon) was the vernacular language, Latin the language of much learned and religious literature. During the early years, the Germanic tribes solidified their hold upon the land held earlier by the Celts, introducing legends and lore from the great store of pagan continental myth, but recording little, for they were essentially illiterate. In Northumbria, in the late seventh and eighth centuries, Christianity and literacy combined with these influences to produce a cultural flowering that ended with the Danish invasions of the ninth century. The Old English literary center then shifted to Wessex in the ninth, tenth, and eleventh centuries, in a kingdom unified under Alfred the Great (849–899). Old English was largely neglected as a literary language after the Norman Conquest, although Latin continued in use alongside the French that served as a vernacular literary language until replaced by Middle English.

Much Old English vernacular literature has been lost, much preserved only in fragments, but what remains is rich and varied. Most of the poetry is found in four manuscripts: the Beowulf MS, Junius MS, Exeter Book, and Vercelli MS. Compiled around A.D. 1000 in the West Saxon dialect, they contain poems of much earlier date, many composed in Northumbria during the period of great cultural activity there. The best Old English prose originated later, and is associated with specific writers of the ninth, tenth, and eleventh centuries.

Some of the earliest Old English poetry stems from the Germanic heroic tradition: *Widsith* (c. 650–700) is a fragmentary account by a SCOP, or minstrel, of masters served and far places visited; *Waldere* (c. 750) and *The Fight at Finnsburg* (c. 750) are fragments of hero tales; *Beowulf* is an EPIC set in a Scandinavian pagan world of the fifth or sixth centuries, overlaid with the Christianity of its anonymous seventh- or eighth-century author. An important second group is made up of elegiac poems, lyrical expressions of loss: *Deor,* a catalog of misfortunes in stanzaic form, each stanza ending with the refrain "That passed, so may this"; *The Wanderer* and *The Seafarer,* lamentations of men far from home; *The Ruin,* a description of a city (probably Bath), formerly splendid, now fallen to ruin; and *The Wife's Lament* and *The Husband's Message,* poems of separation. The heroic tradition continues, transformed to suit English conditions, in poems commemorating tenth-century battles with the invading Danes: *The Battle of Brunanburh* and *The Battle of Maldon.* Other anonymous verse included charms, riddles, and gnomic poems (aphorisms and maxims, often concerning everyday life). Finally, there are the religious poems associated with the two poets whose names are known to us. Caedmon and his school, active in Northumbria in the late seventh and early eighth centuries, produced poems on biblical subjects: *Genesis, Exodus, Daniel, Christ and Satan.* Cynewulf, an Anglican poet of a century later, signed four poems: *The Fates of the Apostles, The Ascension, Juliana,* and *Elene.* Among other poems, Cynewulfian in style but probably not by Cynewulf, is *The Dream of the Rood,* a great religious lyric in DREAM VISION form.

Old English prose first flourished under King Alfred, who translated or encouraged the translation from Latin of such works as Pope Gregory's *Pastoral Care,* the Venerable Bede's *Ecclesiastical History of the English People* and Boethius's *Consolation of Philosophy.* Under his sponsorship was begun *The Anglo-Saxon Chronicle,* a compilation of English history beginning with Caesar's invasion in 55 B.C. and carried through to A.D. 1154. Writers of religious homilies include Aelfric (c. 955–c. 1020) and Wulfstan (d. 1023).

Latin verse and prose of the period is usually didactic, consisting of biblical commentaries; moral, philosophic, and scientific treatises; devotional poems; and histories. The Northumbrian priest Bede (673–735) is the great figure, his *Ecclesiastical History* an important source for later historians. See OLD ENGLISH; OLD ENGLISH VERSIFICATION.

References

Stanley B. Greenfield, **A Critical History of Old English Literature** (1965).
F. M. Stenton, **Anglo-Saxon England**, 3rd ed. (1971).
C. L. Wrenn, **A Study of Old English Literature** (1966).
David M. Zesmer, **Guide to English Literature from Beowulf through Chaucer and Medieval Drama** (1961).

Old English Versification.   Unlike the ACCENTUAL-SYLLABIC VERSE fundamental to English poetry since the fourteenth century, Old English poetry was *accentual* only; it was based on a strict count of accents, or stresses, in each line, with the unstressed syllables varying in number. The ordinary line had four stresses, two on each side of a heavy CAESURA. There was no unit larger than the line, as stanzaic divisions were unusual. In place of end rhyme (at the end of the line), rarely found, Old English poetry used ALLITERATION, with a normal line alliterating on three (or sometimes two or all four) of the stressed syllables:

Grendel gongan,   Godes yrre bær   (*Beowulf*, 711)

Essentially the same system was used in Old Icelandic, Old Saxon, and Old High German poetry. Well suited to the stress patterns of these Germanic languages, it allowed the poet to organize the rhythms of speech into structures easily memorized for recitation or singing in an illiterate age. Evidence from *Beowulf* and other poems suggests that the usual manner of presentation was by a SCOP, or minstrel, who would strike a chord on a harp either in conjunction with the stresses, or at rests between them. In Old English, each line was made up of two verses (half-lines, or *hemistichs*), with two stresses each. The caesura provided a marked break between verses. Ordinarily, the alliteration was keyed to the third stress of the line (the first stress after the caesura), with one or both of the first two stresses usually alliterating, and the fourth sometimes. A consonant alliterated only with itself, a vowel with any vowel. The placing of the stresses in relation to the unstressed portions of each half-line allowed for several basic variations on the fundamental pattern (Sievers counted five). Rarely, a half-line had one stress or, if HYPERCATALECTIC, three.

This system prevailed in English poetry from about A.D. 500 to 1100. The similar alliterative line of Middle English verse (ordinarily longer than the Old English line) was derived from it. See ALLITERATIVE VERSE; METER.

References

Appendix I, **Bright's Anglo-Saxon Reader,** rev. by James R. Hulbert (1935).
A. J. Bliss, **The Metre of Beowulf** (1958).
John C. Pope, **The Rhythm of Beowulf** (1942).

Omnibus. An ANTHOLOGY from one author or of collected pieces on related subjects.

Onomatopoeia. The use of words formed or sounding like what they signify—*buzz, crack, smack, whinny*—especially in an extensive capturing of sense by sound, as in Tennyson's frequently quoted lines from *The Princess:*

> The moan of doves in immemorial elms,
> And murmuring of innumerable bees.

Pope's onomatopoetic tour de force in *An Essay on Criticism* is equally famous:

> 'Tis not enough no Harshness gives Offence,
> The *Sound* must seem an *Eccho* to the *Sense.*
> *Soft* is the strain when *Zephyr* gently blows,
> And the *smooth Stream* in *smoother Numbers* flows;
> But when loud Surges lash the sounding Shore,
> The *hoarse, rough Verse* shou'd like the *Torrent* roar.
> When Ajax strives, some Rock's vast Weight to throw
> The Line too *labours,* and the Words move *slow;*
> Not so, when swift *Camilla* scours the Plain,
> Flies o'er th'unbending Corn, and skims along the Main.
>
> *364–373*

Open Couplet. A couplet, or rhymed pair of lines, in which the sense of the second line runs on to the next couplet for completion. It is the opposite of *CLOSED COUPLET.*

Opera. A musical drama wholly sung to orchestral accompaniment. Opera originated in Florence, Italy, when a group of scholars and musicians tried to recapture the effect of Greek drama with a MONODY sung with little or no accompaniment in 1600. In the same year, the composer Jacopo Peri and the poet Giulio Rospigliosi produced *Eurid-ice,* considered the first opera. In 1656 in England, Sir William D'Av-enant circumvented the Commonwealth's prohibition of stage plays, obtaining permission for an "entertainment after the manner of the ancients" and calling it an "Opera," evidently borrowing from the Ital-ians, and producing *The Siege of Rhodes,* a HEROIC PLAY, "the story sung in recitative music." After the RESTORATION, other native En-glish operas followed, notably John Blow's *Venus and Adonis* (c. 1685) and Henry Purcell's *Dido and Aeneas* (1689), with libretto by Naham Tate. Italian opera entered England in translations sung by English singers, with *Arsinoe, Queen of Cypress* (Drury Lane, 1706) and *Cam-illa* (1706). Soon bilingual operas appeared, with Italians and English each singing in their own language. The first Italian opera completely in Italian was *Almahide* (1710). Also in 1710, George Frederic Handel came to England after writing operas in Italy and then becoming direc-tor of music at the Hanoverian court. In 1711, his *Rinaldo* was highly successful, establishing Italian opera on the English stage for the next 3 decades—he wrote about 40—much to the satirical scorn of many stout Englishmen, notably Henry Fielding. Opera stimulated BALLAD OPERA in satirical response, beginning with John Gay's *Beggar's Opera* (1728), and the convention of orchestral preludes, intermissions, and songs in regular drama. See COMIC OPERA; LIGHT OPERA.

Opéra Bouffe.   Very light French OPERA developed from vaudeville and said to be the forerunner of Gilbert and Sullivan.

Operetta.   Originally a light, one-act OPERA, first mentioned in 1770, but becoming synonymous with COMIC OPERA and LIGHT OPERA by the 1860s.

Oral Transmission.   The oral (rather than written or printed) passing of ballads, proverbs, fairy tales, epics, and other folklore among sing-ers and tellers, sometimes extending from generation to generation through many centuries. Some traditional phrasing, patterns, and mne-monic devices remain, while others change and individuals add touches of their own. Hence the several versions of many ballads, for instance, and the repeated traditional metrical phrases, the catalog of ships and heroes, and the accurate geographical details that Homer preserved concerning places he had never seen and times 500 years in his past.

Oration.   A formal speech. Aristotle in his *Rhetoric* (Chapter 3) de-fined three kinds: (1) deliberative or political, concerned with the fu-ture, urging listeners in parliamentary assemblies to do or not to do something; (2) forensic or legal, concerned with the past, attacking or defending somebody in the law courts; and (3) epideictic or ceremonial, the oratory of display, concerned with present circumstances, praising or blaming someone. The classical oration, as set forth by Cicero, Quintilian, and their followers, has eight parts, with some omitted on occasion, and some occasionally shifted:

1. *Exordium* (or *Proem*): The introduction.
2. *Narratio:* General description of subject and background.
3. *Propositio:* The thesis, the statement of what is to be demonstrated or proved.
4. *Partitio:* Statement of how the thesis will be divided and handled.
5. *Confirmatio* (or *Argumentatio* or *Explicatio*): The chief evidence in support of the thesis.
6. *Reprehensio:* Admission and refutation of the claims of the opposition.
7. *Digressio:* The digression to lighten the load with matters related but not essential, coming anywhere between *exordium* and *peroratio.*
8. *Peroratio:* Conclusion and summary with culminating urging.

Formal oration was taught, practiced and enjoyed through the centuries up to the First World War and a little beyond. Edward Everett, for instance, Orator of the Day who delivered the two-hour analysis of the battles at Gettysburg on 19 November 1863, preceding Lincoln's brief dedication of the National Cemetery there, was considered the greatest orator of his time. By his oration on George Washington, delivered in all parts of the country, he had raised more than $100,000 to buy Mount Vernon for the nation.

Organic Form.   Literary structure seen as growing from an inner germinative principle, as a tree grows to fulfill the innate ideal structure of "tree," rather than being some mechanical form imposed from without. Coleridge originated the idea in defending Shakespeare against charges of haphazardness, a wild tangle of flowers and weeds amid arid patches, "a sort of African nature, rich in beautiful monsters," in his lectures on Shakespeare in 1812. The idea has persisted, most significantly in the NEW CRITICISM, in the metaphor of the growing plant. According to Coleridge, organic form follows "a law which all parts obey," a kind of Aristotelian-Platonic fulfillment of its ideal kind, as in forms of the natural world, with all parts inseparable and the whole greater than the sum of its parts.

No work of true genius dares want its appropriate form, neither indeed is there any danger of this. As it must not, so genius cannot, be lawless; for it is even this that constitutes it genius—the power of acting creatively under laws of its own origination . . . . The true ground for the mistake [of thinking Shakespeare wild, lawless, and formless] lies in the confounding mechanical regularity with organic form. The form is mechanic, when on any given material we impress a pre-determined form, not necessarily arising out of the properties of the material;—as when to a mass of wet clay we give whatever shape we wish it to retain when hardened. The organic form, on the other hand, is innate; it shapes, as it develops, itself from within, and the fulness of its development is one and the same with the perfection of its outward form. Such as the life is, such is the form. Nature, the prime genial artist, inexhaustible in diverse powers, is equally inexhaustible in forms;—each exterior is the physiognomy of the being within,—its true image reflected and thrown out from the concave mirror;—and even such is the appropriate excellence of her chosen poet, of our own Shakespeare,—himself a nature humanized, a genial understanding directing self-consciously a power and an implicit wisdom deeper even than our consciousness.

> *"Shakespeare, A Poet Generally," in*
> *The Literary Remains of Samuel Taylor*
> *Coleridge, vol. 2 (London, 1836), 66–68.*

Ossianic Controversy. The dispute that erupted when the Scottish poet James Macpherson (1736–1796) published *Fingal* (1762) and *Temora* (1763), claiming them to be translations from the Gaelic of a third-century bard named Ossian. Earlier, Macpherson had published *Fragments of Ancient Poetry Collected in the Highlands of Scotland, and Translated from the Gaelic or Erse Language,* (1760). Encouraged by that success, he raised money and toured the Highlands with a group of scholars to find the lost EPIC he claimed could still be recovered. The authenticity of the resulting *Fingal* and *Temora* was soon challenged by Samuel Johnson and others. Macpherson failed to produce his Gaelic originals, although some revised and transcribed MANU-SCRIPTS were made available by the Highland Society in 1807. From the surviving evidence, it seems that Macpherson possessed some Gaelic originals, not necessarily from the third century, but that he created much that he published. His Ossianic poems had a great influence on later European literature, helping foster an interest in the romantic and heroic past. See ROMANTICISM.

Ottava Rima. A STANZA of eight lines of iambic pentameter (see METER), rhyming *abababcc*. Boccaccio first made it popular, and it was used later by Ariosto in *Orlando Furioso* and by Byron in *Don Juan*:

> I want a hero: an uncommon want,
>   When every year and month sends forth a new one,
> Till, after cloying the gazettes with cant,
>   The age discovers he is not the true one;
> Of such as these I should not care to vaunt,
>   I'll therefore take our ancient friend Don Juan—
> We all have seen him, in the pantomime,
> Sent to the devil somewhat ere his time.

More recently, Yeats used it for "Sailing to Byzantium," "Among School Children," and other poems.

Outride. Gerard Manley Hopkins's term for an extra unstressed syllable. Since Hopkins scanned by stresses only, his foot may have as many as three extra *outrides*. See SCANSION.

Overstatement. Exaggeration understood as such, to emphasize a point; also called *hyperbole*. It may be straight: "Heavenly creature! You are a saint." "She is an angel." Or it may be ironic, as when Pope teasingly refers to Belinda's eyes as so dazzling that the sun fears to awaken her and have himself extinguished:

> Sol thro' white Curtains shot a tim'rous Ray,
> And op'd those Eyes that must eclipse the Day.

Straight overstatement may fail by suggesting insincerity or hypocrisy. See AUXESIS.

Oxford Movement. A movement to reform the Anglican church according to the high-church and more nearly Catholic ideals and rituals of the later seventeenth-century church. The Reverend John Keble provided the inspiration, and continuing leadership, first in his widely read poems, *The Christian Year* (1827), then specifically in his sermon, "National Apostasy," preached at the university chapel, Oxford, on 14 July 1833. John Henry Newman, who later converted to Catholicism (1845) and was appointed cardinal, became a leader with his ninety papers, *Tracts for the Times* (1833–1841)—hence the name "Tractarian" for the movement, which emphasized the apostolic succession of the Anglican church from the early Christian (Catholic) church, and freedom from state control. Others active in the movement were R. H. Froude, Isaac Williams, Hugh James Rose (of Cambridge), and especially E. B. Pusey, who, after Newman and some others converted to Catholicism, led the movement along the practical lines of building and beautifying churches, improving church music, reviving ritual, and founding lay guilds. In 1869, Keble College was founded in honor of the movement's leading light, who had also been professor of poetry at Oxford from 1831 to 1841. Pusey, clergyman and professor of Hebrew at Oxford, nominated by the duke of Wellington, was honored by the founding of Pusey House, Oxford, in 1864. Under his leadership, the movement gained the scornful name of "Puseyism." Thomas Carlyle and Matthew Arnold both attacked the movement. Charles Kingsley questioned Newman's sincerity in his conversion, and Newman replied in his moving, candid, and forceful *Apologia pro Vita Sua* (1864). The movement produced a number of novels, among them Newman's *Loss and Gain* (1848) and Charlotte Yonge's *Heir of Redclyffe* (1853). The Episcopal church in the United States owes much to the Oxford Movement.

Oxford Reformers. RENAISSANCE humanists whose friendship began at Oxford in the early reign of Henry VIII, especially John Colet, Sir Thomas More, and Erasmus. Erasmus, a Dutch priest and classical scholar at odds with Scholastic theology, first visited England on invitation in 1499, when he met Colet and More, left in a year, but returned for extended stays. The group believed that humanity would be enhanced through education and improvement of character along classical and rational lines to strengthen unthinking devotion to church and state. Sir Thomas More outlined the perfect society in his *Utopia* (Greek for "no place," 1516); Erasmus, in his *Enchiridion Militis Christiani* (*Education of a Christian Soldier*, 1503), which William Tyndale translated into English under the title *Institutio Christiani Principis*, (*Education of a Christian Prince*). Colet, while dean of St. Paul's Cathedral, founded with his own funds the St. Paul's School, which followed the new classical and rational instruction and included commoners. All three, especially Colet, partook of the new Protestant drive toward the correction of laxity and venality in the clergy, but all remained Catholics. Henry VIII beheaded More for refusing to swear fidelity and thus undermine papal authority. See SCHOLASTICISM.

Oxymoron. A pointed stupidity: *oxy*, "sharp," plus *moron*. One of the great ironic figures of speech—for example, "a fearful joy," as Gray says in his "Ode on a Distant Prospect of Eton College," a phrase picked up by Fanny Burney to conclude her *Evelina* (on the eve of happy marriage), and taken by Joyce Carey for the title of a fine novel. See PARADOX.

P

Paean. (1) A hymn of thanksgiving to Apollo, or another god. (2) Any exulting song of praise or joy. Homer mentions paeans when a fleet sets sail, before attack, and after victory.

Paeon. A Greek and Roman foot of one long syllable and three shorts—the "first paeon": $-\ \cup\ \cup\ \cup$; the "second": $\cup\ -\ \cup\ \cup$; the "third": $\cup\ \cup\ -\ \cup$; the "fourth": $\cup\ \cup\ \cup\ -$. The paeon is virtually unknown in English, except occasionally in Gerard Manley Hopkins, and in some scansions of other poets. See SCANSION.

Pageant. (1) In the twentieth century, an outdoor dramatic spectacle celebrating a historical event. Paul Green's *Lost Colony,* staged every summer since 1937 at Manteo, Roanoke Island, is probably America's oldest; the PASSION PLAY, in which the citizens of Oberammergau, Bavaria, have enacted the Crucifixion since 1634 in thankfulness for the end of the plague, Europe's oldest. (2) A scene, from Latin *pāgina,* "scene," in a medieval MYSTERY PLAY, or the four-wheeled movable stage on which the scene was enacted.

Page Proof. See PROOF.

Paleography. The study and interpretation of ancient handwriting and manuscriptive styles.

Palilogy. Repetition for emphasis: "The Living, the living, he shall praise thee" (Isaiah 38.19); "It is not, believe me, it is not." The device is also called EPIZEUXIS.

Palimpsest. A piece of writing on second-hand vellum, parchment, or other surface carrying traces of previous writings erased; from Greek palimpsēstos, "scraped again." A palimpsest is frequently valuable in recovering lost works or readings from the remaining traces.

Palindrome. A word or phrase reading the same backward and forward (from Greek *palin,* "back," and *dromos,* "a running"). Examples are Adam's greeting to Eve "Madam, I'm Adam," or Napolean's supposed lament "Able was I ere I saw Elba," or "Lewd did I live; evil did I dwel" (with archaic spelling), or "A man, a plan, a canal, Panama!" A glossary for palindromists follows.

Symmetrical: Ada, a haha, a mama, a nana, Anna, a papa, bib, Bob,

bob, boob, bub, civic, dad, deed, deified, did, dud, ecce, eke, ere, esse, Eve, eve, ewe, eye, gag, gig, hah, Hannah, hoh, huh, Idi, Lil, ma'm, madam, mom, mum, Nan, never even, non, noon, nun, oh ho, on no, otto, ovo, pap, pep, peep, pip, pop, poop, pup, radar, redivider, reviver, rotator, rotor, sees, sexes, sis, tat, tenet, Tet, tit, tot, toot, tut, wow.

Asymmetrical: are, avid, bad, bag, ban, bard, bat(s), bur, bus, but(s), deer, dessert, dew, dial, dog, don, draw(s), edit, eel, emir, emit, evil, flog, gal(s), gar, gas, gnat, ha, ho, I saw, I was, leper, lever, liar, (s)loop(s), mad, mat, may, moor, (s)nap(s), net, new, (s)nip(s), no, now, pacer, pal(s), part(s), paws, peels, pets, (s)pot(s), rap(s), rat(s), raw, remit, saw, straw, strop(s), tap(s), tip(s), ton(s), tram(s).

Palinode. An ODE of recantation, or any poem retracting something an author has said earlier. Chaucer's *Legend of Good Women* is an example, showing women more admirable than his earlier Criseyde.

Pamphlet. A small treatise, published separately, unbound, with fewer pages than a book. See BROCHURE.

Pan (or **Pan Shot**). In motion pictures, a movement of the camera from side to side on a stationary pivot to follow action or present a broad sweep of setting. See TRACKING SHOT.

Panegyric. A speech of writing in praise of a person, thing, or achievement. See ENCOMIUM.

Pantheism. A belief that God and the universe are identical, from the Greek words *pan* and *theos,* "all" and "god." God is all; all is God. Some pantheistic teachings emphasize God as the unifying element, as, for Hindus, the Brahman is the supreme reality, present in all things. Other forms of pantheism stress the universe or nature as the single, all-encompassing reality. Since ancient times, pantheism has appeared frequently as a persistent strain in religion, philosophy, and literature. It has colored the work of many writers, including Goethe, Wordsworth, and Emerson. See TRANSCENDENTALISM.

Pantomime. A form of DRAMA presented without words, in a DUMB SHOW. MIME is a larger category of drama, usually silent, but in ancient Greece and Rome sometimes accompanied by words.

Pantoum. A Malayan verse form used by nineteenth-century French poets, including Victor Hugo, and, more rarely, by poets in English. Like a VILLANELLE, a pantoum repeats lines, but unlike a villaneile, it repeats them all. The pantoum is a series of quatrains, or four-line stanzas, beginning with an *abab* RHYME SCHEME. Lines 2 and 4 of the first quatrain become lines 1 and 3 of the next, and so on through a varying number of quatrains. At the end, the pattern is completed by repeating lines 1 and 3 of the first quatrain, in reverse order, as lines 2 and 4 of the last, so that the poem ends on its first line. See VERSE FORMS.

Parabasis. In Greek Old Comedy, a speech made by the CHORUS during intermission, directly to the audience, in the name of the author. The chorus spoke out of character on matters of current concern, unconnected with the play. See COMEDY.

Parable. (1) A short TALE encapsulating a moral or religious lesson, as, for example, the biblical parables of the Laborers in the Vineyard (Matt. xx.1–16) and the Prodigal Son (Luke xv.11–32). (2) Any saying, figure of speech, or narrative in which one thing is expressed in terms of another; an APOLOGUE or ALLEGORY.

Parabola. The technique of illustrating with a slight narrative touch, or PARABLE:

> It is as if a man were to hit the bull's-eye without aiming.
> But this is to count your chickens before they hatch.

Parachresis. The practice of bringing in another's words with new emphasis, usually ironic:

> As Ovid says of the sun: she sees all things.
> He follows her around like Plato's shadow of a shadow.

See IRONY.

Paradiastole. A kind of EUPHEMISM, in which a term remotely similar to the real idea is substituted for ironic effect:

> His driving is rather *playful* [outrageously reckless].
> The general's tactics were *cautious* [downright timid].

Paradiorthosis. A kind of ALLUSION, in which a writer quotes some famous line or phrase without acknowledgment and with a new context or twist, as when Dryden opens his comically satirical *MacFlecknoe* with "All human things are subject to decay," a direct translation of Horace's well-known *Mortalia facta peribunt* (*Ars Poetica*, 68), or when T. S. Eliot twists "the kingdom, the power, and the glory" of the Lord's Prayer into "the boredom, the horror, and the glory of life."

Paradox. An apparently untrue or self-contradictory statement or circumstance that proves true upon reflection or when examined in another light. Examples include Shakespeare's "When my love swears that she is made of truth / I do believe her, though I know she lies," Wordsworth's "The child is father of the man," and Schopenhauer's "The more unintelligent a man is, the less mysterious existence seems to him."

Modern CRITICISM has sometimes stressed paradox as fundamental to literature, just as life itself may be seen as replete with paradoxes.

Reference

Cleanth Brooks, **The Well Wrought Urn** (1947).

Paragoge. The addition of a letter, syllable, or sound to the end of a word. Examples include substandard usages like *drowneded* for *drowned*; the *O* that sometimes fills out the line in a FOLK SONG ("And why so sad gang ye, O?"); and the single syllable pronounced as though it were two to complete the meter in many poems, including Keats's "Ode to a Nightingale": ". . . light-*wingèd* Dryad of the trees."

Paralepsis. See APOPHASIS.

Parallelism. From Greek roots meaning "beside one another," the comparison of things by placing them side by side. As a principle, it is fundamental to literature. Theories of MIMESIS suggest that literature exists by way of its parallels with life. Considerations of METAPHOR reveal that figurative language is based in the identification of parallels. An ALLEGORY is an extended narrative parallel.

When the principle is put into practice, *parallelism* becomes a term for the structural devices that indicate underlying similarities of content. In EXPOSITORY WRITING and in *imaginative*, or *creative writing*, in prose, it is a matter of grammar and rhetoric, as the writer expresses in parallel grammatical form equivalent elements of content—framing words, sentences, and paragraphs to give parallel weight to parallel thoughts. Sometimes, as in the opening of Dickens's *Tale of Two Cities*, it rises almost to poetry as the writer strives for the heightened rhetorical effect of balance and ANTITHESIS:

> It was the best of times, it was the worst of times, it was the age of wisdom, it was the age of foolishness, it was the epoch of belief, it was the epoch of incredulity, it was the season of Light, it was the season of

Darkness, it was the spring of hope, it was the winter of despair, we had everything before us, we had nothing before us, we were all going direct to Heaven, we were all going direct the other way—

In POETRY, parallelism is a fundamental aesthetic device, emphasizing similarities in content, and organizing sounds and rhythms through repetition of words, phrases, and patterns of stress and pronunciation. It comes as a natural adjunct to the rhythms of ACCENTUAL-SYLLABIC VERSE and has been a mainstay of many poets in FREE VERSE. In Walt Whitman's verse it is the single most obtrusive device:

I am the poet of the Body and I am the poet of the Soul,
The pleasures of heaven are with me and the pains of hell are with me,
The first I graft and increase upon myself, the latter I translate into a new tongue.

See ASYNDETON; PARATAXIS; POLYSYNDETON.

Paraphrase.   A rendering in other words of the sense of a text or passage, as of a poem, essay, short story, or other writing; also, a free translation from another language, as distinguished from a literal one.

The *heresy of paraphrase* is a term introduced by Cleanth Brooks in *The Well Wrought Urn* (1947) to give point to his argument that the full meaning of a poem cannot be expressed in any arrangement of words besides the poet's. In this view, poetry is a form of discourse that cannot be paraphrased, as scientific writing, for example, can be. Paraphrase remains, nevertheless, one of the most common and apparently necessary tools of literary CRITICISM.

Parataxis.   The placement of words, phrases, clauses, or sentences in coordinate grammatical constructions: "The white face was gone, the darkness was featureless" (John Updike, "Separating"). ASYNDETON and POLYSYNDETON are forms of parataxis; HYPOTAXIS, the opposite. See PARALLELISM.

Paregmenon.   The technique of playing upon derivatives of a word:

A discrete discretion.
The humble are proud of humility.

Parenthesis.   A word or words included as a deviation from or addition to the primary flow of thought in a sentence or paragraph, usually set apart by *parentheses* (like this), or—as in this instance—by dashes, or [as in this] by brackets. Modern writers, especially when employing STREAM OF CONSCIOUSNESS or influenced by stream-of-consciousness techniques, sometimes insert parenthetical material without supplying traditional punctuation signals. In a broad sense, an INTERLUDE or STORY-WITHIN-A-STORY is also a parenthesis.

Parnassians. A group of French poets prominent from 1865 to the end of the nineteenth century, including Leconte de Lisle, Sully-Prudhomme, François Coppée, Anatole France, and Jules Lemaître. The name derives from the three issues of *Parnasse contemporain* (1866, 1871, 1876), containing poems of the group. Reacting against Romantic excesses, they wrote impersonal poetry, carefully crafted, in fixed forms. Among English poets they influenced are Algernon Swinburne and Austin Dobson (1840–1921).

Parnassus. A mountain in central Greece, formerly sacred to Apollo (god of music, poetry, and prophecy) and Dionysus (god of wine and of ecstatic religious expression). Delphi, seat of the Delphic oracle, lies in a valley on its southern slope. Parnassus is traditionally associated with high poetic achievement. See APOLLONIAN.

Parody. Originally, "a song sung beside" another. From this idea of juxtaposition arose the two basic elements of parody, comedy and criticism. As comedy, parody exaggerates or distorts the prominent features of style or content in a work. As criticism, it mimics the work, borrowing words or phrases or characteristic turns of thought in order to highlight weaknesses of conception or expression. Laughter is often uppermost, but when the element of critical mimicry is stressed, the humor may be slight.

Unsuccessful or unintentional parody is sometimes no more than a feeble imitation of a work, displaying minimal critical insight and arousing no laughter. In this sense, authors sometimes write self-parodies, weak imitations of earlier works. In another form of self-parody, however, authors may undercut the effect of their own creations, intentionally layering their work with parodic reflexive humor, a technique sometimes of BLACK HUMOR and the ANTI-NOVEL. Parody is allied to TRAVESTY and BURLESQUE, but travesty is usually more savagely reductive than parody, and burlesque is generally more broadly aimed at a literary form or at life itself, rather than at a particular author or work.

Dependent upon literary ALLUSION, parody is addressed to a literate audience, one familiar with the work parodied and capable of appreciating the comic and critical commentary. Some parodies, however, such as Lewis Carroll's "Father William" (mimicking Southey's

"The Old Man's Comforts"), assume lives of their own, independent of their originals. See CENTO; PASTICHE; SATIRE.

Paroemia. The application of proverbs to new situations, usually ironically:

> Even the rose has thorns [when a plan has drawbacks].
> Every dog has its day [an opponent has just won the election].
> One cannot live by bread alone [someone has just ordered steak].

Paronomasia. (1) The technique of punning by changing a letter or syllable:

> His *sword* is better than his *word*.
> Bolder in the *buttery* than in the *battery*.
> *Repining* but not *repenting*.

(2) Loosely, any pun.

Parsec. From *parallax* plus *second:* a unit of astronomical distance. Coined in 1913 by the British astronomer Herbert Hall Towner, a *parsec* is equivalent to 3.26 light years. Adopted by SCIENCE FICTION writers, the term is sometimes used erroneously as a measure of speed, not distance.

Partimen. A form of medieval debate poem (also called *joc parti* or *jeu parti*) in which one poet poses a question involving alternatives (as, for example, whether it is better to love a woman or be loved by her), a second responds, and the two exchange opinions until, at the end, the question is resolved by an arbitrator. See TROUBADOUR.

Pasquinade. An anonymous LAMPOON or SATIRE, especially one posted in a public place. The name derives from a Roman statue, disinterred in 1501. Called "Pasquino" and set up near the Piazza Navona, it became a posting place for satires written in conjunction with St. Mark's Day and often signed "Pasquin."

Passion Play. Originally, a play on Christ's Passion; later, one including both Passion and Resurrection. Such plays began in the Middle Ages, performed from the thirteenth century onward, often as part of the pageants presented for the feast of Corpus Christi. After the sixteenth and seventeenth centuries, most were no longer produced, but the one still performed each ten years at Oberammergau in the Bavarian Alps derives from an almost unbroken tradition dating from 1634. See MEDIEVAL DRAMA.

Pastiche. A literary or other artistic work created by assembling bits and pieces from other works. Some pastiches are the result of conscious PLAGIARISM and others of inept and confused borrowing. Still others are skillful constructions—illuminating rather than deceptive—as in passages in Joyce's *Ulysses*. See CENTO; PARODY.

Pastoral. From Latin *pastor*, a shepherd. The first pastoral poet was Theocritus, a Greek of the third century B.C., whose *Idylls*, although written in Ptolemy's court in Alexandria, recalled his boyhood in Sicily. In one of Theocritus's poems, Thyrsis sings of the death of Daphnis, beginning the tradition of PASTORAL ELEGY. In another, the love of Polyphemus for Galatea established the pastoral as a love lyric. In still another, a singing match sets a pattern common later. The Latin poet Virgil (70–19 B.C.) was next, his ten *Eclogues* (or *Bucolics*) celebrating ideal human relationships in beautiful natural surroundings. Later pastorals were generally inspired, at least in part, by these first two poets, and were highly stylized and conventional, repeating names, situations, and techniques from the earlier models.

The pastoral was especially popular in Europe from the fourteenth through the eighteenth centuries, with some fine examples still written in England in the nineteenth century. It flourished as Renaissance HUMANISM gave rise to visions of an idyllic Golden Age and declined when RATIONALISM and the INDUSTRIAL REVOLUTION combined to diminish the imaginative force of such visions. In the fourteenth century in Italy, Dante, Petrarch, and Boccaccio wrote Latin eclogues modeled on Virgil's (see ECLOGUE). In England, Spenser's *Shepheardes Calender* (1579) and Sidney's *Arcadia* (1590) were early examples. Marlowe's "Passionate Shepherd to His Love" ("Come live with me and be my love") is an example of the pastoral as love lyric, a form also written by Shakespeare, Jonson, and Michael Drayton (1563–1631). Shakespeare's *As You Like It* (1600) is a PASTORAL DRAMA. Later, the pastoral elegy retained a stronger tradition than other forms, as in Milton's *Lycidas* (1637), Shelley's *Adonais* (1821), and Arnold's *Thyrsis* (1866).

The pastoral mode is self-reflexive. Typically, the poet echoes the conventions of earlier pastorals in order to put "the complex into the simple," as William Empson observed in *Some Versions of Pastoral* (1935). The poem is not really about shepherds, but about the complex society the poet and readers inhabit, with the friends of the poet, or people like them, disguised by rural dress and flowery aliases, still exhibiting sophisticated sentiments, manners, and speech. The contrast between country and town is sometimes satiric, sometimes melancholy.

It is a mode that leads naturally to ALLEGORY and SYMBOL. With the rise of REALISM, the pastoral fell into disfavor as writers and readers turned to more direct examinations of society. In the self-conscious and ironic inventions of recent writers, however, as well as in their attitudes toward the complex society they inhabit, some hints of the pastoral mode may still be found.

Pastoral Drama. DRAMA using PASTORAL conventions, a form that rose in popularity with the decline of the medieval MIRACLE PLAY. Poliziano's *Orfeo* (1472) was one of the first. Tasso's *Aminta* (1573) had widespread influence, including an imitation by John Fletcher, *The Faithful Shepherdess* (1610). Shakespeare's *As You Like It* (1600) and the shearer's feast in *The Winter's Tale* (1611) show the influence. Allan Ramsay's *Gentle Shepherd* (1725) is a late Scots example in the form of a BALLAD OPERA.

Pastoral Elegy. An ELEGY using PASTORAL conventions. One shepherd mourns the death of another in a formal pattern reflective of the traditions of pastoral poetry and of the society for which the poem is written. So Milton's *Lycidas* repeats imagery dating back to Theocritus (third century B.C.), echoing also the concerns of Cambridge undergraduates of the seventeenth century.

Pastoral Romance. A ROMANCE using PASTORAL conventions. Typically, the pastoral romance was in prose, with lyrics interspersed. The Greek *Daphnis and Chloe* (third century A.D.) influenced later works, as did Boccaccio's *Ameto* (1342). In English, Sir Philip Sidney's *Arcadia* (1590) remains the great example. Thomas Lodge's *Rosalynde* (1590) gave Shakespeare the plot for *As You Like It*.

Pastourelle. A French PASTORAL form of the Middle Ages: a short narrative poem, with dialogue, in which a knight or other man of high social rank courts a shepherdess, sometimes successfully, sometimes not. The Old French play *Robin and Marion* (thirteenth century), by Adam de la Halle, is a dramatized *pastourelle*, and the form perhaps influenced later secular drama as well. See TROUBADOUR.

Patent Theaters. Those licensed, or "patented," by Charles II in 1660. Since the Puritans had banned theaters in 1642, Charles issued "patents" to Sir William Davenant and Thomas Killigrew to organize theatrical companies. The king's brother James, duke of York (afterward James II), sponsored Davenant's company, which acted in a new theater in Dorset Garden after 1671. Killigrew's company, the "King's

Players," occupied the new Theatre Royal in Drury Lane after 1674. The licenses of these two theaters continued to pass to various successors in the eighteenth century.

Pathetic Fallacy.   The attribution of animate or human characteristics to nature, as, especially, when rocks, trees, or weather are portrayed as reacting in sympathy to human feelings or events. John Ruskin coined the term in his chapter "Of the Pathetic Fallacy" in *Modern Painters*, Volume 3 (1856), illustrating his discussion with lines from Charles Kingsley's novel *Alton Locke* (1850):

> They rowed her in across the rolling foam—
> The cruel, crawling foam.

> The foam is not cruel, neither does it crawl. The state of mind which attributes to it these characters of a living creature is one in which the reason is unhinged by grief.

Ruskin qualified the idea by suggesting four human reactions to nature. First is the person who looks at a flower and sees nothing more, one who "perceives rightly because he does not feel." Next is the second-class, or mediocre, poet, "the man who perceives wrongly because he feels," allowing emotion to overpower intellect. Third is the poet of the first order, one "who perceives rightly in spite of his feelings," achieving a balance between emotion and intellect. Fourth is the prophet, an inspired seer, one who recognizes in nature "an animation and pathos of its own," a sense of "the Divine presence." In second-rank poets, the pathetic fallacy is a weakness. In inspired poets it may be a strength, as the imagination transcends any sense of nature as borrowing human feelings.

Pathos.   The feeling of pity, sympathy, tenderness, compassion, or sorrow evoked by someone or something that is helpless. The death of a pet, an Ophelia, or a Cordelia, arouses pathos, as distinct from the tragic depths and heights of Hamlet and Lear.

Pedantry.   Ostentatious book learning: an accusation frequently hurled in scholarly disagreements. Shakespeare's Holofernes (*Love's Labour's Lost*) and Fielding's Partridge (*Tom Jones*) with their misplaced Latin are comic pedants.

Pegasus.   The winged horse of poetry who sprang from the Gorgon Medusa's blood when Perseus beheaded her, and whose hoofstroke on Mt. Helicon brought forth the Muses's inspirational spring of Hippocrene ("horse spring"). See MUSES.

Pelagianism. The early heresy and later theology asserting original innocence as opposed to original sin and salvation through human effort as opposed to salvation through Christ's intermediation and God's grace. Pelagius (c. 354–c. 418), probably born in Britain, became an ascetic spiritual leader in Rome about 378. He blamed the laxity of the clergy on the doctrine of divine grace, which he heard preached from St. Augustine's *Confessions*. Pelagius argued for the essential goodness of humans and their responsibility for choosing asceticism for their own salvation. Augustine wrote to refute him. The church condemned Pelagius's teachings and excommunicated him. In later times, any doctrine opposing CALVINISM by emphasizing good works over faith may be called *Pelagianism*. See AUGUSTINIANISM.

Penny Dreadful. A cheap paperback thriller in England; England's equivalent of the American DIME NOVEL. The term was first recorded in 1884.

Pentameter. A line of five metrical feet. See METER.

Pentastich. A unit of verse in five lines: a CINQUAIN or QUINTAIN (or QUINTET).

Perfectibilitarians. A group of radical thinkers in the 1790s who believed in progress and the perfectibility of human society through rational reform and education. Joseph Priestley's *Letters to the Right Honourable Edmund Burke* (1791) stated clearly for the first time the idea of perfectibility. William Godwin's *Political Justice* (1793), embracing John Locke's theory that outer sensations completely form the human mind, stated an argument that was to become recurrent in sociological thinking well into the twentieth century: if the social environment is rationally improved, good, rational people will result; good education creates good people. Thomas Paine's words "there is a morning of reason rising upon the world" (*The Rights of Man*, 1791) were the creed. Mary Wollstonecraft (1759–1797) Godwin's wife, completed the central group, with whom young William Blake associated.

Perfect Rhyme. See EXACT RHYME.

Periodical. Technically, a publication issued regularly over periods of more than a day, but often including daily newspapers as well—hence, a newspaper, magazine, journal, quarterly, or review. England's first regular newspaper, a single sheet entitled *Corante, or, Newes from Italy, Germany, Hungarie, Spaine, and France* appeared in September 1621. Newspapers proliferated after the RESTORATION of

1660 with the rise of politics. In America, *Publick Occurrences Both Forreign and Domestick*, Boston, 1690, was suppressed after one issue, not to be replaced until 1704 by the government's weekly *Boston News Letter*.

The earliest magazine known is Johann Rist's *Erbauliche Monaths-Unterredungen* (Hamburg, 1663–1668, *Instructive Monthly Discussions*). A French *Journal des Sçavans* and the English Royal Society's *Philosophical Transactions* soon followed in 1665. John Dunton's *Athenian Gazette* (later *Athenian Mercury*, 1690–1697) was England's first general magazine, dealing with "all the most Nice and Curious Questions." In 1693, Dunton brought out *The Ladies' Mercury*, the first women's magazine. Daniel Defoe's newspaper, *A Review of the Affairs of France: And of All Europe* (1704–1713, thrice weekly), launched the political leading article and the PERIODICAL ESSAY, firmly established by Richard Steele's *Tatler* (1709–1711, thrice weekly) and Joseph Addison's and Steele's *Spectator* (1711–1712, 1714, daily). In 1731, Edward Cave started *The Gentleman's Magazine*, originating the term *magazine* (from the Arabic for "storehouse"), since Cave's periodical began as a monthly collection of articles gathered from other sources, under the motto *E pluribus unum*. It continued until 1907. Robert Dodsley, a bookseller, started the first book review, *The Museum*, in 1746, reflecting the rise of the novel and of literacy; this periodical was soon followed by Ralph Griffiths's more famous *Monthly Review* (1749–1845).

Periodical Essay. The brief speculative and chatty essay originating in Daniel Defoe's periodical, *A Review of the Affairs of France: And of All Europe* (1704–1713, thrice weekly), in a section entitled "Advice from the Scandalous Club." Richard Steele, reflecting the social sobering after RESTORATION abandon, established the form in his *Tatler* (1709–1711), "to recommend truth, innocence, honor, virtue, as the chief ornaments of life." He and Joseph Addison confirmed it in *The Spectator* (1711–1712, 1714), which achieved Addison's aim "to enliven morality with wit, and to temper wit with morality," to bring "philosophy out of closets, and libraries, schools, and colleges, to dwell in clubs and assemblies, at tea-tables and in coffee houses" (No. 10). Each essay supposed a fictive author—Mr. Tatler, Mr. Spectator. Other periodicals followed the pattern—*The Guardian, The Englishman, The Female Tatler, The Whisperer*—with Swift, Pope, Berkeley, Joseph Warton, and others contributing. Samuel Johnson's *Rambler* (1750–1752), his contributions to John Hawkesworth's *Adventurer* (1752–1754), and his *Idler* (1758–1760) concluded the genre as the essay moved into the magazines.

Periodic Sentence.   A sentence that suspends its meaning, is gramatically incomplete, until the end. See LOOSE and PERIODIC SENTENCES.

Peripeteia (or **Peripetia, Peripety**).   A sudden change in situation in a drama or fiction, a reversal of luck for good or ill. See PLOT.

Periphrasis.   The practice of talking around the point; a wordy restatement; a circumlocution. Polonius falls amusingly into periphrasis while proclaiming brevity:

> My liege, and madam, to expostulate
> What majesty should be, what duty is,
> Why day is day, night night, and time is time,
> Were nothing but to waste night, day, and time.
> Therefore, since brevity is the soul of wit,
> And tediousness the limbs and outward flourishes,
> I will be brief. Your noble son is mad.
> Mad call I it; for, to define true madness,
> What is't but to be nothing else but mad?
>   *Hamlet II.ii.86–94*

Some periphrasis is ironically effective, as in ANTONOMASIA and ironic EUPHEMISM.

Peroration.   (1) The summative conclusion of a formal ORATION. (2) Loosely, a grandiloquent speech.

Persiflage.   Witty banter.

Persistence of Vision.   The phenomenon of the retina's retaining an image for a moment after the object vanishes, thus making motion pictures possible. This "defect," as Ingmar Bergman has called it, creates the visual illusion of smooth motion from a rapid series of static pictures. GESTALT psychologists call it the *phi-phenomenon.*

Persona.   A mask (in Latin); in poetry and fiction, the projected speaker or narrator of the work—that is, a mask for the actual author. It may be an IMPLIED AUTHOR, who is very similar to the author, or a completely different and ironic projection, like Swift's proposer in *A Modest Proposal* or Browning's duke in "My Last Duchess." Some poets, particularly, seem to speak directly for themselves, with no intervening personae, though critics may insist that even these are projected masks. See NARRATIVE PERSPECTIVE.

Personal Essay.   An INFORMAL ESSAY on a personal subject; a FAMILIAR ESSAY.

Personification. The technique of treating abstractions, things, or animals as persons. A kind of METAPHOR, personification turns abstract ideas, like love, into physical beauties named Venus, or conversely, makes dumb animals speak and act like humans: Mickey Mouse, Donald Duck, Reynard the Fox. Personification engaged the eighteenth-century imagination. Samuel Johnson opens his *Vanity of Human Wishes* (1749) with the lines:

> Let Observation with extensive view,
> Survey mankind, from China to Peru;
> Remark each anxious toil, each eager strife,
> And watch the busy scenes of crowded life;
> Then say how Hope and Fear, Desire and Hate,
> O'erspread with snares the clouded maze of Fate.

Coleridge scoffed at the redundancy of observing with an extensive observation to observe. He missed completely the eighteenth-century's habit of personification. Johnson and his readers would picture a huge being named Observation, who would have a view extensive enough for its detailed survey, after which it could describe how four devious persons named Hope, Fear, Desire, and Hate spread their characteristic snares over the paths, covered with fog, in a maze in a garden owned by a person named Fate. This is an especially pictorial way of saying metaphorically, "Hope and fear are snares; fate is like a foggy maze with snares added."

Persuasion. One of the five modes of composition that nineteenth-century rhetoricians elaborated from Aristotle's three (see ORATION). Persuasion corresponds to Aristotle's first category, *deliberative*, which concerns the future and urges listeners to action, but his second category, *forensic* ARGUMENT, which applies to current legal infractions, generally absorbs the first, leaving the four major modes of prose writing: argument, EXPOSITION, DESCRIPTION, NARRATION.

Petrarchan Conceit. See CONCEIT.

Petrarchan Sonnet. Another name for an ITALIAN SONNET.

Pharmakos. A scapegoat or victim, a STOCK CHARACTER appearing in many forms, always arbitrarily chosen for his or her fate, sacrificed for the good of society. See CHARACTERS.

Phenomenology. A philosophy originated by Edmund Husserl (1859–1938), and its consequent literary criticism, that examines a phenomenon in the consciousness by excluding presuppositions of both objective reality and subjective response. For Husserl, imaginary phenomena have equal status with those taken from the physical world. One realizes the presence of the mental phenomenon, then describes and elucidates its meaning intuitively, eschewing both the empirical analysis of science and that rational deduction of logic. Phenomenology considerably influenced Sartre's EXISTENTIALISM.

Phenomenological criticism includes EXISTENTIAL CRITICISM and the GENEVA SCHOOL OF CRITICISM. Major phenomenologists are Gaston Bachelard, Georges Poulet, Roman Ingarden, and Mikel Dufrenne. According to this approach, the literary work exists only in the reader's consciousness, with reading an intuitive interaction between this aesthetic object in the consciousness and the reader's wider consciousness, a means of personal liberation, a way to freedom. In spite of this intense subjective mentalism, phenomenologists often study all of an author's works to discover intentions behind the creation of the literary object suspended in the reader's consciousness and to describe the way in which the consciousness becomes aware of it. See STRUCTURALISM; POST-STRUCTURALISM.

Philippic. (1) Originally, Demosthenes's three orations (351, 344, 341 B.C.) against the growing threat to Athens of Philip II of Macedon. (2) Cicero's orations against Marc Antony. (3) Any fiery denunciation of someone.

Philistinism. The valuing of material wealth in ignorance or contempt of cultural values. In the 1820s, German students had labeled nonstudents "Philistines" after the biblical enemies of Israel. Several English writers picked up the term and made it current, notably Thomas Carlyle, from whom Matthew Arnold acquired it, to give it enduring currency in his "Sweetness and Light," the first chapter of *Culture and Anarchy* (1869):

> If it were not for this purging effect wrought upon our minds by culture, the whole world, the future as well as the present, would inevitably belong to the Philistines. The people who believe most that our greatness and welfare are proved by our being very rich, and who most give their lives and thoughts to becoming rich, are just the very people whom we call Philistines. Culture says: "Consider these people, then, their way of life, their habits, their manners, the very tones of their voices; look at them attentively; observe the literature they read, the things which give them pleasure, the words which come forth out of their mouths, the thoughts which make the furniture of their minds; would any amount of wealth be worth having with the condition that one was to become just like these people by having it?"

Philology. The study of ancient languages and literatures; also more broadly interpreted from its basic meaning, "love of the word," to include all literary studies; historical linguistics. See LINGUISTICS.

Philosophes. French rationalists of the seventeenth and eighteenth centuries, scientists, religious skeptics, and social reformers—Diderot, d'Alembert, Voltaire, Montesquieu, Buffon, Condillac, Condorcet—most of whom collaborated on the great *Encyclopédie* (1751–1772). See ENLIGHTENMENT.

Phi-Phenomenon. The Gestalt psychologists' name for the PERSISTENCE OF VISION that makes possible motion pictures, as one motionless image is retained by the retina and merges with the next, slightly different, conveying the illusion of movement.

Pibroch. On the bagpipe, a series of variations on traditional dirges and battle music.

Picaresque Novel. A NOVEL chronicling the adventures of a rogue, typically presented as an autobiography, episodic in structure, and panoramic in its coverage of time and place. The term derives from the central character, a *picaro* (from a Spanish word meaning "rogue" or "knave"), because the first picaresque was a widely read Spanish work, the anonymous *Lazarillo de Tormes* (1553).

The picaro gives the picaresque novel its basic qualities. Usually a man (but Defoe's Moll Flanders is a noteworthy exception), he is lowly placed in society, struggling to make his way in a variety of circumstances, serving a number of masters, assisted primarily by his wits. Amoral, concerned first to stay alive, and then, if possible, to prosper, he confronts the institutions of society—government, law, religion, business, military service, marriage, family—with a cynicism justified by his experience. Typically on the move, he wanders from country to city, inn to country house, land to sea, always fleeing the past and in search of the future. Because the world of the picaro is governed more by chance than by an overarching fate, his adventures are incoherent, episodic, and linear in structure as they follow the chronological outline of journey or life. Unlike the hero of many nineteenth- and twentieth-century novels, he does not change in character in response to his adventures, but only adapts to new circumstances. In many respects, he is the LOW MIMETIC counterpart of the HIGH MIMETIC hero of the MEDIEVAL ROMANCE; at odds with a society viewed in his case realistically from its lower levels, he provides a sharp contrast to the romantic hero's loyalty to a society viewed idealistically from higher up. His language, too, contrasts with the language of ROMANCE. A plain man, he adopts a plain style, specifying clearly as he fills his narrative with the everyday descriptive details that are also one of the distinguishing characteristics of the realistic novel.

Popular in the sixteenth, seventeenth, and eighteenth centuries, the picaresque novel provided a prose fiction alternative to the romances, also popular. Thomas Nashe's *Unfortunate Traveller or the Life of Jack Wilton* (1594) was the first important English picaresque. Grimmelshausen's *Simplicissimus* (1669), German, and Le Sage's *Gil Blas* (1715, 1735), French, were important later examples. Cervantes's *Don Quixote* (1605, 1615) owed much to the form. Defoe's *Moll Flanders* (1722), Fielding's *Jonathan Wild* (1743), and Smollett's *Roderick Random* (1748) all show the influence of the picaresque. So, too, do Dickens's *Nicholas Nickleby* (1839), Twain's *Huckleberry Finn* (1884), and, in the twentieth century, Saul Bellow's *Adventures of Augie March* (1953).

References

Robert Alter, **Rogue's Progress: Studies in the Picaresque Novel** (1964).
A. A. Parker, **Literature and the Delinquent: A Study of the Picaresque Novel** (1947).

Picture Frame Stage.   The type of stage most often used for dramatic production in the twentieth century: a BOX SET, with the ACTION behind the PROSCENIUM arch. See ARENA STAGE; THEATERS.

Picture Poem.   See CONCRETE POETRY; SHAPED POEM.

Picturesque, The.   A quality in landscape, and landscaping, admired in the second half of the eighteenth century. The *picturesque* resembled idealized landscape painting, with crags, flaring and blasted trees, a torrent or winding stream, ruins, and perhaps a quiet cottage and cart, with contrasting light and shadow. It was considered an aesthetic mean between the poles of Edmund Burke's "A Philosophical Inquiry into the Sublime and the Beautiful" (1756). In the 1790s, William Gilpin (1724–1804) advocated and described the picturesque, conducting tours to admire it. The scenery in Ann Radcliffe's novels (1790–1797) reflects picturesque painting. In Jane Austen's *Northanger Abbey* (written 1798–1803), Catherine and Henry discuss the picturesque. In America, the Hudson River School of landscapists represented the movement, and critics have noted the picturesque in James Fenimore Cooper's and Washington Irving's writings.

Pièce Bien Faite. See WELL-MADE PLAY.

Pirated Edition. An unauthorized edition printed from an authorized one, frequent in the eighteenth century by Irish printers from popular London books. In the twentieth century, both Russia and Taiwan have pirated numerous books both in the original language and in translation. The first record of the metaphor, which became fully current in the early eighteenth century, is in one J. Hancock's *Brooks' String of Pearls* (1668): "Some dishonest Book-sellers, called Land-Pirates, who make it their Practice to steal Impressions of other mens Copies." Reference to printings of Shakespeare's plays as "pirated" by one actor or another before the FIRST FOLIO (1623) does not appear until the 1880s.

Plagiarism. Literary kidnapping (Latin *plagiārius*, "kidnapper," from *plaga*, "net")—the seizing and presenting as one's own of the ideas or writings of another. The classical concept of MIMESIS, or imitation, encouraged, in Shakespeare's and Spenser's adaptions of the plots and themes of their predecessors, what would now be called *plagiarism*. The widely shared literature of the past also enabled the witty and graceful PARADIORTHOSIS of Jonson, Herrick, Marvell, Dryden, Pope, and others as they tacitly paraphrased poems and lines from the classics where an acknowledgment would seem a sign of stupidity or an insult. Today, even the unconscious borrowing of the words and ideas of others that can creep in from research notes seems *plagiarism*—as Alex Haley acknowledged when he settled out of court for incorporating from his voluminous notes, without citation, some situations from another book on African tribal life in his *Roots* (1976).

Plainsong. The single line of melody with varied nonmetrical phrasing in which celebrants chant in unison the texts of the Latin Roman Catholic mass and canonical hours. St. Gregory the Great, pope from 590 to 604, collected and instituted them (hence the name *Gregorian Chant*, by which they came to be known). "Plainsong" translates the Latin term *cantus plānus*, "level song," which arose in the thirteenth century to distinguish the Gregorian Chant from the newer polyphonic singing, with several harmonically linked melody lines.

Plain Style. The straightforward, unembellished STYLE of preaching favored by seventeenth-century Puritans, as well as by reformers within the Anglican church, as speaking God's word directly from the inspired heart as opposed to the high style of aristocratic oratory and courtliness, the vehicle of subterfuge. Plain style was simultaneously advocated for scientific accuracy by the Royal Society, as Bishop

Thomas Sprat summarizes it in his *History of the Royal Society of London* (1667):

> They have therefore been most rigorous in putting in execution the only Remedy that can be found for this *extravagance,* and that has been a constant Resolution to reject all amplifications, digressions, and swellings of style; to return back to the primitive purity and shortness, when men deliver'd so many *things* almost in an equal number of *words.* They have exacted from all their members a close, naked, natural way of speaking, positive expressions, clear senses, a native easiness, bringing all things as near the Mathematical plainness as they can, and preferring the language of Artizans, Countrymen, and Merchants, before that of Wits and Scholars.

Erich Auerbach, in his *Mimesis: The Representation of Reality in Western Literature* (1953, from German original, 1946), points out that the low style of antiquity, the language of slaves, bumpkins, and commoners used for comedy, as contrasted with the high style of tragedy and epic, became the straightforward middle style as artisans and merchants rose into the middle class and spoke for themselves, with their struggles no longer seen as comic from an aristocratic altitude.

Plaint. A LAMENT or COMPLAINT.

Planh. A medieval Provençal LAMENT, generally on the loss of a patron or other prominent person, but sometimes on a more personal loss.

Plantagenet. See ROYAL HOUSES.

Platonic Criticism. A contemporary (and inaccurate) term for CRITICISM that seeks extraliterary values in literature, in its social significance and philosophical implications, as opposed to "Aristotelian criticism," which explicates aesthetic values and relationships within the work itself. See NEW CRITICISM.

Platonism. Any reflection of Plato's philosophy, particularly the belief in the eternal reality of ideal forms, of which the diversities of the physical world are but transitory shadows. Plato (c. 428–347 B.C.) founded his Academy in Athens about 387. He wrote his earlier dialogues featuring his teacher Socrates (d. 399) before Plato left for Syracuse in 367 for the first of his two visits. Plato's philosophy, developed in dialectic dialogues and covering most of the metaphysical, ethical, and political questions addressed by later thinkers, has been the world's most influential, and debatable. His early dialogues concern Virtue. Those of the middle years—the *Republic, Phaedo, Symposium, Phaedrus, Timaeus, Philebus*—develop his central ideas: questions of Justice and government; the Good as the highest absolute, toward which true lovers ascend toward Beauty, and true philosophers toward Truth, fulfilled in death; the eternal reality of Ideas, and archetypal Forms. The later dialogues deal more with technical philosophic and practical problems.

Plotinus (c. A.D. 205–270), a Hellenistic Greek, imbibed the first revival of Platonism in Alexandria, before he settled in Rome about 245, where he evolved his philosophy that rejected dualism for mystical union with the One, later called NEO-PLATONISM, or, sometimes, the "Alexandrian School" of Neo-Platonism, which considerably influenced Christianity, particularly through St. Augustine (354–430) and St. Thomas Aquinas (c. 1225–1274).

A second surge of Platonism began with Marsilio Ficino (1433–1499), who became head of the Platonic Academy of Florence in 1462 and who dedicated the rest of his life to translating and interpreting Plato into a closer synthesis with Christianity, particularly in *Theologica Platonica* (1482). He profoundly influenced RENAISSANCE thought and literature, and the emerging HUMANISM. He saw the soul as divinely endowed to synthesize the highest with the lowest, the vital center of a universe literally "animated" by the soul. The soul progresses through stages of love and knowledge to contemplative union with God, the One. To Ficino is owed the Renaissance idea of spiritual "Platonic" love. His Neo-Platonism influenced Sidney and Spenser, the seventeenth-century CAMBRIDGE PLATONISTS, and DEISM, especially reflected in the *De Veritate* (1624) of Lord Herbert of Cherbury. Castiglione's *Il Cortegiano* (1528), which Thomas Hoby translated into English as *The Book of the Courtier* (1561), outlines Ficino's Platonic love in Book IV. Spenser's *Fowre Hymnes* (1596—"An Hymne in Honour of Love," "An Hymne in Honour of Beautie," "An Hymne of Heavenly Love," and "An Hymne of Heavenly Beautie") develops Ficino's and Castiglione's Neo-Platonism.

Another wave of Platonism influenced the Romantic poets through the work of the German philosopher G. W. F. Hegel (1770–1831) and the German Idealists and Coleridge's subsequent study of Plotinus and others, and through the militantly anti-Christian writings in England of Thomas Taylor, "The Platonist" (1758–1835), whose commentaries and many translations of Plato and the Neo-Platonists were particularly influential on William Blake. Wordsworth's "Ode: Intimations of Immortality" (1807), Keats's "Ode on a Grecian Urn" (1820), Shelley's

"Mont Blanc," "Hymn to Intellectual Beauty" and *Adonais* (1821) reflect this Romantic expression of Neo-Platonism:

> The One remains, the many change and pass;
> Heaven's light forever shines, Earth's shadows fly;
> Life, like a dome of many-coloured glass,
> Stains the white radiance of Eternity. . . .
>
> *Adonais, LII*

Play. A DRAMA in dialogue to be acted before an audience, or such a work written to be read in private. See CLOSET DRAMA; THEATERS.

Pléiade. The seven stars of the sixteenth-century French literary group that aimed to lift French literature to Greco-Roman eminence: Pierre de Ronsard, the leader; Joachim du Bellay; Jean Dorat; Jean-Antoine de Baïf; Remy Belleau; Pontus de Tyard; and Étienne Jodelle. Charlemagne (reigning 768–814) had designated the first Pléiade of literary lights, presumably taking the name from the seven tragic poets Alexandrian critics, in the reign of Ptolemy Philadelphus (285–247 B.C.), had so designated after the seven stars in the constellation Pleiades. Du Bellay's *Défense et illustration de la langue française* (1549) stated their intention to avoid both new and medieval French, to recover lost words with classical roots and early French ancestry, to coin new ones from Greek and Latin, and to create a new French literature equal to the classics. In England, Spenser's AREOPAGUS had parallel aims. A second Pléiade arose in the reign of Louis XIII (1610–1643) to designate seven poets outstanding in Latin versification.

Pleonasm. Redundancy, "more than enough": for example, "His dialogue is everyday conversation *of common people talking together*"; "She walked *on foot* and waved to them *with her hand*."; a TAUTOLOGY.

Ploce. Emphatic repetition of a word to bring out its literal meaning:

> A man's a man, for 'a that.
> A player who is really a player
> In that battle, Caesar was Caesar.

Plot. The events of a story. The word that Aristotle used for plot in the *Poetics* is *mythos*, which is the origin also of the world MYTH. In its broadest sense *mythos* means narrative or sequential movement, such as any form of verbal structure designed to be read sequentially would possess. But in practice there is a rough distinction between fictions, or narratives that are stories, and thematic narratives, or arguments, as in essays. Aristotle appears to identify the *mythos*, or plot, with his central conception of drama as a *mimesis praxeos,* or imitation of action. The plot is thus the central form, or metaphorically the soul, of the drama.

Such a plot has, Aristotle said, a beginning, middle, and end. This distinguishes the plot from the type of narrative which is merely sequential, starting and stopping arbitrarily, as in a diary or in some of the more naïve forms of ROMANCE. If a plot begins and ends, the beginning must somehow suggest an end, and the end return to the beginning. Thus *Oedipus Rex* begins with the king determined to discover why his land is suffering from a drought: the reader or audience assumes that his discovery of the reason will end the play. He eventually discovers that *he* is the reason; he has killed his father and lives in incest with his mother. Two things are involved here: one is "reversal" (*peripeteia*), or sudden change in fortune; the other is "discovery" (*anagnorisis*). The word *anagnorisis* could also be translated as "recognition," depending on how much of a surprise it is. In some plots, such as those of detective stories, the *anagnorisis* is a discovery, because it is a surprise to the reader; in others, such as those of most tragedies, it is a recognition by members of the audience of something they have come to realize long before, though it may still be a surprise to the chief character.

The plot, then, is not simply an arrangement of events in a straight line. There is always something of a parabola shape about a story that ends in some kind of "recognition" that aligns the end with the beginning. Again, a plot has a shape that, to use a word appropriate to Aristotle's mode of thought, is teleological: it has a purpose in moving as it does, and its purpose is to illuminate the beginning by the end, and vice versa. Plot in this sense is not wholly disconnected from plot in the sense of a planned conspiracy; in fact, most comic and tragic plots include actual conspiracies of one kind or another.

Thus a plot does not simply move with time, but spreads out conceptually in metaphorical space, just as a musical composition has a score that can be studied as a simultaneous unit. This static way of looking at a plot suggests the metaphor of STRUCTURE. Aristotle speaks of *dianoia,* which means "thought" or "meaning," and it seems clear that *mythos* and *dianoia* are really aspects of the same thing, as poetic meaning can never be separated from poetic structure.

Plurisignation. Multiple meaning; a term emphasizing the capacity of a word to carry quite different, sometimes unrelated, messages simultaneously. See AMBIGUITY; CONNOTATION; FOUR SENSES OF INTERPRETATION; POLYSEMOUS MEANING; SEMANTICS; SEMIOTICS.

Poem. An arrangement of words in verse, or any verbal composition characterized by a greater concentration of RHYTHM, sound, and IMAGERY than is usual in PROSE. See POETRY.

Poet. Strictly, the maker of a POEM. Loosely, anyone whose manner of expression suggests the characteristics of POETRY.

Poetaster. A writer of mediocre verse; an inferior poet.

Poetic Diction. Words associated especially with POETRY, or thought particularly suited for poetry, and less common in PROSE. These words come, of course, from the common stock of language available to all writers, but whether and to what extent poets should select from that stock a vocabulary especially suited to poetry as distinct from prose are questions answered in different ways in different times.

In Chapter XII of his *Poetics*, Aristotle defended a poetic diction elevated above the language of common speech by its use of unusual or metaphoric words. As he saw it, however, the poet should refrain from using only such words, as, carried to extremes, they produce riddles and jargon. The best poetic diction is a mixture of the common and the unusual. Since Aristotle's time, poetic diction has most often fallen into the middle range he advocated, although at times it has ranged upward toward the unusual and downward toward the common. For example, poetry in the RENAISSANCE was often lofty, marked by ARCHAISM, Latinisms, and elaborate METAPHOR. Then and later, DECORUM was often a consideration, especially in DRAMA, suggesting that the level of poetic diction should suit the speaker or subject. Poets of the ROMANTIC PERIOD generally approved Wordsworth's aim, announced in the Preface to the *Lyrical Ballads,* to write "in a selection of language really used by men." In the twentieth century, *poetic diction* has sometimes been used as a term of disapproval, as in William Carlos Williams's comment that "there can no longer be serious work in poetry written in 'poetic' diction."

Poetic Drama. DRAMA written in verse. This was the normal way of drama in ancient Greece and Rome, in the medieval MIRACLE PLAY, and in the plays of Marlowe, Shakespeare, and many other RENAISSANCE and seventeenth-century dramatists; PROSE became a medium for imaginative expression only after printed books and literacy began to be widespread. From the eighteenth century onward, when the best new plays were often written in prose, poetic drama retained a living tradition in productions of the classics, although occasionally a play like Shelley's *Cenci* (1819) hearkened back to the older tradition. The twentieth century, however, has seen a number of attempts to create poetic drama as a viable alternative to the prose now more commonly used, the most noteworthy being the plays of Maxwell Anderson, T. S. Eliot, and Christopher Fry. See CLOSET DRAMA, DRAMATIC POETRY.

Poetic Justice.   The rewarding of virtue and the punishing of vice in a work of literature. Used by Thomas Rhymer in *Tragedies of the Last Age* (1678), the phrase has been much repeated since, with considerable discussion as to its desirability as a goal of the writer. Visions of poetic justice have sometimes caused writers to dispense with inner logic or considerations of probability in the real world, as in overtly DIDACTIC writing or in MELODRAMA, the POPULAR ROMANCE, the DETECTIVE STORY, and other forms of POPULAR LITERATURE. Poetic justice may also be found, however, in COMEDY and in the realistic NOVEL, in those situations in which the rewards and punishments seem both suitable and probable results of the credible behavior of the characters. In TRAGEDY and in some twentieth-century literature, poetic justice carries strong overtones of IRONY, as in the successive rewards and punishments, for example, that mark the lives of Oedipus (fifth century B.C.) and Jay Gatsby (1925).

Poetic License.   The liberty taken by a poet who achieves special effects by ignoring the conventions of PROSE with regard to grammar, diction, syntax, pronunciation, punctuation, and the like. It was defined by Dryden as "the liberty which poets have assumed to themselves in all ages, of speaking things in verse, which are beyond the severity of prose." Generally, poetic license is used by major poets as a means of enhancing the poetic communication, as they reject or minimize distortions dictated merely by meter or rhyme.

As a vehicle for illuminating the special nature of language, poetic license may be considered fundamental to poetry, as, in the words of the twentieth-century linguist Roman Jakobson, "The function of poetry is to point out that the sign is not identical with its referent." The same consideration reminds us that poetic license is also a liberty taken by the great imaginative prose writers, who distort conventional language, employing prose as a tool to jar readers out of their complacent sense of what words ordinarily mean.

Poetics.   The theory, art, or science of poetry. Poetics is concerned with the nature and function of poetry and with identifying and explaining its types, forms, and techniques. Aristotle's *Poetics* is the classic treatise. For discussions of poetics, see especially COMEDY; METER; POETRY; RHYME; STANZA; TRAGEDY; VERSE FORMS.

Poet Laureate. Since the seventeenth century, a title conferred by the monarch on English poets. At first, the laureateship carried with it the requirement that the honored poet would write poems to commemorate special occasions, such as royal birthdays, national celebrations, and the like, but since the early nineteenth century the appointment has been for the most part honorary, with no formal duties. Poets Laureate have been John Dryden (1668–1688), Thomas Shadwell (1689–1692), Nahum Tate (1692–1715), Nicholas Rowe (1715–1718), Laurence Eusden (1718–1730), Colley Cibber (1730–1757), William Whitehead (1757–1785), Thomas Warton (1785–1790), Henry James Pye (1790–1813), Robert Southey (1813–1843), William Wordsworth (1843–1850), Alfred, Lord Tennyson (1850–1892), Alfred Austin (1896–1913), Robert Bridges (1913–1930), John Masefield (1930–1967), C. Day Lewis (1968–1972), John Betjeman (1972–1984).

The practice of honoring poets began much earlier than the office of Poet Laureate. Earlier poets associated with the English court, and sometimes called *laureate*, include Chaucer, John Gower, John Lydgate, John Skelton, Ben Jonson, and William Davenant. Still earlier, the Anglo-Saxon SCOP, Scandinavian SKALD, Irish FILID, and Welsh BARD often held positions with similar respect and duties.

The association of laurel with poetry stems from Greek myth. After Daphne escaped from Apollo by turning into a laurel tree, the laurel became the traditional prize for poets and victors. In medieval universities, a student admitted to a degree in grammar, rhetoric, and poetry was crowned with laurel.

Reference

Kenneth Hopkins, **The Poet Laureate** (rev. ed., 1974).

Poetry. Imaginatively intense language, usually in verse. Poetry is a form of FICTION—"the supreme fiction," said Wallace Stevens. It is distinguished from other fictions by the compression resulting from its heavier use of FIGURE OF SPEECH and ALLUSION and, usually, by the music of its patterns of sounds. PROSE POETRY exhibits the qualities of poetry without verse. DOGGEREL exhibits the RHYME and METER of verse without significant imaginative content.

Poetry is a fundamental way of expressing human emotion and thought. Janus-faced, it looks both ways across the ancient chasm between heart and mind, belief and empirical observation, intuition and understanding. Its essential imaginative tools, METAPHOR, SIMILE, and METONYMY, are basic ways of thinking, establishing for primitive societies their myths and religions, assisting today's more sophisticated age to its astonishing insights into the spaces of atom and universe. At the root of all poetry is an emotion or thought that cannot be expressed, or has not yet been, struggling to find concrete embodiment in words. It begins in the images of the preconscious or subconscious mind and is filtered through language toward the precise symbols and syntax of an imaginative construction at first glimpsed only dimly by the poet.

Poets are both seers and makers, defined by characteristics of insight and language, which are often, in finished poems, inseparable. As seers, poets must remain true to the insight. As makers, they must communicate it to others. Speaking in Freudian terms, this is the conflict between the desires of the id and the control of the ego and superego. In any terms, the tensions between emotion and intellect, vision and accomplishment, and self and society are central to the idea of poetry.

The heart-and-mind dichotomy of poetry creates two fundamentally different strains of poetic expression, one of romanticism and one of classicism. The strain that is ROMANTICISM emphasizes the emotional, inspirational, and personal elements of poetry. The romantic poet is first of all a seer, placing most trust in those images that come unbidden, as from the wellsprings of the soul, in dream, reverie, or trance. The ideal of structure is ORGANIC FORM, with the poem assuming the natural shape that comes unbidden from the unconscious. Traditional poetic conventions and community wisdom are viewed with suspicion unless reconfirmed by the bardic vision. The poet speaks with a voice modulated in the deepest wells of personality, or, deeper than that, with the essential wisdom of a pantheistic universe or the God that lies behind it. The strain that is CLASSICISM emphasizes the intellectual, traditional, and communal elements of poetry. The classical poet is above all a maker, asserting the primacy of images carefully crafted to communicate most effectively the deepest insights. Form is preconceived rather than organic, an abstract shape into which the emotion of the poem is poured, containing and transmitting it. Traditional poetic conventions and community wisdom strengthen the poem by supporting it within the cultural architecture of its time. The poet speaks with the voice of priest or teacher, submerging self in an ideal of shared community experience.

The romantic impulse in its purest form has been strongest within the past two hundred years, in poets such as Blake, Wordsworth, Baudelaire, Whitman, Ezra Pound, and William Carlos Williams. The classical impulse ranges from Homer through Dante to Chaucer, Milton, Pope, and T. S. Eliot. Shakespeare wonderfully combined the romantic and classical. More recently, Robert Lowell (1917–1977) shifted in mid-career from a classical to a romantic poetic practice. At bottom, however, the terms *romantic* and *classical* describe tendencies, not firm categories. All true poets combine the vision of the seer with the craft of the maker. The seer without craft writes incoherent babble. The maker without vision polishes the artificial surface of doggerel or empty wit.

Language is the medium of poetry; the poet, of all humans, most the master of language. Through language the vision becomes imaginatively manifest. The content of prose may be expressed in different words, especially if the prose is loose and unpoetic, but the content of poetry cannot be expressed except in the words of the poem. Poetry therefore resists translation. A French or Japanese novel may be read in English with little sense of loss, but not a French or Japanese poem. Robert Frost in Spanish is scarcely Frost. Because of this close tie to language, poetry is significantly shaped by the language and idiom it is written in. The dominant iambics and fundamental four-beat line of English poetry arise naturally from accentual patterns and syntax, or, as the French say, the "thump" of spoken English. Italian, rich in FEMININE RHYME, allowed Dante effects in the TERZA RIMA of *The Divine Comedy* not to be duplicated in English. The tonal qualities of oriental languages make Japanese HAIKU different from haiku in English. Frost's poetry translates with difficulty not only because Frost's language was English but because his idiom is New England. Figures of speech and allusions are a part of this linguistic essence, the poet's voice shaped in part by figures and references common to his or her time and place. Milton's metaphors and allusions are not the metaphors and allusions of Emily Dickinson.

Poetry shares the ancient fictional purpose "to inform and delight." Early poets from Homer to Dante, Chaucer, Milton, and Pope combined both aims. In modern times, poetry has increasingly tended to leave the DIDACTIC and mimetic elements (see MIMESIS) of information to prose fiction and drama, as poets have emphasized delight through the often antithetical aims of aesthetics and popularity. In the nineteenth century, poets like Longfellow and Tennyson could still achieve a popularity rivaling that of novelists. In the twentieth century, however, serious poets from the time of Pound and Eliot have often addressed a smaller audience educated to appreciate their art. For some recent poets the aim of aesthetic delight, or of ART FOR ART'S SAKE, has been everything. "A poem should not mean / But be," wrote Archibald MacLeish, emphasizing the primacy of the created object in a line that unfortunately can be understood as dismissing half of poetry's traditional function. Frost's a poem "begins in delight and ends in wisdom" nicely restores it.

The formal characteristics of poetry arise from its condensation of meaning in patterns of sound. Meter and rhyme serve rhetorical, aesthetic, and mnemonic purposes. Other sound elements such as ALLITERATION, ASSONANCE, and ONOMATOPOEIA help convey meaning and beauty memorably. It is much easier to memorize a passage of poetry than one of prose, and speaking generally, more worthwhile. The STANZA punctuates, like the paragraph in prose, with more precision. Fixed VERSE FORMS like the BALLAD, SONNET, and SESTINA frame varied linguistic constructions. SYLLABIC VERSE provides a unit of measure in languages not heavily accented, or, in English, for poets like Marianne Moore seeking effects outside the usual meters. FREE VERSE is at its best not patternless, but only freed from the patterns of tradition.

The LYRIC poem and the NARRATIVE POEM are the fundamental types, reflecting poetry's primitive origins in song and ritual as the poet expresses an emotion or tells a story. Both are closely related to DRAMA, and plays are frequently written in poetry. Some poems are highly descriptive, however, and others discursive. Subordinate types such as the ELEGY, EPIC, PASTORAL, DRAMATIC MONOLOGUE, and ODE are essentially lyric, narrative, dramatic, descriptive, or discursive or display a combination of those qualities.

References

Alex Preminger, Frank J. Warnke, and O. B. Hardison, eds., **The Encyclopaedia of Poetry and Poetics** (1965).
Herbert Read, **Collected Essays in Literary Criticism** (1938; as **The Nature of Literature,** 1956).
Rene Wellek and Austin Warren, **Theory of Literature** (1942; 2nd ed., 1946).
George Whalley, **Poetic Process** (1953).

Point of Attack. The moment in a play or story that initiates the main action.

Point of View.   See NARRATIVE PERSPECTIVE.

Point of View Shot.   In motion pictures, a shot with the camera positioned next to one of the performers, presenting the scene from that person's perspective. See OBJECTIVE CAMERA; SUBJECTIVE CAMERA.

Polemic.   An argumentative or controversial writing, forcefully presenting the author's viewpoint, from a Greek word meaning "war." Milton's *Areopagitica* is a famous example.

Political Novel.   A NOVEL directly and fundamentally concerned with politics or political issues. Examples include Benjamin Disraeli's *Coningsby* (1844), Anthony Trollope's Palliser novels, Fyodor Dostoevsky's *Possessed* (1871–1872), David Graham Phillips's *Plum Tree* (1905), André Malraux's *Man's Fate* (1933), Arthur Koestler's *Darkness at Noon* (1940), George Orwell's *Nineteen Eighty-Four* (1949), C. P. Snow's *Corridors of Power* (1964), and Philip Roth's *Our Gang* (1971).

Polyphonic Prose.   PROSE especially rich in poetic sound devices, including ALLITERATION, ASSONANCE, RHYME, and RHYTHM. The name is associated particularly with Amy Lowell, whose *Can Grande's Castle* (1918) is an example, a development of an idea she derived from the *Ballades* of the French poet Paul Fort. John Gould Fletcher, a friend of Lowell's, also published pieces in this style in *Breakers and Granite* (1921).

Polyptoton.   "Having many cases." It is the repetition of several words in different grammatical constructions—a multiple PAREGMENON: "My own heart's heart, and ownest own, farewell" (Tennyson).

Polysemous Meaning.   Multiple meaning derived from a single text, each interpretation justified by the different possibilities of signification inherent in words and their arrangements. Dante defined *polysemous* as " 'of more senses than one'; for it is one sense which we get through the letter, and another which we get through the thing the letter signifies; and the first is called literal, but the second allegorical or mystic." SEMIOTICS, STRUCTURALISM, and POST-STRUCTURALISM are modern approaches to literature concerned with polysemous meaning. See AMBIGUITY, ALLEGORY, FOUR SENSES OF INTERPRETATION.

Polysyndeton.   Repetition of conjunctions: "The great thing is to last and get your work done and see and hear and learn and understand; and write when there is something that you know; and not before; and not too damned much after" (Ernest Hemingway, *Death in the After-*

noon). Without conjunctions, the effect is ASYNDETON. See PARALLEL-
ISM; PARATAXIS.

Popular Ballad. Another name for the *traditional ballad* or *folk ballad,* a song of anonymous authorship, transmitted orally. See BALLAD.

Popular Literature. Literature of widespread appeal. Generally, such
literature encapsulates fundamentally simple emotional and intellectual
content in a basic mythological structure. The result may be simple,
or quite complex. Building on ARCHETYPES, popular literature trans-
mutes them into the literary coin of a particular time and place, providing a good index to views widely shared within a society during the
period of popularity.

In primitive societies, popular literature emerges as FOLK TALE and
FOLK SONG, accumulating through oral transmission a representative
store of wisdom and belief. As societies have become more sophisticated, and more literate, transmission by manuscript first, and then by
print, has tended to change the process, with popular literature in recent centuries created by individual authors whose works become popular because they strike responsive chords in the society that reads
them. This popularity may be immediate, widespread, and ephemeral;
it may arise slowly, but continue long; or it may be both immediate
and long-lived.

In common usage, the term *popular literature* has sometimes signified literature immediately popular, widely read, and quickly forgotten. The appeal is often to segments within society that share common
interests, rather than to society as a whole, and in the nineteenth and
twentieth centuries such segments have become large enough to provide the incentive of lucrative markets. A number of GENRES may be
identified, each with its own FORMULA that stretches the simple emotional and intellectual content of all popular literature on an essentially
mythological framework suitable to the interests of the intended audience. For individual discussions, see ADVENTURE STORY, DETECTIVE
STORY, FANTASY, HISTORICAL ROMANCE, MELODRAMA, MYSTERY
STORY, POPULAR ROMANCE, SCIENCE FICTION, and WESTERN. Assured
of an immediate audience, works that fall within these genres are often
unsophisticated in the way they handle essential materials, though they
need not be. When they are well written and challenge the conventions
of the genre, they sometimes rise to a more general and longer-lasting
popularity.

In a less common but equally important usage, *popular literature* is
literature widely read over a long period of time. In contrast to much

popular literature of the ephemeral kind, this type is often very sophisticated, building elaborate structures on simple foundations. Thus, the fundamentally simple story of young lovers divided by family enmity is developed in elaborately different ways in Shakespeare's *Romeo and Juliet* and Scott's *Bride of Lammermoor*, and both versions continue popular in the vastly different, still sophisticated, musical idioms of *Lucia di Lammermoor* and *West Side Story*. Other lasting literary works noteworthy for their popular content, presented with varying degrees of complexity, include the Bible, Dante's *Inferno*, Malory's *Morte Darthur*, Shakespeare's comedies, Milton's *Paradise Lost*, Bunyan's *Pilgrim's Progress*, Richardson's *Clarissa*, Poe's stories, Dickens's *Oliver Twist* and *Great Expectations*, Twain's *Huckleberry Finn*, James's *Turn of the Screw*, Conrad's *Heart of Darkness*, Joyce's *Ulysses*, and Fitzgerald's *Great Gatsby*. See DIME NOVEL; PENNY DREADFUL; PULP MAGAZINES.

Popular Romance.   A popular love story, typically in glamorous or exotic surroundings, such as Venice or the Caribbean. Feminine chastity is a frequent theme. Sensuality is suggested, but explicit sex usually avoided. Young women fall in love with dark, handsome, wealthy, mature men. Troubles follow, but most end happily, in marriage. The GENRE has proved phenomenally successful in recent years, with the Canadian publisher of Harlequin Romances establishing a standard much imitated. In the early 1980s it was estimated that popular romances accounted for as much as 45 percent of the annual paperback sales in the United States. See HISTORICAL ROMANCE; POPULAR LITERATURE.

Pornography.   Literally, writing about prostitutes, derived from Greek words for "prostitutes" and "writing." The term is used to mean any writing emphasizing sex, especially writing calculated to arouse sexual excitement. Works of pornography may be divided into two classes: (1) *erotica*, literature concentrating on physical acts of heterosexual love, and (2) *exotica*, literature presenting perverse or deviant sexuality, including incest, sadism, and masochism.

The term *pornography* generally connotes at least some degree of social disapproval, with expressions such as "soft core" and "hard core" used to indicate the level of objection, as with popular books and magazines and pornographic movies. But the standards change, and many works once banned as indecent, immoral, or illegal are now quite readily available, meeting with far less disapproval than formerly. Major literary works that at times have been considered pornographic, in whole or in part, include Boccaccio's *Decameron*, some of Chaucer's *Canterbury Tales*, and, in the twentieth century, James Joyce's *Ulysses*, D. H. Lawrence's *Lady Chatterley's Lover*, and Vladimir Nabokov's *Lolita*. In court cases involving censorship, issues raised have included the standards of the community, redeeming social value, the perceived intent of the work, and literary quality. In this setting, works have most often been judged pornographic, or obscene, by their effects, as when no purpose can be discovered beyond sexual stimulation or the profit motive—the root concept of prostitution carrying great weight.

Avoiding the negative CONNOTATION of pornography, EROTIC LITERATURE is a term often used for the literature of sensual love treated in a manner generally acceptable to society.

Portmanteau Word. A "suitcase" word, one carrying extra meaning, formed by combining two or more words. A *portmanteau* is a case for carrying clothing and other travel necessities. Lewis Carroll coined the phrase to describe his own practice, as in *Through the Looking-Glass* Humpty Dumpty explains to Alice that the poem "Jabberwocky" employs the word *slithy* to mean both *lithe* and *slimy*. James Joyce used many words of this type, especially in *Finnegans Wake*. See COINED WORDS; NEOLOGISM; NONCE WORD.

Positivism. A movement founded by Auguste Comte (1798–1857) with his *Cours de philosophie positive* (1830–1842), basing knowledge, and eventually conduct, on empirical evidence. He saw knowledge evolving from the theological to the metaphysical to the positive, or scientifically empirical. He classified knowledge on a scale rising from generality to empirical complexity: mathematics, astronomy, physics, chemistry, biology, sociology. LOGICAL POSITIVISM, the twentieth-century outgrowth, emphasizes empirical factuality as the only validity, with all metaphysical concepts, ethics, and evaluations—"value judgments"—as illusions.

References

Joergen Joergensen, **The Development of Logical Positivism,** vol. 2, no. 9, **International Encyclopedia of Unified Science** (1951).
Walter M. Simon, **European Positivism in the Nineteenth Century** (1963).

Post-Modern Period (1965–   ).   The period, after a post-war lull from 1945 to 1965, in which a new generation of talented writers have explored the modern dilemma of self and meaning. But Samuel Beckett, an expatriated Irishman in Paris, a sometime secretary to James Joyce, had already portrayed alienated modern humankind as waiting in a twilight for an uncertain future in his wanly comic play, *Waiting for Godot* (1954), which he had translated from his original French version (1953). Beckett remains the most significant writer of the late twentieth century, as T. S. Eliot was for the earlier. In America, Kurt Vonnegut's and Thomas Pynchon's cryptic nihilism scintillates like fireworks, and John Barth's playful fictions attempt to undermine Aristotelian assumptions that fiction is meaningful as it relates to reality. In England, Doris Lessing established herself with *The Golden Notebook* (1962), an existential *tour de force* about creating one's self through the recorded realities of fiction. Intruding into one's own fiction to ponder its powers became the hallmark of the late 1960s and 1970s, with such outstanding writers as John Fowles (*The French Lieutenant's Woman*, 1969), Margaret Drabble (particularly, *The Waterfall*, 1969), L. P. Hartley (*The Love-Adept*, 1969), Iris Murdoch (*The Black Prince*, 1973), and Dan Jacobson (*The Wonder Worker*, 1973). Other writers of great imaginative power who continued their long productive careers in the 1960s and 1970s are Jorge Luis Borges (1899–   ) and Vladimir Nabokov (1899–1977). With these, and others like Saul Bellow, Fowles, and Drabble, a new good-humored and optimistic stoicism began to affirm some order beneath (or above) the scattered surfaces of accident and bewilderment. Even Beckett's brief and powerful *Not I* (1974), which opens and ends with a voice murmuring in darkness, takes a strangely affirmative turn.

Post-Structuralism.   A mode of literary CRITICISM and thought centered on Jacques Derrida's concept of DECONSTRUCTION, expressed in his three books of 1967: *L'Écriture et al différence* (*Writing and Difference*), *Le Voix et la phénomène* (*Speech and Phenomena*), and *De la gramatologie* (*Of Gramatology*), the major work. Structuralists see language as the paradigm for all structures. Post-structuralists see language as based on differences—hence the analytical deconstruction of what seemed an immutable system. What language expresses is already absent. Like Heraclitus's stream, the present is already past when expressed. In writing, the object is even farther absent, as the word *differs* from what it signifies and *defers* meaning as the utterance lags behind the thought.

Post-structuralism challenges the NEW CRITICISM, which seeks a truth fixed within the "verbal icon," the text, in W. K. Wimsatt's term. Post-structuralism invites interpretations through the spaces left by the way words operate. The New Criticism implies a separate langauge for literature and for criticism. Post-structuralism sees criticism *as* literature, with the same absences and openness, each successive criticism becoming a new literary statement open to further interpretation.

Emphasis shifts from text to reader. In Aristotelian terms, authors communicate through their texts to their audiences. The New Criticism deletes the authors and their intentions, concentrating on the text. Post-structuralism deletes the author and demotes the text, since the loopholes in language itself throw the certainty of both into question. Post-structuralism concentrates on the reader, who is free, according to Roland Barthes, to play with the text's possibilities, producing new texts for subsequent play. Reading and writing are the same kind of enterprise, and all writing is text.

Both literature and philosophy, says Derrida, can only pretend toward truth. Paul de Man agrees, seeing them the same, not separate, as had Plato in denying poets his rational Republic. Literature and philosophy both wrongly assume a fixed presence of reality. Derrida points to the inevitable *absence* of reality in language, and in the perceiver's mind, as each instant moves on. All the reader has is a *trace* of object, or thought, even as the reader tries to find words to express it. Thus reality itself becomes a text, and every text depends on a *pre-text*. For literature, reality has vanished, along with Aristotle's imitated illusion of reality. Meaning depends on intertextuality, as the reader utters new texts in response to old, new pages moving on from their predecessors. Marxist critics see post-structuralism breaking open cultural meanings in which critics have enslaved us, since no writer can present a coherent ideology without the absences and gaps of all linguistic expression. See MARXISM; STRUCTURALISM.

References

Ira Konigsberg, ed., **American Criticism in the Poststructuralist Age** (1981).
Christopher Norris, **Deconstruction: Theory and Practice** (1982).
Robert Young, ed., **Untying the Text: A Post-Structuralist Reader** (1981).

Posy.   An archaic term for a motto, usually in verse, inscribed on a ring or heraldic emblem. The term also refers to a bunch of flowers, or, by extension, an ANTHOLOGY of verse.

Potboiler.   A work written primarily for money, to keep the pot boiling, or food on the table. Frequently the term is used in disparagement, but the work produced is not always inferior. Henry James re-

ferred to *The Turn of the Screw* as "rather a shameless pot-boiler."
Samuel Johnson's *Rasselas* was written in haste to pay the expenses of
his mother's funeral.

Poulter's Measure.   An iambic hexameter line coupled with an iambic heptameter, 12 syllables followed by 14 (a FOURTEENER). In his
Certain Notes of Instruction (1575), George Gascoigne called it "the commonest sort of verse which we use nowadays," dubbing it "poulter's
measure" from the 14 eggs one received as a second dozen. Arthur
Brooke's *Romeus and Juliet* (1562), Shakespeare's source, is in poulter's
measure:

> There is beyond the Alps, a town of ancient fame,
> Whose bright renown yet shineth clear, Verona men it name.

Poulter's measure eventually merged with SHORT METER—a 4-line
STANZA of 2 iambic trimeter lines, a tetrameter, and a trimeter. See
METER.

Practical Criticism.   See CRITICISM.

Pragmatic Criticism.   CRITICISM that emphasizes the relationship of
art to the audience, rather than its relationship to artist or universe.

Pragmatics.   A branch of SEMIOTICS that examines the relation between words (linguistic signs) and their users.

Pragmatism.   In philosophy, the idea that the value of a belief is best
judged by the acts that follow from it—its practical results. Thus,
whatever abstract identities may be claimed for them, truth and reality
are measured concretely, in terms of physical existence. Because prag-
matists choose not to pursue speculations that cannot be verified ex-
perimentally, the truth they accept is relative, changing as scientific
knowledge changes. Reality differs in different times and places, depending upon experience. Religious or ethical beliefs are valid insofar
as they support or fail to support human actions.

  Among philosophers linked to pragmatism are C. S. Peirce, who
developed pragmatism as a formal doctrine (c. 1878); William James;
Henri Bergson; John Dewey; and F. C. S. Schiller. In literature, RE-
ALISM and NATURALISM are in some ways similarly oriented. See IDE-
ALISM; MATERIALISM, REALISM (IN PHILOSOPHY).

Preamble.   An INTRODUCTION, especially to a constitution or other
formal document, setting forth its origin and purpose.

Preciosity. Since the nineteenth century, a term for an affected or overingenious refinement of language. The word was originally used for anything expensive or precious, but is now rare or obsolete in that sense. In French literature, *la préciosité* denotes the refinement of manners and language pursued especially by certain seventeenth-century writers, satirized by Molière in *Les Précieuses ridicules* (1659).

Précis. A brief summary of a work or passage.

Predestination. The belief that an omniscient God, at the Creation, destined all subsequent events, particularly, in Calvinist belief, the election for salvation and the damnation of individual souls. The term also refers to the nontheological belief that everything is fated. See CALVINISM; FATALISM.

Preface. An author's introductory statement of purpose, background, inspiration, debt, and the like. Dryden's Preface to his *Fables Ancient and Modern* (1700), Shaw's prefaces to his plays, and Henry James's to his novels became major critical essays.

Prelude. An introductory piece, originally, in the late sixteenth century, to a play (*praelūdere*, "to play before"), but almost simultaneously signifying preliminary music, the prevailing meaning. Wordsworth's *Prelude; or Growth of a Poet's Mind; An Autobiographical Poem* (finished 1805) adapts the term to poetry, since Wordsworth thought of it as a self-analysis preliminary to a major work, never achieved, to be called *The Recluse*. Although Wordsworth referred to it as "the Ante-chapel . . . to the body of a Gothic Church" (Preface, *The Excursion*), his metaphor in the poem itself is clearly musical: "Matins and vespers of harmonious verse," "harmony dispersed in straggling sounds," "yearning toward some philosophic song / Of Truth . . . / Thoughtfully fitted to the Orphean lyre" (the projected major work). Alice Meynell repeated the musical metaphor in her first volume, *Preludes* (1875), as did T. S. Eliot in his brief "Preludes" (1917).

Pre-Raphaelite. Characteristic of a small but influential group of mid-nineteenth-century painters who hoped to recapture the spiritual vividness they saw in medieval painting before Raphael (1483–1520). In 1848, three young students at the Royal Academy in London— Dante Gabriel Rossetti, William Holman Hunt, John Everett Millais— formed the secret Pre-Raphaelite Brotherhood in protest against what they perceived as the unimaginative and materialistic conventionality of their teachers. They invited James Collinson, F. G. Stephens,

Thomas Woolner (a sculptor), and William Michael Rossetti, a critic and Dante Gabriel's brother, to join them. They exhibited their paintings jointly, signed only with "PRB." In 1850, critics uncovered their identities, and their youth, and lambasted them, particularly as irreverently realistic. John Ruskin defended them as being faithful to natural truth, down to the minute detail that also characterized the pictorial quality of the poetry, especially Dante Gabriel's, influenced by the movement. Their magazine, *The Germ: Thoughts Towards Nature in Poetry, Literature, and Art,* began 1 January 1850, ran for four issues, and published Rossetti's—and the Pre-Raphaelites'—most famous poem, "The Blessed Damozel." The Pre-Raphaelites experimented with light, as their young French contemporaries, the Impressionists, were doing, and achieved a kind of photographic quality, but their spirituality seemed superficial and their themes increasingly sentimental and romantic. Rossetti greatly influenced William Morris (1834–1896) both in Morris's poetry ("Defense of Guenevere," 1858; "Earthly Paradise," 1868–1870) and in his revival of medieval crafts and design. The poetry of Christina Rossetti, sister of D. G. and W. M., is distinguished. See FLESHLY SCHOOL; IMPRESSIONISM.

Presbyterianism. John Calvin's organization of ecclesiastical governance not by bishops representing the pope but by elders representing the congregation (from Greek *presbuteros,* "an older man"). Calvin (1509–1564), on biblical precedent, believed that the church was a community of equals under Christ. Consequently, he replaced the episcopal hierarchy with hierarchies of congregational participation and authority and assemblies of officeholders, pastors, and elders. In England, Puritan Presbyterians were instrumental in the overthrow of Charles I (1648), but a parliamentary minority of Independents (congregationalists), led by Oliver Cromwell, tried and executed him in 1649. John Knox (1505–1572) founded the Presbyterian church in Scotland, which, in the seventeenth and eighteenth centuries, contributed Presbyterian communities in America alongside earlier New England Puritan churches. In the nineteenth century, Scottish Presbyterians, settling in England, formed the nucleus of the Presbyterian church of England, organized in 1876.

Preteritio. See APOPHASIS.

Primitivism. Belief in the superiority of primitive life, and of the earliest periods of history, specifically in a perfect Arcadia (Greek) or Eden (Judeo-Christian) from which humanity has fallen from bad to worse, with civilization spoiling the NOBLE SAVAGE. In classical mythology, humans have fallen from a Golden Age, to a Silver, a Bronze, and an Iron, where they remain in sin and general disorder (see AGES OF THE WORLD). The primitivistic assumption that change means decay prevailed until the idea of PROGRESS, almost of equal antiquity, began to dominate in the late eighteenth century. Seventeenth- and eighteenth-century thinkers, like the third earl of Shaftesbury in his *Characteristics of Men, Manners, Opinions, Times* (1711), argued that primitive humankind was closest to God's nature, hence better. Similarly, they esteemed Homer and Virgil, the "ancients," as closer to nature and literary perfection and thus superior to the "moderns," though, paradoxically, the classics represented the peak of civilization rather than rural simplicity.

Jean Jacques Rousseau applied primitivism to his pursuit of political equality, first in his prize-winning *Discours sur les sciences et les arts* at the Dijon Academy in 1749 (published 1750), which praised humankind's savage state, arguing that sciences, letters, and arts had stifled spiritual liberty, civilizing humans into slavery through luxury. His *Discours sur l'origine et les fondements de l'inégalité parmi les hommes* (1755—known as his *Second Discourse,* on the origin and foundations of inequality among humankind) recasts the Ages of the World as outlined by Hesiod and Ovid. Originally, said Rousseau, humans lived in isolation and hence in equality, avoiding each other as they believed wild animals did. Then earthquakes and other natural upheavals brought humans into communities, and this is the Golden Age, in which humans, nevertheless, learned good and evil, friendship and hate. Then, in the third stage, iron and wheat civilized and ruined humanity, bringing private property and war.

In eighteenth-century England, the two slightly contradictory views of primitivism subsisted side by side and frequently in the same mind, since both revered the past from which modern humankind had fallen. (1) *Chronological primitivism* admired and emulated the classics and distrusted all change as decay; it was especially evident in schemes to stabilize language and in hopes of slowing linguistic change through dictionaries and grammars. (2) *Cultural primitivism* discovered pristine charm, reminiscent of Jean Jacques Rousseau, in ballads, primitive poetry, and untutored writers like Stephen Duck, the "thresher poet" (1705–1752), and Robert Burns (1759–1796). In their poetry "nature" slowly changed from God's cosmic creation to a sublime natural presence in crags and streams. Some writers included a belief in natural freedom as opposed to rational controls.

Primitivism thus transformed itself into the Romantic movement as Wordsworth championed nature, simple language, rustic leach gatherers, and idiot boys, seeing humans as born "trailing clouds of glory" into a golden childhood that declined into the prison-house of society. James Fenimore Cooper's noble Mohicans and their dwindling wilderness reflected primitivism in America, as did Crèvecoeur's *Letters from an American Farmer* (1782).

In art, *primitivism* refers to untrained artists who achieve a naïve and childlike power, like that of Henri Rousseau (1844–1910) and Grandma Moses (1860–1961).

Printing. The production of printed matter. Printing originated in China, after the invention of paper. In about 1041, an alchemist named Pi Sheng devised movable ceramic characters and a method of fusing them to metal plates and afterward removing them for reuse. But CALLIGRAPHY with the brush continued to dominate during centuries punctuated with revivals of printing. In 1234, a Korean invented movable wooden characters, producing books on medicine, agriculture, astronomy, geography, and history. In 1313, in China, an official ordered 60,000 wooden characters to print a history of technology. In 1403, in Korea, King Htai Tjong ordered 100,000 characters cast in bronze.

In 1450, King Sejong of Korea had produced, through his Royal Academy, a new phonetic alphabet and two fonts, almost exactly at the time Johann Gutenberg (c. 1400–1468), in Mainz, Germany, began to print with his newly invented movable type. Printing from carved wooden blocks, or xylography, had begun in Europe about 1275 with the acquisition of paper and paper making from China by way of the Arab world, and Gutenberg's priority as the first printer with movable type was disputed in his own day. But contemporary lawsuits and scholarship pretty well confirm his right.

Gutenberg's earliest printing was of a Letter of Indulgence granted by Pope Nicholas V (1454). The famous Gutenberg Latin Bible appeared in 1455. William Caxton, a wealthy retired English merchant in Flanders, brought printing to England, after learning the new craft and producing, at Bruges, two books he translated from French—the first books printed in English: *Recuyell of the Histories of Troye* (1474) and *The Game and Playe of Chesse* (1476), an allegory about life's gamesmanship. Caxton returned to London and produced his *Dictes or Sayengis of the Philosophres* (18 November 1477), the first book printed in England. Before his death at 70 in 1491, Caxton had printed about a hundred books, 24 his own translations, among them his esteemed edition of Chaucer's *Canterbury Tales* (1483) and his original publication of Malory's *Morte Darthur* (1485). Wynkyn de Worde (died c. 1534), Caxton's apprentice, went on to produce some 800 books. Richard Pynson (flourished, 1490–1530), also associated with Caxton and appointed King's Printer by Henry VIII on his accession (1509), introduced Roman type (as distinct from the earlier BLACK LETTER) into England.

In America, aside from presses in the Spanish colonies, Stephen Daye's press in Boston was the first, producing *The Freeman's Oath* and an almanac, both lost, and the famous *Bay Psalm Book* (1640). William Bradford, the government printer in New York, began printing in Philadelphia about 1683. Sir William Berkeley (c. 1608–1677), king's governor of Virginia under Charles I and again under Charles II, suppressed printing in that colony as an instrument of Puritan subversion.

Various mechanical and steam-powered printing presses evolved throughout the nineteenth century. In the 1880s, Ottmar Mergenthaler, a German immigrant to the United States, invented the Linotype, which could cast a solid line of metallic type from movable letter forms. Presses printing from cylinders followed, and, in the twentieth century, the various means of printing photographically, eventually from signals echoed from satellites. See BLOCK BOOK.

References

T. L. de Vinne, **The Invention of Printing** (1876; reprinted, 1969).
Robert Lechène, "Printing," **Encyclopaedia Britannica** (1980).
D. C. Murtrie, **The Invention of Printing: A Bibliography** (1962).

Private Theaters.   Late Elizabethan theaters catering to an aristocratic audience. Higher prices and, particularly, child actors were among other attractions, like being indoors in rectangular rooms with artificial lighting. *Private* evidently meant "indoors." The Blackfriars theater was referred to as "private" about 1596, though it and other "privates," like the "public" theaters, were open to all. The "private" companies performed at the Blackfriars, St. Paul's, the Inns of Court, and the royal court itself. Shakespeare's company was soon managing both the Blackfriars and the GLOBE THEATER, the leading "private" and "public" theaters. The private theaters featured the MASQUE, increasingly popular with the Stuart court, and became the forerunners of the RESTORATION theater, with its PROSCENIUM stage, screens, and curtain, in contrast to the round Globe with its open Elizabethan stage. See THEATERS.

Prizes and Awards. See AMERICAN ACADEMY AND INSTITUTE OF ARTS AND LETTERS; NOBEL PRIZE; PULITZER PRIZES. See also FELLOWSHIPS AND GRANTS.

Problem Novel. (1) A NOVEL that addresses some social conflict like that between farmers and workers in Steinbeck's *In Dubious Battle* (1936) or between displaced Oklahomans and the California farm establishment in his *Grapes of Wrath* (1939). (2) Loosely, any novel plotted to solve a problem, a "propaganda novel," a "sociological novel," or one with a philosophical thesis, like Santayana's *Last Puritan* (1935) or Mann's *Magic Mountain* (1924).

Problem Play. A play addressed to a social problem, specifically John Galsworthy's *Silver Box* (1906), *Strife* (1909), and *Justice* (1910). Critics cite Ibsen and his English successor, Shaw, as originating the "problem play." It is also called a "thesis play."

Process Shot. In film terminology, a shot of live action taken in front of a screen displaying still or moving images previously filmed.

Proem. An INTRODUCTION, dating in English from Chaucer's "Clerk's Prologue" (c. 1387), in which the Clerk speaks of a "prohemye."

Profile. A biographical article. The term and form originated with *The New Yorker*'s "Profile," still running, of the 1920s.

Progress. Forward movement; as an idea, the belief that civilization is getting better, in contrast to PRIMITIVISM, the belief that civilization has declined. The idea of progress entered the classical Hellenic world, which had conceived only of cyclical ups and downs like a tidal rise and fall, through Hebraic *eschatology*, a concept in which life's "last things" count, and a nation is thought to move from adversity toward promise. St. Augustine, in particular, described life as a progress from sinful birth toward spiritual fulfillment. The eighteenth century—Swift as against the more optimistic Pope, Johnson as against the rising Romantic flow—assumed primitivism, that any change (downhill from Eden) must be for the worse. Somewhere around 1776, with a new nation proclaiming a pursuit of future happiness, and with Gibbon's *Decline and Fall of the Roman Empire* (first volume, 1776) deciding that humankind would never again endure such mayhem, the idea of progress predominated. Such hopefulness was especially evident in the French Revolution of 1789, which declared the past nonexistent and began a new calendar with the year 1. The idea of progress tilted Pope's vertical GREAT CHAIN OF BEING into an upward slant of evolution with its missing link, and an ascending staircase with progressive "steps."

Projective Verse.   A mode of FREE VERSE originating with Charles Olson (1910–1970) and described first in his manifesto "Projective Verse" (1950) and then in his *Projective Verse* (1959). According to Olson, conventional meters and forms are artificial and meaningless, as are the formalist concepts of the NEW CRITICISM. The poet should project a personal vision into the arrangement on the page, measuring phrasing with breath ("breath verse"), drawing vision and form from the cosmos. Olson was an instructor and then rector at the brief experimental Black Mountain College in North Carolina, where Robert Creeley and Robert Duncan joined him. Creeley edited the *Black Mountain Review* (1954–1957), publishing William Carlos Williams (whom the group emulated as they rejected T. S. Eliot) and a number of "Black Mountain poets" including Denise Levertov, Allen Ginsberg, Gary Snyder, and LeRoi Jones (later Imamu Amiri Baraka). See BLACK MOUNTAIN SCHOOL.

Prolegomenon.   An INTRODUCTION stating a purpose or outlining a program.

Prolepsis.   "Anticipation" (Greek). (1) In rhetoric, the technique of anticipating and answering the opposition. (2) A figurative HYPERBOLE anticipating a result: for instance, Hamlet's "Horatio, I am dead"; "She has won the match" (after breaking her opponent's opening service); "Knock him flat."

Proletarian Literature.   Works championing the working class, like Elizabeth Gaskell's novel *Mary Barton* (1848), Galsworthy's plays *The Silver Box* (1906) and *Strife* (1909), and Steinbeck's novels—frequently, though not necessarily, Marxist in theory.

Prologue.   A short speech introducing a play. In Greece, a speaker sketched the background. Latin playwrights continued the tradition as they appropriated and translated Greek plays—some of Plautus's best poetry is in his prologues. The English MYSTERY PLAY and MIRACLE PLAY began with a homily by way of prologue. Thomas Sackville's and

Thomas Norton's *Gorboduc* (1561), the first English tragedy, has a DUMB SHOW for prologue. Various of Shakespeare's plays open with a prologue spoken by a character named "Prologue," "Chorus," "Rumour," and the like, including the "INDUCTION" to *The Taming of the Shrew* (1594), in which a lord picks up the drunken Christopher Sly, takes him home, and stages the play itself for him. Prologues in iambic pentameter couplets reached a peak of tradition in the RESTORATION and eighteenth century, written by the author or a friend and spoken by a principal actor—or actress, preferably—in tights or riding habit or even a cat costume. An EPILOGUE balanced off the performance. The most famous prologue of all time, however, is nondramatic: that to Chaucer's *Canterbury Tales*.

Proof.   A printer's trial sheet, to be corrected by the author or editor before final printing. *Galley proof* (or *galleys*) refers to the long sheet or sheets printed after the type has first been set from MANUSCRIPT, before the work has been laid out in pages. Modern printing frequently eliminates the galley stage. *Page proof* refers to the sheets printed after pages have been made up. *Foul proof* bears marks for correction.

Proparalepsis.   The addition of a syllable: "height," "height*en*."

Propriety.   See DRAMATIC PROPRIETY.

Proscenium.   Originally, in Greece, the whole acting area ("in front of the scenery"); now, that part of the stage projecting in front of the curtain. The proscenium arch, from which the curtain hangs, frames the BOX SET to make the invisible FOURTH WALL of the one-room setting. In the 1560s the Italian theater had introduced a temporary structure, with curtain, to set off a proscenium area. The first permanent proscenium arch was built at the Teatro Farnese, Parma, in 1618–1619. In the RESTORATION and eighteenth century, the proscenium, with curtain to open and close the play, became a permanent feature of stagecraft. See THEATERS.

Prose.   Ordinary writing patterned on speech, as distinct from verse, which has preceded prose in all cultures. English prose began with King Alfred's *Handbook* (887), a commonplace book now lost, and his instigating *The Anglo-Saxon Chronicle*, the translations of the Venerable Bede's *Ecclesiastical History of the English People*, and two works of Pope Gregory the Great. Other early shapers of English prose are Thomas Usk (*The Testament of Love*, 1387); John Wyclif (first translation of the Bible, mostly by his followers, c. 1395); Thomas Malory

(*Morte Darthur*, c. 1470); and William Caxton, who printed Malory in 1485, wrote and printed numerous translations of his own and, in his Preface to his *Eneydos* (1490), pondered on the problems of writing clearly with a changing language. Modern prose is considered as established in 1688, the year of the Bloodless Revolution, particularly under the influence of John Dryden. See ENGLISH LANGUAGE.

Prose Poetry.   Prose rich in cadenced and poetic effects like ALLITERATION, ASSONANCE, CONSONANCE, and the like, and in IMAGERY. See POLYPHONIC PROSE.

Prose Rhythm.   The pulsing effect of similar though irregular spans of phrasing and emphasis that makes some prose seem to approach verse. Some people have attempted systems for scanning rhythmic prose, but with little enlightenment.

Prosody.   The analysis and description of meters; *metrics* (see METER). Linguists apply the term to the study of patterns of accent in a language.

Prosopopeia.   A rhetorical figure in which an orator impersonates an imaginary or absent speaker; a term more loosely applied to any PERSONIFICATION.

Protagonist.   The leading character in a play or story, originally the leader of the CHORUS in the AGON ("contest") of Greek drama, faced with the ANTAGONIST, the opposition. See CHARACTERS.

Protasis.   The conditional clause of an assertion: *"If she works on her game,* she will win." The conclusion is an APODOSIS.

Prothalamion.   A wedding poem. Edmund Spenser coined the term, on the analogy of EPITHALAMIUM, from Greek roots meaning "before the bridal chamber," to use in his title *Prothalamion; or, A Spousal Verse in Honour of the Double Marriage of Lady Elizabeth and Lady Katherine Somerset* (1596).

Prothesis.   In grammar, the addition of a letter or syllable to the beginning of a word, as in *yclad, beloved*. Sometimes in verse, as in "Poor Tom's acold" (*King Lear*, IV.1.52), it helps fill out the METER.

Prototype.   A model for later duplication or imitation; the first of a kind. See ARCHETYPE.

Provenance.   Origin or derivation, as of a MANUSCRIPT, from Latin roots meaning "coming forth."

Proverb. A short, pithy saying, frequently embodying the folk wisdom of a group or nation: "A stitch in time saves nine," "A bird in the hand is worth two in the bush," "When the cat's away, the mice will play." Many ancient ones are collected in the Old Testament book Proverbs. Benjamin Franklin's *Poor Richard's Almanack*, especially in its 1758 Preface, "The Way to Wealth," disseminated large numbers of them, including "Early to bed and early to rise, makes a man healthy, wealthy, and wise." Recent collections include Paul Rosenzweig, ed., *The Book of Proverbs* (1965); W. G. Smith and F. P. Wilson, eds., *The Oxford Dictionary of English Proverbs* (1970); and J. A. Simpson, ed., *The Concise Oxford Dictionary of Proverbs* (1983). See FOLKLORE.

Provincetown Players. American theatrical company associated especially with Eugene O'Neill and the development of twentieth-century American drama. In 1916 O'Neill's first produced play, *Bound East for Cardiff*, was presented in their Wharf Theatre, in Provincetown, Massachusetts, on Cape Cod. Later that year, the group opened the company's new Playwrights' Theater in New York. Others associated with the Provincetown Players included, at first, Robert Edmond Jones and Kenneth Macgowan, and, later, Edna St. Vincent Millay. The Provincetown Players, the Washington Square Players (formed in 1914), the Theatre Guild (formed in 1919), and the Greenwich Village Theatre (1923–1927, managed by Jones, Macgowan, and O'Neill) were instrumental in releasing the burst of creative energy in American drama that centered in New York in the 1920s.

Provincialism. (1) Attachment to the values, ideas, or interests of one's own province, state, or country. The term is customarily used to suggest an outlook overly narrow, naïve, or unsophisticated, in contrast to one more intellectually informed, one that examines issues from a wider perspective. (2) A word, phrase, or manner of speech or behavior peculiar to a certain area; a localism.

Pruning Poem. A poem created by pruning (or cutting) letters from the rhyme words in successive lines, as in these from George Herbert's "Paradise":

> When thou dost greater judgements SPARE
> And with thy knife but prune and PARE
> Ev'n fruitfull trees more fruitfull ARE.

Psalm. From Greek *psalmos*, a song sung to a harp: a sacred song or hymn, as in the Psalms of the Old Testament.

Pseudepigrapha. Jewish writings from 200 B.C. to A.D. 200, falsely attributed to various prophets and kings and excluded from the biblical canon as heretical, as distinct from the APOCRYPHA, books excluded as inappropriate to religious study. The term also refers to any writings falsely attributed.

Pseudonym. A fictitious name adopted by an author for public use, like George Eliot (Mary Ann or Marian Evans), Mark Twain (Samuel Langhorne Clemens), and George Orwell (Eric Blair).

Pseudo-Shakespearean Plays. Plays once attributed to Shakespeare, but no longer generally accepted as his. Considerations of style and attributions on early copies at one time or another suggested Shakespeare's authorship of such plays as *Locrine, The Birth of Merlin, Mucedorus, Sir Thomas More,* and *Arden of Feversham.* The extent of Shakespeare's canon remains in debate, as in 1982 controversy was aroused over a claim for his authorship of *Edmund Ironside.*

Psi Powers. In SCIENCE FICTION, a common abbreviation for *psychic powers* or *psionic powers* ("psychic electronics"). The term covers mental powers (including those that scientists refer to as ESP, or extrasensory perception), such as telepathy, telekinesis, teleportation, precognition, clairvoyance, and levitation.

Psychic Distance. A detachment resulting from a reader's awareness that literature is not life. Psychic distance is small or nonexistent when the reader feels personally touched or even threatened by the events in a book. It is very great when those events seem to bear no relation whatever to the conditions of life. See AESTHETIC DISTANCE; DISTANCE.

Psychoanalytical Criticism. A form of BIOGRAPHICAL CRITICISM that uses the insights of psychology to illuminate a writer's work. See CRITICISM.

Psychological Novel. A NOVEL centered in the psychology of the CHARACTERS, placing heavy emphasis on their inner lives as opposed to the external events that surround them. The psychological novelist displays less interest in what happened than in why it happened and what its effects were on a human psyche.

Such an interest has been important in literature for centuries, and Chaucer's *Troilus and Criseyde,* for example, has been called a psychological novel in verse, but the modern psychological novel arose in the nineteenth century as novelists shifted their emphasis from external action and broad social concerns to close examination of individual characters. George Eliot and George Meredith were forerunners, but Henry James was the great early master, showing the way to the concerns and techniques of the twentieth century, especially in *The Portrait of a Lady* (1881) and in *The Wings of the Dove* (1902), *The Ambassadors* (1903) and *The Golden Bowl* (1904). Joseph Conrad's *Lord Jim* (1900) and *Heart of Darkness* (1902) and other novels display a concern for psychology against a more physically active background than James's, and were also important influences on later writers.

James Joyce's *Portrait of the Artist as a Young Man* (1916) and *Ulysses* (1922), Virginia Woolf's *Mrs. Dalloway* (1925) and *To the Lighthouse* (1927), and William Faulkner's *Sound and the Fury* (1929) are examples of the psychological novel at the height of its development, showing well its use of INTERIOR MONOLOGUE and STREAM OF CONSCIOUSNESS. Later writers have continued an interest in the psychological novel, without developing the methods much further or extending the concerns except to adapt them to later social conditions.

Psychomachia.   A "battle for the soul," the title of a poem by the fourth-century Latin poet Prudentius, a Christian ALLEGORY depicting personified vices and virtues in conflict. The term is also used for medieval allegories on a similar model, the MORALITY PLAY *The Castle of Perseverance* (c. 1425) being a good example.

Ptolemaic Universe.   The universe as perceived by Ptolemy, a Greco-Egyptian astronomer of the second century A.D., whose theories were dominant until the RENAISSANCE produced the COPERNICAN UNIVERSE. In Ptolemy's system, the universe was world-centered, with the sun, moon, planets, and stars understood as rotating around the earth in a series of concentric spheres, producing as they revolved the harmonious "music of the spheres." The spheres outward from the earth were Moon, Mercury, Venus, Sun, Mars, Jupiter, Saturn, Fixed Stars. Long after the formulation of the Copernican theory, the Ptolemaic continued to have imaginative force; it is important, for example, in the cosmology of Milton's *Paradise Lost*.

Public Theaters.   The usual Elizabethan theater. See THEATERS.

Pulitzer Prizes.   Annual awards for achievement in American journalism, literature, and music. The awards, administered by Columbia University, are funded from a bequest made by the newspaper publisher Joseph Pulitzer, and have been given each year since 1917. Categories in journalism include local reporting under deadline and free of deadline, national and international reporting, editorial writing, cartooning, and photography. One prize is given for a composition in music. The prizes in literature are for fiction, poetry, drama, biography, history, and one book in an unlisted category. Differences in opinion between judges making recommendations and the Columbia Board of Trustees, who select the award recipients, have made the prizes sometimes controversial.

Pulp Magazines. Magazines printed on inexpensive, pulp paper. The term is applied especially to the popular magazines of the 1920s and 1930s. Like the earlier DIME NOVEL, they printed escapist fiction. The ADVENTURE STORY, DETECTIVE STORY, MYSTERY STORY, SCIENCE FICTION, and WESTERN accounted for most of their content, with many magazines specializing in particular forms. *Adventure, Amazing Stories, Argosy, Black Mask, Weird Tales,* and, later, *Ellery Queen's Mystery Magazine* were among their number, printing writers like Max Brand and Zane Grey (Westerns), Edgar Rice Burroughs (Tarzan and space fantasies), Dashiell Hammett and Raymond Chandler (detective fiction), and H. P. Lovecraft (tales of fantasy and terror).

Pun. A FIGURE OF SPEECH involving a play on words, usually humorous, but sometimes with serious intent. In one form of punning, a word is repeated, with a shift in meaning: "To England will I steal, and there I'll steal" (*Henry V*, V.1.92). In *paronomasia* (a term also used for puns in general), the repeated word is slightly changed: "A friend turned fiend." In another form, two meanings of a word are suggested simultaneously, as when a court jester is reported to have punned on *laud* (meaning *praise*), angering Archbishop Laud by saying: "Great praise to God, and little laud to the devil." In still another form, a word is used to suggest a second word spelled differently, but sounding the same, as in John Donne's "Hymn to God the Father," where *son* equals *sun* and *done* is pronounced the same as the poet's name:

> I have a sin of fear, that when I have spun
> My last thread, I shall perish on the shore;
> Swear by Thy self, that at my death Thy *Son*
> Shall shine as he shines now and heretofore;
> And, having done that, Thou hast *done*,
> I fear no more.

Pure Poetry. An ideal sometimes sought by poets or critics who imagine a poetry free of the impurities they associate with prosaic uses of language. As more or less rigorously defined by various writers, pure poetry excludes narration, didacticism, ideas, and other elements of content that could be expressed in prose. Essentially lyric, the pure poem stands apart in its poetic essence, an object of beauty, superbly crafted, nonreferential. Frequently, an analogy is made to music, with the emphasis on the poem as a pattern of sounds removed from their prose meanings.

The doctrine of pure poetry belongs primarily to the nineteenth and twentieth centuries, with a number of the ideas first expressed in Poe's "The Poetic Principle" (1850). Later, the French symbolists, including Baudelaire, Mallarmé, Verlaine, Rimbaud, and Valéry, all experimented with the possibilities of pure poetry, greatly influencing twentieth-century verse in English. Wallace Stevens, earlier, and John Ashbery, more recently, may be cited as twentieth-century poets whose verse approaches, at times, the ideal of pure poetry.

Purist. One who aims at or insists upon purity or correctness in diction or STYLE. Extreme purists sometimes attempt to set rigid standards for language, refusing to accept usages that arise outside of prescribed patterns, as when the *Académie Française* set out in the seventeenth century to establish standards for acceptable French. Less extreme purists, acknowledging change and flexibility as principles of linguistic development, encourage precise or graceful communication through careful use of widely accepted conventions of correctness and style.

Puritanism. A Protestant movement arising with the Reformation in England, mid-sixteenth century, particularly influential in forming the New England colonies and their beliefs. Like Luther in Germany and Calvin in Switzerland, Thomas Cartwright (c. 1535–1603), an Anglican clergyman and professor of divinity at Cambridge, wished to purify Anglican ceremony and hierarchy toward something like the original Christian community. He enunciated his attack in a disputation held to celebrate Queen Elizabeth's visitation to Cambridge in 1564. His subsequent disputes and writing crystalized the thinking of those scornfully called "Puritans" by their adversaries, but led to his eventual deposition and exile. Puritans wished to eliminate the surplice from ministerial dress and to take communion sitting down, as at the Last Supper, where it originated. Theocracy—the individual and the congregation governed directly under God through Christ—became primary, reflected in the centrality of the Scriptures and their exposition, direct confession through prayer and public confession to the congregation rather than through priests, and the direct individual experience of God's grace.

The Puritans' drive for representative ecclesiastical and political governance soon allied them with PRESBYTERIANISM and the essentials of CALVINISM. As Hawthorne suggests in *The Scarlet Letter*, the early Puritans, even in the colonies, were a heartier and more worldly breed than popularly supposed, at first not wholly averse to art, music, dancing, fencing, and wine, though more rigorous views soon prevailed. Puritan democratic principles eventually led to civil war, the beheading of Charles I (1649), and the theocratic Puritan COMMONWEALTH under Oliver Cromwell. Puritanism, as such, ended with the RESTORATION of monarchy under Charles II in 1660, but Puritan beliefs continued among those called DISSENTERS, essentially the hard-working middle class opposed to aristocratic frivolity.

Robert Browne (1550–1633) became a leader of Separatist Puritans, emphasizing a religious covenant to separate from "all ungodlie communion and wicked persons" (c. 1580). Browne emphasized each congregation's independence (see CONGREGATIONALISM). One group of Separatists, or Brownists, later fled to Leyden, the Netherlands, to return to England and sail on the *Mayflower* for New England on 6 September 1620 to establish a new theocracy. Of the 120 Pilgrims, only 32 were Separatist Puritans, the rest being hired by the financing company to protect its interests; among them were John Alden, a cooper, and Captain Myles Standish. By 1640, more than 22,000 Puritans had sailed for New England.

Puritanism gave America its first writers: theologians John Cotton, Thomas Hooker, John Eliot (the "apostle of the Indians," the first Protestant missionary), and Cotton Mather; historians William Bradford, John Winthrop, Thomas Hutchinson, and Samuel Sewall; poets Nathaniel Ward, Anne Bradstreet, Michael Wigglesworth, and Edward Taylor. *The Bay Psalm Book* (1640), America's earliest surviving printed book, joined the Bible as the center of every home. Scottish Presbyterians, as William Faulkner's novels indicate, later brought Puritan Calvinism to the Middle Atlantic states and the South, underpinning the essential American Puritan ethics of independence, hard work to prove through success the righteousness of one's calling, and piety.

References

William Haller, **The Rise of Puritanism** (1938).
Alan Simpson, **Puritanism in Old and New England** (1955).
Page Smith, **As a City upon a Hill** (1966).

Purple Patch.   A florid, showy passage of writing, incongruent to its context and perhaps irrelevant to the purpose of the work. In *Ars Poetica*, Horace used the term (literally, a piece of cloth, richly dyed) for something tacked on to catch the eye.

Puseyism.   See OXFORD MOVEMENT.

Pyrrhic.   A Greek and Roman foot of two unstressed syllables: ⌣ ⌣. See METER.

Q

Quadrivium. The more advanced portion of the SEVEN LIBERAL ARTS as studied in medieval universities: arithmetic, geometry, astronomy, and music.

Quantitative Verse. Verse that takes account of the QUANTITY of the syllables (whether they take a long or short time to pronounce) rather than their stress patterns. Classical Greek and Latin verse is quantitative, with a long syllable counted as the equivalent of two shorts; rules govern the different patterns. In contrast, ACCENTUAL-SYLLABIC VERSE has been dominant in English since the fourteenth century, with ACCENTUAL VERSE the rule earlier. In neither is quantity a primary concern, although it is always a consideration as the poet attends to all the sounds of the line.

Quantity. In versification, or the mechanics of poetic composition, the length of time required to pronounce a syllable, varying from short (*a, it, on*) to long (*brakes, stoned, traipsed*). See METER.

Quarterly Review. An English journal espousing Tory principles in answer to the Whiggery of *THE EDINBURGH REVIEW*. Walter Scott, an early mainstay of *The Edinburgh Review*, transferred his allegiance to *The Quarterly Review* upon its founding in 1809.

Quarto. (Abbreviated 4to, 4°): a book made from sheets folded twice, giving signatures of 4 leaves (8 pages). Many Shakespearean plays were first printed individually in quarto editions, designated First Quarto, Second Quarto, etc. See BOOK SIZES; SIGNATURE.

Quatorzian. A poem or STANZA of 14 lines. The term is often reserved for poems that resemble the SONNET in having 14 lines but are unlike it in other ways, as, for example, Frost's "Once by the Pacific." Herrick's "Corinna's Going A-Maying" is in 14-line stanzas.

Quatrain. A STANZA of four lines, rhymed or unrhymed. With its many variations it is the most common stanzaic form in English. Rhymed types include COMMON METER (the BALLAD STANZA), which, with its variations in LONG METER and SHORT METER, is by far the most popular type; the "IN MEMORIAM" STANZA; the CAROL STANZA; the RUBÁIYÁT STANZA; and monorhyme (one-rhyme) stanzas such as that in Dante Gabriel Rossetti's "The Woodspurge."

Quest.   A search or pursuit, one of the most common structural elements in narrative and dramatic literature, frequently rooted in MYTH. The quest was fundamental to Greek and Roman literature and to the MEDIEVAL ROMANCE and has persisted as a MOTIF ever since. In the twentieth century, it is found in works as otherwise dissimilar as Joyce's *Ulysses*, Faulkner's *Light in August*, Tolkien's *Lord of the Rings*, and the popular ADVENTURE STORY and DETECTIVE STORY.

Quibble.   A play on words, as with puns, with the emphasis on minor points, evading substantive issues, as in a debate or a book review.

Quintain (or **Quintet**).   A STANZA of five lines. Many quintains begin with an *abab* QUATRAIN and add a line with an *a* or *b* rhyme, as in George Herbert's "The Pulley" (1633) and Edmund Waller's "Go, Lovely Rose!" (1645). See CINQUAIN.

Quip.   A clever or witty saying; sharp or sarcastic repartee.

R

Raissonneur. French for "reasoner": A character in a play or novel who stands apart from the main action, analyzing and commenting upon it for the benefit of the audience (see CHORUS CHARACTER) or as adviser to a major character (see CONFIDANT).

Ratiocination. The process of reasoning, or a conclusion reached through reasoning. A DETECTIVE STORY emphasizing rational analysis of clues, on the model of "The Murders in the Rue Morgue" or "The Purloined Letter," is sometimes called a "tale of ratiocination," after Poe, who applied the phrase to those stories.

Rationalism. The theory that reason, rather than revelation or authority, provides knowledge, truth, the choice of good over evil, and an adequate understanding of God and the universe. Sixteenth-century HUMANISM (see also OXFORD REFORMERS) praised reason, believing, with the high RENAISSANCE, in humankind's God-given powers to measure the universe. In the seventeenth century, the CAMBRIDGE PLATONISTS merged Renaissance humanism with Christian ethics and scientific discovery by asserting that goodness is essentially rational and free from religious dogma. DEISM stressed the primacy of reason in perceiving the rationally ordered universe. In France, the ENLIGHT-ENMENT emphasized a rational political progress that would eventually eradicate priests and kings. In England, neo-classicism (see NEOCLASS-ICAL PERIOD) held to a rational balance and restraint, and a skeptical awareness of the limits of reason. Whereas the Deists rejected revelation, the "supernatural rationalists," including Newton and Locke, believed revelation necessary to fulfill rational understanding. The idea of a "natural religion" harmonized the gift of reason and natural goodness with God's rationally ordered nature.

Reference

W. E. H. Lecky, **History of the Rise and Influence of the Spirit of Rationalism in Europe** (1865).

Rationalization. The concoction of innaccurate but self-satisfying reasons for one's conduct.

Realism. In literature, faithful representation of life. Realism carries the conviction of true reports of phenomena observable by others. It may be contrasted with ROMANTICISM, IMPRESSIONISM, and EXPRESSIONISM, which are less true to external phenomena, although each carries its own kind of truth. Realism is a slippery term, sometimes used too loosely to be of value except as an indicator of a reader's reaction. What seems real to one reader seems preposterous to another, and the common reader's idea of reality is quite different from the professional philosopher's. Realism is most useful here when understood in the context of the nineteenth-century movement that first applied it to literature, discussed its qualities, and in the end gave it the widespread currency it still enjoys.

Nineteenth-century realism was in part a reaction against the excesses of Romanticism, and in part a turning away from the philosophic underpinnings of classical and Romantic literature. Early examples of realism include Balzac's *La Comédie humaine* (begun in the 1830s), Turgenev's *Sportsman's Sketches* (1852), and Flaubert's *Madame Bovary* (1856). Although some of the materials and methods of realism are prominent in English novels even in the eighteenth century, realism as a movement began in that country with George Eliot, whose discussion of her aims in Chapter XVII of *Adam Bede* (1859) is still frequently cited. In the United States, the chief spokesman was William Dean Howells, whose best effort was *The Rise of Silas Lapham* (1885). Other realistic novelists of the period were, in Russia, Dostoevsky and Tolstoy; in England, Trollope, Meredith, and Hardy; and, among Americans, Twain and James. Within a group so diverse, there were wide differences, and by the end of the century realism as a movement was dead, although its influence continues in the literature and criticism of today.

"Realism," wrote Howells, "is nothing more and nothing less than the truthful treatment of material." This statement summarizes nicely the aims of the realists from 1830 to 1890: realism does not exaggerate or play down, but looks at life squarely, reporting it as it is. Realists often thought of their art as a mirror, convinced that if they reflected the surface of life accurately, they would also reflect it truthfully. Underlying their practice was a materialistic belief that truth is a commodity accessible on the surface of things, perceptible to the senses. Permanent truths may exist apart from the material world—in the mind of God, the ideal forms of Plato, or the mental constructions of other humans—but they are manifest in the physical details of the here and now. Therefore, the realists turned away from the models of the past to embrace examples in the present. They replaced the classical and Neoclassical emphasis on traditional form and content with an exploratory and contemporary aesthetic. In place of the noble and heroic abstractions of romance, they presented detailed particularizations of the lives of ordinary people. Nature was the model, not art. The typical subject was the ordinary life closest to the experience of the writer.

At least as important as their aims were the techniques the realists used to further them. In Howells's brief definition, one of the most important words is "treatment." Rigid selectivity comes first. In the best realistic practice, the mirror is never placed at random, but positioned to reflect scenes carefully selected to be representative. The emphasis is on ordinary people, settings, and events. The extraordinary is carefully defined as unrepresentative, placed against a backdrop of the everyday in order to avoid the species of untruth that presents the unusual as though it were normal. VERISIMILITUDE is sustained by masses of detail accurately observed from life: houses, furniture, clothing, train stations, seasonal changes, social habits, speech patterns. Diction and sentence structure tend toward a PLAIN STYLE, highlighting the story rather than the teller. Typically, great care is taken to select a NARRATIVE PERSPECTIVE capable of presenting the best window on the truth. Often in the third person, the perspective tends to downplay the subjective privileges available to third-person omniscience, enhancing the illusion of reality, especially in later realism, by removing the telltale signs of authorial presence evident in a biased commentary. Sometimes, as notoriously in the work of Henry James, a narrative perspective is selected that will in the end leave much of the story untold, reflecting in the form of the novel the truth that our perspectives upon life are also severely limited. Similarly, some James novels and the SLICE OF LIFE stories by others end without the traditional formal closure of earlier tales and novels, again in reflection of the failure of life to present itself in neat packages for our inspection. Deemphasizing plot as a contrivance imposed by artists upon life, the realists tended toward probing explorations of character. As a result, when realistic novels are tightly plotted, they are usually so because events are made to seem the inevitable result of choices made by characters so thoroughly examined that we can imagine them acting in no other way. This tendency toward extensive internal examination of characters in the nineteenth-century novel led directly to the PSYCHOLOGICAL NOVEL and to STREAM OF CONSCIOUSNESS, both heirs of realism.

Some characteristics of nineteenth-century realism can be seen in

other periods and in other genres. Petronius, Boccaccio, and Chaucer
are often cited as early examples of realism. The PICARESQUE NOVEL
displays realistic qualities absent from the ROMANCE. Burns, Wordsworth, Whitman, Frost, and William Carlos Williams were in some
respects realists in verse. Nineteenth-century stage realism is evident
in plays by Ibsen and Chekhov. In the twentieth century, many novels,
short stories, and plays have been fundamentally realistic.

Realism used for propaganda has sometimes been called *critical realism*, for works generally critical of society, like those of Upton Sinclair and the MUCKRAKERS, or *socialist realism*, for works using realism
in the service of MARXISM.

NATURALISM is sometimes used in ways synonymous with realism,
but it has also a more specialized meaning discussed here under its own
heading. See MIMESIS; SURREALISM.

References

Erich Auerbach, **Mimesis: The Representation of Reality in Western Liter-
ature** (trans. 1953).
George J. Becker, **Documents of Modern Literary Realism** (1963).
Georg Lukács, **Studies in European Realism** (trans. 1964).
Donald Pizer, **Realism and Naturalism in Nineteenth-Century American Fic-
tion** (1960).

Realism (in Philosophy).   (1) In the Middle Ages, the belief that universal concepts possess real existence apart from particular things and
the human mind. They exist either as entities like Platonic forms or
else as concepts in the mind of God. Medieval realism was opposed to
NOMINALISM. (2) In later epistemology, the belief that things exist
apart from our perception of them. In this sense, realism is opposed to
IDEALISM, which locates all reality in our minds.

Reason, Age of.   See NEOCLASSICAL PERIOD and ENLIGHTENMENT.

Recognition.   The moment at which a chief character recognizes the
happy or awful truth, usually of his or her own or another's identity,
of which the audience (or reader) is frequently aware. Aristotle, in his
Poetics, first named it, and prized it, citing *Oedipus Rex* as the greatest
instance.

Redaction.   (1) A revised version. (2) A rewriting or condensing of an
older work.

Reductio ad Absurdum. "Reduction to absurdity"—the technique of disproving an assertion by showing the absurdity in which it must logically conclude. "Still waters run deep"—"Yes, just like a mud puddle."

Redundancy. "Overflowing"—wordy, verbose, repetitive, tautological, pleonastic expression, using many more words than necessary.

Reflector. A term used by Henry James to designate a character in a story whose observations and comments are important in shaping the reader's understanding of the other characters. James's *Wings of the Dove* (1902) illustrates the method, as a portrait of Milly Theale gradually emerges from the observations of a number of reflectors. See CHARACTERIZATION; NARRATIVE PERSPECTIVE.

Reform Bill of 1832. The law that eliminated 56 seats in Parliament from "rotten" buroughs (those with only a few voters), replaced them with 156 new constituencies, and considerably spread the right to vote among the middle class. Lord Grey (Charles Grey, second Earl Grey, created Lord Howick in 1806), prime minister of a Whig government formed in 1830 when the duke of Wellington's Tory ministry collapsed, led the movement for reform with King William IV's approval. Young Charles Dickens earned his spurs as parliamentary reporter during the debates. The bill led to further reforms, notably the abolition of slavery in the British colonies (1833). Writers like Dickens, Elizabeth Gaskell, Carlyle, Ruskin, Charles Kingsley, Disraeli, and George Eliot reflected growing liberalism. Pressed by the Liberals, the Conservative government passed a second Reform Bill (1867) expanding the franchise. The third Reform Bill (1884) gave suffrage to virtually all adult males. In 1918, suffrage expanded to include all men and women over 30; in 1928, the age was lowered to 21. See CHARTISM; INDUSTRIAL REVOLUTION.

Refrain. A set phrase, or chorus, recurring throughout a song or poem, usually at the end of a STANZA or other regular interval. Some refrains take a new meaning with each repetition, like Poe's famous "Nevermore." A REPETEND is a refrain somewhat rephrased with each repetition.

Regionalism. See LOCAL COLOR WRITING.

Reification. The "thing-ification" of abstract concepts, treating them as if they had material existence (from Latin *rēs*, "thing"). It is a frequent metaphor: "Honor is a burden"; "Silence so thick you could cut it with a knife." In MARXISM, *reification* refers to Marx's belief that metaphysics must be boiled down to material reality, that humans must realize that "all that is called history is nothing else than the process of creating man through human labour, the becoming of nature for man. Man has thus evident and irrefutable proof of his own creation by himself" (*Economic and Philosophic Manuscripts of 1844,* 1959).

Relativism. The philosophical belief that nothing is ABSOLUTE, that values are relative to circumstances. In CRITICISM, relativism is either personal or historical. The *personal relativist* believes that all standards of judgment are individual, that there is no disputing taste. The *historical relativist* believes that standards differ with time and place, observing how the aesthetic values of the ENLIGHTENMENT, for example, are different from those of the ROMANTIC PERIOD, and rejecting notions of more permanent standards.

Reliable Narrator. One whose attitudes and judgments concerning the story may be taken as no different from those of the author. See UNRELIABLE NARRATOR.

Relief Scene. A scene in a TRAGEDY that eases the emotional intensity, usually in the FALLING ACTION. See DRAMATIC STRUCTURE.

Religious Drama. See RELIGIOUS LITERATURE; MEDIEVAL DRAMA; MIRACLE PLAY; MORALITY PLAY; MYSTERY PLAY.

Religious Literature. Literature with significant religious content. Religion and imaginative literature overlap because both are codified in words, preserved in the oral traditions of preliterate societies and in the manuscripts and print of literate societies. This connection is obvious, and applies also to politics and literature, medicine and literature, manners and literature, philosophy and literature, aesthetics and literature, and all other areas of human knowledge and belief. But religion and imaginative literature also share qualities not so evident in other forms of verbal communication, as both rely heavily on FIGURATIVE LANGUAGE and MYTH. POETRY is particularly close to religion in this respect, but other forms of FICTION display the same tendencies. This does not mean that religion is fiction, or fiction religion, but only that they employ the same tools to communicate their truths. For this reason, a religious text may be considered as religion, or it may be considered as literature. Similarly, a work of fiction dealing with compelling human concerns (as all lasting fiction seems to) may be considered as fundamentally religious. The term *religious literature*, however, is most useful when reserved for works that achieve a substantial part of their meaning by dealing directly or indirectly with religious matters.

If the consideration is limited to sacred and imaginative writing, and if the vast literature of primarily sectarian commentary and history is excluded, five major categories of religious literature may be distinguished. (1) *Primary texts fundamental to religious belief.* This literature is often revered as transmitted to humans by divine revelation, accepted as the writing of inspired teachers and prophets. Examples are the Bible, the Torah, the Talmud, the Koran, the Bhagavad Gita, the Book of Mormon, and the sacred myths of tribal cultures. (2) *The literature of personal religious statement.* Sometimes this is devotional, sometimes doubtful and questioning. Within this category, Dante's *Divine Comedy* and Milton's *Paradise Lost* stand apart in Western tradition in their power to give personal but permanent mythic shape to the thought of later readers. Less comprehensive works expressive of personal visions include the *Confessions* of St. Augustine; the meditations of religious mystics in the Middle Ages; *Piers Plowman;* poems by John Donne, George Herbert, Gerard Manley Hopkins, and T. S. Eliot; the sermons of Jonathan Edwards; Robert Frost's *A Masque of Mercy* and *A Masque of Reason;* Archibald MacLeish's *J.B.;* T. S. Eliot's *Murder in the Cathedral.* (3) POPULAR LITERATURE *on religious themes.* This includes SAINTS' LIVES, the MIRACLE PLAY, the MORALITY PLAY, popular devotional poetry, *Pilgrim's Progress,* and modern novels such as Lloyd C. Douglas's *Robe.* (4) *Philosophical and quasiphilosophical works touching on religious questions.* Examples are St. Augustine's *City of God,* Sir Thomas More's *Utopia,* Thomas Paine's *Age of Reason,* Carlyle's *Sartor Resartus,* Emerson's *Nature* and *Essays,* Newman's *Apologia pro Vita Sua,* and Nietzsche's *Thus Spake Zarathustra.* (5) *Imaginative works not primarily religious, but heavy with religious content.* Elegies frequently assuage mourning with religious consolation. Greek tragedies must be understood in the context of Greek belief. *Beowulf* mixes pagan themes with Christianity. Arthurian legends, *The Faerie Queene,* and Romantic works generally, down to the present day, utilize religious motifs. Light and dark symbolism, powerfully rendered in the Bible, also enriches works as varied as *Macbeth, The Scarlet Letter, Moby-Dick,* and *Hard Times,* all with religious overtones. Specifically Christian allusions or symbols are important to the understanding of Tolstoy's "Death of Ivan Ilych," the stories of Flannery O'Connor, and Faulkner's *Light in August* and *A Fable.* Sartre's

No Exit and Beckett's *Waiting for Godot* are twentieth-century dramas directly and indirectly referential to religious belief. Traditional religious themes underlie the allegories of C. S. Lewis and such fantasies as Tolkien's *Lord of the Rings*.

Relique. A relic; a term preserved only in Bishop Thomas Percy's *Reliques of Ancient English Poetry* (1765), the basic collection of English ballads.

Renaissance (1500–1660, in England). The rebirth of art and literature from the rediscovery of ancient Greece and Rome, and a turning against medieval mortification and contempt for this world to see humanity as the full measure to which knowledge, achievement, beauty, and enjoyment might expand. It began in Italy with Dante (1265–1321), who forged a new national language and consciousness, with Virgil at his side, in his new Christian epic, *The Divine Comedy* (1300–1320). Soon Petrarch (1304–1374) termed the Middle Ages "dark" and called for an awakening into the radiance of the Greek and Roman past.

The Renaissance, though glimmering in Chaucer's day, reached England over a century later with the arrival of Erasmus, the Dutch "Prince of Humanists," on his first visit in 1499, and with the scholars whom young Henry VIII began to attract to his court in 1509. The discovery of America and further voyages of discovery and commerce, Copernicus's new astronomy (1543), Caxton's new printing press at Westminster (1476), the Protestant Reformation, which turned from ecclesiastical authority toward individual consciousness, all stimulated an optimistic excitement as to what humans could achieve, an optimism which flowered in the Elizabethans.

The English Renaissance really ended with Elizabeth in 1603. Skepticism entered with the dour Scot James I, and exuberance faded before the rising Puritans, who closed the theaters in 1642. Nevertheless, Francis Bacon's *Advancement of Learning* (1605) and *Novum Organum* (1620), his "new instrument" of empirical science, continued the Renaissance quest toward expanding horizons. In France, Descartes's immensely influential *Discours* (1637), rendered into Latin in 1644, carried the Renaissance to its ego-centric extremity: *cogito ergo sum*, "I think; therefore, I am." Even the repressive COMMON-WEALTH, which killed a king to set up a government of legislators (1649), was a late Renaissance expression. Hence historians close the English Renaissance at 1660, the RESTORATION, when the cheerful Charles II changed the Puritan dirge, and Milton's *Paradise Lost*

(1667), the last great Renaissance accomplishment, revived the epic past in new Christian magnitude. See ENGLISH LITERATURE, PERIODS OF and the "Chronology of Literature and World Events."

Rendering. Henry James's term for scenic depiction, with dialogue, as against authorial narration. See SCENIC METHOD.

Repartee. A quick turn of wit, or series of quick turns, in conversation (from French fencing, "to turn back again").

Repetend. (1) That which is repeated—a sound, word, phrase, or REFRAIN. (2) A partial repetition, a PAREGMENON: "He *looped* the *loop*." (3) A refrain that varies with each occurrence, like the second line of each stanza in Shakespeare's song in *The Winter's Tale:*

> When daffodils begin to peer,
>   With heigh! the doxy over the dale,
> Why, then comes in the sweet o' the year,
>   For the red blood reigns in the winter's pale.
>
> The white sheet bleaching on the hedge,
>   With heigh! the sweet birds, oh, how they sing!
> Doth set my pugging tooth on edge,
>   For a quart of ale is a dish for a king.
>
> The lark, that tirra-lyra chants,
>   With heigh! with heigh! the thrush and the jay,
> Are summer songs for me and my aunts,
>   While we lie tumbling in the hay.

Repetition. Restatement, either exact or approximate, of a sound, word, line, and the like. It is an essential of rhetorical and poetic emphasis. See ALLITERATION; ANADIPLOSIS; ANAPHORA; ANTIMETABOLE; ANTISTROPHE; ASSONANCE; EPANALEPSIS; EPANADOS; EPISTROPHE; POLYPTOTON; POLYSYNDETON; REPETEND; SYMPLOCE. See also PLEONASM; REFRAIN.

Requiem. A mass for the dead, or a song or poem, taking title from the mass's opening line *Requiem aeternam dona eis, Domine:* "Give them eternal rest, O Lord."

Resolution. The unwinding of the plot; the DENOUEMENT.

Resolved Stress. Another name for DISTRIBUTED STRESS.

Restoration (1660–1700). The period that restored peace, monarchy, and the Stuarts to the throne after the Puritan COMMONWEALTH, the first modern attempt at democracy, which had beheaded Charles I. A new *pax Romana* under a new Augustus, Charles II, was the hope, a new Virgilian and Horatian England, with the HEROIC COUPLET balancing extremes toward a GOLDEN MEAN. French manners, and wigs, followed Charles across the English Channel. Witty, lubricious comedy took the stage as the theaters reopened, with real actresses instead of boys for the first time. Restoration comedy, the COMEDY OF MANNERS, was the period's hallmark, under George Etherege, William Wycherley, and William Congreve. Satire and dialectical poetry, like Dryden's *Absalom and Achitophel* (1681), faced the political and religious uncertainties. The HEROIC PLAY emerged, with its exotic and romantic dream of magnificence in strife, and its standard conflict of love and honor. In the new Royal Society (already meeting, but not chartered by Charles until 1662), science triumphed in Newton's discoveries of gravity, the calculus, and the prism, and in Halley's comet. In 1688, after severe religious conflict, William of Orange and Mary Stuart ascended the throne in England's first and only balanced monarchy, husband and wife both holding the golden orb of authority. This "Glorious Revolution" (1688) is also taken as the watershed into modern English prose, under Dryden's pen. See ENGLISH LITERATURE, PERIODS OF and the "Chronology of Literature and World Events."

Revenge Tragedy. The popular Elizabethan mode initiated by Thomas Kyd's *Spanish Tragedy* (c. 1586), wherein a father or son must revenge a murder of son or father by a present ruler. *Hamlet* (1602) is the greatest. Others, with varying motives for revenge, are Shakespeare's *Titus Andronicus* (1594), Henry Chettle's *Tragedy of Hoffman* (1602), George Chapman's *Bussy D'Ambois* (1607), John Marston's *Antonio's Revenge* (1607), and Cyril Tourneur's *Atheist's Tragedy* (1611). See SENECAN TRAGEDY; TRAGEDY OF BLOOD.

Reversal. The thrilling change of luck for the PROTAGONIST at the last moment in comedy or tragedy—the *peripeteia*, which Aristotle first described in his *Poetics*, along with the DISCOVERY that usually sparks it. See DRAMATIC STRUCTURE.

Review. (1) A journalistic critique of a new play or book. (2) A magazine reviewing the current literary and political scene: *The Saturday Review of Literature, The Partisan Review*. (3) A musical show of song and dance with the satirical excuse of "reviewing" the contemporary scene. See REVUE.

Revue. A BURLESQUE or satirical and topical song-and-dance show "reviewing" contemporary events, a form borrowed from France in the late nineteenth and early twentieth centuries.

Rhapsody. In ancient Greece, a portion of an EPIC poem recited by a wandering minstrel, from a Greek word meaning "stitch song," since lines from memory were stitched together with improvisations. A *rhapsody* has come to mean any set of lyric passages, loosely connected, or, sometimes, a single emotional or ecstatic utterance, loose in thought or form. Since the nineteenth century, the term has been applied also to emotional musical compositions.

Rhetoric. From Greek *rhētōr*, "orator": the art of persuasion in speaking or writing. For some, since ancient times, rhetoric has been understood as a system of persuasive devices divorced from considerations of the merits of the case argued. In this usage, some writings become "mere rhetoric," ornamentation devoid of substance. For others, rhetoric is seen from an Aristotelian perspective as the art of expressing truth clearly and logically. In this usage, an understanding of rhetoric is a necessary part of education.

In textbooks such as Aristotle's *Rhetoric* (c. 320 B.C.), Cicero's *De Inventione* (84 B.C.), and Quintilian's *Institutio Oratoria* (c. A.D. 90), classical writers devised systems that led to rhetoric as one of the *trivium* studied, along with grammar and logic, in the medieval university. Without much change from classical times, the rules of rhetoric survived well into the nineteenth century, emphasizing a five-part process for an oration: INVENTION, arrangement, STYLE, memory, and delivery. In the twentieth century, study of rhetoric has generally placed more emphasis on writing than on speech.

Rhetorical Accent. Emphasis for the sake of meaning, either where English naturally puts it ("The house is green") or where the speaker puts the meaning ("Are you going?" "Are you going?"), as distinct from *word accent,* which is fixed in polysyllabic words like *going* and *potentate.* The poet fits both word accent and rhetorical accent to the metrical frame, using the metrical accents to bring out the rhetorical ones.

Rhetorical Criticism. CRITICISM that emphasizes the writer's RHETORIC, the tools for communicating with the audience.

Rhetorical Figure. A FIGURE OF SPEECH based on stylized patterning, as in ANAPHORA, in which successive phrases begin with the same words, or other kinds of REPETITION; or on a dramatic pretense, as in APOSTROPHE, in which a nonpresent being or person is addressed; or ANACOLUTHON, in which a sentence is broken off to conclude in another way.

Rhetorical Question. A question posed for rhetorical effect, usually with a self-evident answer: "Will we stand up for our rights? Will we allow our freedoms to be taken from us?" Shylock's series in *The Merchant of Venice* is memorable:

> Hath not a Jew eyes? Hath not a Jew hands, organs, dimensions, senses, affections, passions? Fed with the same food, hurt with the same weapons, subject to the same diseases, healed by the same means, warmed and cooled by the same winter and summer as a Christian is? If you prick us, do we not bleed? If you tickle us, do we not laugh? If you poison us, do we not die? And if you wrong us, shall we not revenge?

> *III.i.60–69*

Rhopalic Verse. Verse thicker at one end than the other (from a Greek word meaning "club-like"), as, for example, when each word in a line is a syllable longer than the one before ("a cudgel thickening enormously"), or each line in a STANZA is a foot longer:

> Who'er she be,
> That not impossible she
> That shall command my heart and me;
> *Richard Crashaw, "Wishes to His Supposed Mistress"*

Rhyme (sometimes **Rime,** an older spelling). The effect created by matching sounds at the end of words. Ordinarily, this includes the last accented vowel and the sounds that follow it, but not the sound of the preceding consonant. *Masculine rhyme* falls on one syllable: *fat, cat; defeat, repeat. Feminine rhyme (double rhyme)* includes two syllables: *better, setter; defeated, repeated. Triple rhyme,* often reserved for LIGHT VERSE and DOGGEREL, involves three syllables: *clerical, spherical.*

Rhymes may be classified according to sound. The rhymes given above are *exact rhymes (full, true, perfect, complete, whole),* repeating end sounds precisely. *Slant rhyme (half, approximate, imperfect, near, off, oblique)* provides an approximation of the sound: *cat, cot; hope, cup; defeated, impeded. Identical rhyme* repeats the entire sound, including the initial consonant, sometimes by repeating the same word in a rhyme position, sometimes, as in *rime riche,* by repeating the sound with two senses: *two, too. Eye rhymes* look alike, but sound different, and may be intentional poetic variations, or the result of a dialect or a change in pronunciation over time: "If this be error, and upon me *proved,* / I never writ, nor no man ever *loved.*" *Apocopated rhyme* pairs a masculine and a feminine ending, rhyming on the stress: *cope, hopeless; kind, finder.* In *mosaic rhyme* two words rhyme with one, or two with two: *master, passed her; chorus, before us; went in, sent in.* Broken *rhyme* divides a word (not a rhyme) at line end to create a rhyme, as in Gerard Manley Hopkins's "Windhover," where *king-* / *dom* is broken at the end of the first line to rhyme with *wing* in the fourth. In *linked rhyme*, borrowed by Hopkins from Welsh verse, the sound of one word in a rhyming pair at the end of a line is completed by adding the consonant beginning the next line, as in this example from "The Wreck of the Deutschland": "She drove in the dark to *leeward*, / . . . night *drew her* / *D*ead. . . ."

Rhymes may also be classified by position. Most rhyme is *end rhyme (terminal rhyme)*, found at the end of a line of poetry. *Initial rhyme* comes at the beginning, and is sometimes combined with end rhyme, as in these lines from Sidney Lanier's "Symphony": "*Vainly* might Plato's brain *revolve it:* / *Plainly* the heart of a child could *solve it.*" *Internal rhyme* occurs within one line or in successive middles: "And *wears* man's smudge and *shares* man's smell. . . ." *Leonine rhyme,* a type of internal rhyme, is, strictly speaking, a disyllabic rhyme pairing the last word before the CAESURA with the end word of a hexameter or pentameter line in Latin (see METER). In English, half-lines often rhyme, giving a balanced leonine effect: "The splendor *falls* on castle *walls.*" *Crossed rhyme (interlaced rhyme)* combines internal and end rhyme in an interlaced pattern, giving a long-line COUPLET the sound of a short-line QUATRAIN, as in Swinburne's "Hymn to Proserpine": "Laurel is green for a *season,* and love is sweet for a *day*; / But love grows bitter with *treason,* and laurel outlives not *May.*" *Enclosed rhyme* envelops a couplet with rhyming lines in the pattern *abba*. In *interlocking rhyme* a word unrhymed in a first STANZA is linked with the words rhymed in the next to create a continuing pattern, as in TERZA RIMA: *aba bcb cdc*, and so on.

The functions of rhyme are essentially four: pleasurable, mnemonic, structural, and rhetorical. Like meter and FIGURATIVE LANGUAGE, rhyme provides a pleasure derived from fulfillment of a basic human desire to see similarity in dissimilarity, likeness with a difference. As a mnemonic aid, it couples lines and thoughts, imprinting poems and passages on the mind in a manner that assists later recovery. As a structural device, it helps to define line ends and establishes the patterns of couplet, quatrain, stanza, BALLAD, SONNET and other poetic units and forms. As a rhetorical device, it helps the poet shape the poem and the reader understand it. Because rhyme links sound, it also links thought, pulling the reader's mind back from the new word to the word that preceded it. This linking can provide an artful inevitability in poetic communication, as when Shakespeare uses a couplet to close a sonnet or provide a snap to the end of a scene: ". . . The play's the thing / Wherein I'll catch the conscience of the king." As a rhetorical tool, rhyme may link unusual images or illogical or ironic thoughts, overpowering sense with sound, as the poet imposes a private vision on a reader who accepts unchallenged the argument behind the rhyme.

The effect of rhyme in a poem depends to a large extent on its association with meter. Rhymes gain emphasis in sound and rhetoric when they are heavily stressed—as is end rhyme, for example, in poems with insistent meter and heavily END-STOPPED LINES. Internal rhyme gains emphasis when it falls on a heavy stress immediately before a caesura. Conversely, end rhyme in RUN-ON LINES and internal rhyme with no caesura sound less thumpingly on the ear, especially when the poem's meter is unobtrusive. Rhyme in FREE VERSE or SYLLABIC VERSE passes sometimes unnoticed except by careful observers.

Rhyme as thus far considered is frequent in the poetry of many languages, but not all. Rare in Greek and Latin and in Old English, it has been common in English since the fourteenth century. By a more extended definition, covering the sound patterns of the poetry of all languages, rhyme includes any sound echo, including ALLITERATION, ASSONANCE, CONSONANCE, and the *reiteration* in lines like "*Tiger, tiger,* burning bright" and "*Heard* melodies are *sweet,* but those un*heard* / Are *sweete*r. . . ."

Ordinarily a feature of poetry, rhyme may be found also, at times, as a special effect in prose, especially POLYPHONIC PROSE. In a common secondary usage, the term *rhyme* is employed to mean a poem in rhymed verse, as, for example, a NURSERY RHYME.

Rhyme Royal.   A STANZA of seven lines of iambic pentameter, rhyming *ababbcc* (see METER). Although its name derives from its use by James I of Scotland in *The Kingis Quair (The King's Book),* it had been used earlier by Chaucer in *The Parlement of Foules, Troilus and Criseyde,* and other poems, and it is therefore sometimes called the *Chaucerian stanza.* Other examples include Wyatt's "They Flee from Me" and Shakespeare's *Rape of Lucrece.* The following is a nineteenth-century example, from William Morris's *The Earthly Paradise:*

> Of Heaven or Hell I have no power to sing,
> I cannot ease the burden of your fears,
> Or make quick-coming death a little thing,
> Or bring again the pleasure of past years,
> Nor for my words shall ye forget your tears,

> Or hope again for aught that I can say,
> The idle singer of an empty day.

Rhyme Scheme. The pattern created by the rhyming words of a STANZA or poem. In the most common method of describing end rhyme (at the end of lines), each ending sound is designated by a letter. For example, *abcb* is the rhyme scheme of the BALLAD STANZA, in which the second and fourth lines rhyme, but the first and third do not. Rhyming couplets (paired lines), TERZA RIMA, and various types of QUATRAIN display different rhyming possibilities within the space of two, three, or four lines. Some rhyme schemes, like those for the TRI-OLET and VILLANELLE, require the repetition not just of rhymes but of entire lines. See VERSE FORMS and alphabetical entries of the forms listed there.

Rhyming Slang. See SLANG.

Rhythm. The measured flow of repeated sound patterns, as, for example, the heavy stresses of ACCENTUAL VERSE, the heavy and light stresses of ACCENTUAL-SYLLABIC VERSE, the long and short syllables of QUANTITATIVE VERSE, the counted syllables of SYLLABIC VERSE, the balanced syntactical arrangements of PARALLELISM in either verse or prose, and the effects created in either verse or prose by other repetitions and alternations, including such structural elements as long or short clauses, sentences, paragraphs, and stanzas. See CADENCE; METER; SPRUNG RHYTHM; STANZA.

Riddle. An ingenious problem, puzzle, or conundrum, typically a METAPHOR with one element of the implied comparison expressed and the other left for guessing. The most famous riddle from ancient times is the Sphinx's question to Oedipus: "What walks on four legs in the morning, two at noon, and three in the evening?" (answer: a human being—on all fours as an infant, erect as an adult, supported by a cane in old age). One children's riddle goes like this:

> Twenty white horses on a red hill:
> Now they prance,
> Now they dance,
> Now they stand still

The answer is teeth and gums, with a child's twenty "milk teeth" moving as the riddle is spoken, standing still as it ends. Some riddles turn on a PUN: "When is a door not a door?" "When it's a jar."

Many riddles are anonymous, the earliest collection in English being the poems of the Old English *Exeter Book* (eighth century). In tribal cultures, they are often connected with magic and ritual. For children and as an element of FOLKLORE, they are often primarily for entertainment. For sophisticated poets, they offer one variety of the delight that arises from surprising resemblances, as when Emily Dickinson, in "A Route of Evanescence," disguises her description of a hummingbird in images that include "a revolving Wheel" and "The mail from Tunis."

Reference

Archer Taylor, **English Riddles from Oral Tradition** (1951).

Rime Couée.   A French term for TAIL-RHYME.

Rime Riche.   RHYME on identical sounds with different senses (*sea, see*); a form of IDENTICAL RHYME.

Rising Action.   In a play, the events preceding the CLIMAX. See DRAMATIC STRUCTURE; FALLING ACTION; FREYTAG'S PYRAMID.

Rising Meter.   A METER beginning unstressed, running from light to heavy, as Coleridge describes it:

> Iambics march from short to long.
> With a leap and a bound the swift Anapests throng.

Robot.   An artificial man or woman. The term derives from the Czech word for "worker" and was first given widespread currency in Karel Capek's play *R.U.R.* (*Rossum's Universal Robots*, 1921). In SCIENCE FICTION, the term *robot* is frequently applied to a mechanical person, as distinct from an *android*, an artificial human of organic material, but the terms are also used interchangeably. See CYBORG.

Robotics, Three Laws of.   In SCIENCE FICTION, a set of principles attributed to Isaac Asimov and observed by many writers, especially in the 1940s and 1950s, but not by all: a robot (1) may not injure a human, or allow harm to a human through inaction; (2) must obey all commands of a human except those that would conflict with the first law; and (3) must protect its own existence, except where self-protection would conflict with the first or second law.

Rocking Rhythm.   RHYTHM in lines built on the AMPHIBRACH: ◡ — —. It is rare in English and frequently scannable otherwise. Some of Swinburne shows rocking rhythm, frequently irregular:

Ŏ daughter | of earth, of | my mother, |

her crown and | blossom | of birth, |

Ĭ am also, | Ĭ also, | thy brother; | Ĭ go as |

Ĭ came | unto earth. |

"Hymn to Proserpine"

Rococo. Ornate, elaborate style in art, architecture, or literature. Rococo is sometimes described as a lighter, more fanciful successor to BAROQUE style. The term is perhaps derived from French *rocaille* ("rock work") and *coquille* ("shell"). The word suggested originally the elaborate ornamentation in eighteenth-century grottoes, as well as the architectural scrollwork and entwined leaves, branches, and flowers of interior decoration of the same period.

Rodomontade. Extravagant or vainglorious boasting, in the manner of Rodomonte, a bragging Saracen king in Ariosto's *Orlando Furioso* (1516 –1532). See BOMBAST.

Roman à Clef. French for "novel with a key," one depicting real persons under fictitious names, in German a *Schlüsselroman*. The genre began in seventeenth-century France, in novels like Madeleine de Scudéry's *Le Grand Cyrus* (1649–1653). Examples of the "key novel" in English include Thomas Love Peacock's *Nightmare Abbey* (1818), Nathaniel Hawthorne's *Blithedale Romance* (1852), Aldous Huxley's *Point Counter Point* (1928), W. Somerset Maugham's *Cakes and Ale* (1930), and Saul Bellow's *Humboldt's Gift* (1975).

Romance. In its broadest possible meaning, a continuous narrative in which the emphasis is on what happens in the plot, rather than on what is reflected from ordinary life or experience. Thus a central element in romance is adventure; at its most primitive, romance is an endless sequence of adventures—endless in the sense that the story simply stops, with no structural ending built into it. However, a life capable of continuous adventure is clearly for young people, and is in fact a sublimated form of eroticism. Hence today there are two popular forms of romance, one an ADVENTURE STORY, such as the spy thriller or the DETECTIVE STORY, the other a highly conventionalized love story (see POPULAR ROMANCE).

Romance began historically in the Western tradition with late Greek fictions, the most elaborate being Heliodorus's *Ethiopiaca*, in which the themes of continuous adventure and the postponement of the sexual union of hero and heroine until the end of the story are obvious enough. More sentimental stories with more continuous erotic interest, such as Longus's *Daphnis and Chloe*, remind us that a PAS-TORAL, idealized setting is very common in quieter forms of romance, and in fact varieties of pastoral may appear in other romance forms: the WESTERN story, for instance, is a modern form of pastoral. In the Middle Ages romance became absorbed into the chivalric and courtly-love codes of a feudal society: the hero is often a knight-errant who destroys giants, robbers, and other disturbers of the peace as tributes to his inspiring lady. Here and there, as notably in the Grail romances, we can see that romance is closely related to MYTH. The chief charac-ters are human beings, if sometimes magicians or disguised animals, but the setting is a world in which the laws of nature do not consis-tently operate. Again, the central Christian myth includes a romance pattern in which Christ destroys the dragon of death and hell and re-deems his bride the Church, just as in the romance of St. George, the hero kills a dragon, releases a lady threatened by it, dies himself and revives, and succeeds to the kingdom. Such proximity to myth, even to sacred myth, gives a dimension of dream and wish fulfillment.

Thus in Spenser's *Faerie Queene*, which is related not directly to MEDIEVAL ROMANCE but to RENAISSANCE developments of it, espe-cially Ariosto's *Orlando Furioso*, the first book shows St. George set-ting off to kill his dragon as an imitator of Christ. In the first canto he and his lady disappear into a dreamy magical forest so dense that no light from the sky can penetrate it. In this first canto, too, St. George kills a dragon called Error, as a kind of rehearsal for his supreme achievement. Bunyan's *Pilgrim's Progress* is a simpler example of a ro-mance which is a continuous allegory of the Christian life.

In later centuries a greater demand for some similarity to ordinary experience caused various modifications in romance patterns. Some ro-mances became simply love stories, often of great length. In 1764 Hor-ace Walpole's *Castle of Otranto* started a vogue for fantastic or GOTHIC elements in story telling: the setting is pushed back to an earlier age, where the intrusion of ghosts, magicians, and similar apparatus seems more appropriate (see GOTHIC NOVEL). In Scott, the historical setting, because of its greater distancing, helps the romancer to emphasize the adventurous plot, with its intrigues and mysteries and exciting epi-sodes. Scott was not an allegorical writer, but the possibilities for AL-LEGORY in the romance form interested later nineteenth-century writ-ers, including Nathaniel Hawthorne and Bulwer Lytton, the latter having strong occult interests. The ghost story, which is mainly a nine-teenth-century phenomenon, was a byproduct of this fashion.

The later Victorian William Morris marks a further development of romance. Morris collected a great number of traditional romances, which he versified or translated or adapted, most of them in the book called *The Earthly Paradise*. Later in his life he turned to a form of prose romance in which the setting, though vaguely medieval, was in fact purely imaginary, both the history and the geography being invented, as the titles suggest ("The Wood Beyond the World"; "The Well at the World's End," and so on). These stories were out of fashion at the time, but after a remarkable mid-twentieth-century success in somewhat the same idiom—Tolkien's *Lord of the Rings*—a good deal of what is sometimes known as SCIENCE FICTION began to take on romance themes. A strange, magical, even miraculous setting seems appropriate enough when the setting is another planet, and what relation the story still has to our own experience contributes the allegorical dimension. See NOVEL.

Romantic Comedy. A COMEDY with love as the primary theme. Shakespeare's *Midsummer Night's Dream, As You Like It*, and *Twelfth Night* are the classic examples.

Romantic Epic. A term sometimes used to describe a kind of long NARRATIVE POEM popular in the RENAISSANCE, combining qualities of the MEDIEVAL ROMANCE and the classical EPIC. Examples include Ariosto's *Orlando Furioso* (1516–1532), Tasso's *Jerusalem Delivered* (1581), and Spenser's *Faerie Queene* (1590–1596).

Romanticism. A term describing qualities that colored most elements of European and American intellectual life in the late eighteenth and early nineteenth centuries, from literature, art, and music, through architecture, landscape gardening, philosophy, and politics. Although expressions of Romanticism arose at different times and were manifested in different ways in Europe and America, a few broad tendencies were common in literature and in politics. (1) Romanticism celebrated the individual. Within the social, political, and intellectual structures of society, it stressed the separateness of the person. In literature, this was evident in a turn toward common humanity as a proper subject for art and an increased acceptance of experimentation from writers determined to express their individuality through their choices of subjects and techniques. (2) Romantics demonstrated a strong faith in the fundamental goodness and eventual perfectibility of humankind. For them a human was born not in sin, as Calvinists would have it; instead, the newborn infant came "trailing clouds of glory . . . / From God, who is our home," as Wordsworth puts it. Imperfect society would be perfected through individual good released, encouraged, and made all-en-compassing. (3) Romanticism embraced nature as a model for harmony in society and art. Ideas of PRIMITIVISM suggested that earlier societies and artistic forms were more satisfactory than later ones. Jean Jacques Rousseau's NOBLE SAVAGE encapsulated an idealized vision of humanity freed from the limiting restraints of civilization. The grounds of great country estates were carefully arranged to imitate picturesque natural scenes. In literature, a lyrical looseness replaced formal, closed structures such as the HEROIC COUPLET. (4) The Romantic view was egalitarian. Equal at birth in the eye of the Maker, inherently good, valued as individuals, all people were encouraged toward self-development. The social structure was perceived as a medium for protecting and encouraging individual aspirations. (5) Romanticism stressed the value of expressive abilities common to all, inborn rather than developed through training. Emotional, intuitional, and sensual elements of artistic, religious, and intellectual expression were counted in some ways more valid than the products of education and reason. The heart versus the head became one of the great conflicts of the nineteenth century, with Romanticism raising the issue and pointing the way.

These qualities were not unique to the late eighteenth century and the beginning of the nineteenth, but in earlier and later times they were less dominant. Romanticism marked a sharp turn away from the characteristics of the NEOCLASSICAL PERIOD. Another sharp turn, not much later, produced the characteristics of REALISM.

For literature, a few more tendencies and specific examples may be cited. Romantic nostalgia for earlier and simpler times frequently found inspiration in the Middle Ages. Thomas Percy's *Reliques of Ancient English Poetry* (1765) began the vogue for serious BALLAD, FOLK SONG, and FOLKLORE study that spread rapidly throughout Europe. The CELTIC REVIVAL of the eighteenth century sprang from a fascination with the early inhabitants of the British Isles, evident also in the OSSIANIC CONTROVERSY. Complementing a nostalgia for the past was a view of the present tinted at some times with SENTIMENTALISM and at other times obsessed with images of death and decay, as in the poems of the GRAVEYARD SCHOOL. Emphasis on individualism was fed by the growth of the NOVEL, which early absorbed characteristics of Romanticism, as in Samuel Richardson's *Clarissa* (1747–1748), Oliver Goldsmith's *Vicar of Wakefield* (1766), Laurence Sterne's *Sentimental Journey* (1768), and Henry Mackenzie's *Man of Feeling* (1771). An offshoot, the GOTHIC NOVEL stressed the fantastic and grotesque, with stories often set in the Middle Ages. In another manifestation of interest in the past, the HISTORICAL NOVEL was born in the works of Sir Walter Scott. CHILDREN'S LITERATURE arose as a separate genre, as children began to be perceived as entities different from adults, or as small primitives as yet unspoiled by society. Writers turned inward, stressing spontaneity and self, as in the visions of Blake, Wordsworth's *Prelude*, and Coleridge's "Kubla Khan." The simple lives of the lower orders were elevated in respect, as in Burns's "The Cotter's Saturday Night" and Wordsworth's "Michael."

At the beginning of the nineteenth century, generally in the years between 1798 and 1832, Romanticism in England reached its most complete expression in the work of the great Romantic poets: Wordsworth, Coleridge, Byron, Shelley, and Keats. Slightly later, on the other side of the Atlantic, the same broad characteristics were dominant between 1820 and 1860 in the period of America's first great literary flowering, in the works especially of Washington Irving, James Fenimore Cooper, Emerson, Hawthorne, Poe, Thoreau, Melville, and Whitman. See ROMANCE; ROMANTIC PERIOD; TRANSCENDENTALISM.

References

M. H. Abrams, **The Mirror and the Lamp** (1953).
Harold Bloom, ed., **Romanticism and Consciousness: Essays in Criticism** (1970).
Northrop Frye, ed., **Romanticism Reconsidered** (1963).
A. O. Lovejoy, **Essays in the History of Ideas** (1944).

Romantic Period (1798–1832). The span of years from Wordsworth and Coleridge's *Lyrical Ballads* (1798) to the year of the parliamentary REFORM BILL OF 1832 and the beginning of Dickens's career. The era rejected the eighteenth-century belief in rational control, emphasizing instead "the spontaneous overflow of powerful feelings" (Wordsworth) and the inner individual consciousness and imagination, valuing even irrational states like ecstasy and fantasy. Nature was thought to be pantheistic, reflecting God and truth with divine inspirational power:

> One impulse from a vernal wood
>   May teach you more of man,
> Of moral evil and of good,
>   Than all the sages can.

> Sweet is the lore which nature brings;
>   Our meddling intellect
> Misshapes the beauteous forms of things:—
>   We murder to dissect.

Here in "The Tables Turned" (1798), Wordsworth is calling his hypothetical friend away from the books and the past, which the eighteenth century had reverenced; he is emphasizing both the present and its emotive experience, and voicing the Romantic's distrust of rationalism, oddly borrowing from the Age of Reason itself as he does so, indeed from Pope, who expressed only the difficulty in analyzing a person's motives:

> Like following life thro' creatures you dissect,
> You lose it in the moment you detect.
> *"Epistle to Cobham," 39–40*

For Wordsworth and his contemporaries, instinct, emotion, and imagination were truer than the meddling intellect. The simple rustic, close to nature, speaking in simple language, is the new NOBLE SAVAGE, complete with Jean Jacques Rousseau's PRIMITIVISM, but in a new natural Eden of the present. Henry Mackenzie recognized and championed Robert Burns on these grounds, and introduced German Romantic literature to the Royal Society in Edinburgh, and consequently to England, in a paper he read in 1788. That essay fired young Walter Scott to emulate Goethe and Schiller in Romantic novels about the Scottish and British past, carrying forward the impulse of the GOTHIC NOVEL and romancers. In his Preface to *Waverley* (1814), Scott also claims that the seventeenth-century French romances of La Calprenède and Madeleine de Scudéry, still known and read throughout the eighteenth century, first set his mind romancing. Optimism prevailed, and faith in PROGRESS, even proclaiming paradoxically, in Tom Paine's words, "a morning of reason rising upon the world" as rational self-government threw off the shackles of monarchs and priests. Poetry was preeminent in the hands of Wordsworth, Coleridge, Keats, Shelley, and Byron. See ENGLISH LITERATURE, PERIODS OF and the "Chronology of Literature and World Events."

Romany. The language of the gypsies. Belonging to the Indo-Iranian subfamily of the Indo-European group of languages, Romany has absorbed much vocabulary from the countries in which the gypsies have lived since migrating from India to Europe in the Middle Ages. George Borrow's *Zincali* (1841) described the life of Spanish gypsies and included a dictionary of their language. His *Romano Lavo-Lil* (1874) was a pioneering study of the language of English gypsies. The same author's *Lavengro* (1851) and *The Romany Rye* (1857) are loosely fictional accounts of English gypsy life.

Rondeau. A French verse form, characteristically in 15 lines divided into 3 stanzas of 5, 4, and 6 lines, with a short REFRAIN (usually taken from the poem's first half-line) forming the last line of stanzas 2 and 3. Except for the refrain, only two rhymes are used: *aabba aabR aabbaR*. Austin Dobson's "In After Days" shows the pattern:

> In after days when grasses high
> O'ertop the stone where I shall lie,
>   Though ill or well the world adjust
>   My slender claim to honored dust,
> I shall not question or reply.
>
> I shall not see the morning sky;
> I shall not hear the night-wind sigh;
>   I shall be mute, as all men must
>   In after days!
>
> But yet, now living, fain were I
> That someone then should testify,
>   Saying—"He held his pen in trust
>   To Art, not serving shame or lust."
> Will none?—Then let my memory die
>   In after days!

See STANZA; VERSE FORMS.

Rondeau Redoublé. A French verse form in 6 quatrains, using 2 rhymes. The first 4 lines are used in succession as the last lines of stanzas 2, 3, 4, and 5. The last QUATRAIN is followed by a REFRAIN taken from the poem's first half-line. The RHYME SCHEME is thus *abab baba abab baba abab babaR*. The form is rare in English, though some poets have used it. See STANZA; VERSE FORMS.

Rondel. In modern usage, a term for a French verse form in 13 lines (sometimes 14), using the first 2 lines as a REFRAIN, with line 1 repeated as line 7 and 13, and line 2 repeated as line 8 (and sometimes line 14). The RHYME SCHEME is *abba abab abba(b)*. The following lines by W. E. Henley give the form:

> Beside the idle summer sea
> And in the vacant summer days,
> Light Love came fluting down the ways,
> Where you were loitering with me.
>
> Who has not welcomed, even as we,
> That jocund minstrel and his lays

Beside the idle summer sea
And in the vacant summer days?

We listened, we were fancy-free;
And lo! in terror and amaze
We stood alone—alone at gaze
With an implacable memory
Beside the idle summer sea.

"Merciless Beauty," attributed to Chaucer, is a triple rondel in a variant pattern, with the first three lines of each section providing the refrain for each. ROUNDEL was an earlier spelling. The RONDEAU and TRIOLET have also been termed rondels. See VERSE FORMS.

Round Character.   One possessing the depth and complexity of a living person, the opposite of a FLAT CHARACTER. See CHARACTERS.

Roundel.   A term now usually restricted to the verse form used by Swinburne in *A Century of Roundels* (1883), but formerly a spelling for RONDEL. A roundel is composed of 3 3-line stanzas, using 2 rhymes, with a short REFRAIN, taken from the poem's first half-line, coming at the end of stanzas 1 and 3: *abaR bab abaR*. Swinburne's "The Roundel" is an example:

A roundel is wrought as a ring or a starbright sphere,
With craft of delight and with cunning of sound unsought,
That the heart of the hearer may smile if to pleasure his ear
    A roundel is wrought.

Its jewel of music is carven of all or of aught—.
Love, laughter, or mourning—remembrance of rapture or fear—
That fancy may fashion to hand in the ear of thought.

As a bird's quick song runs round, and the hearts in us hear
Pause answer to pause, and again the same strain caught,
So moves the device whence, round as a pearl or tear,
    A roundel is wrought.

See STANZA; VERSE FORMS.

Roundelay.   A term from Old French *rondelet*, used for any short, simple song with a REFRAIN, for singing or dancing.

Roundheads.   Adherents of the Parliamentary, or Puritan, party in the English Civil War, so called from their short haircuts, as opposed to the fashionable long wigs of the Cavaliers, supporters of King Charles I. See CAVALIER POETS.

Royal Houses.   The families of the kings and queens of England. Since the twelfth century, these have been the following: *Plantagenet* (or *Angevin*), from 1154 to 1399, including Henry II (1154–1189), Richard I (1189–1199), John (1199–1216), Henry III (1216–1272), Edward I (1272–1307), Edward II (1307–1327), Edward III (1327–1377), Richard II (1377–1399). *Lancaster,* from 1399 to 1461, including Henry IV (1399–1413), Henry V (1413–1422), Henry VI (1422–1461). *York,* from 1461 to 1485, including Edward IV (1461–1483), Edward V (1483), Richard III (1483–1485). *Tudor,* from 1485 to 1603, including Henry VII (1485–1509), Henry VIII (1509–1547), Edward VI (1547–1553), Mary I (1553–1558), Elizabeth I (1558–1603). *Stuart,* from 1603 to 1649 and 1660 to 1714, including James I (1603–1625), Charles I (1625–1649), Charles II (1660–1685), James II (1685–1688), Mary II (1689–1694) and William III (1689–1702), Anne (1702–1714). *Hanover,* from 1714 to 1901, including George I (1714–1727), George II (1727–1760), George III (1760–1820), George IV (1820–1830), William IV (1830–1837), Victoria (1837–1901). *Saxe-Coburg-Gotha* (or *Wettin*), from 1901 to 1917, including Edward VII (1901–1910) and George V (1910–1936), who changed the name to Windsor in 1917. *Windsor,* from 1917 to the present, including George V, Edward VIII (1936), George VI (1936–1952), Elizabeth II (1952–   ).

Rubáiyát.   From an Arabic word for QUATRAINS: a collection of quatrains, as in Edward FitzGerald's *The Rubáiyát of Omar Khayyám* (1859).

Rubáiyát Stanza.   The STANZA used by Edward FitzGerald in his translation of *The Rubáiyát of Omar Khayyám:* a QUATRAIN in iambic pentameter (see METER), rhyming *aaba:*

> Come, fill the Cup, and in the Fire of Spring
> Your Winter-garment of Repentance fling:
>   The Bird of Time has but a little way
> To flutter—and the Bird is on the Wing.

Rubric.   From Latin *rubrica,* "red earth" (for coloring): in a book or MANUSCRIPT, a heading, marginal notation, or other section distinguished for special attention by being printed in red ink or in distinctive type.

Rules, The.   Principles of Neoclassical criticism believed to be basic to drama and poetry because reflecting nature and epitomizing Aristotle. Nicolas Boileau's *L'Art poétique* (1674) was the basic inspiration, augmented by René le Bossu's *Traité du poème épique* (translated 1675).

The Rules required faithfulness to the three UNITIES—unity of action, of time, and of place—and to the twofold concept of DECORUM: (1) that characters should be consistent to type in speech and action, kings kings and beggars beggars; (2) that style should be consistent to its GENRE, high for TRAGEDY and EPIC, lower in proper proportion for the lesser genres of COMEDY, PASTORAL, ELEGY, and so forth.

Unity of action required causal consistency aimed at a single end. Unity of time required the action to imitate chronological time, unfolding as it actually would in reality, preferably in the light of one day, but at most in no more than 24 hours. This goes beyond Aristotle's remark that ideally a tragedy should take place in "one revolution of the sun." Unity of place, about which Aristotle said nothing, requires that all the action occur in one place, one setting. John Dennis's *Grounds of Criticism in Poetry* (1704) is England's most vigorous championship of the Rules, though they considerably influenced both writing and criticism, especially as Alexander Pope rationalized them, with becoming permissiveness, in *An Essay on Criticism* (1711):

> Those RULES of old *discover'd*, not *devis'd*,
> Are *Nature* still, but *Nature Methodiz'd*.
>   88–89

Rune. (1) A letter in the Germanic alphabet of northern Europe, Scandinavia, and Britain. The alphabet arose sometime in the second century A.D. and continued as late as the seventeenth, though the Roman alphabet of Christianity, and Latin, competed early and eventually displaced it for everything but inscriptions and charms. The Goths probably derived the Germanic alphabet from the Etruscan alphabet in northern Italy, which had derived from the Greek. The most common form had 24 runes; the Anglo-Saxon, 28 and, after c. 900 A.D., 33. The earliest full sentence known is that on the Golden Horn of Gallehus, a village in Jutland where the horn was excavated in 1734, on which the goldsmith inscribed his name, or that of his lord, in the early 400s, running out of space on the last word:

Ek H l e w a g a s t i R ⦙ H o l t i j a R⦙ h o r na ⦙tawi d o⦙

I, HlewagastiR HoltijaR, horna tawido.

I, Lee-guest, of Woods, made [had made] this horn.

Most surviving runes are inscribed on stone, but our word *book* comes from Old English *boc*, "beech," for the beechwood staffs that evidently carried the first runic lettering.

(2) A charm, magical spell, or any secret message, since any written message seemed magical and secret, and since runes were frequently inscribed to cast spells. (3) A Finnish poem, or, loosely, any ancient Scandinavian poem, or, metaphorically, any poem at all.

Run-on Line.   A line of poetry whose sense does not stop at the end, with punctuation, but runs on to the next line. The opposite of END-STOPPED LINE. See ENJAMBMENT.

S

Saga. An Icelandic prose narrative of historic and legendary deeds, written in the twelfth and thirteenth centuries, or any similar heroic tale. The Grettis Saga (c. 1320, translated as *The Saga of Grettir the Strong*), telling of a noble hero outlawed at age 14 for killing a man in a quarrel and outlawed a second time for accidental deaths in a fire, is one of the latest and greatest. Grettir's major exploit, returning to free his people from the ravaging ghost of Glam the shepherd, derives from the same remote oral source behind Beowulf's slaying of Grendel. John Galsworthy adopted the title of his *Forsyte Saga* (1906–1921, 1924–1929) from the Icelandic family sagas, of which the Grettis Saga is one, as Grettir's brother finally avenges Grettir's lonely death.

Saints' Lives. Medieval biographies of saints legendizing their miracles and martyrdom in verse or prose, especially the many such stories appearing throughout the twelfth and thirteenth centuries. See HAGIOGRAPHY.

Saltic Fables. Librettos for pantomimes concerning nymphs and satyrs, said to be composed by Lucan (A.D. 39–65).

Sans Serif. See SERIF.

Sapphics. Verse in a STANZA used by Sappho, from whom it takes its name. Much used by Catullus also, it was later imitated in other languages in which the metrics come less easily than in Greek and Latin. Essentially, it is a QUATRAIN of three eleven-syllable lines (‒ ◡ ‒ ◡ ‒ ◡ ◡ ‒ ◡ ‒ ◡, with the fourth and last syllables either long or short) and one five-syllable line (‒ ◡ ◡ ‒ ◡, with the last syllable either long or short). A stanza from Swinburne's "Sapphics" illustrates:

> All the night sleep came not upon my eyelids,
> Shed not dew, nor shook nor unclosed a feather,
> Yet with lips shut close and with eyes of iron
> Stood and beheld me.

Sarcasm. A cutting personal remark, from Greek *sarkazein*, "to tear flesh." Because the tearing is frequently ironic, people often misapply the term to any ironic statement. "You ugly little thing" addressed to a dwarf would be sarcastic but not ironic. See IRONY.

Satanic School. Byron, Shelley, Leigh Hunt, and their group, so designated in Southey's "Preface," *A Vision of Judgment* (1821) for their radical ideas and conduct. The LAKE SCHOOL of Wordsworth, Coleridge, and Southey held contrasting ideas about poetry. Later unconventional groups have been similarly designated as "satanic."

Satanism. Worship of Satan. St. Augustine and others considered magic a remnant of paganism to be cured by conversion and education, and satanism indeed seems to derive both from orgiastic fertility rites and the Zoroastrian concept of a dualistic struggle between Ormazd (Ahura Mazda), the power of light and good, and Ahriman, the power of darkness and evil. In the third century A.D. the Persian seer Mani originated MANICHAEISM, synthesizing Zoroastrian polarity with Christianity, which became a major heresy. In the Balkans, from the tenth to the fifteenth centuries, a neo-Manichaeism flourished among the Bogomils (named for the priest Bogomil, the founder)—a belief that the devil created the material world, which was to be spurned abstemiously. The Albigensians in southern France, in the twelfth and thirteenth centuries, held the same doctrine. The church attacked these heresies as satanic. In 1320, a papal bull declared all magic as heresy, and the Inquisition began to mention the Witches' Sabbath and Black Mass, orgiastic midnight parodies of orthodox rituals. The Saturday night revel (before sober Sunday), Halloween (midnight deviltry before All Saints' Day), and Mardi Gras (Fat Tuesday before Ash Wednesday) are modern survivals. Hawthorne frequently depicts the satanism presumed to flourish in early Puritan America, most notably in "Young Goodman Brown." Satanism revived during the reign of Louis XIV (1643–1715) and emerged again in the 1890s. It persists in scattered parts of the world.

Satire. Literature that ridicules vices and follies. The term comes from *satura*, a mixed dish or, metaphorically, a medley, although a derivation from *satyra*, and the belief that satire had developed from the Greek SATYR PLAY has influenced its history. Satire arose as a specific verse form in Latin literature, practiced by Horace, Juvenal, and Persius. It has no real counterpart in Greek literature, but another form of satire, in prose with verse interludes, or simply in prose, was allegedly invented by the Greek cynic Menippus, whose works are lost, and was the form (without the verse) used by Lucian. It is called the MENIPPEAN SATIRE, or sometimes the *Varronian satire* (from the Latin writer Varro, whose works are also lost except for fragments).

Verse satire, as the specific form of that name, was revived in English literature by Joseph Hall in *Virgidemiarum* (1597). Hall claimed to be the first English satirist, though he had been preceded by Gascoigne's *Steel Glass* (1576). His followers John Marston (1576–1634) and John Donne emphasized the harsh, rugged, obscure style of Persius, and wrote in a deliberately irregular meter. This tendency survived in satire with the intentional doggerel and comic rhymes of Samuel Butler's *Hudibras*, Byron's *Don Juan*, and W. S. Gilbert in Victorian times. With the RESTORATION, and partly under the influence of Boileau in France, satire acquired the more Horatian characteristics of strict meter and a prevailing tone of urbanity and good temper, sometimes deepening to harsh and ferocious condemnation of social evils in imitation of Juvenal. This type of satire is the form most frequently employed by Dryden and Pope. Pope even rewrote two of Donne's satires in a more regular meter, to make them more acceptable to the taste of his time.

Menippean satire in prose also revived with Erasmus and others in the humanist period, and continues through Swift and Voltaire to Thomas Love Peacock (who revived the use of verse interludes), thence to Aldous Huxley and others in our day. But before long, satire changed its meaning. It now means, not two specific genres or subgenres of narrative, but a tone of antagonism between the writer and the material which may be found in any genre. Thus we speak of satire in Chaucer or Ibsen or Evelyn Waugh without regard to the genre in which it occurs. Satire in this sense is a type of IRONY which is normally in a comic context, in contrast to tragic irony, and is more militant in tone than the irony which depends on the suppression of all attitudes of commitment or engagement on the part of the writer. Direct satire—that is, personal or individualized attack—is certainly found in literature, as in Byron's early satire, *English Bards and Scotch Reviewers*. But most personal satire belongs to the pamphlet wars in religion and politics that fall outside the normal orbit of literature.

Indirect or more purely literary satire seems to be a combination of the ironic with the fantastic: Swift's fantasy settings in *Gulliver's Travels* and the romantic adventures of Voltaire's characters and of Byron's *Don Juan* are typical. Pure fantasy without the tone of antagonism is at one extreme: the Alice books appear to be straightforward fantasy, but the fact that their interspersed poems are often parodies of well-known writers dips them lightly into satire. Pure irony, where the attitude is too detached for the characteristic antagonistic tone of satire to appear, is at the other extreme. Of the two words derived from the metaphor of the masked actor, *hypocrite* and *person*, the former carries a moral charge, and what the satirist sees is normally a society in which all forms of personality are more or less hypocritical. Satire is usually what is called obscene—that is, outspokenly scatological—because under the hypocrisy of dressing up there is a democracy of the body usually concealed in public. It also includes parodies of literary form itself, which again is a way of allowing one's creative efforts to appear in a conventional dress. Many satires are anonymous, fragmentary, or deliberately disorganized and chaotic in structure. It is also characteristic of satire, especially in the Menippean tradition, to present people as representatives of certain intellectual attitudes, the social consequences of which are ridiculed by their sponsorship of them.

Perhaps the most concentrated form of fantasy is the presentation of the imaginary ideal state known as the UTOPIA, where all activity is ritualized and where every individual fits perfectly into the social mold. And perhaps the most concentrated form of satire is what is now called the DYSTOPIA, the Utopian parody of a world turned by malice or cunning into a nightmarish hell, as in Orwell's *Nineteen Eighty-Four*, Yevgeny Zamyatyn's *We*, or Aldous Huxley's *Brave New World* and *Ape and Essence*. A good deal of SCIENCE FICTION is based on dystopian allegories (for example Ray Bradbury's *Fahrenheit 451* and Walter M. Miller's *A Canticle for Leibowitz*), where the relation to the social pitfalls in contemporary technology is close enough for frightening plausibility in the fantasy. See HORATION SATIRE; JUVENALIAN SATIRE; SATIRIC POETRY.

Satiric Poetry. Poetry that ridicules vices and follies. Horace (65–8 B.C.), the genial and general, and Juvenal (A.D. 60?–140?), the pungent and particular, were the chief begetters. They were the models for the burst of satiric poetry in English that ran from the RESTORATION to the middle of the eighteenth century—the NEOCLASSICAL PERIOD. Rochester (1648–1680) wrote the first imitations of Horace, from which his masterpiece *A Satyr against Mankind* (1675) was derived. Dryden translated Juvenal (1693); his major satires, *Absalom and Achitophel* (1681) and *MacFlecknoe* (1682) are Juvenalian in their biting personal portraiture. Some of Pope's best writing is in his *Imitations of Horace* (1733–1738), wherein he "stoop't to Truth, and moraliz'd his song" (*Arbuthnot*, 341). Johnson's major poem, *The Vanity of Human Wishes* (1749), imitates Juvenal's tenth satire. Byron's *Don Juan* (1819–1824) and *The Vision of Judgment* (1821) are England's last major satiric poems. In America, James Russell Lowell's *Biglow Papers* (1848, 1867) and *A Fable for Critics* (1848) stand out, as do more recently Don

Marquis's *archy and mehitabel* (1927) and Ogden Nash's long stream of verses that flowed through *The New Yorker* and elsewhere from 1930 until his death in 1971.

Saturday Club. A literary-scientific group meeting irregularly around Boston in the mid-nineteenth century. Louis Agassiz, Emerson, Longfellow, William Hickling Prescott, Whittier, and Oliver Wendell Holmes—who celebrated it in his poem "At the Saturday Club"—were members. Hawthorne, John Lothrop Motley, and Charles Sumner were also included. Emerson's youngest son, Dr. Edward Waldo Emerson, wrote its history.

Satyr Play. One of the elements, along with three tragedies, in the traditional Greek program. The satyr play's structure was tragic; its matter, serious mythology; its treatment, grotesquely comic, with CHORUS of satyrs with horse tails. The only one extant is Euripides's *Cyclops*.

Saxe-Coburg-Gotha. See ROYAL HOUSES.

Scansion. A system for analyzing and marking poetical meters and feet. Two prevail: (1) marking short and long, light and accented, syllables thus ⌣ —; (2) marking unstressed and stressed syllables so as to include secondary stress thus ⌣ ´ | ⌣ ⸜.

(1) Ă sūn, | ă shad- | ow of | ă mag- | nĭtude. |

(2) Ă sún, | ă shad- | ow of | ă mag- | nĭtude. |

Scanners sometimes add an accent mark to the macron (—), particularly in classical prosody, to indicate the ictus, or patterned point of stress, as in the spondee: — ´. Classical patterns may combine the breve (⌣) and macron to indicate that the syllable may be either long or short: ≍. Other symbols are | (a vertical bar to mark feet); ⫶ (ANACRUSIS); ‖ (CAESURA); ∧ (pause other than caesura).

Sidney Lanier (1842–1881) and others have tried musical notation, ♪♪♩ , to indicate the varying lengths of syllables, but with only temporary success, since such detail obscures the basic metrical pattern. Gerard Manley Hopkins (1844–1878) devised SPRUNG RHYTHM, a system for scanning his unique metrics. See METER.

Scenario. (1) An outline of a play. (2) A *screenplay*, or script for a film.

Scene. (1) A continuous episode in a play, novel, or film. (2) The place of action. (3) An item in Kenneth Burke's "pentad" (see DRAMATISM).

In the Greek theater, the *skene* ("tent") was the central hut representing the setting. ELIZABETHAN DRAMA made no clear division of scenes, but denoted them effectively by entrances, exits, and clearings of the stage. In the RESTORATION and eighteenth century, playwrights numbered a new scene with each entrance or exit. Modern writers group scenes by continuous episode.

Scène à Faire. See OBLIGATORY SCENE.

Scenic Method. The presentation of a NOVEL or SHORT STORY (or a part of one) in scenes, as though it were a PLAY. In a common use of scenic method, frequent in the novels of Henry James, the author alternates scenic passages with nonscenic ones. In the latter, the author may summarize action or dialogue, rather than presenting it dramatically, thus passing quickly over hours, months, or years, or may present the mind of a character reflecting on events. See DRAMATIC METHOD; NARRATIVE PERSPECTIVE; SUMMARY NARRATION.

Scheme. Obsolete synonym for FIGURE OF SPEECH.

Schlüsselroman. German for "key novel." See ROMAN À CLEF.

Scholasticism. The logical reconciliation of Christian theology to rational questions, originating in the religious schools founded in the ninth and tenth centuries. The teacher, the *doctor scholasticus*, gave the movement its name, along with the synonym *Schoolman*. In the first era (twelfth century), Anselm (1033–1109), "father of Scholasticism," diverged with tighter logic from the older "patristic" thinkers, whose followers included Abelard (1079–1142) and Bernard of Clairvaux (1090?–1153). In the second era, the major one, Aristotelian logic and the syllogism predominated in the thinking of the great opposing camps, that of Thomas Aquinas (1225–1274), the "Thomists," and that of Duns Scotus (c. 1265–1308), the "Scotists." The third era dwindled away to nothing in the fifteenth century until, in the sixteenth (earliest record 1530), the brilliant name of Duns had become synonymous with "hair-splitter" and "dullard"—a *dunce*. Scholastic deductive logic gave way to the wider reasoning of Renaissance HUMANISM. John Colet presumably persuaded Erasmus to give up Scholastic deduction. A century later, Francis Bacon's *Novum Organum* (1620) proclaimed the new inductive method, the way of science, that has prevailed ever since. See OXFORD REFORMERS.

Scholiast.   A commentator, usually unknown, writing explanations and interpretations (*scholia*) in the margins of Greek and Latin manuscripts.

Schoolman.   See SCHOLASTICISM.

School of Night.   Presumably, a group of young nobles and intellectuals led by Sir Walter Raleigh in studying astronomy and occult lore. The only reference to it is in Shakespeare's *Love's Labour's Lost* (c. 1597):

> Black is the badge of hell,
> The hue of dungeons and the schoole of night.
> *IV. III.254–255*

Long considered a misprint and emended to "suit of night," the phrase was restored in 1903 by Arthur Acheson, who argued for the existence of the clique, satirized by Shakespeare in the young nobles in the play. A pamphlet in 1592 refers to "Sir Walter Rauley's Schoole of Atheisme." The group presumably included Henry Percy, ninth earl of Northumberland; Thomas Harriot, mathematician; and poets Matthew Roydon and George Chapman. Chapman's poem *The Shadow of Night* (1594) praises blackness, night, study, and contemplation as against frivolous dalliance with women.

References

Arthur Acheson, **Shakespeare and the Rival Poet** (1903).
Muriel C. Bradbrook, **The School of Night: A Study in the Literary Relationships of Raleigh** (1936).

School Plays.   Plays in Latin or English written in imitation of the Roman comedies of Plautus and Terence and performed in schools and colleges in England in the sixteenth century. The earliest extant example, also the first English comedy, is *Ralph Roister Doister*, written about 1553 by Nicholas Udall, headmaster at Eton and Westminster. These plays preserved classical notions of structure and may have influenced Elizabethan dramatists who became acquainted with them in school, as they did also with the models for the school plays, the classical dramas themselves.

Science Fiction.   FICTION in which new and futuristic scientific developments propel the plot. Traces of the scientific speculation that would inspire science fiction began with the scientific awakening of the

RENAISSANCE. Roger Bacon (c. 1214–1294) believed that human beings might achieve flight. Leonardo da Vinci (1452–1519) drew an airplane. Bishop John Wilkins, first secretary of the Royal Society, published *The Discovery of a World in the Moon* (c. 1638), with an appendix (1640), "The possibility of a passage thither." Wilkins, watching birds glide with wings motionless, thought that humans could work out the proportions and means to imitate nature. Swift satirized the new scientific aspirations in *Gulliver's Travels* (1726) with his flying island controlled by a loadstone, or magnet. Robert Paltock's *Peter Wilkins* (1751) made his Cornishman a general among beautiful bat people, conducting a war in the air.

Mary Shelley's *Frankenstein, or The Modern Prometheus* (1818) was the first novel projected wholly on scientific speculation. But Jules Verne was the true originator of modern science fiction with *Voyage au centre de la terre* (*Voyage to the Center of the Earth*, 1864), *Vingt mille lieus sous les mers* (*Twenty Thousand Leagues Under the Sea*, 1869), and *Le Tour du monde en quatre-vingt jours* (*Around the World in Eighty Days*, 1873), soon to be followed by H. G. Wells's *Time Machine* (1895), *The Wonderful Visit* (1895), and *The Invisible Man* (1897). Kurd Lasswitz's popular *Auf Zwei Planeten* (*On Two Planets*, 1897) contained the first description of an invasion from Mars, immediately topped by Wells's famous *War of the Worlds* (1898). The science-fiction DYSTOPIA of Aldous Huxley, *Brave New World* (1932), and George Orwell, *Nineteen Eighty-Four* (1949), are classics. Isaac Asimov, Ray Bradbury, Arthur C. Clarke, Robert Heinlein, and Ursula Le Guin have strengthened not only the technical plausibility of science fiction but its moral import.

Scop. An Anglo-Saxon bard, or court poet, a kind of poet laureate. A scop was both composer and singer, or reciter. Some scops moved from court to court, like the GLEEMAN, the Irish FILID, and the Welsh BARD, still holding the honored position.

Scots Makars. The Scottish "Makers," or poets, of the fifteenth and sixteenth centuries, frequently called "Scottish Chaucerians" because of their use of Chaucerian forms and materials. Most important are James I, Robert Henryson, William Dunbar, and Gavin Douglas. See SCOTTISH LITERATURE.

Scottish Chaucerians. See SCOTS MAKARS.

Scottish Literature. The writings native to Scotland. Besides the Latin, mostly ecclesiastical, writings common to European countries in the Middle Ages, Scottish literature exists primarily in three languages, Gaelic, Scots, and English.

Scottish Gaelic, close kin to Irish Gaelic, had almost no separate literary tradition before the eighteenth century. Never much spoken outside the Highlands, the language first flowered as a literary medium in response to the defeat of Jacobite hopes in Bonnie Prince Charlie's campaign of 1745 and because of a growing interest in ANTIQUARIAN-ISM in Scotland. One of the famous literary controversies of the eighteenth century erupted when James Macpherson (1736–1796) published *Fingal* (1762) and *Temora* (1763) as supposed translations from Gaelic epic poems by a third-century bard named Ossian. Macpherson doubtless collected fragments, but most likely created most of what he printed (see OSSIANIC CONTROVERSY). Poets of stature who have written in Scottish Gaelic include Alexander MacDonald (c. 1700–1770) and Duncan Ban Macintyre (1724–1812) in the eighteenth century and Sorley Maclean (1911–   ) and George Campbell Hay (1915–   ) in the twentieth. Iain Crichton Smith (1928–   ) has written in Gaelic and English and has translated Macintyre's *Ben Dorain* and Maclean's *Poems to Eimhir* into English.

Scots has a much richer tradition. This is the language of Lowland Scotland and the Borders, direct descendant of the Northern English of the Middle Ages, and now the Lallans (i.e., Lowland Scots) of the twentieth-century Scottish Renaissance. Most vernacular literature that has survived from Scotland prior to the seventeenth century is in Scots: songs and ballads such as "Waly, Waly," "Sir Patrick Spens," "Edward," "Lord Randal," "The Wife of Usher's Well," and "The Twa Corbies" (most were collected later); *The Bruce* of John Barbour (c. 1320–1395); Blind Harry's *Wallace* (c. 1460); anonymous poems such as *Colkelbie Sow* (?c. 1450) and *Rauf Coilyear* (?c. 1480); and the poems of the Scots Makars (or Scottish Chaucerians), James I (1394–1437), Robert Henryson (c. 1420–c. 1490), William Dunbar (c. 1460–c. 1513), Gavin Douglas (c. 1475–1522), Sir David Lyndsay (?1490–?1555), Alexander Scott (?c. 1520–c. 1590), and Alexander Montgomerie (?1545–?1610). Of the Makars, Dunbar is generally ranked highest, counted with Burns and MacDiarmid as one of the three greatest Scots poets. His "Lament for the Makaris" powerfully recalls admired poets taken by death. "The Twa Maryit Wemen and the Wedo" satirizes women as they discuss their men, utilizing an unrhymed alliterative style abandoned much earlier in England. Henryson's principal works are versions of Aesop's *Fables* and *The Testament of Cresseid*, in which he continues the story begun by Chaucer through the heroine's leprosy and death. *The Kingis Quair* (*The King's Book*) of James I describes his captivity in England and his love of Lady Joan Beaufort. Douglas's *Aeneid*, in Scots heroic couplets, was the first complete translation of that poem in either Scots or English.

After James VI of Scotland became James I of England in 1603, the language of Scottish literature was generally English until the Scottish Revival of the eighteenth century renewed interest in Scots and Gaelic. As lyrical and popular forerunners of Burns, Allan Ramsay (1686–1758) and Robert Fergusson (1750–1774) kept Scots alive, as did such anthologies as James Watson's *Choice Collection of Comic and Serious Scots Poems* (1706–1711) and Ramsay's *Tea-Table Miscellany* (1724–1732). Robert Burns (1759–1796), who wrote in Scots, has been the Scottish poet most admired outside of Scotland. A poetic genius, well read, but with little formal education, he shares with Sir Walter Scott the distinction of creating much of the picture of Scottish people and manners held in the minds of non-Scottish readers around the world. His verse ranges from universally known songs like "Auld Lang Syne" and "John Anderson My Jo," frequently adapted from folk originals, through sentimental and humorous poems such as "To a Mouse" ("The best-laid schemes o' Mice an' Men/Gang aft agley") and "To a Louse: On Seeing One on a Lady's Bonnet at Church," to the mock-heroic witch tale "Tam o' Shanter," the rollicking cantata "The Jolly Beggars," and the brilliant genre piece "The Cotter's Saturday Night." After Burns, Scottish literature was again generally in English until the Scottish Renaissance that followed World War I. Here the great poet, seen by some as the equal of Burns, is Hugh MacDiarmid, pseudonym for Christopher Murray Grieve (1892–1978). MacDiarmid's Lallans is a synthetic mixture of older Scots and contemporary vernacular first forged into the lyrics of *Sangschaw* (1925) and *Penny Wheep* (1926) and later forming the basis for his lyrical, satiric, and comic masterpiece, *A Drunk Man Looks at the Thistle* (1926). A constant rebel, politically as well as aesthetically, he wrote in numerous styles and, later, more and more frequently in English. A major late effort, in 6000 lines, is *In Memoriam James Joyce* (1955). His *Complete Poems 1920–1976* (1978) suggests comparison with such other modern masters as Yeats, Frost, and T. S. Eliot. Other recent poets in Scots (or Scots and English) include William Soutar (1898–1943), Robert Garioch (1908–   ), and Sydney Goodsir Smith (1915–   ). Literary prose in Scots has been mostly limited to dialect passages in such writers as Tobias Smollett, Scott, John Galt, George MacDonald, Stevenson, and J. M. Barrie.

Much Scottish literature is in English, some clearly Scottish, some indistinguishable from the literature of England. Among earlier writers, James Thomson (1700–1748), writing in England, produced *The Seasons* (1730), one of the most popular poems of its time. The novels of Tobias Smollett (1721–1771), of which *Humphry Clinker* (1771) is best, ramble over land and sea in eighteenth-century picaresque fashion. The philosopher David Hume (1711–1776) and the economist Adam Smith (1723–1790) rank with the most influential thinkers of recent centuries. Lives of Johnson by James Boswell (1740–1795) and Scott by John Gibson Lockhart (1794–1854) are arguably the best biographies in English, at least before the twentieth century. Thomas Carlyle (1795–1881) and Thomas Babington Macaulay (1800–1859), Scots active in England, were among the great nineteenth-century historians. Lord Byron (1788–1824) was half Scottish and attended grammar school in Aberdeen, but belongs primarily to the English poetic tradition.

Sir Walter Scott (1771–1832) was one of the creative giants of the nineteenth century. A great antiquary and editor, in *Minstrelsy of the Scottish Border* (1802) he preserved many Border ballads in the form now most familiar. Turning to the creation of verse, he earned worldwide fame depicting Scotland as a country of splendid scenery, romantic traditions, and high adventure in long works including *The Lay of the Last Minstrel* (1805), *Marmion* (1808), and *The Lady of the Lake* (1810). As a writer of fiction, he changed the history of the novel with a series of brilliant combinations of history, realism, romance, and significant themes in works that ranged from his own time backward into the Middle Ages and from Scotland through England and France into the Holy Land. *Waverley* (1814), a story of the Jacobite uprising of 1745, came first and set the pattern for the rest. *The Heart of Midlothian* (1818) is perhaps most evenly successful.

Most important as a novelist after Scott is Robert Louis Stevenson (1850–1894), whose *Kidnapped* (1886) and *The Master of Ballantrae* (1889) are not much inferior to the better-known *Treasure Island* (1883). His *Dr. Jekyll and Mr. Hyde* (1886) is a classic tale of a double. John Galt (1779–1839), a contemporary of Scott's, depicted Scottish country life in *Annals of the Parish* (1821) and Scottish immigrants in Canada and upstate New York in *Lawrie Todd* (1830) and *Bogle Corbet* (1831). James Hogg (1770–1835), the "Ettrick Shepherd," poet and friend of Scott, is most remembered today for the disturbing psychology of his novel *The Private Memoirs and Confessions of a Justified Sinner* (1824). The fantasies of George MacDonald (1824–1905), especially *At the Back of the North Wind* (1870) and *Lilith* (1895) are powerfully evocative in their dreamlike and nightmarish reality. So, too, is *A Voyage to Arcturus* (1920), by David Lindsay (1878–1945). John Buchan (1875–1940), novelist and civil servant who became governor general of Canada, wrote many novels, among them the thrillers *The Thirty-Nine Steps* (1915) and *Greenmantle* (1916). Lewis Grassic Gibbon, pseudonym for James Leslie Mitchell (1901–1935), combined Scots vernacular and English in a haunting trilogy, *A Scots Quair* (1932–1934). Muriel Spark (1918–   ) fictionalized life in a Scottish girls' school in *The Prime of Miss Jean Brodie* (1961).

There have been few Scottish dramatists. J. M. Barrie (1860–1937) is remembered chiefly for the plays *The Admirable Crichton* (1902) and *Peter Pan* (1903). Among twentieth-century Scottish poets writing in English, Edwin Muir (1887–1959) stands apart as challenging MacDiarmid for supremacy, with poems such as "The Horses" and "The Brothers."

References

Alan Bold, **Modern Scottish Literature** (1983).
Maurice Lindsay, **History of Scottish Literature** (1977).
Trevor Royle, **The Macmillan Companion to Scottish Literature** (1983).

Screenplay.   A script for a film, a *scenario*.

Scriblerus Club.   A club formed to satirize "all false taste in learning," proposed by Pope and joined by Swift, John Arbuthnot, John Gay, Thomas Parnell, and Robert Harley, the prime minister and earl of Oxford. It existed only from February to June 1714, but eventually produced *Memoirs of the Extraordinary Life, Works, and Discoveries of Martinus Scriblerus*, published in the second volume of Pope's prose *Works* (1741), as the work of Pope and Arbuthnot, who had been the principal writer and inventor of satiric deviltry. Pope served as gatherer and polisher of the papers from Arbuthnot, who had died in 1735. Three of the eighteenth century's greatest works sprang from the Scriblerian matrix: Swift's *Gulliver's Travels* (1726), Gay's *Beggar's Opera* (1728), Pope's *Dunciad* (1728, 1742, 1743).

Scriptural Drama.   See MYSTERY PLAY.

Secondary Stress.   A stress lighter than the major stress, as in the second foot below:

The kíng | sits ín | Dum fér- | ling Tówn |

See METER; SCANSION.

Second Law of Thermodynamics.   See ENTROPY.

Self-Effacing Author.   A writer whose subjective presence in a work of FICTION has been effectively eliminated. The term describes especially those late nineteenth- and twentieth-century novelists and short story writers who have worked at eliminating commentary that can be ascribed to the author, providing the reader a direct and immediate relationship to the speeches, thoughts, and actions of the CHARACTERS. See NARRATIVE PERSPECTIVE.

Semantics.   The study of the way language signals meanings and their changes, including the way words relate to what they signify, the way they relate to each other (syntax), the way they relate to general meanings (symbolic logic), and the way they relate to those who interpret them.

Semiotics.   In anthropology, sociology, and linguistics, the study of signs, including words, other sounds, gestures, facial expressions, music, pictures, and other signals used in communication between people, between people and animals, between animals, and so on. As a form of SEMANTICS, semiotics consists of (1) syntactics—how syntax signals meaning, (2) semantics—how words signal meanings, and (3) pragmatics—how users and their words relate in meaning.

Senecan Style.   The highly rhetorical, hyperbolic style of Seneca (c. 4 B.C.–A.D. 65) in his tragedies, detailed in description, exaggerated in comparisons, yet aphoristic and epigrammatic with much STICHO-MYTHIA turned sharply line for line. The Senecan style is considered the opposite of Cicero's suave and balanced prose; its iambic pentameter verse was very influential in both English and French tragedies of the sixteenth and seventeenth centuries.

Senecan Tragedy.   The bloody and bombastic tragedies of revenge inspired by Seneca's nine closet dramas, which had been discovered in Italy in the mid-sixteenth century and soon translated into English. Seneca revised Euripides, and some Aeschylus and Sophocles, into windy and gory descriptions of horror and meditative soliloquys, interspersed with line for line stichomythic dialogue, and a thrilling ghost or witch. Sackville and Norton's *Gorboduc* (1561), the first English tragedy, imitates Seneca, and the line passes through Kyd's *Spanish Tragedy* (c. 1586) and on to *Hamlet* (1602). The countess of Pembroke promoted plays closer to Seneca by copying the French versions of Robert Garnier–Kyd's translation of Garnier's *Cornelie* as *Cornelia* (1594), Samuel Daniel's *Tragedy of Cleopatra* and *Philotas* (1605).

Sensibility. Sensitive feeling, emotion. The term arose early in the eighteenth century to denote the tender undercurrent of feeling in the NEOCLASSICAL PERIOD and continued through Jane Austen's *Sense and Sensibility* (1811)—with the reasonable Elinor and the emotional Marianne—to the present. T. S. Eliot believed that in the seventeenth century "a dissociation of sensibility set in, from which we have never recovered," aggravated by the powerful influence of Dryden and Milton. Donne and other writers of METAPHYSICAL POETRY had "a direct sensuous apprehension of thought, or recreation of thought into feeling." But early in the eighteenth century, Eliot said, thought became dissociated from feeling. Poets "thought and felt by fits, unbalanced," and "the feeling, the sensibility becomes crude and sentimental" ("The Metaphysical Poets," 1921).

Oddly, sensibility, valuing benevolence and feeling, arose from rational DEISM, which rendered divinity remote and threw individuals back on their feelings for guidance, with sensitivity the sign of goodness. Altamont, in Nicholas Rowe's tremendously influential *The Fair Penitent* (1703)—staged through most of the century—was an early example: Altamont faints three times from emotion, exhibiting his sensibility and excellence. The earl of Shaftesbury's *Characteristics of Men, Manners, Opinions, Times* (1711), countering Hobbes's theory of humankind's essential selfishness by postulating innate "affections" for virtue, beauty, and the good of oneself and society, considerably stimulated the valuing of sensibility. See DISSOCIATION OF SENSIBILITY; SENTIMENTALISM; SENTIMENTAL NOVEL.

Sensuous and **Sensual.** *Sensuous* writing is heavy with IMAGERY. Its appeal is to the perceptions of the five senses: sight, hearing, touch, smell, and taste. The term *sensual*, which also describes writing heavy with imagery, generally suggests a greater concern for gratification of the senses, especially the appetites for sex, food, and drink. See IMAGE; IMAGINATION.

Sentence. In older usage, *SENTENTIA*: a pointed saying, MAXIM, or opinion, as in "Full of high sentence, but a bit obtuse" (T. S. Eliot, "The Love Song of J. Alfred Prufrock"). Now, more commonly, *sentence* refers to any series of words comprising a grammatically complete expression.

Sententia. A Latin term for a pointed saying or opinion: an APHORISM, APOTHEGM, or MAXIM. The plural is *sententiae.*

Sentimental Comedy. An early eighteenth-century embodiment on stage of the new SENTIMENTALISM; a response to the witty cynicism of

RESTORATION COMEDY demonstrating the effect of such righteous attacks as Jeremy Collier's *Short View of the Immorality and Profaneness of the English Stage* (1698). Richard Steele led the way with *The Funeral* (1701), *The Lying Lover* (1703), *The Tender Husband* (1705), and especially *The Conscious Lovers* (1722), wherein the lovers "consciously" and conscientiously quaver over everyone's feelings. A similar tenderness, with happy reward, glowed anew in Hugh Kelly's *False Delicacy* (1768), Richard Cumberland's *West Indian* (1771), and many other dramas, flourishing onward in nineteenth-century MELODRAMA well into the twentieth century. Goldsmith's *Good-natur'd Man* (1768) and *She Stoops to Conquer* (1773) made good comedy of the popular hypersensitivity while nevertheless affirming the value of tenderness.

Sentimentalism.   An indulgence in pity and tears to enjoy one's benevolence or self-pity without paying the psychic debt exacted by Aristotle's tragic terror. It arose in the eighteenth century with the belief in humanity's inherent benevolence, affirmed by the earl of Shaftesbury against Hobbes's assumption of essential selfishness and the Calvinists' of the depravity of humankind after the Fall. In 1749, the term *sentimental* was new, referring to a general quickness of perceptions, opinions, and feelings. Lady Bradshaigh wrote to Samuel Richardson:

> Pray, Sir, give me leave to ask you (I forgot it before) what, in your opinion, is the meaning of the word *sentimental*, so much in vogue amongst the polite, both in town and country? In letters and common conversation, I have asked several who make use of it, and have generally received for an answer, it is—it is—sentimental. Every thing clever and agreeable is comprehended in that word; but [I] am convinced a wrong interpretation is given, because it is impossible everything clever and agreeable can be so common as this word. I am frequently astonished to hear such a one is a *sentimental* man; we were a *sentimental* party; I have been taking a *sentimental* walk.
>
> Richardson's *Correspondence*
> *(1804)*, IV. 282

Laurence Sterne, in 1740, writing to Elizabeth Lumley, his bride of a year hence, provides the earliest specimen of the word in its present tender sense:

> One solitary plate, one knife, one fork, one glass!—I gave a thousand pensive, penetrating looks at the chair thou hadst so often graced, in those quiet and sentimental repasts—then laid down my knife and fork, and took out my handkerchief, and clapped it across my face, and wept like a child.

Sterne's *Sentimental Journey* (1768) made the meaning secure.

The sentimental movement arose early. Addison wrote of frequently visiting Westminster Abbey, "where the gloominess of the place" fills "the mind with a kind of melancholy, or rather thoughtfulness, that is not disagreeable" (*Spectator* 26, 30 March 1711). Steele's play *The Conscious Lovers* (1722) and Thomas Parnell's *Night Piece on Death* (1722), the first poem of the GRAVEYARD SCHOOL, are other early symptoms. Joseph Warton's blank-verse poem *The Enthusiast* (1744) includes most of the elements: a primitivistic nostalgia for a simpler, more innocent, more rustic past, with a pleasant, melancholy sigh. The sentimental attention to inner individual feelings forecast ROMANTICISM. See SENSIBILITY.

Sentimentality. The practice of maundering in emotion. Dickens has been accused of it, and many a tender tale of the late nineteenth and early twentieth centuries is guilty, like Kate Douglas Wiggins's famous *The Old Peabody Pew* (1907), with frontispiece of the heroine "In the old pew darning the faded cushion," or Myrtle Reed's *The Flower of Dusk* (1908). See SENTIMENTALISM.

Sentimental Novel. One reflecting the sentimental movement in the eighteenth century, indulging in pity and tears to gratify benevolence. It evolved directly from the comic novel, though Richardson's tragic *Clarissa* luxuriates in the heroine's demise. Fielding's *Tom Jones* cites warm feeling as the reward for benevolent virtue. Sterne's *Tristram Shandy* keeps the sentimental under comic wraps, but it spills out in his *Sentimental Journey* (1768). Goldsmith's *Vicar of Wakefield* (1766) begins comically but lapses into sentiment and "pleasing melancholy," enjoyed amid distress. Mackenzie's *Man of Feeling* (1771), with its hypersensitive benevolist as hero and a tear on every page, begins comically in Sterne's style, complete with comic gaps in the manuscript.

Septenary. A seven-stress line; a FOURTEENER. See METER.

Septet. A seven-line STANZA. RHYME ROYAL produces one of the few septets in English.

Septuagint. The oldest extant Greek translation of the Old Testament, originating in the third century B.C., so called (from Latin *septuaginta*, "seventy") because, according to tradition, it was completed by 70 (or 72) scholars in 72 days. Later additions include the APOCRYPHA. Its importance to biblical scholarship stems from the fact that it was translated from texts later lost. It was the version used by New Testament writers such as St. Paul, and is still in use in the Greek church. See BIBLE, TRANSLATIONS OF.

Sequel.   A literary work that explores later events in the lives of characters introduced elsewhere. *Oedipus at Colonus* is a sequel to *Oedipus Rex*. John Updike's *Rabbit Redux* and *Rabbit Is Rich* are sequels to *Rabbit, Run*.

Serenade.   An evening song, traditionally for singing outside a lady's window, or a literary imitation of one.

Serif.   In printing, a fine cross stroke at the top or bottom of a letter. *Sans serif* designates a style of printing without these lines. This type is with serifs. This is sans serif.

Servantois.   Medieval lyric in couplets on a serious subject.

Sesquipedalian.   Latin for "a foot and a half": a humorous term for polysyllabic verse or prose.

Sestet.   (1) the second unit of an Italian SONNET, following the OC-TAVE. To the *abbaabba* rhyme of the octave, the sestet adds six lines rhyming *cdecde, cdcdcd*, or in some variant pattern. (2) A STANZA of six lines. See SEXAIN.

Sestina.   A VERSE FORM from medieval France, consisting of six stanzas of six lines each, followed by a three-line ENVOY. In place of rhyme, ordinarily not used, six key words are selected for systematic repetition. In strict form, these six words, to which we may assign the order 1, 2, 3, 4, 5, 6 in the first stanza, are repeated in the second stanza, weaving back and forth from last to first to give a new order 6, 1, 5, 2, 4, 3. This pattern is repeated in stanzas 3 through 6, giving 3, 6, 4, 1, 2, 5; 5, 3, 2, 6, 1, 4; 4, 5, 1, 3, 6, 2; 2, 4, 6, 5, 3, 1. In the envoy the six key words appear again, three within the lines and three at line ends, in varying patterns, but most often 2, 4, 6 within the lines and 5, 3, 1 at the ends, repeating the order of the last stanza. Kipling's "Sestina of the Tramp-Royal" and John Ashbery's "The Painter" provide excellent examples. See STANZA; VERSE FORMS.

Setting.   (1) The time and place of a STORY or PLAY; its LOCALE. In a broader sense, setting includes also such elements as the moral, intellectual, and social MILIEU in which the characters move. (2) Also, in the theater, the scenery and props used on stage. See *MISE EN SCÈNE*.

Seven Ages of Man.   The traditional medieval division of a lifetime into seven stages, best known by the summary of the melancholy Jaques in Shakespeare's *As You Like It* (II.vii.139–166):

> All the world's a stage,
> And all the men and women merely players.
> They have their exits and their entrances,
> And one man in his time plays many parts,
> His acts being seven ages. At first, the infant,
> Mewling and puking in the nurse's arms.
> Then the whining schoolboy, with his satchel
> And shining morning face, creeping like snail
> Unwillingly to school. And then the lover,
> Sighing like furnace, with a woeful ballad
> Made to his mistress' eyebrow. Then the soldier,
> Full of strange oaths and bearded like a pard,
> Jealous in honour, sudden and quick in quarrel,
> Seeking the bubble reputation
> Even in the cannon's mouth. And then the justice,
> In fair round belly with good capon lin'd,
> With eyes severe and beard of formal cut,
> Full of wise saws and modern instances;
> And so he plays his part. The sixth age shifts
> Into the lean and slipper'd pantaloon,
> With spectacles on nose and pouch on side;
> His youthful hose, well sav'd, a world too wide
> For his shrunk shank, and his big manly voice,
> Turning again toward childish treble, pipes
> And whistles in his sound. Last scene of all,
> That ends this strange eventful history,
> Is second childishness and mere oblivion,
> Sans teeth, sans eyes, sans taste, sans everything.

Seven Cardinal Virtues. In the Middle Ages, the four Greek virtues stressed by Plato, sometimes called *natural virtues*—wisdom (or prudence), courage (or fortitude), temperance, and justice—and also three *theological virtues* derived from Christian teaching—faith, hope, and charity (or love).

Seven Deadly Sins. In the Middle Ages, pride, envy, wrath, sloth, avarice, gluttony, and lust. Pride was the worst, the sin that led to Satan's downfall.

Seven Liberal Arts. The subjects studied in medieval universities, consisting of the *trivium* (grammar, logic, and rhetoric), for the B.A., and the *quadrivium* (arithmetic, geometry, astronomy, and music), for the M.A.

Sexain. A STANZA of six lines. Examples include the BURNS STANZA, the VENUS AND ADONIS STANZA, the first six stanzas of a SESTINA, and the SESTET of an Italian SONNET. A sexain is frequently made by combining a QUATRAIN and a COUPLET, as in the Venus and Adonis stanza, in iambic pentameter, and in the following poems, all in LONG METER: Thomas Campion's "There is a Garden in Her Face," Wordsworth's "I Wandered Lonely as a Cloud," Matthew Arnold's "To Marguerite," and W. D. Snodgrass's "April Inventory."

Shakespearean Sonnet (or **English Sonnet**). A SONNET in three quatrains and a COUPLET, rhyming *abab cdcd efef gg*. See QUATRAIN.

Shanty (or **Chantey**). Perhaps derived from French *chantez*, "to sing": a sailor's work song, to accompany such tasks as hoisting sails or hauling in the anchor. Most shanties are from the nineteenth century, but "Haul on the Bowline" dates from Tudor times. Collections include W. M. Doerflinger, *Shantymen and Shantyboys* (1951) and Stan Hugill, *Shanties from the Seven Seas* (1961). See FOLK SONG.

Shaped Poem. English for Latin *carmen figuratum*, a poem constructed so that its shape on a page presents a picture of its subject. Examples include George Herbert's "The Altar" and "Easter Wings" (1633) and John Hollander's "Swan and Shadow" (1969). See CONCRETE POETRY.

Short Couplet. An iambic tetrameter COUPLET. See METER.

Short Meter. A STANZA (abbreviated S. M. in hymn books) shortening the first line of COMMON METER to make a 3/3/4/3 stress pattern in iambic METER. Examples include Dickinson's "The Heart Asks Pleasure—First," and Hardy's "I Look into My Glass," which begins:

> I look into my glass,
> And view my wasting skin,
> And say, "Would God it came to pass
> My heart had shrunk as thin!"

See POULTER'S MEASURE.

Short Story. A fictional prose narrative read comfortably in a single sitting. In length, it falls between the short short story of under 2,000 words and the NOVELETTE of over 15,000. Although any brief narrative is by some definitions a short story, in common literary usage the term refers most often to fictions of the nineteenth and twentieth centuries.

Like other forms of FICTION, the short story is an imaginative construction, shaping the elements of experience into an artful composition. Often it imitates the texture of ordinary life close to home, as in the stories of Anton Chekhov, Katherine Mansfield, John Cheever, or John Updike. Nineteenth-century American LOCAL COLOR stories exploited an interest in the regional differences of a large country, as in the works of Bret Harte, George Washington Cable, and Sarah Orne Jewett. In the twentieth century, a similar interest continues, more often transcending time and place, as in the stories of William Faulkner and Flannery O'Connor. At times, the material of short stories remains so close to reality as to require few changes to pass as the truth telling of autobiography, as in F. Scott Fitzgerald's "Babylon Revisited." At other times, the imitation is of life exotic or adventurous, as in many of the stories of Rudyard Kipling or Ernest Hemingway. Sometimes the imaginative basis is less mimetic, or imitative, than fanciful or self-reflexive, as in the stories of Edgar Allan Poe, Jorge Luis Borges, Stanislaw Lem, or Ursula Le Guin.

Characteristically close to poetry and drama, but distinct from them, the short story may be defined as a brief narrative in prose. Its prose distinguishes it from the stories told in the popular BALLAD and in literary ballads like *The Rime of the Ancient Mariner*, with their heavily stylized verse narration. Because it is narrated, not acted, it differs from the short play. Yet both distinctions require qualification. Early verse stories such as Chaucer's bawdy, comic "Miller's Tale" resemble modern short stories in much apart from the verse. Poets occasionally still remind us of this ancient closeness, trying to tell short stories in verse, as in Robinson Jeffers's "Roan Stallion." The dramatic method of writing fiction (see NARRATIVE PERSPECTIVE) produces short stories that read like plays and are easily adapted to the stage. Indeed, the length of the short story fosters both poetic and dramatic effects, driving the writer toward the heavy use of FIGURATIVE LANGUAGE and the reliance on sound and RHYTHM characteristic of poetry and the heightened reality and dramatic focus characteristic of the role playing of the stage.

The short story is narrative. It tells a story: there is general agreement on this point, but disagreement as to what constitutes a story. In earlier times, a story was a series of events, with a beginning, middle, and end: this happened, and then that happened, and the result was such-and-such. Stories thus broadly defined are older than the oldest human records and appear quite early in the histories of the world's literatures. The purpose is the ancient fictional purpose of information and delight. In such forms as ANECDOTE, TALE, PARABLE, EPIC, and ROMANCE, earlier short fictions artfully combined incidents in narrative sequence. Some writers of modern short stories have stressed incidents as well, but others have so varied the older patterns, and so stressed elements other than events, that the modern short story stands apart as a distinctive genre.

Egyptian papyri from 3000 B.C. record the tale telling of the sons of Cheops. The Bible is a repository of ancient stories: Noah, Job, the parables of Christ. Epics such as the *Odyssey* string separate stories on a loose biographical thread. The Arab world, India, China, and Japan all have their collections of early stories. In the West, the FRAME NARRATIVE such as *The Decameron* or *The Canterbury Tales* contains traditional materials reshaped by the inspiration of individual genius. The native hero legends of North America and Africa were preserved through generations of ORAL TRANSMISSION until collected and printed. All these stories interpret humanity to itself, serving as models to the modern short story, which in our time serves the same function.

The rise of literacy, expansion of printing, and growth of the middle class gave rise to the modern short story, which depends upon an extensive reading public with the leisure to pursue its interest in varieties of experience and expression. In the eighteenth century, the episodic chapters in the typical NOVEL and the brief narratives in journalistic ventures like *The Spectator* helped to point the way. In the nineteenth century, the form burst into flower in the years between Irving and Poe. Washington Irving blended a lucid style, folk materials, evocative natural settings, perceptive character analysis, and skillfully developed plots in "Rip Van Winkle" and "The Legend of Sleepy Hollow." Sir Walter Scott's "Wandering Willie's Tale" (from *Redgauntlet*) exploited a contemporary interest in legends, and his "Two Drovers" explored the influence of place and cultural bias on human affairs in a masterly account of bloody conflict between friends. Nathaniel Hawthorne's *Twice-Told Tales* and Edgar Allan Poe's *Tales of the Grotesque and Arabesque* introduced new dimensions of verbal craftsmanship and allegoric and symbolic intensity. After this initial flowering, the form flourished throughout the nineteenth century, with some of the major writers appearing in continental Europe: Prosper Merimée, Guy de Maupassant, and Anton Chekhov. In the late nineteenth century, a concern for plot began to give way to a concern for character, in the stories of Chekhov and Henry James, especially, that has continued important in the work of many later writers, who seem less interested in an event than in its effect on a personality.

In the twentieth century, the short story and novel have been the dominant forms of literary expression. The dramatic growth of magazines, from those catering to the mass market in the center to the LITTLE MAGAZINES on one hand and the PULP MAGAZINES on the other, has provided support to short story writers of all kinds. Nationalistic literary movements such as the IRISH RENAISSANCE have given impetus to the short story also, both in older nations and in newly emergent ones. Subgenres, most with roots in the nineteenth century, have proliferated: the DETECTIVE STORY, WESTERN, ADVENTURE STORY, "true" romance, tale of terror, SCIENCE FICTION, FANTASY. Writers most widely admired for their literary quality have usually written realistic fiction, accurately portraying their own times and places, emphasizing either plot or character, with frequently a sharp focus on a moment of illumination or EPIPHANY, as in James Joyce's "Araby." SYMBOL and ALLEGORY have also proved important, however, as in the stories of Franz Kafka and, more recently, in the fantastic fictions of writers like Borges and Donald Barthelme. In some of the greatest stories, REALISM and symbol are closely wedded: Joyce's "The Dead," Katherine Mansfield's "Bliss." See POPULAR LITERATURE.

Sigmatism. From Greek *sigma*, the letter *s*: heavy use of the letter *s*, sometimes combined with the hissing sounds of other sibilants (*sh*, *z*, *zh*, *ch*, *j*): "When to the sessions of sweet silent thought" (Shakespeare, Sonnet 30); "All shod with steel, / We hissed along the polished ice in games" (Wordsworth, *The Prelude*).

Signature. In printing, the unit (or GATHERING) formed by one printed sheet after it has been folded to form the pages of a book. In one common book size, OCTAVO, each signature contains 8 leaves (16 pages). The term *signature* also refers to the printer's mark that often appears at the bottom of the first page of each signature, helping to keep each in its proper order in the book. See BOOK SIZES.

Signified, Signifier. In structural LINGUISTICS, the *signified* is the idea in mind when a word is used, an entity separate from the *signifier*, the word itself. Ferdinand de Saussure (1857–1913) originated the terms in *Course in General Linguistics*, lectures at the University of Geneva, 1906–1907, 1908–1909, 1910–1911, published posthumously by his students in 1915. See CONNOTATION; DENOTATION; STRUCTURALISM.

Silver Age. (1) The second of the AGES OF THE WORLD. (2) The period of Latin literature from A.D. 14 to 180, including Martial, Tacitus, Juvenal, and Pliny the Younger.

Silver Fork School.   Disparaging name applied to nineteeth-century English writers of popular novels on the life of the aristocracy. Among those who fall at least at times into this class are Frances Trollope, Catherine Gore, Theodore Edward Hook, Bulwer-Lytton, and Disraeli.

Simile.   A METAPHOR containing *like, as,* or *as if*:

> She swims *like* a fish.
> She swims *as* a fish swims.
> She swims *as if* she were a fish.

Sirventes.   A medieval Provençal poem of personal or political invective or satire. See TROUBADOUR.

Situation.   The position with respect to others and to the past and future of one or more CHARACTERS at a given point within a PLOT— as, for example, Laura's situation as *The Glass Menagerie* ends; or the situation in *Hamlet* that prompts the soliloquy "To be or not to be. . . ." See DRAMATIC SITUATION.

Sixteenmo.   (Abbreviated 16mo, 16°): a book made from sheets folded to give signatures of 16 leaves (32 pages). See BOOK SIZES; SIGNATURE.

Sixty-fourmo.   (Abbreviated 64mo, 64°): a book made from sheets folded to give signatures of 64 leaves (128 pages). See BOOK SIZES; SIGNATURE.

Skald (or Scald).   A Scandinavian court poet of the ninth through eleventh centuries who sang of the deeds of kings and chieftains, much like the Celtic BARD and Anglo-Saxon SCOP.

Skeltonics.   The poetry of John Skelton (c. 1460–1529) and his imitators. An intentional doggerel (clumsy, trivial verse) of strongly stressed, usually two-beat, irregular lines rhymed in two's, three's, and four's with occasional unrhymed lines. Skelton derived his verse from medieval Latin student doggerel to satirize the times and the new humanistic learning.

> And if ye stand in doubt
> Who brought this rime about,
> My name is Colin Clout.
> I purpose to shake out
> All my cunning bag. . . .

Sketch. (1) An unpretentious work in prose, a brief or offhand description, narration, or ESSAY. Sometimes such a work attains considerable polish, as in Washington Irving's *Sketch Book* and Charles Dickens's *Sketches by Boz*. (2) A short dramatic work; a SKIT.

Skit. A short dramatic work, often a PARODY or SATIRE, frequently presented as part of a longer entertainment like a musical REVUE or stage or television variety show.

Slack Syllable. Unstressed syllable.

Slang. The special vocabulary of a class or group of people (as, for example, truck drivers, jazz musicians, salespeople, drug dealers), generally considered substandard, low, or offensive when measured against formal, educated usage. At least some slang, however, is familiar to all, especially during the periods when it is in vogue, and is used by even the highly educated in conversation, and sometimes in writing, for its humor or pointedness. Frequently faddish (*grody to the max*) and ephemeral, slang is also sometimes very long-lived, and sometimes passes into standard usage (*movie*). English is rich in slang, from single words (*bughouse, grifter, groovy, hassle, heist, sloshed, vamoose*), through miscellaneous phrases (*doing her thing, three sheets in the wind, drunk as a fiddler's bitch*), to the COCKNEY *rhyming slang* recorded in literature in books like George Orwell's *Down and Out in Paris and London* (*hit or miss* for *kiss*; *plates of meat* for *feet*). See CANT; COLLOQUIALISM; DIALECT; JARGON.

References

H. L. Mencken, **The American Language** (3 vols., 1936–1948).
Eric Partridge, **A Dictionary of Slang and Unconventional English,** 8th ed. (2 vols., forthcoming).

Slant Rhyme. Also called *half, approximate, imperfect, near, off, oblique.* It provides an approximation of the sound: *up, step; peer, pare.* See RHYME.

Slapstick. Loud farcical comedy often featuring pies thrown in the face and much whacking, originally with a double paddle that made the whack louder.

Slave Narrative. Autobiographical descriptions by escaped slaves, appearing from 1830 to 1860 as part of the Abolition movement, most notably *A Narrative of the Life of Frederick Douglass: An American Slave* (1845). See AFRO-AMERICAN LITERATURE.

Slice of Life. The English translation of *tranche de vie*, describing the NATURALISM (2) of Zola and other French novelists.

Slick Magazine. A magazine like *The Saturday Evening Post, The Ladies' Home Journal,* or *Collier's,* mass-circulated cheaply before World War II because of extensive advertising, so called because it was printed on glossy, or "slick," paper.

Social Drama. DRAMA stressing the social world, with emphasis on the individual's place in the society of his or her time. Examples include Ibsen's *Enemy of the People,* Strindberg's *Miss Julie,* Chekhov's *Cherry Orchard,* and Miller's *Death of a Salesman.*

Socialist Realism. REALISM in the service of MARXISM, placing the social effect above artistic considerations.

Society Verse. See *VERS DE SOCIÉTÉ* and LIGHT VERSE.

Sock. (1) A light low-heeled shoe worn by actors in Greek and Roman comedy, matching their low status as slaves and bumpkins. See BUSKIN. (2) A METONYMY for comedy itself.

Socratic. Describing a method of eliciting a logical or interpretive point by questions, feigning ignorance as Socrates does in Plato's *Dialogues.* The stance is called Socratic irony.

Solecism. A nonstandard usage or grammatical mistake. See BARBARISM.

Soliloquy. "Talking alone" (from Latin *solus*) in a play, wherein the character reveals his or her thoughts and, frequently, informs the audience of attitudes and background.

Solution. See CATASTROPHE; DENOUEMENT.

Song. A LYRIC poem, especially one written for music. Examples of songs are those in Shakespeare's plays, or Jonson's "Drink to Me Only with Thine Eyes," conceived with music in mind.

Sonnet. A verse form of fourteen lines, in English characteristically in iambic pentameter and most often in one of two rhyme schemes: the *Italian* (or *Petrarchan*) or *Shakespearean* (or *English*). An *Italian sonnet* is composed of an OCTAVE, rhyming *abbaabba,* and a SESTET, rhyming *cdecde* or *cdcdcd,* or in some variant pattern, but with no closing COUPLET. A *Shakespearean sonnet* has three quatrains and a couplet, and rhymes *abab cdcd efef gg.* In both types, the content tends to follow the formal outline suggested by rhyme linkage, giving two divisions to the thought of an Italian sonnet and four to a Shakespearean one. The Italian sonnet develops an idea through eight lines and then pauses, creating a turn or VOLTA, before the concluding six. A Shakespearean sonnet frequently introduces a subject in the first quatrain, expands it in the second, and once more in the third, and concludes in the couplet. Both patterns of development are subject to variation, however, as when an Italian sonnet does not observe the volta or a Shakespearean sonnet treats the first two quatrains together in thought, like an octave.

Named variations on the sonnet include the Spenserian and Miltonic. A *Spenserian sonnet* (or *link sonnet*) employs three quatrains linked by rhyme, followed by a couplet: *abab bcbc cdcd ee*. A *Miltonic sonnet* is simply an Italian sonnet that eliminates the pause between octave and sestet, as in "On His Blindness." Other variations include blendings of the two forms, as in Yeats's "Leda and the Swan" (two Shakespearean quatrains followed by an Italian sestet) and Frost's "Design" (an Italian octave followed by a Shakespearean quatrain and couplet). Wordsworth frequently employed an easier version of the Italian octave, changing it to *abbaacca*, as in "Mutability."

Although usually in iambic pentameter in English (iambic hexameter in French), sonnets can be found in other meters. Sidney's "Loving in Truth," the first sonnet in *Astrophel and Stella*, is in hexameter. In "Spelt from Sibyl's Leaves" Gerard Manley Hopkins expanded each line to eight feet of SPRUNG RHYTHM, but kept an Italian rhyme scheme. See CROWN OF SONNETS; CURTAL SONNET; METER; QUATORZAIN; QUATRAIN; RHYME SCHEME; SONNET SEQUENCE; VERSE FORMS.

Sonnet Sequence.   A group of sonnets thematically unified to create a longer work, although generally, unlike the STANZA, each sonnet so connected can also be read as a meaningful separate unit. Sonnet sequences in English include Sidney's *Astrophel and Stella*, Spenser's *Amoretti*, Shakespeare's sonnets, Donne's *Holy Sonnets*, Elizabeth Barrett Browning's *Sonnets from the Portuguese*, Longfellow's *Divina Commedia*, and Edna St. Vincent Millay's *Fatal Interview*.

Sons of Ben.   Followers of Ben Jonson, particularly the playwrights Francis Beaumont, John Fletcher, Philip Massinger, Nathan Field, Richard Brome, and James Shirley. The designation overlaps with the TRIBE OF BEN, applied to his lyrical followers.

Sound-Over. In film, the bridging from one scene to the next by dialogue or other sound. See VOICE-OVER.

Source. The model or inspiration for a literary work, like Bandello's romance and Arthur Brooke's poem *The Tragicall Historye of Romeus and Juliet* (1562) behind Shakespeare's *Romeo and Juliet*. These are *primary sources*. A *secondary source* would be someone telling Shakespeare about the story in Bandello and Brooke.

Spasmodic School. A group of overwrought and ranting poets of the 1850s: Sydney Dobell, Alexander Smith, P. J. Bailey, George Gilfillan, and others. W. E. Aytoun parodied them in *Firmilian: A Spasmodic Tragedy* (1854), whence the name. The early Robert Browning, Elizabeth Barrett Browning, and Tennyson's *Maud* were thought "spasmodic."

Spatial Form. Joseph Frank's term for what he sees as a major shift in literary perception in the twentieth century. T. S. Eliot, Pound, Proust, Joyce, and Djuna Barnes, he says, "ideally intend the reader to apprehend their work spatially, in a moment of time, rather than as a sequence" ("Spatial Form in Modern Literature," *Sewanee Review* [Spring 1945], expanded as the first chapter in his *Widening Gyre: Crisis and Mastery in Modern Literature*, 1963).

Spectacle. A grand and lavish scene, like those in the films of Cecil B. DeMille. The large theaters and the star system of the nineteenth century invited spectacles in staging. Scenes in novels, like the glittering ball before Waterloo in Thackeray's *Vanity Fair*, are sometimes called spectacles. Aristotle mentions spectacle in his *Poetics*, considering it the least artistic of the six elements of a tragedy (the others are plot, character, thought, diction, and song).

Spenserian Sonnet (or **Link Sonnet**). A SONNET in three quatrains linked by rhyme, followed by a COUPLET: *abab bcbc cdcd ee* (see QUATRAIN).

Spenserian Stanza. The STANZA invented by Edmund Spenser for *The Faerie Queene:* nine lines in iambic METER, with the first eight in pentameter and the ninth in hexameter (an alexandrine), rhyming *ababbcbcc*. The form is remarkable for its flexibility, the interwoven rhymes providing a pattern short enough for lyric expression or for the stages of a longer narrative movement, and long enough for thoughtful commentary, with the added length of the last line allowing extra room for summary. Burns's "The Cotter's Saturday Night," Byron's *Childe*

Harold's Pilgrimage, and Shelley's *Adonais* all use this stanza, shown here in the opening of Keats's "The Eve of St. Agnes":

> St. Agnes's Eve—Ah, bitter chill it was!
> The owl, for all his feathers, was a-cold;
> The hare limp'd trembling through the frozen grass,
> And silent was the flock in woolly fold:
> Numb were the Beadsman's fingers, while he told
> His rosary, and while his frosted breath,
> Like pious incense from a censer old,
> Seem'd taking flight for heaven, without a death,
> Past the sweet Virgin's picture, while his prayer he saith.

Spondee.   A metrical foot of two long, or stressed, syllables: $-\ -$. See METER.

Spoonerism.   An amusingly inadvertent exchange of sounds, usually initial: *a blushing crow* for "a crushing blow"; *a half-warmed fish* for "a half-formed wish." It was named after the Rev. William Archibald Spooner (1844–1930), warden of New College, Oxford, notorious for such nervous slips. Many jokes depend on intentional spoonerisms.

Sprung Rhythm.   Gerard Manley Hopkins's term to describe his variations of iambic METER to avoid the "same and tame." His feet, he said, vary from one to four syllables, with one stress per foot, on the first syllable. Hence "four sorts of feet, a monosyllable and the so-called accentual Trochee, Dactyl, and the First Paeon" ($-\ |\ -\ \smile\ |\ -\ \smile\ \smile\ |\ -\ \smile\ \smile\ \smile$). Hopkins said that it is "the most natural of things." But his description overlooks how much of the basic iambic framework remains in his sonnets:

I caught | this morn- | ing morn- | ing's min- | ion, king- |

dom of day- | light's dau- | phin, dap- | ple-dawn- | drawn Fal- | con, in |

his rid-ing |

His scheme is ambivalent, for dapple-dawn-drawn | Falcon | also scans as a First Paeon and Trochee.

Standard Edition.   An authoritative edition of the works of a prominent writer, frequently in one volume and continuing year after year as the basic textbook. Examples include the Cambridge Editions of "Complete Poetical Works"—Browning (1895), Spenser (1908), Chaucer (1933)—published by Houghton Mifflin Company, at the Riverside

Press, Cambridge, Massachusetts, and the competing "Oxford Standard Editions" by the Oxford University Press. Some of these editions also remain *definitive*: established as the text closest to the author's original product and most inclusive in canon, through exhaustive textual collation and historical research, not yet superseded by subsequent discoveries.

Stanislavsky Method. An acting method taught by the Russian director, actor, and teacher Konstantin Stanislavsky (Konstantin Sergeyevich Alekseyev, 1863–1938), widely influential on modern schools of acting, notably in the Actor's Studio, New York City. Stanislavsky stressed emotional fidelity and deep identification with a character followed by natural movements and voice rather than accurate representation of a historical period. He also stressed ensemble acting and total effect of all details. With Vladimir Nemirovich-Danchenko, he founded the Moscow Art Theater in 1898, producing a number of Chekhov's plays. His *An Actor Prepares* (translated 1936), *Building a Character* (translated 1950), and *Creating a Role* (translated 1961) are basic to much modern acting.

Stanza. A term derived from an Italian word for "room" or "stopping place" and used, loosely, to designate any grouping of lines in a separate unit in a poem: a VERSE PARAGRAPH. More strictly, a stanza is a grouping of a prescribed number of lines in a given METER, usually with a particular RHYME SCHEME, repeated as a unit of structure. Poems in stanzas provide an instance of the aesthetic pleasure in repetition with a difference that also underlies the metrical and rhyming elements of poetry; as structural units, stanzas stand apart like rooms in the house of the poem, each worthy of separate consideration, but each bound structurally to the whole. From this twin interest, in the small and the large, comes an artistic tension missing in nonstanzaic poems, which elicit a different aesthetic response.

Common names for stanzas are listed below, by line length. For definitions and examples, see the individual headings.

4 lines: ALCAIC STROPHE; BALLAD STANZA; CAROL STANZA; COMMON METER; ELEGIAC STANZA; HEROIC QUATRAIN; "IN MEMORIAM" STANZA; LONG METER; QUATRAIN; RUBÁIYÁT STANZA; SAPPHICS; SHORT METER.

5 lines: CINQUAIN; QUINTAIN.

6 lines:	BURNS STANZA; SEXAIN; TAIL-RHYME; VENUS AND ADONIS STANZA.
7 lines:	RHYME ROYAL.
8 lines:	OCTAVE; OTTAVA RIMA.
9 lines:	SPENSERIAN STANZA.
14 lines:	QUATORZAIN.

The COUPLET and the TERCET, considered by some too short to qualify as stanzas, are sometimes printed as separate units and used by poets in ways that seem to qualify them as stanzas. An ENVOY is a stanza defined by its position and function at the end of a poem.

Stave. Archaic or poetic synonym for *stanza,* particularly in songs (from the musical *staff*).

Stereotype. A character representing generalized racial or social traits repeated as typical from work to work, with no individualizing traits (from the solid metal mold used to mass-produce duplicates of printer's type). See TYPE CHARACTERS.

-Stich. A line of poetry (Greek *stikhos*), principally in *hemistich,* a half-line, and *distich,* a couplet.

Stichomythia. Dialogue in alternate lines, favored in Greek tragedy and by Seneca and his imitators among the Elizabethans—including Shakespeare—and Corneille (1606–1684) and Racine (1639–1699) in France:

> *Hamlet:* Now, mother, what's the matter?
> *Queen:* Hamlet, thou hast thy father much offended.
> *Hamlet:* Mother, you have my father much offended.
> *Queen:* Come, come, you answer with an idle tongue.
> *Hamlet:* Go, go, you question with a wicked tongue.
> *Queen:* Why, how now, Hamlet?
> *Hamlet:*   What's the matter now?
> *Queen:* Have you forgot me?
> *Hamlet:*   No, by the rood not so!
> You are the Queen. . . .
>
> *III.iv.8–15*

Stock Characters. Familiar types repeated in literature to become the stock in trade of a particular GENRE, like the strong, silent HERO of the WESTERN or the hard-boiled hero of the DETECTIVE STORY. Some few stock characters appear in many guises in different times and

places, as, for example, the *alazon*, or bragging imposter. See CHAR-
ACTERS.

Stock Response.   An uncritical response aroused by considerations
external to a literary work. For example, a movie audience may ap-
plaud the waving of a flag or the appearance of the cavalry on the
horizon, without considering whether in this particular film the flag or
the cavalry deserves applause.

Stock Situation.   A recurrent situation in literature. The love triangle
and confusions based on mistaken identity are stock situations frequently repeated in different types of literature. Some stock situations
belong to a particular GENRE, as, for example, in a WESTERN, a stock
situation is the enmity between homesteaders and cattle ranchers. See
ARCHETYPE.

Stoicism.   (1) Generally, fortitude, repression of feeling, indifference
to pleasure or pain. (2) Specifically, the philosophy of the Stoics, originally followers of Zeno of Citium (c. 334 – c. 262 B.C.), who earned
their name from the Stoa Poecile ("painted porch") in Athens, where
they gathered for lectures and discussion. In Stoic philosophy, logic
teaches that all knowledge derives from sense perceptions; physics
teaches that all reality is material. Force (or God) pervades all things,
shaping both material reality and the reason and soul of animate existence. Both logic and physics subserve ethics, where virtue is the highest good, pursued in congruence with an understanding derived from
logical and physical necessity. The virtuous learn "to live consistently
with nature." Cultivating endurance and self-control, they accept necessity, restraining passions such as joy and grief that place them in
conflict with nature's dictates.
     Among greek philosophies, Stoicism was especially attractive to the
Romans, as seen in the works or teachings of Cicero (106 – 43 B.C.),
Seneca (c. 3 B.C.– A.D. 65), Epictetus (c. 50 – c. 138), and Marcus
Aurelius (121–180). Stoic qualities underly much imaginative literature, including, in the twentieth century, the attitudes of the typical
Hemingway hero. See CYNICISM.

Stop Frame.   See FREEZE FRAME.

Story.   From Latin *historia*, "history": a narrative, or sequence of
events. A story may be true or false, long or short, complete or incomplete, oral or written, possible or impossible. Any series of events arranged by people as a record or imitation of life, or a diversion from

it, is a story, even when no words are used, as in story paintings, PANTOMINE, or silent movies. The main story genres, or types, in literature, in FICTION, POETRY, and DRAMA, are discussed under their alphabetical entries. See ALLEGORY; AUTOBIOGRAPHY; BALLAD; BIOGRAPHY; CHRONICLE; EPIC; FABLE; FOLK TALE; HISTORY AS LITERATURE; LEGEND; MYTH; NOVEL; NOVELETTE; NOVELLA; PARABLE; POPULAR LITERATURE; ROMANCE; SHORT STORY; STORY-WITHIN-A-STORY.

Using the word in a much more specialized sense, critics sometimes distinguish a *story* from a PLOT, with the story defined as the sequence of events as they happened, or are imagined to have happened, in their proper chronological order, and the plot defined as the author's arrangement of the events of the story, which is sometimes quite different. See FABULA; *SUJET*.

Story-Within-a-Story. A story told within the framework of a longer story. Examples include Scott's "Wandering Willie's Tale" in *Redgauntlet* and Melville's "The Town Ho's Story" in *Moby-Dick*. See ENVELOPE CONSTRUCTION; FRAME NARRATIVE; *MISE EN ABYME*.

Straight Man. In a comedy team, the person who delivers the serious line that sets up the comic response.

Stream of Consciousness. The term first applied to the human mind by William James in *Principles of Psychology*, 1890, and useful since then in describing the subject matter and technique of literary works that emphasize the mental processes of characters. As METAPHOR, it suggests the mind's similarity to a stream: continually flowing, sometimes swift, sometimes slow, eddying in currents back upon itself, varying in depth, accessible on the surface, darker and more obscure below, carrying a mixed freight of natural and foreign objects picked up along its journey. Conveniently, it was introduced at a time when writers of fiction had already begun to shift their emphasis from plot to character and were beginning to explore, along with the infant psychology of the day, the inner workings of the mind.

As a description of subject matter, stream of consciousness may be applied to any fictional passage in which the author attempts a fluid representation of a character's consciousness, including sensory perceptions, conscious thought, unconscious associations, and memories. Typically, such passages reflect the disorder of the mind through a contrived disorder of presentation, avoiding logical progression and narrative unity and making much use of fragmentary sentences and fractured syntax. Other characteristics are unorthodox punctuation, heavy with dashes and ellipses; unusual capitalization; frequent italics and boldface type; or sometimes a lack of punctuation or of distinguishing typefaces altogether. Some of the most famous examples are found in Dorothy Richardson's *Pilgrimage*, Joyce's *Ulysses*, Virginia Woolf's *Mrs. Dalloway* and *To the Lighthouse*, and Faulkner's *Sound and the Fury* and *As I Lay Dying*. Joyce's *Finnegans Wake* carries the subject matter further, into the subconscious levels of sleep. Poets, too, have used the material or been influenced by it: E. E. Cummings in many of his lyrics, John Berryman in his *Dream Songs*.

Stream-of-consciousness technique involves an attempt to suit the narrative style to the contents of the mind under examination. Mimetic, or imitative, devices, springing from the subject matter, are apparent in sentence structure, punctuation, and typography. Other techniques are primarily structural, involving a respect for the chronological order of presentation of a mind in flux and a careful consideration of NARRATIVE PERSPECTIVE. Thus, in Molly Bloom's soliloquy at the end of *Ulysses*, the chronology requires Molly's mind to become increasingly incoherent as she drifts from consciousness toward sleep. In this and other works, the contents of the mind, flowing in apparently chaotic order through time, are dictated in part by such structural devices as the repetition of key images and motifs, or by the author's imposition of external stimuli to jar the mind back into a pattern it had lost. The unity of logical progression and coherent thought traditional to narration is replaced in stream-of-consciousness writing by a unity threaded on time and composed of IMAGERY, theme, and the close focus of a carefully controlled narrative perspective.

As a form of narrative perspective, stream-of-consciousness technique extends the possibilities of both first-person and third-person narration. For the third-person narrator, it extends the privileges of omniscience to include the most hidden recesses of the mind, including unconscious associations and private symbols that remain forever beyond the conscious understanding of the character involved. Joyce's *Ulysses* is an example. Within the conventions of first-person narration, stream of consciousness provides a method of telling a story conceived but unspoken, as conscious thoughts, memories, and repressed verbalizations mingle in the interior monologues of a work like Faulkner's *As I Lay Dying*. See INTERIOR MONOLOGUE.

References

Dorrit Cohn, **Transparent Minds: Narrative Modes for Presenting Consciousness in Fiction** (1978).

Melvin Friedman, **Stream of Consciousness: A Study in Literary Method** (1955).

Robert Humphrey, **Stream of Consciousness in the Modern Novel** (1954).

Stream-of-Consciousness Novel. One making significant use of STREAM OF CONSCIOUSNESS; for example, Joyce's *Ulysses*, Virginia Woolf's *To the Lighthouse*, Faulkner's *Sound and the Fury*.

Stress. In poetry, the ACCENT or emphasis given to certain syllables, indicated in SCANSION by a *macron* ($-$). In a trochee, for example, the stress falls on the first syllable: summer. See METER.

Strong Curtain. A powerful conclusion to an ACT in a PLAY. See CURTAIN.

Strophe. Part of the choral ODE in classical Greek DRAMA. The strophe was chanted by the CHORUS, as it moved in one direction. An ANTISTROPHE, chanted while the chorus reversed the first movement, and an EPODE, chanted while the chorus stood still, completed the ode. Later, the term was applied to a STANZA of any ode and to stanzaic units of irregular length in other poems, as, for example, in poems in FREE VERSE.

Structural Criticism. A general term for any approach that examines a work in terms of the relationship between its parts. See CRITICISM; DRAMATIC STRUCTURE; SEMIOTICS; STRUCTURALISM; POST-STRUCTURALISM.

Structuralism. The study of social organizations and myths, of language, and of literature as structures. Each part is significant only as it relates to others in the total structure, with nothing meaningful by itself. Social anthropologist Claude Lévi-Strauss (1908–   ) originated structuralism with his *Les Structures élémentaires de la parenté* (1949, translated as *The Elementary Structures of Kinship*, 1969), a study patterned after the structural LINGUISTICS of Ferdinand de Saussure. The other leading structuralists, like Lévi-Strauss, are French: Jacques Lacan, Michel Foucault, Roland Barthes, and Jacques Derrida. All apply the concepts of structural linguistics to their particular interests, especially Saussure's SIGNIFIER (the uttered word) and SIGNIFIED (the idea in mind). Lacan, a psychoanalyst, describes in linguistic terms how the human mind operates, signifying and expressing its unconscious and conscious concepts. The others emphasize the linguistic relativism of each experience. All stand against authority, and metaphysics, and even the central self, or ego, as archaic formulations inhibiting freedom and the plurality of the individual and momentary view. The literary text, or "lexicon of signification," in Barthes's terms, is disjunct from the author and his or her intention, as in the earlier NEW CRITICISM, and open to each reader's, and each reading's, response. Such a response emphasizes the synchronic or present-moment structure for analysis and interpretation, "deconstructing," in Derrida's term, all *a priori* assumptions to get at the fluid structures in the text itself.

References

Geoffrey H. Hartman, "Structuralism: The Anglo-American Adventure," **Yale French Review** 36–37 (1966).
Michael Land, ed., **Introduction to Structuralism** (1970).
Jean Piaget, **Structuralism** (English trans., 1970).
John Sturrock, ed., **Structuralism and Since: From Lévi-Strauss to Derrida** (1979).

Structural Linguistics.   Analysis and description of the grammatical structures of a spoken language. See LINGUISTICS.

Structure.   The construction or organization of a literary work. This word is a METAPHOR from architecture, and hence can hardly be applied to an art that moves in time, as literature does, without making allowance for its origin. Aristotle spoke of the importance of PLOT in tragedy: if we examine a tragedy or any other literary construction in terms of its plot, we soon see that we can look at the entire work simultaneously, "frozen," as it were, just as we can examine the score of a musical composition. At the same time the effect of its movement must be kept in mind, and so a structure cannot be static even if the metaphor is. According to Jean Piaget (*Structuralism*, English translation 1970), the conception of structure includes three aspects: wholeness, transformation, and self-regulation. All these aspects are characteristic of literature: the necessity for wholeness or UNITY in a literary work has been recognized since Plato; transformations are seen in the endless retellings of familiar stories and in the persistence of certain genres, or types, along with the typical characters (comedy and such comic types as the braggart, parasite, etc.); self-regulation is evident in the fact that literature is not dependent on factors external to itself. As this reference to Piaget shows, structure became the basis of the critical movement known as STRUCTURALISM, which derived largely from the work of the anthropologist Lévi-Strauss, who suggested that kinship in tribal communities corresponded to certain elements in their language. His work was influential in leading to the conception of the "linguistic model," of finding in language the key to other social structures that were also forms of communication.

The emphasis on structure in literary CRITICISM first arose in the twentieth century (although of course the conception itself had been there from the beginning) as a reaction against the emphasis on "texture" among the so-called new critics (John Crowe Ransom, Cleanth Brooks, and others—see NEW CRITICISM). For them, a text was also a *textus*, or fabric of verbal interrelationships; but such elements as the genre the literary work belonged to, the conventions it employed, the totality of the impression its ambiguities and overlapping meanings led up to, were less clearly brought out. Study of structure thus increased the critic's awareness of the importance of historical setting and social conditioning in literature.

Stuart. See ROYAL HOUSES.

Sturm und Drang. German for "storm and stress": a German literary movement of the late eighteenth century. It emphasized the freedoms of ROMANTICISM, rejecting the moderation of CLASSICISM and the RATIONALISM of the ENLIGHTENMENT, and was heavily nationalistic, as displayed in its fondness for German materials, including FOLKLORE. Among authors associated with the movement were Goethe, Schiller, and Friedrich Klinger, whose romantic drama *Wirrwarr, oder Sturm und Drang* (1776) gave it its name.

Style. An author's personal manner of expression. This may be highly individualistic or idiosyncratic, so that we understand rather quickly by the manner, without much consideration, that we have come upon a passage, say, by Faulkner or Dickens—or at least that the passage was written by someone using a Faulknerian or Dickensian style. A style may also be without telltale marks of a strong personality—the PLAIN STYLE of much good expository prose.

Style is the result of the choices an author makes, with respect not to subject matter but to its presentation. A style may be ABSTRACT or CONCRETE, heavy with CONNOTATION or essentially denotative, characterized by particular uses of FIGURATIVE LANGUAGE or largely free of them. Indeed, all elements of diction (word choice), syntax, paragraph construction, and organization are proper subjects for stylistic analysis in prose, as are, in verse, such elements as METER and RHYME.

A style is individual, personal to the writer, but it is also marked by characteristics derived from circumstances. Hence, it is possible to

speak of period styles—see RENAISSANCE; AUGUSTAN AGE; GEOR-
GIAN; of styles appropriate to a particular occasion, as formal, informal, or colloquial; of styles distinguished by their uses, as satiric, journalistic, literary, scientific. See DEMOTIC STYLE; HIERATIC STYLE;
RHETORIC; SEMIOTICS; STRUCTURALISM; POST-STRUCTURALISM.

Subjective Camera.   Film terminology used to describe a camera positioned to enhance a viewer's sense of subjective participation in a
scene, as when the camera seems to represent an actor, with the performers acting toward it as toward a person. See OBJECTIVE CAMERA;
POINT OF VIEW SHOT.

Subjectivity.   Personal or emotional expression of taste or opinion, as
opposed to OBJECTIVITY, impersonal expression. Both terms are used
to describe an author's attitude toward a work, the behavior of a CHAR-
ACTER within it, or the reaction of a reader or critic. For example,
writers may describe a love affair subjectively, communicating clearly
their personal attitudes toward it, or objectively, revealing nothing of
their feelings as authors. Similarly, a character within a novel may
react to others with passionate subjectivity, or with cold objectivity.
Subjective readers and critics stress intuitive, internally felt reactions,
distrusting intellectual analysis based on external considerations. See
ABSOLUTE; DRAMATIC METHOD; OBJECTIVE CORRELATIVE; OBJECTIVE
METHOD; RELATIVISM.

Sublime.   Latin, *sublimis* (literally, "up to the lintel"): in literature, a
quality attributed to lofty or noble ideas, grand or elevated expression,
or (the ideal of sublimity) an inspiring combination of thought and
language. In nature or art, it is a quality, as in a landscape or painting,
that inspires awe or reverence. The concept owes its long currency to
the influence of the rhetorical treatise *On the Sublime*, a work of the
first century A.D. assigned to the otherwise unknown Longinus. According to Longinus, the sublime derives from five sources, the first
two essentially natural, or innate with the writer, the last three
achieved through art: (1) mental elevation, (2) inspired passion, (3)
figurative language, (4) noble diction, (5) dignified and harmonious arrangement. The eighteenth century was much taken with ideas of sublimity; Edmund Burke's *Philosophical Inquiry into the Origin of our
Ideas of the Sublime and the Beautiful* (1757) was an important statement. In Immanuel Kant's *Critique of Judgment* (1790), beauty is finite,
the sublime associated with the infinite.

Subplot. A sequence of events subordinate to the main story in a narrative or dramatic work. Frequently a subplot involves secondary characters in actions separate from the central action, adding another dimension to the work and sometimes presenting a second illustration of, or ironic commentary on, the main theme. See PLOT.

Subscription Publication. A method of publishing by which a publisher or author accepts orders for a book not yet in print, supplying copies after publication to those who have subscribed. See VANITY PRESS.

Substitution. The insertion of another kind of foot into the regular metrical pattern; EQUIVALENCE. See METER. The opening line of Shakespeare's Sonnet 116 is a beautiful example of substitutions in his basic *iambic pentameter* line—two *trochees* and an IONIC DOUBLE FOOT:

$$\overline{\text{Let}} \; \breve{\text{me}} \mid \overline{\text{not}} \; \breve{\text{to}} \mid \breve{\text{the}} \; \overline{\text{mar}} \mid \breve{\text{riage}} \; \breve{\text{of}} \mid \overline{\text{true}} \; \overline{\text{minds}} \mid$$

Sujet. The events or motifs of a narrative considered in the order of presentation by the author, the order in which the reader encounters them. See *FABULA*; *MOTIF*.

Summary Narration. Narration of ACTION or DIALOGUE in summary fashion, without details: "The next few days passed pleasantly away"; "Further discussion led them to no conclusion." See DRAMATIC METHOD; SCENIC METHOD.

Surrealism. French, literally "above or out of realism": originally, a French literary and artistic movement of the 1920s, aimed at liberating artistic works from the control of logic and reason. André Breton issued the first surrealist manifesto in 1924, appropriating a term coined earlier by Guillaume Apollinaire. Surrealists experimented with techniques such as AUTOMATIC WRITING, sometimes under hypnosis, and were much influenced by the insights of Freudian psychology as they sought to express in print or paint the incoherent language and unfettered images of the subconscious mind. Their influence was soon worldwide. Painters who have been described as surrealistic include Giorgio de Chirico, Max Ernst, Yves Tanguy, Salvador Dali and René Magritte. In film, the works of Jean Cocteau are good examples. In literature, the influence can be seen in the works of Samuel Beckett, William Burroughs, Jean Genêt, and Eugène Ionesco. See ABSURD, THEATER OF THE; DADAISM; EXPRESSIONISM.

Suspense. A state of uncertainty, anticipation, or curiosity concerning the outcome of a PLOT or the resolution of a CONFLICT. Suspense is in some measure a part of the effect of all stories, as the reader is impelled forward by the questions "What will happen?" "When?" "In what manner?"

Suspension of Disbelief. The attitude toward literature that allows at least temporary acceptance of propositions that might be questioned in a more reflective mood. The phrase comes from Coleridge's *Biographia Literaria,* in which he wrote of "that willing suspension of disbelief for the moment, which constitutes poetic faith."

Suzhet. See SUJET.

Sweetness and Light. Beauty and intelligence. The phrase is central to Matthew Arnold's *Culture and Anarchy* (1869), where it is the title of the first chapter and the theme of much that follows, as Arnold argues for the importance to society of intellectual and aesthetic pursuits. Arnold derived the phrase from Jonathan Swift's *Battle of the Books* (1704), in which Swift compares the writers of his time to spiders spinning intricate webs from the dirt within themselves, unlike the classical writers of Greece and Rome, who were like bees, extracting nature's wealth from its flowers: "Instead of dirt and poison we have rather chosen to fill our hives with honey and wax; thus furnishing mankind with the two noblest of things, which are sweetness and light." See ANCIENTS AND MODERNS, QUARREL OF THE; HEBRAISM; HELLENISM.

Sword Dance. A medieval folk ritual, probably celebrating the death and resurrection of the year at the winter solstice, or Christmastide. The two principal characters are a Fool, dressed in an animal skin, and Bessy, a man in woman's clothes. They are introduced in rhymed speeches. Other dancers surround one of the characters with their swords, and sometimes slay him. This is the origin of *The Mummers' Play* (see MUMMING), and hence one of the origins of English drama (see MEDIEVAL DRAMA).

Syllabic Verse. Poetry in which METER has been set aside and the line is controlled by an arbitrary number of syllables, regardless of stress. Marianne Moore and other twentieth-century writers have preferred this form. It is standard in the unstressed Romance languages and in Japanese verse forms such as HAIKU.

Syllabus. An outline, ABSTRACT, or summary, as of the contents of a book, a course of study, or a series of lectures.

Syllepsis. Greek for "taking together": a figure of speech in which one word links two constructions expressing quite different senses, as in Dickens's "Miss Bolo went home in a flood of tears and a sedan chair." See PARALLELISM; ZEUGMA.

Syllogism. Greek for "reckoning together": a formula used in logic to arrive at precise solutions to problems by accepting two premises that lead inevitably to a conclusion. Within the two premises are three terms, one unique to each and one common to both. If both premises are valid, the conclusion must also be valid, as in the stock example of the simplest form of syllogism:

> *Major premise:* All men are mortal.
> *Minor premise:* Socrates is a man.
> *Conclusion:* Therefore, Socrates is mortal.

"Mortal" is the *major term,* the large category in the major premise that appears also in the conclusion. "Socrates" is the *minor term;* its relation to the major term becomes apparent in the conclusion. "Men" is the *middle term,* linking major and minor terms by means of the two premises accepted as valid.

Symbaritic Fables. Comic erotic tales originating in the Roman town of Sybaris, destroyed by Crotona in 510 B.C.; none is extant. Ovid in *Tristia* (II.417), Priscian in *Praeexercitamenta Rhetorica* (I), and others mention them as the most lascivious stories of all.

Symbol. Any unit of any verbal structure that may be isolated for critical attention. The word has been used in such a bewildering variety of contexts in literary CRITICISM that it seems most helpful to give it the broadest possible meaning for itself and then look into the different relationships implied by that variety. The smallest units, in an alphabetical language, are the letters; next come words, to which we shall confine ourselves here.

A symbol is a SIGNIFIER: it has a potential relation to something being SIGNIFIED. In that relation there are three aspects of particular importance. First, it conveys to the mind the sense of something specific which is signified; second, its relation to the signified is an arbitrary and conventionally assumed relation; third, it is intelligible only because it is different from every other signifier. Thus in reading we are, first, trying to unite the human consciousness with some aspect of experience which the verbal structure brings into signification. Second, we are continually searching in our memories for the conventional and socially agreed-upon significance of the verbal units. If we are reading something in a language we know imperfectly and have to keep looking words up in a dictionary, we soon see how urgent this aspect of reading is. Third, we are trying to make sense out of what we read—that is, we are building bridges between the differences that each unit has from the others.

In some tendencies in literature, such as the French movement known as *symbolisme,* stress is placed on relating the verbal units to one another, turning away from description or any aspect of words that seems to be fixed by convention in the interests of greater fluidity. On the other hand, there are other tendencies that lay stress on the descriptive aspect of symbols, their generally understood meanings that convey to the reader some experience through words with the least possible difficulty. This is the tendency often spoken of as "REALISM" using words in a context of externalized MIMESIS. Or a symbol may recall similar symbols previously used in similar contexts within literature; this use of a symbol may be called an ARCHETYPE, or recurring unit of literary convention. Or certain words may appear to us as keys to a whole complex of verbal meaning, as a philosopher's total meaning may be suggested by some such word as *form, time, substance,* or *being.* This last usually means that the word has a great variety of significations, and in literature more particularly double or multiple meanings of words play a major role in unifying the work. Thus in Horatio's first words to the ghost in *Hamlet:* "What art thou that usurp'st this time of night?" the word *usurp* introduces the ambiguity on which so much of the play as a whole turns: the question of the reality of the relationship between the ghost and Hamlet's father. Such variety in approaching the term *symbol* is evidence of the fact that literary structures in particular have POLYSEMOUS MEANING—that is, have many aspects of meaning, and can be approached from many points of view. See SYMBOLISM.

Symbolism.   A term ordinarily applied to self-conscious uses more common in literature than in written or oral communication generally. In this sense, symbolism is a heightened use of SYMBOL, presenting the word first for its ordinary signification (as when the word *rose* stands for the flower rose) and then for some idea lying behind the ordinary signification (as when the word *rose* stands for the flower rose, which stands for beauty).

Symbols used in this way fall into three classes. (1) *Natural symbols* present things not for themselves, but for the ideas people commonly associate with them: a star for hope, a cloud for despair, night for death, a sunrise for a new beginning. (2) *Conventional symbols* present things for the meanings people within a particular group have agreed to give them: a national flag for the ideas of home or patriotism associated with it, or a Christian cross or star of David for the associations hey evoke in people familiar with the appropriate religion. (3) *Literary ymbols* sometimes build upon natural or conventional symbols, adding meanings appropriate primarily within the work at hand, but sometimes they also create meanings within a work for things that have no natural or conventional meaning outside it, as Melville does with his white whale, for instance.

From the nineteenth century onward, writers have been increasingly self-conscious in their use of symbols. American writers of RO-MANTICISM and TRANSCENDENTALISM—Emerson, Hawthorne, Poe, Thoreau, Melville—found symbols valuable for expressing the inner truth they stressed. French symbolists—Baudelaire, Rimbaud, Mallarmé, Valery—followed; influenced especially by Poe, they stressed the power of the symbol to convey internal emotions and imaginings that seemed neglected by the concern of nineteenth-century REALISM with physical surfaces. French symbolism, in turn, greatly influenced Yeats, Pound, and T. S. Eliot, and through them most literature since.

Sympathy. Greek for "feeling together". (1) A likeness of feeling between people, a community of ideas or sharing of interests. (2) An understanding of another's situation, as, for example, pity for another's suffering. Sympathy suggests an intellectual awareness, whereas EM-PATHY suggests emotional identification.

Symploce. A combination of the rhetorical figures ANAPHORA and EPISTROPHE. It is the repetition of one word or phrase at the beginning and of another at the end of successive clauses or lines:

> *Justice* came down from heaven to view the *earth; Justice* returned to heaven and left the *earth.*

> *Clear and sweet* is my *soul*, and *clear and sweet* is all that is not my *soul*.

Symposium. Greek for "drinking together": a gathering for drinking and friendly discussion. Echoing the title of Plato's diagloue *The*

Symposium, the term is used for scholarly gatherings and, by extension, for collections of papers on one subject or for one occasion.

Synaesthesia. Greek for "perceiving together": close association or confusion of sense impressions. The result is essentially a METAPHOR, transferring qualities of one sense to another, as in common phrases like "blue note" and "cold eye" or in lines of poetry: "The dawn comes up like thunder" (Kipling); "How hot the scent is of the summer rose" (Robert Graves). Synaesthesia is more marked in some writers than in others, as some seem to perceive synaesthetically. Vladimir Nabokov, for example, claimed a synaesthetic response even to letters of the alphabet: "The *a* of the English alphabet . . . has for me the tint of weathered wood, but the French *a* evokes polished ebony" *(Speak, Memory).*

Synchoresis. The technique of conceding something, usually ironically, to retort with greater force:

> I admit that we have no business in their affairs, except the business of helping them, at their request, toward freedom and justice.

Synchronic. Together in time; simultaneous. Synchronic analysis of linguistic structures considers the structures of the present, ignoring those of the past. See DIACHRONIC; LINGUISTICS.

Syncopation. The effect produced in verse or music when two STRESS patterns play off against one another. Thus, in a line of verse, the stresses established by the METER may run contrary to those of normal speech:

ˇ — ˇ — ˇ — ˇ — ˇ — ˇ
To be or not to be, that is the question

as opposed to

ˇ — ˇ — ˇ ˇ — ˇ ˇ — ˇ
To be or not to be, that is the question.

See COUNTERPOINT RHYTHM.

Syncope. Greek for "cutting short": omission of one or more letters or sounds from the middle of a word: *ev'ry, ne'er, o'er.* Syncope is frequently used to bring a line of poetry to metrical regularity, as in Milton's "On His Having Arrived at the Age of Twenty-Three," where the last word in the fourth line rhymes with "truth": "But my late spring no bud or blossom shew'th." See ELISION.

Syncretism. (1) Reconciliation or combination of differing beliefs or approaches in philosophy, religion, or CRITICISM. (2) In LINGUISTICS, the merging of differently inflected forms.

Synecdoche. The understanding of one thing by another—a kind of METAPHOR in which a part stands for the whole, or the whole for a part: *a hired hand* meaning "a laborer," or *the law* meaning "a police officer."

Synonyms. Words in the same language denoting the same thing, usually with different connotations: *female, woman, lady, dame; male, masculine, macho.*

Synonymy. Repetition of synonyms for emphasis:

A miserable, wretched, depressed neighborhood.

Synopsis. A summary of a play, a narrative, or an argument.

Synthetic Language. One that expresses syntax by inflections, or word endings, as in Latin or German. OLD ENGLISH was synthetic, but Modern English is an ANALYTICAL LANGUAGE expressing syntax primarily through word order.

Syzygy. (1) In Greek metrics, two feet combined as one. (2) The technique of making one word follow its predecessor harmoniously without consonantal tangles in pronunciation, according to Poe and Sidney Lanier.

T

Tableau. (1) *Tableau vivant*—"living picture" (French). A scene on stage, on a float, or in a parlor entertainment in which costumed actors pose motionless in imitation of a famous painting or some literary, historical, or mythical event; popular in the nineteenth century. Parlor games often asked guests to identify the representation and characters. (2) Also arising in the nineteenth century, a similar freezing of action, in the midst of a scene, with action then resuming, usually before the curtain closed the scene or the play.

Tabula Rasa. A blank mind; literally, "a scraped tablet," from the Greek and Roman wax-coated wooden tablet erased by smoothing it over with the flat end of the stylus. The term most frequently refers to John Locke's conception of the mind as a blank, with no innate ideas, upon which the sensory world writes its impressions. But Locke never used the term, though he referred to wax taking an impression, and a blank sheet of paper. Aristotle compared the mind to a "tablet on which nothing has been written" (*De Anima* 3.4.11). Plutarch said that the soul at birth is a card or sheet ("khartes") ready for writing (*Placita Philosophorum* 4.11). The phrase first appeared in English in David Lindsay's *Ane Pleasant Satyre of the Thrie Estaitis* (1535): "Because I have bene, to day, *Tanquam tabula rasa*." Robert South, a preacher widely read in the eighteenth century, gave the term a certain currency in a sermon preached in 1662 but not printed until 1727: "Aristotle . . . affirms the Mind to be first a mere *Rasa Tabula*" (*Sermons* I.52).

Tagelied. A dawn song, a medieval German love lyric in imitation of the Provençal ALBA. See AUBADE.

Tail-Rhyme. A STANZA, in the Middle Ages called *rime couée*, characterized by a series of longer lines followed by a shorter "tail." A common pattern in medieval romances is a six-line tail-rhyme stanza composed of a couplet, or rhymed pair, a tail, another couplet, and a second tail, rhyming *aabccb*, as in the Middle English "Sir Launfal" and Chaucer's "Tale of Sir Thopas." Other patterns are also found, with the tail sometimes rhymed with one or more of the longer lines, sometimes not. Post-medieval variations may be seen in Michael Drayton's "To the Cambro-Britons and Their Harp," Keats's "La Belle Dame sans Merci," Longfellow's "Excelsior," and poems in the BURNS STANZA, such as "To a Mouse."

Tale. A simple short narrative with a story teller's air.

Tall Tale. A humorous account of superhuman capers popular on the nineteenth-century American frontier, many concerning Mike Fink and Davy Crockett. Rudolphe Erich Raspe's *Baron Münchhausen: Narrative of his Marvellous Travels* (1785) is the earliest example, though unrelated to the American frontier. Münchhausen (c. 1720–1797), a German in the Russian army fighting the Turks, told extravagant tales of his exploits. Raspé, an adventurer who fled to England after a theft, retold and elaborated Münchhausen's tales in English.

Tanka. A Japanese verse form with 31 syllables arranged in 5 lines to give a count of 5/7/5/7/7. Less influential in English than the HAIKU, it has been imitated occasionally, by Amy Lowell among others. See VERSE FORMS.

Taste. Discernment of literary and aesthetic excellence. The metaphor transferring gustatory to aesthetic taste appears in medieval Latin—*De gustibus non est disputandum:* "There's no disputing tastes." The term arose in English after 1660: "With *Sion's* songs, to all true tastes excelling / Where God is praised" (*Paradise Regained* IV.347–348, 1671); "No, no, hang him, he has no taste" (Congreve, *Double Dealer* I.ii, 1964). In 1712, Addison addressed *Spectator* 409 to the subject, since "this word arises very often in conversation." He stated that "Most Languages make use of this Metaphor, to express that Faculty of Mind, which distinguishes all the most concealed Faults and nicest Perfections in Writing," and went on to define it as "that Faculty of the Soul, which discerns the Beauties of an Author with Pleasure and the Imperfections with Dislike." He believed that taste, though partly innate, is to be cultivated by wide reading, conversation, and knowledge of "the best Critics both ancient and modern"—a view hardly altered to the present day, as we find T. S. Eliot claiming that the purpose of criticism is "the elucidation of works of art and the correction of taste" (*Collected Essays*, 1932, p. 13).

Tautology. Useless repetition of ideas in different words; redundancy. "He [*vocally*] sang [*by himself*] a solo [*song*]"; "first comes [*the letter*] A, then [*it is followed by the letter*] B, then [*after that comes the letter*] C."

Technique. A systematic method, as in the following examples of literary analysis: "E. E. Cummings's technique of fracturing and spacing language to elicit meaning," or "The technique of merging fragmentary sentences to suggest the stream of consciousness." The term is frequently overused, or misused, as in "The symbolic journey is a major technique in Joyce's *Ulysses.*"

Telestich. An ACROSTIC using the last letter of each line.

Tenor and Vehicle. I. A. Richards's terms for the two aspects of METAPHOR, *tenor* being the actual thing projected figuratively in the *vehicle:* "She [tenor] is a rose [vehicle]." Richards cites Hamlet's "What should such fellows as I do crawling between heaven and earth?" in which Hamlet is the *tenor* and "crawling" things the *vehicle* (*The Meaning of Meaning,* 1923).

Tension. Allen Tate's term for a poem's successful unification of the opposites of abstract and concrete, DENOTATION and CONNOTATION. He tailors his term from two in logic: *extension,* a word's denotation, the class of things it specifies, and *intension,* a word's relevant connotations. The extension of *chair* is the class "all chairs"; the intension of *chair* is "a vehicle used by the gentry in the eighteenth century," or "a leader of a meeting," and so forth. According to Tate, good poetry is the "full, organized body of all the extension and intension that we can find in it." The New Critics adopted Tate's tension in discussing PARADOX, IRONY, and the CONCRETE UNIVERSAL. His "Tension in Poetry" appeared in 1938, reprinted in *Collected Essays* (1959).

Tenson (or *Tenzone*). A poetic form, originating in Provençe in the twelfth century, in which two poets debate a subject of general interest. The *tenson* is distinguished from the PARTIMEN, or *joc parti,* in which one poet poses a question and another responds to it. See TROUBADOUR.

Tercet (or **Triplet**). A verse unit of three lines, sometimes rhymed, sometimes not. Common varieties include TERZA RIMA; poems in MONORHYME tercets, such as Herrick's "Upon Julia's Clothes," Tennyson's "The Eagle," and Frost's "Provide, Provide"; and the tercets occasionally interspersed in poems using the HEROIC COUPLET. The term is also used to designate half of the SESTET of an Italian SONNET. William Carlos Williams's VARIABLE FOOT, as seen in "The Ivy Crown" and "The Sparrow," is an arrangement of unrhymed tercets.

Terminal Rhyme. Another name for END RHYME.

Terza Rima. A verse form composed of TERCETS with interlocking RHYME (*aba bcb cdc,* and so on), usually in iambic pentameter. Invented by Dante for his *Divine Comedy,* it is difficult in English be-

cause of the demands made by the RHYME SCHEME. Shelley's "Ode to
the West Wind" is a famous example, beginning:

> O wild West Wind, thou breath of Autumn's being,
> Thou, from whose unseen presence the leaves dead
> Are driven, like ghosts from an enchanter fleeing.
>
> Yellow, and black, and pale, and hectic red,
> Pestilence-stricken multitudes: O thou,
> Who chariotest to their dark wintry bed. . . .

In the second section of part II of "Little Gidding," Eliot attempted a
variation, alternating, in a terza rima pattern, feminine and masculine
endings in place of rhyme.

Testament.   (1) A humorous, ribald, satiric "last will and testament"
in verse originating in late Roman times and developed in medieval
and Renaissance France, particularly in François Villon's *Le Petit Testament* (c. 1457) and *Le Testament* (his major work, called *Le Grand
Testament* because of its 2023 lines, c. 1462). In England, a number of
testaments appeared in the early 1500s: the anonymous *Jyl of Breynt-
ford's Testament* and *Colin Blowbol's Testament* and Humphrey Powell's
Wyll of the Devil (c. 1550). Robert Henryson's *The Testament of Cresseid* (1593), a serious version, describes in the third person Cressida's
end as a leper. "The Testament of Hawthorne" in *Tottel's Miscellany*
(1557) is a love COMPLAINT. (2) A work testifying to something, like
Thomas Usk's prose allegory *The Testament of Love*, actually not testifying to love but to his own vindication just before execution in 1388.
Robert Bridges's *The Testament of Beauty* (1929), published on his
eighty-fifth birthday, summed up his poetic philosophy in "loose alex-
andrines" derived from his admiration of Gerard Manley Hopkins.

Tetralogy.   (1) In Greek drama, three tragedies and a SATYR PLAY.
(2) Any four related plays, novels, or operas—Shakespeare's *Richard
II*, *Henry IV*, Parts One and Two, and *Henry V*, for instance.

Tetrameter.   Four-foot lines. See *METER*.

Textual Criticism.   The endeavor to establish and edit a definitive
literary text. The textual critic attempts to establish as nearly as possible what the author wrote. Even a manuscript in the author's handwriting must be collated word for word against the first edition, and
then the first edition collated against each succeeding one in the au-

thor's lifetime, to determine which changes the author probably made during the process of printing and reprinting and which are printer's errors or unauthorized editing. The textual editor lists in appendices all changes in all editions so that readers may check both text and judgment. A textual critic working from manuscripts made by scribes before the advent of printing must establish which manuscript seems closest to the author's lost original and the order of transmission and priority among the manuscripts. See CRITICISM.

Texture.   According to the New Critics, all details of incident, imagery, tone, style, meter, rhyme, and the like as distinct from *structure*. An analysis of texture concentrates on surface rather than shape or substance. See NEW CRITICISM.

Theater in the Round.   Dramatic productions in an area surrounded by the audience. See ARENA STAGE.

Theater of the Absurd.   See ABSURD, THEATER OF THE

Theaters.   In general, the buildings in which plays, concerts, and the like are performed. The earliest Greek theater was a circular dancing area, the *orchēstra*, around a small raised platform holding the altar of Dionysus. Beyond the rim opposite the audience, the *skēnē* ("tent")— a tent, hut, or low wall—concealed the actors while they changed masks and costumes. As tragedy progressed, the central stand and altar disappeared. Where possible, a semicircular hillside held curving rows of stone benches. After the classical period of Aeschylus, Sophocles, and Euripides (c. 470–406 B.C.), a long raised platform held an elongated *skēnē*, now a building with three doors, and provided a stage, the *logeion* ("speaking place"), for the principal actors while the CHORUS remained in the circular orchestra. A *machina*, a derrick for lowering gods (the origin of the term DEUS EX MACHINA) and hoisting heroes, now topped the *skēnē*, sometimes built into two stories. Canvases on wooden frames with painted scenery were leaned against the *skēnē* (whence our word *scene*), and platforms on wheels were rolled out to depict events indoors—a king on a throne, an altar, murdered corpses. The Theater of Dionysus in Athens, the most revered, probably evolved from the simple *orchēstra*. Its present remains are renovations of the fourth century B.C. rebuilt by Nero in the first century A.D., and again altered in the third.

   The Roman theater cut the *orchēstra* to a semicircle, extended the stage, and absorbed the *skēnē* into a substantial building that backed the entire semicircular amphitheater with its tiers of seats and supporting arches and passageways. The stage alone held the action. Privileged spectators in litters and portable chairs occupied the orchestra. After the reign of Augustus (c. A.D. 14 onward), the smaller roofed theater, the *odeum* ("place for odes"), or music hall, began to appear.

Christianity suppressed theaters in the fifth century, and the theater evolved anew from the church, first with platforms, called *mansions*, within the church for scenes from the Nativity and the Passion, then in the churchyard, then on movable wagons, or *pageants*, for the mystery and miracle plays. Renaissance Italy rediscovered the classics and the theater, through Vitruvius's *De Architectura* (c. 27 B.C.). After a number of temporary indoor stagings, Palladio's Teatro Olimpico at Vicenza, completed in 1585, five years after his death, became the first modern indoor theater.

The Elizabethan theater arose from the innyard and the bear-baiting pit—round or octagonal structures open to the air with boxes ranging up the straight inner walls like an inn's balconies and a stage jutting into the yard where the crowd, the "groundlings," could stand or sit on benches on its three sides. A stage house, with curtained inner stage and a balcony with curtain above, and sometimes a third story, backed the open stage. A canopy on two pillars, the "heavens," protruded part way from the stage house, and a trapdoor or two emitted ghosts.

In 1576, James Burbage built London's first public theater, called the Theater, at Shoreditch, north of the old City and beyond reach of its magistrates. When Burbage died in 1597, his sons Cuthbert and Richard, leading actors in Shakespeare's company, dismantled it, dividing half the ownership among Shakespeare and four others, and from its timbers built the Globe (1599) at Bankside, south of the Thames, where the Rose (c. 1586) and the Swan (1594) already flourished. Edward Alleyn built the square Fortune (1599) at what is now Fortune Street, between Golden Lane and Whitecross Street, central London. In St. John Street, two streets to the west, the Red Bull, refurbished from an actual innyard, was evidently already in business. It managed to stage an occasional play or entertainment throughout the COMMONWEALTH, which had closed the theaters in 1642, and it housed the new Theatre Royal company from 1660 to 1663. Philip Henslowe, who managed the Rose until 1603, built the Hope nearby in 1614.

Beginning with the Blackfriars in 1596, indoor PRIVATE THEATERS began their competition. In 1604, Inigo Jones returned to England with Italian ideas and firmly established the PROSCENIUM arch, perspective scenery, and elaborate machinery for the court MASQUE, including one with a globe that turned on an invisible axle to reveal eight dancers sitting inside. The PATENT THEATERS of the RESTORATION adopted the indoor, proscenium plan, but retained a considerable proscenium jut from the Elizabethan stage. The curtain, as in the Italian and private theaters, if used at all, was raised after the prologue, or introductory speech, and lowered only to close the last act, with scenes shifted before the audience's eyes. After 1750, the "act drop" curtain became standard.

The nineteenth century expanded size, improved acoustics and lighting, and democratized seating. The twentieth century's major innovation is the ARENA THEATER, the theater in the round, moving back toward the open staging of Shakespeare and of Palladio's Teatro Olimpico in which the action moved forward from the proscenium into a horseshoe of tiered benches. See DRAMA; MIRACLE PLAY; MYSTERY PLAY.

References

George Freedley and John A. Reeves, **A History of Theatre,** 3rd ed. rev. (1968).

Phyllis Hartnoll, ed., **The Oxford Companion to the Theatre,** 3rd. ed. (1967).

Allardyce Nicoll, **The Development of the Theatre,** 5th ed. rev. (1966).

Theme. (1) A central idea. (2) A topic for discussion. (3) An expository essay written for class.

Theoretical Criticism. See CRITICISM.

Thermodynamics. See ENTROPY.

Thesis. (1) The central proposition of an argumentative essay, a dissertation, or a book. (2) A master's or doctoral dissertation. (3) In ancient Greek prosody, a stressed syllable ("a placing") as against an unstressed syllable, an ARSIS ("a raising"). Originally the terms referred to the placing and raising of the dancing feet that paced the verses. Later prosodists, thinking that the raising referred to the voice, switched the meanings, which now prevail, with *arsis* for a stressed syllable and *thesis* for an unstressed.

Thesis Play. See PROBLEM PLAY.

Third-Person Limited Omniscience. A method sometimes adopted in modern story telling, whereby the omniscience of the traditional story teller is constrained in some significant way. For instance, the narrator may present only the knowledge that is available to the protagonist, or main character, keeping other information hidden. See NARRATIVE PERSPECTIVE.

Third-Person Narration. Method of story telling in which someone who is not involved in the story, but stands somewhere outside it in space and time, tells of the events. See NARRATIVE PERSPECTIVE.

Third-Person Omniscience. The traditional way of telling a story by a THIRD-PERSON NARRATOR, who is not involved in the events. By story-telling CONVENTION, the narrator possesses the powers of omniscience, knowing all there is to know, but revealing it in the manner of Scheherazade in the *Thousand and One Nights*—in the way that will make the story most interesting. See NARRATIVE PERSPECTIVE.

Thirty-Twomo. (Abbreviated 32mo, 32°): a book made from sheets folded to give signatures of 32 leaves (64 pages). See BOOK SIZES; SIGNATURE.

Three Decker. A three-volume novel, a form that had become customary toward the end of the eighteenth century, with volumes issued at intervals.

Three-Dimensional Character. A *round character*, one possessing the depth and complexity of an actual person. See CHARACTERS.

Three Laws of Robotics. See ROBOTICS, THREE LAWS OF.

Threnody. A song of lamentation; a DIRGE.

Tin Pan Alley. The popular-music industry around Times Square, New York, and its products; from musician's slang *tin pan* for a tinny piano, around 1900.

Tone. In modern criticism, following I. A. Richards, the author's attitude toward subject and audience—playful, serious, ironic, formal, somber, and the like; a work's MOOD.

Tone Color. Musical resonance, as distinct from meaning, in language; an experience derived primarily from sound. See CACOPHONY; EUPHONY; ONOMATOPOEIA; SIGMATISM; SYNAESTHESIA; SYZYGY.

Topographical Poetry. Poetry celebrating some topographical location, originated by Sir John Denham's *Cooper's Hill* (1642), as Johnson says in his *Life of Denham:* "a species of composition that may be denominated *local poetry,* of which the fundamental subject is some particular landscape, to be poetically described, with the addition of such embellishments as may be supplied by historical retrospection or incidental meditation." A number of topographical poems followed in the seventeenth and early eighteenth centuries, all reflecting the landscape painting newly flourishing—Edmund Waller's *Poem on St. James's Park* (1661) and Sir Samuel Garth's *Claremont* (1715) among them. Pope's *Windsor Forest* (1713), celebrating the Treaty of Utrecht, world peace, and Britain's future glory, is most notable. John Dyer, himself a painter, is most painterly in *Grongar Hill* (1726), with views along the river Towy in Wales. See UT PICTURA POESIS.

Topos. A commonplace, from Greek *topos* (plural *topoi*), "place." (1) A topic for argument, remembered by the classical system of placing it, in the mind's eye, in a place within a building and then proceeding mentally from one place to the next. (2) A rhetorical device, similarly remembered as a commonplace. (3) E. R. Curtius's term for common themes in medieval literature: CARPE DIEM, the lover's lament, the poet's decrying a sense of insufficiency, and the like (*European Literature and the Latin Middle Ages*, 1948, tr. 1853).

Touchstone. (1) Matthew Arnold's term for "lines and expressions of the great masters" by which one may test the quality of other poetry, especially as to its "high seriousness." (2) A smooth black stone (basalt or jasper) on which one tested gold or silver by comparing a streak against a streak left by a piece of standard quality.

Tour de Force. "A turn of strength"—the ingenious handling of something apparently too difficult. Joyce's *Ulysses*, James's *Turn of the Screw*, Faulkner's *Sound and the Fury*, and Cummings's pictorially fractured poems have been called *tours de force*. Sometimes the term implies qualified praise, suggesting that the critic has discerned technical proficiency in a work in other respects of lesser value.

Tracking Shot. In motion pictures, a shot made by moving the camera and its support to follow after the subject. See PAN.

Tract. A political, religious, or philosophical pamphlet. See OXFORD MOVEMENT.

Tractarian Movement. See OXFORD MOVEMENT.

Tradition. The handing down from generation to generation of stories, sayings, beliefs, literary conventions, and the like. The BALLAD prevails through *oral tradition;* the matter of MEDIEVAL ROMANCE through *written*, though doubtless with an oral background. The many romances about Alexander the Great, for instance, all derive from a Greek prose account by "pseudo-Callisthenes" (second century A.D.); those about the Trojan War, from two accounts in Latin prose purportedly by eyewitnesses, Dares Phrygius (sixth century) and Dictys Cretensis (fourth century), Homer being completely unknown to the Middle Ages. The conventions of PASTORAL poetry traveled down the ages from Theocritus (third century B.C.) to Alexander Pope (1709).

Traditional Ballad. Another name for the *popular ballad* or *folk ballad*, a song of anonymous authorship, transmitted orally. See BALLAD.

Tragedy. Fundamentally a serious FICTION involving the downfall of a HERO or HEROINE. In ancient Greece the ritual of the dying god Dionysus included the singing of a choral ode, known as the *dithyramb*, in his honor. The dithyramb contained among other things the tone of passionate lamentation appropriate to the story of a dying god. The semilegendary Thespis is said to have amplified this ode into a potentially dramatic form by including a narrative from the leader of the chorus. Aeschylus, by adding a second actor (a third, apparently introduced by Sophocles, appears also in Aeschylus's later plays) brought in dialogue, and with it a fully matured dramatic form. Tragedies were acted mainly during the spring festival of Dionysus, and the priest of Dionysus was present. Three dramatists competed each year for a prize, and presented, at least at first, a group of three tragedies (trilogy) on related themes, followed by a SATYR PLAY which was lighter in tone, the four plays together making a tetralogy.

Greek tragedy was strongly influenced by the conception of a contract of order and stability in which gods, human society, and nature all participated. An act of aggression (Greek *hybris*, often spelled *hubris*) throws this cosmic machinery out of gear, and hence it must make a countermovement to right itself. This countermovement is usually called *nemesis*, and a number of words often translated "fate" (*heimarmene, moira, ananke*) also refer to this recovery of order, which makes the tragic action seem inevitable. The conception of a contract is a moral conception, but the particular action called tragic that happens to the hero does not depend on moral status. Aristotle spoke of a tragic *hamartia*, usually translated "flaw," as essential to the hero, but this flaw, despite the fact that *hamartia* is the ordinary New Testament word for sin, is not necessarily a moral defect, but rather a matter of being in a certain place exposed to a tragic action. According to Aristotle, a tragic action should, by raising pity and terror, effect a *cathar-sis*, or purification of these emotions. Whatever Aristotle meant by this, in dramatic experience this catharsis appears to be essentially a detachment of the spectator from feelings of attraction or repulsion toward the characters, particularly the hero.

Thus in Sophocles's *Oedipus Rex* the king of Thebes, an able and responsible ruler, attempts to discover the reason for the drought that has been causing famine in his land, and learns that he has unknowingly killed his father and is living in incest with his mother. In his horror at this discovery he tears out his eyes. A second Oedipus play, *Oedipus at Colonus*, shows Oedipus's reconciliation to and acceptance by the gods at his death: that does not make the play a comedy, but manifests the order and stability that caused the earlier tragedy. Similarly, in Aeschylus's trilogy the *Oresteia*, we first see the murder of Agamemnon by his wife and her lover, then the revenge of Agamemnon's son Orestes on the murderers, then the pursuit of Orestes by the Furies, who in that form are agents of a mechanical or automatic form of nemesis. In the third play of the series, *The Eumenides*, the Furies are incorporated into the more flexible and humane contract announced by Athene, so that that play, again, manifests the basis of order for tragedy and is not a comedy, even though it ends in great serenity. In Euripides, on the other hand, some of the actions, notably those of *Alcestis* and *Ion*, seem to move in the direction of COMEDY.

In these examples three main themes of tragedy are evident. One is the theme of isolation, in which a hero, a character of greater than ordinary human size, becomes isolated from the community. Mortal heroes of divine ancestry, like many Greek heroes, must discover the limitations of their humanity; if they are gods, like Aeschylus's Prometheus, they are isolated by the power of the much stronger god Zeus. Then there is the theme of the violation and reestablishment of order, in which the neutralizing of the violent act may take the form of a revenge. Finally, a character may embody a passion too great for the cosmic order to tolerate, such as the passion of sexual love. This theme is more conspicuous in Euripides (e.g. *Hippolytus*).

In Roman literature tragedy was cultivated by Seneca, whose plays may not have been intended for the theater of his time. When drama revived in the Renaissance, Seneca was the only classical model directly available to Shakespeare and to most of his contemporaries. Renaissance tragedy seems to be essentially a mixture of the heroic and the ironic. It tends to center on heroes who, though they cannot be of divine parentage in Christianized Western Europe, are still of titanic size, with an articulateness and social authority beyond anything in our normal experience. In Shakespeare the theme of the social isolation of the hero appears at its most powerful and concentrated in *King Lear*, where the king's abdication of royal power leaves him exposed to the malignancy of the two of his three daughters who supplant him. RE-VENGE TRAGEDY, a common Elizabethan and Jacobean form, appears in *Hamlet*, with revenge being imposed on the hero as a moral obliga-tion. The tragedy of passion, in its commonest form of sexual love, is the mode of *Romeo and Juliet*, and a different form of it appears in Racine's *Phèdre*.

After the Renaissance, the most notable development of tragic drama was in Germany, with the works of Schiller and the younger Goethe, especially the first part of *Faust*. Many other tragic dramas were literary imitations of the great classical and Renaissance models, and have not worn well on the stage. Prose fiction (*Crime and Punish-ment, Anna Karenina, Moby-Dick, Madame Bovary*) has been the genre of most of the really powerful modern tragedies. Even here the ironic component of tragedy predominates over the heroic one, because of the difficulty of assuming the convention of a tragic hero who is larger than life size. Such a figure as Willy Loman in Arthur Miller's *Death of a Salesman*, for example, gains his heroic aura only through being a representative of a specific social development, the emphasis on hustling and hard-selling capitalism which at one time, at least, formed a prominent part of what is called the American dream. Lo-man's isolation in itself is simply ironic: it is the collapse of the dream he embodies that is tragic. See DOMESTIC TRAGEDY; MELODRAMA; TRAGIC FLAW; TRAGIC IRONY; TRAGICOMEDY.

Tragedy of Blood.   An Elizabethan TRAGEDY offering the thrills of bloody mutilation. See REVENGE TRAGEDY; SENECAN TRAGEDY.

Tragic Flaw.   Greek *hamartia:* in a TRAGEDY, the defect in the HERO that leads to a downfall.

Tragic Irony.   The essence of TRAGEDY, in which the most noble and most deserving person, because of the very grounds of his or her ex-cellence, dies in defeat. See IRONY.

Tragicomedy.   (1) A tragedy with happy ending, frequently with penitent villain and romantic setting, disguises, and discoveries, partic-ularly the Jacobean plays originated by Beaumont and Fletcher in *Phi-laster* (1611) and *A King and No King* (1611). Fletcher coined and de-fined the term: "A tragi-comedy is not so called in respect of mirth and killing, but in respect it wants deaths, which is enough to make it no tragedy, yet brings some near it, which is enough to make it no comedy, which must be a representation of familiar people, with such kind of trouble as no life be question'd; so that a god is as lawful in this as in tragedy, and mean people as in a comedy" ("To the Reader," *The Faithful Shepherdess*, 1610, a romantic pastoral not itself a tragicomedy). The earliest example of a tragicomedy is Richard Edwards's *Damon and Pythias* (1564), designated a "tragical comedy" in its prologue. (2) A tragedy with an independent comic subplot interspersed, like Thomas Southerne's *Fatal Marriage* (1694) and *Oroonoko* (1696). Although tragicomedy faded out at the beginning of the eighteenth century, its sentimentality and devices continued in nineteenth- and twentieth-century MELODRAMA.

Transcendental Club. The group of Concord and Boston friends that, together with the publication of Emerson's *Nature* (1836), initiated New England TRANSCENDENTALISM; originally called the *Hedge Club*.

Transcendentalism. In its Latin roots, essentially a "passing over" or a "climbing beyond." The term has been applied to the philosophy of Immanuel Kant and others who give priority to preexisting truth, or truth accessible through thought, over that based in the particular experiences of the senses. More important to literary studies, however, is its use as the name for a short-lived but major phenomenon in New England that began with the publication of Emerson's *Nature* in 1836 and ended, as a movement, with the beginning of the Civil War in 1860.

New England transcendentalism found its sources in Kant; later German transcendentalism and IDEALISM; the English Romantics, especially Wordsworth and Coleridge; Carlyle; oriental mysticism; and UNITARIANISM. Its first significant statement, and one of its most important, was *Nature*, published the same year that a small group of friends from Concord and Boston, later to be known as the *Transcendental Club*, began meeting for intellectual discussion. In time, the membership included George Ripley, Bronson Alcott, Margaret Fuller, Theodore Parker, Emerson, and Thoreau. The effects on American literature and society were enormous.

Transcendentalism in the United States was never a coherent philosophy, even within the works of Emerson, its chief spokesman. Like a religion, it subscribed to articles of faith, not proven, that had great practical effect in the lives and works of its believers. Among these, the most important were the divinity of human beings and the unity of God. All people were perceived as partaking of the spark of the eternal Divine. God was seen as everywhere immanent in the Creation, as the "Over-Soul" that animated all. From this basis, much followed, including the crucial idea that humans have not lost their ability to commune directly with the central Divinity, but have only allowed it to fall into disuse. Humans can receive direct inspiration from God, without the mediation of priests or printed texts of religion, through an "inner light," like that of the Quakers, that is common to all, or through reading signs of eternal truth everywhere present in nature. Beyond these central ideas, there was much division of opinion and contradiction, especially concerning the practical effects of transcendentalism, as indeed there was bound to be in any system of thought that left so much open to individual understanding and interpretation. Nor was even Emerson consistent. Transcendentalism was a philosophy particularly open to growth and change, especially in a country changing as rapidly as was the United States in the middle years of the nineteenth century. "A foolish consistency," wrote Emerson in "Self-Reliance," "is the hobgoblin of little minds."

The practical consequences, some of those contradictory also, can hardly be overstated. Emerson's *American Scholar,* the Harvard Phi Beta Kappa address for 1837, was received as a declaration of independence for American literature and thought, casting aside bondage to Europe. The two series of his *Essays* (1841, 1844) helped shape the thought of generations and became American literary classics. Thoreau's *Walden* and "Civil Disobedience" became models of individualism in practice. Hawthorne and Melville reflected transcendental ideas in their works. Whitman proved in many ways the poet of the new world that Emerson had predicted. But the effects moved far beyond literature. In its insistence on the fundamental dignity and worth of common humanity, transcendentalism provided powerful support to the American ideal of a broadly based democratic society, building national good on a foundation of individual value. This belief in an ultimate ideal, however, did not mean that the present could not be improved. The transcendental magazine THE DIAL (1840–1844), edited first by Margaret Fuller and then by Emerson, served as an exchange of ideas for social reform. Experiments in communal living were tried at BROOK FARM and Fruitlands. Many transcendentalists were active abolitionists and feminists. Some were conservationists, early ecologists, vegetarians, celebrating the oneness of nature and humanity. Above all, perhaps, transcendentalism fostered the strong traits of

American individualism and self-reliance important to social and political history down to the present.

References

Paul F. Boller, Jr., **American Transcendentalism, 1830–1860: An Intellectual Inquiry** (1974).
Perry Miller, ed. **The Transcendentalists: An Anthology** (1950).

Transferred Epithet. See EPITHET.

Transformational Grammar. A system of grammatical analysis assuming a deep unverbalized structure in language from which several alternative surface structures, or verbal utterances, may emerge. It is also called *transformational-generative grammar,* since it establishes rules by which surface sentences may be generated and transformed from a basic grammatical kernel. A kernel sentence might be "The teachers expected a raise." Its transformations may be "A raise was expected by the teachers" and "Did the teachers expect a raise?"

Zellig S. Harris suggested the kernel and its generated alternatives in *Methods of Structural Linguistics* (1951). His student, Noam Chomsky, in his doctoral dissertation "Transformational Analysis" (University of Pennsylvania, 1955), refined and deepened Harris's concepts, giving the new analysis its name. His *Syntatic Structures* (1957) put his theory before the world. His *Cartesian Linguistics* (1966), reviving seventeenth-century assumptions, proposed a DEEP STRUCTURE innate in all humans and common to all languages. Hence Chomsky has proposed two deep structures, without clearly distinguishing them: a deep universal one and an operational one in each language, which can be conveniently worked out by rules and verbalized in each language.

References

J. P. B. Allen and Paul Van Buren, eds., **Chomsky: Selected Readings** (1971).
Suzette Haden Elgin, **A Primer of Transformational Grammar for Rank Beginners** (1975).
Ronald W. Langacker, **Language and Its Structure** (1973).
Robert H. Robins, **General Linguistics: An Introductory Survey,** 2nd ed. (1971).

Translation. The process of changing from one language to another. Because of differences in vocabulary, syntax, and idiom, something of the sense or effect is always different in a translation, as is suggested by the Italian proverb *traduttore, traditore* ("translator, traitor"). This is especially true of poetry, where a *literal translation* (an attempt to present the word-for-word meaning of the original) must necessarily lose much sound and rhythm important to the poetic effect. A *loose translation* keeps the tone and spirit of a work, but loses precise word-for-word meaning. Looser still, an *adaptation* takes its inspiration from another language, but turns it to a new use, as in Robert Lowell's *Imitations* (1961), versions of poems from various times and places, in which Lowell attempted to "do what my authors might have done if they were writing their poems now and in America."

Famous translations in English include King Alfred's, of Boethius's *Consolation of Philosophy* and Bede's *Ecclesiastical History* (ninth century); Thomas North's *Plutarch's Lives* (1579); George Chapman's *Iliad* (1598–1611); the King James Bible: the Authorized Version (1611); Dryden's *Virgil* (1687); Pope's *Iliad* (1715–1720); and Edward Fitz-Gerald's *Rubáiyát of Omar Khayyám* (1859–1879).

Travesty. Literally a "cross-dressing": a literary work so clothed, or presented, as to appear ludicrous; a grotesque image or likeness. See BURLESQUE.

Tribe of Ben. The younger lyricists, particularly Robert Herrick, who drank with, rhymed with, and modeled themselves on Ben Jonson: Thomas Randolph, William Cartwright, Thomas Carew, Sir John Suckling, John Cleveland, Richard Lovelace—the CAVALIER POETS. See SONS OF BEN.

Trilogy. Originally a set of three tragedies performed together in ancient Greece; hence, any three literary works, related to one another, but each capable of standing alone. See TETRALOGY.

Trimeter. Three-foot lines. See METER.

Triolet. A verse form of 8 lines, with 2 rhymes: *abaaabab*. The entire first line is repeated as line 4, and the first and second lines are repeated as lines 7 and 8. This example is by Robert Bridges:

> When first we met we did not guess
> That Love would prove so hard a master;
> Of more than common friendliness
> When first we met we did not guess.
> Who could foretell this sore distress
> This irretrievable disaster
> When first we met?—We did not guess
> That Love would prove so hard a master.

See VERSE FORMS.

Triple Meter.   Lines of three-syllable feet, either anapestic or dactylic. See METER.

Triple Rhyme.   The matching of three final syllables, the accented plus two unaccented: *listening / glistening; syllable / killable*. It is a variation of FEMININE RHYME.

Triplet.   See TERCET.

Tripos.   At Cambridge University, the final honors examination for the B.A. degree. Originally, the tripos (so named from the three-legged stool this person sat on) was a graduate appointed to debate the candidate. Later the term was applied to a set of humorous verses composed by the tripos, and also to the list of candidates for the degree. Once limited to degrees in mathematics, the term was later extended to her subjects.

Tristich.   A unit of verse in three lines. See TERCET.

Trite Expression.   A CLICHÉ.

Trivium.   The first three of the SEVEN LIBERAL ARTS as studied in medieval universities: grammar, logic, and rhetoric (including oratory).

Trochee.   A metrical foot going — ‿. See METER.

Trope.   Greek *tropos* for "a turn": a word or phrase turned from its usual meaning to an unusual one; hence, a figure of speech, or an expression turned beyond its literal meaning. Ancient, medieval, and Renaissance RHETORIC distinguished various types, with some, such as METAPHOR and METONYMY, classed as tropes of words, and others, such as ALLEGORY, IRONY, and HYPERBOLE, classed as tropes of sentences. In earlier times, tropes were considered as ornaments or embellishments to language. More recently, beginning as early as the eighteenth century, they have been considered as fundamental ways of thinking, and therefore necessary to precise communication.

In relation to medieval music, a trope was a brief elaboration on a Gregorian chant. In relation to medieval literature, the term is used to designate a phrase or passage inserted into the authorized liturgy. The most famous of these is the *Quem quaeritis?* trope often cited as the earliest instance of MEDIEVAL DRAMA.

Tropological Meaning.   The moral application of a work; in the Middle Ages one of FOUR SENSES OF INTERPRETATION.

Troubadour. From Provençal *trobador*, "finder" or "inventor". The troubadours were lyric poets of southern France who wrote in Provençal (*langue d'oc*) from the twelfth through the mid-fourteenth centuries. Court poets, they wrote love songs in the form of the CANZONE, which were usually sung not by the poet but by a professional MINSTREL or JONGLEUR. Among other poetic types they favored are the *TENSON* and *PARTIMEN* (or *joc parti*)—forms of debate or dialogue; *PASTOURELLE*; *ALBA* (dawn song); *PLANH* (lament); and *SIRVENTES* (personal or political invective or satire). Masters of intricate meters and rhymes, they developed such forms as the SESTINA. Among those whose names are still known are Guillaume d'Aquitaine, Arnaut Daniel, and Bertrand de Born. They influenced a good deal of later poetry, including that of Dante and Petrarch.

Trouvère. From Old French *trovere*, "finder" or "inventor": the TROUBADOUR of northern France, contemporary with the southern troubadours and much influenced by them. They wrote in *langue d'oïl*, the antecedent of modern French, composing love lyrics, romances, and the CHANSON DE GESTE.

True Rhyme. See EXACT RHYME.

Truncation. The dropping of a syllable or two at the beginning or end of a metrical line. See CATALEXIS.

Tudor. See ROYAL HOUSES.

Tudors, the Early (1485–1558). The period marking the beginnings of the RENAISSANCE in England, during the reigns of Henry VII and Henry VIII. William Caxton introduced printing in English, first at Bruges, Flanders (1474), then at London (1476). John Colet, Lyly, and Erasmus created HUMANISM with the revival of Greek and Roman learning. SCOTTISH LITERATURE became significant through the poets Dunbar, Douglas, and Lindsay. For the next four centuries, all English schoolchildren, including Shakespeare, Fielding, Johnson, and Matthew Arnold, began learning their Latin from Lyly's *Grammar* (1513). Thomas More's *Utopia* (1516), the lyrics of Wyatt and Surrey, and John Skelton's bumptious poems and satires were notable. See ENGLISH LITERATURE, PERIODS OF and the "Chronology of Literature and World Events."

Tumbling Verse. Irregular, strongly stressed, usually two-beat verse. See SKELTONICS.

Twelvemo. See DUODECIMO.

Two-Dimensional Character.   Flat character, lacking the depth and complexity of a living person. See CHARACTERS.

Type.   (1) A literary GENRE. (2) One of the TYPE CHARACTERS. (3) A SYMBOL or EMBLEM. Hawthorne used the word in this sense in the penultimate paragraph of *The Scarlet Letter* when he called Hester's scarlet A a "symbol" and also "a type of something to be sorrowed over." (4) In theology and literary CRITICISM, an event in early Scriptures or literature that is seen as prefiguring an event in later Scriptures or in history or literature generally. Everything that happens in the Old Testament may thus be seen as a type for something that happens in the New Testament, and many events in the Bible as types for events in later history and literature. In this usage, the type occurred in the past. The event prefigured is an *antitype*. See ANAGOGY; ARCHETYPE; MYTH.

Type Characters.   Ones endowed with traits that mark them more distinctly as representatives of a type or class than as individuals standing apart from a type: the typical doctor or housewife, for example. Type characters are the opposite of INDIVIDUALIZED CHARACTERS. They are common in ROMANCE, ALLEGORY, and the various forms of POPULAR LITERATURE. See CHARACTERS.

Typescript.   A typed copy of a literary work. See MANUSCRIPT.

Typology.   The study of *types;* see TYPE (4). Typology springs from a theory of literature or history that recognizes events as duplicated in time. In literary CRITICISM, the student of typology examines works in the light of the organization of their typical elements, considering the author's manipulation of these elements as a branch of RHETORIC. See ANAGOGY; ARCHETYPE; MYTH.

U

Ubi Sunt. Latin for "where are"? The phrase refers to a poetic theme especially popular in the Middle Ages, as in the Middle English poem *"Ubi Sunt Qui Ante Nos Fuerunt?"* ("Where Are Those That Were Before Us?"). François Villon's "Ballad of Dead Ladies," in the nineteenth-century translation by Dante Gabriel Rossetti, gave to the theme a formulation popular in modern times: "Where are the snows of yesteryear?" *Ubi sunt* poems, from all times and places, lament the loss of things past. See BALLADE; CARPE DIEM; ELEGY.

Ultima Thule. A phrase meaning "farthest Thule" and sometimes used figuratively for the outermost limits of exploration. Thule was the name given to a northern island (perhaps Iceland, the Shetland Islands, or Norway) discovered and described in the fourth century B.C. by a Greek navigator, Pytheas.

Ultraists (or **Ultráismo**). A Spanish and Spanish-American movement in poetry following the French Symbolists in FREE VERSE, metrical innovation, and extreme imagery and symbolism. It was founded in Madrid in 1919 by Guiliermo de Torre, and published in the periodicals *Grecia* (1919–1920) and *Ultra* (1921–1922). Jorge Luis Borges, an Argentinian who emigrated to Europe with his family in 1914, at age 15, joined the group in 1920 and took Ultráismo back to Buenos Aires in 1921, from where it spread through South America, influencing Chileans Pablo Neruda and Vicente Huidobro and Mexicans Jaime Torres Bodet and Carlos Pellicer. The movement has continued in avant-garde writers after World War II.

Underground Literature. (1) In countries with strict government controls of the means of publication, literature produced and circulated illegally, as, for example, in manuscript or typescript copies, printed on clandestine presses, or smuggled outside the country to be printed. (2) More loosely, any literature subversive of the majority views in the environment where it is produced, especially when it is printed outside the regular publishing channels and for a limited audience.

Understatement. An ironic minimizing of a fact in order to emphasize it. See MEIOSIS.

Unitarianism. A form of Christianity that stresses the unity of God and denies the doctrine of the Trinity. Unitarianism emerged as a distinct belief with numerous adherents in England and the United States in the first half of the nineteenth century, though its roots go back much earlier than that. Especially important in the United States, it was in some ways a natural development of CONGREGATIONALISM and DEISM, emphasizing the primacy of reason and the individual conscience in matters of faith and morals, with Jesus seen as a great man rather than as the son of God. James Martineau, in England, and Ralph Waldo Emerson, Theodore Parker, and William Ellery Channing, in the United States, were prominent early leaders. See TRANSCENDENTALISM.

Unities.   With reference to DRAMA, the three traditional unities: PLOT, time, and place. The idea stems from Aristotle's discussion of TRAGEDY in his *Poetics*, where he stresses the importance of unity of plot. Critics of the sixteenth and seventeenth centuries insisted also upon the importance of unity of time and place, which some assumed as necessary corollaries to the idea of a unified plot. Of time, Aristotle suggested only that the ideal tragedy should occur within "a single revolution of the sun," or little more. Of place, he said nothing. His definition of a unified plot emphasized continuous ACTION, from beginning through middle to end, with each event the necessary or probable result of the one that preceded it, and with no irrelevant EPISODE. See RULES, THE.

Unity.   The quality of an artistic work that allows it to stand as a complete and independent whole, with each part related to each other part and no part irrelevant or superfluous. Plato, in the *Phaedrus*, first proposed the principle of unity as an important aesthetic consideration, holding up the organic unity of nature as a model for human effort. For Aristotle, unity of PLOT was central to TRAGEDY, and other writers expanded that to include the three UNITIES of plot, time, and place. By the same reasoning, other forms of unity are important to other GENRES—as, for example, an EPIC or a BIOGRAPHY is unified by focus on an individual life, or a LYRIC poem by its expression of a single dominant emotion. Among other sources of unity are theme, STYLE, and, for narrative works, NARRATIVE PERSPECTIVE.

Universality.   The quality of broad appeal in a work of art, making it attractive to all people in all times and places. See CONCRETE UNIVERSAL; POPULAR LITERATURE.

University Wits.   Oxford and Cambridge men, active contributors to London literary life in the last two decades of the sixteenth century. Among their number were Christopher Marlowe, Robert Greene, John

Lyly, Thomas Lodge, and Thomas Nashe. They were important in the development of the characteristic forms and techniques of the age, including especially BLANK VERSE, ELIZABETHAN DRAMA, the PASTORAL ROMANCE, and the PICARESQUE NOVEL.

Unreliable Narrator. A narrator, or story teller, who displays attitudes toward the story, or judgments about it, markedly different from those we know or assume to belong to the author. The PERSONA of an unreliable narrator is therefore an important part of our consideration of the story as we strive to understand the differences between what we have been told and what we might have been told by a more reliable witness. In Henry James's *Turn of the Screw*, the governess who narrates is perhaps reliable in her report of events as she has perceived them: we have little reason to suppose she misrepresents what she has seen. On the other hand, she is perhaps unreliable as a guide to the facts as they would have been given by an objective witness: what she sees is not necessarily what others would see or what the author would have us believe. Similarly, a NAÏVE NARRATOR like Huckleberry Finn is reliable as to events and his understanding of them, but unreliable in the moral judgments that stem from his naïveté: Huck's view of slavery, for example, is not the author's. The term *unreliable narrator* owes its currency to Wayne C. Booth's *The Rhetoric of Fiction* (1961). See NARRATIVE PERSPECTIVE.

Upstage. The rear of a stage. An actor "upstages" another by moving toward the rear and forcing the other actor to turn his or her back to the audience.

Ur-. Prefix, from German, meaning "primitive," "original," or "earliest." *Ursprache*, for example, is a term used in philology for an original language reconstructed from the evidence of various cognate languages that arose from it. An *ur-text* is the earliest form of a literary work, a hypothetical ancestor of later forms.

Usage. The way a society uses its language, as verbal habits, particularly in speech, attain public acceptance and change mannerisms, expressions, and grammar. Horace (65–8 B.C.) was the first to describe the process:

> Mortalia facta peribunt,
> nedum sermonum stet honos et gratia vivax.
> Multa renascentur quae iam cecidere, cadentque
> quae nunc sunt in honore vocabula, si volet usus,
> quem penes arbitrium est et ius et norma loquendi.
>
> *Ars Poetica, 68–72*

Mortal works will perish; even less will the dignity and charm of speech live long. Many words that now drop out will be reborn, and those now respected will fall, if so willed by usage, which has the decision, and the law and measure of speaking.

Structural linguists, who argue that structure gives meaning and that speech is supreme, maintain that differing usages are equally good. The traditionalist and the PURIST, arguing that words have intrinsic meanings, maintain that the choices made by writers are preferable to the spoken alternatives, since they reflect more careful judgment and practice. For instance, the linguist argues that usage has established *none of them are* on an equal footing with *none of them is*. Purists prefer *none of them is;* since *none* ("no one") is intrinsically singular and the subject of singular *is*; they see *of them* as mistakenly attracting the plural *are*.

Utilitarianism.   In ethics, a theory proposing that human actions should be judged good or bad in terms of their social utility. Utilitarianism was founded in England toward the end of the eighteenth century by Jeremy Bentham, who held that the fundamental basis for morality is "the greatest happiness for the greatest number." For Bentham, happiness was primarily pleasure, with social welfare inevitably bound to individual self-interest. Later, John Stuart Mill argued that a true utilitarianism recognizes the importance of qualitative and not merely quantitative pleasure. Utilitarianism formed an important part of the intellectual ferment that led to nineteenth-century political and social reforms, and it was much discussed, and sometimes attacked, by writers such as Carlyle and Dickens.

Utopia.   A word from Greek roots (*outopia,* meaning "no place," or else "eutopia," meaning "good place"), pointing to the idea that a utopia is a nonexistent land of social perfection. As Thomas More expressed it in his *Utopia* (1516), a Latin work contrasting sixteenth-century England with an imaginary island of the New World, "to find citizens ruled by good and wholesome laws, that is an incredible and rare thing."

Utopian literature is as old as the *Republic* of Plato (429?–347 B.C.), an outline of an ideal society, ruled by a philosopher-king. Francis Bacon's *New Atlantis* (1627) is a seventeenth-century example. In the nineteenth century, visions of the benefits of industrialization spawned many examples of the genre, including, in England, Samuel Butler's *Erewhon* (1872), with its title an ANAGRAM for *nowhere,* and William Morris's *News from Nowhere* (1891). In the United States, Edward Bellamy's *Looking Backward* (1888) had a phenomenal success (300,000 copies were printed in less than two years), rivaled earlier only by *Uncle Tom's Cabin* and certain of the DIME NOVEL genre. Widely read around the world in English and numerous translations, Bellamy's work was followed by a flood of utopian literature, including W. D. Howells's *Traveler from Altruria* (1894) and *Through the Eye of a Needle* (1907) and H. G. Wells's *Modern Utopia* (1905). In the twentieth century, utopian literature has sometimes taken the form of the *dystopia* (Greek for "bad place"), or anti-utopia, as seen in Aldous Huxley's *Brave New World* (1932) and George Orwell's *Nineteen Eighty-Four* (1949).

Utopian literature is related to attempts to discover utopias, such as Atlantis, the Fortunate Isles, or El Dorado; to describe the conditions of an earthly paradise attainable in the future, as in St. Augustine's *City of God;* or to create the conditions of a better society now, as in the many ideal communities founded in nineteenth-century America, including BROOK FARM, the Oneida community, and New Harmony.

References

Joyce O. Hertzler, **The History of Utopian Thought** (1923).
Mark Holloway, **Heavens on Earth: Utopian Communities in America 1680–1880**, 2nd ed. (1966).
Lewis Mumford, **The Story of the Utopias**, rev. ed. (1966).

Ut Pictura Poesis. "As with a picture, so with poetry": a belief, arising in the seventeenth century with TOPOGRAPHICAL POETRY and prevailing in the eighteenth, that poetry should be like a painting. Although Horace's phrase was used as a justification for the belief, the Latin poet actually said only that poems, like pictures, have varying qualities to be variously judged:

> Ut pictura poesis: erit quae, si propius stes,
> te capiat magis, et quaedam, si longius abstes.
> haec amat obscurum, volet haec sub luce videri,
> iudicis argutum quae non formidat acumen;
> haec placuit semel, haec deciens repetita placebit.
> *Ars Poetica 361–365*

As with a picture, so with poetry. One will captivate you more the nearer you stand, and another the farther. This loves the shade; that will want to be seen under light, not dreading the judge's lively penetration. This pleased once; that ten times reviewed will please.

V

Vade Mecum.   Latin for "go with me": a handbook or manual carried about for frequent reference.

Vanity Press.   A firm that accepts and publishes books of doubtful commercial value, deriving its income from charging the costs of publication to the author. See SUBSCRIPTION PUBLICATION.

Variable Foot.   In FREE VERSE, a unit with one primary stress, and a variable number of unstressed or lightly stressed syllables. William Carlos Williams used the term frequently, applying it especially to the stepped-down TERCET of *The Desert Music and Other Poems* (1954) and *Journey to Love* (1955), as in the opening lines of "Asphodel, That Greeny Flower":

> Of asphodel, that greeny flower,
> > like a buttercup
> > > upon its branching stem—
> save that it's green and wooden—
> > I come, my sweet,
> > > to sing to you.

Count one beat (one foot) to each line.

Variorum Edition.   "With notes of various persons," from the Latin *cum notis variorum*. A variorum EDITION collects in one place many notations, commentaries, and interpretations of a work, by a variety of scholars. The term is also used for an edition gathering the different versions of a work from previous printings, author's revisions, and so on. Examples include *The New Variorum Shakespeare*, edited by H. H. Furness and others, and *The Variorum Edition of the Poems of W. B. Yeats*, edited by Peter Allt and Russell K. Alspach.

Varronian Satire.   See MENIPPEAN SATIRE.

Vatic.   Divinely inspired, oracular (from Latin *vates*, "prophet"). Ancient poets considered themselves divinely inspired, or hoped to be, as they called for INSPIRATION from the Muse. Some modern poets, like Blake and Whitman, have been called *vatic*.

Vaudeville.   A stage show of unrelated songs, skits, acrobatics, dances, jokes, and the like, thriving particularly in America from 1881, when Tony Pastor staged his first big show in New York, until 1932, when the Palace Theatre closed. Many famous entertainers began on the vaudeville circuits that moved from New York to other cities: George M. Cohan, Harry Houdini, W. C. Fields, Will Rogers, Eddie Cantor, Jimmy Durante, Jack Benny. Such variety shows originated in eighteenth-century London with farces, especially those staged by John Rich, and songs and acrobatics between the acts of other plays.

The term originated with the light topical songs attributed to Olivier Basselin, who lived in the fifteenth-century in the Vau de Vire, the Vire Valley in Normandy: *chanson du Vau de Vire*. In a letter to Richard West from Paris, 18 June 1739, Horace Walpole furnished the first recorded usage in English: "I will send you one of the vaudevilles or ballads which they sing at the comedy after their *petites pièces*." The first appearance of the term to mean "stage entertainment" was in 1833.

Vehicle.   See TENOR AND VEHICLE.

Venus and Adonis Stanza.   The STANZA of Shakespeare's "Venus and Adonis": six iambic pentameter lines, combining a quatrain and a couplet (as at the end of a Shakespearean SONNET), rhyming *ababcc*. Other poets have used it as well, including Chidiock Tichborne in his "Elegy" and Thomas Campion in "My Sweetest Lesbia."

Verisimilitude (*Vraisemblance* in French).   The appearance of actuality. "Swift possesses the art of verisimilitude," wrote Scott (*Life of Swift*, 1814). Poe valued the term and the effect of actuality in his fantastic tales. Defoe wrote *A Journal of the Plague Year* with such verisimilitude that many took it for an authentic eyewitness account.

Vers de Société.   "Society verse"—witty, polished, and suave light verse written to amuse polite society. Anacreon, Catullus, Martial, and Horace among the ancients, Jean Froissart of the fourteenth century, and Herrick, Carew, and Lovelace of the early seventeenth wrote many short verses that qualify. But the term originated with the playful and sophisticated lyrics of the seventeenth-century French salons, particularly that of Catherine de Vivonne, marquise de Rambouillet, with Vincent Voiture (1597–1648) the preeminent writer. In England, Matthew Prior (1664–1721) was outstanding, and Pope's *Rape of the Lock*, though large for the genre in its MOCK-EPIC dimensions, the all-time masterpiece. William Ernest Henley and Austin Dobson revived the form in the late nineteenth century, and Sir John Betjeman in the twentieth. In America, Ogden Nash created his unique unpolished mode.

Verse. (1) One line of poetry. (2) A STANZA, particularly with a refrain. (3) Poetry in general. (4) Light poetry as opposed to serious.

Verse Forms. The characteristic shapes or structures of different kinds of poems. The form of a poem is determined by such structural elements as the number of lines, the METER, the RHYME SCHEME, and the characteristic STANZA. These elements may be rigidly prescribed, as for *fixed forms* like the sonnet and the villanelle, or more loosely defined, as for the ballad and the ode. Forms defined in their alphabetical place in this book are listed here according to the number of lines in each:

3 lines:	HAIKU
4 lines:	CLERIHEW
5 lines:	LIMERICK; TANKA
8 lines:	TRIOLET
10 lines (and tail):	CURTAL SONNET
11 lines:	ROUNDEL
13 or 14 lines:	RONDEL
14 lines:	SONNET
15 lines (usually):	RONDEAU
19 lines:	VILLANELLE
25 lines:	RONDEAU REDOUBLÉ
28 lines (usually):	BALLADE
39 lines:	SESTINA
Varying line counts:	BALLAD; ODE; PANTOUM

Forms without names listed here may be described by their most prominent structural elements, as for example, a poem in TERZA RIMA, or in HEROIC COUPLETS, or in three QUATRAINS. See also CONCRETE POETRY; FREE VERSE; SHAPED POEM.

Verse Paragraph. A paragraphed unit of thought in a long poem in BLANK VERSE or couplets. Irregular FREE VERSE units, like those of Whitman, are sometimes considered verse paragraphs.

Versification. The mechanics of poetic composition. See METER; SCANSION.

Vers Libre. See FREE VERSE.

Vice. A stock character from the medieval MORALITY PLAY, a mischief-making tempter, like Puck or Ariel. See CHARACTERS; STOCK CHARACTERS.

Victorian Period (1837–1901). The reign of Queen Victoria. Popularly considered an age of earnest propriety in manners, language, and literature, with the ideal delicacy and purity of women cloaking a masculine hypocrisy that exploited the poor, plundered the colonies, and filled the brothels. The middle class was coming into prominence. The industrial revolution girdled the globe in prosperity and optimism. By the end of Victoria's reign, the railroad, the steamship, the dynamo, the electric streetcar, and the incandescent lamp had transformed the Western world. The automobile was on the road. In 1901, France, the inventer and leader, produced 5386 cars and the United States about 2500. The Automobile Club of Great Britain competed in French city-to-city races that would soon improve highways and accelerate transportation.

Aside from the middle-class complacency and hypocrisy attacked by contemporaries as well as by moderns, a considerable commitment to Christian duty toward one's fellows prevailed in personal life and public reform. Parliament passed laws against slavery and abusive child labor. Founded in 1836, the London Working Men's Association drew up a Charter (1838)—in a movement soon called CHARTISM—petitioning for expanded suffrage and other parliamentary reforms, most of them eventually enacted later in the century. The European revolutions of 1848 gained much sympathy in England, and the socialist movement reached London personally in 1849 with Karl Marx, expelled from both Prussia and France. The botched Crimean War with Russia (1854–1855) exposed governmental inefficiency, brought reforms, and demonstrated through Florence Nightingale, founder of modern nursing, the professional ability of women.

Religion and science, mutually supportive in the eighteenth century, fell into open conflict. In 1854, Pope Pius IX proclaimed the IMMACULATE CONCEPTION, freeing "the Blessed Virgin Mary, from the first instant of her conception, . . . from all stain of Original Sin" because she was destined to become the mother of Christ. In 1859, Darwin's *Origin of Species* denied divine purpose in the evolution of life. In 1867, in "Dover Beach," Matthew Arnold heard the Sea of Faith pouring away over the rocky edges of the world. In 1882, Nietzsche's madman declared God dead (*Die fröhliche Wissenschaft, The Joyful Knowledge*).

The novel continued to flourish with Dickens, Thackeray, and Trollope. George Eliot and Hardy brought it to new tragic and realistic heights. Shaw, and Ibsen in translation, brought the drama to new social consciousness. Tennyson and Browning dominated poetry. The

PRE-RAPHAELITE MOVEMENT harked back to the Middle Ages and early Italian RENAISSANCE for renewed inspiration in pictorial nature. The DECADENTS put art for art's sake above any natural representation or moral purpose. The modern world was emerging in persistent experiments rejecting all previous modes, freeing verse, looking for the logical positivism of factuality, to stand as symbols and images, without comment and interpretation.

The "Late Victorian Period" dates from 1870, when the Prussian War raised Germany into an international threat, and uncertainty and pessimism eroded the earlier Victorian confidence.

Vignette. (1) A brief, subtle, and intimate literary portrait, named for *vignette portraiture*, which is unbordered, shading off into the surrounding color at the edges, with features delicately rendered. (2) A short essay, sketch, or story, usually less than five hundred words.

Villain. From Old French *vilain*, a peasant or churl. The term now denotes a CHARACTER of evil purpose set in opposition to a HERO or PROTAGONIST. Some villains, however, usurp the role of protagonist, or come close to it, Milton's Satan being a famous example. See CHARACTERS.

Villanelle. One of the French VERSE FORMS, in 5 TERCETS, all rhyming *aba*, and a QUATRAIN, rhyming *abaa*. The entire first and third lines are repeated alternately as the final lines of tercets 2, 3, 4, and 5, and together to conclude the quatrain. Examples include E. A. Robinson's "The House on the Hill," William Empson's "Missing Dates," Theodore Roethke's "The Waking," and Dylan Thomas's "Do Not Go Gentle into That Good Night."

Virelay. (1) A medieval French poem or song with nine-line stanzas patterned like the LAY with two rhymes only per STANZA. The rhyme goes *aabaabaab*, the *a* lines having five feet and the *b* lines two, but, unlike the lay, the end rhyme of the first stanza becomes the opening long-line rhyme of the second stanza, and so on until the last stanza uses the *a* rhyme as its concluding short-line rhyme. A three-stanza virelay would thus rhyme *aabaabaab bbcbbcbbc ccaccacca*. (2) Loosely, other similar French forms and songs.

Virgule. A "little rod"—the diagonal mark or slash used to indicate line ends in poetry printed continuously in running prose:

> As Marvell says, "The grave's a fine and private place, / But none I think do there embrace."

Visual Rhyme.   See EYE RHYME.

Voice-Over.   In film, the voice of an unseen speaker commenting "over" a scene, filling in background, and the like. Occasionally, as in Sir Laurence Olivier's *Hamlet,* it is the voice of silent thought. See SOUND-OVER.

Volta.   The turn of thought occurring after the OCTAVE of an Italian SONNET. A Miltonic sonnet is characterized by the absence of this turn, as the thought continues uninterrupted from octave to sestet. The term may also be applied to other places where a turn of thought occurs, as sometimes after the first two QUATRAINS of a Shakespearean sonnet.

Vorticism.   A brief literary-artistic movement centered on the magazine *Blast* (1914–1915), founded and edited by Ezra Pound and Wyndham Lewis, painter and writer. A vortex of creative energy, stationary yet dynamic, like a whirlpool, found expression in cubistic, futuristic, and abstract forms. The French sculptor Henri Gaudier-Brzeska was the chief originator, but Joyce and T. S. Eliot partook.

Vraisemblance.   See VERISIMILITUDE.

Vulgate.   (1) A people's common vernacular language (Latin *vulgus,* "common people"). (2) The Vulgate Bible, translated by St. Jerome c. 383–405 from the Hebrew Masoretic text, with advice from rabbis and support from the Old Latin (the Itala) and Greek texts; the official Roman Catholic Bible. (3) The "Vulgate Romances," Old French prose versions of Arthurian stories, from the thirteenth century.

Wandering Jew. A man who, according to legend, urged Jesus to go faster as he carried the cross to Calvary and who, consequently, must wander the earth until the Second Coming. The story first appeared in Matthew Paris's *Chronica Majora*, which continued the work of Roger of Wendover, chronicler to the monastery of St. Albans, England, whom Paris succeeded as chronicler in 1236. The chronicle tells of an Armenian archbishop who visited St. Albans in 1228 (therefore in Wendover's part) and told of dining recently with a Christian named Joseph who, as Pontius Pilate's porter Cartaphilus, had urged Jesus on, had been told to "tarry till I come," had converted to Christianity, and now testified to the new faith by his longevity. In 1602, a pamphlet published at Leyden tells that Paulus von Eizen, bishop of Schleswig, met a Jew named Ahasuerus in 1542 who admitted to being the famous wanderer. The story was popular from the sixteenth to nineteenth centuries. Shelley's *Queen Mab* (1821) is one version. Joyce's Leopold Bloom in *Ulysses* (1922) is another.

Wardour Street English. An artificial, archaistic style—a criticism of William Morris's translated *Odyssey* (1887). Wardour Street, London, sold antiques, some spurious.

War of the Theaters. Competitive satirizing among Elizabethan dramatists, beginning with Ben Jonson's *Every Man out of His Humour* (1599), a satire against social pretentiousness dedicated to the gentlemen of the INNS OF COURT. Young John Marston, a lawyer of the Middle Temple, took offense, attacking Jonson's egotistical self-portrait in *Cynthia's Revels* (1600) with a satirical caricature in *Histriomastix* (1600). The war continued in Marston's *Jack Drum's Entertainment* (1600), Thomas Dekker's (with Chettle and Haughton) *Patient Grissel* (1600), Jonson's *Poetaster* (1601), and Dekker's *Satiromastix, or The Untrussing of the Humourous Poet* (1601). Because Jonson had sold *Cynthia's Revels* to the Queen's Revels, the boy actors at the Blackfriars theater, and because the boys of Paul's (choristers from St. Paul's Cathedral) and the Queen's Revels (in whom Marston had a considerable financial stake) acted Marston's plays, the war broadened to include rivalry between children and the established companies, the "common stages" mentioned in *Hamlet* (II.ii). An anonymous students' satire at Cambridge, *The Return from Parnassus* (c. 1602) declared that

Shakespeare had bested Jonson, indicating Shakespeare's involvement and prompting the theory that *Troilus and Cressida* (c. 1602) represents Shakespeare's part in the war. See SCHOOL PLAYS.

Watermark. (1) A translucent logo—a fleur-de-lis, for instance,—left in seventeenth- and eighteenth-century laid paper to denote the manufacturer. (2) One of the widely spaced perpendicular CHAIN LINES or narrowly spaced horizontal WIRE LINES left by the metal grid on which the pulp of laid paper settles to form a sheet.

Weak Ending. A line end not normally stressed but lifted into stress by the METER, as in *-ges* and *-mer* in Shakespeare's lines from *Henry IV*, Part I:

> Glittering in golden coats like images;
> As full of spirit as the month of May
> And gorgeous as the sun in the midsummer;
> Wanton as youthful goats, wild as young bulls.

Well-Made Novel. A neatly constructed novel, so termed from the expression WELL-MADE PLAY.

Well-Made Play. An ingeniously plotted play, with neat dialectical repartee, asides, and a climactic scene (the OBLIGATORY SCENE). The concept derives from MELODRAMA and the French *pièce bien faite* ("well-made play") of Eugène Scribe (1791–1861) and Victorien Sardou (1831–1908). English examples included Dion Boucicault's *London Assurance* (1841), Tom Taylor's *The Ticket-of-Leave Man* (1863), Henry Arthur Jones's *Silver King* (1882), and Arthur Wing Pinero's *The Second Mrs. Tanqueray* (1893). Ibsen and Shaw both perfected the well-made play.

Welsh Literature. The writings of the people of Wales. Welsh literature began in the sixth century with northern heroic bards composing to intricate rules of meter and rhyme. The "Four Ancient Books of Wales"—*The Book of Taliesin, The Book of Aneurin, The Black Book of Caemarthen,* and the *Red Book of Hergest*—contain, among others, the major work of Taliesin, Aneurin, Myrddin (Merlin), and Llywarch Hen. The *englyn,* a short poem perhaps influenced by Latin epigrams, appeared in central and eastern Wales. The *Red Book of Hergest* contains five tales connected with Arthur, three coming from French originals.
 Under King Gruffud ap Cynan (1054–1137), court poets (*gogynfeirdd*) developed a mannered archaistic style culminating in the work of Cynddelw Brydydd Mawr (fl. 1155–1200), called "The Great Poet,"

probably because of his physical stature. From the same period comes the *Four Branches of the Mabinogi,* prose tales compiled eventually in the fourteenth and fifteenth centuries and in the nineteenth century given the name the MABINOGION.

In the fourteenth century, Dafydd ap Gwilym, the greatest Welsh poet and Chaucer's contemporary, initiated the "Golden Age" of Welsh poetry in south Wales, abandoning the stilted style for the more colloquial, recognizing the natural world, elevating love poetry, and inaugurating the *Cywyddwyr* period, named for the *cywydd* meter he made famous—seven-syllable couplets rhyming alternate masculine and feminine endings, the unaccented syllable matching the accented, as in *sing, blowing.* The *Cywyddwyr* period culminated in the fifteenth and declined in the sixteenth centuries as Tudor England dampened local interest in Welsh culture. But Bishop William Morgan translated the Bible (1583), and theological-educational interests produced some prose. Poetry revived in the eighteenth century as religious writers adapted the *cywydd* and the *awdl,* another ancient form, along with some free verse, to modern times and hymnody. Other theological writers developed a clear and elegant prose.

Wales awoke politically in the nineteenth century, especially in the work of Daniel Owens, the "Welsh Dickens." In 1819, the twelfth-century Eisteddfod, an annual bardic and choral competition, was revived and continues down to the present. The founding of the University of Wales in 1872 stimulated further pride in Welsh language and literature. Significant twentieth-century writers are: (poetry) William John Gruffydd, T. Gwynn-Jones, Saunders Lewis; (short story) Dewi Williams, Islywn Williams, Kate Roberts; (novel) Kate Roberts, Tegla Davies, T. Rowland Hughes, Islwyn Ffowc Ellis; (drama) R. G. Berry, D. T. Davies, Saunders Lewis, Huw Lloyd Edwards, T. Parry, Gwilym R. Jones.

References

Thomas Parry, **A History of Welsh Literature** (1955).
Gwyn Williams, **An Introduction to Welsh Poetry** (1953).
Ifor Williams, **The Beginnings of Welsh Poetry** (1972).

Weltanschauung. "World view" (German), especially from a particular standpoint—pessimistic, optimistic, romantic, and so forth.

Weltschmerz. "World pain" (German). A romantic, pessimistic anguish over the ills of the world.

Western. A novel, story, or film about cowboys and gunslingers of the nineteenth-century American frontier. Westerns arose in the DIME NOVEL and PULP MAGAZINES. The itinerant cowhand or the town marshal, facing the deadly gun of the outlaw on behalf of innocence and justice, has become America's knight in denim armor. Owen Wister's *Virginian* (1902) lifted the Western into significant literature, as did Walter Van Tilburg Clark's *Ox-Bow Incident* (1940). Zane Grey's many stereotypic Westerns, most notably *Riders of the Purple Sage* (1912), sold thirteen million copies during his life (1875–1939). See POPULAR LITERATURE.

West Indian Literature. See COMMONWEALTH LITERATURE.

Wettin. See ROYAL HOUSES.

Wheel. See BOB AND WHEEL.

Whole Rhyme. See EXACT RHYME.

Widow. A short line (perhaps the end of a paragraph) printed at the beginning of a page or column. Generally widows are discovered in PROOF and eliminated by resetting before the final printing.

Windsor. See ROYAL HOUSES.

Wire Line. One of the thin, translucent, horizontal lines, about a sixteenth of an inch apart, left by the metal grid on which the pulp of laid paper settle to form a sheet. See CHAIN LINE; WATERMARK.

Wisdom Literature. Books of the Bible and Apocrypha concerning ethics, religion, and the law, as distinguished from the prophetic and liturgical literature. Wisdom literature consists chiefly of Job, Proverbs, Ecclesiasticus, Ecclesiastes, Wisdom of Solomon.

Wit and Humor. Wit is intellectual acuity; humor, an amused indulgence of human deficiencies. Wit now denotes the acuity that produces laughter. It originally meant mere understanding, then quickness of understanding, then, beginning in the seventeenth century, quick perception coupled with creative fancy. Humor (British *humour,* from the four HUMORS) was simply a disposition, usually eccentric. In the eighteenth century, which, with the seventeenth, had debated the terms, *humour* came to mean a laughable eccentricity and then a kindly amusement at such eccentricity. Ben Jonson's comic satires on fixated eccentricities, *Every Man in His Humour* (1958) and *Every Man out of His Humour* (1599), show the way in which early *humor* indicated the laughable.

Women as Actors. Females in dramatic roles. In Greece, men took the female roles. In Roman comedy, the future Empress Theodora (d. 548) could make her mark as comic slave and naked pornographer in Constantinople. Beginning in 1545, the Italian COMMEDIA DELL'ARTE involved a female Inamorata and her servant, or soubrette, Columbine, and subsequent French and Italian companies included actresses. England maintained only male companies until the RESTORATION (1660), when Charles II, returning from exile in France, licensed two theaters and brought the French custom of actresses with him. Jacobean masques, however, drawing amateur performers from the court, had frequently included women, and a French company with actresses had played in London in 1629, but to a cold reception. Sir William D'Avenant's ground-breaking *Siege of Rhodes* (1656) featured one Mrs. Coleman, the first English actress, as the heroine, Ianthe. Conversely, some boys continued to appear in female roles on the Restoration stage.

Word Accent. The stress fixed in a word by normal usage, as in $\overline{\text{rip}}\breve{\text{ple}}$. See ACCENT and RHETORICAL ACCENT.

Wrenched Accent. An accent shifted from normal word accent ($\overline{\text{la}}\breve{\text{dy}}$ becoming $\breve{\text{la}}\overline{\text{dy}}$), by meter or rhyme, as in Blake's "I asked a thief." An angel comes along:

> Had a peach from the tree,
> And 'twixt earnest & joke
> Enjoy'd the Lady.

See ACCENT.

Y

Yale Critics. Literary critics influential in the 1970s and 1980s. Of the Yale Critics, Paul de Man (*Allegories of Reading*), Geoffrey Hartman (*Deconstruction and Criticism*), and J. Hillis Miller (*Fiction and Repetition*) have been associated especially with the POST-STRUCTURALISM of Jacques Derrida. Like Derrida, they perceive a literary work as a set of conflicting signs, with a fixed meaning undecidable because of the elusive, ambiguous nature of language. Their more pragmatic colleague Harold Bloom (*The Anxiety of Influence* and *A Map of Misreading*) has been more Freudian (see FREUDIAN CRITICISM), with his vision of the history of poetry as an Oedipal struggle in which each new "strong" poet, the spiritual offspring of an earlier poet, attempts in poetry to murder the precursor. It follows for Bloom (*Agon: Towards a Theory of Revisionism*) that the "strong reading" (or "misreading") of an individual critic provides persuasive understanding of a text that might otherwise be seen as a jumble of incoherent possibilities. See DECONSTRUCTION.

York. See ROYAL HOUSES.

Young Man from the Provinces. Lionel Trilling's term, coined in an introduction to James's *The Princess Casamassima* in 1948, to describe a genre of novels in which a rural youth seeks achievement in the city like a "questing knight," there to be tested. Trilling cited, as predecessors to *The Princess Casamassima*, Stendahl's *Red and the Black*, Balzac's *Père Goriot* and *Lost Illusions*, Dickens's *Great Expectations*, Flaubert's *Sentimental Education*, and, as a later example, Fitzgerald's *Great Gatsby*. He included this essay in *The Liberal Imagination* (1950).

Z

Zeugma. The technique of using one word to yoke two or more others for ironic or amusing effect, achieved when at least one of the yoked is a misfit, as in Pope's "lose her Heart, or Necklace, at a Ball," or Gibbon's "laws the wily tyrant dictated and obeyed." It is also called SYLLEPSIS, with *zeugma* sometimes restricted to grammatical misfits only: "He lay down and carpets."

Zoom Shot. Something filmed by moving the camera, or its zoom lens, swiftly in or out, described *zoom in* or *zoom out*.

CHRONOLOGY
OF LITERATURE
AND WORLD EVENTS

Barbara M. Perkins

CHRONOLOGY OF LITERATURE AND WORLD EVENTS

WORLD	BRITAIN	THE AMERICAS
B.C.		
c. 3500 First pictographs, Sumeria		
3500–2631 Old Kingdom, Egypt		
c. 3200 Cuneiform ideographs, Sumeria		
c. 3000 Egyptian hieroglyphics; urban culture in India		
2680 Great Pyramid of Cheops		**c. 2500** Earliest remains of agricultural village sites at Huaca Prieta, Peru, and Cuello on the Yucatán peninsula
2375–1800 Middle Kingdom, Egypt		
c. 2100–c. 2000 Reign of Hammurabi, Babylonian lawgiver		
Before 2000 *Epic of Gilgamesh*		
c. 1850 Semitic syllabic writing at Sinai		
1650–1220 Hebrew captivity in Egypt		
1580–1090 Egyptian Empire	**c. 16th century** Building of Stonehenge	
1500 Cities in Hwang Valley, China; alphabetical script in Nile and Euphrates Valleys		
c. 1400? Phoenician syllabary from Sinai		
1380–1362 Reign of Amenhotep IV (Ikhnaton)		
1360–1350 Reign of Tutankhamon		

c. 1250 Trojan War
1250?–900 Greek alphabet from Phoenician syllabary
1122–255 Chou Dynasty, China
1010–974 Reign of David, king of the Jews

800–500 *The Upanishads*
8th to 2nd centuries Old Testament texts
753–509 Roman Kingdom
c. 750? Homer
7th century Zoroaster; Sappho (born c. 630)
6th century Solon; Anacreon (born c. 570); Lao Tzu (born c. 604)
Siddharta Gautama Buddha (563?–483)
Confucius (c. 551–478)
c. 522 Pindar born
521–485 Reign of Darius I of Persia
509–29 Roman Republic; Aeschylus (525–456)
5th century Golden Age of Greek tragedy; Phidias
5th to 1st centuries *The Mahabharata*
500–449 Persian wars

c. 1000–A.D. 300 Mayan civilization in Yucatán; development of calendar, hieroglyphics

495

WORLD	BRITAIN	THE AMERICAS

WORLD

Sophocles (496?–406)
490 Battle of Marathon
Herodotus (c. 485–425)
485–464 Reign of Xerxes I, Persia
Euripides (480?–406?)
Socrates (469–399)
c. 460 Hippocrates born
Thucydides (c. 460–c. 399)
458 Sophocles's *Oresteia* wins first prize
Aristophanes (448?–380?)
441 Sophocles, *Antigone*
431 Euripides, *Medea*
Plato (429–347)
411 Aristophanes, *Lysistrata*
404 Fall of Athens
Aristotle (384–322)
Demosthenes (384?–322)
Alexander the Great (356–323)
332 Founding of Alexandria
323–330 The Ptolemys of Egypt
3rd century Great Wall of China begun;
Euclid, foundations of geometry;
Aristarchus of Samos, sun-centered
universe
255–206 Ch'in Dynasty
206–A.D. 221 Han Dynasty

496

124 Chinese found Grand College to
    train rulers
Cicero (106–43)
1st century *The Bhagavad-Gita*
Julius Caesar (100–44)
Lucretius (99–55)
Catullus (84–54)
Virgil (70–19)
73 Roman slave uprising
Cleopatra (69–30)
Horace (65–8)

55 Julius Caesar's conquest of Britain

Ovid 43–A.D. 17
Augustus Caesar (30–A.D. 14)
Jesus Christ (c. 6 B.C.–A.D. 27)

A.D.

14–476 Roman Empire

43 Emperor Claudius visits Britain

Juvenal (50?–after 127)
Tacitus (55–120)
65 Death of Petronius
67 Coming of Buddhism to China
79 Destruction of Pompeii
c. 100 First known manufacture of
    paper in China
Ptolemy (fl. 127–151), earth-centered
    theory of the universe

122–127 Building of Hadrian's wall

WORLD

A.D.

200–400 Tartar invasion of China

4th century *The Kamasutra*
St. Jerome (c. 347–420)
St. Augustine (354–430)

c. 400 Kalidasa, *Shakuntala*, Indian
drama

Attila the Hun (406?–453)

410 Fall of Rome to Alaric the Hun

Boethius (c. 475–525), *De Consolatione
Philosophiae*

522 Buddhism enters Japan

Mohammed (570–632)
590–604 Papacy of St. Gregory the
Great

BRITAIN

407 Romans evacuate Britain
c. 432 St. Patrick arrives in Ireland

(449–early twelfth century) **OLD
ENGLISH LITERATURE**

449 Angles, Saxons invade England

Gildas (516?–570?), first mention of
prototype of King Arthur

563 St. Columba from Ireland lands on
Iona, Hebrides, to establish monastery
c. 565 St. Columba converts Pictish
king, Scotland

597 Augustine of Canterbury arrives as
missionary

THE AMERICAS

7th century The Koran

618–905 T'ang Dynasty
622 The Hegira (flight of Mohammed from Mecca, year 1 of Islamic calendar)
630–800 Golden Age of Tibet

Wang Wei **(699–759)**, Chinese painter
Li Tai Po **(c. 700–762)**, Chinese poet of T'ang Dynasty
Tu Fu **(712–770)**, Chinese poet
Po Chu-i **(722–846)**, Chinese poet

Charlemagne **(742–814)**, king of the Franks and Holy Roman Emperor

c. 615 Angles in power in Northumbria, beginning first literate culture of any Germanic people

633 St. Aidan from Iona brings Celtic Christianity to Northumbria
Aldhelm **(640?–709)**
c. 650–700 *Widsith*
650–750 *Beowulf*
Caedmon **(fl. 657–680)**
664 Synod of Whitby reinstates Roman Christianity
The Venerable Bede **(c. 673–735)**, *The Ecclesiastical History of the English People*

735 Archbishopric of York founded
Alcuin **(735–804)**
c. 750 *Waldere; The Fight at Finnsburg*

700–1100 Wari Empire, Peru

WORLD	BRITAIN	THE AMERICAS
751 Papermaking reaches Samarkand from China	Offa II, King of Mercia (757–796)	
781 Alcuin invited to set up school in Charlemagne's court	787 First recorded Danish raid	
793 First paper made in Baghdad, under Harun-al Rashid	Cynewulf (late 8th or early 9th century)	
	c. 800 *Andreas*	
	9th century *Judith*	
	Egbert, king of Wessex (802–839)	
	856–875 Height of Danish raids	
	Late 9th or early 10th century	
	Deor; The Wanderer; The Seafarer; The Ruin; The Wife's Lament and The Husband's Message	
	Alfred the Great (849–899), king of Wessex 871–899	
c. 900 *Quem quaeritis* trope; Invention of gun powder	878 Peace of Wedmore; England divided between Alfred and Guthrun the Dane	
910 Monastery founded at Cluny	c. 891 *Anglo-Saxon Chronicle* begins	
	924–939 Ethelstan completes conquest of Danelaw	
	c. 937 *Battle of Brunanburh*	
950 First appearance of paper money in China	Aelfric (c. 955–c. 1020)	

960–1279 Sung Dynasty

Lady Murasaki Shikibu (978?–1031?), *The Tale of Genji*

Ibn Sina [Avicenna] (980–1037), Islamic philosopher and physician

993 Founding of Delhi

St. Anselm (1033?–1109), named to Canterbury by William the Conqueror

1041 Chinese develop movable type

959–975 Reign of Edgar (943?–975), king of the English

c. 990–998 Heptateuch, first seven books of the Bible

c. 991 *The Battle of Maldon*

late 10th century Manuscript of *Beowulf*

978–1016 Reign of Aethelred the Redeless; Danish raids resume under Sven I; tribute paid

1003–1023 Wulfstan, Archbishop of York

1013–1016 Sven I acknowledged as king; Aethelred flees

1017–1035 Reign of King Canute

1042–1066 Reign of King Edward the Confessor

1066 Harold Godwinson elected king

1066 Norman Conquest: Harold killed at the Battle of Hastings; William, duke of Normandy, takes throne

1066–1087 Reign of William I

c. 1000 Leif Ericson reaches North American coast

WORLD

Pierre Abelard (1079–1142)

Bernard of Clairvaux (1090?–1153)

1095–1099 First Crusade
c. 1100 *Song of Roland*

1120 Knights Templar founded
1123 Death of Omar Khayyám

Frederick Barbarossa (1123–1190)
Holy Roman Emperor

Averroës (1126–1298), Spanish–Arabian philosopher, author of commentaries on Aristotle

BRITAIN

1086 The Great Domesday Census
1087–1100 Reign of William Rufus

1093 Anselm named archbishop of Canterbury

1100–1350 ANGLO-NORMAN PERIOD
1100–1135 Reign of Henry I
Thomas à Becket (1118–1170)

Robert Wace (c. 1124–1174), *Roman de Brut* (1155)

1125 William of Malmesbury, *Gesta Regum Anglorum*

1128 Cistercian order established in Britain

THE AMERICAS

1135–1154 Rivalry of Matilda and Stephen for crown
After 1135 Geoffrey of Monmouth, *Historia Regum Briamniae (History of the Kings of Britain)*
Walter Map (c. 1140–c. 1209) introduced Grail story to Arthurian cycle

1147–1149 Second Crusade
1150 Building of Angkor Wat
Benoit de Sainte-More, *Roman de Troie*, c. 1150–1160
Provençal troubadours flourished 1150–1200
1152 Henry Plantagenet marries Eleanor of Aquitaine

1150–1500 MIDDLE ENGLISH LITERATURE

1154–1399 House of Plantagenet
1154–1189 Reign of Henry II
Marie de France (fl. 1155–1190)

1161 First known use of gunpowder in war
Genghis Khan (1162–1227)
Chrétien de Troyes (fl. 1170)
Wolfram von Eschenbach, (c. 1170–1220), *Parzival*

1164 Thomas à Becket made archbishop of Canterbury
1170 Becket martyred

1175 Building of Canterbury Cathedral begins

503

WORLD

St Francis of Assisi (11822-1226)
1185–1336 Rise of Zen Buddhism, Samurai class
1187 Capture of Jerusalem by Saladin

Late 12th century Song of el Cid

1189–1192 Third Crusade

1190 Teutonic Knights founded

1200 Charter of the University of Paris

1202–1204 Fourth Crusade
1204 Sack of Constantinople; great library burned
1208 Albigensian Crusade

Gottfried von Strassburg (fl. 1210), Tristan
1212 Children's Crusade; Genghis Khan invades China

BRITAIN

John of Salisbury (d. 1180), pupil of Abelard, Policratus

Layamon (fl. 1189–1207)

1189–1199 Reign of Richard I, Coeur de Lion

1199–1216 Reign of King John

c. 1200 Ancrene Riwle; the Katherine group of saints' lives; The Owl and the Nightingale

c. 1205 Layamon, Brut

13th century Founding of Cambridge and Oxford Universities

THE AMERICAS

Late 12th century Aztecs arrive in Mexico

Kublai Khan (1216–1294)

c. 1225 *Roman de la Rose* begun by
  Guillaume de Lorris
Thomas Aquinas (1225–1294)
1233 Inquisition established

Dante Alighieri (1265–1321)
Giotto (c. 1266–1337)
1269–1295 Travels of Marco Polo

c. 1275 *Roman de la Rose* completed by
  Jean de Meun

1288–1293 Polo in India

1291 Kublai Khan invades Japan

1215 Signing of Magna Carta
1216–1272 Reign of Henry III
1220 Dominican order arrives in
  England
1224 Franciscan order arrives

c. 1240 *The Bestiary*
c. 1250 *Havelock the Dane; King
  Horn; Floris and Blancheflour*
c. 1250–1300 *Debate of the Body and the
  Soul*
1258 Provisions of Oxford Institute
  Great Council to advise the king

1272–1307 Reign of Edward I

1280s Edward's wars against the Welsh;
  building of coastal castles in Wales
1290 Expulsion of the Jews
Late 13th century *Amis and Amiloun;
  Land of Cockayne*
1290–1314 Wars against the Scots

---

c. 1250 Incas enter Cuzco, Peru

WORLD

13th to 16th centuries *1001 Nights* stories compiled

c. 1300 Paper mills operating in Spain, Italy, France, and Germany

St. Brigit of Sweden (**1303–1373**)

Petrarch (**1304–1374**)

1306 Expulsion of Jews from France

Giovanni Boccaccio (**1313–1375**)

Tamerlane (**1336?–1405**)

1337 Outbreak of the Hundred Years War

BRITAIN

13th and 14th centuries Secular and religious lyrics and ballads

Richard Rolle (**c. 1300–1349**)

c. 1300 *Richard Coeur de Lion; Guy of Warwick; Bevis of Hampton*

1303 *Handlyng Synne*

1307–1349 Reign of Edward II

1314 Battle of Bannockburn; Scots led by Robert the Bruce win independence

c. 1320 *Sir Orfeo*

1327 Parliament forces Edward II to abdicate; he is murdered in prison

1327–1377 Reign of Edward III

John Wyclif (**c. 1328–1384**)

William Langland (**c. 1332–c. 1400**)

John Gower (**c. 1330–1408**)

c. 1330 The Chester cycle of drama

THE AMERICAS

c. 1325 Building of Aztec capital, Tenochtitlan

Jean Froissart (1337–1410), *Chronicles*

1339–1349 Parliament divides into Houses of Commons and Lords

Geoffrey Chaucer (c. **1343–1400**)

1345 Founding of the Order of the Garter

1346 English victory at Crécy

St Catherine of Siena (**1347–1380**)
Boccaccio, *Decameron* (**1348–1353**)
1350–1650 Nō plays of Japan

1348–1349 Black Death

c. **1350** *William of Palerne; Tale of Gamelyn; Sir Launfal*

c. **1356** Sir John Mandeville, *Travels*

c. **1360** *Alliterative Morte Arthur*

Gawain Poet (fl. **1360–1400**)

1362 English designated official language of the courts

c. **1362–c. 1390** Langland's *Piers Plowman*

Thomas Hoccleve (c. **1368–c. 1437**)

1368–1644 Ming Dynasty

1369–1400 AGE OF CHAUCER
1369–1370 Chaucer, *The Book of the Duchess*

John Huss (**1369–1415**)

John Lydgate (c. **1370–c. 1450**)
Last quarter 14th century York cycle of plays

1377 First mention of Robin Hood
1377–1399 Reign of Richard II

WORLD

Filippo Brunelleschi (1377–1446),
   Florentine architect
1378–1417 Papal Schism
Thomas à Kempis (1379?–1471),
   Imitation of Christ

Jan Van Eyck (c. 1390–1441), credited
   with discovery of oil paint

Masaccio (1401–1428?), Florentine
   painter
Fra Filippo Lippi (c. 1406–1469),
student of Masaccio, teacher of
Botticelli

BRITAIN

c. 1379 Chaucer, *The House of Fame*
1379–1382 Chaucer, *Parliament of Fowls*
1381 Peasants' Revolt
1385 Chaucer, *Troilus and Criseyde*
c. 1385 *The Second Shepherds' Play*
1386 Chaucer, *Legend of Good Women*
1387 Chaucer, Prologue to *The
   Canterbury Tales*

c. 1392 *The Cuckoo and the Nightingale*
c. 1394 *Piers the Plowman's Creed*
1399 Richard II forced to abdicate
1399–1461 House of Lancaster
1399–1413 Reign of Henry IV
c. 1400 manuscript of *Sir Gawain and
   the Green Knight, Pearl, Purity,* and
   Patience

Sir Thomas Malory (c. 1410–1471)

THE AMERICAS

508

Joan of Arc (1412–1431)

1415 Battle of Agincourt; Treaty of Troyes: Henry V of England designated regent of France and successor to Charles VI

1428–1429 Joan of Arc's army triumphs
François Villon (1431–1463?)

Sandro Botticelli (c. 1444–1510), Florentine painter
1448 Charles VII retakes most of France from English
Lorenzo di Medici (1449–1492), Renaissance art patron
Hieronymus Bosch (c. 1450–1516), Dutch painter

Juliana of Norwich (d. 1413), *Revelations of Divine Love*
1413–1422 Reign of Henry V

Robert Henryson (c. 1420–c. 1490)
1422–1461 Reign of Henry VI
William Caxton (c. 1422–1491), First English printer
1422–1509 *The Paston Letters*
c. 1425 *The Castle of Perseverance*
After 1425 The Wakefield cycle of plays

c. 1438 *The Golden Legend* translated into English
Margery Kempe (d. 1440), English mystic

1450 Cade's Rebellion

WORLD	BRITAIN	THE AMERICAS
	c. 1450 *The Squire of Low Degree*	
Leonardo da Vinci (1452–1519), painter and scientist		
1453 Turks led by Mohammed II take Constantinople	1453–1456 Richard of York regent during Henry VI's insanity	
1455 Gutenberg Bible, first book printed with movable type	1455–1485 War of the Roses	
	William Dunbar (c. 1460–c. 1513)	
	John Skelton (c. 1460–1529)	
	1461–1485 House of York	
	1461–1483 Reign of Edward IV	
	1471 Queen Margaret's army defeated; Henry VI dies	
Desiderius Erasmus (1466?–1536), *In Praise of Folly*		
Niccolò Machiavelli (1469–1527), *The Prince*	1474 William Caxton prints his translation of Le Fevre, *Recuyell of the Histories of Troye* at Bruges, first book printed in English	
Albrecht Dürer (1471–1528), German artist		
Nicolaus Copernicus (1473–1543) Polish astronomer		
1473 First printed music		
Ludovico Ariosto (1474–1533), *Orlando Furioso*		
Michelangelo Buonarroti (1475–1564), sculptor, painter, architect, poet		

1476 Caxton establishes first printing press in England at Westminster
1477 Caxton's *Dictes and Sayenges of the Philosophers*, first book printed in England
Sir Thomas More (1478–1535)

1483 Edward V crowned, imprisoned, murdered
1483–1485 Reign of Richard III
1485 Caxton prints *Morte Darthur*
1485 Henry Tudor defeats Richard at Bosworth Field, is crowned Henry VII
1485–1603 House of Tudor
1485–1509 Reign of Henry VII
c. 1485 *Everyman*
1491–1547 Reign of Henry VIII

1500–1600 **RENAISSANCE PERIOD**
1485–1558 Early Tudor

1492–1504 Voyages of Columbus
1497 John Cabot lands on coast of North America

1478 Spanish Inquisition established
Baldassare Castiglione (1478–1529)
Martin Luther (1483–1546)

Raphael (1483–1520)
Ulrich Zwingli (1484–1531)

Titian (**c. 1490–1576**)
Ignatius Loyola (**1491–1556**)
1492 Expulsion of Jews from Spain
François Rabelais (**1494?–1553**)
1498 Vasco da Gama reaches Calcutta, India, and sails around Africa

WORLD

Pierluigi da Palestrina (1526?–1594)
Tulsi Das (1532–1623), Hindu poet
Michel de Montaigne (1533–1592)

1536 Calvin, *Institutes of the Christian Religion*
1540 Loyola founds Society of Jesus
El Greco (c. 1541–1614)

1543 Copernicus, *De Revolutionibus Orbium Coelestium*, theory of sun-centered universe
Torquato Tasso (1544–1595), *Jerusalem Delivered*

Miguel de Cervantes (1547–1616)

BRITAIN

1529 More named chancellor

1534 Act of Supremacy; English Reformation begins
1536 Tyndale's translation of the Bible

1547–1553 Reign of Edward VI
1551 Thomas Cranmer (1489–1556), *Articles of Religion*, basis for Anglicanism
Edmund Spenser (1552?–1599)
Sir Walter Raleigh (1552?–1618)
1553 Edward VI names Lady Jane Grey his heir; she is beheaded in 1554

THE AMERICAS

1528 Expedition including Cabeza de Vaca (Álvar Núñez) reaches Florida
c. 1530–1536 Núñez de Vaca and two companions explore the Southwest
1533 Pizarro expedition plunders Incan city of Cuzco

1542 Juan Cabrillo leads expedition to San Diego Bay area; Núñez de Vaca, *Los Naufragios (The Shipwrecked Men)* tells of wandering adventures in Southwest

Matteo Ricci (1552–1610), Jesuit missionary to China

1556–1598 Reign of Philip II of Spain

1560 Geneva Bible

Lope de Vega (1562–1635)

Galileo (1564–1642)

Johannes Kepler (1571–1630)
1571 Spanish take the Philippines; Battle of Lepanto, Christian galleys destroy Ottoman fleet, Cervantes wounded
Peter Paul Rubens (1577–1640)
1577–1580 Sir Francis Drake circumnavigates the world

513

1553–1558 Reign of Mary I; restoration of Catholic bishops, persecution of Protestants, Cranmer burned at stake
Sir Philip Sidney (1554–1586)
John Lyly (1554?–1606)

1558–1603 ELIZABETHAN AGE (REIGN OF ELIZABETH I)

1558 Loss of Calais
Thomas Kyd (1558–1594)
1559 Mary Stuart assumes title of Queen of Scotland and England

Francis Bacon (1561–1626)
Samuel Daniel (1562–1619)
Michael Drayton (1563–1631)
William Shakespeare (1564–1616)
Christopher Marlowe (1564–1593)
Thomas Nashe (1567–1601)
Thomas Campion (1567–1620)

John Donne (1572–1631)
Ben Jonson (1572–1637)

1577 Holinshed, *Chronicles*
Robert Burton (1577–1640), *The Anatomy of Melancholy*

North American Colonies

1565 Founding of St. Augustine

WORLD	BRITAIN	NORTH AMERICAN COLONIES
	William Harvey (1578–1657), first to demonstrate circulation of blood	1579 Sir Francis Drake lands north of San Francisco and claims the area for Elizabeth I
	1579 Spenser, *Shepheardes Calender*; Lyly, *Euphues*	
	John Fletcher (1579–1625)	Captain John Smith (c. 1580–1631)
	John Webster (c. 1580–c. 1630)	
1581 Dutch repudiate Spanish rule Hugo Grotius (1583–1645), Dutch jurist and statesman	1582 University of Edinburgh founded Francis Beaumont (c. 1585–1616)	1585 English colonize Roanoke Island
	c. 1586 Kyd, *The Spanish Tragedy*	
	1587 Mary Queen of Scots executed	
	1588 Spanish Armada destroyed; Thomas Harriot, *A Brief and True Report of the New Found Land of Virginia*	John Winthrop (1588–1649)
	c. 1588 Marlowe, *Dr. Faustus*	
	Thomas Hobbes (1588–1679)	
	1589 Richard Hakluyt, *Principal Navigations*	
	1590 Spenser, *Faerie Queene*, Parts I–III	William Bradford (1590–1657)
	1591 Sidney, *Astrophel and Stella*	
	Robert Herrick (1591–1674)	

Nicolas Poussin (1594–1665), French painter
René Descartes (1596–1650)
Anthony Van Dyke (1599–1641)
Calderon de la Barca (1600–1681)
1602 Dutch East India Company founded

1605 Cervantes, *Don Quixote*, Part I

Rembrandt (1606–1669)
Pierre Corneille (1606–1684)

Izaak Walton (1593–1683)
George Herbert (1593–1633)
Thomas Carew (c. 1595–1640)

1596 Essex's rebellion
1599 Globe Theater built
1600 Charter of the East India Company
1602 Shakespeare, *Hamlet*

1603–1625 JACOBEAN PERIOD

1603–1649 House of Stuart
1603–1625 Reign of James I
1604 Shakespeare, *Othello*
1605 Shakespeare, *Macbeth, King Lear;* the Gunpowder Plot
Sir Thomas Browne (1605–1682)
Edmund Waller (1606–1687)

John Milton (1608–1674)

Sir John Suckling (1609–1642)
1611 Shakespeare, *The Tempest;* King James Version of *Bible*
Samuel Butler (1612–1680)

Roger Williams (c. 1603–1683)

1606 Charters of the Virginia and Plymouth Colonies
1607 Jamestown Colony founded
1608 French settle Quebec City; John Smith, *A True Relation . . . of Virginia*
1609 Champlain is first European to navigate Lake Champlain; Henry Hudson explores Hudson River

Anne Bradstreet (1612?–1672)

1630 University of Tokyo founded

Benedict de Spinoza (1632–1677)
1632–1653 Building of the Taj Mahal
1635 Founding of Academie Française

1636 Corneille, *The Cid*
1637 Descartes, *Discourse of the Method of Rightly Guiding the Reason*
Jean Racine (1639–1699)

1640–1688 Reign of Frederick the Elector

1643–1715 Reign of Louis XIV
Antonio Stradivari (1644–1737)

John Dryden (1631–1700)

John Locke (1632–1704)
Samuel Pepys (1633–1703)
1633 First collection of poems of John Donne

Thomas Traherne (1637–1674)

1639 English East India Company buys and settles Madras, India

1642–1648 Civil War
1642 Theaters closed; Sir John Denham, *Cooper's Hill*
Sir Isaac Newton (1642–1727)

1644 Milton, "Areopagitica"

1630 Massachusetts Bay Colony founded; Bradford begins *History of Plymouth Plantation*.
1630–1649 Winthrop journal (published as *History of New England from 1630 to 1649*)

Michael Wigglesworth (1631–1705)

1634 First settlement in Maryland
1635 Boston Latin School founded
1636 Roger Williams founds Providence, R.I.; Harvard College founded

Mary Rowlandson (1636?–1678?)
1637 Thomas Morton, *New English Canaan*
1638 First printing press; Anne Hutchinson banished.

Increase Mather (1639–1723)
1640 *Bay Psalm Book*, first book printed in America
1642 Montreal founded

1644 Williams, *Bloudy Tenent of Persecution*

WORLD	BRITAIN	THE AMERICAS
Gottfried von Leibniz (1646–1716)		William Penn (1644–1718) Edward Taylor (1452?–1729)
	John Wilmot, earl of Rochester (1647–1680)	
	1649–1660 COMMONWEALTH	
	1649 Execution of Charles I John Churchill, duke of Marlborough (1650–1722)	**1650** Bradstreet, *The Tenth Muse* Samuel Sewall (1652–1730)
	1651 Hobbes, *Leviathan* **1656** D'Avenant, *Siege of Rhodes*, first "opera," first heroic play	**1656** Quakers arrive in Massachusetts
1656 Invention of pendulum clock	**1658** Death of Cromwell	**1659** John Eliot, *The Christian Commonwealth*
1657 Great Fire of Tokyo	**1660–1800 NEOCLASSICAL PERIOD (AGE OF REASON)**	
Mid-17th century Building of Versailles Palace	**1660–1700 RESTORATION PERIOD**	
	1669–1714 House of Stuart **1660** Restoration; **1660–1685** reign of Charles II	

1666 Founding of French Academy of Science
1667 French invade Spanish Netherlands
Giovanni Vico (1668–1774), Italian philosopher and jurist
1672–1725 Reign of Peter the Great of Russia

Jean Watteau (1684–1721)
Johann Sebastian Bach (1685–1750)

George Frideric Handel (1685–1759)

1660–1669 Pepys, *Diary*
Daniel Defoe (1660–1731)
1662 Founding of Royal Society
1665 Plague Year
1666 Great Fire of London

Jonathan Swift (1667–1745)
1667 Milton, *Paradise Lost*
1668 Dryden made Poet Laureate
William Congreve (1670–1729)
Joseph Addison (1672–1717)
Sir Richard Steele (1672–1729)

1678 Bunyan, *Pilgrim's Progress;*
Dryden, *All for Love*
1685–1688 Reign of James II

John Gay (1685–1732)
1687 Newton, *Principia*
Alexander Pope (1688–1744)
1688 Aphra Behn, *Oroonoko, or The Royal Slave*, first antislavery novel

1662 Wigglesworth, *Day of Doom*
Cotton Mather (1663–1728)
Sarah Kemble Knight (1666–1727)

1673 Marquette and Joliet are first Europeans to navigate Mississippi River
William Byrd (1674–1744)
1674–1729 Sewall, *Diary*
1675–1676 King Philip's War
1678 Bradstreet, *Poems*
1682 William Penn (1644–1718) settles Pennsylvania, founds Philadelphia; Robert LaSalle (1643–1687) explores Mississippi River; Rowlandson, *Captivity and Restoration*

WORLD	BRITAIN	NORTH AMERICAN COLONIES
		1689–1697 King William's War
	1688 Glorious Revolution	
	1689 Bill of Rights restricts power of the crown	
	1689–1702 Reign of William and Mary II	
	Samuel Richardson (1689–1761)	
	Lady Mary Wortley Montagu (1689–1762)	
1690 British found Calcutta	1690 Locke, *Essays Concerning Human Understanding*	
		1692 Salem witch trial executions
		1693 Founding of William and Mary College; Cotton Mather, *Wonders of the Invisible World*
	1694 Founding of Bank of England	John Bartram (1699–1777), American botanist
1695 Dictionary published by Academie Française	William Hogarth (1697–1764)	
Voltaire (1694–1778)		
	1700–1750 AUGUSTAN AGE	
	James Thomson (1700–1749)	1701 Yale University founded; Detroit settled
	1701 Act of Settlement defines limited monarchy	1702 Cotton Mather, *Magnalia Christi Americana*
	1702 *The Daily Courant*, first daily paper	
	1702–1714 Reign of Anne	

520

1703 Fahrenheit thermometer system accepted
1704–1713 War of the Spanish Succession
Carolus Linnaeus (1707–1778), Swedish botanist and taxonomist

Jean Jacques Rousseau (1712–1778)
Denis Diderot (1713–1784)
1713 Treaty of Utrecht
1715 Death of Louis XIV
1715–1774 Reign of Louis XV
1715, 1735 Le Sage, *Gil Blas*

John Wesley (1703–1791)
1704–1710 Duke of Marlborough leads allied army against France

1707 Union of England and Scotland
Henry Fielding (1707–1754)
Samuel Johnson (1709–1784)
1709–1711 Addison and Steele, *The Tatler*
1710 Handel comes to England
1710–1713 Swift, *Journal to Stella*
1711 Pope, *Essay on Criticism*
1711–1712, 1714 Addison and Steele, *The Spectator*
David Hume (1711–1776)

1714–1901 House of Hanover
1714–1727 Reign of George I

Thomas Gray (1716–1771)
Horace Walpole (1717–1797)
David Garrick (1717–1779)

1719 Defoe, *Robinson Crusoe*
1721 Ministry of Robert Walpole
William Collins (1721–1759)
Tobias Smollett (1721–1771)

Jonathan Edwards (1703–1758)
1704 First newspaper, *Boston News Letter*; Knight, *Journal of a Journey*
Benjamin Franklin (1706–1790)

1708 Cook, *Sot-Weed Factor*

1710 Mather, *Bonifacius*

1713 Increase Mather, *A Plain Discourse Showing Who Shall and Who Shall Not Enter Heaven*

1718 New Orleans founded

John Woolman (1720–1772)

Immanuel Kant (1724–1804)

1731 Abbé Prévost, *Manon Lescaut*

Jean Fragonard (1732–1806)
Franz Joseph Haydn (1732–1809)

1735 Linnaeus, *System of Nature*

BRITAIN

1722 Defoe, *Journal of the Plague Year;
Moll Flanders*
Christopher Smart (1722–1771)
Adam Smith (1723–1790)
Sir Joshua Reynolds (1723–1792)

1726–1730 Thomson, *The Seasons*
1727 Swift, *Gulliver's Travels*
1727–1760 Reign of George II
Thomas Gainsborough (1727–1788)
1728 Gay, *The Beggar's Opera*
Oliver Goldsmith (c. 1728–1774)
1729 Swift, *A Modest Proposal*
Edmund Burke (1729–1797)

William Cowper (1731–1800)
1732 Covent Garden Theater built
1733 Pope, *Essay on Man*
Joseph Priestley (1733–1804)

NORTH AMERICAN COLONIES

1722 Franklin, *Silence Dogood*
Samuel Adams (1722–1803)

1729 Byrd, *History of the Dividing Line*

George Washington (1732–1799)
1733–1757 Franklin, *Poor Richard's
Almanack*
1733 Georgia settled by Oglethorpe,
Byrd, *Journal*
Daniel Boone (1734–1820)
John Adams (1735–1826)
1735 Wesley brothers visit America;
Peter Zenger found not guilty in first
freedom of press suit

1740–1780 Reign of Maria Theresa of Austria
1740–1786 Reign of Frederick the Great of Prussia
1740–1748 War of the Austrian Succession
Antoine Houdon (1741–1828), French sculptor

Antoine Lavoisier (1743–1794)

Francisco Goya (1746–1828)
Jacques David (1748–1825)

Johann Goethe (1749–1832)
1749, Jean Jacques Rousseau, *Discourse on the Arts and Sciences*

Edward Gibbon (1737–1794)
1737 Theater Licensing Act

1740 Richardson, *Pamela*
James Boswell (1740–1795)

1742 Fielding, *Joseph Andrews*

1745 Jacobite rebellion

1747–1748 Richardson, *Clarissa;*
1748 Hume, *Inquiry Concerning Human Understanding*
Jeremy Bentham (1748–1832)
1749 Fielding, *Tom Jones;* Johnson, *Vanity of Human Wishes*

Paul Revere (1735–1818)
St. Jean de Crèvecoeur (1735–1813)
Patrick Henry (1736–1799)
Thomas Paine (1737–1809)
John Singleton Copley (1737–1815)
William Bartram (1739–1823)

1740–1748 King George's War
1741 Edwards, *Sinners in the Hands of an Angry God*

Charles Wilson Peale (1741–1827)

Thomas Jefferson (1743–1826)

King George's War (1745–1748)

1749 University of Pennsylvania founded; First American dramatic company at Philadelphia

WORLD

1755 Lisbon earthquake
Wolfgang Amadeus Mozart (1756–1791)
1756–1763 Seven Years' War
1757 British Empire in India founded on
Clive's victories

Antonio Canova (1759–1822)

1759 Voltaire, *Candide*

Friedrich von Schiller (1759–1805)

1762 Jean Jacques Rousseau, *The Social
Contract*
1762–1796 Reign of Catherine the Great
of Russia

BRITAIN

1750–1789 AGE OF JOHNSON

1751 Gray, "Elegy Written in a Country
Churchyard"
Richard Brinsley Sheridan (1751–1816)

1753 British Museum founded
George Crabbe (1754–1832)

1755 Johnson, *Dictionary*

William Blake (1757–1827)

Horatio, Lord Nelson (1758–1805)

1759–1767 Sterne, *Tristram Shandy*

Robert Burns (1759–1796)
Mary Wollstonecraft (1759–1797)
1760–1820 Reign of George III

NORTH AMERICAN COLONIES

1751 Franklin, *Experiments and
Observations in Electricity*; John
Bartram, *Observations on American
Plants*; James Madison (1751–1836)
Philip Freneau (1752–1832)

Joel Barlow (1754–1812)
1754–1763 French and Indian War
Phillis Wheatley (1754?–1784)
1754 Edwards, *The Freedom of the Will*
Alexander Hamilton (1755–1804)
1755 Acadians expelled from Nova
Scotia
Royall Tyler (1757–1826)

1758 Edwards, *The Great Christian
Doctrine of Original Sin Defended*
1759 Forts Niagara and Ticonderoga
taken by British; Quebec captured

1762 St. Louis founded

1763 Mason-Dixon Survey

524

	1764 Horace Walpole, *The Castle of Otranto*	1764 James Otis, *Rights of British Colonies*
	1765 Percy, *Reliques of Ancient English Poetry*	1765 Stamp Act
	1765 Invention of the steam engine by Watt	
	1766 Goldsmith, *The Vicar of Wakefield* Thomas Malthus (1766–1854)	1766 Franklin, *Examination Before the House of Commons*
		1767 Godfrey, *Prince of Parthia*, first American play to be acted Andrew Jackson (1767–1845)
François de Chateaubriand (1768–1848)	1768 Spinning machine invented	1768 Dickinson, *Letters from a Farmer in Pennsylvania*
Napoleon Bonaparte (1769–1821)	Duke of Wellington (1769–1852)	1769 Samuel Adams and others, *Appeal to the World*; Gaspar de Portola establishes San Diego Bay Colony
Ludwig van Beethoven (1770–1827) Georg W. F. Hegel (1770–1831)	William Wordsworth (1770–1850)	1770 Boston Massacre; Friar Junipero Serra founds first of California missions
	1771 Mackenzie, *The Man of Feeling*; Smollett, *Humphry Clinker* Sir Walter Scott (1771–1832)	1771 Franklin *Autobiography* begins Charles Brockden Brown (1771–1810)
1772 First partition of Poland; French *Encyclopédie* completed	Samuel Taylor Coleridge (1772–1834)	1772 Freneau, *Rising Glories of America*
	1773 Goldsmith, *She Stoops to Conquer*	1773 Boston Tea Party; Wheatley, *Poems*

WORLD	BRITAIN	NORTH AMERICAN COLONIES
1774 Goethe, *The Sorrows of Young Werther*	Robert Southey (1774–1843)	1774 Closing of Boston Harbor; Jefferson, *Summary View of Rights of British America;* Woolman, *Journal;* Convening of Continental Congress
		Meriwether Lewis (1774–1809)
	1775–1783 War with colonies	1775–1783 Revolutionary War
	Jane Austen (1775–1817)	1775 Battles of Lexington, Concord, and Bunker Hill
	Joseph Turner (1775–1851)	
	Charles Lamb (1775–1834)	
	Walter Savage Landor (1775–1864)	
	1775 Sheridan, *The Rivals;* Burke, *Speech on Conciliation*	
	1776 Gibbon, *Decline and Fall of the Roman Empire;* Smith, *Wealth of Nations*	1776 Paine, *Common Sense;* first of *The American Crisis* pamphlets; Jefferson, Declaration of Independence; San Francisco founded
	John Constable (1776–1837)	
	1777 Sheridan, *School for Scandal*	
	William Hazlitt (1778–1830)	1778 Freneau, *American Independence;* Articles of Confederation
José de San Martín (1778–1850), liberator of Chile and Peru	1778 Burney, *Evelina*	1779 Ethan Allen, *Narrative of the Captivity;* John Paul Jones's naval victories
	1779 Johnson, *Lives of the Poets*	
	Thomas Moore (1779–1852)	
Jean Ingres (1780–1867)		
1781 Kant, *Critique of Pure Reason*		1781 Surrender of Cornwallis at Yorktown; Articles of Confederation ratified

1782 Crèvecoeur, *Letters from an American Farmer*
1783 Treaty of Paris ends war
Washington Irving (1783–1859)
1783 Noah Webster, *Elementary Spelling* helped standardize American orthography; *Grammar* and *Reader* appear in subsequent years
1784 England recognizes American independence
John J. Audubon (1785–1851)
1786 Freneau, *Poems*
1787 Royall Tyler *The Contrast*, first American comedy done by professional actors; Constitutional Convention
1787–1788 Hamilton and others, *The Federalist*

James Fenimore Cooper (1789–1851)
1789–1797 George Washington, president

1791 Bill of Rights; William Bartram, *Travels through North and South Carolina*
1791–1792 Paine, *Rights of Man*

Leigh Hunt (1784–1859)

Thomas De Quincey (1785–1859)
Thomas Love Peacock (1785–1866)
1786 Burns, *Poems*

George Gordon, Lord Byron (1788–1824)

1789 Blake, *Songs of Innocence*; Bentham, *Principles of Morals and Legislation*

1791 Boswell, *Life of Johnson*

Simón Bolívar (1783–1830)
Stendhal (Marie-Henri Beyle) (1783–1842)

Felix Mendelssohn (1786–1847)

1788 First transportation of British convicts to Australia
1789 (July 14) Storming of the Bastille; French Revolution begins

Alphonse de Lamartine (1790–1869)
1791 Marquis de Sade, *Justine*

527

WORLD	BRITAIN	UNITED STATES
1792 Proclamation of the French Republic	1792 Wollstonecraft, *Rights of Women;* Percy Bysshe Shelley **(1792–1822)**	
Gioacchino Rossini **(1792–1868)**		
1793 Execution of Louis XVI	1793 War with France	
	John Clare **(1793–1864)**	William Cullen Bryant **(1794–1878)**
1794 Reign of Terror	1794 Blake, *Songs of Experience*	1794–1795 Paine, *Age of Reason*
	John Keats **(1795–1821)**	1796 Barlow, *Hasty Pudding*
	Thomas Carlyle **(1795–1881)**	
	George Darley **(1795–1846)**	
Camille Corot **(1796–1875)**	1796 Jenner demonstrates vaccination	1796 Washington, Farewell Address
	1796–1798 Austen writes *Pride and Prejudice, Sense and Sensibility,* and *Northanger Abbey*	William H. Prescott **(1796–1859)**
Franz Schubert **(1797–1828)**	Mary Wollstonecraft Shelley **(1797–1851)**	1797–1801 John Adams, president
Heinrich Heine **(1797–1856)**		
	1798–1832 **ROMANTIC PERIOD**	
1798–1799 Napoleon's campaign in Egypt	1798 Wordsworth and Coleridge, *Lyrical Ballads;* Malthus, *Essay on the Principle of Population*	1798 Brown, *Wieland*
Giacomo Leopardi **(1798–1837)**		
Eugène Delacroix **(1798–1863)**		
Alexander Pushkin **(1799–1837)**		
Honoré de Balzac **(1799–1850)**		

1800 Volta invents electric battery

Victor Hugo (1802–1885)

Hector Berlioz (1803–1869)
1803–1805 French Empire
George Sand (1804–1876)
1804 Napoleon crowns himself emperor

1806–1809 Defeat of Prussia by France

Giuseppe Garibaldi (1807–1882)

Gerard de Nerval (1808–1855)
Honoré Daumier (1808–1879)
1808 Goethe, *Faust*, Part I

Nikolai Gogol (1809–1852)

Thomas Macaulay (1800–1859)
1800 Maria Edgeworth, *Castle Rackrent*
John Henry, Cardinal Newman (1801–1890)
1802 Scott, *Minstrelsy of the Scottish Border; Edinburgh Review* founded
Thomas L. Beddoes (1803–1849)
Edward Bulwer-Lytton (1803–1873)
Benjamin Disraeli (1804–1881)
1805 Wordsworth, *Prelude;* Scott, *The Lay of the Last Minstrel;* Battle of Trafalgar
Elizabeth Barrett Browning (1806–1861)
John Stuart Mill (1806–1873)
1807 Abolition of the slave trade; Byron, *Hours of Idleness;* Charles and Mary Lamb, *Tales from Shakespeare*

1808 Scott, *Marmion*

1809 Byron, *English Bards and Scotch Reviewers;* first issue of *Quarterly Review*
Charles Darwin (1809–1882)
Alfred, Lord Tennyson (1809–1892)
William Gladstone (1809–1898)

1800 Weems, *Life of Washington;* Library of Congress founded; Washington, D.C., becomes capital
1801–1809 Thomas Jefferson, president

1803 Louisiana Purchase
Ralph Waldo Emerson (1803–1882)
Nathaniel Hawthorne (1804–1864)
1804 J. Q. Adams, *Letters;* Burr-Hamilton duel; Lewis & Clark Expedition (1804–1806)
1806 Noah Webster, *Dictionary*
William G. Simms (1806–1870)
John Greenleaf Whittier (1807–1892)
Henry Wadsworth Longfellow (1807–1882)
1807 Barlow, *Columbiad;* first voyage of Fulton's steamboat

1809 Irving, *Knickerbocker's History*
Edgar Allan Poe (1809–1849)
Oliver Wendell Holmes (1809–1894)
Abraham Lincoln (1809–1865)
1809–1817 James Madison, president

WORLD

Frédéric Chopin (1810–1849)
Alfred de Musset (1810–1857)
1811, 1812 Napoleon's Russian
  campaign
Franz Liszt (1811–1886)

Richard Wagner (1813–1883)
Giuseppe Verdi (1813–1901)
Søren Kierkegaard (1813–1855)
1814 Napoleon exiled to Elba

1815 Battle of Waterloo
Otto von Bismarck (1815–1898)

BRITAIN

1810 Scott, *Lady of the Lake*; Porter,
  Scottish Chiefs
1811 Austen, *Sense and Sensibility*
  published
William Makepeace Thackeray (1811–
  1863)

1812 Byron, *Childe Harold*, Cantos I, II
Charles Dickens (1812–1870)
Robert Browning (1812–1889)

1813 Byron, *Bride of Abydos*; Austen,
  Pride and Prejudice published; Southey
  made Poet Laureate
1814 Scott, *Waverley*; Wordsworth,
  Excursion

1815 Scott, *Guy Mannering*
Anthony Trollope (1815–1882)

1816 Coleridge, *Christabel*; Byron,
  Prisoner of Chillon
Charlotte Brontë (1816–1855)

1817 Keats, *Poems*; Coleridge,
  Biographia Literaria; Mary Shelley,
  Frankenstein; first issue *Blackwood's
  Magazine*

UNITED STATES

Margaret Fuller (1810–1860)

Harriet Beecher Stowe (1811–1896)

1812–1815 War with England

1815 Freneau, *Poems on American
  Affairs; North American Review*
  established

1817–1825 James Monroe, president
1817 Bryant, "Thanatopsis"
Henry David Thoreau (1817–1862)
Frederick Douglass (c. 1817–1895)

Ivan Turgenev (1818–1883)
Karl Marx (1818–1883)
1819 First Atlantic steamship crossing

Friedrich Engels (1820–1895)

Gustave Flaubert (1821–1880)
Charles Baudelaire (1821–1867)
Fyodor Dostoevsky (1821–1881)
1822 Independence for Spanish colonies in South America; Greek independence

1825–1834 Era of Santa Anna in Mexico

1818 Keats, *Endymion*; Scott, *The Heart of Midlothian*
Emily Brontë (1818–1848)
1819 Byron, *Don Juan* I, II; Shelley, *The Cenci*
Mary Ann Evans [George Eliot] (1819–1880)
John Ruskin (1819–1900)
Charles Kingsley (1819–1875)
1820–1830 Reign of George IV
1820 Scott, *Ivanhoe*; Shelley, *Prometheus Unbound*
Herbert Spencer (1820–1903)
1821 Scott, *Kenilworth*; Shelley, *Adonais*

Matthew Arnold (1822–1888)

1825 First railroad completed

James Russell Lowell (1819–1891)
Herman Melville (1819–1891)
Walt Whitman (1819–1892)

1820 Missouri Compromise; Irving, *The Sketch Book*
Susan B. Anthony (1820–1906)

1821 Cooper, *The Spy*; Bryant, *Poems*

1823 Monroe Doctrine; Cooper, *The Pioneers*; E. Everett, *Progress of Literature in America*
Francis Parkman (1823–1893)
1825–1829 John Quincy Adams, president
1825 Erie Canal opens; Italian opera introduced

WORLD

Count Leo Tolstoy (1828–1910)
Henrik Ibsen (1828–1906)

1830 July Revolution in France
1830–1848 Reign of Louis Philippe

1831 Stendhal, *The Red and the Black*

Édouard Manet (1832–1883)

Edgar Degas (1834–1917)

BRITAIN

Dante Gabriel Rossetti (1828–1882)
George Meredith (1828–1909)

1830–1837 Reign of William IV

1832 First Reform Bill
Lewis Carroll [C. L. Dodgson] (1832–1898)

1833–1834 Carlyle, *Sartor Resartus*
1833–1841 Oxford Movement
William Morris (1834–1896)

UNITED STATES

1826 Cooper, *Last of the Mohicans*
John W. DeForest (1826–1906)
1827 Cooper, *The Prairie*; Poe, *Tamerlane*
1828 Audubon, *Birds of America*; Hawthorne, *Fanshawe*; Webster, *An American Dictionary*
1829–1837 Andrew Jackson, president
1829 Irving, *Conquest of Granada*
Henry Timrod (1829–1867)
1830 Holmes, "Old Ironsides"; *Godey's Lady's Book* founded; Capitol building completed
Emily Dickinson (1830–1886)
1831 Poe, *Poems*; McCormick demonstrates reaper; New England Anti-Slavery Society founded
1832 Tales by Poe appear in *Philadelphia Saturday Courier*
Louisa May Alcott (1832–1888)
1833 Poe, *Manuscript Found in a Bottle*

James Whistler (1834–1903)

1834 Davy Crocket, A Narrative of the Life of David Crockett; Southern Literary Messenger established
Mark Twain [Samuel Clemens] (1835–1920)
1835 Simms, The Partisan; The Yemasee; Longstreet, Georgia Scenes
Bret Harte (1836–1902)
Winslow Homer (1836–1910)
1836 Emerson, Nature; Holmes, Poems; McGuffy, Eclectic Readers
1837–1841 Martin Van Buren, president
1837 Hawthorne, Twice-Told Tales; Whittier, Poems; Emerson, American Scholar
William Dean Howells (1837–1920)
1838 Morse demonstrates telegraph; Underground Railroad established; DeTocqueville, Democracy in America
Henry Adams (1838–1918)
1839 Longfellow, Hyperion; Voices of the Night

1840 The Dial established; Cooper, Pathfinder; Dana, Two Years Before the Mast; Poe, Tales of the Grotesque and Arabesque

---

1834 Bulwer-Lytton, Last Days of Pompeii
1835 Robert Browning, Paracelsus
Samuel Butler (1836–1902)
1836 Dickens, Pickwick Papers
William S. Gilbert (1836–1911)
1837–1901 VICTORIAN PERIOD
1837–1901 Reign of Victoria
1837 Carlyle, French Revolution; Lockhart, Life of Scott
Algernon Swinburne (1837–1909)
1838 Ocean steamships connect England and America
1838–1848 Chartist Movement to extend the vote

Walter Pater (1839–1894)

Thomas Hardy (1840–1928)
1840 Dickens, Old Curiosity Shop; Robert Browning, Sordello; Marriage of Victoria and Albert

---

Paul Cézanne (1839–1906)
1839 Daguerreotype pictures
1839–1842 First Opium War
Auguste Rodin (1840–1917)
Claude Monet (1840–1926)
Émile Zola (1840–1902)
1840 British sovereignty over Australia

WORLD	BRITAIN	UNITED STATES
Auguste Renoir (1841–1919)	1841 British win Hong Kong; Carlyle, *Heroes and Hero Worship*	1841 William Harrison, president
		1841–1845 John Tyler, president
		1841 Cooper, *The Deerslayer*; Emerson, *Essays*; Longfellow, *Ballads*
		1841–1846 Brook Farm
Stéphane Mallarmé (1842–1898)	1842 Robert Browning, *Dramatic Lyrics*; Tennyson, *Poems*; Dickens, *American Notes*	1842 Longfellow, *Poems on Slavery*
		Sidney Lanier (1842–1881)
		Ambrose Bierce (1842–1914?)
	1843 Wordsworth made Poet Laureate; Dickens, *A Christmas Carol*	Henry James (1843–1916)
Henri Rousseau (1844–1910)	1844 Thackeray, *Barry Lyndon*; Elizabeth Browning, *Poems*; Disraeli, *Coningsby*	Thomas Eakins (1844–1916)
Paul Verlaine (1844–1896)	Robert Bridges (1844–1900)	George Washington Cable (1844–1925)
	Gerard M. Hopkins (1844–1889)	1844 Morse demonstrates telegraph; Emerson, *Essays: Second Series*
	1845 Repeal of the Corn Laws	1845 Annexation of Texas; Margaret Fuller, *Women in the Nineteenth Century*
		1845–1849 James Polk, president
		1846–1847 Mexican War
	1846 Brontë sisters, *Poems*	1846 Hawthorne, *Mosses from a Old Manse*; Holmes; *Poems*; Melville, *Typee*; Poe, "Philosophy of Composition"; Smithsonian Institution founded
1847 Joule, first law of thermodynamics	1847 E. Brontë, *Wuthering Heights*; C. Bronte, *Jane Eyre*; Tennyson, *The Princess*	1847 Emerson, *Poems*; Longfellow, *Evangeline*; Prescott, *Conquest of Peru*; Melville, *Omoo.*

Joel Chandler Harris (1848–1908)

1848 Lowell, *Biglow Papers*; *A Fable for Critics*; Melville, *Mardi*; discovery of gold in California

1849 Parkman, *The Oregon Trail*; Thoreau, *Week on the Concord and Merrimac Rivers*

1849–1850 Zachary Taylor, president

Sarah Orne Jewett (1849–1909)

1850–1853 Millard Fillmore, president

1850 Hawthorne, *The Scarlet Letter*; Poe, "The Poetic Principle"; *Harper's Magazine* founded; Melville, *White Jacket*

1851 Hawthorne, *House of the Seven Gables*; Melville, *Moby-Dick*

Kate Chopin (1851–1904)

1852 Hawthorne, *Blithedale Romance*; Stowe, *Uncle Tom's Cabin*; Melville, *Pierre*

Mary E. Wilkins Freeman (1852–1930)

1853–1857 Franklin Pierce, president

1854 Thoreau, *Walden*; founding of Republican Party

1855 Whitman, *Leaves of Grass*; Longfellow, *The Song of Hiawatha*

1847–1848 Thackeray, *Vanity Fair*

1848 Mill, *Political Economy*

1849–1850 Dickens, *David Copperfield*

1850 Tennyson made Poet Laureate; E. B. Browning, *Sonnets from the Portuguese*; Tennyson, "In Memoriam"; Thackeray, *Pendennis*; Robert Louis Stevenson (1850–1894)

1851 Ruskin, *Stones of Venice*; Borrow, *Lavengro*; Great Exposition

1852 Thackeray, *Henry Esmond*; Tennyson, *Ode on the Death of the Duke of Wellington*

George Moore (1852–1933)

1853 Dickens, *Bleak House*; Elizabeth Gaskell, *Cranford*; Arnold, *Poems*; C. Brontë, *Villette*

1854 Dickens, *Hard Times*

Oscar Wilde (1854–1900)

Paul Gauguin (1848–1903)

1848 February Revolution, France; Marx and Engels, *Communist Manifesto*; Failure of German Revolution leads to emigration of intellectuals to U.S.

1851–1870 Australian gold rush

1852–1870 French Second Empire

Vincent van Gogh (1853–1890)

1853–1855 Crimean War

WORLD

1856   Flaubert, *Madame Bovary*
Sigmund Freud (1856–1939)
1856–1860   Second Opium War
1857   Baudelaire, *Les Fleurs du Mal*

1858–1866   Transatlantic cable
1858–1860   U.S. trade treaty with Japan

Georges Seurat (1859–1891)

BRITAIN

1855   Robert Browning, *Men and Women*; Tennyson, *Maud*; Trollope, *The Warden*
Oscar Wilde (1856–1900)
George Bernard Shaw (1856–1950)

1857   Trollope, *Barchester Towers*; Dickens, *Little Dorrit*
Joseph Conrad (1857–1924)
1858   G. Eliot, *Scenes of Clerical Life*

1859   Tennyson, *Idylls of the King*; Dickens, *Tale of Two Cities*; G. Eliot, *Adam Bede*; Meredith, *Ordeal of Richard Feverel*; FitzGerald, *Rubáiyát of Omar Khayyám*; Darwin, *Origin of Species*; J. S. Mill, *On Liberty*
Alfred E. Housman (1859–1936)
Arthur Conan Doyle (1859–1930)
Francis Thompson (1859–1907)

UNITED STATES

John Singer Sargent (1856–1925)

Louis Sullivan (1856–1924)

1857–1861)   James Buchanan, president
1857   *Atlantic Monthly* founded; *Dred Scott* decision
1858   Holmes, *Autocrat of the Breakfast Table*; Longfellow, *Courtship of Miles Standish*; Lincoln-Douglas Debates; first transatlantic cable
Charles W. Chesnutt (1858–1932)
1859   John Brown's raid on Harper's Ferry

Hamlin Garland (1860–1940)

Anton Chekhov (1860–1904)

Aristide Maillol (1861–1944)
Rabindranath Tagore (1861–1941)

1863–1870 Emancipation of serfs in Russia

1864 Pasteur develops germ theory
1864–1869 Tolstoy, *War and Peace*
Italo Svevo (1864–1928), Italian fiction writer

Wassily Kandinsky (1866–1944)
Sun Yat-sen (1866–1925)
Benedetto Croce (1866–1952)
Romain Rolland (1866–1949)

1860 G. Eliot, *Mill on the Floss*; Collins, *Woman in White*

1861 G. Eliot, *Silas Marner*; Reade, *The Cloister and the Hearth*
1862 Ruskin, *Unto This Last*; Spencer, *First Principles*; Meredith, *Modern Love*
1863 G. Eliot, *Romola*; T. H. Huxley, *Man's Place in Nature*; Kingsley, *Water Babies*

1864 Robert Browning, *Dramatis Personae*; Tennyson, *Enoch Arden*; Newman, *Apologia pro Vita Sua*
1864 Lewis Carroll, *Alice in Wonderland*; Dickens, *Our Mutual Friend*; Arnold, *Essays in Criticism*
Rudyard Kipling (1865–1936)
William Butler Yeats (1865–1939)

H. G. Wells (1866–1946)

1860 Bessemer develops converter for steel manufacture; Emerson, *Conduct of Life*; Hawthorne, *The Marble Faun*
1861 Confederacy established; Civil War begins
1861–1865 Abraham Lincoln, president
1862 Browne, *Artemus Ward, His Book*; Battle of Shiloh; clash of Monitor and Merrimac; Siege of Vicksburg
Edith Wharton (1862–1937)
1863 Lincoln, Gettysburg Address; Emancipation Proclamation; Longfellow, *Tales of a Wayside Inn*; L. M. Alcott, *Hospital Sketches*; first military draft
1864 Bryant, *Thirty Poems*; Lowell, *Fireside Travels*; Thoreau, *The Maine Woods*; Whittier, *In War Times*; Sherman's march to the sea
1865 End of Civil War; Thoreau, *Cape Cod*; Whitman, *Drum Taps*; Lincoln assassinated; Thirteenth Amendment outlaws slavery
1865–1869 Andrew Johnson, president
1866 Whittier, *Snow Bound*; Howells, *Venetian Life*; Civil Rights Act and Fourteenth Amendment

WORLD

1867–1894 Marx, *Das Kapital*
1867 Nobel invents dynamite
Luigi Pirandello (1867–1936)
Maxim Gorky (1868–1936)
1868 Restoration of Japanese empire
Henri Matisse (1869–1954)
André Gide (1869–1951)
Mohandas Gandhi (1869–1948)
1869 Suez Canal opens; doctrine of papal
     infallibility

1870–1871 Franco-Prussian War

Georges Rouault (1871–1958)
Marcel Proust (1871–1922)
Paul Valéry (1871–1945)
1871 Abolition of feudalism in Japan
Piet Mondrian (1872–1944)

Colette (1873–1954)

BRITAIN

Arnold Bennet (1867–1931)
John Galsworthy (1867–1933)
Ernest Dowson (1867–1900)
1868 Collins, *The Moonstone;* Disraeli,
     prime minister
1869 Trollope, *Phineas Finn;*
     Blackmore, *Lorna Doone;* Arnold,
     Culture and Anarchy; Robert
     Browning, *The Ring and the Book*

1870 D. G. Rossetti, *Poems*

John Synge (1871–1909)

1871 Darwin, *Descent of Man*

1872 G. Eliot, *Middlemarch*

1873 Pater, *Studies in the Renaissance;*
     Newman, *The Idea of a University*
Ford Madox Ford (1873–1939)
Winston Churchill (1874–1965)
G. K. Chesterton (1874–1936)
1874–1880 Disraeli, Prime Minister

UNITED STATES

1867 Alaska bought from Russia;
     DeForest, *Miss Ravenel's Conversion*

1868 L. M. Alcott, *Little Women*
Edgar Lee Masters (1868–1950)
1869–1877 Ulysses S. Grant, president
1869 Twain, *Innocents Abroad;*
     Transcontinental railroad completed
Edwin Arlington Robinson (1869–1935)
William Vaughn Moody (1869–1910)
Frank Lloyd Wright (1869–1959)
1870 Harte, *Luck of Roaring Camp*
Frank Norris (1870–1902)
1871 Whitman, *Democratic Vistas;*
     Howells, *Their Wedding Journey*
Stephen Crane (1871–1900)
Theodore Dreiser (1871–1945)
1872 Twain, *Roughing It*
Paul Laurence Dunbar (1872–1906)
Willa Cather (1873–1947)

Amy Lowell (1874–1925)
Robert Frost (1874–1963)
Ellen Glasgow (1874–1945)

1875–1877 Tolstoy, *Anna Karenina*
Thomas Mann (1875–1955)
Rainer Marie Rilke (1875–1926)
Constantin Brancusi (1876–1957)

1877 Victoria made Empress of India

Paul Klee (1879–1940)
1879 Ibsen, *A Doll's House*

Guillaume Apollinaire (1880–1918)

Pablo Picasso (1881–1973)
Fernand Léger (1881–1955)

1874 Hardy, *Far from the Madding Crowd*

1876 G. Eliot, *Daniel Deronda*

1878 Hardy, *Return of the Native*

1879 Meredith, *The Egoist*; Robert Browning, *Dramatic Idylls*

Gertrude Stein (1874–1946)

1876 Twain, *Tom Sawyer*; James, *Roderick Hudson*; invention of the telephone
Sherwood Anderson (1876–1941)
Jack London (1876–1916)

1877–1881 Rutherford B. Hayes, president
1877 Edison, phonograph; James, *The American*; Lanier, *Poems*
1878 James, *The Europeans*
Carl Sandburg (1878–1967)
Upton Sinclair (1878–1968)
1879 Howells, *The Lady of the Aroostook*; Cable, *Old Creole Days*; James, *Daisy Miller*; Edison, light bulb
Wallace Stevens (1879–1955)
H. L. Mencken (1880–1956)
Joseph Stella (1880–1946)
1880 Longfellow, *Ultima Thule*; Harris, *Uncle Remus*
1881 James Garfield, president
1881–1885 Chester A. Arthur, president

WORLD	BRITAIN	UNITED STATES
	1881 D. G. Rossetti, *Ballads and Sonnets*	1881 James, *Portrait of a Lady*; *Washington Square*; Cable, *Madame Delphine*
		1882 Twain, *The Prince and the Pauper*; Howells, *A Modern Instance*; Whitman, *Specimen Days*
Georges Braque (1882–1963)	James Joyce (1882–1941)	1882–1898 Child, *English and Scottish Popular Ballads*
1882–1914 British occupation of Egypt	Virginia Woolf (1882–1941)	Franklin D. Roosevelt (1882–1945)
		Margaret Sanger (1883–1966)
Walter Gropius, (1883–1969)	1883 Stevenson, *Treasure Island*	1883 Twain, *Life on the Mississippi*; Brooklyn Bridge completed
Franz Kafka (1883–1924)		1884 Twain, *Huckleberry Finn*
1884–1914 Sino-French war over Indochina		William Carlos Williams (1884–1963)
		1885–1889 Grover Cleveland, president
Nikos Krazantzakis (1883?–1957)	1885 Gilbert and Sullivan, *The Mikado*; Pater, *Marius the Epicurean*	1885 First gasoline internal combustion engine; Howells, *The Rise of Silas Lapham*
	D. H. Lawrence (1885–1930)	Ezra Pound (1885–1972)
		Elinor Wylie (1885–1928)
		Sinclair Lewis (1885–1951)
		Ring Lardner (1885–1933)

Oskar Kokoschka (1886–1965)

Marcel Duchamp (1887–1968)
Mies van der Rohe (1887–1969)

Adolf Hitler (1889–1945)
1889 Eiffel Tower built to demonstrate use of steel

Boris Pasternak (1890–1960)
Charles de Gaulle (1890–1970)

Max Ernst (1891–1976)

1886 Hardy, *Mayor of Casterbridge*; Stevenson, *Dr. Jekyll and Mr. Hyde*; *Kidnapped*; Tennyson, *Locksley Hall Sixty Years After*; Kipling, *Departmental Ditties*
Siegfried Sassoon (1886–1967)
Rupert Brooke (1887–1915)
Edwin Muir (1887–1959)
Edith Sitwell (1887–1964)

1888 Kipling, *Plain Tales from the Hills*
Katherine Mansfield (1888–1923)

1889 Stevenson, *The Master of Ballantrae*

1890 Bridges, *Shorter Poems*

1891 Hardy, *Tess of the D'Urbervilles*; Doyle, *Adventures of Sherlock Holmes*; Kipling, *The Light that Failed*; Barrie, *The Little Minister*; start of the "Little Theatre" movement

1886 Howells, *Indian Summer*; James, *The Bostonians*; *Princess Casamassima*; Jewett, *A White Heron*
H. D. [Hilda Doolittle] (1886–1961)

Robinson Jeffers (1887–1962)
Marianne Moore (1887–1972)
Irving Berlin (1888–   )
Maxwell Anderson (1888–1959)
Eugene O'Neill (1888–1953)
T. S. Eliot (1888–1965)
John Crowe Ransom (1888–1974)
1888 James, *The Aspern Papers*
1889–1893 Benjamin Harrison, president
1889 Twain, *A Connecticut Yankee in King Arthur's Court*
Conrad Aiken (1889–1973)
Allen Tate (1889–1979)
Katherine Anne Porter (1890–1980)
1890 Dickinson, *Poems*; Howells, *A Hazard of New Fortunes*
1891 Garland, *Main-Travelled Roads*; Bierce, *Tales of Soldiers and Civilians*; Howells, *Criticism and Fiction*; International Copyright Act passed
Henry Miller (1891–1980)

WORLD	BRITAIN	UNITED STATES
		Archibald MacLeish (1892–1982)
		Edna St. Vincent Millay (1892–1950)
		Pearl Buck (1892–1973)
	1892 Kipling, *Barrack Room Ballads*	**1893–1897** Grover Cleveland, president
Joan Miró (1893–1983)	Hugh MacDiarmid (1892–1978)	**1893** Crane, *Maggie: A Girl of the Streets*; James, *The Real Thing and Other Stories*
	1893 Thompson, *Poems*; Shaw, *Mrs. Warren's Profession*	**1894** Howells, *A Traveler from Altruria*; Twain, *Pudd'nhead Wilson*; annexation of Hawaii; Chopin, *Bayou Folk*
1894–1895 Sino-Japanese War	Wilfred Owen (1893–1918)	
	1894 Yeats, *Land of Heart's Desire*; Kipling, *Jungle Book*	E. E. Cummings (1894–1963)
	Aldous Huxley (1894–1963)	James Thurber (1894–1961)
1895 Roentgen discovers X-ray; Marconi invents wireless (radio)	**1895** Wells, *The Time Machine*; Conrad, *Almayer's Folly*	**1895** Crane, *The Red Badge of Courage*
	Robert Graves (1895–)	Edmund Wilson (1895–1972)
	F. R. Leavis (1895–1978)	
	1896 Housman, *A Shropshire Lad*; Hardy, *Jude the Obscure*	**1896** Edison, motion picture; Jewett, *Country of the Pointed Firs*; Harold Frederic, *The Damnation of Theron Ware*; Twain, *Joan of Arc*
		F. Scott Fitzgerald (1896–1940)
		John Dos Passos (1896–1970)
1897 First Zionist Congress	**1897** Conrad, *The Nigger of the Narcissus*; Kipling, *Captains Courageous*	**1897–1901** William McKinley, president
1897–1899 Dreyfus case		**1897** James, *What Maisie Knew*; *Spoils of Poynton*; Robinson, *Children of the Night*
Erich Maria Remarque (1897–1970)		

Louise Bogan (1897–1970)
William Faulkner (1897–1962)
Thornton Wilder (1897–1975)
George Gershwin (1898–1937)
Alexander Calder (1898–1976)

1898 Puerto Rico becomes part of U. S.
1899 Edwin Markham, *The Man with the Hoe*; Chopin, *The Awakening*

Hart Crane (1899–1932)
Ernest Hemingway (1899–1961)
Vladimir Nabokov (1899–1977)
E. B. White (1899–   )

1900 Dreiser, *Sister Carrie*

Thomas Wolfe (1900–1938)

1901–1909 Theodore Roosevelt, president
1901 Moody, *Poems*; Norris, *The Octopus*; Booker T. Washington, *Up From Slavery*; James, *The Sacred Fount*
1902 Glasgow, *The Battle Ground*; James, *The Wings of the Dove*; Wister, *The Virginian*; Wharton, *Valley of Decision*

Langston Hughes (1902–1967)
John Steinbeck (1902–1968)
Nathanael West (1903–1940)

Henry Moore (1898–   )

1899 Irish Literary Theatre founded in Dublin

Elizabeth Bowen (1899–1973)

1900 Conrad, *Lord Jim*

1901 Kipling, *Kim*
1901–1910 Reign of Edward VII
1901–1914 EDWARDIAN PERIOD
1901–1919 House of Saxe-Coburg-Gotha
1902 Bennett, *Anna of the Five Towns*; Conrad, *Youth*; Masefield, *Saltwater Ballads*; Yeats, *Cathleen ni Houlihan*

Stevie Smith (1902–1971)

1898 Curies discover radium

1899–1900 Boxer Rebellion
1899–1902 Boer War
1899 Chekhov, *Uncle Vanya*

Federico Garcia Lorca (1899–1936)
Jorge Luis Borges (1899–   )

1900 Planck, quantum theory; Freud, *Interpretation of Dreams*; Pavlov experiments with conditioned reflex

Alberto Giacometti (1901–1966)
André Malraux (1901–1976)

George Orwell (1903–1950)

Marguerite Yourcenar (1903–   )

WORLD	BRITAIN	UNITED STATES
	Evelyn Waugh (1903–1966)	Countee Cullen (1903–1946)
	1903 Butler, *The Way of All Flesh*; Conrad, *Typhoon and Other Stories*; Shaw, *Man and Superman*	Mark Rothko (1903–1973)
		1903 James, *The Ambassadors*; London, *The Call of the Wild*; Norris, *The Pit*; Wright brothers flight
Arshile Gorky (1904–1948)	1904 Barrie, *Peter Pan*; Synge, *Riders to the Sea*	1904 O. Henry, *Cabbages and Kings*; James, *The Golden Bowl*; London, *The Sea-Wolf*; Adams, *Mont-Saint-Michel and Chartres*
Willem de Kooning (1904–)	C. Day Lews (1904–1972)	
1904–1905 Russo-Japanese War	Graham Greene (1904–)	
		James T. Farrell (1904–1979)
		Richard Eberhart (1904–)
		Isaac B. Singer (1904–)
Jean-Paul Sartre (1905–1980)	C. P. Snow (1905–1980)	1905 Einstein, theory of relativity; Wharton, *House of Mirth*
Mikhail Sholokhov (1905–)		Robert Penn Warren (1905–)
	Samuel Beckett (1906–)	1906 Sinclair, *The Jungle*; beginning of the "Little Theater" movement; San Francisco earthquake
		Clifford Odets (1906–1963)
Alberto Moravia (1907–)	1907 Synge, *The Playboy of the Western World*; Kipling, Nobel Prize	1907 Adams, *The Education of Henry Adams*
	Wystan Hugh Auden (1907–1973)	
	Louis MacNeice (1907–1963)	
Simone de Beauvoir (1908–)	1908 Bennet, *Old Wives' Tale*	1908 O. Henry, *The Voice of the City*
		Richard Wright (1908–1960)
		Theodore Roethke (1908–1963)

1909 Gide, *Strait Is the Gate*

1910 Japan annexes Korea

1911 Revolution in China; Sun Yat-sen sets up Republic; Maurice Maeterlinck, Nobel Prize

Eugène Ionesco (1912–   )
Patrick White (1912–   )
1912 Gerhart Hauptmann, Nobel Prize
Albert Camus (1913–1960)
1913 Rabindranath Tagore, Nobel Prize

1914–1918 World War I
1914–1917 Mexican Revolution

1909 Galsworthy, *Plays*
Stephen Spender (1909–   )

1910–1936 Reign of George V
1910 Noyes, *Collected Poems*; Bennett, *Clayhanger*; Galsworthy, *Justice*

Lawrence Durrell (1912–   )
1912 Shaw, *Pygmalion*
1913 D. H. Lawrence, *Sons and Lovers*; Robert Bridges made Poet Laureate

Dylan Thomas (1914–1953)

1909–1913 William Howard Taft, president
1909 Stein, *Three Lives*; Ford begins assembly line
Eudora Welty (1909–   )
James Agee (1909–1955)
1910 Robinson, *Town Down the River*; NAACP founded
1911 Dreiser, *Jennie Gerhardt*; Wharton, *Ethan Frome*; Bierce, *Devil's Dictionary*
Elizabeth Bishop (1911–1979)
J. V. Cunningham (1911–   )
Tennessee Williams (1911–1983)
1912 Dreiser, *The Financier*
Jackson Pollock (1912–1956)
John Cheever (1912–1982)
1913–1921 Woodrow Wilson, president
1913 Cather, *O Pioneers!*; Frost, *A Boy's Will*
Delmore Schwartz (1913–1966)
1914 Frost, *North of Boston*; Panama Canal opened
Randall Jarrell (1914–1965)
Ralph Ellison (1914–   )
John Berryman (1914–1972)
William Stafford (1914–   )

1915 Romain Rolland, Nobel Prize; sinking of the Lusitania

Heinrich Böll (1917–   )
1917 Russian Revolution; Balfour Declaration

1918–1933 German Republic
Aleksandr Solzhenitsyn (1918–   )
Armistice
1919 League of Nations founded; Treaty of Versailles

1915 Conrad, *Victory*; Brooke, *Collected Poems*; Maugham, *Of Human Bondage*; Lawrence, *The Rainbow*

1916 Joyce, *Portrait of the Artist as a Young Man*; Moore, *The Brook Kerith*; Wells, *Mr. Britling Sees It Through*

1917 to present House of Windsor
1917 Shaw, *Heartbreak House*; Barrie, *Dear Brutus*

1918 Lawrence, *New Poems*; Hopkins, *Poems*

1919 Conrad, *The Arrow of Gold*; Maugham, *The Moon and Sixpence*; Hardy, *Collected Poems*
Iris Murdoch (1919–   )
Doris Lessing (1919–   )

1915 James Branch Cabell, *The Rivet in Grandfather's Neck*; Masters, *Spoon River Anthology*
Saul Bellow (1915–   )
Arthur Miller (1915–   )
1916 Frost, *Mountain Interval*; Amy Lowell, *Men, Women and Ghosts*; Robinson, *Man Against the Sky*; Twain, *The Mysterious Stranger*; Sandburg, *Chicago Poems*
Walker Percy (1916–   )
Robert Lowell (1917–1977)
1917 U.S. enters war; Garland, *Son of the Middle Border*; T. S. Eliot, *Prufrock*
John F. Kennedy (1917–1963)
Carson McCullers (1917–1967)
1918 Cather, *My Ántonia*; Sandburg, *Cornhuskers*; O'Neill, *Moon of the Caribees*; Theater Guild established
1919 Sherwood Anderson, *Winesburg, Ohio*; Cabell, *Jurgen*; Pound, *First Cantos*; Prohibition amendment (Eighteenth)
Lawrence Ferlinghetti (1919–   )

1920 de la Mare, *Collected Poems*; Mansfield, *Bliss*; Wells, *The Outline of History*; Lawrence, *Women in Love*

1921 A. Huxley, *Chrome Yellow*

1921 Irish Free State founded; Anatole France, Nobel Prize

1922 Joyce, *Ulysses*; Galsworthy, *Forsyte Saga*; Housman, *Last Poems*; Mansfield, *The Garden Party*; Woolf, *Jacob's Room*
Philip Larkin (1922–   )
Donald Davie (1922–   )
1923 Hardy, *Collected Poems*; A. Huxley, *Antic Hay*; Shaw, *Saint Joan*; Lawrence, *Studies in Classic American Literature*; Yeats, Nobel Prize

1922 Mussolini's fascists seize Italy
Alain Robbe-Grillet (1922–   )

1920 Eliot, *Poems*; Fitzgerald, *This Side of Paradise*; Sinclair Lewis, *Main Street*; Millay, *A Few Figs from Thistles*; O'Neill, *Emperor Jones*; Robinson, *Lancelot*; Wharton, *The Age of Innocence*; Women's Suffrage Amendment (Nineteenth)
Howard Nemerov (1920–   )
1921–1923 Warren G. Harding, president

1921 Dos Passos, *Three Soldiers*; O'Neill, *Anna Christie*; Wylie, *Nets to Catch the Wind*; Sacco and Vanzetti found guilty (executed 1927); Robinson, *Collected Poems*
Richard Wilbur (1921–   )
1922 Cummings, *The Enormous Room*; Eliot, *The Waste Land*; Lewis, *Babbitt*; O'Neill, *The Hairy Ape*
Kurt Vonnegut (1922–   )

1923–1929 Calvin Coolidge, president
Cather, *A Lost Lady*; Frost, *New Hampshire*
James Dickey (1923–   )

WORLD	BRITAIN	UNITED STATES
		Denise Levertov (1923–) Norman Mailer (1923–)
	1924 Forster, *A Passage to India*	**1924** Hemingway, *in our time* (Paris); Jeffers, *Tamar and Other Poems*; Ransom, *Chills and Fever*; Melville's *Billy Budd* first published; Emily Dickinson, *Complete Poems*
		George Segal (1924–) James Baldwin (1924–) William Gass (1924–)
1925 Gide, *The Counterfeiters*; Kafka, *The Trial*	**1925** Shaw, Nobel Prize; Woolf, *Mrs. Dalloway*	**1925** Cather, *The Professor's House*; Cummings, *XLI Poems*; Dos Passos, *Manhattan Transfer*; Dreiser, *An American Tragedy*; Fitzgerald, *The Great Gatsby*; Glasgow, *Barren Ground*; Hemingway, *In Our Time*; Lewis, *Arrowsmith*; O'Neill, *Desire Under the Elms*
		Truman Capote (1925–1984) Flannery O'Connor (1925–1964)
	1926 Kipling, *Debits and Credits*; Lawrence, *The Plumed Serpent*; T. E. Lawrence (of Arabia), *The Seven Pillars of Wisdom*; MacDiarmid, *A Drunk Man Looks at the Thistle*	**1926** Hemingway, *The Sun Also Rises*; Glasgow, *The Romantic Comedians*; O'Neill, *The Great God Brown*
		A. R. Ammons (1926–) Robert Bly (1926–)

1927–1928 Chiang Kai-shek unites Nationalist China
1927 Henri Bergson (1859–1941), Nobel Prize
Gunther Grass (1927–   )

1928 Stalin purges; Sigrid Undset (1882–1949), Nobel Prize

1929 Thomas Mann, Nobel Prize; Remarque, *All Quiet on the Western Front*

1927 Woolf, *To the Lighthouse*
Molly Holden (1927–   )

1928 A. Huxley, *Point Counter Point*; Lawrence, *Lady Chatterley's Lover*

1929 Bridges, *The Testament of Beauty*; Galsworthy, *A Modern Comedy*; Graves, *Goodbye to All That*; Woolf, *A Room of One's Own*
Thom Gunn (1929–   )

Allen Ginsberg (1926–   )
James Merrill (1926–   )
W. D. Snodgrass (1926–   )
1927 Cather, *Death Comes for the Archbishop*; Jeffers, *The Women at Point Sur*; O'Neill, *Marco Millions*; Robinson, *Tristram*; Wilder, *The Bridge of San Luis Rey*; Lindbergh New York–Paris flight
John Ashbery (1927–   )
Galway Kinnell (1927–   )
W. S. Merwin (1927–   )
James Wright (1927–1980)
1928 Benét, *John Brown's Body*; Frost, *West-Running Brook*; MacLeish, *The Hamlet of A MacLeish*; Tate, *Mr. Pope and Other Poems*
Anne Sexton (1928–1974)
Edward Albee (1928–   )
1929–1933 Herbert Hoover, president
1929 Stock market crash; Faulkner, *The Sound and the Fury*; Hemingway, *A Farewell to Arms*; Lewis, *Dodsworth*; Wolfe, *Look Homeward, Angel*; Glasgow, *They Stooped to Folly*; Museum of Modern Art founded
Adrienne Rich (1929–   )
Martin Luther King, Jr. (1929–1968)

WORLD

1930 Gandhi's "Salt March"

1931 Japan invades Manchuria; Spain becomes a republic; Reichstag fire
Andre Voznesensky (1931–   )

1933–1945 German Third Reich
1933 André Malraux, *La Condition Humaine*

BRITAIN

1930 Maugham, *Cakes and Ale*; Coward, *Private Lives*; Waugh, *Vile Bodies*; Masefield made Poet Laureate
Elaine Feinstein (1930–   )
Ted Hughes (1930–   )
Harold Pinter (1930–   )
Jon Silken (1930–   )

1931 Galsworthy, *Maid in Waiting*; Woolf, *The Waves*

1932 Galsworthy, Nobel Prize; Auden, *The Orators*; Huxley, *Brave New World*
Geoffrey Hill (1932–   )
1933 Auden, *Dance of Death*; Spender, *Poems*; Yeats, *Collected Poems*

UNITED STATES

1930 Sinclair Lewis, first American Nobel Prize; T. S. Eliot, *Ash Wednesday*; Maxwell Anderson, *Elizabeth the Queen*; Hart Crane, *The Bridge*; Dos Passos, *The 42nd Parallel*; Faulkner, *As I Lay Dying*
John Barth (1930–   )
Jasper Johns (1930–   )
Gary Snyder (1930–   )
1931 Cather, *Shadows on the Rock*; Faulkner, *Sanctuary*; O'Neill, *Mourning Becomes Electra*
Toni Morrison (1931–   )
1932 Caldwell, *Tobacco Road*; Dos Passos, *1919*; Faulkner, *Light in August*; Farrell, *Young Lonigan*; MacLeish, *Conquistador*
Sylvia Plath (1932–1963)
John Updike (1932–   )
1933–1945 Franklin Delano Roosevelt, president
1933 Caldwell, *God's Little Acre*;

Yevgeny Yevtushenko (1933–   )

1934 Pirandello, Nobel Prize; "Long March" of Mao Tse-tung

1936–1939 Spanish Civil War; Mussolini conquers Ethiopia

1934 Graves, *I, Claudius*; Waugh, *A Handful of Dust*

1935 MacNeice, *Poems*; Spender, *The Destructive Element*

1936 Edward VIII abdicates;
1936–1952 Reign of George VI
1936 Auden, *Look, Stranger*; Housman, *More Poems*; A. Huxley, *Eyeless in Gaza*; D. Thomas, *25 Poems*

1937 Woolf, *The Years*
1938 Auden, *Selected Poems*

Cozzens, *The Last Adam*; MacLeish, *Frescoes for Mr. Rockefeller's City*; Stein, *The Autobiography of Alice B. Toklas*

Philip Roth (1933–   )
John Gardner (1933–1982)
1934 Farrell, *The Young Manhood of Studs Lonigan*; Fitzgerald, *Tender Is the Night*; O'Hara, *Appointment in Samarra*; Henry Roth, *Call It Sleep* Imamu Amiri Baraka [LeRoi Jones] (1934–   )

Joan Didion (1934–   )
N. Scott Momaday (1934–   )
1935 Maxwell Anderson, *Winterset*; T. S. Eliot, *Murder in the Cathedral*; Stevens, *Ideas of Order*; Wolfe, *Of Time and the River*; Steinbeck, *Tortilla Flat*

1936 O'Neill, Nobel Prize; Frost, *A Further Range*; Faulkner, *Absalom, Absalom!*; Dos Passos, *The Big Money*; Mitchell, *Gone with the Wind*; Sandburg, *The People, Yes*

1937 Millay, *Conversations at Midnight*; Steinbeck, *Of Mice and Men*; *The Red Pony*; Stevens, *The Man with the Blue Guitar*; Hemingway, *To Have and Have Not*

WORLD

1938-1975 Francisco Franco, caudillo of Spain

1938 Hitler annexes Austria; Kazantzakis, *The Odyssey: A Modern Sequel*; Jean-Paul Sartre, *Nausea*

1939-1945 World War II

1939 Hitler seizes Czechoslovakia

1941 Ho Chi Minh founds Vietminh to drive French out of Indochina; Rommel North African campaigns

1942 Japanese occupation of Philippines; Albert Camus, *The Myth of Sisyphus*; *The Stranger*

BRITAIN

1938 Graves, *Collected Poems*, Richardson, *Pilgrimage* novel cycle completed

1939 Joyce, *Finnegan's Wake*; D. Thomas, *The World I Breathe*; Cary, *Mr. Johnson*
Seamus Heaney (1939–   )

1940 C. P. Snow begins *Strangers and Brothers* sequence; Yeats, *Last Poems and Plays*; Graham Greene, *The Power and the Glory*

1941 Cary, *Herself Surprised*; de la Mare, *Bells and Grass*; Spender, *Ruins and Visions*

1942 Cary, *To Be a Pilgrim*; Coward, *Blithe Spirit*; E. Waugh, *Put Out More Flags*

UNITED STATES

Thomas Pynchon (1937–   )
1938 Hemingway, *The Fifth Column and the First Forty Nine Stories*; Wilder, *Our Town*; Pearl Buck, Nobel Prize
Joyce Carol Oates (1938–   )

1939 Edward Taylor, *Poetical Works* (first publication); Porter, *Pale Horse, Pale Rider*; Steinbeck, *The Grapes of Wrath*; Wolfe, *The Web and the Rock*; Nathanael West, *The Day of the Locust*

1940 Hemingway, *For Whom the Bell Tolls*; Faulkner, *The Hamlet*; Pound, *Cantos*; Wolfe, *You Can't Go Home Again*; Wright, *Native Son*
Bobbie Ann Mason (1940–   )

1941 (Dec. 7) Pearl Harbor attack; Fitzgerald, *The Last Tycoon*; Glasgow, *In This Our Life*; Jeffers, *Be Angry at the Sun*; Welty, *A Curtain of Green*
Anne Tyler (1941–   )

1942 Cozzens, *The Just and the Unjust*; Faulkner, *Go Down, Moses*; Jarrell, *Blood for a Stranger*

1943 Sartre, *Being and Nothingness*	1943 Coward, *This Happy Breed*; H. Green, *Caught*	1943 Dos Passos, *Number One*; T. S. Eliot, *Four Quartets*; Warren, *At Heaven's Gate*
1944 Allied troops land in Normandy; Sartre, *No Exit*	1944 Cary, *The Horse's Mouth*; A. Huxley, *Time Must Have a Stop*	1944 Robert Lowell, *Land of Unlikeliness*; Porter, *The Leaning Tower*; Karl Shapiro, *V-Letter and Other Poems*; Bellow, *Dangling Man* Alice Walker (1944–)
		1945–1953 Harry S. Truman, president
1945 Atomic bombs dropped on Hiroshima and Nagasaki; United Nations Charter signed; Germany divided	1945 H. Green, *Loving*; E. Waugh, *Brideshead Revisited*; Orwell, *Animal Farm*; Auden, *Collected Poetry*	1945 Frost, *A Masque of Reason*; Jarrell, *Little Friend, Little Friend*; Ransom, *Selected Poems*; T. Williams, *The Glass Menagerie*; Wright, *Black Boy*
1945–1949 Greek Civil War		
1946 Hesse, Nobel Prize; Peron elected president of Argentina; Kazantzakis, *Zorba the Greek*; first meetings of the UN	1946 Spender, *European Witness*; D. Thomas, *Deaths and Entrances*; Churchill, "Iron Curtain" Speech	1946 Jeffers, *Medea*; O'Neill, *The Iceman Cometh*; Warren, *All the King's Men*; Welty, *Delta Wedding*; William Carlos Williams, *Paterson, I*; R. Lowell, *Lord Weary's Castle* Tim O'Brien (1946–)
1947 British rule in India ends; Partition of Pakistan; Gide, Nobel Prize	1947 Auden, *The Age of Anxiety*; George Barker, *Love Poems*; Spender, *Poems of Dedication*; Ivy Compton-Burnett, *Manservant and Maidservant*	1947 Marshall Plan begins; Kinsey report on sexuality; Dreiser, *The Stoic*; Frost, *A Masque of Mercy*; Stevens, *Transport to Summer*; T. Williams, *A Streetcar Named Desire*; Michener, *Tales of the South Pacific* Ann Beattie (1947–)

WORLD

1948 State of Israel founded; Paton, *Cry, the Beloved Country*

1949 North Atlantic Treaty Organization founded; West German Republic founded; People's Republic of China founded

1949–1950 Simone de Beauvoir, *The Second Sex*

1950–1953 Korean War

1950 Eugène Ionesco, *The Bald Soprano*

1951 Beckett, *Malone Meurt*

BRITAIN

1948 Fry, *The Lady's Not for Burning*; Graham Greene, *The Heart of the Matter*; A. Huxley, *Ape and Essence*; E. Waugh, *The Loved One*; Graves, *The White Goddess*; Sidney Smith, *Under the Eildon Tree*

1949 Cary, *A Fearful Joy*; Orwell, *Nineteen Eighty-Four*; Spender, *The Edge of Being*

1950 Auden, *The Enchafèd Flood*; de la Mare, *Inward Companion*; D. Thomas, *Twenty-six Poems*; V. S. Pritchett, *Mr. Beluncle*; Bertrand Russell, Nobel Prize

1951 Auden, *Nones*; G. Greene, *The End of the Affair*; Spender, *World Within World*; Beckett, *Molloy*; A. Powell begins *A Dance to the Music of Time* sequence

UNITED STATES

1948 Faulkner, *Intruder in the Dust*; Jarrell, *Losses*; Mailer, *The Naked and the Dead*; Pound, *Pisan Cantos*; Capote, *Other Voices, Other Rooms*; T. S. Eliot, Nobel Prize

1949 Dos Passos, *The Grand Design*; Miller, *Death of a Salesman*; Welty, *The Golden Apples*; Faulkner, Nobel Prize

1950 Cummings, *XAIPE*; T. S. Eliot, *The Cocktail Party*; Hemingway, *Across the River and into the Trees*; William Inge, *Come Back, Little Sheba*; Singer, *The Family Moskat*; Stevens, *Auroras of Autumn*; National Book Awards established

1951 Faulkner, *Requiem for a Nun*; Jarrell, *Seven-League Crutches*; James Jones, *From Here to Eternity*; R. Lowell, *Mills of the Kavanaughs*; Carson McCullers, *The Ballad of the Sad Cafe*; James Merrill, *First Poems*;

1952 Amos Tutuola, *The Palm Wine Drinkard*; Egyptian King abdicates, Nasser named president

1953 Truce in Korean War

1954 British evacuate Suez Canal; first hydrogen bomb; French troops withdraw from Indochina

1955 Warsaw Pact signed; birth control pill introduced; J. P. Donleavy, *The Ginger Man*; Nabokov, *Lolita* (Paris)

1952 Reign of Queen Elizabeth II begins; Betjeman, *First and Last Loves*; Beckett, *Waiting for Godot*; Cary, *Prisoner of Grace*; Dylan Thomas, *Collected Poems*

1953 Cary, *Except the Lord*; Hartley, *The Go-Between*; Beckett, *Watt*; E. Waugh, *Love Among the Ruins*; Winston Churchill, Nobel Prize for Literature

1954 MacNeice, *Autumn Sequel*; D. Thomas, *Under Milk Wood*; Kingsley Amis, *Lucky Jim*; Tolkien, *Lord of the Rings* trilogy; William Golding, *Lord of the Flies*; John Wain, *Hurry on Down*

1955 Auden, *The Shield of Achilles*; Cary, *Not Honour More*; D. Thomas, *Adventures in the Skin Trade*; Golding, *The Inheritors*

J. D. Salinger, *Catcher in the Rye*; Styron, *Lie Down in Darkness*; W. C. Williams, *Autobiography*

1952 Hemingway, *The Old Man and the Sea*; Steinbeck, *East of Eden*; Ellison, *Invisible Man*

1953–1961 Dwight Eisenhower, president

1953 Baldwin, *Go Tell It on the Mountain*; Bellow, *Augie March*; Cheever, *The Enormous Radio*; Roethke, *The Waking*; Salinger, *Nine Stories*; Warren, *Brother to Dragons*; T. Williams, *Camino Real*; Miller, *The Crucible*; Inge, *Picnic*

1954 Supreme Court outlaws racial segregation in schools; Hemingway, Nobel Prize; T. S. Eliot, *The Confidential Clerk*; Faulkner, *A Fable*; Stevens, *Collected Poems*

1955 Elizabeth Bishop, *North and South—A Cold Spring*; T. Williams, *Cat on a Hot Tin Roof*; Baldwin, *Notes of a Native Son*; William Gaddis, *The Recognitions*; W. C. Williams, *Journey*

WORLD

1956 Russia crushes Hungarian Revolution; Patrick White, *Tree of Man*

1957 European Common Market established; first satellite, Sputnik, launched; Albert Camus, Nobel Prize; Boris Pasternak's *Doctor Zhivago* printed in Milan, Italy

1958 Boris Pasternak declines Nobel Prize; Chinua Achebe, *Things Fall Apart*; Khrushchev becomes Russian premier; de Beauvoir, *Memoirs of a Dutiful Daughter*

1959 Castro revolution in Cuba; St. Lawrence Seaway opened

BRITAIN

1956 O'Casey, *Mirror In My House*; John Osborne, *Look Back in Anger*; Angus Wilson, *Anglo-Saxon Attitudes*; Golding, *Pincher Martin*

1957 John Braine, *Room at the Top*; L. P. Hartley, *The Hireling*; Hughes, *Hawk in the Rain*; Joyce, *Letters*; Osborne, *The Entertainer*; Edith Sitwell, *Collected Poems*; Elizabeth Taylor, *Angel*; E. Waugh, *The Ordeal of Gilbert Pinford*

1958 Beckett, *Endgame*; Alan Sillitoe, *Saturday Night and Sunday Morning*; T. H. White, *The Once and Future King*; Wilson, *The Middle Age of Mrs. Eliot*

1959 Cary, *The Captive and the Free*; Golding, *Free Fall*; Laurie Lee, *Cider with Rosie*; Harold Pinter, *The Birthday Party*; Sillitoe, *Loneliness of*

UNITED STATES

to Love; Alabama bus boycott led by M. L. King; Salk polio vaccine

1956 O'Neill, *Long Day's Journey into Night*; Pound, *Section: Rock Drill*; Baldwin, *Giovanni's Room*; Bellow, *Seize the Day*; Berryman, *Homage to Mistress Bradstreet*; Ginsberg, *Howl*; John Ashbery, *Some Trees*

1957 James Agee, *A Death in the Family*; Cozzens, *By Love Possessed*; Cheever, *The Wapshot Chronicle*; Faulkner, *The Town*; Jack Kerouac, *On the Road*; Nabokov, *Pnin*; O'Neill, *A Touch of the Poet*; Singer, *Gimpel the Fool and Other Stories*.

1958 Cummings, *95 Poems*; Bernard Malamud, *The Magic Barrel*; MacLeish, J. B.; Pound, *Pavanes and Divagations*; Updike, *The Poorhouse Fair*; Alaska admitted as forty-ninth state

1959 Edward Albee, *The Zoo Story*; Bellow, *Henderson the Rain King*; T. S. Eliot, *The Elder Statesman*; Faulkner, *The Mansion*; Lorraine

the Long Distance Runner; Keith Waterhouse, *Billy Liar*; Arnold Wesker, *The Kitchen*

1960 Amis, *Take a Girl Like You*; Durrell completes *Alexandria Quartet*; Powell, *Casanova's Chinese Restaurant*; Pinter, *The Caretaker*

1961 Beckett, *Happy Days*; Muriel Spark, *The Prime of Miss Jean Brodie*; Hughes, *The Fox in the Attic*; Murdock, *A Severed Head*; Osborne, *Luther*; Wain, *Weep Before God*; Gunn, *My Sad Captains*

1962 Graves, *New Poems 1962*; Powell, *The Kindly Ones*; Lessing, *The Golden Notebook*; T. Burgess, *A Clockwork Orange*

1961 Berlin Wall built; V. S. Naipaul, *A House for Mr. Biswas*

1962 Cuban missile crisis; Aleksandr Solzhenitsyn, *One Day in The Life of Ivan Denisovich*

Hansberry, *Raisin in the Sun*; John Knowles, *A Separate Peace*; Lowell, *Life Studies*; Philip Roth, *Goodbye Columbus*; Snodgrass, *Heart's Needle*; Warren, *The Cave*; Hawaii admitted as fiftieth state

1960 Barth, *The Sot-Weed Factor*; Lillian Hellman, *Toys in the Attic*; Jarrell, *The Woman in the Washington Zoo*; O'Connor, *The Violent Bear It Away*; Pound, *Thrones*; Snyder, *Myths and Texts*; Stafford, *West of Your City*; Updike, *Rabbit, Run*

1961–1963 John F. Kennedy, president
1961 First manned suborbital space flight; Peace Corps created; Dos Passos, *Midcentury*; Joseph Heller, *Catch-22*; Salinger, *Franny and Zooey*; Albee, *The American Dream*; Ginsberg, *Kaddish*; Hawkes, *The Lime Twig*; Walker Percy, *The Movie Goer*; Tillie Olsen, *Tell Me a Riddle*

1962 Albee, *Who's Afraid of Virginia Woolf?*; Robert Bly, *Silence in the Snowy Fields*; Faulkner, *The Reivers*; Frost, *In the Clearing*; Porter, *Ship of Fools*; T. Williams, *Night of the Iguana*; Nabokov, *Pale Fire*; Roth,

WORLD	BRITAIN	UNITED STATES
		Letting Go; Stafford, *Traveling Through the Dark*; W. C. Williams, *Pictures from Brueghel*; Reynolds Price, *A Long and Happy Life*; Steinbeck, Nobel Prize
1963 Fall of Diem government in Vietnam; ban on atmospheric testing of nuclear weapons	**1963** John Fowles, *The Collector*; G. Greene, *A Sense of Reality*; Margaret Drabble, *A Summer Bird-Cage*; David Storey, *This Sporting Life*	**1963** Kennedy assassination; Cummings, *73 Poems*; Jeffers, *The Beginning and the End*; Salinger, *Raise High the Roof Beam, Carpenters*; Malamud, *Idiots First*; Mary McCarthy, *The Group*; Pynchon, *V.*; Ken Kesey, *One Flew Over the Cuckoo's Nest*; Updike, *The Centaur*
		1963–1967 Lyndon Johnson, president
1964 Jean-Paul Sartre declines Nobel Prize; Brezhnev becomes Russian premier; Martin Luther King, Jr., receives Nobel Peace Prize	**1964** Larkin, *The Whitsun Wedding*; Powell, *The Valley of Bones*; Peter Shaffer, *The Royal Hunt of the Sun*; Golding, *The Spire*	**1964** Bellow, *Herzog*; Berryman, *77 Dream Songs*; Hemingway, *A Moveable Feast*; O'Neill, *More Stately Mansions*; Roethke, *The Far Field*; Lowell, *For the Union Dead*; Barthelme, *Come Back, Dr. Caligari*; Hawkes, *Second Skin*; LeRoi Jones, *Dutchman*; Burroughs, *The Naked Lunch*; Elkin, *Boswell*; Rechy, *City of Night*
1965 U.S. intervention in Vietnam begins	**1965** C. D. Lewis, *The Room*; E. Waugh, *Sword of Honor* trilogy; Pinter, *The Homecoming*	**1965** Albee, *Tiny Alice*; Mailer, *American Dream*; O'Connor, *Everything That Rises Must Converge*; Jerzy Kosinski,

1967 Arab–Israeli War

1968 Tet offensive in Vietnam; D. O. Fagunwa, *Forest of a Thousand Daemons* (first English edition)

1968 Vietnam peace talks begin

1966 Fowles, *The Magus*; G. Greene, *The Comedians*; MacNeice, *One for the Grave*

1967 Christopher Isherwood, *A Meeting by the River*; MacDiarmid, *A Lap of Honour*; Wilson, *No Laughing Matter*; Tom Stoppard, *Rosencrantz and Guildenstern Are Dead*

1968 Auden, *Collected Longer Poems*; Thomas Kinsella, *Nightwalker and Other Poems*; Edwin Morgan, *The Second Life*

1969 Fowles, *The French Lieutenant's Woman*; Lessing, *Children of Violence*; Storey, *In Celebration*; Samuel Beckett, Nobel Prize

Painted Bird; Ammons, *Corson's Inlet*; Snyder, *Riprap and Cold Mountain Poems*; Berger, *Little Big Man*

1966 Albee, *A Delicate Balance*; Barth, *Giles Goat-Boy*; Malamud, *The Fixer*; Plath, *Ariel*; Pynchon, *The Crying of Lot 49*; Kesey, *Sometimes a Great Notion*; Selby, *Last Exit to Brooklyn*; Watts riots; anti-war protests

1967 Moore, *Complete Poems*; Merwin, *The Lice*; Styron, *Confessions of Nat Turner*; Wilder, *The Eighth Day*; Gass, *Omensetter's Luck*

1968 Martin Luther King and Robert Kennedy assassinated; Baldwin, *Tell Me How Long the Train's Been Gone*; Barth, *Lost in the Funhouse*; Gass, *In the Heart of the Heart of the Country*; Mailer, *Armies of the Night*; Kosinski, *Steps*; Sukenick, *Up*; Updike, *Couples*

1969–1974 Richard Nixon, president

1969 First landing of astronauts on moon; Cheever, *Bullet Park*; Berryman, *The Dream Songs*; R. Lowell, *Notebook, 1967–1968*; Oates, *them*; Nabokov, *Ada*; Kurt Vonnegut, *Slaughterhouse-Five*

WORLD

1970 Solzhenitsyn, Nobel Prize

1971 Pablo Neruda, Nobel Prize; Mordecai Richler, *St. Urbain's Horseman*

1972 Heinrich Böll, Nobel Prize; A. D. Hope, *Collected Poems 1930–1970*; U.S. troops leave Vietnam

BRITAIN

1970 Ted Hughes, *Crow*

1971 Forster, *Maurice*; Thom Gunn, *Moly*; Geoffrey Hill, *Mercian Hymns*; Mary Lavin, *Collected Stories*

1972 Auden, *Epistle to a Godson*; Drabble, *The Needle's Eye*; Lessing, *The Story of a Non-Marrying Man*; Donald Davie, *Collected Poems 1950– 1970*; Richard Adams, *Watership Down*

UNITED STATES

1970 Hemingway, *Islands in the Stream*; Bellow, *Mr. Sammler's Planet*; Dickey, *Deliverance*; Merwin, *The Carrier of Ladders*; Welty, *Losing Battles*; Richard Brautigan, *Trout Fishing in America*; four student anti-war protesters killed by National Guard at Kent State University

1971 Voting age lowered to 18; J. V. Cunningham, *Collected Poems and Epigrams*; Joan Didion, *Play It as It Lays*; Ernest Gaines, *The Autobiography of Miss Jane Pitman*; John Hawkes, *The Blood Oranges*; Galway Kinnell, *The Book of Nightmares*; Kosinski, *Being There*; O'Connor, *Collected Stories*; Walker Percy, *Love in the Ruins*; Updike, *Rabbit Redux*

1972 Ammons, *Collected Poems, 1951– 1971*; Berryman, *Delusions, Etc.*; John Gardner, *The Sunlight Dialogues*; Welty, *The Optimist's Daughter*; Sam Shepard, *The Tooth of Crime*; Ishmael Reed, *Mumbo Jumbo*; Watergate break-in; Nixon re-elected

1973 Earle Birney, *The Bear on the Delhi Road*; Derek Walcott, *Another Life*; Patrick White, Nobel Prize; End of Vietnam War

1974 Western publication of Solzhenitsyn's *The Gulag Archipelago*; Solzhenitsyn exiled

1975 Birney, *Collected Poems*; Nadine Gordimer, *Selected Stories*

1976 Margaret Atwood, *Selected Poems*

1973 Graham Greene, *The Honorary Consul*; Iris Murdoch, *The Black Prince*; Lessing, *Collected African Stories*; Peter Shaffer, *Equus*; Kinsella, *Notes from the Land of the Dead*; Morgan, *From Glasgow to Saturn*

1974 Fowles, *Ebony Tower*; Philip Larkin, *High Windows*; Stoppard, *Travesties*; Davie, *The Shires*

1975 Seamus Heaney, *North*; Lessing, *Memoirs of a Survivor*; Powell completes *A Dance to the Music of Time* sequence; Graves, *Collected Poems*; Stevie Smith, *Collected Poems*

1976 Amis, *The Alteration*; Hughes, *A Season of Songs*; E. Waugh, *Diaries*; Powell, *Hearing Secret Harmonies*; J. B. Priestley, *Found, Lost, Found*

1973 Ginsberg, *The Fall of America*; R. Lowell, *The Dolphin*; Pynchon, *Gravity's Rainbow*; Vonnegut, *Breakfast of Champions*; Agnew resigns; Gerald Ford appointed vice-president

1974 Ammons, *Sphere*; Baldwin, *If Beale Street Could Talk*; Heller, *Something Happened*; Kinnell, *The Avenue Bearing the Initial of Christ . . .* ; Reed, *Last Days of Louisiana Red*; Erica Jong, *Fear of Flying*; Nixon impeachment hearings begin; Nixon resigns presidency

1974–1977 Gerald Ford, president

1975 Ashbery, *Self-Portrait in a Convex Mirror*; Bellow, *Humboldt's Gift*; E. L. Doctorow, *Ragtime*; Gaddis, *JR*; Kosinski, *Cockpit*; Ursula Le Guin, *The Wind's Twelve Quarters*; John A. Williams, *Mothersill and the Foxes*; Larry Woiwode, *Beyond the Bedroom Wall*

1976 Judith Guest, *Ordinary People*; Alex Haley, *Roots*; Merrill, *Divine Comedies*; Sexton, *45 Mercy Street*; Vonnegut, *Slapstick*; Gardner, *October Light*; Bellow, Nobel Prize; U.S. Bicentennial

WORLD	BRITAIN	UNITED STATES
		1977–1981 Jimmy Carter, president
1977 Patrick White, *Fringe of Leaves*	**1977** Fowles, *Daniel Martin*; Tolkien, *Silmarillion*; Drabble, *The Ice Age*; Hughes, *Gaudete*; Percy H. Newby, *Kith*	**1977** Cheever, *Falconer*; Didion, *A Book of Common Prayer*; R. Lowell, *Day by Day*; Percy, *Lancelot*
	1978 G. Greene, *Human Factor*; Murdoch, *The Sea, The Sea*; MacDiarmid, *Complete Poems*; T. H. White, *Book of Merlin*	**1978** Cheever, *Stories of John Cheever*; John Irving, *The World According to Garp*; Morrison, *Song of Solomon*; Updike, *The Coup*; Tim O'Brien, *Going After Cacciato*; Isaac B. Singer, Nobel Prize
1979 Naipaul, *A Bend in the River*; American citizens taken hostage in Iran; U.S. and China establish diplomatic relations	**1979** Burgess, *Abba Abba*; Hughes, *Remains of Elmet*; G. Fielding, *Pretty Doll Houses*; Wain, *The Pardoner's Tale*; Golding, *Darkness Visible*	**1979** Barth, *Letters*; Heller, *Good as Gold*; Merrill, *Mirabell: Books of Number*; Baldwin, *Just Above My Head*; Malamud, *Dubin's Lives*; Ashbery, *As We Know*
1980 Hazzard, *The Transit of Venus*; Mphahlele, *Chirundu*; Richler, *Joshua Then and Now*; P. White, *The Twyborn Affair*	**1980** Beckett, *Company*; Burgess, *Earthly Powers*; Drabble, *The Middle Ground*; Golding, *Rites of Passage*; G. Greene, *Doctor Fischer of Geneva or the Bomb Party*; Sillitoe, *The Storyteller*; A. Wilson, *Setting the World on Fire*	**1980** Doctorow, *Loon Lake*; Kosinski, *Passion Play*; Beattie, *Falling in Place*; Kinnell, *Mortal Acts, Mortal Words*
		1981– Ronald Reagan, president
1981 Atwood, *Bodily Harm*; Gordimer, *July's People*	**1981** Geoffrey Household, *Summon the Bright Water*; Lessing, *The Sirian Experiments*; Murdoch, *Nuns and*	**1981** Ammons, *A Coast of Trees*; Ashbery, *Shadow Train*; Bly, *The Man in the Black Coat Turns*; Hemingway,

Soldiers; Spark, Loitering with Intent; Waterhouse, Maggie Muggins

1982 Atwood, Dancing Girls and Other Stories; de Beauvoir, When Things of the Spirit Come First

1982 Beckett, Ill Seen Ill Said; Fowles, Mantissa

1983 William Golding, Nobel Prize; Burgess, The End of the World News; Lessing, Documents Relating to the Sentimental Agents in the Volyen Empire; Murdoch, The Philosopher's Pupil; Powell, How the Wheel Becomes It; Sillitoe, The Lost Flying Boat; Storey, A Prodigal Child; Waterhouse, In the Mood

Letters; Irving, The Hotel New Hampshire; Morrison, Tar Baby; Moore, Complete Poems; Plath, Collected Poems; Sexton, Complete Poems; Updike, Rabbit Is Rich

1982 Barth, Sabbatical; Barthelme, Sixty Stories; Bellow, The Dean's December; Cheever, Oh, What A Paradise It Seems; Elkin, George Mills; Malamud, God's Grace; Singer, The Collected Stories; Tyler, Dinner at the Homesick Restaurant; Updike, Bech Is Back; Vonnegut, Deadeye Dick; Alice Walker, The Color Purple

1983 Bishop, Complete Poems 1927–1979; Didion, Salvador; H. D. [Hilda Doolittle] Collected Poems 1912–1944; Mailer, Ancient Evenings; Merrill, From the First Nine; The Changing Light at Sandover; Stafford, A Glass Face in the Rain